The Practical Guide to Writing

with Readings and Handbook

EIGHTH EDITION

Sylvan Barnet
Tufts University

Marcia Stubbs
Wellesley College

Pat Bellanca
Harvard University

 LONGMAN

An Imprint of Addison Wesley Longman, Inc.

New York • Reading, Massachusetts • Menlo Park, California • Harlow, England
Don Mills, Ontario • Sydney • Mexico City • Madrid • Amsterdam

English Editor: Lynn M. Huddon
Supplements Editor: Donna Campion
Marketing Manager: Renée Ortbals
Project Manager: Donna DeBenedictis
Design Manager/Cover Designer: Rubina Yeh
Cover Photo: Paul Klee, "Twittering Machine" (Zwitscher–Maschine), 1922.
  Watercolor, and pen and ink on oil transfer drawing on paper, mounted on
  cardboard, 25 1/4 x 19" (63.8 x 48.1 cm). The Museum of Modern Art,
  New York. Purchase. Photograph copyright © 1999 The Museum of Modern
  Art, New York.
Photo Researcher: Julie Tesser
Technical Desktop Manager: Heather A. Peres
Electronic Production Specialist: Sarah Johnson
Senior Print Buyer: Hugh Crawford
Electronic Page Makeup: Allentown Digital Systems, Inc.
Printer and Binder: The Maple-Vail Book Manufacturing Group
Cover Printer: Coral Graphic Services, Inc.

For permission to use copyrighted materials, grateful acknowledgment is made
to the copyright holders on pp. 575–578, which are hereby made part of this
copyright page.

Library of Congress Cataloging-in-Publication Data

Barnet, Sylvan
    The practical guide to writing: with readings and handbook/
Sylvan Barnet, Marcia Stubbs, Pat Bellanca.—8th edition.
      p.   cm.
    Includes index.
    ISBN 0-321-02391-9 (pbk.)
    1. English language—Rhetoric. 2. College readers. 3.Report
writing.   I. Barnet, Sylvan.   II. Bellanca, Pat.   III. Title.
PE1408.L4314 1999
808'.0427—dc21   99-40170
                                                        CIP

Please visit our website at http://www.awlonline.com

ISBN 0-321-02391-9

12345678910—MA—020100099

Contents

Preface

The book is designed for college courses in which students write essays, instructors read them, and students and instructors together discuss them. We hope we offer a practical guide to all three activities. The student, looking for information about choosing a topic, writing an analysis, constructing a paragraph, using a semicolon, can use the text as a guide to the week's writing assignment. The instructor can suggest chapters or passages the student should consult in revising a draft or in starting the next assignment. Students and instructors together can discuss the exercises, the techniques used in the reprinted essays, the assumptions we make, and the suggestions we offer.

Although we include discussions and examples of description and narration, we emphasize analysis, exposition, and argument because those are the chief activities, usually rolled into one, that we all engage in, both in school and later. When students write papers, or professors write articles, or social workers write case studies, most of what they write explains ideas and how the writers arrived at them. Because they want to be believed, they present their ideas and evidence persuasively.

In addition to including many examples from the writing of our students, we have included more than fifty short essays—a third of them new to this edition—as well as numerous paragraphs from books and essays, the work for the most part of first-rate contemporary writers, both academic and popular. There are also a sample book review, a sample music review, a summary, two essays based on interviews, and two research papers. We include all these readings both to illustrate ways of writing and to provide students with something to write about. The suggested topics for writing often require the students to write about something outside of themselves. Some writing topics do present opportunities for introspection, and all of them in fact require it, but we think that much of a student's writing should be directed outward, not solely a look into the heart but a look around—at people, at places, and especially at ideas.

We have tried therefore to balance the advice "Trust your feelings," "Ask yourself questions," with prescriptions: "Keep your reader in mind," "Avoid clichés." We have tried to increase the student's awareness that writing is both an exploration of self ("Choose a topic you can write about honestly") and a communication with others ("Revise for clarity").

Chapter 1 includes three essays by students, a brief article by Philip Roth, and some informal exercises. Chapter 2 focuses on revision; it includes an example of peer review and a case history of a student paper from assignment through several revisions; it also offers a series of notes, drafts, and revisions by a professional writer. Instructors may find these chapters useful for the first few class meetings. During the first week of the semester, we commonly suggest that students browse through the book from beginning to end, reading what interests them, skimming the rest, and generally familiarizing themselves with the book's contents and organization. But because each chapter can stand by itself, the instructor can assign chapters for study in whatever seems a suitable order. Similarly the student can consult whatever passages seem most relevant to drafting, revising, or editing a particular essay.

A NOTE ON THE EIGHTH EDITION

We've streamlined and updated the book throughout, pruning discussions, adding more student writing, and presenting advice in what we believe is a more accessible way than ever. (Readers familiar with previous editions will notice more bulleted lists, more photographs, and more white space this time around.) In addition:

- We've extensively revised Chapter 2, "Drafting and Revising," which (in addition to the peer review case history) now includes a series of drafts and revisions by the journalist and historian Frances FitzGerald.
- We've added new student writing and new stories (by Charlotte Perkins Gilman and Isabel Allende) to Chapter 17, "Writing about Literature." We've also added to this chapter a brief discussion of the range of critical approaches that students may encounter as they begin to study literature in their college courses.
- Chapter 16, "The Research Essay," has been completely updated, and now provides essential information on using online library catalogs and indexes, and other electronic and Internet sources.
- A new Chapter 7, "The Writer's Voice," offers students concrete advice on developing style; it also includes a discussion of stylistic differences among the academic disciplines.
- We've included recent essays by such writers as Nicholas Negroponte, Patricia J. Williams, Debra Dickerson, and Steve Martin.
- We've also included compelling academic writing on such topics as the Buffalo Bill Museum, medieval manuscripts, the Internet, and plagiarism.

ACKNOWLEDGMENTS

In this revision we have responded to requests from many loyal users of our book and are indebted to many colleagues, students, editors, and other friends. These include Ronald Ashcroft, SUNY, College at Cortland; Michael Carrino, SUNY Plattsburgh; Darren Chiang-Schultheiss, Fullerton College; Phyllis Cox, Ivy Tech State College Region 7; David Espey, University of Pennsylvania; Margaret Griffith, Chadron State College; Karen Hattaway, San Jacinto College North; Lynn Huddon, Addison Wesley Longman; David Neas, Southwestern Community College; Maria Notarangelo, California State University, San Bernardino; John Orr, Fullerton College; Gerald Richman, Suffolk University; Kathi Shay, Southwestern Community College; Suzanne Shepard, Broome Community College; Matt Smith, Chattanooga State Technical Community College; Scott Stankey, Anoka-Ramsey Community College.

We are deeply grateful to Frances FitzGerald for giving us permission to reprint portions of her notes and manuscript for *Fire in the Lake.* We also thank

Dr. Howard Gotlieb, Director of Special Collections at Boston University's Mugar Library, and Sean D. Noël, Public Service and Fiscal Administrator at Special Collections, for their generosity in making those materials available to us

We also remain indebted to: John Ambrose, Jeannine Atkins, Richard Audet, Lois Avery, Barbara Balfour, Judith Barisonzi, Hannah Barrett, Tim Barretto, James Beaton, Pat Bellanca, Kay Berenson, Helle Bering-Fensen, Barbara Jane Berk, Morton Berman, Phyllis Braumlich, Gary Brienzo, Daniel V. Brislane, Lillian Broderick, James Brothers, Pearl L. Brown, Peter Brunette, Carroll Burcham, Pat Burnes, William Burto, A. Butrym, Terry P. Caesar, Patricia A. Cahill, William E. Cain, Joan Carberg, Susan Carlisle, Thomas Carnicelli, Sally Carson, David Cavitch, Cynthia Chapin, Charles H. Christensen, Sandra Christianson, Sarah Clark, Michael Cleary, John M. Clum, James Cobb, Phyllis Cole, William F. Coles, S. Cooney, Shirley Corvo, John Covell, Don Richard Cox, Claire Crabtree, Leslie Crabtree, Mary Ann Creadon, Mary Bryan H. Curd, Michael Curley, Leopold Damrosch, Carol A. David, Marlene Baldwin Davis, Robert Dees, Tom De Palma, Imogene De Smet, Aviva Diamond, T. Di Paolo, Pat Dorazio, Nicholas Durso, James Early, Janet Ellerby, Nathaniel Elliott, Doris Eyges, Marina Femmer, Denise Ferguson, Cathy Fiore, Nancy E. Fischer, Terry Flaherty, Thomas F. Flynn, Jan Fontein, C. Dennyy Freese, John Fugate, Krin Gabbard, Cynthia Galivan, Cinthia Gannett, Thomas J. Gasque, Walker Gibson, David Giele, James Gifford, Walker Gilmer, David Goldfaden, Margaret Gooch, Brenda Gotthelf, Christopher Gould, John Grass, Maggie Griffith, Jack Guillon, Stephen Hahn, Steve Hamelman, Nigel Hampton, James Hauser, Owen Hawley, Mark Heidmann, Thomas W. Herzing, Gervase Hittle, Robert Hosmer, Viki Hull, Susan Jamison, Owen Jenkins, Peter M. Johnson, Ronna C. Johnson, Mary D. Jones, George Kearns, Joseph Keefe, Robert Keefe, Kathryn Keller, Dr. Frank Kelly, Nancy Kneeland, Judith Kohl, Molly Moore Kohler, Roberta Kramer, George Kugler, Richard L. Lane, Andrea La Sane, Jonathan Lawson, Elsie Leach, Helen M. Lewis, Peter Lindblom, E. Darlene Lister, Marget Livesay, Jane Lump, Kathryn Lynch, Nancy Mackay, Ian C. Mackenzie, D'Ann Madewell, Teruko Maki, George Marcopoulos, Sr. Lynda Martin-Boyle, H.O.O.M., Victoria McCabe, Leo McCauley, Lisa J. McClure, Joan McCoy, Patricia McGowan, Ken McLaurin, Celeste A. Meister, Michael Meyer, George Miller, Eva Mills, Melodie Monahan, Joan Moon, Betty Morgan, Denise Muller, Margaret A. Murphy, Richard Muth, Robert A. Myers, Charles Nash, Barbara Nelson, Thomas Newkirk, J. Stephan Newmann, Donald Nontelle, Jo Anna Norris, Richard D. Olson, John O'Neill, Mary O'Sullivan, Julie Owen-Streit, Joan Patrie, Donald Pattow, Mary Mocsary Pauli, Douglas Peterson, Russell O. Peterson, Bill Pierce, Elaine Plasberg, Carolyn Potts, Maureen Potts, Charles Quagliata, S. Quiroz, Hope Rajala, John Rath, Martha Reid and her colleagues at William and Mary, Stephen Reid, Gerald Richman, Alice Robertson, Leo Rockas, Judith Root, Hephzibah Roskelly, Zelda Rouillard, Melissa Ruchhoeft, Scott Ruescher, John Rusciewitz, Richard Sandler, Stephen Sapious, Frances W. Sauers, Carl Schaffr, Gerald Schiffhorst, Sybil Schlesinger, Carmen Schmersahl, Charles Schuster, William Scott, Patrick W. Shaw, Suzanne Sheppard, Sally Bishop Shigley, James M. Siddens, Earl Sigmund, Joyce Monroe Simmons, Martha Simonsen, Edward Sims, Mark Slater, James Slattery, Audrey Smith, John Smolens, James Sodon, Jay Soldner, David Solheim, Nancy Sommers, Dr. Harold Spicer, Judith Stanford, Robert Stein, Ann Steinmetz, Frances M. Stowe, Kay Sturdivant, Elaine Supowitz, John Swan, Ann M. Tarbell, Ruth Thomas, Luther T. Tyler, Larry Uffelman, Kathy

Valdespino, Kerry Walk, Allison Warriner, Barbara Weaver, Renita Weems, Adrienne Weiss, Melinda Westbrook, Dorothy Widmayer, Lisa Wien, Lance Wilcox, Anita C. Wilson, Mary Ann Wilson, Howard Winn, Donald Winters, Elizabeth Wood, Winifred J. Wood, Strohn Woodard, Arthur P. Wooley, Hae Yong Yi, Mallory Young, and all our students.

Sylvan Barnet

Marcia Stubbs

Pat Bellanca

Ancillaries

Longman is pleased to offer the following selected ancillaries to teachers and students using *The Practical Guide to Writing with Readings and Handbook,* Eighth Edition:

- An updated Instructor's Manual features abundant practical advice on using the book as well as new suggestions for collaborative exercises and additional topics for critical thinking and writing. The Instructor's Manual is available to adopters of this edition.
- In cojunction with Penguin Putnam, Inc., Longman is proud to introduce "The Penguin Program." This program allows us to offer a wide variety of Penguin titles at a significant discount when they're packaged with any Longman title. Popular Penguin titles include Mike Rose's *Lives on the Boundary* and *Possible Lives,* and Neil Postman's *Amusing Ourselves to Death.*
- *Researching Online,* Third Edition, by David Munger, is an indispensable media guide that gives students detailed, step-by-step instructions for performing electronic searches; using e-mail, listservs, Usenet newsgroups, IRCs, and MU*s to do research; and assessing the validity of electronic sources.
- *The Essential Research Guide* is a two-page, handy laminated card, featuring a table with guidelines for evaluating different kinds of print and online sources, a list of editing and proofreading symbols, and a list of cross-curricular website resources.
- *The Longman Guide to Columbia Online Style* is a 32-page booklet that includes an overview of Columbia Online Style, guidelines for finding and evaluating electronic sources, and many examples for citing electronic sources.
- *Model Research Papers from Across the Disciplines,* Fifth Edition, (Diane Gould, Shoreline Community College) is a collection of student papers illustrating the most recent MLA, APA, CBE, Chicago, and Columbia Online Style documentation systems. Annotations highlight important considerations for writing in each field.
- *Daedalus Online* is the next generation of the highly awarded Daedalus Integrated Writing Environment (DIWE), uniting a peer-facilitated writing pedagogy with the inherently cooperative tools of the World Wide Web. This web-based writing environment allows students to explore online resources, employ pre-writing strategies, share ideas in real-time conferences, and post feedback to an asynchronous discussion board. As they collaborate online, students are learning to improve the organization, style and expression of their writing. *Daedalus Online* also offers instructors a suite of interactive management tools to guide and facilitate their students' interaction. Specifically, instructors can:
  - Effortlessly create and post assignments.
  - Link these assignments to online educational resources.
  - Tie these lessons to selected Longman textbooks.
  - Customize materials to fit with any instructional preference.

- *The English Pages* at ⟨http://www.awlonline.com/englishpages⟩. *The English Pages* website provides instructors and students with continuously updated resources for reading, writing, and research practice in four areas: composition, literature, technical writing, and basic skills. Features include simulated Internet search activities to help students learn the process of finding and evaluating information on the WWW, and annotated links that provide the best information on the widest variety of writing issues and research topics.

PART ONE

An Overview of the Writing Process

The Balloon of the Mind

Hands, do what you're bid:
Bring the balloon of the mind
That bellies and drags in the wind
Into its narrow shed.

—William Butler Yeats

1

Discovering Ideas

All there is to writing is having ideas. To learn to write is to learn to have ideas.

—Robert Frost

To know what you want to draw, you have to begin drawing.

—Picasso

STARTING

How to Write: Writing as a Physical Act

"One takes a piece of paper," William Carlos Williams wrote, "anything, the flat of a shingle, slate, cardboard and with anything handy to the purpose begins to put down the words after the desired expression in mind." Good advice, from a writer who produced novels, plays, articles, book reviews, an autobiography, a voluminous correspondence, and more than twenty-five books of poetry, while raising a family, enjoying a wide circle of friends, and practicing medicine in Rutherford, New Jersey. Not the last word on writing (we have approximately 85,000 of our own to add), but where we would like to begin: "One takes a piece of paper . . . and . . . begins to put down the words. . . ."

Writing is a physical act, like swimming, and like most physical acts, to be performed skillfully, to bring pleasure to both performer and audience, it requires practice. Talent helps. Perhaps few of us are born to become great writers, just as few of us are born to become great swimmers. Nevertheless, we can learn to write, as we can learn to swim, for all practical purposes, including pleasure.

In this book we offer some suggestions, definitions, rules, and examples to help you learn not simply to write, but to write well. We hope they will help you to avoid some of the trials and errors—and the fear of drowning—that sometimes accompany uninstructed practice.

Why Write? Writing as Thinking

In life (as opposed to school), people are motivated by their jobs and other interests to put their ideas in writing. To secure contracts and research funding, scientists and engineers must put their proposals in writing, and then must report, again in writing, the results of their work to their sponsors and colleagues. Parents petition school boards and lawmakers; through prepared talks and newsletters, volunteers reach the communities they serve. In short, anyone who is engaged with ideas or who wants to influence the course of events finds it necessary to convert what Williams called "the desired expression in mind" into words on paper.

As a student, you may not always see a connection between the assignment you receive today and the need you will have several years from now to put your ideas in writing. The rewards of seeing your proposal accepted or of serving your community are probably a bit distant to motivate you to write five hundred words on an assigned topic this week. There is, though, a closer reward. "To be learning something new," said Aristotle, "is ever the chief pleasure of humankind." We believe that. We also believe that writing is not simply a way to express ideas, but a way to discover them.

We emphasize ideas because we are making some assumptions about you: that you are an adult, that you're acquiring an education, either in school or on your own, and that the writing skill you need most help with is not grammar or punctuation—though you may need help with them too—but the expression of ideas in clear and interesting expository essays. We begin, then, with some ideas about ideas.

Some Ideas About Ideas: Invention

Would-be writers have one of two complaints: either "I have the ideas but I don't know how to express them," or "I have nothing to say." When we are faced with a blank page, ideas and even words may elude us. We must actively seek them out. Since classical times the term "invention" has been used to describe the active search for ideas. ("Invention" comes from the Latin word *invenire,* "to come upon," or "to find.") Invention includes activities with which you may already be familiar, such as freewriting, brainstorming, listing, and clustering. A related activity is the practice of keeping a journal. In the following pages we'll briefly describe several invention strategies and provide guidelines for keeping a journal. All of these activities have one step in common: starting to write by writing.

Starting to Write by Writing Suppose your assignment is to choose and respond to a recent editorial. You've chosen one, read it several times, underlined a few key sentences, made a few notes. You have some ideas, but they don't seem connected; you don't know how to begin. Here are five suggestions for getting started.

1. Sit down and start writing. If you have the ideas but don't know how to express them, start writing anyway. Resist the temptation to check your e-mail, to make a cup of soup, to call your mother. Now is *not* the time to do your laundry or to make your bed. Sit down and start putting one word after another.

2. Start with something easy. Start anywhere. Start with what comes to mind first. You might, for example, start by summarizing the editorial you're responding to or by sketching any one of your ideas about it. *Don't think you* *must start with an introductory paragraph;* you can write an introduction later, once your ideas have become better defined. It doesn't matter where you begin, only that you do begin. Start anywhere, and keep going.

3. Try freewriting. Put your hands on the keyboard or pick up a pen and *just start writing.* Forget the rules for a while. Forget about the five-paragraph essay; don't worry about grammar or spelling or punctuation. If you can't think of the right word, write something close to it, or leave a blank space and move on. If you find yourself going in a direction you hadn't anticipated, keep writing anyway. Maybe there's something worth thinking about down the road—you won't know until you get there. If, for example, you're writing about why you disagree with one argument in the editorial, a point on which you agree with the author may occur to you. Fine. Write it down now, while you're thinking of it. You can organize your points of agreement and disagreement later. But if you reach what appears to be a dead end, simply move on, or start again someplace else. You are writing to discover what you think, and it's a good idea to work as quickly as you can. (Take Satchel Paige's advice: Don't look back; something might be gaining on you.)

4. Plan to stop writing. Give yourself a time limit. If you tend to procrastinate (many writers do), try keeping your first sessions short. Promise yourself that you'll stop working after twenty minutes—or thirty, or fifteen—and *keep that promise*. If at the start you limit your writing sessions, you accomplish two things. You reduce anxiety: the thought of working at your desk for twenty minutes is not nearly as daunting as the thought of writing four or five pages. And after twenty minutes you'll have *something* down on paper. You can gradually increase the length of the sessions—to an hour, or three, or whatever is reasonable, given the assignment and your schedule. Of course, you can follow this advice only if you have started to work on an assignment reasonably soon after receiving it—but setting a time limit for the initial stages of writing will help you to get an early start.

5. Revise later. After a few false starts (and probably more than one session), your ideas will begin to take form on the page. But don't expect them to appear at this early stage in final form, beautifully organized and in polished sentences. Ideas rarely exist that way in one's mind. In fact, until we put them into words, ideas are usually only rough impressions or images, not clear thoughts at all. (As E. M. Forster wrote, "How do I know what I think until I see what I say?") Once you do get some ideas down on paper, you can begin to see which ones must be developed or deleted, where connections need to be made, where details and examples need to be added. At this stage, you may be close to having a first draft. Whether or not you like what you've written (your response probably depends more on your temperament than on your actual accomplishment), take a rest from it. Do something else: make your bed, or if you like, just climb into it.

Listing Listing is a way to discover ideas or to pin them down by writing. Like freewriting (which we discuss above), and like the other invention exercises we discuss below, listing may help those who believe they have nothing to say. The process is something like making a shopping list. You write down "soap" and are immediately reminded that you also must pick up some laundry. Similarly, if you plan to argue for a course of action, listing one reason for it may bring others to mind.

Listing is especially useful when you are making a comparison—of two figures in a photograph, for example, or two characters in a story, or two positions on an issue. Start writing by listing the similarities, and then list the differences. Or, start writing both lists at once, making brief entries, as they occur to you, in parallel columns.

Listing can help you discover and develop ideas; it can also help you to find a topic to write about. Suppose, for example, you have been assigned to write an essay on a form of popular culture that interests you. You can begin simply by listing some of the first forms of popular culture that occur to you as you think about the subject:

Popular Culture

movies, sci-fi, sci-fi movies?

TV movies, detective serials

soap operas (why are they called operas? Why <u>soap</u> operas?)

music videos

cop shows--<u>NYPD Blue, Homicide</u>

male/female detectives

the blues

But having written "the blues" above, you begin to think of the words to a song:

When a woman takes the blues
She tucks her head and cries
But when a man catches the blues
He catches a freight and rides

By the time you have written these lyrics out from memory, you have pretty much decided that you'll write on the blues. You're interested in the blues and already know something about them; you have some CDs and tapes at hand; and an idea for an essay is beginning to form:

"He catches a freight and rides . . ."

Why all this talk of traveling? (It's worth remembering that an unanswered question is an essay topic in disguise.) You begin to search your memory, perhaps you play some tapes, maybe take some notes. The blues are full of travel, you find, but of different kinds. You begin, once again, to make a list, to jot down words or phrases:

disappointed lover	back to the South
travel to a job	life is a trip
from the South	jail
fantasy travel	

Your new list provides more than a topic; you are now several steps closer to a draft of an essay that you think you may be able to write, on the reason for (or meaning of?) travel in the blues.

Clustering Clustering (or **mapping**) is similar to listing, though it takes a different visual form. Sometimes ideas don't seem to line up vertically, one after another. Instead, they seem to form a cluster, with one idea or word related to a group of several others. It may be useful then to start by putting a key word or phrase (let's stay with TRAVEL IN THE BLUES) in a circle in the center of a page, and then jotting down other words as they occur, encircling them and connecting them appropriately. A map or cluster might look like the diagram shown here.

If you start writing by putting down words that occur to you in a schematic way—in a map or cluster—it may help you to visualize the relationship between ideas. The visualization may also prompt still other ideas and the connections between them.

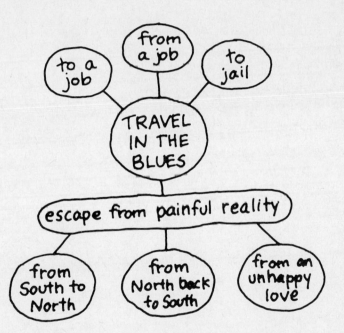

Asking Questions (and Answering Them) Almost the first thing a journalist learns to do in getting a story is to ask six questions:

- who?
- what?
- when?
- where?
- why?
- how?

If you borrow this approach, asking yourself questions and answering them, you will often find that you can get a start on a writing project. The questions that journalists ask are appropriate to their task: to report what happened, who made it happen, how it happened, and so on. Learning to write academic essays is largely learning to ask—and to answer—questions appropriate to academic disciplines.

In analyzing a painting or a sculpture, for example, an art historian might answer certain basic questions:

- When, where, and by whom was the work made?
- Where would the work originally have been seen?
- What purpose did the work serve?
- In what condition has the work survived?

and then, depending on the work, more detailed questions. If, for example, the work is a landscape painting, the following questions might be appropriate:

- What is the relation between human beings and nature?
- What does the medium (oil paint or watercolor, for instance) contribute?
- What is the effect of light in the picture?
- What is the focus of the composition?
- How does the artist convey depth?

Similarly, a social scientist writing a review of research on a topic might ask about each study under review:

- What major question is posed in this study?
- What is its chief method of investigation?
- What mode of observation was employed?
- How is the sample of observations defined?

Students in all disciplines—art history and social science are given here only as examples—learn what questions matter by listening to lectures, participating in class discussions, and reading assigned books and articles. The questions differ from discipline to discipline, as the list above suggests, but the process—of asking and answering the questions that matter—is common to all of them.

An Exercise in Critical Reading: Philip Roth, "Reflections on the Death of a Library"

In a writing course, the subject is writing—not art history, sociology, or anything else. Nevertheless, writing assignments, like the assignments in other disciplines, are designed to give students practice in critical reading, that is, practice in such skills as summarizing, analyzing, and evaluating written texts. We explain these skills in some detail in several places in this text. Here by way of introduction, we take you through a brief exercise in discovering ideas about a text *by asking questions and answering them*—an exercise that combines invention and critical reading.

First read the following article from *The New York Times*. The author, Philip Roth, was born in Newark, New Jersey, in 1933. Although Roth is primarily known as a novelist, he also writes occasional essays. (We have numbered the paragraphs to facilitate reference to them.)

 **PHILIP ROTH[1]**

Reflections on the Death of a Library

1   What will the readers of Newark do if the City Council goes ahead with its money-saving plan to shut down the public library system on April 1? Will they loot the stacks as Newarkers looted furniture and appliance stores in the riot of 1967? Will police be called in to Mace down thieves racing off with the *Encyclopaedia Britannica?* Will scholars take up sniping positions at reference room windows and school children "seize" the main Washington Street building in order to complete their term papers? If the City Council locks up the books, will library card holders band together to "liberate" them?

2   I suppose one should hope not. Apparently there must be respect for Law and Order, even where there is none for aspiration and curiosity and quiet pleasure, for language, learning, scholarship, intelligence, reason, wit, beauty, and knowledge.

3   When I was growing up in Newark in the forties we assumed that the books in the public library belonged to the public. Since my family did not own many books, or have much money for a child to buy them, it was good to know that solely by virtue of my municipal citizenship I had access to any book I wanted from that grandly austere building downtown on Washington Street, or from the branch library I could walk to in my neighborhood. No less satisfying was the idea of communal ownership, property held in common for the common good. Why I had to care for the books I borrowed, return them unscarred and on time, was because they weren't mine alone, they were everybody's. That idea had as much to do with civilizing me as any I was ever to come upon in the books themselves.

4   If the idea of a *public* library was civilizing so was the place, with its comforting quiet, its tidy shelves, its knowledgeable, dutiful employees who weren't teachers. The library wasn't simply where one had to go to get the books, it was a kind of exacting haven to which a city youngster willingly went for his lesson in restraint and his training in self-control. And then there was the lesson in

[1]In February 1969, after riots had already destroyed much of Newark's black slum neighborhoods, the Newark City Council voted to strike from the city budget the $2.8 million required to finance the Newark Museum and the Newark Public Library. Hundreds of Newark residents vehemently opposed this move, which would have shut down two exceptional civic institutions. In the face of the protest, the Council eventually rescinded their decision. This article appeared on the editorial page of *The New York Times,* March 1, 1969, about two weeks after the Council had announced the budget cutback [Roth's note].

order, the enormous institution itself serving as instructor. What trust it inspired—in both oneself and in systems—first to decode the catalogue card, then
to make it through the corridors and stairwells into the open stacks, and there to
discover, exactly where it was supposed to be, the desired book. For a ten-year-
old to find he actually can steer himself through tens of thousands of volumes to
the very one he wants is not without its satisfactions. Nor did it count for nothing to carry a library card in one's pocket; to pay a fine if need be; to sit in a
strange place, beyond the reach of parent and school, and read whatever one
chose, in anonymity and peace; finally, to carry home across the city and even
into bed at night a book with a local lineage of its own, a family-tree of Newark
readers to which one's name had now been added.

5   In the forties, when Newark was mostly white and I was being raised there,
it was simply an unassailable fact of life that the books were "ours" and that the
public library had much to teach us about the rules of civilized life, as well as civilized pleasures to offer. It is strange, to put it politely, that now when Newark is
mostly black, the City Council (for fiscal reasons, we are told) has reached a decision that suggests that the books don't really belong to the public after all, and
that the lessons and pleasures a library provides for the young are no longer essential to an education. In a city seething with social grievances there is, in fact,
probably little that could be *more* essential to the development and sanity of the
thoughtful and ambitious young than access to those libraries and books. For the
moment the Newark City Council may, to be sure, have solved a fiscal problem:
it is too bad, however, that they are unable to calculate the frustration, cynicism,
and rage that such an insult must inevitably generate, or to imagine what shutting down the libraries may cost the community in the end.

 ## Questions

Now answer the following questions.

1. a. What was the occasion for this article?
    b. What was Roth's response?
2. a. How does Roth support his position in paragraph 3? Why does he
        mention his childhood?
    b. What are the two main reasons he gives in paragraph 3 in support of
        his position?
3. What does Roth mean by "civilizing" in paragraphs 3 and 4?
4. In paragraph 5, what new reasons does he state or imply in support of his
    position?
5. How does he engage our interest in his first two paragraphs? How does
    he enlist our support for his point of view?
6. Optional: How successful is he?

If you were to write out your answers and then to review and revise them a
bit, you would probably have a draft of an essay something like the student's
essay that follows. (Numbers in parentheses refer to the questions.)

On Philip Roth's "Reflections"

The City Council of Newark introduced a plan to shut down the public library system in order to save money. (la) Philip Roth in his article (The New York Times, March 1, 1969) argues that the closing of the libraries will be a costly mistake, and that the action will be an insult to the citizens of Newark. (1b)

He supports his position by telling how the library helped him when he was young. (2a) He says that the public library gave him a chance to use books that his family couldn't afford, but more important, the very idea of a public library, of the communal ownership of books, played a part in civilizing him. (2b) By civilizing Roth means socializing. The quiet and orderly fashion in which the library was arranged and run taught him restraint, and taught him to value solitude, privacy, and self-control. Looking for books was itself a lesson in order: he learned, for example, that he could find, through the card catalog, one book among the many thousands there. (3)

Roth suggests that since Newark has become predominantly black, the City Council's attitude toward the library's functions and importance has changed. He implies that the Council's plan is irresponsible and discriminatory. He points out that in a city with as many social problems as Newark's the lessons and pleasures given to the young by the library are more, not less, essential to their education. He says that although the Council's move may solve an immediate fiscal problem, it will in the end create greater social problems because of the frustration and rage it will generate. (4)

He questions what the readers might do if the library is shut down. He hypothesizes that they might riot and loot the library, or they might seize the library and liberate the books. His questions are, of course, ironic. By overdramatizing the possible reactions, he gains the interest of the reader, and he shows the senselessness of the Council's plan. Through

sarcasm, he discloses a further irony: the City Council, whose members are

the first to insist on respect for law and order, have no respect themselves

for communal as opposed to private property, or for the civilized qualities

law and order should foster and support: beauty, knowledge, pleasure,

aspiration. (5)

To develop ideas about a text, then, become a critical reader of it by asking questions and answering them. Approach it, especially on rereading it, asking such questions as:

- Who wrote this?
- When was it written?
- Why and for what audience was it written?
- What point or argument does the author make?
- How does the author make it?
- How successful (believable, interesting, persuasive) do I find it?

Keeping a Journal

Writing daily in a journal helps writers to remain fluent. As we said at the start, writing is a physical act, and to keep in trim, you should practice daily—or as close to daily as you can manage. Many writers also keep journals both to stimulate ideas and to record ideas for future use. We recommend that you keep a journal, and that you use it to record your responses—however vague or fleeting—to the things you're reading and writing about in your courses. Rereading such journal entries can be a good way to get started on a new project.

Guidelines

1. Where to write: Your instructor may ask you to write in a loose-leaf notebook—so that you can turn in pages occasionally, and your instructor won't have to stagger home with twenty or thirty notebooks. If you keep a journal strictly for your own use, write with whatever materials feel comfortable: pen, pencil, computer; loose sheets, bound notebook, or whatever. (Dr. William Carlos Williams often wrote poems on prescription blanks.)

2. When to write: Any time; ten to fifteen minutes a day if possible. Some people find it helpful to establish a regular time for writing, just before they go to sleep, for example. Habits can be helpful; but not all of us can or should lead well-regulated lives. Writing for a minute or two several times a day may work best for you.

3. How long is an entry? An entry may be a few words, a line or two, a few pages. There's no special length, but do keep writing until you've put into words at least one thought or observation or question.

4. Form. Date each entry but then write freely. Don't correct or revise. Don't worry about spelling, vocabulary, punctuation. Use whatever language,

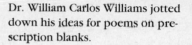

Phone: RUtherford 2-0669   Reg. No. 3810
WILLIAM C. WILLIAMS, M. D.
9 Ridge Road   Rutherford, N. J.
Office Hours: 1 to 2 P.M. Except Friday
Evenings 7 to 8 P.M., Monday and Thursday

Name _____ *Age* ____

Address _____ *Date* _____

Dr. William Carlos Williams jotted down his ideas for poems on prescription blanks.

idiom, voice you wish. It's a good way to keep in touch with yourself and with the friends and family you've temporarily left. (You *can* go home again.)

5. As for content, write about anything that comes to mind. You can think of your journal as a record of your life now, which you might read with pleasure some years from now when many of the rich details of your daily experience would otherwise be forgotten. Write down your thoughts, feelings, impressions, responses, dreams, memories. May Sarton once said, "The senses are the keys to the past." If you have a strong sensory memory of something—the mixed smell of saltwater, sand, and machinery oil, for example—try to describe it in words, and then to track it down. You may find a buried scene from your childhood that you can rescue from your memory by a train of associations. If you keep tracking, and writing, you may discover why that scene is important. Likewise, if you have a strong response to something you're reading—anger, perhaps, or confusion, try to explain it, to get it down on paper. Doing so may help you begin to develop an idea for an essay.

Examples: Journal Entries by Students

1. It is difficult to believe that not understanding a physics problem isn't the worst problem in the world.

2. 9/20 Lab was a trip today. Right before my eyes, I observed an egg cell being invaded by an army of sperm cells. Think of it. That's how I began. I used to be a nothing, and now I'm something, an "I." (I was only looking at a sea urchin's egg, but that sure beats not looking at a sea urchin's egg.)

3. Intro to Women's Studies upset me today. We talked about the role of women in religion. We discussed how feminist theologians (thealogians?) believe that God is not necessarily a man but could be a woman. Their argument is that the Bible was translated and interpreted by men for their own purposes. They wanted to utilize the Bible to give women a subordinate role to men. I do believe that, or at least I think all this is worth questioning. But it's hard for me--no, sad--to think of God as a woman when I have grown to love him as a man, a father.

4. "Teruko-san! How come you don't understand what I am saying to you!! How come you are repeating these errors so many times!! One! Two! Three! Go!!" My arms, hands, fingers and even my brain are frozen. Tears are running down my cheek. My both hands are sitting on the keyboard frighteningly. Silence. I hear my heart, beating thump thump thump. With a deep sigh, Mrs. Ikebuchi closes the page of a score which is blackened with fingering numbers, circles and crosses. Without saying any words, she leaves the room, and goes to the kitchen. The lesson is over. I sigh and wipe off my tears with the back of my hands, pick up the scores, go to the living room and sit on the tatami-floor stiffly. "By the way Teruko-san, did you see my gardenia? It is so beautiful! Come! come and see it!" She comes out from the kitchen with a big round black lacquer tray with tea and cookies on it. She puts the tray on the table and walks out to the garden to the gardenia bush. "Isn't this pretty?" "Yes." "Isn't this a nice smell?" "Yes." Mrs. Ikebuchi walks back to the living room and I follow her three steps behind and sit on the tatami-floor stiffly again. Mrs. Ikebuchi pours tea and asks me merrily, "How much sugar do you want? how much cream do you want? which cookie do you want? rabbit? elephant? or duck?" I answer politely, "two sugars, please? (it is cube sugar), that's enough, thank you (for cream). May I have a rabbit?" "Oh you like the rabbit! Good! By the way do you know the story about the rabbit? Ah--what was it? Ah, Peter Rabbit!" Her story is going on and on and on. Meanwhile I finish my tea and cookie. "Well, Teruko-san, see you next Monday." I stand up, my legs are numb from sitting on the tatami-floor, and start to walk slowly, my toes are tickling. I pick up my scores and bow and say "Thank you very much." Walk out the sliding door. Release! I skip home.

5. A belief I had when I was small: For some reason I thought every person was allowed only a certain number of words per lifetime. Of course, at that time in my life I was quiet, except when I was mad and all reason left me.

6. Anticipating something is like falling off a cliff and never reaching the bottom.

7. "Civilizing." That word bugs me. Roth says that the public library "civilized him." I wonder about this. Was he UNcivilized before he started going there? (Not likely, I think.) Just who is

this argument supposed to persuade--and of what? Isn't he just playing into whites' fears about African Americans? Maybe not. I'll have to think more about this.

FOCUSING

What to Write About: Subject, Topic, Thesis

If you're taking a course in composition, you will probably receive assignments to write on something you are reading or on something out of your personal experience, which may include your experience of books. In other courses, it's usually up to you to choose a *subject* from those covered in the course, to focus on a *topic* within the subject, and to narrow the topic by formulating a *thesis*. Any assignment requires you to narrow the subject so that you can treat it thoroughly in the allotted space and time. Therefore you write not on *Time* magazine, but on the political bias of *Time*, or on a comparison of *Time* and *Newsweek*, based on one or two issues of each, arguing for the superiority of one over the other; not on political primaries (a subject), but on a specific proposal to abolish them (a topic); not on penguins (a subject), but on the male penguin's role in hatching (a topic). A good general rule in finding a topic is to follow your inclinations: focus on something about the subject that interests you.

Suppose your assignment is to read the Book of Ruth in the Hebrew Bible and to write an essay of 500 to 1000 words on it. If you start with a topic like "The Book of Ruth: A Charming Tale" you're in trouble. The topic is much too vague. In writing about it you'll find yourself hopping around from one place in the book to another, and in desperation saying things like "The Book of Ruth is probably one of the most charming tales in all literature," when you haven't read all literature, and couldn't define *charm* precisely, if your life depended on it.

What to do? Focus on something that interested you about the book. (If you read the book with pencil in hand, taking some notes, underlining some passages, putting question marks at others, you'll have some good clues to start with.) The book is named after Ruth, but perhaps you find Naomi the more interesting character. If so, you might jot down: "Although the Book of Ruth is named after Ruth, I find the character of Naomi more interesting."

Stuck again? Ask yourself some questions. *Why* do you find her more interesting? To answer that question, reread the book, focusing your attention on all the passages in which Naomi acts or speaks or is spoken of by others. Ruth's actions, you may find, are always clearly motivated by her love for Naomi. But Naomi's actions are more complex, more puzzling. If you're puzzled, trust your feeling—*there is something puzzling there. What* motivated Naomi? Convert your question to "Naomi's Motivation" and you have a *topic*.

With this topic in mind, if you explore Naomi's actions one by one you may conclude that "Although Naomi shows in many of her actions her concern for her daughter-in-law, her actions also reveal self-interest." Now you have a *thesis*, that is, a brief statement of your main point. It's a bit awkwardly worded but you can work on a smoother, more natural expression later.

"Naomi's Motivation" is a topic in literary criticism, but if your special interest is, for example, economics, or sociology, or law, your topic might be one of these:

Economic Motivation in the Book of Ruth

Attitudes toward Intermarriage in the Book of Ruth

The Status of Women in the Book of Ruth

Any one of these topics can be managed in 500 to 1000 words. But remember, you were assigned to write on the Book of Ruth. Formulate a thesis with evidence from that book. Suppress the impulse to put everything you know about economics or intermarriage or the-status-of-women-through-the-ages in between two thin slices, an opening sentence and a concluding sentence, on the Book of Ruth.

Let's take another example. Suppose that in a course on Modern Revolutionary Movements you're assigned a term paper on any subject covered by the readings or lectures. A term paper is usually about three thousand words and requires research. You're interested in Mexican history, and after a preliminary search you decide to focus on the Revolution of 1910 or some events leading up to it. Depending on what is available in your library, you might narrow your topic to one of these:

Mexican Bandits—The First Twentieth Century Revolutionists

The Exploits of Joaquin Murieta and Tiburcio Vasquez—Romantic Legend and Fact

In short, it is not enough to have a subject (the Book of Ruth, revolutions); you must concentrate your vision on a topic, a significant part of the field, just as a landscape painter or photographer selects a portion of the landscape and then focuses on it. Your interests are your most trustworthy guides to the portion of the landscape on which to focus.

As you think about your topic and information relating to it, try to formulate a *tentative* or working thesis. Think of your tentative sentence—which may not appear in your final paper—as a working hypothesis, a proposition to be proved, disproved, or revised in light of information you discover.

Naomi's character is more interesting than Ruth's.

Murieta and Vasquez were in the vanguard of a revolution.

Your "working thesis" will help you to maintain your focus, to keep in mind the points that you must support with evidence: quotations, facts, statistics, reasons, descriptions, and illustrative anecdotes. But be prepared to modify your working thesis, perhaps more than once, and perhaps substantially. Once you begin amassing evidence and arguments, you may find that they support a different thesis. Your best ideas on your topic may turn out to be radically different from the ideas with which you began. As we pointed out earlier, writing is not simply a way to express ideas you already have, it is also a way to discover them.

Although essays based on substantial research almost always include an explicit thesis sentence in the finished essay, short essays based on personal experience often do not. An essay recounting a writer's experience of racism, for example, or conveying the particular atmosphere of a neighborhood, is likely to have a central idea or focus, a *thesis idea*, rather than a *thesis sentence*. But whether stated or implied, the thesis idea must be developed (explained, supported, or proved) by evidence presented in the body of the essay. The kind of evidence will vary, of course, not only with your topic but also with your audience and purpose.

DEVELOPING IDEAS

Materials that writers use to develop ideas, to explain and support a thesis, are largely by-products of the reading, note-taking, freewriting, questioning, and remembering that are part of the writing process from beginning to end. Materials for developing an essay on Naomi's motivation will be passages from the Book of Ruth, brief quotations that the writer introduces and explains. Similarly, materials for an essay on the blues will be quotations from a thoughtful selection of lyrics. An essay on a memorable experience, one that led to an interesting idea, will rely on the writer's memory of that experience, examined with a reader in mind. In all of these instances, in fact, imagining a reader helps a writer develop ideas.

Thinking About Audience and Purpose

Thinking about your audience, about what you want your readers to understand and believe, is central to the revision process. You read over a draft you have written to see if it will be clear and interesting to someone else, to someone who is not you, who does not know what you know, and does not necessarily share your beliefs. If you use a technical term, will a likely reader understand it? Should you define the term, or can you substitute a more familiar word? Have you identified the source of a quotation? And is it clear why you are using the quotation at this point in your essay? Are the paragraphs arranged in a clear sequence? Have you provided effective transitions? And so on. Reading your draft (preferably aloud), imagining an audience, you can often spot unclear patches, and then revise them. Reading your draft to an actual audience, a friend or classmate, is even better.

But thinking about audience and purpose can be helpful at earlier stages of writing too, when you are trying to develop an idea and to work up evidence to support it. If you are uncertain how to begin, or if, on the other hand, you are overwhelmed by the materials you have unearthed and don't know how to sort them out, try asking yourself these questions:

- Who are my readers?
- What do they need to know?
- What do I want them to believe?

When you ask, "Who is my reader?" the obvious answer—the teacher who assigned the essay—is, paradoxically, the least helpful. To learn to write well, you'll have to force that fact out of your mind, pretend it isn't true, or you're likely to feel defeated from the beginning. Write instead for someone who understands your material less well than you. Remember: *When you write, you are the teacher*. It's probably easier to assume the role of the teacher if you imagine your reader to be someone in your class, that is, someone intelligent and reasonably well informed who shares some of your interests but who does not happen to be you, and who therefore can't know your thoughts unless you organize them and explain them clearly and thoroughly.

Writing from Experience:
Two Essays by Students

Let's look at two essays, each written by a student during the first week of the semester in a composition course. Both students were asked to write from their own experience; the assignment was to describe or explain something they knew well to others who were unfamiliar with it. Perhaps you're familiar with such an assignment. You try to think of something interesting you've done, but you've led a most unremarkable life. Your classmates, all strangers, seem to know more than you do about almost everything. They've all been to France or Mexico or Hong Kong—well, some of them. All you did last summer was file cards and run errands in an office full of boring people. Here is the first student's essay, on, as it happens, a boring job.

Example 1

A Lesson

As I look back at it, my first thought is that my job was a waste of time. It consisted of compiling information from the files of the Water and Assessor's Department in a form suitable for putting on the city's computer. Supposedly this would bring the water billing and property taxing to an efficient level. If the job sounds interesting, don't be deceived. After the first week of work, I seriously doubted that I would survive through the summer.

But I was able to salvage a lesson in the self-discipline of coping with people. Of course we all know how to succeed with friends, family, acquaintances, and employers. But try it in a situation where you have a distinct disadvantage, where you are the seller and they are the customers. And remember, the customer is always right.

By observing the situation, though I was not a participant, I learned that patience, kindness, and understanding can remove the difficulties you cross at the time.

Not a bad topic, really. One can learn something valuable from a boring, menial, frustrating job. Or if not, one can examine boredom (what exactly is it? is it the same as impatience? how does it come about? how does it feel?) and write about it without boring the reader. But this essay doesn't teach us anything about boredom. It doesn't allow us through concrete, specific details to feel with the writer that we too would have doubted we could survive the summer. Instead, it offers generalizations such as "compiling information from our files" and "a form suitable for putting on the city's computer," which give us no sense of the tedium of daily transferring numbers from 500 manila index cards to 500 gray index cards. In fact, the essay gives us almost no sense of the job. The second paragraph ends with the words "the customer is always right," but nothing in the essay suggests that the writer (whose work "consisted of compiling information from the files") had any contact with customers. We really don't know what she did. Nor does the essay present any evidence that the experience was redeemed by a lesson in "patience, kindness, and understanding."

As it turns out, there was no such lesson. In class discussion, the student admitted that the job was a waste of time. She had, out of habit, tried to come up with some pious thought to please the instructor. The habit had short-circuited the connection between the student's feelings and the words she was writing. The class discussion led to some genuinely interesting questions. Why, for example, are we reluctant to admit that something we've done was a waste of time? "The job was a waste of time" would have been, for most of us, a more productive thesis than "I was able to salvage a lesson." What experiences lead to the conclusions: I must write what the instructor expects; the instructor expects a pious thought? (We'd like to hear from a student willing to explore that topic in 500 to 1000 words.)

The class discussion, as we said, revealed the student's real attitude toward her job. The questions that, as readers, the class asked also provided a focus for the writer, which helped her to formulate a more productive thesis. It's helpful to imagine such a discussion with real readers in the early stages of writing as you grope for what you have to say. For although it would be tidy if writers could simply, and in the following order, (1) choose a subject, (2) focus on a topic, (3) formulate a thesis, (4) support the thesis in the body of the essay, things don't often work out that way. More commonly, writers discover their topic, formulate their thesis and develop support for their thesis in the act of writing and revising, in asking questions and in answering them, in discarding the answers, or even the questions, and starting again.

Now look at the second essay, again on a common experience. Ask yourself as you read it, or reread it, what makes it uncommonly interesting.

Example 2

Dedication Doth Not a Good Teacher Make

The worst teacher I ever had was a brilliant and charming man. Fergy (it was short for Mr. Ferguson) had written the textbook we used for Chemistry. He had designed his house and built it himself, getting professional help only for the electricity and plumbing. He could remember the scores of all the football games he'd seen, and the names of the players on each team. He never kept lists--"Lists rot the memory," he said--so he memorized which type of lab implement he kept in which of fifty drawers, and he could tell you instantly, without pause. Sometimes we would ask him where a certain type of obscure bottle could be found just to test him, but he never failed. "Middle left-hand drawer in Lab Station Six," would say old Fergy, and in that middle left-hand drawer it would be. I never knew him to forget a name, a face, or a formula, either.

That, I think, was his failing as a teacher. Because he had no trouble grasping or recalling a concept, he had trouble in understanding how we could. The one thing his extraordinary mind seemed unable to comprehend was that it was extraordinary, that not everyone could think as completely and as easily as he. If the class had questions he would try to answer them, but he tended to complicate and expand on ideas, rather than to simplify them. He could not believe that we needed not expansion but explanation, with the result that we soon learned not to ask too many questions for fear of extra material to learn. And it did become a fear of learning, because, try as we would, we somehow never managed to pin down concepts like electron shells and the wave theory of gravitation, but we would still have to answer for them on tests--and, ultimately, at home. (I never decided which was worse, knowing that once again I had made a complete fool of myself by taking a chem test, or having to listen to my parents sigh and claim that I could have done better if I'd tried.)

Fergy would have been horrified to know that he had this discouraging effect on us. He loved us and he loved teaching and he loved chemistry. He was always available for outside help, not only for chemistry, but for any problem, whether in English or your social life. He tried to make class interesting by telling little anecdotes and playing with the chemicals. Actually, he was funny, and interesting, and charming, and he kept us hoping that we'd understand chem so that he would approve of us and so we could relax and enjoy him. But although he is one of the best people it has been my good fortune to have known, he never did manage to teach me a lick of chemistry.

As you study this book, you'll frequently find questions following examples of writing. Critical reading and writing are closely intertwined. If you practice asking and answering questions as you read, as well as when you write, the skills you develop will reinforce each other. Try answering the following questions on "Dedication Doth Not a Good Teacher Make":

- What is the writer's thesis?
- How does she support the thesis?
- If you found the essay interesting, what makes it interesting?
- If you found it convincing, what makes it convincing?

The Groucho Marx Complex Clearly—examining these essays should make it clear—there is no such thing as an uninteresting life, or moment in life. There are only uninteresting ways to talk about them. It's also clear that some people are more interested in introspection and in talking and writing about their personal experiences than others. The others may be suffering from the Groucho Marx Complex: as Groucho put it, "I don't want to belong to any club that would have me as a member." Students who freeze at the notion of writing about themselves often feel that everything they have done is so ordinary, no one else could possibly be interested in it; anything they know is so obvious, everyone else must know it already. If this is your problem, remember that no one else knows exactly what you know; no one else can know what it feels like to live inside your skin. If you work at summoning up from your memory concrete and specific details, you can turn the most ordinary experience into a first-rate essay.

Remember too that writing from your own experience does not necessarily mean writing about private experience. We all have areas of experience we'd rather keep private, and we have a right to remain private about them. The important thing in writing about experience is, as Marianne Moore said, that "we must be as clear as our natural reticence allows us to be." Think, then, of experiences that you are willing to share and to be clear about. If, for example, you have just learned in a psychology course what "operant conditioning" means, define it for someone unfamiliar with the term. You might find yourself narrating an experience of your own to exemplify it; to be clear, you will have to provide an example. Or if an object in a local museum or craft exhibit or store interests you, ask yourself a question—why do I like it?—and you'll probably be able to turn an object into an experience. You'll also be turning an experience into an object—an essay—that will interest your readers.

Writing academic papers usually requires examining and evaluating texts and other evidence beyond your personal experience or previous knowledge. Nevertheless, you still must trust your own ideas. Trusting your own ideas does not, of course, mean being satisfied with the first thought that pops into your head. Rather, it means respecting your ideas enough to examine them thoughtfully; it means testing, refining, and sometimes changing them. But it is always your reading of a text, your conduct of an experiment, your understanding of an issue that your essay attempts to communicate.

AN OVERVIEW: FROM SUBJECT TO ESSAY

We each must work out our own procedures and rituals (John C. Calhoun liked to plow his farm before writing), but the following suggestions may help. The rest of the book will give you more detailed advice.

1. If a topic is assigned, write on it; if a topic is not assigned, turn a subject into a topic. Get an early start, preferably the day you receive the assignment. Do this by employing any or all of the strategies—freewriting, listing, clustering, asking questions, keeping a journal—that we have discussed. When you look over your jottings, note what especially interests you, and decide what topic you can sensibly discuss in the assigned length. Unfortunately, few of us can in a few pages write anything of interest on a large subject. We simply cannot in 500 words say anything readable (that is, true and interesting to others) on subjects as broad as music, sports, ourselves. Given such subjects, we have nothing to say, probably because we are desperately trying to remember what we have heard other people say. Trying to remember blocks our efforts to look hard and to think. To get going, we must narrow such subjects down to specific topics: from music to country music, from sports to commercialization of athletics, from ourselves to a term with a roommate.

2. Get a focus. Once you have turned a subject into a topic, you need to shape the topic by seeing it in a particular focus, by having a thesis, an attitude, *a point*:

Country music is popular because . . . ;

College athletes are exploited because . . . ;

Problems between roommates can be avoided if . . .

Probably you won't find your exact focus or thesis immediately, but you can begin to refine your thinking by *asking some questions* about your topic. For example:

Why is country music popular?

What kind of people like it?

Why are some performers more successful than others?

If you ask yourself questions now, you may be able to answer them a day or two later. And you'll likely find that reading what you have jotted down leads to something else—something that wouldn't have occurred to you if you hadn't written down the first thing. Few of us have good ideas about a topic at the start, but as we put our ideas into words, better ideas may begin to emerge.

Keeping your audience and your purpose in mind will help too. If, for example, you're writing about country music to interest a reader who doesn't listen to it, you will begin to find things that you must say.

3. Turn your reveries into notes. Put aside, for a day or two, what you've written so far (assuming you have a week to do the essay), but be prepared to add to it. Useful thoughts—not only ideas, but details—may come to you while you are at lunch, while you read a newspaper or magazine, while your mind wanders in your other classes. Write down these thoughts—in your journal, perhaps—don't assume that you will remember them when you come to draft your essay.

   4. Sort things out. About two days before the essay is due, look over what you've written so far, and see if you can discover a workable thesis. This might be a good moment to practice free writing on your topic, or to arrange your notes into what looks like a reasonable sequence. To help keep your thesis in focus, give your essay a provisional title. Don't be afraid to be obvious. If you look back at some of the titles of sections in this book, you will see such things as

   "Why Write?"

   "Starting to Write by Writing," and

   "Developing Ideas."

Simple as they are, these titles helped to keep us focused as we drafted and revised the chapter. And they tell you something about the topic at hand. Sometimes wordplay produces an attractive but still informative title—for example, a student's "If You Have *Time,* read *Newsweek.*"

   5. Write. Even if you're unsure that you have a thesis and an organization, start writing. Don't delay. You've already begun to capture and organize some of your ideas, and you have a mind that, however casually, has already been thinking. Don't worry about writing an effective opening paragraph (your opening paragraph will almost surely have to be revised later anyway); just try to state and develop your point, based on the phrases or sentences you have accumulated, adding all of the new details that flow to mind as you write. If you get stuck, *ask yourself questions.*

   Have I supported my assertions with examples?

   Will a comparison help to clarify the point?

   Which quotation best illustrates this point?

Keep going until you have nothing left to say.

   6. Save what you can. Immediately after writing the draft, or a few hours later, look it over to see how much you can salvage. Don't worry about getting the exact word here or there; just see whether or not you have a thesis, whether or not you keep the thesis in view, and whether or not the points flow reasonably. Delete irrelevant paragraphs, however interesting (you can save them in a separate file if you can't bear to throw them away); move paragraphs that are relevant but that should be somewhere else. Don't assume that tomorrow you will be able to remember that the paragraph near the bottom of page 3 will go into the middle of page 2. Move the block, now, so that when you next read the essay you will easily be able to tell whether in fact the paragraph does belong in the middle of page 2. Finally, settle on a title. Then put the draft aside until tomorrow.

   7. Revise. Reread your draft, first with an eye toward large matters. Revise your opening paragraph or write one to provide the reader with a focus; make sure each paragraph grows out of the previous one, and make sure you keep the thesis in view. Remember, *when you write, you are the teacher.* As you revise, make sure that assertions are supported by evidence; try to imagine a reader (the person who sits next to you in class, perhaps), and let this imagined reader tell you where you get off the point, where you are illogical, where you need an example—in short, where you are in any way confusing.

Next, after making the necessary large revisions, read the draft with an eye toward smaller matters: make sure that each sentence is clear and readable. (You can do this only by reading slowly—preferably aloud, unless you have developed the ability to hear each sentence, each word, in the mind's ear.) Let's say that in telling a reader how to handle disks for a word processor, you have written, "When you write the label for the disk, use a felt pen." You notice, in revising, that the reader may wonder *why* a pencil or a ball-point pen should not be used, and so you'll alter the sentence to "Because the pressure of a pencil or a ball-point pen can damage the surface of the disk, label the disk with a felt pen."

Cross out extra words; recast unclear sentences. Keep pushing the words, the sentences, the paragraphs into shape until they say what you want them to say from the title onward. (This contest between writers and their words is part of what Muhammad Ali had in mind when he said, referring to his work on his autobiography, "Writing is fighting.") Correct anything that disturbs you—for instance, awkward repetitions that grate.

8. Edit. When your draft is as good as you can make it, take care of the mechanical matters: spell-check your document, double-checking in a dictionary if you have any doubts about a particular word; if you are unsure about a matter of punctuation, check it in this book. You will also find instructions about such things as title placement and margin size in Chapter 21, "Manuscript Form." And be sure to acknowledge the sources not only of quotations but also of any ideas that you borrowed, even though you summarized or paraphrased them in your own words. (On plagiarism, see pages 318–21.)

9. Prepare the final copy. If you are on schedule, you will be doing this a day before the essay is due. But wait a few hours before you proofread it, because right now you are too close to your essay. If you put the essay aside for a while and then reread it, again aloud, you will be more likely to catch omitted words, transposed letters, inconsistent spelling of names, and so forth. If you have time to print out a final corrected copy, do it. If not, you may make corrections—neatly, and in black ink—right on the page. (See pages 471–72.)

10. Hand the essay in on time. In short, the whole business of moving from a subject to a finished essay on a focused topic adds up to Mrs. Beeton's famous recipe: "First catch your hare, then cook it."

Exercises

1. Quickly scan several editorials or op-ed pieces in *The New York Times* (or another newspaper or newsmagazine) until you find one that you really want to read. Read it. Then for each paragraph, or group of paragraphs, write one or two questions that call for a summary of the paragraph's content or an explanation of the paragraph's purpose. Overall, your questions should explore why the editorial is particularly interesting or effective.

2. Write journal entries on two or three assignments (of writing, reading, lab work, or problem sets) made in your courses in the first two weeks of classes.

3. Write a journal entry recalling, in as much detail as you can, your earliest memory.
4. Narrow the following subjects to a topic. Then for each find a more specific focus for a 500-word essay.

Example:

Mental Retardation

  Housing for the mentally retarded

    A controversial proposal to house mentally retarded adults in my neighborhood

Homelessness

Athletic scholarships

The Internet

The Olympics

Gun control

Animal rights

AIDS

The writing requirement

5. Formulate a thesis sentence for two topics derived from Exercise 4.

Suggestions for Writing

1. Write a piece somewhat like Roth's (pages 9–10) in which you respond to a current proposal in your college community. (Suggested length: 500 words.) Or, respond to Roth's article. (Perhaps something he says reminds you of something you have read or experienced; or maybe you agree or disagree strongly with some point he makes.)
2. Explain something clearly—a process, a concept, a place, an experience—that you know well but that others in your class may not know about or may understand less well than you. (Suggested length: 500 words.

CHAPTER
2
Drafting and Revising

I have never thought of myself as a good writer. Anyone who wants reassurance of that should read one of my first drafts. But I'm one of the world's great revisers.

—James Michener

READING DRAFTS

In Chapter 1, we focused on how to have ideas and how to get them down on paper. We suggested that from the start of a project the writer is almost simultaneously both inventing ideas and refining them. But we also advised that, particularly at the start, it's best to suspend critical judgment until you have begun to capture your thoughts, however roughly expressed, on paper. In this chapter, we will focus on ways to improve and refine rough drafts. First, we want to make what may seem like an obvious point: to improve the draft you have written, *you must first read it.* Moreover, you must try to read it objectively and critically.

Imagining Your Audience and Asking Questions

To read your draft objectively, to make sure that you have said what you intended to say, first put it aside for a day, or at least for a couple of hours. Then read it through thoughtfully, as if you were not the writer, but someone reading if for the first time. As you read, try to imagine the questions such a reader might want or need to ask you to understand what you meant. Then, read your draft again, asking yourself the following questions:

1. Does the draft present an idea? Does it have a focus or make a unified point?
2. Is the idea or are the ideas clearly supported? Is there convincing evidence? Are there sufficient specific details?
3. Is the material effectively organized?

There are, of course, many other questions you might ask, and we'll suggest some before we're done. But let's start with these.

1. Does the draft present an idea? Does it have a focus or make a unified point? If, on reading your draft objectively, you find that it doesn't have an idea, a point to develop, then there's probably no reason to tinker with it (or to hand it in). It may be best to start again, using the invention techniques we discussed earlier. (Rereading the assignment is probably a good idea too.)

Let's suppose, however, that you do find some interesting material in your draft but that you're not yet sure what it adds up to. The chances are that some extraneous material is getting in your way—some false starts, needless repetition, or interesting but irrelevant information. Some pruning is probably in order.

Picasso said that in painting a picture he advanced by a series of destructions. A story about a sculptor makes a similar point. When asked how he had made such a lifelike image of an elephant from a block of wood, the sculptor answered, "Well, I just knocked off everything that didn't look like elephant." Often, revising a draft begins with similar "destruction." Having identified the main point that you want to pursue, don't be afraid to hack away competing material until you can see that point clearly in its bold outline. Of course you must have a lot of stuff on paper to begin with (at the start, nothing succeeds like excess). But often you must remove some of it before you can see that you have in fact roughly formulated the main point you want to make, and even produced some evidence to support it.

2. Is the idea (or are the ideas) clearly supported? Is there convincing evidence? Are there sufficient specific details? Writers are always reluctant to delete. Students with an assignment to write 500 or 1000 words by a deadline are, understandably, among the most reluctant. But, almost certainly, once you have settled on the focus of your essay, you will be adding material as well as deleting it. It isn't enough simply to state a point; you must also prove or demonstrate it.

If you argue, for example, that smoking should be banned in all public places, including parks and outdoor cafes, you must offer reasons for your position and also meet possible objections with counterarguments; perhaps you will cite some statistics. If you are arguing that in Plato's *Apology* Socrates' definition of truth goes beyond mere correspondence to fact, you will need to summarize relevant passages of the *Apology* and introduce quotations illuminating Socrates' definition. Almost always a draft needs the addition of specific details and examples to support and clarify its generalizations.

3. Is the material effectively organized? As you prune away the irrelevancies and add the specific details and examples that will clarify and strengthen your point, as your draft begins more and more to "look like elephant," ask yourself if the parts of your draft are arranged in the best order. If you have given two examples, or stated three reasons, with which one is it best to begin? Ask yourself if paragraphs are in a reasonable sequence. Will the relationship of one point to the next be clear to your reader? Does the evidence in each paragraph support the point of that paragraph? (The same evidence may be more appropriate to a different paragraph.) Does your opening paragraph provide the reader with a focus? Or, if it performs some other important function, such as getting the reader's attention, does the essay provide the reader with a focus soon enough?

In general, in working on the organization of drafts, follow two rules:

- Put together what belongs together.
- Put yourself in the position of your reader; make it as easy as possible for the reader to follow you.

Peer Review: The Benefits of Having a Real Audience

Occasionally a writing assignment will specify the reader you should address. For example: "Write a letter to the editor of your hometown newspaper arguing that . . ." More often, your reader must be imagined. We usually suggest imagining someone in your class who has not thought about your topic or considered the specific evidence you intend to examine.

In many writing classes students routinely break up into small groups to read and discuss each other's work. Peer review (as this practice is commonly called) is useful in several ways.

First, peer review gives the writer a real audience, readers who can point to what puzzles or pleases them, who ask questions and make suggestions, who may often disagree (with the writer or with each other) and who frequently, though not willfully, misread. Though writers don't necessarily like everything they hear (they seldom hear, "This is perfect. Don't change a word!"), reading and discussing their work with others almost always gives them a fresh perspective on their work, and a fresh perspective may stimulate thoughtful revision. (Having your intentions misread, because your writing isn't clear enough, can be particularly stimulating.)

Moreover, when students write drafts that will be commented on, they are doing what professional writers do. Like journalists, scholars, engineers, lawyers—anyone whose work is ordinarily reviewed many times, by friends and spouses, by colleagues, and by editors, before the work is published—students who write drafts for peer review know they will have a chance to discuss their writing with their colleagues (other students) before submitting a final version for evaluation. Writers accustomed to writing for a real audience are able, to some extent, to internalize the demands of a real audience. Even as they work on early drafts, they are sensitive to what needs to be added, or deleted, or clarified. Students who discuss their work with other students derive similar benefits. They are likely to write and revise with more confidence, and more energy.

The writer whose work is being reviewed is not the sole beneficiary. When students regularly serve as readers for each other, they become better readers of their own work, and consequently better revisers. Learning to write is in large measure learning to read.

Peer review in the classroom takes many forms; we'll look in a moment at an example as we trace a student's essay that is revised largely as a result of peer review. But even if peer review is not part of your writing class, you may want to work with a friend or another student in the class, reading each other's drafts.

When you work on your essay with your classmates or your friends, good manners *and* academic practice require that you thank them for their help, that you **document** their contributions. You can offer a sentence or two of general thanks at the end of the essay—something like this:

> I'd like to thank the members of my peer revision group, Rebecca Sharp and Isabella Thorpe, for helping me to clarify the main idea of my essay and for suggesting ways to edit my sentences.

Or you can thank your peer reviewers for their specific contributions by inserting a footnote or endnote at the end of the sentence that contains an idea or words you wish to acknowledge, and then writing a sentence like this:

Kevin Doughten drew my attention to the narrator's play on words here; I wish to thank him for helping me develop this point.

From Assignment to Essay: A Case History

On September 12, Suki Hudson was given the following assignment: Write an essay (roughly 500 words) defining racism or narrating an experience in which you were either the victim or the perpetrator of a racist incident. Bring a first draft with two copies to class on September 16 for peer review. Revised essay due September 26.

Suki kept no record of her first thoughts and jottings on the topic, but what follows is an early attempt to get something down on paper. Because it was far from the finished essay she would write, not yet even a first draft, we label it a Zero Draft:

Zero Draft. Sept. 13

It was a warm sunny day in the playground. My three-year-old

brother and other children were playing gaily until one of the boys'

mothers interrupted. She called her son, whispered something, and when

he went back to the playground he excluded my brother from playing

together. I didn't know what to call the incident, but my heart ached as I

watched my little brother enviously looked at the other kids. I immediately

left the playground with him, and the playground has never been the same

since that day.

At that point, having reached the end of the anecdote, Suki stopped. What she had written was not yet an essay, and it was far short of the suggested 500 words, but it was a start, which is all she had hoped to accomplish on this first try.

Later she read what she had written, and asked a friend to read it and see if he had any suggestions. It was a frustrating conversation. The friend didn't understand why Suki thought this was a "racist incident." Why did Suki leave the playground? Why hadn't she just asked the boy's mother for an explanation? The questions took her by surprise; she felt annoyed, then miserable. So she changed the subject.

But "the subject" didn't go away. Still later, she wrote the following account of the conversation in her journal:

Sept. 13:

I asked J to read my paper and he thought I was being paranoid.

Why didn't I just ask the boy's mother what was the matter? But I could

not have even thought of going up to the woman to question her motives.

It was beyond my control if she wanted to be ignorant and cruel to a

different race. (Or was it really my ignorance to walk away from a simple

explanation?)

The following day, looking over what she had written, it occurred to her to
try adding the journal entry to the anecdote. Maybe in a concluding paragraph
she could explain why what happened in the playground was obviously a racist
incident.

Here is the conclusion:

Sept. 14

Most people in modern society don't recognize the more subtle cases

of racism. People feel if they are not assaulting physically they are not

violating the law, and as long as they are living according to the law,

racism is not committed. However, the law or the constitution does not

protect the human heart from getting hurt, and without a doubt the most

critical racist action could be committed by close friends or their loved

ones.

But having written that last line Suki was struck by something odd about it. The
woman in the playground was not a loved one, nor was she a close friend. Still,
it was true that racist acts can be committed by friends, and even if the acts are
undramatic, they should be recognized as racist acts. At this point, she thought
that she had a thesis for her essay, but she also realized that she had begun to recall a different experience. Starting again, she wrote the following account:

In Korea, I had a very close friend whose father was Chinese.

Although her mother was a Korean woman, they were treated as foreign

people in town, and they were singled out on many occasions. Her father

died when she was little but everyone in town knew she was a half

Chinese. Her mother ran a Chinese restaurant, and they lived very quietly.

My family knew her mother well and I was close friends with the girl and

for many years I was the only friend she ever had. However, as I entered

junior high school my new group of friends didn't approve of her

background, and I drifted away from her. She was a very quiet, shy person

and although I stopped calling or visiting her, she always remembered me

on holidays to send presents. After graduating from junior high school she went to Taiwan to live with her grandparents, whom she had never met. I gathered she could not stand the isolation any longer at her age. Many years later I realized how cruel I had been to her, and I tried to locate her without success.

The following day Suki combined the two drafts (hoping to come closer to the 500 words), added a new concluding paragraph, and (rather disgusted with the whole assignment) typed up her first draft to hand in the next day. She photocopied it, as instructed, for peer review in class.

As we said earlier, peer review in the classroom takes many forms. Ordinarily, the instructor distributes some questions to be answered by both the writer and the readers. Typically the writer is asked to speak first, explaining how far along he or she is in writing the essay, and what help readers might give. The writer might also be asked, "What are you most pleased with in your writing so far?"

Readers are then asked to respond. Instructions may vary, depending on the particular assignment, but the questions distributed in Suki's class, shown here, are fairly typical.

Questions for Peer Review   Writing 125R

Read each draft once, quickly. Then read it again, with the following questions in mind:

1. What is the essay's topic? Is it one of the assigned topics, or a variation from it? Does the draft show promise of fulfilling the assignment?
2. Looking at the essay as a whole, what thesis (main idea) is stated or implied? If stated, where is it stated? If implied, try to state it in your own words.
3. Looking at each paragraph separately:
   What is the basic point (the topic sentence or idea)? How does the paragraph relate to the essay's main idea or to the previous paragraph?
   Is each sentence clearly related to the previous sentence?
   Is the paragraph adequately developed? Are there sufficient specific details or examples?
   Is the transition from one paragraph to the next clear?
4. Look again at the introductory paragraph. Does it focus your attention on the main point of the essay? If not, does it effectively serve some other purpose? Does the opening sentence interest you in the essay? Do you want to keep reading?
5. Is the conclusion clear? Is the last sentence satisfying?
6. Does the essay have a title? Is it interesting? Informative?

First Draft What follows is first the draft Suki gave the two members of her group, and then a summary of the group's discussion. Before reading her draft aloud (the procedure the instructor recommended for this session), Suki explained how she had happened to narrate two experiences and asked which narrative she should keep, or if she could keep both.

First Draft

S. Hudson

Sept. 16

It was a warm sunny day in the playground. My three-year-old brother and other children were playing gaily until one of the boys' mothers interrupted. She called her son to whisper something and when he went back to the playground he excluded my brother from playing together. I didn't know what to call the incident, but my heart ached as I watched my little brother enviously looked at other kids. I immediately left the playground with him, and the playground has never been the same since that day.

A friend of mine said I was being paranoid. It would have been appropriate to ask the boy's mother what was the matter, or if she had anything to do with the kids excluding my brother from playing. But I could not have even thought of going up to the woman to question her motives. It was beyond my control if she wanted to be ignorant and cruel to a different race, or perhaps my ignorance to walk away from a simple explanation.

Most people in modern society recognize only the dramatic instances of racism, and on a daily basis people don't recognize the more subtle cases of racism. People feel if they are not assaulting physically they are not violating the law, and as long as they are living according to the law, the racism is not committed. However, the law or the constitution does not protect the human heart from getting hurt, and without a doubt the most critical racist action could be committed by close friends or their loved ones.

In Korea, I had a very close friend whose father was Chinese. Although her mother was a Korean woman they were treated as foreign people in town, and they were singled out on many occasions. Her father died when she was little, but everyone in town knew she was a half Chinese. Her mother ran a Chinese restaurant, and they lived very quietly. My family knew her mother well and I was close friends with the girl and for many years I was the only friend she ever had. However, as I entered junior high school my new group of friends didn't approve of her background and I drifted away from her. She was a very quiet, shy person, and although I stopped calling or visiting her, she always remembered me on holidays to send presents. After graduating from junior high school she went to Taiwan to live with her grandparents whom she had never met. I gathered she could not stand the isolation any longer at her age. Many years later, I realized how cruel I have been to her, and I tried to locate her without success.

She was a victim in a homogeneous society, and had to experience the pain she did not deserve. It is part of human nature to resent the unknown, and sometimes people become racist to cover their fears or ignorance.

Summary of Peer Group Discussion

1. The group immediately understood why the friend (in the second paragraph) had difficulty understanding that the first incident was racist. It might well have been racist, but, they pointed out, Suki had said nothing about the racial mix at the playground. It does become clear by the fourth paragraph that the writer and her brother are Korean, but we don't get this information early enough, and we know nothing of the race of the woman who whispers to her son. Suki had neglected to say—because it was so perfectly obvious to her—that she and her brother were Korean; the mother, the other child, in fact all others in the playground, were white.

2. Suki's readers confirmed her uneasiness about the third paragraph. They found it confusing. (a) Suki had written "people don't recognize the more subtle cases of racism." Did she mean that the mother didn't recognize her action as racist, or that Suki didn't? (b) In the first paragraph Suki had written "I didn't know what to call the incident." But then the second paragraph is contradictory. There she seems to accuse the mother of being "cruel to a different race." (c) And the last sentence of the third paragraph, they agreed, in which Suki writes of racist acts "committed by close friends," did not tie in at all with the first part of the essay, although it did serve to introduce the second anecdote.

3. Her group was enthusiastic, though, about Suki's telling of the two stories and advised her to keep both. Both were accounts of more or less subtle acts of racism. One student thought that they should appear in chronological order: first the Korean story and then the more recent story, set in the playground. But both readers were sure that she could find some way to put them together.

4. They were less sure what the essay's thesis was, or whether it even had one. One student proposed:

> Subtle racist acts can be as destructive as dramatic instances (implied in paragraph 3).

The other proposed combining:

> It is part of human nature to resent the unknown

and

> . . . sometimes people become racist to cover their fears or ignorance (from the final paragraph).

All three members of Suki's group (Suki included) thought that the ideas in the essay were supported by the narratives. But the draft didn't yet hang together: Suki would have to work on the way the separate parts connected.

5. One member of the group then pointed out that the second paragraph could be deleted. The friend mentioned in it (who called Suki "paranoid") had been important to Suki's thinking about her first draft, but served no useful purpose in the draft they were looking at, and other details in that paragraph were murky.

6. On the other hand, the first paragraph probably needed additional details about the setting, the people involved, what each did. How does a three-year-old know he's been excluded from a play group? What happened? What did the other children do? What did he do? And, as the group had seen at once, some details were needed to establish the racist nature of the incident. They also reminded Suki that her essay needed a title.

7. Finally, some small details of grammar. Suki's English is excellent, although English is her second language (her third actually). But the other two in her group, being native speakers of English, were able to catch the slightly odd diction in

> she always remembered me on holidays to send presents

and the error in

> my heart ached as I watched my little brother enviously looked at other kids.

Suki asked if the past tense was right in

> I realized how cruel I have been to her

and the others supplied:

> I realized how cruel I had been to her

(though they could not explain the difference).

Several days later Suki consulted her notes and resumed work on her draft, and by September 25, the night before it was due, she was able to print the final version, which now included a title.

Suki Hudson

Ms. Cahill

Writing 125R

September 28, 1999

Two Sides of a Story

It was a warm sunny day in the playground. My three-year-old

brother and two other small boys were playing together in the sandbox.

My brother was very happy, digging in the sand with a shovel one of the

other boys had brought, when one of the mothers sitting on a bench across

from me called to her son. She bent over and whispered something to him, and he went right over to my brother and pulled the shovel out of his hand. He pushed my brother aside and moved to the other side of the sandbox. The other boy followed him, and they continued to play. My heart ached as I watched my little brother enviously looking at the other kids. I didn't fully understand what had happened. I looked across at the mother, but she turned her head away. Then I picked up my brother and immediately left the playground with him.

I thought the woman was extremely rude and cruel, but I didn't think then that she was behaving in a racist way. We had only recently come here from Korea, and although I had been told that there was much racism in America, I thought that meant that it was hard for some people, like blacks, to find jobs or go to good schools. In some places there were street gangs and violence. But I didn't understand that there could be subtle acts of racism too. I was aware, though, in the playground that my brother and I were the only Koreans, the only nonwhites. When the woman turned her face away from me it felt like a sharp slap, but I was ignorant about her motives. I only guessed that she told her child not to play with my brother, and I knew that the playground was never the same since that day.

That incident was several months ago. When I started to think about it again recently, I thought also of another time when I was ignorant of racism.

In Korea, I had a very close friend whose father was Chinese. Although her mother was a Korean woman they were treated as foreign people in town, and they were singled out on many occasions. Her father died when she was little, but everyone in town knew she was half Chinese. Her mother ran a Chinese restaurant, and they lived very quietly. My family knew her mother well and I was close friends with the girl, and for many years I was the only friend she ever had. However, as I entered junior high school my new group of friends didn't approve of her background and I drifted away from her. She was a very quiet, shy person, and although I stopped calling or visiting her, she always remembered to send me presents on holidays. After graduating from junior high school, she went to Taiwan to live with her grandparents, whom she had never met. I gathered she could not stand the isolation any longer at her age. Many years later, I realized how cruel I had been to her, and I tried to locate her without success.

She was a victim in a homogeneous society, and had to experience pain she did not deserve. There was no law to protect her from that, just as there was no law to protect my little brother. Perhaps the woman in the playground did not realize how cruel she was being. She probably didn't think of herself as a racist, and maybe she acted the way I did in Korea, without thinking why. It isn't only the dramatic acts that are racist, and maybe it isn't only cruel people who commit racist acts. It is part of human nature to fear the unknown, and sometimes people become racist to cover their fears, or ignorance.

Acknowledgments

I would like to thank Ann Weston and Tory Chang for helping me to develop my main point, and to organize and edit my essay.

Notes, Drafts, Revisions: An Historian Revises Her Work

As we face the empty computer screen, we imagine that other, better, more experienced writers are efficiently filling up *their* computer screens with lucid sentences, organized paragraphs, brilliant ideas. Not so—or at least, not usually so. For most writers, most of the time, ideas emerge through the revision process; focus, organization, and clarity result from rereading and rewriting. Drafts written by experienced writers can be as messy and apparently unpromising as drafts written by the rest of us.

By way of illustration (and, perhaps, inspiration), we reprint here an excerpt from *Fire in the Lake: The Vietnamese and the Americans in Vietnam*, by the journalist and historian Frances FitzGerald. FitzGerald went to South Vietnam as a reporter in 1966, just a few years after she graduated from college; reports she wrote that year for *The New York Times, The Atlantic Monthly,* and other publications were the basis of *Fire in the Lake*, which was published in 1972. In this book, FitzGerald argues in part that cultural differences and racial biases doomed from the start the American mission, the goal of which was to prevent the spread of Communism by supporting South Vietnam in the war against Communist North Vietnam.

In the passage that follows, FitzGerald discusses some of the consequences of American policy in Vietnam, policy that required American officials to aid the Saigon government, which they knew to be corrupt. Following the excerpt, we reprint portions of FitzGerald's drafts of the beginning of the piece. The drafts are typewritten, of course, but because they are, it is possible to trace the writer's revision process, a process that can be obscured by the word processor's cut-and-paste function and delete key. At the end of the chapter, we reprint some advice FitzGerald received on an early version of *Fire in the Lake* from one of her editors.

 **FRANCES FITZGERALD**

Prospero's Army[1]

The effort of trying to hold reality and the official version of reality together finally took its toll on the Americans in Vietnam. When added to all the other strains of war, it produced an almost intolerable tension that expressed itself not in a criticism of American policy so much as in a fierce resentment against the Vietnamese. The logic of that anger was a simple one, combined of guilt and illusions destroyed. The nature of those illusions was even less apparent to Americans than it had been to the French, but the illusions were nonetheless powerful. At the Senate Foreign Relations Committee hearings in 1965, General Maxwell Taylor, just returned from the ambassadorship in Saigon, said in describing the pacification program: "We have always been able to move in the areas where the security was good enough. But I have often said it is very hard to plant the corn outside the stockade when the Indians are still around. We have to get the Indians farther away in many of the provinces to make good progress." In Vietnam American officers liked to call the area outside GVN[2] control "Indian country." It was a joke, of course, no more than a figure of speech, but it put the Vietnam War into a definite historical and mythological perspective: the Americans were once again embarked upon a heroic and (for themselves) almost painless conquest of an inferior race. To the American settlers the defeat of the Indians had seemed not just a nationalist victory, but an achievement made in the name of humanity—the triumph of light over darkness, of good over evil, and of

---

[1]Editors' note. The title refers to two characters in Shakespeare's *The Tempest;* Prospero, a duke who was ousted from his dukedom, arrives at an island, where he enslaves Caliban, its only inhabitant other than Ariel, a spirit. Prospero regards Caliban (whose name is a corruption of *cannibal*) as a brute.

[2]Government of South Vietnam; the American-supported Saigon Government.

Frances FitzGerald's Department of Defense ID card.

civilization over brutish nature. Quite unconsciously, the American officers and officials used a similar language to describe their war against the NLF.[3] According to the official rhetoric, the Viet Cong did not live in places, they "infested areas"; to "clean them out" the American forces went on "sweep and clear" operations or moved all the villagers into refugee camps in order to "sanitize the area." Westmoreland spoke of the NLF as "termites." The implications of this language rarely came to consciousness (some of the American field commanders actually admired the Front as a fighting force), but they were nonetheless there. The Americans were white men in Asia, and they could not conceive that they might fail in their enterprise, could not conceive that they could be morally wrong.

Beyond all the bureaucratic and strategic interests in the war, it was this "can do" attitude, this sense of righteous mission that had led the U.S. government deeper and deeper into Vietnam. Moral infallibility, military invincibility—the two went together and were not to be differentiated, not in Vietnam, in any case, where the enemy was not only Communist but small, yellow, and poor. The difficulty was that the "allies" of the United States belonged within almost the same category—the same category with the one term of Communism removed. The distinction—Communist, non-Communist—so obvious in theory, became an elusive one in practice when juxtaposed with the much greater contrast between Americans and Vietnamese.

[3]The National Liberation Front, a South Vietnamese guerrilla organization opposed to the Saigon government.

In coming to Vietnam, most American advisers, for instance, expected their "counterparts" to render them their due as members of a more "advanced" society. The expectation was not, after all, unreasonable, since the U.S. government sent them out to advise the Vietnamese. But the advisers tended to see themselves in the roles of teacher and older brother, and when the Vietnamese did not respond to them in the expected manner—when they did not even take their advice—few succeeded in reconstructing the truth of the matter. Few saw that the Vietnamese were not the pupils of the Americans, but people with a very different view of the world and with interests that only occasionally coincided with their own. For those few who succeeded there were an equal number of others [. . .] who took an extreme parochial view, looking upon the Vietnamese as savages or children with empty heads into which they would pour instruction. Covered with righteous platitudes, theirs was an essentially colonialist vision, born out of the same insecurity and desire for domination that had motivated many of the French. When their "counterparts" did not take their instruction, these advisers treated the Vietnamese like bad pupils, accusing them of corruption or laziness, and attempted to impose authority over them. And when the attempt at coercion failed, they retreated from the Vietnamese entirely, barricading themselves in behind American weapons and American PX[4] goods, behind the assumption of American superiority and the assumption that the Vietnamese were not quite human like themselves.

"Don't you realize," exploded one young embassy officer, "don't you realize that everything the Americans do in Vietnam is founded on a hatred of the Vietnamese?" His outburst was shocking, for he, of all Americans in Vietnam, had managed to preserve a sense of balance. He understood the point of view of the Vietnamese officials as well as the Americans, and because of his own success at reconciling the two, he had believed that the best in both would prevail. Two years earlier he had confidence that the two could find some common ground for cooperation against the NLF. But he, the diplomat *par excellence,* had seen his compatriots turn into spineless bureaucrats and frustrated proconsuls. And into murderers.

5   In 1969 an incident came to the attention of the U.S. Congress that had occurred a year and a half before in the wake of the Tet[5] offensive. On a routine search and destroy operation a company from the American Division had walked into the village of My Lai and without provocation had gunned down three hundred and forty-seven civilians, most of them women and children. A photographer had taken pictures of screaming women, dead babies, and a mass of bodies piled up in a ditch. Even once substantiated, the story seemed incredible to many people. How could American soldiers have committed such an atrocity? The congressional subcommittee investigating the incident wrote much later, "What obviously happened at My Lai was wrong. In fact it was so wrong and so foreign to the normal character and actions of our military forces as to immediately raise a question as to the legal sanity at the time of those men involved." But

---

[4]Post Exchange; located on a military base or installation, a store that serves military personnel.
[5]The Tet Offensive, named after the Vienamese Lunar New Year holiday, took place in January 1966; it was a large-scale offensive operation by the NLF during which 30 provincial capitals in the South were attacked.

as teams of psychiatrists were later to show, Lieutenant William Calley and the other men involved were at the time quite as "sane" as the members of the congressional committee who investigated them. The incident was not exceptional to the American war.

Young men from the small towns of America, the GIs who came to Vietnam found themselves in a place halfway round the earth among people with whom they could make no human contact. Like an Orwellian army, they knew everything about military tactics, but nothing about where they were or who the enemy was. And they found themselves not attacking fixed positions but walking through the jungle or through villages among small yellow people, as strange and exposed among them as if they were Martians. Their buddies were killed by land mines, sniper fire, and mortar attacks, but the enemy remained invisible, not only in the jungle but among the people of the villages—an almost metaphysical enemy who inflicted upon them heat, boredom, terror, and death, and gave them nothing to show for it—no territory taken, no visible sign of progress except the bodies of small yellow men. And they passed around stories: you couldn't trust anyone in this country, not the laundresses or the prostitutes or the boys of six years old. The enemy would not stand up and fight, but he had agents everywhere, among the villagers, even among the ARVN[6] officers. The Vietnamese soldiers were lazy and the officials corrupt—they were all out to get you one way or another. They were "gooks," after all. Just look how they lived in the shacks and the filth; they'd steal the watch off your arm.

And the stories of combat were embellished: about how the enemy attacked Alpha Company one night and hundreds of them were killed, but they kept on coming in "human waves," screaming like banshees. It didn't matter how many you killed because they were fanatics who didn't know the value of human life. In boot camp or in the barracks late at night, an experienced sergeant would tell about how the VC[7] killed women and children and tortured their prisoners, cutting off the ears of their victims, or their genitals. And how the ARVN soldiers did the same when their American advisers weren't around.

There was terror in these stories, but also a kind of release, since if the Vietnamese did not act like human beings, then they did not have to be treated as such. All the laws of civilization were suspended. "And when you shot someone you didn't think you were shooting at a human. They were a gook or a Commie and it was okay, 'cause, like, they [the American officers] would tell you they'd do it to you if they had the chance." The expressiveness of the soldiers' language made even more explicit the fact that these stories were largely fantasies—and fantasies of exactly the same sort that the Americans had created about the Indians and Prospero about Caliban. Like the French soldiers before them, GIs mentally stripped the Vietnamese of their humanity in order to deliver themselves of their own guilty desires. The war brought out their latent sadism, as perhaps all wars between races (and particularly guerrilla wars) have brought it out of all armies. The Americans were no different—that was the shock. "You'll look at your enemy and these people that you're sort of a visitor to. You'll look at them as animals and at the same time you're just turning yourself into an animal, too."

---

[6]Army of the Republic of South Vietnam; the American-supported South Vietnamese Army.
[7]Viet Cong; Communist guerrillas.

A moving account—focused, lucid, persuasive. Each paragraph develops an aspect of the central idea of the passage and is carefully linked to the paragraphs that precede and follow it. The eight paragraphs are packed with information, with vivid quotations from the American officials, with careful analysis of the language those officials used to talk about the Vietnamese and of the stories American soldiers told about them.

FitzGerald's early jottings and drafts look very different from the finished piece of writing. In her notes for the section, for example, she seems almost to be talking to herself, reminding herself of what to do and when to do it ("just report here"; "show this rather than analyse") and asking the questions the passage will answer: "What are aims?"; "What becomes of Americans in Vietnam so long exposed to the contraditiction [*sic*] between aims (apparently being reached) and reality."

[A]

Just report here

Sense of superirority (show this rather than analyse —
can include MaxwellTaylor) And like early settlers -- sense
of moral superiority as well as technological. (Here the military
briefer and Pike.)

    Above -- technological and money superiority that makes
them completely insensitive to the requirements of the situation.
Thus Kahn, Mang Thit, etc.

    They think what is wanted is better life -- not realizing that
VC program is almost entirely political -- power to the people
(not to sonoi Americans and bourg middle-men)

    Wisfulfillment
    All the way from lowest prov rep to Johnson (look what
Clifford says about reading the reports) The system is slanted
that way, from the begin ing by "progress reports" -- by
measurement of input rather than the whole situation. That is
what Komer speaks of
a. how it happens
b. what are aims?
c. What becomes of Americans in Vietnam so long exposed to the
contraditiction betweeen aims (apparently being reached) and
reality.
    American policy as a projection of own values -- has nothing
to do with the Vietnamese, but what they have been brought
up believing about themselves. They cannot see the harshness
of the political conflict -- expect VC to come in when business
is good, when democracy in place. They do not realize that to
do this requires fundamental change. Confusion is that they
speak of "rev" and they do not mean it any more than "rev
new soap".

From the Frances FitzGerald Collection, Department of Special Collections, Boston University.

It's worth noting how this question, the central idea of the piece ("What becomes of Americans in Vietnam so long exposed to the contraditiction [*sic*] between aims . . . and reality"), evolves as FitzGerald revises. It becomes, in the first sentence of the published version,

The effort of trying to hold reality and the official version of reality together finally took its toll on the Americans in Vietnam,

a much more precise and concise version of the sentence that appears in a draft of the section that we label [E] and reprint on page 46:

Though the fiction of "progress" and "reform" could have continued forever, the burden of supporting it was considerable, particularly for those Americans who had to deal with the daily reality.

And in a rough outline of the passage, reprinted below, this central idea is stated at the top of the page in the rather abstract (even vague) phrase,

[B]

3.

The reaction of people caught between reality and illusion
  a. Take on side of Saigon govt agst interests of the Americans
  b. Hatred

the metaphor of the Indians -- put the war in a definite historical context.

Treatment of Viets in country as noble savages)

(⁽ᵇᵘ⁾) Also sense of moral superiority -- mil briefer and Pike. Directed agst the enemy -- but also by a kind logic, agst other Viets. Eorzthe (by many)

For the soldiers -- very simple -- they had come to find Comms only to find that all Viets are "gooks". This is the end of the logic of Rusk.

For the civilians and others -- more complicated. They had come expecting a relationship -- if not commander, then older brother -- only to find that the Viets do not reciprocate. They do not obey and they have no interest in xxx becoming Americans. Therefore frustration and hatred.

Result is that no one in the country speaks out against the inhumanity -- against the violation of all the R Genva Treaty.

Here again, as with the French, the psychology of terror -- feeling that what the other side does is obscene. They are filthy savages and therefore it does not matter what is done to them. (same as with the Indians)
    The tortures
    The My Lai and other massacres
    The soldiers carr.ing around obscen picture

But more than that -- the systematic killing and harassment of civilian population as outlined by Westmoreland.

(Above This a. of taking side with Saigon is should come before invicibility -- attempt to reconcile their own desires with the reality. A part of the involvement. Reason that they cannot see what they are doing is myth of invincibility.

For soldiers -- contact supposedly only with the enemy. For civilians, vv. But those are the wateforis rather than soldier and civilian.

Moral superiority -- the logic is that what they do is bad because it is on purpose, whereas all our killiings are 'scientific' or due to techno accident. Or in the last nrat (Pike) by mistake. And this is dearly not true.

It's worth noting too that the list of points above forms a *working* outline. FitzGerald moves the discussion of "moral superiority" from place to place; the sequence of ideas corresponds only partly to the final order in which they appear. Ideas sketched in this outline—the similarity between the "early settlers" of the American frontier and the Americans in Vietnam, for example—become central to the revision. And of course other ideas (about technology, for example) are deleted as FitzGerald refines her focus.

In the notes above [B] and in the draft page below [C], FitzGerald appears to be writing quickly and freely: she abbreviates words, leaves sentences unfinished, and is unconcerned with spelling and punctuation. It's clear that her purpose is simply to get her ideas into words on paper. She refines and develops some of those ideas in subsequent drafts; she drops others completely as she sharpens her focus. One of FitzGerald's goals here (as she notes above) is to provide a "definite historical context" for American attitudes toward the Vietnamese. In the excerpt below, she begins tentatively to provide that context—with references to Calvinists and Cotton Mather (a seventeenth-century New England Puritan) and to the strength of the American "community."

[C]

```
            Spiritual
Conference. Moral infallibility, secular infallibility -- it was
in a sense the same connection that had been made by the Papacy
in the 16th? century    the two went together
The United States was the most powrful nation on earth
because it had the best system of government, the best way of
life. Or vica versa -- for it was the fact that the United States
was the most powerful that convinced the Americans that they
                     Though
had the best possible system. Buried deep -- and deeper in such
                                        conjunction
intellects as  erman Khanh, it was much the same correlation
that the  hinese and the Vietnamese had tradically made between
the morality and science. And by no coincidence? for it was
the strain of puritanism in both cultures that had aduced this
sttange combination of moraliz pragmatism and absolutism.
             Calvinists
According to Cotton Mather? the community was strong because
they believed in inized    not just because the people believed in
God but because they followed a certain way of life ,- and
conversely the fact that the community was strongvproved that
their way of life was the best of all possible worlds.
In the 50s and the 60s it was just this confirmation that had
                     half-
held a vast and diverse continent together -- the metaphysics
                                        faith
of liveralism -- a belie  the conviction that made out of
diversity an absolute virtue and so permitted no diversity,
     faith
a belief inprogres that made an aboslute virute out of
progress and so permitted no progress except except that made
                                        though
within the prescribed model for it -- a blief that waszfi
it seemed to be scienfic was in fact as much based in morality
as thezGz Marzism-Leninism. (Confuscianism and). Moral infallibility,
```

In a subsequent version of the section, FitzGerald's idea about "historical context" begins to shift. In the annotated draft page reprinted below and labelled [D], she drops the references to Cotton Mather and begins invoking ideas about the frontier and about the "early settlers." She refers to "noble savages" (and then changes her mind and crosses out the sentence in which this term appears); between the lines, near the middle of the page, she writes the phrase "Indian country?" In the margins are other notes as well, notes she seems to have written to herself on rereading the draft: "Enlarge"; "could expand and improve"; "What he is really doing is colonialist."

[D]

||

Go into rank of superiority.

making progress in the war could, perhaps, go on forever, it the effort of supporting ti took its toll on the Americans, particularly on those in the lower ranks who had to deal with the day-to-day reality. The conflict (between their their expectations and the reality)produced in soldiers and civilians alike an intense resentment — a resentment not against the or the war policy   For the GIs American command but against the Vietnamese. The logic was a simple one for the GIs. They had come to Vietnam (so they had been told by Dean Rusk among others) to defend out valiant Free World Allies against the totalitarian Cimmunists

The logic was a simple one: America is the greatest country on earth and therefore it must be our Vietnamese 'allies' who are causing all the trouble abd preventing us from winning this war. For the civilians and advisors the often logic was confirmed by their personal experiences with their counterparts.

These Americans had come to Vietnam with certain expectations of their "counterparts"; or rather, of their relationship to them. They had seen themselves in the role of older brother, or teacher — they had expected the Vietnamese to render them their due as members of a more "advanced" society. They had expected gratitude for their efforts, and when they had got neither gratitude nor "cooperation" or obedeience, they had failed to reconstruct the Vietnamese point of view. They had failed to see that the Vietnamese were not "noble savages" empty of ideas and   For some the deception was even more pronounced, for they   For the men like the Marine colonel with his would find carpentry sets, the deception would be all the more pronounced, for they had looked upon the Vietnamese   Vietnam as a blank page and the Vietnamese as pupils with empty heads waiting for their know how" and their democratic principles to be poured in. When the Vietnamese showed them that they were not   How could one explain that the Vietnamese were not pulls but people with a very different view of the world and interests that only occasionally

could + improve

Enlarge

Expand this perhaps looks like a guide book?

What he is really doing is colonialist

They found Viets completely unmatched

Though covered in self-righteous platitudes, it was the version of a colonialist. And he could not let it go - could not see that the Viet....

FitzGerald begins expanding on these ideas about the frontier, Indians, and colonialism in a subsequent revision, two portions of which are reprinted below. The first excerpt, [E], begins to develop the analogy hinted at in the page reprinted above, the parallel between Americans in Vietnam and settlers on the frontier. FitzGerald develops the analogy further—with quotations and specific evidence—in the second excerpt, [F], where she begins to consider the implications of the language Americans in Saigon used to describe the Viet Cong. She'll combine these two passages in a subsequent draft of the piece. This draft, in the meantime, is still several steps from the version FitzGerald submitted to her publishers, but it has begun to look like a focused piece of writing.

[E]

```
          Though the fiction of "progress" and "reform" could have continued
          burden                   took its toll
forever, the effort of supporting it was considerable, particularly for those

Americans who had to deal with the daily reality.sixthexxxx. When added to

all the other pressures of the war and of working with the Vietnamese

it monaisdizes it produced an almost intolerable tension that expressed
          often      nerortic behavior      often in
itself sometimes in internal battles, sometimes in a fierce resentment of

the Vietnamese      some times in anger against the Vietnamese.

The logic of that anger was a simple one: the United States is ghe greates

country on earth and therefore it must be out allies who are creating all
                    (The apparent truth of the statement head all the innter
the difficulties  (but it had      complexities  force behind it.

 ..historical or mythological perspective: the Americans were once again

setting out on a heroci nut for them almost painless conquest of an inferior

face. The defeat of the indidians had seemed not just a nationalist victory

but an achievement made in the name of the whole human race — the triumph
                                                            of
of light over darkness, of good over evil and a step a.xistaryzfor civilization
raw
over nature. Asxwhitexmenxizasiayzthez Though the parallel   analogy was

rarely came to consciousness, it was nonetheless there. As white men in Asia,

the Americans did not conceive they could fail in their enterprise, did not

conceive they could be wrong. Moral infallibility, military invicibility —

the two went together and had not to be reconciled — not in VN in any case,

where the enemy was not only Communist but small, yellow and poor. And behind
                                                            sense of a
(Above. Behind all the diplomatic it was this "can do" attitude, this sense
righteous mission               further and further
of superiority that led the US government into the war   (Perhaps here note

on CIA man —reflecting opinion in the country
```

From the Frances FitzGerald Collection, Department of Special Collections, Boston University.

[F]

                                          Before the wave of
Xrevisionist movies showing the Indians as brave and noble people,
       merely
thez Hollywood had transcribed -- and quite accurately -- what
the frontiersmen had thought of the Indians at the time: that
thye were 'saxagss dirty savages, tricky and untrustworthy
pagan sagages. The defeat of the Indians was seen not just as
a nationalist victory (the way the Vietnamese had regarde their
defeat of the Chinese) but an achieve triumph of light over
                  good
darkness, of virtue over evil and step towards the provress of
the whole human race. Quite zoas unconsciously -- for their
remakrs often showed no real hostility -- the Americanx soldiers
and officials adopted the same kind of rhetoric in speaking of
the Viet Gong. The Viet Cong "infested areas", etc....clear
operations The image of America as a disingectant for germ-
ridden feces.(Also trickery -- they would not "stand up and fight"
they were cowardly
for the Americans as well as the French, the Vietnam war was
"la sale guerre".) And they were bound to win. Moral infallibility,
military invicibility -- the two had not to be distinguished, --
not in Vietnam, in any case, where the enemy was not only
Communist, but small, poor and yellow. (later, irony for GIs)

From the Frances FitzGerald Collection, Department of Special Collections, Boston University.

Finally, we reprint here a close-to-finished version of the opening paragraphs of "Prospero's Army."

[G]

As reality and official reality moved farther and farther apart,
the effort of trying to hold the two together finally took its toll on the
Americans. When added to all the other strains of war, it produced an almost
intolerable tension that expressed itself not in a criticism of American
policy so much as in a fierce resentment against the Vietnamese. The logic of
that anger was a simple one, combined of guilt and illusions destroyed. The
nature of those illusions was even less pa apparant thanzitzkax to Americans
than it had been to the French, but it they were nonetheless powerful.
At the Senate Foreign Relations Committee Hearings in 1965 General Maxwell
Taylor, just returned from the ambassadorship in Saigon, said in describing
the pacification program: "We have always been able to move in areas where
the security was good enough. But I have often said it is very hard to
plant corn outside the stockade when the Indians are still around. We have
to get the Indians farther way away in many of the provinces in order to
make good progress." (Note 12) In Vietnam American officers liked to call
the area outside GVN control "Indian country". It was a joke, of course, no
more than a figure of speech, but it put the Vietnam war into a definite
historical and mythological persepective: the Americans were once again embarked
upon an heroic and (for themselves) almost painless conquest of an inferior
race. To the American settlers the defeat of the Indians had seemed not just
a nationalist victory, but an achievement made in the name of humanity —
the triumph of light over darkness, of good over evil, and of civilization
over brutish nature. Quite unconsciously the American officers and officials
used a similar language to describe their war against the NLF. According to
the official rhetoric, the Viet Cong did not live in places, they "infested
areas"; to "clean them out" the American forces went on "sweep and clear"
operations or moved all the villagers into refugee camps in order to
Westmoreland spoke of the NLF as "termites."
"sanitize the area". The implications of this language rarely came to
consciousness (some of the American field commanders actually admired the
Front as a fighting force), but they were nonetheless there. The Americans
were white men in Asia, and they could not conceive they might fail in their
enterprise, could not conceive they could be morally wrong.

From the Frances FitzGerald Collection, Department of Special Collections, Boston University.

The revision process for FitzGerald was hard work—for both the author and her editors. At one point during the early stages of writing the draft, one of her editors wrote to her in frustration:

> So far in our working together on this book, I have suggested that you keep working and regard the completed material as first-draft only. I now begin to see I was wrong. The present material is *pre* first draft; it has not yet got to the point where an editor can do anything with it. It is so rough, so lacking in clarity, that all we can do is throw up our hands. Frankie, you have to solve the problem of articulating the Vietnam problem, both in the organization and the style of your book. I think you have a lot of work to do before solving it. If you believe you should keep forging ahead before you solve it, simply to cover the area you want the book eventually to cover, by all means do so; but when that is done, I am afraid you have another task ahead of you that is at least as daunting.

Fire in the Lake went on to win the Bancroft Prize for History, the National Book Award, and the Pulitzer Prize.

Topics for Critical Thinking and Writing

1. Look again at FitzGerald's early notes [A]. Which ideas on this page make their way into the published version of the piece? Which ideas does FitzGerald drop?
2. How much of the freewriting [C] reprinted on page 44 does FitzGerald use in the final version of the piece? Why do you think she chose not to include the material she cut?
3. At what point in the revision process does FitzGerald seem to begin imagining a reader reading what she's written? What kinds of changes does she make as a result of imagining her audience?
4. Based on the notes and jottings and on the rough outline, what would you say is FitzGerald's attitude toward Americans in Vietnam? How would you describe her attitude toward American soldiers in the final version of the piece? (Which sentences seem especially revealing?)
5. FitzGerald began the process of writing the piece by asking herself a question: "What becomes of Americans in Vietnam so long exposed to the contraditiction [*sic*] between aims (apparently being reached) and reality?" How, finally, does she answer this question? What makes her answer persuasive?

Suggestions for Writing

1. Write an essay in response to the assignment Suki Hudson received: In 500 words, narrate an experience in which you were either the victim or the perpetrator of a racist incident.

2. Write an essay on "Prospero's Army." In about 500 words, tell your reader what FitzGerald's main point is, briefly summarize the steps of her argument, and then explain what makes the piece persuasive. (Consider the evidence she uses as well as the attitude she expresses toward her topic.)

3. Think about how you usually respond to a writing assignment—or how you responded to a particular assignment. Try to trace, step by step, your thoughts, actions, and feelings from the moment you receive an assignment to the moment you turn in a finished essay.

   Looking back, what experiences have you had as a writer, in class or out, that have led to your current practice and to your attitude toward writing? Do you find writing under some circumstances (writing letters, for example, or writing for a school newspaper) easier than others?

   Turn your reflections into an essay of about 500 words.

3

Shaping Paragraphs

PARAGRAPH FORM AND SUBSTANCE

It is commonly said that a good paragraph has

- *unity* (it makes one point, or it indicates where one unit of a topic begins and ends);
- *organization* (the point or unit is developed according to some pattern); and
- *coherence* (the pattern of development, sentence by sentence, is clear to the reader).

We will say these things too. Moreover, we will attempt to demonstrate that, generally speaking, they are true. Along the way we also hope to show you how to shape your ideas into effective paragraphs. But first we feel obliged to issue this warning: you can learn to write a unified, organized, coherent paragraph that no one in his or her right mind would choose to read. Here is an example:

Charles Darwin's great accomplishments in the field of natural science resulted from many factors. While innate qualities and characteristics played a large part in leading him to his discoveries, various environmental circumstances and events were decisive factors as well. Darwin himself considered his voyage on the Beagle the most decisive event of his life, precisely because this was to him an educational experience similar to if not more valuable than that of college, in that it determined his whole career and taught him of the world as well.

Notice that the paragraph is unified, organized, and coherent. It has a **topic sentence** (the first sentence). It uses **transitional devices** ("while," "as well," "Darwin himself") and, as is often helpful, it **repeats key words**. But notice also that it is wordy, vague, and inflated ("in the field of," "many factors," "qualities and characteristics," "circumstances and events," "precisely because," "educational experience," "similar to if not more valuable than"). It is, in short, thin and boring. To whom does it teach what?

Consider, by contrast, these paragraphs from of another essay on Darwin:

> Charles Darwin's youth was unmarked by signs of genius. Born in 1809 into the well-to-do Darwin and Wedgwood clans (his mother was a Wedgwood, and Darwin himself was to marry another), he led a secure and carefree childhood, happy with his family, indifferent to books, responsive to nature. The son and grandson of impressively successful physicians, he eventually tried medical training himself, but found the studies dull and surgery (before anesthesia) too ghastly even to watch. So, for want of anything better, he followed the advice of his awesome father (6'2", 336 pounds, domineering in temperament) and studied for the ministry, taking his B.A. at Christ's College, Cambridge, in 1831.
>
> Then a remarkable turn of events saved Darwin from a country parsonage. His science teacher at Cambridge, John Stevens Henslow, arranged for Darwin the invitation to be naturalist on H.M.S. *Beagle* during a long voyage of exploration. Despite his father's initial reluctance, Darwin got the position, and at the end of 1831 left England for a five-year voyage around the globe that turned out to be not only a crucial experience for Darwin himself, but a passage of consequence for the whole world.
>
> —PHILIP APPLEMAN

Notice how full of life these paragraphs are, compared to the paragraph that begins by asserting that "Charles Darwin's great accomplishments in the field of natural science resulted from many factors." These far more interesting paragraphs are filled with specific details, facts, and names that combine to convey ideas. We finish reading them with a sense of having learned something worth knowing, from someone fully engaged not only with the topic, but also with conveying it to someone else.

The one indispensable quality of a good paragraph, the quality that the first paragraph on Darwin lacks, is **substance.** A paragraph may define a term, describe a person or a place, make a comparison, tell an anecdote, summarize an opinion, draw a conclusion; it may do almost anything provided that it holds the readers' attention by telling them something they want or need to know, or are reminded of with pleasure.

But even a substantial paragraph, as we shall soon see, does not guarantee that you'll hold the attention of your readers, because readers (like writers) are often lazy and impatient. The important difference is that readers can afford to be. If they find that they must work too hard to understand you, if they are puzzled or confused by what you write, if the effort they must expend is greater than their reward, they can—and will—stop reading. The art of writing is in large part the art of keeping your readers' goodwill while you teach them what you want them to learn. Now, experienced writers can usually tell—not so much while they are writing as while they are revising—what does or does not make a satisfactory unit, and their paragraphs do not always exactly follow the principles we are going to suggest. But we think that by following these principles, more or less as you might practice finger exercises in learning how to play the piano, you will develop a sense of paragraphing. Or, to put it another way, you will improve your sense of how to develop an idea.

PARAGRAPH UNITY:
TOPIC SENTENCES, TOPIC IDEAS

The idea developed in each paragraph often appears, briefly stated, as a **topic sentence**. Topic sentences are most useful, and are therefore especially common, in paragraphs that offer arguments; they are much less common, because they are less useful, in narrative and descriptive paragraphs.

The topic sentence usually is the first sentence in the paragraph—or the second, following a transitional sentence—because writers usually want their readers to know from the start where the paragraph is going. Sometimes, though, you may not wish to forecast what is to come; you may prefer to put your topic sentence at the end of the paragraph, summarizing the points that earlier sentences have made, or drawing a generalization based on the earlier details. Even if you do not include a topic sentence anywhere in the paragraph, the paragraph should have a topic idea—an idea that holds the sentences together.

Examples of Topic Sentences at Beginning and at End, and of Topic Ideas

1. The following paragraph begins with a topic sentence.

The Marx Brothers' three best films at Paramount—*Monkey Business* (1931), *Horse Feathers* (1932), and *Duck Soup* (1933)—all hurl comic mud at the gleaming marble pillars of the American temple. The target of *Monkey Business* is money and high society, the rich society snobs merely happen to be gangsters who made their money from bootlegging. The target of *Horse Feathers* is the university; knowledge and the pursuit of it are reduced to thievery, bribery, lechery, and foolishness. The target of *Duck Soup* is democracy and government itself; grandiose political ceremonies, governmental bodies, international diplomacy, the law courts, and war are reduced to the absurd. All three films also parody popular "serious" genres—gangster films, college films, and romantic European-kingdom films. The implication of this spoofing is that the sanctified institution is as hollow and dead as the cinematic cliché; the breezy, chaotic, revolutionary activities of the comic anarchists give society's respectable calcifications a much-deserved comeuppance.

—Gerald Mast

The first sentence announces the topic. Everything that follows this topic sentence develops or amplifies it, first by commenting one by one on the three films named at the outset, then by speaking of the three films as a group, and then by offering a closely related generalization (the films spoof serious films) and a comment on the implications of this generalization. The writer begins by stating or summarizing his idea, then offers specific evidence to support it, and then offers a related idea. (In a sense, the paragraph delivers on the promise the writer makes in its first sentence.) The development is from the general to the particular and then again to the general.

2. The next paragraph has its topic sentence at the end:

If we try to recall Boris Karloff's face as the monster in the film of *Frankenstein* (1931), most of us probably think of the seams holding the pieces together, and if we cannot recall other details we assume that the face evokes horror. But when we actually look at a picture of the face rather than recall a memory of it, we are perhaps chiefly impressed by the high, steep forehead (a feature often associated with intelligence), by the darkness surrounding the eyes (often associated with physical or spiritual weariness), and by the gaunt cheeks and the thin lips slightly turned down at the corners (associated with deprivation or restraint). The monster's face is of course in some ways shocking, but probably our chief impression as we look at it is that this is not the face of one who causes suffering but of one who himself is heroically undergoing suffering.

—LESLIE RODRIGUEZ

When the topic sentence is at the end, the paragraph usually develops from the particular to the general, the topic sentence serving to generalize or summarize the information that precedes it. Such a topic sentence can be especially effective in presenting an argument: the reader hears, considers, and accepts the evidence before the argument is explicitly stated, and if the evidence has been effectively presented the reader willingly accepts the conclusion.

3. The next paragraph has no topic sentence:

A few years ago when you mentioned Walt Disney at a respectable party—or anyway this is how it was in California, where I was then—the standard response was a headshake and a groan. Intellectuals spoke of how he butchered the classics—from *Pinocchio* to *Winnie the Pooh,* how his wildlife pictures were sadistic and coy, how the World's Fair sculptures of hippopotamuses were a national if not international disgrace. A few crazies disagreed, and since crazies are always the people to watch, it began to be admitted that the early Pluto movies had a considerable measure of *je ne sais quoi,* that the background animation in *Snow White* was "quite extraordinary," that *Fantasia* did indeed have *one* great sequence (then it became two; now everyone says three, though there's fierce disagreement on exactly which three).

—JOHN GARDNER

The topic here is, roughly, "Intellectuals used to scorn Disney, but recently they have been praising him." Such a sentence could easily begin the paragraph, but it is not necessary because even without it the reader has no difficulty following the discussion. The first two sentences talk about Disney's earlier reputation; then the sentence about the "crazies" introduces the contrary view and the rest of the paragraph illustrates the growing popularity of this contrary view. The paragraph develops its point so clearly and consistently (it is essentially a narrative, in chronological order) that the reader, unlike the reader of a complex analytic paragraph, does not need the help of a topic sentence either at the beginning, to prepare for what follows, or at the end, to pull the whole together.

UNIFYING IDEAS INTO PARAGRAPHS

Although we emphasize **unity** in paragraphs, don't assume that every development or refinement or alteration of your thought requires a new paragraph. Such an assumption would lead to an essay consisting entirely of one-sentence paragraphs. A good paragraph may, for instance,

- ask a question and answer it, or
- describe an effect and then explain the cause, or
- set forth details and then offer a generalization.

Indeed, if the question or the effect or the details can be set forth in a sentence or two, and the answer or the cause or the generalization can be set forth in a sentence or two, the two halves of the topic should be pulled together into a single paragraph. Only if the question (for example) is long and complex and the answer equally long or longer, will you (or, more precisely, your reader) need two or more paragraphs.

Let's consider three paragraphs from an essay on ballooning. In the essay from which the following paragraphs are taken, the writer has already explained that ballooning was born in late eighteenth-century France and that almost from its start there were two types of balloons, gas and hot air. Notice that in the paragraphs printed below the first is on gas, the second is chiefly on hot air (but it helpfully makes comparisons with gas), and the third is on the length of flights of both gas and hot-air balloons. In other words, each paragraph is about one thing—gas balloons, hot-air balloons, length of flight—but each paragraph also builds on what the reader has learned in the previous paragraphs. That the third paragraph is about the flights of gas *and* of hot-air balloons does not mean that it lacks unity; it is a unified discussion of flight lengths.

> Gas balloons swim around in air like a sleeping fish in water, because they weigh about the same as the fluid they're in. A good, big, trans-Atlantic balloon will have 2,000 pounds of vehicle, including gas bag and pilot, taking up about 30 cubic feet (as big as a refrigerator), plus 300 pounds of a "nothing" stuff called helium, which fills 30,000 cubic feet (as big as three houses). Air to fill this 30,000 cubic feet would also weigh 2,300 pounds, so the balloon system averages the same as air, floating in it as part of the wind.
>
> Hot-air balloons use the same size bag filled with hot air instead of helium, kept hot by a boot-sized blowtorch riding just over the pilot's head. Hot air is light, but not as light as helium, so you can't carry as much equipment in a hot-air balloon. You also can't fly as long or as far. Helium will carry a balloon for days (three and a half days is the record), until a lot of gas has leaked out. But a hot-air balloon cools down in minutes, like a house as soon as its heat source runs out of fuel; and today's best fuel (heat-for-weight), propane, lasts only several hours.
>
> A good hot-air flight goes a hundred miles, yet the gas record is 1,897 miles, set by a German in 1914 with the junk (by today's standards) they had then. Unmanned scientific gas balloons have flown half a million miles, staying up more than a year. Japan bombed Oregon in World War II with balloons. Two hot-air balloonists, Tracy Barnes and Malcolm Forbes, have made what they called transcontinental flights, but each was the sum of dozens of end-to-end hops, trailed by pick-up trucks, like throwing a frisbee from Hollywood to Atlantic City.
>
> —DAVID ROYCE

Now contrast the unity of any of the previous three paragraphs on ballooning with the lack of focus in this paragraph from a book on athletic coaching.

> Leadership qualities are a prerequisite for achievement in coaching. A leader is one who is respected for what he says and does, and who is ad-

mired by his team. The coach gains respect by giving respect, and by possessing knowledge and skills associated with the sport. There are many "successful" coaches who are domineering, forceful leaders, gaining power more through fear and even hate than through respect. These military-type men are primarily from the old school of thought, and many younger coaches are achieving their goals through more humanistic approaches.

Something is wrong here. The first half of the paragraph tells us that "a leader is one who is respected for what he says and does," but the second half of the paragraph contradicts that assertion, telling us that "many" leaders hold their position "more through fear and even hate than through respect." The trouble is *not* that the writer is talking about two kinds of leaders; a moment ago we saw that a writer can in one paragraph talk about two kinds of balloons. The trouble here is that we need a unifying idea if these two points are to be given in one paragraph. The idea might be: There are two kinds of leaders, those who are respected and those who are feared. This idea might be developed along these lines:

> Leadership qualities are a prerequisite for achievement in coaching, but these qualities can be of two radically different kinds. One kind of leader is respected and admired by his team for what he says and does. The coach gains respect by giving respect, and by possessing knowledge and skills associated with the sport. The other kind of coach is a domineering, forceful leader, gaining power more through fear than through respect. These military-type men are primarily from the old school of thought, whereas most of the younger coaches achieve their goals through the more humane approaches of the first type.

ORGANIZATION IN PARAGRAPHS

A paragraph needs more than a unified point; it needs a reasonable **organization** or sequence. After all, a box containing all of the materials for a model airplane has unity (all the parts of the plane are there), but not until the parts are joined in the proper relationship do we get a plane. In the following paragraph, a sentence is out of place.

> Leonardo da Vinci's *Mona Lisa* has attracted and puzzled viewers for almost five hundred years, and I don't suffer from the delusion that I can fully account for the spell the picture casts. Still, I think it is easy enough to account for at least part of the mystery. The most expressive features of a face are the mouth and the eyes, and we notice that Leonardo slightly blurred or shaded the corners of the mouth so that its exact expression cannot be characterized, or, if we characterize it, we change our mind when we look again. Lisa herself is something of a mystery, for history tells us nothing about her personality or about her relationship to Leonardo. The corners of her eyes, like the corners of her mouth, are slightly obscured, contributing to her elusive expression.

Which sentence is out of place in the paragraph you have just read? How might you work it into its proper place?

Leonardo da Vinci. *Mona Lisa.*

Exactly how the parts of a paragraph will fit together depends, of course, on what the paragraph is doing.

1. If it is *describing* a place, it may move from a general view to the significant details—or from immediately striking details to some less obvious but perhaps more important ones. It may move from near to far, or from far to near, or from the past to the present.

2. If it is *explaining,* it may move from cause to effect, or from effect to cause, or from past to present; or it may offer an example.

3. If it is *arguing,* it may move from evidence to conclusion, or from a conclusion to supporting evidence; or it may offer one piece of evidence, for instance an anecdote (a short narrative) that illustrates the argument.

4. If it is *narrating*, it will likely move chronologically; in the following paragraph, written by a student, we move from waking at 7:00 A.M., to washing and combing, to readiness for the day's work, and then to a glance at the rest of the day that will undo the 7:00 A.M. cleanup.

I can remember waking at seven to Ma's call. I'd bound out of bed because Ma just didn't allow people to be lazy. She'd grab me and we'd rush to the bathroom for the morning ritual. Bathing, toothbrushing, lotioning, all overseen by her watchful eyes. She didn't let anything go by. No missing behind the ears, no splashing around and pretending to bathe. I bathed and scrubbed and put that lotion on till my whole body was like butter on a warm pan. After inspection it was back to my room and the day's clothes were selected. A bit of tugging and I was dressed. Then she'd sit me down and pull out the big black comb. That comb would glide through my hair and then the braiding would begin. My head would jerk but I never yelled, never even whimpered. Finally I was ready. Ready to start the day and get dirty and spoil all of Ma's work. But she didn't care. She knew you couldn't keep a child from getting dirty but you could teach it to be respectable.

5. If a paragraph is *classifying* (dividing a subject into its parts) it may begin by enumerating the parts and go on to study each, perhaps in climactic order. Here is an example:

The chief reasons people wear masks are these: to have fun, to protect themselves, to disguise themselves, and to achieve a new identity. At Halloween, children wear masks for fun; they may, of course, also think they are disguising themselves, but chiefly their motive is to experience the joy of saying "boo" to someone. Soldiers wore masks for protection, in ancient times against swords and battle-axes, in more recent times against poison gas. Bank robbers wear masks to disguise themselves, and though of course this disguise is a sort of protection, a robber's reason for wearing a mask is fairly distinct from a soldier's. All of these reasons so far are easily understood, but we may have more trouble grasping the reason that primitive people use masks in religious rituals. Some ritual masks seem merely to be attempts to frighten away evil spirits, and some seem merely to be disguises so that the evil spirits will not know who the wearer is. But most religious masks are worn with the idea that the wearer achieves a new identity, a union with supernatural powers, and thus in effect the wearer becomes--really becomes, not merely pretends to be--a new person.

Notice that the first sentence offers four reasons for wearing masks. The rest of the paragraph amplifies these reasons, one by one, and in the order indicated in the first sentence. Since the writer regards the last reason as the most interesting and the most difficult to grasp, he discusses it at the greatest length, giving it about as much space as he gives to the first three reasons altogether.

The way in which a paragraph is organized, then, will depend on what the writer is trying to do—what the writer's purpose is. Almost always one of the writer's purposes is to make something clear to a reader. Among the common methods of organizing a paragraph, and keeping things clear, are the following:

1. General to particular (topic sentence usually at the beginning)
2. Particular to general (topic sentence usually at the end)
3. Enumeration of parts or details or reasons (probably in climactic order)
4. Question and answer
5. Cause and effect
6. Comparison and contrast
7. Analogy
8. Chronology
9. Spatial order (e.g., near to far, or right to left)

The only rule that can cover all paragraphs is this: readers must never feel that they are stumbling as they follow the writer to the end of the paragraph. They

Vladimir Koziakin. *Spaghetti.*

should not have to go back and read the paragraph again to figure out what the writer had in mind. A paragraph is not a maze; it should be organized so that readers can glide through it in seconds, not minutes.

COHERENCE IN PARAGRAPHS

In addition to having a unified point and a reasonable organization, a good paragraph is **coherent;** that is, the connections between ideas in the paragraph are clear. Coherence can often be achieved by inserting the right transitional words or by taking care to repeat key words.

Transitions

Richard Wagner, commenting on his work as a composer of operas, once said "The art of composition is the art of transition," for his art moved from note to note, measure to measure, scene to scene. **Transitions** establish connections between ideas; they alert readers to what will follow. Here are some of the most common transitional words and phrases.

1. **amplification or likeness:** similarly, likewise, and, also, again, second, third, in addition, furthermore, moreover, finally
2. **emphasis:** chiefly, equally, indeed, even more important
3. **contrast or concession:** but, on the contrary, on the other hand, by contrast, of course, however, still, doubtless, no doubt, nevertheless, granted that, conversely, although, admittedly
4. **example:** for example, for instance, as an example, specifically, consider as an illustration, that is, such as, like
5. **consequence or cause and effect:** thus, so, then, it follows, as a result, therefore, hence
6. **restatement:** in short, that is, in effect, in other words
7. **place:** in the foreground, further back, in the distance
8. **time:** afterward, next, then, as soon as, later, until, when, finally, last, at last
9. **conclusion:** finally, therefore, thus, to sum up

Consider the following paragraph:

Folklorists are just beginning to look at Africa. A great quantity of folklore materials has been gathered from African countries in the past century and published by missionaries, travelers, administrators, linguists, and anthropologists incidentally to their main pursuits. No fieldworker has devoted himself exclusively or even largely to the recording and analysis of folklore materials, according to a committee of the African Studies Association reporting in 1966 on the state of research in the African arts. Yet Africa is the continent supreme for traditional cultures that nurture folklore. Why this neglect?

—RICHARD M. DORSON

The reader gets the point, but the second sentence seems to contradict the first: the first sentence tells us that folklorists are just beginning to look at Africa, but the next tells us that lots of folklore has been collected. An "although" between these sentences would clarify the author's point, especially if the third sentence were hooked on to the second, thus:

Folklorists are just beginning to look at Africa. Although a great quantity

of folklore materials has been gathered from African countries in the past

century by missionaries, travelers, administrators, linguists, and

anthropologists incidentally to their main pursuits, no fieldworker has

devoted himself . . .

But this revision gives us an uncomfortably long second sentence. Further revision would help. The real point of the original passage, though it is smothered, is that although many people have incidentally collected folklore materials in Africa, professional folklorists have not been active there. The contrast ought to be sharpened:

Folklorists are just beginning to look at Africa. True, missionaries,

travelers, administrators, linguists, and anthropologists have collected a

quantity of folklore materials incidentally to their main pursuits, but

folklorists have lagged behind. No fieldworker . . .

In this revision the words that clarify are the small but important words "true" and "but." The original paragraph is like a jigsaw puzzle that's missing some tiny but necessary pieces.

Repetition

Coherence is also achieved through the **repetition** of key words. When you repeat words or phrases, or when you provide clear substitutes (such as pronouns and demonstrative adjectives), you are helping the reader to keep step with your developing thoughts. Grammatical constructions too can be repeated, the repetitions or parallels linking the sentences or ideas.

In the following example, notice how the repetitions provide continuity.

Sir Kenneth Clark's *The Nude* is an important book; and, luckily, it is also most readable; but it is not a bedside book. Each sentence needs attention because each sentence is relevant to the whole, and the incorrigible skipper will sometimes find himself obliged to turn back several pages, chapters even in order to pick up the thread of the argument. Does this sound stiff? The book is not stiff because it is delightfully written. Let the student have no fears; he is not going to be bored for a moment while he reads these 400 pages; he is going to be excited, amused, instructed, provoked, charmed, irritated, and surprised.

Notice not only the exact repetitions ("each sentence," "stiff") but also the slight variations, such as "an important book," "not a bedside book"; "he is not going," "he is going"; and the emphatic list of participles ("excited, amused, instructed," and so on) at the conclusion.

LINKING PARAGRAPHS TOGETHER

Since each paragraph in an essay generally develops a single idea, a single (new) aspect of the main point of the essay, as one paragraph follows another, readers should feel they are getting somewhere—smoothly and without stumbling. As you move from one paragraph to the next—from one step in the development of your main idea to the next—you probably can keep your readers with you if you link the beginning of each new paragraph to the end of the paragraph that precedes it. Often a single transitional word (such as those listed on page 60) will suffice; sometimes repeating key terms will help connect a sequence of paragraphs together and make your essay (as many writers put it) "flow."

Consider the movement of ideas in the following essay written in response to an assignment that asked students to analyze a family photograph.

Cheryl Lee

Writing 125

Ms. Medina

April 1, 1999

The Story Behind the Gestures

1   At the close of my graduation ceremony, my entire family gathered together to immortalize the special moment on film. No one escaped the flash of my mother's camera because she was determined to document every minute of the occasion at every possible angle. My mother made sure that she took pictures of me with my hat on, with my hat off, holding the bouquet, sitting, standing, and in countless other positions. By the time this family picture was taken, my smile was intact, frozen on my face. This is not to say that my smile was anything less than genuine, for it truly was a smile of thankfulness and joy. It is just that after posing for so

many pictures, what initially began as a spontaneous reaction became a
frozen expression.

2   The viewer should, however, consider not so much the frozen
expressions of those in the photograph, but rather the fact that the picture
is posed. A posed picture supposedly shows only what the people in the
picture want the viewer to see--in this case, their happiness. But ironically
the photograph reveals much more about its subjects than the viewer first
imagines. The photograph speaks of relationships and personalities. It
speaks about the more intimate details that first seem invisible but that
become undeniable through the study of gestures.

3   In the photograph, the most prominent and symbolic of gestures is
the use and position of the arms. Both my father and mother place an arm
around me and in turn around each other. Their encircling arms, however,
do more than just show affection; they unify the three figures into a close
huddle that leads the viewer's eye directly to them as opposed to the
background or the periphery. The slightly bended arms that rest at their
sides act as arrows that not only reinforce the three figures as the focal

point but also exclude the fourth figure, my brother, from sharing the "spotlight." Unlike the other members of the family whose arms and hands are intertwined, Edwin stands with both hands down in front of him, latching onto no one. The lack of physical contact between the huddled figures and Edwin is again emphasized as he positions himself away from the viewer's eye as he stands in the periphery.

4   Edwin's position in the photograph is indicative of him as a person, for he always seems to isolate himself from the spotlight, from being the center of attention. Thus, it is his decision to escape public scrutiny, not the force of my parents' arms that drives him to the side. His quiet, humble nature directs him away from even being the focal point of a picture and leads him towards establishing his own individuality and independence in privacy. His long hair and his "hand-me-down" clothes are all an expression of his simply being himself. The reason behind his physical independence is the emotional independence that he already possesses at the age of sixteen. He stands alone because he can stand alone.

5   While Edwin stands apart from the other three figures, I stand enclosed and protected. The lock of arms as well as the bouquet restrain me; they dissuade me from breaking away in favor of independence. Although my mother wants me to achieve the same kind of independence that Edwin has achieved, she works to delay the time when I actually will move away to the periphery. Perhaps my being the only daughter, the only other female in the family, has something to do with my mother's desire to keep me close and dependent as long as possible. Her arm reaches out with bouquet in hand as if to shield me from the world's unpleasantness. Even though my father also holds onto me with an encircling arm, it is my mother's firm grip that alone persuades me to stay within the boundary of their protective arms.

6   Her grip, which proves more powerful than my father's hold,

restrains not only me but also my father. In the picture, he falls victim to

the same outstretched hand, the same touch of the bouquet. Yet this time,

my mother's bouquet does more than just restrain; it seems to push my

father back "into line" or into his so-called place. The picture illustrates

this exertion of influence well, for my mother in real life does indeed

assume the role of the dominant figure. Although my father remains the

head of the household in title, it is my mother around whom the household

revolves; she oversees the insignificant details as well as the major ones.

But my father doesn't mind at all. Like me, he also enjoys the protection

her restraining arm offers. It is because of our mutual dependence on my

mother that my father and I seem to draw closer. This dependence in turn

strengthens both of our relationships with my mother.

7   At the time the picture was taken, I seriously doubt that my mother

realized the significance of her position in the picture or the import of her

gestures. All of us in fact seem too blinded by the festivity of the occasion

to realize that this photograph would show more than just a happy family

at a daughter's graduation. The family photograph would inevitably

become a telling portrait of each member of the family. It would, in a

sense, leave us vulnerable to the speculative eyes of the viewer, who in

carefully examining the photograph would recognize the secrets hidden in

each frozen expression.

A few observations on these paragraphs may be useful. First, notice that each paragraph in the sequence examines a different aspect of the photograph and introduces a new point into the discussion. The first paragraph gives background information (the photograph was taken at Lee's graduation); the second paragraph states the writer's point—that studying the gestures of her family members enables us to understand their "personalities and relationships." Each succeeding paragraph treats one of these gestures (paragraph 2, for example, considers the encircling arms) or one of the personalities or relationships. Paragraph 4 focuses on the writer's brother Edwin; paragraph 5 focuses on Lee's relationship to her mother; paragraph 6 focuses on her mother and father. We might think that symmetry requires that each family member get a single paragraph, but given the complexity of their relationships to each other, and given the mother's dominance in the family, it makes sense that things don't break down so neatly and that Lee devotes two paragraphs to her mother.

Second, notice how Lee makes the essay cohere. Although she uses some transitional words ("however" at the beginning of the second paragraph; "while" at the beginning of the fifth paragraph), she establishes coherence in this essay primarily by repeating the key terms of her discussion. The first sentence of each new paragraph picks up a word or phrase from the last sentence of the paragraph preceding it. The phrase "frozen expressions" links the beginning of the second paragraph to the end of the first; "gesture" links the second paragraph to the third; "position" links the third to the fourth; "stand" links the fourth to the fifth; and so on. These links are hardly noticeable on a first reading, but because Lee uses transitions and repetition effectively, the writing flows, and the reader never stumbles.

PARAGRAPH LENGTH

There are no hard-and-fast rules about paragraph length, but most good paragraphs are between 100 and 200 words, consisting of more than one or two but fewer than eight or ten sentences. It is not a matter, however, of counting words or sentences; paragraphs are coherent blocks, substantial units of your essay, and the spaces between them are brief resting places allowing the reader to take in what you have said. One double-spaced, word-processed page of writing (approximately 250 words) is about as much as the reader can take before requiring a slight break. On the other hand, a single page with half a dozen paragraphs is probably faulty because the reader is too often interrupted with needless pauses and because the page has too few *developed* ideas: an assertion is made, and then another, and another. These assertions are unconvincing because they are not supported with detail. To put it another way, a paragraph is a room in the house you are building. If your essay is some 500 words long (about two double-spaced word-processed pages) you probably will not break it down into more than four or five rooms or paragraphs; if you break it down into a dozen paragraphs, readers will feel they are touring a rabbit warren rather than a house.

The Use and Abuse of Short Paragraphs

A short paragraph can be effective when it summarizes a highly detailed previous paragraph or group of paragraphs, or when it serves as a transition between two complicated paragraphs, but unless you are sure that the reader needs a break, avoid thin paragraphs. A paragraph that is nothing but a transition can usually be altered into a transitional phrase or clause or sentence that starts the next paragraph. But of course there are times when a short paragraph is exactly right. Notice the effect of the two-sentence paragraph between two longer paragraphs:

> After I returned to prison, I took a long look at myself and, for the first time in my life, admitted that I was wrong, that I had gone astray— astray not so much from the white man's law as from being human, civilized—for I could not approve the act of rape. Even though I had some

insight into my own motivations, I did not feel justified. I lost my self-respect. My pride as a man dissolved and my whole fragile moral structure seemed to collapse, completely shattered.

That is why I started to write. To save myself.

I realized that no one could save me but myself. The prison authorities were both uninterested and unable to help me. I had to seek out the truth and unravel the snarled web of my motivations. I had to find out who I am and what I want to be, what type of man I should be, and what I could do to become the best of which I was capable. I understood that what had happened to me had also happened to countless other blacks and it would happen to many, many more.

—ELDRIDGE CLEAVER

If the content of the second paragraph were less momentous, it would hardly merit a paragraph. Here the brevity contributes to the enormous impact; those two simple sentences, set off by themselves, seem equal in weight, so to speak, to the longer paragraphs that precede and follow. They are the hinge on which the door turns.

When used for emphasis, short paragraphs can be effective.

Often, though, short paragraphs (like the one directly above) leave readers feeling unsatisfied, even annoyed. Consider these two consecutive paragraphs from a draft of a student's essay on Leonardo's *Mona Lisa*.

Leonardo's "Mona Lisa," painted about 1502, has caused many people to wonder about the lady's expression. Different viewers see different things.

The explanation of the puzzle is chiefly in the mysterious expression that Leonardo conveys. The mouth and the eyes are especially important.

Sometimes you can improve a sequence of short paragraphs merely by joining one paragraph to the next. But unsatisfactory short paragraphs usually cannot be repaired so simply. The reason is that the source of the problem is usually not that sentences have been needlessly separated from each other, but that generalizations have not been supported by details, or that claims haven't been supported by evidence. Here is the student's revised version, strengthening the two thin paragraphs of the draft.

Leonardo's "Mona Lisa," painted about 1502, has caused many people to wonder about the lady's expression. Doubtless she is remarkably life-like but exactly what experience of life, what mood, does she reveal? Is she sad, or gently mocking, or uncertain or self-satisfied, or lost in daydreams? Why are we never satisfied when we try to name her emotion?

Part of the uncertainty may of course be due to the subject as a whole. What can we make out of the combination of this smiling lady and that utterly unpopulated landscape? But surely a large part of the explanation lies in the way that Leonardo painted the face's two most expressive features, the eyes and the mouth. He slightly obscured the corners of these, so that we cannot precisely characterize them: and although on one viewing we may see them one way, on another viewing we may see them slightly differently. If today we think she looks detached, tomorrow we may think she looks slightly threatening.

This revision is not simply a padded version of the earlier paragraphs; it is a necessary clarification of them, for without the details the generalizations mean almost nothing to a reader.

INTRODUCTORY PARAGRAPHS

As the poet Byron said, at the beginning of a long part of a long poem, "Nothing so difficult as a beginning." Woody Allen thinks so too. In an interview he said that the toughest part of writing is "to go from nothing to the first draft."

Almost all writers—professionals as well as amateurs—find that the first paragraphs in their drafts are false starts. As we suggest in Chapter 1, we think you shouldn't worry too much about the opening paragraph of your draft; you'll almost surely want to revise your opening later anyway. (Surprisingly often your first paragraph may simply be deleted; your second, you may find, is where your essay truly begins.)

When writing a first draft you merely need something—almost anything may do—to break the ice. But in your finished paper the opening cannot be mere throat-clearing. The opening should be interesting. Among the commonest *un*interesting openings are:

1. A dictionary definition ("Webster says . . .")
2. A restatement of your title. The title is (let's assume) "Anarchism and the Marx Brothers," and the first sentence says, "This essay will study the anarchic acts of the Marx Brothers." True, the sentence announces the topic of the essay, but it gives no information about the topic beyond what the title already offers, and it provides no information about you either—that is, no sense of your response to the topic, such as might be present in, say, "The Marx Brothers are funny, but one often has the feeling that under the fun the violence has serious implications."
3. A broad generalization, such as "Ever since the beginning of time, human beings have been violent." Again, such a sentence may be fine if it helps you to start drafting, but it should not remain in your final version: it's dull—and it tells your readers almost nothing about the essay they're

about to read. (Our example, after all, could begin anything from an analysis of *Pulp Fiction* to a term paper on World War II.) To put it another way, the ever-since-the-beginning-of-time opening lacks substance—and if your opening lacks substance, it will not matter what you say next. No one will bother to read more.

What is left? What *is* a good way for a final version to begin? Your introductory paragraph will be at least moderately interesting if it gives information, and it will be pleasing if the information provides focus; that is, if it lets the reader know exactly what your topic is, and where you will be going. Remember, when you write, *you* are the teacher; it won't do to begin,

George Orwell says he shot the elephant because . . .

We need some information, identifying the text you are writing about.

George Orwell, in "Shooting an Elephant," says he shot the elephant

because . . .

Even better is,

In "Shooting an Elephant," George Orwell sets forth his reflections on

his service as a policeman in Burma. He suggests that he once shot an

elephant because . . . but his final paragraph suggests that we must look

for additional reasons.

Compare, for example, the opening sentences from three essays written by students on Anne Moody's *Coming of Age in Mississippi.* The book is the autobiography of an African-American woman, covering her early years with her sharecropper parents, her schooling, and finally her work in the civil rights movement.

The environment that surrounds a person from an early age tends to

be a major factor in determining their character.

This is what we call a **zonker** (see page 82), an all-purpose sentence that serves no specific purpose well. Notice also the faulty reference of the pronoun (the plural "their" refers to the singular "a person"), the weaseling of "tends to be a major factor," and the vagueness of "early age" and "environment" and "character." These all warn us that the writer will waste our time.

It is unfortunate but true that racial or color prejudice shows itself

early in the life of a child.

Less pretentious than the first example, but it labors the obvious, and sounds annoyingly preachy.

Anne Moody's autobiography, <u>Coming of Age in Mississippi</u>, vividly illustrates how she discovered her identity as an African-American.

Surely this is the best of the three openings. Informative and focused, it identifies the book's theme and method, and it offers an evaluation. The essayist has been considerate of her readers: if we are interested in women's autobiographies or life in the South, we will read on. If we aren't, we are grateful to her for letting us off the bus at the first stop.

Let's look now not simply at an opening sentence but at an entire first paragraph, the opening paragraph of an analytic essay. Notice how the student provides the reader with the necessary information about the book she is discussing (the diary of a man whose son is brain-damaged) and also focuses the reader's attention on the essay's topic (the quality that distinguishes this diary from others).

Josh Greenfeld's diary, <u>A Place for Noah</u>, records the attempts of a smart, thoughtful man to reconcile himself to his son's autism, a severe mental and physical disorder. Most diaries function as havens for secret thoughts. And Greenfeld's diary does frequently supply a voice to Greenfeld's darkest fears about who will ultimately care for Noah. It provides, too, an intimate glimpse of a family striving to remain a coherent unit despite their tragedy. But beyond affording such urgent and personal revelations, <u>A Place for Noah</u>, in chronicling the isolation of the Greenfelds, reveals how inadequate and ineffectual our medical and educational systems are in responding to families victimized by catastrophic illness.

This example is engaging, although fairly direct—but of course you can provide interest and focus by other, more indirect means, among them the following:

- A quotation
- An anecdote or other short narrative
- An interesting fact (a statistic, for instance, showing the reader that you know something about your topic)
- A definition of an important term—but not merely one derived from a desk dictionary
- An assertion (in an essay offering a proposal) that a problem exists
- A glance at a view different from your own
- A question—but an interesting one, such as "Why do we call some words obscene?"

Many excellent opening paragraphs do not use any of these devices, and you need not use any of them if they feel forced. But in your reading you may observe that these devices are used widely. Here is an example of the second device, **an anecdote** that makes an effective, indeed an unnerving, introduction to an essay on aging.

> There is an old American folk tale about a wooden bowl. It seems that Grandmother, with her trembling hands, was guilty of occasionally breaking a dish. Her daughter angrily gave her a wooden bowl, and told her that she must eat out of it from now on. The young granddaughter, observing this, asked her mother why Grandmother must eat from a wooden bowl when the rest of the family was given china plates. "Because she is old!" answered her mother. The child thought for a moment and then told her mother, "You must save the wooden bowl when Grandma dies." Her mother asked why, and the child replied, "For when you are old."
>
> —SHARON R. CURTIN

The third strategy, **an interesting detail**, shows the reader that you know something about your topic and that you are worth reading. We have already seen (page 52) a rather quiet example of this device, in a paragraph about Charles Darwin, which began "Charles Darwin's youth was unmarked by signs of genius." Here is a more obvious example, from an essay on blue jeans:

> That blue jeans or denims are not found only in Texas is not surprising if we recall that jeans are named for Genoa (Gene), where the cloth was first made, and that denim is cloth de Nîmes, that is, from Nîmes, a city in France.

(Such information is to be had by spending about thirty seconds with a dictionary.)

The fourth strategy, **a definition**, is fairly common in analytic essays; the essayist first clears the ground by specifying the topic. (For more on definition, see Chapter 11, "Defining.") Here is the beginning of an essay on bilingual education.

> Let's begin by defining "bilingual education." As commonly used today, the term does *not* mean teaching students a language other than English (almost everyone would agree that foreign-language instruction should be available, and that it is desirable for Americans to be fluent not only in English but also in some other language); nor does "bilingual education" mean offering courses in English as a second language to students whose native language is, for example, Chinese, or Spanish or Navajo or Aleut. (Again, almost everyone would agree that such instruction should be offered where economically possible.) Rather, it means offering instruction in such courses as mathematics, history, and science *in the student's native language,* while also offering courses in English as a second language. Programs vary in details, but the idea is that the non-native speaker should be spared the trauma of total immersion in English until he or she has completed several years of studying English as a

second language. During this period, instruction in other subjects is given in the student's native language.

—Tina Bakka

The fifth strategy, **the assertion that a problem exists**, is common in essays that make proposals. The following example is the first paragraph of a (successful) grant proposal written by engineers seeking government funding for their research project, a new method for treating liver cancer. Notice that the paragraph does not in fact offer the authors' proposal; it simply points out that there really is an unsolved problem, and the reader infers that the proposal will offer the solution.

Liver cancer, especially metastatic colorectal cancer, is a significant and increasing health concern. In the United States, half of the 157,000 new cases of colorectal cancer will develop metastases in the liver. These metastases will lead to over 17,000 deaths annually. And while not as significant a health risk as colorectal metastasis, hepatocellular carcinoma is being diagnosed with increasing frequency. The current standard of practice for treating liver cancer is surgical resection, but only 10% of patients are eligible for this procedure. (Circumstances limiting eligibility include the tumor location, the number of lobes affected by the cancer, the patient's general poor health, and cirrhosis.) Further, less than 20% of those patients who undergo resection survive for three years without recurrence. Transplantation is an alternative to resection, but this technique is not appropriate for metastatic disease or for larger cancers, and the shortage of liver grafts limits the usefulness of this technique. Systemic chemotherapy has been shown to have a therapeutic effect on metastases, but it has also been shown to have no effect on long-term survival rates.

—Michael Curley and Patrick Hamilton

The sixth strategy, **a glance at the opposition**, is especially effective if the opposing view is well-established, but while you state it, you should manage to convey your distrust of it. Here is an example:

One often hears, correctly, that there is a world food crisis, and one almost as often hears that not enough food is produced to feed the world's entire population. The wealthier countries, it is said, jeopardize their own chances for survival when they attempt to subsidize all of the poorer countries in which the masses are starving. Often the life-boat analogy is offered: There is room in the boat for only X people, and to take in $X + 1$ is to overload the boat and to invite the destruction of all. But is it true that the world cannot and does not produce enough food to save the whole population from starving?

—V. Nagarajan

The seventh strategy, **a question**, is briefly illustrated by the opening paragraph of an essay about whether it is sometimes permissible for doctors to lie to their patients.

Should doctors ever lie to benefit their patients—to speed recovery or to conceal the approach of death? In medicine as in law, government, and other lines of work, the requirements of honesty often seem dwarfed by greater needs: the need to shelter from brutal news or to uphold a promise of secrecy; to expose corruption or to promote the public interest.

—Sissela Bok

Clearly, there is no one way to write an opening paragraph, but we want to add that you cannot go wrong in beginning your essay—especially if it's an analytic essay written for a course in the humanities—with a paragraph that includes **a statement of your thesis**. A common version of this kind of paragraph

- offers some background (if you're writing about a novel, for example, you'll give the author and title as well as relevant information about the novel's plot);
- suggests the problem or question the essay will address (in the paragraph below, the problem is implied: In *Frankenstein* similar characters meet very different fates; how can we account for the difference?); and;
- ends with a sentence that states the main point, or thesis, of the essay.

In Frankenstein, Mary Shelley frames the novel with narratives of two similar characters who meet markedly different fates. Frankenstein, the medical researcher, and Walton, the explorer, are both passionately determined to push forward the boundaries of human knowledge. But while Walton's ambition to explore unknown regions of the earth is directed by reason and purpose, Frankenstein's ambition to create life is unfocussed and misguided. This difference in the nature of their ambitions determines their fates. Walton's controlled ambition leads him to abandon his goal in order to save the lives of his crew members. When we last see him, he is heading toward home and safety. Frankenstein's unchecked ambition leads to his own death and the self-destruction of his creature.

CONCLUDING PARAGRAPHS

Concluding paragraphs, like opening paragraphs, are especially difficult if only because they are so conspicuous. Fortunately, you are not always obliged to write one. Descriptive essays, for example, may end merely with a final paragraph, not with a paragraph that draws a conclusion. In an expository essay explaining a process or mechanism you may simply stop when you have finished. Just check to see that the last sentence is a good one, clear and vigorous, and stop. In such essays there is usually no need for a crescendo signaling your farewell to the reader. Persuasive essays are more likely to need concluding paragraphs, not merely final paragraphs. But even persuasive essays, if they are short enough, may end without a formal conclusion; if the last paragraph sets forth the last step of the argument, that may be conclusion enough.

But if you do have to write a concluding paragraph, say something interesting. It is not of the slightest interest to say "Thus we see . . ." and then echo your title and first paragraph. There is some justification for a summary at the end of a long essay because the reader may have half forgotten some of the ideas presented thirty pages earlier, but an essay that can easily be held in the mind needs something different, something more. A good concluding paragraph rounds out the previous discussion. Such a paragraph may offer a few sentences that summarize (without the obviousness of "We may now summarize"); but it will probably also draw an inference that has not previously been expressed. To draw such an inference is not to introduce an entirely new idea—the end of an essay is hardly the place for that. Rather it is to see the previous material in a fresh perspective, to take the discussion perhaps one step further.

Because all writers have to find out what they think about any given topic, and have to find the strategies appropriate for presenting these thoughts to a particular audience, we hesitate to offer a do-it-yourself kit for final paragraphs, but the following simple devices often work:

- End with a quotation, especially a quotation that amplifies or varies a quotation used in the opening paragraph.
- End with some idea or detail from the beginning of the essay and thus bring it full circle.
- End with a new (but related) point, one that takes your discussion a step further.
- End with an allusion, say to a historical or mythological figure or event, putting your topic in a larger framework.
- End with a glance at the readers—not with a demand that they mount the barricades, but with a suggestion that the next move is theirs.

If you adopt any of these devices, do so quietly; the aim is not to write a grand finale, but to complete or round out a discussion.

Here are the beginning and the end of an essay on change in Emily Dickinson's poetry. (We reprint the beginning as well as the end of the essay to illustrate the first two suggestions above.) Note the way the writer begins the last paragraph with a quotation that amplifies the opening paragraph's point about Dickinson's troubled response to change in the opening paragraphs; note also that the word "palsy," found in the opening paragraph, appears again in the last paragraph.

Emily Dickinson's life knew little change of the conventional sort. As

her sister-in-law Susan wrote in an 1886 obituary, "Miss Emily Dickinson

of Amherst,"

The death of Miss Emily Dickinson, daughter of the late Edward
Dickinson, at Amherst on Saturday, makes another sad inroad on the
small circle so long occupying the old family mansion. It was for a
long generation overlooked by death, and one passing in and out of
there thought of old-fashioned times, when parents and children
grew up and passed maturity together, in lives of singular
uneventfulness, unmarked by sad or joyous crises.

Dickinson lived in the same house all her years but the one she spent at
seminary; she never married; she never worked. Yet in spite of this
permanence--or because of it--change seemed to fascinate her and to
inspire much of her poetry. She says as much in a June 1862 letter to her
mentor T. W. Higginson, whom she tells that when "a sudden light on
Orchards, or a new fashion in the wind trouble my attention," she feels a
"palsy" that "the Verses just relieve" (Selected 174). Indeed Dickinson is
probably best known for her many verses on the most troubling of all
changes: "Because I could not stop for Death / He kindly stopped for me."
Yet changes--deaths, seasonal changes, shifts in the quality of light (as at
sunset or sunrise)--both trouble and charm Dickinson. A remark from a
letter of April 1873 to her cousins Louise and Frances Norcross reveals the
dichotomy in her attitude. . . .

Now for the final paragraph:

"Poetry is what Dickinson did to her doubts and incomprehension,"
writes critic David Porter (328), and she surely felt doubt about things
she knew or feared would change. "Because I could not say it--I fixed it in
the Verse--for you to read--when your thought wavers," she wrote in an
1862 letter to Samuel Bowles (Selected 170). Dickinson wrote about change
to give it the kind of order she understood, to control it and to fix it and
so relieve her "palsy." To this extent, poetry for her must have had an

immortal quality, like the wine of Indian Summer, and writing it must

have been an ultimate act of faith.

And here are the beginning and end of a review, by Salman Rushdie, of Kazuo Ishiguro's *Remains of the Day*. The conclusion sets the novel into the context of Ishiguro's other fiction; it also introduces, in its final sentence, a new point (that England and Japan may be surprisingly similar), a point connected to the discussion of "formality" and "dignity" in the opening.

The beginning:

> The surface of Kazuo Ishiguro's novel, *The Remains of the Day,* is almost perfectly still. Stevens, a butler well past his prime, is on a week's motoring holiday in the West Country. He tootles around, taking in the sights and encountering a series of green-and-pleasant country folk who seem to have escaped from one of those English films of the 1950s in which the lower orders doff their caps and behave with re-spect towards a gent with properly creased trousers and flattened vow-els. It is, in fact, July 1956; but other, timeless worlds, the world of Jeeves and Bertie Wooster, the upstairs-downstairs world of Hudson, Mrs. Bridges and the Bellamys, are also in the air. . . .

The end:

> Ishiguro's first novel, *A Pale View of Hills,* was set in postwar Nagasaki but never mentioned the Bomb; his new book is set in the very month that Nasser nationalized the Suez Canal, but fails to mention the crisis, even though the Suez debacle marked the end of a certain kind of Britain whose passing is a subject of the novel. Ishiguro's sec-ond Japanese novel, *An Artist of the Floating World,* also dealt with themes of collaboration, self-deception, self-betrayal and with certain notions of formality and dignity that recur here. It seems that England and Japan may not be so very unlike one another, beneath their rather differently inscrutable surfaces.

All essayists will have to find their own ways of ending each essay; the five strategies we have suggested are common but they are not for you if you don't find them useful. And so, rather than ending this section with rules about how to end essays, we suggest how not to end them: don't merely summarize, don't say "in conclusion," don't introduce a totally new point, and don't apologize.

✓ A Checklist for Revising Paragraphs

- ✔ Does the paragraph *say* anything? Does it have substance?
- ✔ Does the paragraph have a topic sentence? If so, is it in the best place? If the paragraph doesn't have a topic sentence, might one improve the paragraph? Or does it have a clear topic idea?
- ✔ If the paragraph is an opening paragraph, is it interesting enough to at-tract and to hold a reader's attention? If it is a later paragraph, does it eas-ily evolve out of the previous paragraph, and lead into the next para-graph?
- ✔ Does the paragraph contain some principle of development, for instance from cause to effect, or from general to particular?

✔ Does each sentence clearly follow from the preceding sentence? Have you provided transitional words or cues to guide your reader? Would it be useful to repeat certain key words, for clarity?

✔ What is the purpose of the paragraph? Do you want to summarize, or tell a story, or give an illustration, or concede a point, or what? Is your purpose clear to you, and does the paragraph fulfill your purpose?

✔ Is the closing paragraph effective, and not an unnecessary restatement of the obvious?

Exercises

1. Reread the paragraph on page 53, in which a topic sentence (about three films by the Marx Brothers) begins the paragraph. Then write a paragraph with a similar construction, clarifying the topic sentence with details. You might, for example, begin thus: "When facing a right-handed batter, a left-handed pitcher has a distinct advantage over a right-handed pitcher." Another possible beginning: "All three major television networks offer pretty much the same kinds of entertainment during prime time."

2. Reread the paragraph on page 54, discussing the face of Frankenstein's monster, and then write a paragraph on some other widely known face, ending your paragraph with a topic sentence. The cover of a recent issue of *Time* or *Newsweek* may provide you with the face you need.

3. The following paragraph is unified, but incoherent. How could it be reorganized?

Abortion, the expulsion of a fetus which could not develop and function alone successfully, is an issue which has caused much discussion in the past decade. There exist mainly two opposing groups concerning this subject, but many people's opinions lie somewhere in the middle. Some believe that abortions should be legalized unconditionally throughout the United States, while others believe that abortions should be illegal in all cases.

4. The following paragraph is both unified and fairly well organized, but it is still lacking in coherence. What would you do to improve it?

The cyclist must also master prerace tactics. Not only what to wear and what food to bring are important, but how to strip the bike of unnecessary weight. Cycling shoes are specially designed for bike racing. They have a metal sole that puts the energy directly to the pedal, thus efficiently using one's power. The food that one brings is important in a long-distance race. It must not only be useful in refueling the body, but it must be easily eaten while pedaling. Candy bars and fruit, such as bananas, satisfy both requirements. The bike must be stripped of all unnecessary weight, including saddlebags and reflectors. Some cyclists drill holes in parts of the frame, saddle post, and handlebars to lessen the weight of the bike.

5. On pages 56–57 we printed a paragraph on athletic coaching and we also printed a more unified revision of the paragraph. But the revision is still weak, for it lacks supporting details. Revise the revision, giving it life.

6. Here is a newspaper report—chiefly in paragraphs of one sentence each—of an unfortunate happening. Imagine how it could be reorganized into one paragraph, into two paragraphs, and into three. Decide which organization would be most effective and revise the report accordingly.

REUTERS

Fish Eat Brazilian Fisherman

1   MANAUS, BRAZIL.—Man-eating piranha fish devoured fisherman Zeca Vicente when he tumbled into the water during a battle with 300 farmers for possession of an Amazon jungle lake.

2   Vicente, a leader of a group of 30 fishermen, was eaten alive in minutes by shoals of the ferocious fish lurking in Lake Januaca.

3   He died when the farmers—packed in an armada of small boats—attacked the fishermen with hunting rifles, knives, and bows and arrows after they refused to leave.

4   The farmers, who claimed the fishermen were depleting the lake's fish stocks, one of their main sources of food, boarded the fishing vessels and destroyed cold storage installations.

5   Last to give way was Vicente, who tried to cut down the farmers' leader with a knife. But farmers shot him and he fell wounded into the water, and into the jaws of the piranhas.

6   Fifteen persons have been charged with the attack which caused Vicente's death and the injury of several other fishermen.

7   Lake Januaca, about four hours from this Amazon River town by launch, is famous for its pirarucu and tucunare fish which are regarded as table delicacies.

7. Here is the opening paragraph of an essay (about 750 words) on the manufacture of paper in the fifteenth century, the days of the earliest printed books. On the whole it is very good, but the unity and the organization can be improved. Revise the paragraph.

We take paper for granted, but old as it is it did not always exist. In fact, it was invented long after writing was invented, for the earliest writing is painted or scratched on cave walls, shells, rocks, and other natural objects. Paper was not even the first manufactured surface for writing; sheets made from papyrus, a reed-like plant, were produced about 2500 B.C., long before the invention of paper. Although the Chinese may have invented paper as early as the time of Christ, the oldest surviving paper is from early fifth-century China. The Arabs learned the secret of paper-making from the Chinese in the eighth century, but the knowledge traveled slowly to Europe. The oldest European paper, made by the Moors in Spain, is of the twelfth century. Early European paper is of poor quality and so not until the quality improved, around the fourteenth century, did paper become widely used. Most writing was done on parchment, which is the skin of a sheep or goat, and vellum, which is the finer skin of a lamb, kid, or calf. Whatever the animal, the skin was washed, limed, unhaired, scraped, washed again, stretched, and rubbed with pumice until a surface suitable for writing was achieved. Until it was displaced by paper, in the fourteenth century, parchment was the chief writing surface in Europe.

8. Here is the concluding paragraph of a book review. What repetitions do you find? What is their effect?

Mr. Flexner's book is more than a political argument. He has written so vividly and involved us so deeply that there are moments when we yearn to lean over into the pages, pull Hamilton aside, and beg him to reconsider, to pity, to trust, to wait, or merely to shut up. Yet the book's effect is not melodramatic. It is tragic—a tragedy not of fate but of character, the spectacle of an immensely gifted man who tried to rule a nation and could not rule himself.

—NAOMI BLIVEN

4

Revising Sentences for Conciseness

Excess is the common substitute for energy.

—MARIANNE MOORE

All writers who want to keep the attention and confidence of their audience revise for conciseness. The general rule is to say everything relevant in as few words as possible. The conclusion of the Supreme Court's decision in *Brown v. the Board of Education of Topeka,* for example—"Separate educational facilities are inherently unequal"—says it all in six words.

The writers of the following sentences talk too much; they bore us because they don't make every word count.

There are two pine trees which grow behind this house.

On his left shoulder is a small figure standing. He is about the size of the doctor's head.

The judge is seated behind the bench and he is wearing a judicial robe.

Compare those three sentences with these revisions:

Two pine trees grow behind this house.

On his left shoulder stands a small figure, about the size of the doctor's head.

The judge, wearing a robe, sits behind the bench.

We will soon discuss in some detail the chief patterns of wordiness, but here it is enough to say that if you prefer the revisions you already have a commendable taste for conciseness. What does your taste tell you to do with the following sentences?

A black streak covers the bottom half. It appears to have been painted with a single stroke of a large brush.

The time to begin revising for conciseness is when you think you have an acceptable draft in hand—something that pretty much covers your topic and comes reasonably close to saying what you believe about it. As you go over it, study each sentence to see what can be deleted without loss of meaning or emphasis. Read each paragraph, preferably aloud, to see if each sentence supports the topic sentence or idea and clarifies the point you are making. Leave in the concrete and specific details and examples that support your ideas (you may in fact be adding more) but cut out all the deadwood that chokes them:

- extra words
- empty or pretentious phrases
- weak qualifiers
- redundancies
- negative constructions
- wordy uses of the verb *to be*
- other extra verbs and verb phrases.

We'll discuss these problems in the next pages, but first we offer some examples of sentences that cannot be improved on; they're so awful there's nothing to do but delete them and start over. Zonker, in Garry Trudeau's cartoon, is a master of what we call Instant Prose (stuff that sounds like the real thing, but isn't).

DOONESBURY   by Garry Trudeau

INSTANT PROSE (ZONKERS)

Here are some examples of Instant Prose from students' essays:

> Frequently a chapter title in a book reveals to the reader the main point that the author desires to bring out during the course of the chapter.

We could try revising this, cutting the twenty-seven words down to seven:

> A chapter's title often reveals its thesis.

But why bother? Unless the title is an exception, is the point worth making?

> The two poems are basically similar in many ways, yet they have their significant differences.

True, all poems are both similar to and different from other poems. Start over with your next sentence, perhaps something like: "The two poems, superficially similar in rough paraphrase, are strikingly different in diction."

> Although the essay is simple in plot, the theme encompasses many vital concepts of emotional makeup.

> Following a transcendental vein, the nostalgia in the poem takes on a spiritual quality.

> Cassell only presents a particular situation concerning the issue, and with clear descriptions and a certain style sets up an interesting article.

Pure zonkers. Not even the writers of these sentences now know what they mean.

Writing Instant Prose is an acquired habit, like smoking cigarettes or watching soap operas; fortunately it's easier to kick. It often begins in high school, sometimes earlier, when the victim is assigned a ten-page paper, or is told that a paragraph *must* contain at least three sentences, or that a thesis is stated in the introduction to an essay, elaborated in the body, and repeated in the conclusion. If the instructions appear arbitrary, and the student is bored or intimidated by them, the response is likely to be, like Zonker's, meaningless and mechanical.

Students like Zonker have forgotten, or have never learned, the true purpose of writing—the discovery and communication of ideas, attitudes, and judgments. They concentrate instead on the word count: stuffing sentences, padding paragraphs, stretching and repeating points, and adding flourishes. Rewarded by a satisfactory grade, they repeat the performance, and in time, through practice, develop some fluency in spilling out words without thought or commitment, and almost without effort. Such students enter, as Zonker would say, the college of their choice, feeling somehow inauthentic, perhaps even aware that they don't really mean what they write: symptoms of habitual use of, or addiction to, Instant Prose.

How to Avoid Instant Prose

1. Trust yourself. Writing Instant Prose is not only a habit; it's also a form of alienation. If you habitually write zonkers you probably don't think of what you write as your own but as something you produce on demand for someone else. (Clearly Zonker is writing for that unreasonable authority, the teacher, whose mysterious whims and insatiable appetite for words he must somehow satisfy.) Breaking the habit begins with recognizing it, and then acknowledging the possibility that you can take yourself and your work seriously. It means learning to respect your ideas and experiences (unlearning the passive habits that got you through childhood) and determining that when you write you'll write what you mean—nothing more, nothing less. This involves taking some risks, of course; habits offer some security or they would have no grip on us. Moreover, we all have moments when we doubt that our ideas are worth taking seriously. Keep writing honestly anyway. The self-doubts will pass; accomplishing something—writing one clear sentence—can help make them pass.

2. Learn to recognize Instant Prose Additives when they crop up in your writing, and in what you read. And you *will* find them in what you read—in textbooks and in academic journals, notoriously.

Here's an example from a recent book on contemporary theater:

> One of the principal and most persistent sources of error that tends to bedevil a considerable proportion of contemporary literary analysis is the assumption that the writer's creative process is a wholly conscious and purposive type of activity.

Notice all the extra stuff in the sentence: "principal and most persistent," "tends to bedevil," "considerable proportion," "type of activity." Cleared of deadwood the sentence might read:

> The assumption that the writer's creative process is wholly conscious bedevils much contemporary criticism.

3. Acquire two things: a new habit, Revising for Conciseness; and what Isaac Singer calls "the writer's best friend," a wastebasket.

EXTRA WORDS AND EMPTY WORDS

Extra words should, by definition, be eliminated; vague, empty, or pretentious words and phrases may be replaced by specific and direct language.

Wordy

> However, it must be remembered that Ruth's marriage could have positive effects on Naomi's situation.

Concise

Ruth's marriage, however, will also provide security for Naomi.

In the second version, the unnecessary "it must be remembered that" has been eliminated; for the vague "positive effects" and "situation," specific words communicating a precise point have been substituted. The revision, though briefer, says more.

Wordy

In high school, where I had the opportunity for three years of working with the student government, I realized how significantly a person's enthusiasm could be destroyed merely by the attitudes of his superiors.

Concise

In high school, during three years on the student council, I saw students' enthusiasm destroyed by insecure teachers and cynical administrators.

Again, the revised sentence gives more information in fewer words. How?

Wordy

The economic situation of Miss Moody was also a crucial factor in the formation of her character.

Concise

Anne Moody's poverty also helped to form her character.

"Economic situation" is evasive for poverty; "crucial factor" is pretentious. Both are Instant Prose.

Wordy

It creates a better motivation of learning when students can design their own programs involving education. This way students' interests can be focused on.

Concise

Motivation improves when students design their own programs, focused on their own interests.

Now revise the following wordy sentences:

1. Perhaps they basically distrusted our capacity to judge correctly.
2. The use of setting is also a major factor in conveying a terrifying type atmosphere.

Notice how, in the examples provided, the following words crop up: "basically," "significant," "situation," "factor," "involving," "effect," "type." These words have legitimate uses, but are often no more than Instant Prose Additives. Cross them out whenever you can. Similar words to watch out for: *aspect, facet, fundamental, manner, nature, ultimate, utilization, viable, virtually, vital.* If they make your writing sound good, don't hesitate—cross them out at once.

Weak Intensifiers and Qualifiers

Words like *very, quite, rather, completely, definitely,* and *so* can usually be struck from a sentence without loss. Paradoxically, sentences are often more emphatic without intensifiers. Try reading the following sentences both with and without the bracketed words:

At that time I was [very] idealistic.

We found the proposal [quite] feasible.

The remark, though unkind, was [entirely] accurate.

It was a [rather] fatuous statement.

The scene was [extremely] typical.

Both films deal with disasters [virtually] beyond our control.

The death scene is [truly] grotesque.

What she did next was [completely] inexcusable.

The first line [definitely] establishes that the father had been drinking.

Always avoid using intensifiers with *unique.* Either something is unique—the only one of its kind—or it is not. It can't be very, quite, so, pretty, or fairly unique.

Circumlocutions

Roundabout ways of saying things enervate your prose and tire your reader. Notice how each circumlocution in the first column is matched by a concise expression in the second.

I came to the realization that	I realized that
She is of the opinion that	She thinks that
The quotation is supportive of	The quotation supports
Concerning the matter of	About
During the course of	During
For the period of a week	For a week
In the event that	If
In the process of	During, while
Regardless of the fact that	Although
Due to the fact that	Because
For the simple reason that	Because
The fact that	That
Inasmuch as	Since
If the case was such that	If
It is often the case that	Often
In all cases	Always
I made contact with	I called, saw, phoned, wrote
At that point in time	Then
At this point in time	Now

Now revise this sentence:

> These movies have a large degree of popularity for the simple reason that they give the viewers insight in many cases.

Wordy Beginnings

Vague, empty words and phrases clog the beginnings of some sentences. They're like elaborate windups before the pitch.

Wordy

> By analyzing carefully the last lines in this stanza, you find the connections between the loose ends of the poem.

Concise

> The last lines of the stanza connect the loose ends of the poem.

Wordy

> What the cartoonist is illustrating and trying to get across is the greed of the oil producers.

Concise

> The cartoon illustrates the greed of the oil producers.

Wordy

> Dealing with the crucial issue of the year, the editorial is expressing ironical disbelief in any of the possible solutions to the Middle East crisis.

Concise

> The editorial ironically expresses disbelief in the proposed solutions to the Middle East crisis.

Wordy

> In the last stanza is the conclusion (as usual) and it tells of the termination of the dance.

Concise

> The last stanza concludes with the end of the dance.

Wordy

> In opposition to the situation of the younger son is that of the elder who remained in his father's house, working hard and handling his inheritance wisely.

Concise

> The elder son, by contrast, remained in his father's house, worked hard, and handled his inheritance wisely.

Notice that when the deadwood is cleared from the beginning of the sentence, the subject appears early, and the main verb appears close to it:

The last lines . . . connect. . . .

The cartoon illustrates. . . .

The editorial . . . expresses. . . .

The last stanza concludes. . . .

The elder son . . . remained. . . .

Locating the right noun for the subject, and the right verb for the predicate, is the key to revising sentences with wordy beginnings. Try revising the wordy beginnings in the following sentences:

1. The way that Mabel reacts toward her brother is a fine representation of her nature.
2. In Langston Hughes's case he was "saved from sin" when he was going on thirteen.

Empty Conclusions

Often a sentence that begins well has an empty conclusion. The words go on but the sentence seems to stand still; if it's not revised, it requires another sentence to explain it.

Empty

"Those Winter Sundays" is composed so that a reader can feel what the poet was saying.

(How is it composed? What is he saying?)

Concise

"Those Winter Sundays" describes the speaker's anger as a child, and his remorse as an adult.

Empty

In both Orwell's and Baldwin's essays the feeling of white supremacy is very important.

(Why is white supremacy important?)

Concise

Both Orwell and Baldwin trace the insidious consequences of white supremacy.

Empty

Being the only white girl among about ten black girls was quite a learning experience.

(What did she learn?)

Concise

As the only white girl among about ten black girls, I began to understand the experiences of isolation, helplessness, and rage regularly reported by minority students.

Wordy Uses of the Verbs *To Be,* *To Have,* and *To Make*

Notice that in the preceding unrevised sentences a form of the verb *to be* introduces the empty conclusion: "*was* saying," "*is* very important," "*was* quite a learning experience." In each revision, the right verb added and generated substance. In the following sentences, substitutions for the verb *to be* both invigorate and shorten otherwise substantial sentences. (The wordy expressions are italicized, and so are the revisions.)

Wordy

The scene *is taking place* at night, in front of the capitol building.

Concise

The scene *takes place* at night, in front of the capitol building.

Wordy

In this shoeshining and early rising *there are indications* of church attendance.

Concise

The early rising and shoeshining *indicate* church attendance.

Wordy

The words "flashing," "rushing," "plunging," and "tossing" *are suggestive of* excitement.

Concise

The words "flashing," "rushing," "plunging," and "tossing" *suggest* excitement.

The rule is, whenever you can, replace a form of the verb *to be* with a stronger verb.

To Be	Strong Verb
and a participle ("is taking")	takes
and a noun ("are indications")	indicate
and an adjective ("are suggestive")	suggest

Try revising the following sentence:

The rising price of oil is reflective of the spiraling cost of all goods.

Sentences with the verbs *to have* and *to make* can similarly be reduced:

Wordy

The Friar *has knowledge* that Juliet is alive.

Concise

The Friar *knows* that Juliet is alive.

Wordy

The stanzas *make a vivid contrast* between Heaven and Hell.

Concise

The stanzas *vividly contrast* Heaven and Hell.

Like all rules, this one has exceptions. We don't list them here; you'll discover them by listening to your sentences.

Redundancy

The word *redundancy,* derived from a Latin word meaning "overflowing, over-lapping," refers to unnecessary repetition in the expression of ideas. "Future plans," after all, are only plans, and "to glide smoothly" or "to scurry rapidly" is only to glide or to scurry. Unlike repetition, which often provides emphasis or coherence (for example, "government of the people, by the people, for the people"), redundancy can always be eliminated.

Redundant

Any student could randomly sit anywhere. (If the students could sit any-where, the seating was random.)

Concise

Students could sit anywhere.

Students chose their seats at random.

Redundant

I have no justification with which to excuse myself.

Concise

I have no justification for my action.

I can't justify my action.

I have no excuse for my action.

I can't excuse my action.

Redundant

In the orthodox Cuban culture, the surface of the female role seemed de-grading. (Perhaps this sentence means what it says. More probably "surface" and "seemed" are redundant.)

Concise

In the orthodox Cuban culture, the female role seemed degrading.

In the orthodox Cuban culture, the female role was superficially degrading.

Redundant

In "Araby" the boy feels alienated emotionally from his family.

Concise

In "Araby" the boy feels alienated from his family.

Try eliminating redundancy from the following sentences:

1. The reason why she hesitates is because she is afraid.
2. Marriage in some form has long existed since prehistoric times.

What words can be crossed out of the following phrases?

a. throughout the entire article
b. her attitude of indifference
c. a conservative type suit
d. all the different tasks besides teaching
e. his own personal opinion
f. elements common to both of them
g. emotions and feelings
h. shared together
i. falsely padded expense accounts
j. alleged suspect

Many phrases in common use are redundant. For example, there is no need to write "blare noisily," since the meaning of the adverb "noisily" is already in the verb "blare." Watch for phrases like these when you revise:

round in shape	resulting effect
purple in color	close proximity
poetic in nature	connected together
tall in stature	prove conclusively
autobiography of her life	must necessarily
basic fundamentals	very unique
true fact	very universal
free gift	the reason why is because

Negative Constructions

Negative constructions are often wordy and sometimes pretentious.

Wordy

Housing for married students is *not unworthy of* consideration.

Concise

Housing for married students is worth considering.

Better

The trustees should earmark funds for married students' housing. (Probably what the author meant.)

"See what I mean? You're never sure just where you stand with them."

Wordy

After reading the second paragraph *you aren't left with* an immediate reaction as to how the story will end.

Concise

The first two paragraphs create suspense.

The following example from a syndicated column is not untypical:

Although it is not reasonably to be expected that someone who fought his way up to the Presidency is less than a largely political animal and sometimes a beast, it is better not to know—really—exactly what his private conversations were composed of.

The Golden Rule of writing is "Write for others as you would have them write for you," not "Write for others in a manner not unreasonably dissimilar to the manner in which you would have them write for you." (But see the discussion of *not . . . un-* in the Glossary, page 464, for effective use of the negative.)

EXTRA SENTENCES, EXTRA CLAUSES: SUBORDINATION

Sentences are sometimes wordy because ideas are given more elaborate grammatical constructions than they need. In revising, these constructions often can be reduced. Two sentences, for example, may be reduced to one, or a clause may be reduced to a phrase.

Wordy

The Book of Ruth was probably written in the fifth century B.C. It was a time when women were considered the property of men.

Concise

The Book of Ruth was probably written in the fifth century B.C., when women were considered the property of men.

Wordy

The first group was the largest. This group was seated in the center of the dining hall.

Concise

The first group, the largest, was seated in the center of the dining hall.

Wordy

The colonists were upset over the tax on tea and they took action against it.

Concise

The colonists, upset over the tax on tea, took action against it.

Who, Which, That   Watch particularly for clauses beginning with *who, which,* and *that.* Often they can be shortened.

Wordy

George Orwell is the pen name of Eric Blair, *who was* an English writer.

Concise

George Orwell is the pen name of Eric Blair, an English writer.

Wordy

They are seated at a table *which* is covered with a patched and tattered cloth.

Concise

They are seated at a table covered with a patched and tattered cloth.

Wordy

There is one feature *that is* grossly out of proportion.

Concise

One feature is grossly out of proportion.

It Is, This Is, There Are   Also watch for sentences and clauses beginning with *it is, this is, there are* (again, wordy uses of the verb *to be*). These expressions often lead to a *which* or a *that,* but even when they don't they may be wordy.

Wordy

> The trail brings us to the timberline. This is the point where the trees become stunted from lack of oxygen.

Concise

> The trail brings us to the timberline, the point where the trees become stunted from lack of oxygen.

Wordy

> This is a quotation from Black Elk's autobiography which discloses his prophetic powers.

Concise

> This quotation from Black Elk's autobiography discloses his prophetic powers.

Wordy

> It is frequently considered that *Hamlet* is Shakespeare's most puzzling play.

Concise

> *Hamlet* is frequently considered Shakespeare's most puzzling play.

Wordy

> In Notman's photograph of Buffalo Bill and Sitting Bull there are definite contrasts between the two figures.

Concise

> Notman's photograph of Buffalo Bill and Sitting Bull contrasts the two figures.

Try revising the following sentences:

1. There are many writers who believe that writing can't be taught.
2. Always take more clothes than you think you will need. This is so that you will be prepared for the weather no matter what it is.
3. This is an indication that the child has a relationship with his teacher which is very respectful.

(For further discussion of subordination see pages 130–33. On *which* clauses, see also Chapter 20, "Usage," page 469.)

SOME CONCLUDING REMARKS ABOUT CONCISENESS

We spoke earlier about how students learn to write Instant Prose and acquire other wordy habits—by writing what they think the teacher has asked for. We haven't forgotten that instructors assign papers of a certain length in college too.

But the length given is not an arbitrary limit that must be reached—the instructor who asks for a five-page or twenty-page paper is probably trying to tell you the degree of elaboration expected on the assignment. Such, apparently, was the intention of William Randolph Hearst, the newspaper publisher, who cabled an astronomer, "Is there life on Mars? Cable reply 1000 words." The astronomer's reply was, "Nobody knows," repeated 500 times.

What do you do when you've been asked to produce a ten-page paper and after diligent writing and revising you find you've said everything relevant to your topic in seven and a half pages? Our advice is, hand it in. We can't remember ever counting the words or pages of a substantial, interesting essay; we assume that our colleagues elsewhere are equally reasonable and equally overworked. If we're wrong, tell us about it—in writing, and in the fewest possible words.

Exercises

1. First identify the fault or faults that make the following sentences wordy, and then revise them for conciseness.
    a. There were quite a number of contrasts that White made between the city school and the country school which was of a casual nature all throughout.
    b. The study of political topics involves a careful researching of the many components of the particular field.
    c. Virtually the most significant feature of any field involving science is the vital nature of the technical facilities, the fundamental factor of all research.
    d. Like a large majority of American people, I, too, have seen the popular disaster films.
    e. Something which makes this type of film popular (disaster) is the kind of subconscious aspect of "Can man overcome this problem?" Horror films, on the other hand, produce the aspects of whether or not man can make amends for his mistakes.
    f. The average American becomes disappointed and downtrodden due to the fact that he can't help himself and is at the mercy of inflation and unemployment.
    g. Some relationships have split up because of the simple fear of having an abnormal child, while perhaps there might have been other alternatives for these couples.
    h. Reading has always been a fascinating and exciting pastime for me for as long as I can remember.
    i. This cartoon appeared in the 17 September 1999 issue of *Newsweek*. This political cartoon was originally taken from the *Tulsa Tribune*. The cartoonist is Simpson.
    j. Only once in the first two sentences does the author make reference to the first person.
    k. The length of the sentences are similar in moderation and in structural clarity.
    l. The magnitude of student satisfaction with the program ranged from total hatred to enthusiastic approval.

m. Taking a look at the facial expressions of the man and the woman in both pictures one can see a difference in mood.

n. One drawing is done in watercolor and the other is done in chalk which is a revision of the watercolor.

o. The dialogue places the role of the two gods on a believable basis.

p. Senseless crimes such as murder and muggings are committed on a daily basis.

q. One must specify that the current heavy metal craze which is so very popular today is not considered to be African-American music.

r. The two major aspects behind the development of a performer are technique and musicianship.

s. I remember my first desire to smoke cigarettes as I watched my father smoke. My father often sat in his favorite easy chair idly smoking cigarettes.

t. Christopher Stone's article "Putting the Outside Inside the Fence of Law" is concerning the legal rights of the environment. He comments on the legal rights of other inanimate entities which seem to be acceptable. Just as these entities are represented, so should the environment be represented.

2. In the following paragraph, from a student essay on Charlotte Perkins Gilman's short story "The Yellow Wallpaper," circle all forms of the verbs *to be, to have,* and *to make.* Then, wherever possible, eliminate these verbs by reducing clauses or by substituting stronger, more exact, or active verbs.

Charlotte Perkins Gilman's story "The Yellow Wallpaper" is about a woman who has been diagnosed with a "temporary nervous depression" and who is moved by her husband to a house in the country so that she may have the opportunity to rest and recuperate from her illness. As the story progresses, however, her depression is combined with her isolated situation, and her mental state is made more fragile as a result. Gradually, her ability to make distinctions between reality and fantasy is lost, and she is overcome with madness. Her madness is reflected in her descriptions of the yellow wallpaper with which the walls of her bedroom is covered. At first the wallpaper is simply described as "ugly" and "repellent." By the end of the story, though, the narrator is seeing a figure of a woman who is trapped behind the wallpaper, a woman who shakes and pulls at the wallpaper and who seems to be making an effort to free herself from its confinement.

3. When you complete the draft of the essay you're currently writing, identify and circle all forms of the verbs *to be, to have,* and *to make.* Replace as many of them as possible with stronger verbs.

5

Revising Sentences for Clarity

Here's to plain speaking and clear understanding.

—SIDNEY GREENSTREET, in *The Maltese Falcon*

CLARITY

We have seen new realities created by the advance of physics. But this chain of creation can be traced back far beyond the starting point of physics. One of the most primitive concepts is that of an object. The concepts of a tree, a horse, any material body, are creations gained on the basis of experience, though the impressions from which they arise are primitive in comparison with the world of physical phenomena. A cat teasing a mouse also creates, by thought, its own primitive reality. The fact that the cat reacts in a similar way toward any mouse it meets shows that it forms concepts and theories which are its guide through its own world of sense impressions.

—ALBERT EINSTEIN AND LEOPOLD INFELD

Skills constitute the manipulative techniques of human goal attainment and control in relation to the physical world, so far as artifacts or machines especially designed as tools do not yet supplement them. Truly human skills are guided by organized and codified *knowledge* of both the things to be manipulated and the human capacities that are used to manipulate them. Such knowledge is an aspect of cultural-level symbolic processes, and, like other aspects to be discussed presently, requires the capacities of the human central nervous system, particularly the brain. This organic system is clearly essential to all of the symbolic processes; as we well know, the human brain is far superior to the brain of any other species.

—TALCOTT PARSONS

Why is the first passage easier to understand than the second?

Both passages discuss the relationship between the brain and the physical world it attempts to understand. The first passage, by Einstein and Infeld, is, if anything, more complex both in what it asserts and in what it suggests than the second, by Parsons. Both passages explain that the brain organizes sense impressions. But Einstein and Infeld further explain that the history of physics can be understood as an extension of the simplest sort of organization, such as we all make in distinguishing a tree from a horse, or such as even a cat makes in teasing a mouse. Parsons only promises that "other aspects" will "be discussed presently." How many of us are eager for those next pages?

Good writing is clear, not because it presents simple ideas, but because it presents ideas in the simplest form the subject permits. A clear analysis doesn't falsely reduce a complex problem to a simple one; it breaks it down into its simple, comprehensible parts and discusses them, one by one, in a logical order. A clear paragraph explains one of these parts coherently, thoroughly, and in language as simple and as particular as the reader's understanding requires and the context allows. Where Parsons writes of "organized and codified *knowledge* of . . . the things to be manipulated," Einstein and Infeld write simply of the concept of an object. And even "object," a simple but general word, is further clarified by the specific, familiar examples, "tree" and "horse." Parsons writes of "the manipulative techniques of . . . goal attainment and control in relation to the physical world, so far as artifacts or machines especially designed as tools do not yet supplement them." Einstein and Infeld show us a cat teasing a mouse.

Notice also the clear organization of Einstein and Infeld's paragraph. The first sentence, clearly transitional, refers to the advance of physics traced in the preceding pages. The next sentence, introduced by "But," reverses our direction: we are now going to look not at an advance, but at primitive beginnings. And the following sentences, to the end of the paragraph, fulfill that promise. We move back to primitive human concepts, clarified by examples, and finally to the still more primitive example of the cat. Parson's paragraph is also organized, but the route is much more difficult to follow.

Why do people write obscurely? Surely some students learn to write obscurely by trying to imitate the style of their teachers or textbooks. The imitation may spring from genuine admiration for these authorities. Or students may feel that a string of technical-sounding words is what the teacher expects. If this thought has crossed your mind, we can't say you're entirely wrong. Learning a new discipline often involves acquiring a specialized vocabulary. But we add the following cautions:

- Teachers expect your writing to show thought and make sense. They are likely to be puzzled by the question "Do you want me to use technical terms in this paper?"
- If you try to use technical terms appropriate to one field when you write about another, you are likely to write nonsense. Don't write "the machine was viable" if you mean only that it worked.
- When you do write for specialists in a particular field, use technical terms precisely. Don't write in an art history paper "This print of Van Gogh's *Sunflowers*" if you mean "This reproduction of Van Gogh's *Sunflowers.*"
- No matter what you are writing, don't become so enamored of technical words that you can't write a sentence without peppering it with *input, interface, death-symbol, parameter, phallocentric, feedback,* and so on.

But to return to the question, "Why do people write obscurely?" It's difficult to write clearly.[1] Authorities may be obscure not because they want to tax you with unnecessary difficulties, but because they don't know how to avoid such difficulties. If you have ever tried to assemble a mechanical toy or to install a computer upgrade by following the "easy instructions," you know that the simplest kind of expository writing, giving instructions, can foil the writers most eager for your goodwill (that is, those who want you to use their products). Few instructions, unfortunately, are as unambiguous as "Go to jail. Go directly to jail. Do not pass Go. Do not collect $200."

You can, though, learn to write clearly, by learning to recognize common sources of obscurity in writing and by consciously revising your own work. We offer, to begin with, three general rules:

1. Use the simplest, most exact, most specific language your subject allows.
2. Put together what belongs together, in the essay, in the paragraph, and in the sentence.
3. Keep your reader in mind, particularly when you revise.

Now for more specific advice, and examples—the cats and mice of revising for clarity.

CLARITY AND EXACTNESS: USING THE RIGHT WORD

Denotation

Be sure the word you choose has the right *denotation* (explicit meaning). Did you mean sarcastic or ironic? Fatalistic or pessimistic? Disinterested or uninterested? Biannual or semiannual? Enforce or reinforce? Use or usage? If you're not sure, check the dictionary. You'll find some of the most commonly misused words discussed in Chapter 20, "Usage" pp. 454-470. Here are examples of a few others.

1. Daru faces a dilemma between his humane feelings and his conceptions of justice. (Strictly speaking, a dilemma requires a choice between two equally unattractive alternatives. "Conflict" would be a better word here.)
2. However, as time dragged on, exercising seemed to lose its charisma. (What is charisma? Why is it inexact here?)
3. Ms. Wu's research contains many symptoms of depression which became evident during the reading period. (Was Ms. Wu depressed by her research? We hope not. Probably she described or listed the symptoms.)

[1]Our first draft of this sentence read "Writing clearly is difficult." Can you see why we changed it?

"I'm not quite clear on this, Fulton. Are you moaning about
your prerequisites, your requisites, or your perquisites?"

4. When I run I don't allow myself to stop until I have reached my destiny.
   (Which word is inexact?)

Connotation

Be sure the word you choose has the right *connotation* (association, implication). As Mark Twain said, the difference between the right word and the almost
right word is the difference between lightning and the lightning bug.

1. Boston politics has always upheld the reputation of being especially
   crooked. ("Upheld" inappropriately suggests that Boston has proudly
   maintained its reputation. "Has always had" would be appropriate here,
   but pale. "Deserved" would, in this context, be ironic, implying—accurately—the writer's scorn.)
2. This book, unlike many other novels, lacks tedious descriptive passages.
   ("Lacks" implies a deficiency. How would you revise the sentence?)
3. New Orleans, notorious for its good jazz and good food. . . . (Is "notorious" the word here? or "famous"?)

4. Sunday, Feb. 9. Another lingering day at Wellesley. (In this entry from a student's journal, "lingering" strikes us as right. What does "lingering" imply about Sundays at Wellesley that "long" would not?)

Because words have connotations, most writing—even when it pretends to be objective—conveys attitudes as well as facts. Consider, for example, this passage by Jessica Mitford, describing part of the procedure used today for embalming:

> A long, hollow needle attached to a tube . . . is jabbed into the abdomen, poked around the entrails and chest cavity, the contents of which are pumped out. . . .

Here, as almost always, the writer's *purpose* in large measure determines the choice of words. Probably the sentence accurately describes part of the procedure, but it also, of course, records Mitford's contempt for the procedure. Suppose she wanted to be more respectful—suppose, for example, she were an undertaker writing an explanatory pamphlet. Instead of the needle being "jabbed" it would be "inserted," and instead of being "poked around the entrails" it would be "guided around the viscera," and the contents would not be "pumped out" but would be "drained." Mitford's words would be the wrong words for an undertaker explaining embalming to apprentices or to the general public, but, given her purpose, they are exactly the right ones because they convey her attitude with great clarity.

Notice, too, that many words have social, political, or sexist overtones. We read for example of the *children* of the rich, but the *offspring* of the poor. What is implied by the distinction? Consider the differences in connotation in each of the following series:

1. friend, boyfriend, young man, lover (What age is the speaker?)
2. dine, eat (What was on the menu? Who set the table?)
3. spinster, bachelor (Which term is likely to be considered an insult?)
4. underdeveloped nations, developing nations, emerging nations
5. preference, bias, prejudice
6. upbringing, conditioning, brainwashing
7. message from our sponsor, commercial, ad, plug
8. intelligence gathering, espionage, spying
9. emigrate, defect, seek asylum
10. antiabortion, pro-life; pro-abortion, pro-choice

Reprinted with permission of King Features Syndicate.

Quotation Marks as Apologies

When you have used words with exact meanings (denotations) and appropriate associations (connotations) for your purpose, don't apologize for them by putting quotation marks around them. If the words *copped a plea, ripped off,* or *kids* suit your purpose better than *plea-bargained, stolen,* or *children,* use them. If they are inappropriate, don't put them in quotation marks; find the right words.

Being Specific

In writing descriptions, catch the richness, complexity, and uniqueness of things. Suppose, for example, you are describing a scene from your childhood, a setting you loved. There was, in particular, a certain tree . . . and you write: "Near the water there was a big tree that was rather impressive." Most of us would produce something like that sentence. Here is the sentence Ernesto Galarza wrote in *Barrio Boy:*

> On the edge of the pond, at the far side, there was an enormous walnut tree, standing like an open umbrella whose ribs extended halfway across the still water of the pool.

We probably could not have come up with the metaphor of the umbrella because we wouldn't have seen the similarity. (As Aristotle observed, the gift for making metaphors distinguishes the poet from the rest of us.) But we can all train ourselves to be accurate observers and reporters. For "the water" (general) we can specify "pond"; for "near" we can say how near, "on the edge of the pond," and add the specific location, "at the far side"; for "tree" we can give the species, "walnut tree"; and for "big" we can provide a picture, its branches "extended halfway across" the pond: it was, in fact, "enormous."

Galarza does not need to add limply, as we did, that the tree "was rather impressive." The tree he describes *is* impressive. That he accurately remembered it persuades us that he was impressed, without his having to tell us he was. For writing descriptions, a good general rule is: show, don't tell.

Be as specific as you can be in all forms of exposition too. Take the time, when you revise, to find the exact word to replace vague, woolly phrases or clichés. In the following examples we have to guess or invent what the writer means.

Vague

The clown's part in *Othello* is very small.

Specific

The clown appears in only two scenes in *Othello.*

The clown in *Othello* speaks only thirty lines. (Notice the substitution of the verb "appears" or "speaks" for the frequently debilitating "is." And in place of the weak intensifier "very" we have specific details to tell us how small the role is.)

Vague

He feels uncomfortable at the whole situation. (Many feelings are uncomfortable. Which one does he feel? What's the situation?)

Specific

He feels guilty for having distrusted his father.

Vague

The passage reveals a somewhat calculating aspect behind Antigone's noble motives. ("A somewhat calculating aspect" is vague—and wordy—for "calculation." Or did the writer mean "shrewdness"? What differences in connotation are there between "shrewd" and "calculating"?)

Vague

She uses simplicity in her style of writing. (Do we know, exactly, what simplicity in style means?)

Specific

She uses familiar words, normal word order, and conversational phrasing.

Vague cliché

Then she criticized students for living in an ivory tower. (Did she criticize them for being detached or for being secluded? For social irresponsibility or studiousness?)

Specific

Then she criticized students for being socially irresponsible.

Using Examples

In addition to exact words and specific details, illustrative examples make for clear writing. Einstein and Infeld, in the passage quoted on page 96, use as an example of a primitive concept a cat teasing not only its first mouse, but also "any mouse it meets." Here are two paragraphs that clarify their topic sentences through examples; the first is again from *Barrio Boy.*

> In Jalco people spoke in two languages—Spanish and with gestures. These signs were made with the face or hands or a combination of both. If you bent one arm and tapped the elbow with the other hand, it meant "He is stingy." When you sawed one arm across the other you were saying that someone you knew played the fiddle terribly. To say that a man was a tippler you made a set of cow's horns with the little finger and the thumb of one hand, bending the three middle fingers to the palm and pointing the thumb at your mouth. And if you wanted to indicate, without saying so for the sake of politeness, that a mutual acquaintance was daffy, you tapped three times on your forehead with your middle finger.
>
> —Ernesto Galarza

In the next paragraph, Northrop Frye, writing about the perception of rhythm, illustrates his point:

> Ideally, our literary education should begin, not with prose, but with such things as "this little pig went to market"—with verse rhythm rein-

forced by physical assault. The infant who gets bounced on somebody's knee to the rhythm of "Ride a cock horse" does not need a footnote telling him that Banbury Cross is twenty miles northeast of Oxford. He does not need the information that "cross" and "horse" make (at least in the pronunciation he is most likely to hear) not a rhyme but an assonance. . . . All he needs is to get bounced.

Frye does not say our literary education should begin with "simple rhymes" or with "verse popular with children." He says "with such things as 'this little pig went to market,'" and then he goes on to add "Ride a cock horse." We know exactly what he means. Notice, too, that we do not need a third example. Be detailed, but know when to stop.

Your reader is likely to be brighter and more demanding than Lady Pliant, who in a seventeenth-century play says to a would-be seducer, "You are very alluring—and say so many fine Things, and nothing is so moving to me as a fine Thing." "Fine Things," of course, are what is wanted, but only exact words and apt illustrations will convince intelligent readers that they are hearing fine things.

Now look at a paragraph from a student's essay whose thesis is that rage can be a useful mechanism for effecting change. Then compare the left-hand paragraph with the same paragraph, revised, at the right. Note the specific ways, sentence by sentence, the student revised for clarity.

In my high school we had little say in the learning processes that were used. The subjects that we were required to take were irrelevant. One had to take them to earn enough points to graduate. Some of the teachers were sympathetic to our problem. They would tell us about when they were young, how they tried to oppose their school system. But when they were young it was a long time ago, for most of them. The principal would call assemblies to speak on the subject. They were entitled "The Value of an Education" or "Get a	In my high school we had little say about our curriculum. We were required, for example, to choose either American or European History to earn enough points for graduation. We wanted, but were at first refused, the option of Black History. Some of our teachers were sympathetic with us; one told me about her fight opposing the penmanship course required in her school. Nor was the principal totally indifferent—he called assemblies. I remember one talk he gave called "The Value of an Education in Today's World," and

Good Education to Have a Bright Future." The titles were not inviting. They had nothing to do with our plight. Most students never came to any agreements with the principal because most of his thoughts and views seemed old and outdated.

another, "Get a Good Education to Have a Bright Future." I don't recall hearing about a Black History course in either talk. Once, he invited a group of us to meet with him in his office, but we didn't reach any agreement. He solemnly showed us an American History text (not the one we used) that had a whole chapter devoted to Black History.

Jargon and Technical Language

Most dictionaries give three meanings for *jargon:* technical language, meaningless language, and inflated or pretentious language.

The members of almost every profession or trade—indeed, almost all people who share any specialized interest—use technical language. Composition teachers talk of conjunctions, misplaced modifiers, and writer's block; baseball fans talk of southpaws, the hit-and-run, and the hat trick; Freudians talk of cathect, libido, and the oral phase; magicians talk of the French drop, double-lifts, and second-dealing.

Properly used, technical language communicates information concisely and clearly, and it can create a comfortable bond between speakers, or between the writer and the reader. But to the outsider it may seem meaningless, hence the second definition of the word, meaningless talk. In fact, *jargon* originally meant (some six hundred years ago) the twittering of birds—and this is what the language of specialists sounds like to the outsider's ear. The third meaning, pretentious language, comes from the outsider's impatience with other people's technical language. We wonder if all of that twittering—all of the mysterious vocabulary—really is necessary, and we suspect that perhaps the speaker is making a big deal out of what can be said much more simply, maybe in an effort to impress us.

Consider, for instance, a twenty-eight-page manual issued in Dallas to parents of children in kindergarten through the third grade. The manual, intended to help parents decipher their children's report cards, is titled *Terminal Behavioral Objectives for Continuous Progression Modules in Early Childhood Education.* Terminal objectives, it seems, means goals. What does the rest mean? If you were one of the parents, would you expect much help from the manual? It was intended to be helpful, but it sounds like a parody, doesn't it?

And finally, a deliberate parody. A. P. Herbert in his book *What a Word!* tells us how a social scientist might write a familiar biblical command:

DILBERT reprinted by permission of United Feature Syndicate, Inc.

>   In connection with my co-citizens, a general standard of mutual good
>   will and reciprocal non-aggression is obviously incumbent upon me.

What is the command? (See Leviticus 19.18.)

   In general, when you write for nonspecialists, avoid technical terms; if you must use them, define them. If you use a technical term when writing for specialists, be sure you know its precise meaning. But whenever you can, even among specialists, use plain English.

Clichés

Clichés (literally, in French, molds from which type is cast) are trite expressions, mechanically—that is, mindlessly—reproduced. Since they are available without thought they are great Instant Prose Additives (see pages 82-93). Writers who use them are usually surprised to be criticized: they find the phrases attractive, and may even think them exact. (Phrases become clichés precisely because they have wide appeal and therefore wide use.) But clichés, by their very nature, cannot communicate the uniqueness of your thoughts. Furthermore, because they come instantly to mind, they tend to block the specific detail or exact expression that will let the reader know what precisely is in your mind. In revising, when you strike out a cliché, you force yourself to do the work of writing clearly. The following example is full of clichés:

>   Finally, the long awaited day arrived. Up bright and early. . . . She peered at
>   me with suspicion; then a faint smile crossed her face.

Other examples:

first and foremost	time honored
the acid test	bustled to and fro
fatal flaw	short but sweet
budding genius	few and far between
slowly but surely	D-day arrived
little did I know	sigh of relief
the big moment	last but not least

In attempting to avoid clichés, however, don't go to the other extreme of wildly original, super-vivid writing—"'Well then, say something to her,' he roared, his whole countenance gnarled in rage." It's often better simply to say, "he said." (Anyone who intends to write dialogue should memorize Ring Lardner's intentionally funny line, "'Shut up!' he explained.") Note also that such common expressions as "How are you?" "Please pass the salt," and "So long" are not clichés; they make no claim to be colorful.

Metaphors and Mixed Metaphors

Ordinary speech abounds with metaphors. We speak or write of the foot of a mountain, the germ (seed) of an idea, the root of a problem. Metaphors so deeply embedded in the language that they no longer evoke pictures in our minds are called *dead metaphors*. Ordinarily, they offer us, as writers, no problems: we need neither seek them nor avoid them; they are simply there. (Notice, for example, "embedded" two sentences back.) Such metaphors become problems, however, when we unwittingly call them back to life. Howard Nemerov observes: "That these metaphors may be not dead but only sleeping, or that they may arise from the grave and walk in our sentences, is something that has troubled everyone who has ever tried to write plain expository prose."

Dead metaphors are most likely to haunt us when they are embodied in clichés. Since we use clichés without attention to what they literally say or point to, we are unlikely to be aware of the dead metaphors buried in them. But when we attach one cliché to another, we may raise the metaphors from the grave. The result is likely to be a mixed metaphor; the effect is almost always absurd.

Water seeks its own level whichever way you want to slice it.

Traditional liberal education has run out of gas and educational soup kitchens are moving into the vacuum.

The low ebb has been reached and hopefully it's turned the corner.

Her energy, drained through a stream of red tape, led only to closed doors.

We no longer ask for whom the bell tolls but simply chalk it up as one less mouth to feed.

As comedian Joe E. Lewis observed, "Show me a man who builds castles in the air and I'll show you a crazy architect."

Fresh metaphors, on the other hand, imaginatively combine accurate observations. They are not prefabricated ideas; they are a means of discovering or inventing new ideas. They enlarge thought and enliven prose. Here are two examples from students' journals:

"You're right as rain. It's the dawn of history, and there are no clichés as yet. I'll drink to that."

I have some sort of sporadic restlessness in me, like the pen on a polygraph machine. It moves along in curves, then suddenly shoots up, blowing a bubble in my throat, making my chest taut, forcing me to move around. It becomes almost unbearable and then suddenly it will plunge, leaving something that feels like a smooth orange wave.

Time is like wrapping papers. It wraps memories, decorates them with sentiment. No matter (almost) what's inside, it's remembered as a beautiful piece of past time. That's why I even miss my high school years, which were filled with tiredness, boredom, confusion.

And here is a passage from an essay in which a student analyzes the style of a story he found boring:

Every sentence yawns, stretches, shifts from side to side, and then

quietly dozes off.

Experiment with metaphors, let them surface in the early drafts of your essays and in your journals, and by all means, introduce original and accurate comparisons in your essays. But leave the mixed metaphors to politicians and comedians.

Euphemisms

Euphemisms are words substituted for other words thought to be offensive. In deodorant advertisements there are no armpits, only *underarms*, which may *perspire,* but not sweat, and even then they don't smell. A parent reading a report card is likely to learn not that his child got an F in conduct, but that she "experiences difficulty exercising self-control: (a) verbally (b) physically." And where do old people go? To Sun City, "a retirement community for senior citizens."

Euphemisms are used for two reasons: to avoid giving offense, and, sometimes unconsciously, to disguise fear or animosity. We do not advise you to write or speak discourteously; we do advise you, though, to use euphemisms consciously and sparingly, when tact recommends them. It's customary in a condolence letter to avoid the word *death,* and, depending both on your own feelings and those of the bereaved, you may wish to follow that custom. But there's no reason on earth to write "Hamlet passes on." You should be aware, moreover, that some people find euphemisms themselves offensive. Margaret Kuhn, for instance, argues that the word *old* is preferable to *senior.* "Old," she says "is the right word. . . . I think we should wear our gray hair, wrinkles, and crumbling joints as badges of distinction. After all, we worked damn hard to get them." She has organized a militant group called the Gray Panthers to fight ageism.

In revising, replace needless euphemisms with plain words. Your writing will be sharper, and you might, in examining and confronting them, free yourself of a mindless habit, an unconscious prejudice, or an irrational fear.

A Digression on Public Lying

There is a kind of lying which, in the words of Walker Gibson, we may call *public lying.* Its rules are to avoid substance, direct answers, and plain words. Its tendency is to subvert the English language. It employs and invents euphemisms, but the public liar intends to protect not his listeners, but himself and his friends, and he misleads and deceives consciously. Public lying was not invented during the Vietnam War (in 1946 George Orwell had already written what some people call the definitive essay on it, "Politics and the English Language"). But the war produced some classic examples, from which we select a few.

Feiffer

© 1979 Jules Feiffer. Reprinted with permission of Universal Press Syndicate. All rights reserved.

The war in Vietnam, of course, was not a war, but a "conflict" or an "era." "Our side" never attacked "the other side," we made "protective reaction raids"; we didn't invade, we "incursed." We didn't bomb villages, we "pacified" them; peasants were not herded into concentration camps, but "relocated." We didn't spray the countryside with poisons, destroying forests, endangering or killing plant, animal, and human life, we "practiced vegetation control." When American intelligence agents drowned a spy, they referred to their action as "termination with extreme prejudice."

There is a Gresham's law in rhetoric as there is in economics: bad language drives out good. Bad language is contagious; learn to detect the symptoms: use of vague words for clear words; use of sentences or phrases where words suffice; evasive use of the passive voice; and outright lying.

Passive or Active Voice?

1. I baked the bread. (active voice)
2. The bread was baked by me. (passive voice)
3. The bread will be baked. (passive voice)

Although it is the verb that is in the active or the passive voice, notice that the words *active* and *passive* describe the subjects of the sentences. That is, in the first sentence the verb "baked" is in the active voice; the subject "I" acts. In the second and third sentences the verbs "was baked" and "will be baked" are in the passive voice; the subject "bread" is acted on. Notice also the following points:

- The *voice* of the verb is distinct from its *tense*. Don't confuse the passive voice with the past tense. (Sentence 2 above happens to be in the past tense, but 3 is not; both 2 and 3 are in the passive voice.)
- The passive voice uses more words than the active voice. (Compare sentences 1 and 2.)
- A sentence with a verb in the passive voice may leave the doer of the action unidentified. (See sentence 3.)
- Finally, notice that in each of the three sentences the emphasis is different.

In revising, take a good look at each sentence in which you have used the passive voice. If the passive clarifies your meaning, retain it; if it obscures your meaning, change it. More often than not, the passive voice obscures meaning.

Passive voice

The revolver given Daru by the gendarme *is left* in the desk drawer. (Left by whom? The passive voice here obscures the point.)

Active voice

Daru leaves the gendarme's revolver in the desk drawer.

Passive voice

Daru serves tea and the Arab *is offered* some. (Confusing shift from the active voice "serves" to the passive voice "is offered.")

Active voice

Daru serves tea and *offers* the Arab some.

Avoid what has been called the Academic Passive: "In this essay it has been argued that . . ." This cumbersome form used to be common in academic writing (to convey scientific objectivity) but "I have argued" is usually preferable to such stuffiness.

When is the passive voice appropriate? The passive is appropriate when (1) the doer is obvious ("Clinton was elected president in 1992"), or (2) the doer is unknown ("The picture was stolen between midnight and 1:00 A.M."), or (3) the doer is unimportant ("Unexposed film should be kept in a light-proof container").

The Writer's "I"

It is seldom necessary in writing an essay (even on a personal experience) to repeat "I think that" or "in my opinion." Your reader knows that what you write is your opinion. Nor is it necessary, if you've done your job well, to apologize. "After reading the story over several times I'm not really sure what it is about, but . . ." Write about something you are reasonably sure of. Occasionally, though, when there is a real problem in the text, for example the probable date of the Book of Ruth, it is not only permissible to disclose doubts and to reveal tentative conclusions; it may be necessary to do so.

Note also that there is no reason to avoid the pronoun *I* when you are in fact writing about yourself. Attempts to avoid *I* ("this writer," "we," expressions in the passive voice such as "it has been said above" and "it was seen") are noticeably awkward and distracting. And sometimes you may want to focus on your subjective response to a topic in order to clarify a point. The following opening paragraph of a movie review provides an example:

> I take the chance of writing about Bergman's *Persona* so long after its showing because this seems to me a movie there's no hurry about. It will be with us a long time, just as it has been on my mind for a long time. Right now, when I am perhaps still under its spell, it seems to me Bergman's masterpiece, but I can't imagine ever thinking it less than one of the great movies. This of course is opinion; what I know for certain is that *Persona* is also one of the most difficult movies I will ever see; and I am afraid that in this case there is a direct connection between difficulty and value. It isn't only that *Persona* is no harder than it has to be; its peculiar haunting power, its spell, and its value come directly from the fact that it's so hard to get a firm grasp on.
>
> —ROBERT GARIS

Students who have been taught not to begin sentences with *I* often produce sentences that are eerily passive even when the verbs are in the active voice. For example:

1. Two reasons are important to my active participation in dance.
2. The name of the program that I enrolled in is the Health Careers Summer Program.
3. An eager curiosity overcame my previous feeling of fear to make me feel better.

But doesn't it make more sense to say:

1. I dance for two reasons.
2. I enrolled in the Health Careers Summer Program.
3. My curiosity aroused, I was no longer afraid.

A good rule: **Make the agent of the action the subject of the sentence.**

CLARITY AND COHERENCE

Writing a coherent essay is hard work; it requires mastery of a subject and skill in presenting it; it always takes a lot of time. Writing a coherent paragraph often takes more fussing and patching than you expect, but once you have the hang of it, it's relatively easy and pleasant. Writing a coherent sentence requires only that you stay awake until you get to the end of it.

We all do nod sometimes, even over our own prose. But if you make it a practice to read your work over several times, at least once aloud, you give yourself a chance to spot the incoherent sentence before your reader does, and to revise it. Once you see that a sentence is incoherent, it's usually easy to recast it.

Cats Are Dogs

Looking at a picture of a woman, a man once said to the painter Henri Matisse, "That woman's arm is too long." "That's not a woman," Matisse replied, "it's a painting."

In some sentences a form of the verb *to be* mistakenly asserts that one thing is in a class with another. Is a picture a woman? Are cats dogs? Students did write the following sentences:

Incoherent

X. J. Kennedy's poem "Nothing in Heaven Functions as It Ought" is a contrast between Heaven and Hell. (As soon as you ask yourself the question "Is a poem a contrast?" you have, by bringing the two words close together, isolated the problem. A poem may be a sonnet, an epic, an ode—but not a contrast. The writer was trying to say what the poem does, not what it is.)

Coherent

X. J. Kennedy's poem "Nothing in Heaven Functions as It Ought" contrasts Heaven and Hell.

Incoherent

Besides, he tells himself, a matchmaker is an old Jewish custom. (Is a matchmaker a custom?)

Coherent

Besides, he tells himself, consulting a matchmaker is an old Jewish custom.

Try revising the following:

The essay is also an insight into imperialism.

In a related problem, one part of the sentence doesn't know what the other is doing.

Incoherent

Ruth's devotion to Naomi is rewarded by marrying Boaz. (Does devotion marry Boaz?)

Coherent

Ruth's marriage to Boaz rewards her devotion to Naomi.

Incoherent

He demonstrates many human frailties, such as the influence of others' opinions upon one's actions. (Is influence a frailty? How might this sentence be revised?)

Items in a Series

If you were given a shopping list that mentioned apples, fruit, and pears, you would be puzzled and possibly irritated by the inclusion of "fruit." Don't puzzle or irritate your reader with a **false series** of this sort. Analyze sentences containing items in a series to be sure that the items are of the same order of generality. For example:

False series

His job exposed him to the "dirty work" of the British and to the evils of imperialism. ("The 'dirty work' of the British" is a *specific* example of the more *general* "evils of imperialism." The false series makes the sentence incoherent.)

Revised

His job, by exposing him to the "dirty work" of the British, brought him to understand the evils of imperialism.

In the following sentence, which item in the series makes the sentence incoherent?

Why should one man, no matter how important, be exempt from investigation, arrest, trial, and law-enforcing tactics?

Modifiers

A modifier should appear close to the word it modifies (that is, describes or qualifies). Three kinds of faulty modifiers are common: misplaced, squinting, and dangling.

Misplaced Modifiers If the modifier seems to modify the wrong word, it is called *misplaced.* Misplaced modifiers are often unintentionally funny. The judo parlor that advertised "For $20 learn basic methods of protecting yourself from an experienced instructor" probably attracted more amused readers than paying customers.

Misplaced

Orwell shot the elephant under pressured circumstances. (Orwell was under pressure, not the elephant. Put the modifier near what it modifies.)

Revised

Orwell, under pressure, shot the elephant.

Misplaced

Orwell lost his individual right to protect the elephant as part of the imperialistic system. (The elephant was not part of the system; Orwell was.)

Revised

As part of the imperialistic system, Orwell lost his right to protect the elephant.

Misplaced

Amos Wilder has been called back to teach at the Divinity School after ten years retirement due to a colleague's illness. (Did Wilder retire for ten years because a colleague was ill? Revise the sentence.)

Revise the following:

1. Sitting Bull and William Cody stand side by side, each supporting a rifle placed between them with one hand.
2. Complete with footnotes the author has provided her readers with some background information.

Sometimes other parts of sentences are misplaced:

Misplaced

We learn from the examples of our parents who we are. (The sentence appears to say we are our parents.)

Revised

We learn who we are from the examples of our parents.

Misplaced

It is up to the students to revise the scheme, not the administrators. (We all know you can't revise administrators. Revise the sentence.)

Squinting Modifiers If the modifier is ambiguous, that is, if it can be applied equally to more than one term, it is sometimes called a *squinting modifier:* it seems to look forward, and it seems to look backward.

Squinting

Being with Jennifer more and more enrages me. (Is the writer spending more time with Jennifer, or is she more enraged? Probably more enraged.)

Revised

Being with Jennifer enrages me more and more.

Squinting

Writing clearly is difficult. (Is this sentence about "writing" or about "writing clearly"?)

Revised

It is clearly difficult to write.

Revised

It is difficult to write clearly.

Squinting

Students only may use this elevator. (Does "only" modify students? If so, no one else may use the elevator. Or does it modify elevator? If so, students may use no other elevator.)

Revised

Only students may use this elevator.

Students may use only this elevator.

Note: The word *only* often squints, seeming to look in two directions. In general, put *only* immediately before the word or phrase it modifies. Often it appears too early in the sentence. (See the Glossary.)

Dangling Modifiers   If the term being modified appears nowhere in the sentence, a modifier is called *dangling.*

Dangling

Being small, his ear scraped against the belt when his father stumbled. (The writer meant that the boy was small, not the ear. But the boy is not in the sentence.)

Revised

Because the boy was small his ear scraped against the belt when his father stumbled.

Being small, the boy scraped his ear against the belt when his father stumbled.

Dangling

A meticulously organized person, his suitcase could be tucked under an airplane seat. (How would you revise the sentence?)

The general rule: **When you revise sentences, put together what belongs together.**

Reference of Pronouns

A pronoun is used in place of a noun. Because the noun usually precedes the pronoun, the noun to which the pronoun refers is called the *antecedent* (Latin: "going before"). For example:

antecedent   **pronoun**
When *Sheriff Johnson* was on a horse, *he* was a big man.

But the pronoun can also precede the noun:

pronoun   **noun**
When *he* was on a horse, *Sheriff Johnson* was a big man.

The word *antecedent* can be used here too. In short, the antecedent is the word or group of words referred to by a pronoun.

Whenever possible, make sure that a pronoun has a clear reference. Sometimes it isn't possible: *it* is commonly used with an unspecified reference, as in "It's hot today," and "Hurry up please, it's time"; and there can be no reference for interrogative pronouns: "What's bothering you?" and "Who's on first?" But otherwise always be sure that you've made clear what noun the pronoun is standing for.

Vague Reference of Pronouns

Vague

Apparently, they fight physically and it can become rather brutal. ("It" doubtless refers to "fight," but "fight" in this sentence is the verb, not an antecedent noun.)

Clear

Their fights are apparently physical, and sometimes brutal.

Vague

I was born in Colón, the second largest city in the Republic of Panama. Despite this, Colón is still an undeveloped town. ("This" has no specific antecedent. It appears to refer to the writer's having been born in Colón.)

Clear

Although Colón, where I was born, is the second largest city in Panama, it remains undeveloped. (On *this,* see also Glossary, page 468.)

Revise the following sentence:

They're applying to medical school because it's a well-paid profession.

Shift in Pronouns This common error is easily corrected.

1. In many instances the child was expected to follow the profession of your father. (Expected to follow the profession of whose father, "yours" or "his"?)
2. Having a tutor, you can get constant personal encouragement and advice that will help me budget my time. (If "you" have a tutor will that help "me"?)

Revise the following sentences:

1. Schools bring people of the same age together and teach you how to get along with each other.

2. If asked why you went to the dance, one might say they were simply curious.

Ambiguous Reference of Pronouns   A pronoun normally refers to the first appropriate noun or pronoun preceding it. Same-sex pronouns and nouns, like dogs, often get into scraps.

Ambiguous

Her mother died when she was eighteen. (Who was eighteen, the mother or the daughter?)

Clear

Her mother died when Mabel was eighteen.

Her mother died at the age of eighteen. (Note the absence of ambiguity in "His mother died when he was eighteen.")

Ambiguous

Daru learns that he must take an Arab to jail against his will. (Both Daru and the Arab are male. The writer of the sentence meant that Daru learns he must act against his will.)

Clear

Daru learns that he must, against his will, take an Arab to jail.

The general rule: **Put together what belongs together.**

Agreement

Noun and Pronoun   Everyone knows that a singular noun requires a singular pronoun, and a plural noun requires a plural pronoun, but writers sometimes slip.

Faulty

singular   **plural**
A *dog* can easily tell if people are afraid of *them.*

Correct

singular   **singular**
A *dog* can easily tell if people are afraid of *it.*

Faulty

singular   **plural**
Every student feels that Wellesley expects *them* to do their best.

Correct

singular   **singular**
Every student feels that Wellesley expects *her* to do her best.

Each, everybody, nobody, no one, and *none* are especially troublesome. See the entries on these words in Chapter 20, "Usage."

Subject and Verb A singular subject requires a singular verb, a plural subject a plural verb.

Faulty

      plural   **singular**

Horror *films* bring to light a subconscious fear and *shows* a character who succeeds in coping with it.

Correct

      plural   **plural**

Horror films bring to light a subconscious fear and *show* a character who succeeds in coping with it.

The student who wrote "shows" instead of "show" thought that the subject of the verb was "fear," but the subject really is "Horror films," a plural.

Faulty

The manager, as well as the pitcher and the catcher, were fined.

Correct

The manager, as well as the pitcher and the catcher, was fined.

If the sentence had been "The manager and the pitcher . . . ," the subject would have been plural and the required verb would be *were:*

The manager and the pitcher were fined.

But in the sentence as it was given, "as well as" (like *in addition to, with,* and *together with*) does *not* add a subject to a subject and thereby make a plural subject. "As well as" merely indicates that what is said about the manager applies to the pitcher and the catcher.

Revise the following:

About mid-morning during Spanish class the sound of jeeps were heard.

Three Additional Points

1. A **collective noun**—that is, a noun that is singular in form but that denotes a collection of individuals, such as *mob, audience, jury*—normally takes a *singular* verb:

Correct

The mob is at the gate.

Correct

An audience of children *is* easily bored. (The subject is "an audience," *not* "children.")

Correct

The jury is seated.

But when the emphasis is on the individuals within the group—for instance when you are calling attention to a division within the group—you can use a plural verb:

The jury disagree.

Still, because this sounds a bit odd, it is probably better to recast the sentence:

The jurors disagree.

2. Sometimes a sentence that is grammatically correct may nevertheless sound awkward:

One of its most noticeable features is the lounges.

Because the subject is "one"—*not* "features"—the verb must be singular, "is," but "is" sounds odd when it precedes the plural "lounges." The solution: **Revise the sentence.**

Among the most noticeable features are the lounges.

3. When a singular and a plural subject are joined by *or, either* ... *or,* or *neither* ... *nor,* use a verb that agrees in number with the subject closest to the verb. Examples:

Correct

Either the teacher *or the students are* mistaken.

Correct

Either the students *or the teacher is* mistaken.

The first version uses "are" because the verb is nearer to "students" (plural) than to "teacher" (singular); the second uses "is" because the verb is nearer to "teacher" than to "students."

Repetition and Variation

1. Don't be afraid to repeat a word if it is the best word. The following paragraph repeats "interesting," "paradox," "Salinger," "What makes," and "book"; notice also "feel" and "feeling." Repetition, a device necessary for continuity and clarity, holds the paragraph together.

> The reception given to *Franny and Zooey* in America has illustrated again the interesting paradox of Salinger's reputation there: great public enthusiasm, of the *Time* magazine and Best Seller List kind, accompanied by a repressive coolness in the critical journals. What makes this a paradox is that the book's themes are among the most ambitiously highbrow, and its craftsmanship most uncompromisingly virtuoso. What makes it an interesting one is that those who are most patronizing about the book are those who most resemble its characters: people whose

ideas and language in their best moments resemble Zooey's. But they feel they ought not to enjoy the book. There is a very strong feeling in American literary circles that Salinger and love of Salinger must be discouraged.

—MARTIN GREEN

2. Use pronouns, when their reference is clear, as substitutes for nouns. Notice Green's use of pronouns; notice also his substitution of "the book," for *"Franny and Zooey,"* and then "its" for "the book's." Substitutions that neither confuse nor distract keep a paragraph from sounding like a broken phonograph record.

3. Do not, however, confuse the substitutions we have just spoken of with the fault called Elegant Variation. A groundless fear of repetition sometimes leads students to write first, for example, of "Salinger," then of "the writer," then of "our author." Such variations strike the reader as silly. They can, moreover, be confusing. Does "the writer" mean "Salinger," or the person writing about him? Substitute "he" for "Salinger" if "he" is clear and sounds better. Otherwise, repeat "Salinger."

4. But don't repeat a word if it is being used in two different senses.

Confusing

My theme focuses on the theme of the book. (The first "theme" means "essay"; the second means "underlying idea" or "motif.")

Clear

Green's essay focuses on the theme of the book.

Confusing

Caesar's character is complex. The comic characters, however, are simple. (The first "character" means "personality"; the second means "persons" or "figures in the play.")

Clear

Caesar is complex; the comic characters, however, are simple.

5. Finally, eliminate words repeated unnecessarily. Use of words like *surely, in all probability, it is noteworthy* may become habitual. If they don't help your reader to follow your thoughts, they are Instant Prose Additives. Cross them out.

In general, when you revise, decide if a word should be repeated, varied, or eliminated, by testing sentences and paragraphs for both sound and sense.

Euphony

The word is from the Greek, "sweet voice," and though you need not aim at sweetness, try to avoid cacophony, or "harsh voice." Avoid distracting repetitions of sound, as in "The story is marked by a remarkable mystery," and "This is seen in the scene in which . . ." Such echoes call attention to themselves, getting in the way of the points you are making. When you revise, tune out irrelevant sound effects.

Not all sound effects are irrelevant; some contribute meaning. James Baldwin, in his essay "Stranger in the Village," argues that the American racial experience has permanently altered black and white relationships throughout the world. His concluding sentence is

This world is white no longer, and it will never be white again.

As the sentence opens, the repetition of sounds in "*w*orld is *w*hite" binds the two words together, but the idea that they are permanently bound is swiftly denied by the most emphatic repetition of sounds in *no, never, again,* as the sentence closes. Or take another example:

America, Love It or Leave It.

If it read, "America, Love It or Emigrate," would the bumper sticker still imply, as clearly and menacingly, that there are only two choices, and for the patriot, only one?

Transitions

Repetition holds a paragraph together by providing continuity and clarity. Transitions such as *next, on the other hand,* and *therefore* also provide continuity and clarity. Because we discuss transitions at length on pages 60–61, in our chapter on paragraphs, we here only remind you to make certain that the relation between one sentence and the next, and one paragraph and the next, is clear. Often it will be clear without an explicit transition: "She was desperately unhappy. She quit school."

But do not take too much for granted; relationships between sentences may not be as clear to your readers as they are to you. You know what you are talking about; they don't. After reading the passage readers may see, in retrospect, that you have just given an example, or a piece of contrary evidence, or an amplification, but readers like to know in advance where they are going; brief transitions such as *for example, but, finally* (readers are keenly interested in knowing when they are getting near the end) are enormously helpful.

CLARITY AND SENTENCE STRUCTURE: PARALLELISM

Make the structure of your sentence reflect the structure of your thought. This is not as formidable as it sounds. If you keep your reader in mind, remembering that you are explaining something to someone who understands it less well than you, you will almost automatically not only say *what* you think but also show *how* you think.

Almost automatically. In revising, read your work as if you were not the writer of it, but your intended reader. If you reach a bump or snag, where the shape or direction of your thought isn't clear, revise your sentence structure. Three general rules help:

- Put main ideas in main (independent) clauses.
- Subordinate the less important elements in the sentence to the more important.
- Put parallel ideas and details in parallel constructions.

The time to consult these rules consciously is not while you write, but while you revise. (The first two rules are amplified in the next chapter, "Revising for Emphasis." Clarity and emphasis are closely related, as the following discussion of parallel construction makes evident.)

Consider the following sentence and the revision:

Awkward

He liked eating and to sleep.

Parallel

He liked to eat and to sleep.

In the first version, "eating" and "to sleep" are not grammatically parallel; the difference in grammatical form blurs the writer's point that there is a similarity. Use parallel constructions to clarify relationships—for instance to emphasize similarities or to define differences.

I divorce myself from my feelings and immerse myself in my obligations.

—FROM A STUDENT JOURNAL

She drew a line between respect, which we were expected to show, and fear, which we were not.

—ERNESTO GALARZA

I will not accept if nominated and will not serve if elected.

—WILLIAM TECUMSEH SHERMAN

Fascist art glorifies surrender; it exalts mindlessness; it glamorizes death.

—SUSAN SONTAG

In the following examples, the parallel construction is printed in italic type.

Awkward

The dormitory rules needed revision, a smoking area was a necessity, and a generally more active role for the school in social affairs were all significant to her.

Parallel

She recommended that the school *revise* its dormitory rules, *provide* a smoking area, and *organize* more social activities.

Awkward

Most Chinese parents disapprove of interracial dating or they just do not permit it.

Parallel

Most Chinese parents *disapprove* of interracial dating, and many *forbid* it.

Revise the following sentence:

The rogallo glider is recommended for beginners because it is easy to assemble, to maintain, and it is portable.

In parallel constructions, be sure to check the consistency of articles, prepositions, and conjunctions. For example, "He wrote papers on a play by Shakespeare, a novel by Dickens, and a story by Oates," *not* "He wrote papers on a play by Shakespeare, a novel of Dickens, and a story by Oates." The shift from "by" to "of" and back to "by" serves no purpose and is merely distracting.

Let's study this matter a little more, using a short poem as our text.

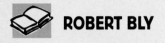 **ROBERT BLY**

Love Poem

When we are in love, we love the grass,
And the barns, and the lightpoles,
And the small mainstreets abandoned all night.

Suppose we change "Love Poem" by omitting a conjunction or an article here and there:

When we are in love, we love the grass,
Barns, and lightpoles,
And the small mainstreets abandoned all night.

We've changed the rhythm, of course, but we still get the point: the lover loves all the world. In the original poem, however, the syntax of the sentence, the consistent repetition of "and the . . ." "and the . . ." makes us feel, without our thinking about it, that when we are in love we love the world, everything in it, equally. The list could extend infinitely, and everything in it would give us identical pleasure. In our altered version, we sacrifice this unspoken assurance. We bump a little, and stumble. As readers, without consciously being aware of it, we wonder if there's some distinction being made, some qualification we've missed. We still get the point of the poem, but we don't feel it the same way.

To sum up:

> A pupil once asked Arthur Schnabel (the noted pianist) whether it was better to play in time or to play as one feels; his characteristic mordant reply was another question: "Why not feel in time?"
>
> —DAVID HAMILTON

Exercises

1. In the following sentences, underline phrases in which you find the passive voice. Recast the sentences, using the active voice:
    a. The phrases in which the passive voice is found should be underlined.
    b. The active voice should be used.

   c. In the letter from Mrs. Mike advice was sought regarding her problem with her tenant.

   d. The egg is guarded, watched over, and even hatched by the male penguin.

   e. After the Industrial Revolution, the workers' daylight hours were spent in factories.

   f. Tyler found that sexual stereotyping was reinforced in the kindergarten: the girls were encouraged to play with dolls and the boys with Mack trucks.

   g. Insufficient evidence was given in the report to prove her hypothesis that reading problems originate in peer relationships.

2. Revise the following sentences to eliminate faults in modifiers:

   a. At the age of ten years, my family moved to Zierenberg, West Germany.

   b. Without knowing the reason, my father's cheeks became red with embarrassment.

   c. Buffalo Bill became friends with Sitting Bull while performing together in the Wild West Show.

   d. During a drought, annual plants will succumb without help.

   e. Looking out from my window, the sky was inky black.

   f. Mr. Von Karajan conducted the orchestra three times during the weekend before returning to his home in the Alps to the delight of the audience.

3. In the following sentences, locate the errors in agreement and correct them.

   a. Locate the error and correct them.

   b. One must strive hard to reach their goal.

   c. I would recommend the book to anyone who wants to improve their writing.

   d. Her collection of antique toys fill the house.

4. Recast the following sentences, using parallel constructions to express parallel ideas:

   a. Jacoby's aim in writing is to disgrace the passively committed and opposition to feminism.

   b. The boys segregated themselves less, the girls showed broader career interests, and unromantic, cross-sex relationships were achieved.

   c. The study shows parents and educators that it is important to change and it can be done.

   d. I do believe that there should be equality between men and women: equal pay for equal work; everybody should have an equal chance to attain whatever goals they may have set for themselves; and everybody should share the same responsibilities toward society.

5. Identify the specific faults that make the following sentences unclear, then revise each sentence for clarity. (Note that you will often have to invent what the writer thought he or she had said.)

   a. Actually, she was aging, and quite average in other respects.

   b. If technology cannot sort out its plusses and minuses, and work to improve them, man must.

   c. Brooks stresses the farm workers' strenuous way of life and the fact that they have the bare necessities of life.

   d. Instead of movable furniture, built-in ledges extend into the center of the room to be used as tables or to sit on.

 e. The issue has been saved for my final argument because it is controversial.

 f. I am neither indifferent nor fond of children.

 g. When the students heard that their proposal was rejected a meeting was called.

 h. A viable library is the cornerstone of any college campus.

 i. Her main fault was that she was somewhat lacking in decision-making capabilities.

 j. After industrialization a swarm of immigrants came bantering to our shores.

 k. Each group felt there was very personal rapport and thus very candid feedback resulted.

 l. He can tolerate crowding and pollution and seems disinterested or ignorant of these dangers.

 m. The wooden door occupies the majority of the stone wall.

 n. Yale students frequently write to Ann Landers telling her fictional stories of their so-called troubles as a childish prank.

 o. At my grandmother's house vegetables were only served because meat was forbidden.

 p. My firm stand seemed to melt a little.

 q. The conclusion leaves the conflict neatly tied in smooth knots.

 r. The paragraph reeks of blandness.

6. The following sentences, published in *AIDE,* a magazine put out by an insurance company, were written to the company by various policyholders. The trouble is that the writers mean one thing but their sentences say another. Make each sentence clearly say what the writer means.

 a. The other car collided with mine without giving warning of its intentions.

 b. I collided with a stationary truck coming the other way.

 c. The guy was all over the road; I had to swerve a number of times before I hit him.

 d. I pulled away from the side of the road, glanced at my mother-in-law, and headed over the embankment.

 e. In my attempt to kill a fly, I drove into a telephone pole.

 f. I had been driving for forty years when I fell asleep at the wheel and had the accident.

 g. To avoid hitting the bumper of the car in front, I struck the pedestrian.

 h. The pedestrian had no idea which direction to run, so I ran over him.

 i. The indirect cause of this accident was a little guy in a small car with a big mouth.

7. In 1983, while conflicting reports were being broadcast about an invasion of Grenada by U.S. troops, Admiral Wesley L. McDonald, in the Pentagon, answered a reporter's question thus: "We were not micromanaging Grenada intelligencewise until about that time frame." Bruce Felknor, director of yearbooks for the *Encyclopaedia Britannica,* says that he was "inspired" by that answer to translate "a small selection of earlier admirals' heroic prose for the edification, indeed enjoyment, of our young." Below we list Felknor's translations and, in parentheses, the names of the admirals, the battles, and the dates of their heroic prose. What were the original words?

 a. "Combatwise, the time frame is upcoming." (John Paul Jones, off the English coast, September 23, 1779)

b. "Area accessed in combat mode; mission finished." (Oliver Hazard Perry, after the Battle of Lake Erie, September 10, 1813)

c. "Disregard anticipated structural damage. Continue as programmed." (David Farragut, Mobile Bay, August 5, 1864)

d. "Implementation of aggressive action approved; time frame to be selected by fire control officer." (George Dewey, Manila Bay, May 1, 1898)

8. Translate the following euphemisms into plain English:

a. revenue enhancement

b. atmospheric deposition of anthropogenically derived acidic substances

c. resize our operations to the level of profitable opportunities (spoken by a business executive)

d. reconcentrate (or redeploy) our forces

CHAPTER

6

Revising Sentences for Emphasis

In revising for conciseness and clarity we begin to discover what we may have been largely unaware of in the early stages of writing: what in our topic most concerns us and precisely why it interests us. That moment of discovery (or those several discrete moments) yields more pleasure than any other in writing. From there on we work, sometimes as if inspired, to make our special angle of vision seem as inevitable to our readers as it is to us. Now as we tighten sentences or expand them, as we shift the position of a word or a paragraph, or as we subordinate a less important idea to a more important one, we are assigning relative value and weight to each of our statements. The expression of value and weight is what is meant by emphasis.

Inexperienced writers may *try* to achieve emphasis as Queen Victoria did, by a style consisting *almost entirely* of italics and—dashes—and—exclamation marks!!! Or they may spice their prose with clichés ("little did I realize," "believe it or not") or with a liberal sprinkling of intensifiers ("really beautiful," "definitely significant," and so on). But experienced writers abandon these unconvincing devices, preferring to exploit the possibilities of position, of brevity and length, of repetition, and of subordination.

EMPHASIS BY POSITION

First, let's see how a word or phrase may be emphasized. If it appears in an unusual position it gains emphasis, as in "This course he liked." Because in English the object of the verb usually comes after the verb as in "He liked this course," if the object appears first, it gains emphasis. But this device is tricky; words in an unusual position often seem ludicrous, the writer fatuous: "A mounted Indian toward the forest raced."

Let's now consider a less strained sort of emphasis by position. The beginning and the end of a sentence or a paragraph are emphatic positions; of these two positions, the end is usually the more emphatic. What comes last is what stays most in the mind. Compare these two sentences:

The essay is brief but informative.

The essay is informative but brief.

The first sentence leaves the reader with the impression that the essay, despite its brevity, is worth looking at. The second, however, ends more negatively, leav-

126

ing the reader with the impression that the essay is so brief that its value is fairly slight. Because the emphasis in each sentence is different, the two sentences say different things.

The rule: It usually makes sense to put the important point near the end, lest the sentence become anticlimactic. Here is a sentence that properly moves to an emphatic end:

> Although I could not read its six hundred pages in one sitting, I never willingly put it down.

If the halves are reversed the sentence trails off:

> I never willingly put it down, although I could not read its six hundred pages in one sitting.

This second version straggles away from the real point—that the book was interesting.

Anticlimactic

> Besides not owning themselves women also could not own property.

Emphatic

> Women could not own property; in fact, they did not own themselves.

The commonest anticlimaxes are caused by weak qualifiers (*in my opinion, it seems to me, in general, etc.*) tacked on to interesting statements. Weak qualifiers usually can be omitted. Even useful ones rarely deserve an emphatic position.

Anticlimactic

> Poodles are smart but they are no smarter than pigs, I have read.

Emphatic

> Poodles are smart, but I have read that they are no smarter than pigs.

The rule: Try to bury dull but necessary qualifiers in the middle of the sentence.

EMPHASIS BY BREVITY AND LENGTH: SHORT AND LONG SENTENCES

How long should a sentence be? One recalls Lincoln's remark to a heckler who asked him how long a man's legs should be: "Long enough to reach the ground." No rules about length can be given, but be careful not to bore your reader with a succession of short sentences (say, under ten words) and be careful not to tax your reader with a monstrously long sentence. In *Les Misérables* Victor Hugo wrote a sentence containing 823 words and punctuated by ninety-three commas, fifty-one semicolons, and four dashes—not a good model for beginners.

Consider this succession of short sentences:

The purpose of the refrain is twofold. First, it divides the song into stanzas. Second, it reinforces the theme of the song.

These sentences are clear, but since the points are simple, readers may feel they are being addressed as if they were children. There is too much emphasis (too many heavy pauses) on too little. The reader can take all three sentences at once:

The purpose of the refrain is twofold: it divides the song into stanzas and it reinforces the theme.

The three simple sentences have been turned into one compound sentence, allowing the reader to keep going for a while.

Now compare another group of sentences with a revision.

Hockey is by far the fastest-moving team sport in America. The skaters are constantly on the go. They move at high speeds. The action rarely stops.

These four sentences, instead of suggesting motion, needlessly stop us. Here is a revision:

Hockey is by far the fastest-moving team sport in America. The skaters, constantly on the go, move at high speeds, and the action rarely stops.

By combining the second, third, and fourth sentences, the writer keeps the reader on the go, like the players.

Next, a longer example that would be thoroughly delightful if parts of it were less choppy.

Conceit

At my high school graduation we had two speakers. One was a member of our class, and the other was a faculty member. The student speaker's name was Alva Reed. The faculty speaker's name was Mr. Williams. The following conversation took place after the graduation ceremony. Parents, relatives, faculty, and friends were all outside the gymnasium congratulating the class of 1989. Alva was surrounded by her friends, her parents, and some faculty members who were congratulating her on her speech. Not standing far from her was Mr. Williams with somewhat the same crowd.

"Alva dear, you were wonderful!"

"Thanks Mom. I sure was scared though: I'm glad it's over."

At that moment, walking towards Alva were her grandparents. They both were wearing big smiles on their faces. Her grandfather said rather loudly, "That was a good speech dear. Nicely done, nicely done." walking past them at that moment was Mr. Williams.

  He stuck his head into their circle and replied, "Thank you," and walked away.

The first four sentences of this amusing anecdote seem to be written in spurts. They can easily be combined and improved thus:

> At my high school graduation we had two speakers. One was a member of our class, Alva Reed, and the other was a faculty member, Mr. Williams.

If we think that even this version, two sentences instead of four, is a little choppy, we can rewrite it into a single sentence:

> At my high school graduation we had two speakers, Alva Reed, a member of our class, and Mr. Williams, a faculty member.

or:

> The two speakers at my high school graduation were Alva Reed, a member of our class, and Mr. Williams, a faculty member.

The rest of the piece is less choppy, but reread it and see if you don't discover some other sentences that should be combined.

Sometimes, however, the choppiness of a succession of short sentences is effective. Look at this description of the methods by which George Jackson, in prison, resisted efforts to destroy his spirit:

> He trains himself to sleep only three hours a night. He studies Swahili, Chinese, Arabic and Spanish. He does pushups to control his sexual urge and to train his body. Sometimes he does a thousand a day. He eats only one meal a day. And, always, he is reading and thinking.
>
> —JULIUS LESTER

These six sentences add up to only fifty-one words. The longest sentence—the one about pushups—contains only thirteen words. That the author is at ease also with longer and more complicated sentences is evident in the next paragraph, which begins with a sentence of forty-two words.

> Yet, when his contact with the outside world is extended beyond his family to include Angela Davis, Joan, a woman who works with the Soledad defense committee, and his attorney, he is able to find within himself feelings of love and tenderness.

Can we account for the success of the passage describing Jackson's prison routine? First, the short sentences, with their repeated commonplace form (subject, verb, object) in some degree imitate Jackson's experience: they are almost monotonously disciplined, almost as regular as the pushups the confined Jackson does.

> He trains himself. . . .

He studies Swahili. . . .

He does pushups. . . .

Sometimes he does a thousand. . . .

He eats only one meal a day.

Later, when Jackson makes contact with Angela Davis and others, the long sentence (forty-two words) helps to suggest the expansion of his world. Second, the brevity of the sentences suggests their enormous importance, certainly to Jackson and to Julius Lester and, Lester hopes, to the reader.

Keep in mind this principle: **Any one sentence in your essay is roughly equal to any other sentence.** If a sentence is short, it must be relatively weighty. A lot is packed into a little. Less is more. (The chief exceptions are transitional sentences such as, "Now for the second point.") Consider the following passage:

> It happened that in September of 1933 Lord Rutherford, at the British Association meeting, made some remark about atomic energy never becoming real. Leo Szilard was the kind of scientist, perhaps just the kind of good-humored, cranky man, who disliked any statement that contained the word "never," particularly when made by a distinguished colleague. So he set his mind to think about the problem.
>
> —Jacob Bronowski

The first two sentences are relatively long (twenty-three words and thirty-one words); the third is relatively short (ten words), and its brevity—its weight or density—emphasizes Szilard's no-nonsense attitude.

EMPHASIS BY REPETITION

Don't be afraid to repeat a word if it is important. The repetition will add emphasis. Notice in these lucid sentences by Helen Gardner the effective repetition of "end" and "beginning."

> *Othello* has this in common with the tragedy of fortune, that the end in no way blots out from the imagination the glory of the beginning. But the end here does not merely by its darkness throw up into relief the brightness that was. On the contrary, beginning and end chime against each other. In both the value of life and love is affirmed.

The substitution of "conclusion" or "last scene" for the second "end" would be worse than pointless; it would destroy Miss Gardner's point that there is *identity* or correspondence between beginning and end.

EMPHASIS BY SUBORDINATION

Five Kinds of Sentences

Before we can discuss the use of subordination for emphasis, we must first talk about what a sentence is, and about five kinds of sentences.

If there is an adequate definition of a sentence, we haven't found it. Perhaps the best definition is not the old one, "a complete thought," but "a word or group of words that the reader takes to be complete." This definition includes such utterances as "Who?" and "Help!" and "Never?" and "Maybe." Now, in speaking, "While he was walking down the street" may be taken as a complete thought, if it answers the question "When did the car hit him?" In writing, however, it would be a sentence fragment that probably should be altered to, say, "While he was walking down the street he was hit by a car." We will discuss intentional fragments on page 132. But first we should take a closer look at complete sentences.

Usually a sentence names someone or something (this is the subject) and it tells us something about the subject (this is the predicate); that is, it "predicates" something about the subject. Let us look at five kinds of sentences: simple, compound, complex, compound-complex, and sentence fragments.

1. A **simple sentence** has one predicate, here italicized:

Shakespeare *died.*

Shakespeare and Jonson *were contemporaries.*

The subject can be elaborated ("Shakespeare and Jonson, England's chief Renaissance dramatists, were contemporaries"), or the predicate can be elaborated ("Shakespeare and Jonson were contemporaries in the Renaissance England of Queen Elizabeth"); but the sentence remains technically a simple sentence, consisting of only one main (independent) clause with no dependent (subordinate) clause.

2. A **compound sentence** has two or more main clauses, each containing a subject and a predicate. It is, then, two or more simple sentences connected by a coordinating conjunction (*and, but, for, nor, or, so, yet*) or by *not only . . . but also,* or by a semicolon or colon or, rarely, by a comma.

Shakespeare died in 1616, and Jonson died in 1637.

Shakespeare not only wrote plays, but he also acted in them.

Shakespeare died in 1616; Jonson died twenty-one years later.

3. A **complex sentence** has one main (independent) clause and one or more subordinate (dependent) clauses. The main clause (here italicized) can stand as a sentence by itself.

Although Shakespeare died, *England survived.*

Jonson did not write a commemorative poem when Shakespeare died.

The parts not italicized are subordinate or dependent because they cannot stand as sentences by themselves.

4. A **compound-complex sentence** has two or more main clauses (here italicized) and one or more subordinate clauses.

In 1616 Shakespeare died and *his wife inherited the second-best bed* because he willed it to her.

Each of the two italicized passages could stand by itself as a sentence, but "because he willed it to her" could not (except as the answer to a question). Each italicized passage, then, is a main (independent) clause, and "because he willed it to her" is a subordinate (dependent) clause.

We will return to subordination, but let us first look at the fifth kind of sentence, the sentence fragment.

5. A **sentence fragment** does not fit the usual definition of a sentence, but when the fragment is intended the thought is often clear and complete enough. Intentional fragments are common in advertisements:

> Made of imported walnut. For your pleasure. At finer stores.

> More native than the Limbo. More exciting than the beat of a steel drum. Tia Maria. Jamaica's haunting liqueur.

And yet another example, this one not from an advertisement but from an essay on firewood:

> Piles of it. Right off the sidewalk. Split from small logs of oak or ash or maple. Split. Split again.
>
> —JOHN MCPHEE

All these examples strike us as pretentious in their obviously studied efforts at understatement. Words are hoarded, as though there is much in little, and as though to talk more fully would demean the speaker and would desecrate the subject. A few words, and then a profound silence. Here less is not more; it is too much. The trouble with these fragmentary sentences is not that they don't convey complete thoughts but that they attract too much attention to themselves; they turn our minds too emphatically to their writers, and conjure up images of unpleasantly self-satisfied oracles.

Here, however, is a passage from a student's essay, where the fragmentary sentences seem satisfactory to us. The passage begins with a simple sentence, and then gives three fragmentary sentences.

> The film has been playing to sellout audiences. Even though the
>
> acting is inept. Even though the sound is poorly synchronized. Even
>
> though the plot is incoherent.

If this passage is successful, it is because the emphasis is controlled. The author is dissatisfied, and by means of parallel fragments (each beginning with the same words) she conveys a moderately engaging weariness and a gentle exasperation.

Then, too, we see that if the first three periods were changed to commas we would have an orthodox complex sentence. In short, because the fragments are effective we find them acceptable.

For ways to correct ineffective or unacceptable fragments, see pages 431–32 in Chapter 19.

Subordination

Having surveyed the kinds of sentences, we can at last talk about using subordination to give appropriate emphasis.

Make sure that the less important element is subordinate to the more important. Consider this sentence, about the painter Vincent van Gogh, who was supported by his brother Theo.

Supported by Theo's money, van Gogh painted at Arles.

The writer puts van Gogh in the independent clause ("Van Gogh painted at Arles"), subordinating the relatively unimportant Theo.

Had the writer wished to give Theo more prominence, the passage might have run:

Theo provided money, and van Gogh painted at Arles.

Here Theo (as well as van Gogh) stands in an independent clause, linked to the next clause by "and." The two clauses, and the two people, are now of approximately equal importance.

If the writer had wanted to emphasize Theo and to deemphasize van Gogh, he might have written:

While van Gogh painted at Arles, Theo provided the money.

Here van Gogh is reduced to the subordinate clause, and Theo is given the dignity of the only independent clause.

In short, though simple sentences and compound sentences have their place, they make everything of equal importance. Since everything is not of equal importance, you must often write complex and compound-complex sentences, subordinating some things to other things.

Exercises

1. Here is one way to test your grasp of the relationship of independent and subordinate elements in a sentence. This *haiku* (a Japanese poetic form) consists of one sentence that can be written as prose: "After weeks of watching the roof leak, I fixed it tonight by moving a single board."

   ### Hitch Haiku

   After weeks of watching the roof leak
   I fixed it tonight
   by moving a single board.

   —GARY SNYDER

   a. Identify the independent clause and the subordinate elements in the poem.
   b. The "I" in the poem's sentence does or has done three things. Write three simple sentences, each expressing one of the actions.
   c. Write one sentence in which all three of the poem's actions are expressed, but put in the independent clause one of the two actions that appear in a subordinate element in the poem.
   d. Compare your sentence with the poem's. Both sentences should be clear. How do they vary in emphasis?
   e. Optional: Compare the original sentence written as poetry and written as prose.

2. First identify the fault or faults that make the following sentences unemphatic, and then revise them for emphasis.

    a. He lists some of the rights given to humans and to nonhumans and both admits and accounts for the oddity of his proposal well by citing examples.

    b. Rights for women, African-Americans and the insane were granted though many couldn't see the value in it and so now our environment should be granted rights even though it takes some getting used to the idea.

    c. Thus Creon's pride forces Antigone's death which drives his son to suicide and then his wife.

    d. Stock breeding will give the same result as population evolution, defenders of positive eugenics claim.

    e. The family today lacks the close relationship it had before the industrial age, for example.

    f. The woman's face is distraught, her hair is unkempt, and her dress is rumpled.

    g. There is probably no human being who would enjoy being eaten by a shark.

3. Analyze the ways Theodore Roosevelt achieved emphasis in the following passage on Grand Canyon.

In Grand Canyon Arizona has a natural wonder which, so far as I know, is in kind absolutely unparalleled throughout the rest of the world. . . . Leave it as it is. You cannot improve upon it. The ages have been at work on it, and man can only mar it. What you can do is to keep it for your children, your children's children, and for all those who come after you as one of the great sights which every American, if he can travel at all, should see.

CHAPTER

7
The Writer's Voice

The friends that have it I do wrong
When ever I remake a song,
Should know what issue is at stake:
It is myself that I remake.

—WILLIAM BUTLER YEATS

DEFINING STYLE

Style is not simply a flower here and some gilding there; it pervades the whole work. Van Gogh's style, or Walt Disney's, let us say, consists in part of features recurring throughout a single work and from one work to the next: angular or curved lines, hard or soft edges, strong or gentle contrasts, and so on. Pictures of a seated woman by each of the two artists are utterly different, and if we have seen a few works by each, we can readily identify who did which one. Artists leave their fingerprints, so to speak, all over their work. Writers leave their voiceprints.

The word *style* comes from the Latin *stilus,* a Roman writing instrument. Even in Roman times *stilus* had acquired a figurative sense, referring not only to the instrument but also to the writer's choice of words and arrangement of words into sentences. But is it simply the choice and arrangement of words we comment on when we speak of a writer's style, or are we also commenting on the writer's mind? Don't we feel that a piece of writing, whether it's on Civil War photographs or on genetics and intelligence, is also about the writer? The writing, after all, sets forth the writer's views of his or her topic. It sets forth perceptions and responses to something the writer has thought about. The writer has, from the start, from the choice of a topic, revealed that he or she found it worth thinking about. The essay, in attempting to persuade us to think as the writer does, reveals not only how and what the writer thinks, but also what he or she values.

When we write about things "out there," our writing always reveals the form and likeness of our minds, just as every work of art reveals the creator as well as the ostensible subject. A portrait painting, for example, is not only about the sitter, it is also about the artist's perceptions of the sitter; hence the saying that every portrait is a self-portrait. Even photographs are as much about the photographer as they are about the subject. Richard Avedon said of his portraits of famous people, "They are all pictures of me, of the way I feel about the people I photograph." A student's essay similarly, if it is truly written, is not exclusively about "*La Causa* and the New Chicana"; it is also about her perceptions and responses to both racism and sexism.

STYLE AND TONE

> *The style is the man.*
> —BUFFON

> *The style is the man. Rather say the*
> *style is the way the man takes himself.*
> —ROBERT FROST

Suppose we take a page of handwriting, or even a signature. We need not believe that graphology is an exact science to believe that the shape of the ink-lines on paper (apart from the meaning of the words) often tells us something about the writer. We look at a large, ornate signature, and we sense that the writer is confident; we look at a tiny signature written with the finest of pens, and we wonder why anyone is so self-effacing.

More surely than handwriting, the writer's style reveals, among other things, his or her attitude toward the self (as Frost's addition to Buffon's epigram suggests), toward the reader, and toward the subject. The writer's attitudes are reflected in what is usually called *tone.* It is difficult to separate style from tone but we can try. Most discussions of style concentrate on what might be thought of as ornament: figurative language ("a sea of troubles"), inversion ("A leader he is not"), repetition and parallelism ("government of the people, by the people, for the people"), balance and antithesis ("It was the best of times, it was the worst of times"). Indeed, for centuries style has been called "the dress of thought," implying that the thought is something separate from the expression; the thought, in this view, is dressed up in stylistic devices. But in most of the writing that we read with interest and pleasure, the stylistic devices are not ornamental and occasional but integral and pervasive. When we talk about wit, sincerity, tentativeness, self-assurance, aggressiveness, objectivity, and so forth, we can say we are talking about style, but we should recognize that style now is not a matter of ornamental devices that dress up some idea, but part of the idea itself. And "the idea itself" includes the writer's unified yet appropriately varied tone of voice.

To take a brief example: the famous English translation of Caesar's report of a victory,

> I came, I saw, I conquered,

might be paraphrased thus:

> After getting to the scene of the battle, I studied the situation. Then I devised a strategy that won the battle.

But this paraphrase loses much of Caesar's message; the brevity and the parallelism of the famous version, as well as the alliteration (came, conquered), convey tight-lipped self-assurance—convey, that is, the tone that reveals Caesar to us. And this tone is a large part of Caesar's message. Caesar is really telling us not only about what he did, but also about what sort of person he is. He is perceptive, decisive, and effective. The three actions, Caesar in effect tells us, are (for a man like Caesar) one. (The Latin original is even more tight-lipped and more unified by alliteration: *veni, vidi, vici.*)

Let's look now at a longer sentence, the opening sentence of Lewis Thomas's essay "On Natural Death":

> There are so many new books about dying that there are now special shelves set aside for them in bookstores, along with the health, diet and home-repair paperbacks and the sex manuals.

This sentence could have ended where the comma is placed: the words after "bookstores" are, it might seem, not important. One can scarcely argue that by specifying some kinds of "special shelves" Thomas clarifies an otherwise difficult or obscure concept. What, then, do these additional words do? They tell us nothing about death and almost nothing about bookshops, but they tell us a great deal about Thomas's *attitude* toward the new books on death. He suggests that such books are faddish and perhaps (like "the sex manuals") vulgar. After all, if he had merely wanted to call up a fairly concrete image of a well-stocked bookstore, he could have said "along with books on politics and the environment," or some such thing. His next sentence runs:

> Some of them are so packed with detailed information and step-by-step instructions for performing the function you'd think this was a new sort of skill which all of us are now required to learn.

Why "you'd think" instead of, say, "one might believe"? Thomas uses a colloquial form, and a very simple verb, because he wants to convey to us his common-sense, homely, down-to-earth view that these books are a bit pretentious—a pretentiousness conveyed in his use of the words "performing the function," words that might come from the books themselves. In short, when we read Thomas's paragraph we are learning as much about Thomas as we are about books on dying. We are hearing a voice, perceiving an attitude, and we want to keep reading, not only because we are interested in death but also because Thomas has managed to make us interested in Thomas, a thoughtful but unpretentious fellow.

Now listen to a short paragraph from John Szarkowski's *Looking at Photographs.* Szarkowski is writing about one of Alexander Gardner's photographs of a dead Confederate sharpshooter.

> Among the pictures that Gardner made himself is the one reproduced here. Like many Civil War photographs, it showed that the dead of both sides looked very much the same. The pictures of earlier wars had not made this clear.

Try, in a word or two, to characterize the tone (the attitude, as we sense it in the inflection of the voice) of the first sentence. Next, the tone of the second, and then of the third. Suppose the second and third sentences had been written thus:

> It showed that the dead of both sides looked very much the same. This is made clear in Civil War photographs, but not in pictures of earlier wars.

How has the tone changed? What word can you find to characterize the tone of the whole, as Szarkowski wrote it?

Now another passage from Szarkowski's book:

> Jacob A. Riis was a newspaper reporter by occupation and a social reformer by inclination. He was a photographer rather briefly and apparently rather casually; it seems beyond doubt that he considered photography a useful but subservient tool for his work as reporter and reformer. It is clear that he had no interest in "artistic" photography, and equally clear that the artistic photographers of his time had no interest in him.

Do you find traces of Szarkowski's voiceprint here?

Finally, a longer passage by the same writer. After you read it, try to articulate the resemblances between this and the other—qualities that allow us to speak of the writer's tone.

> There are several possible explanations for the fact that women have been more important to photography than their numbers alone would warrant. One explanation might be the fact that photography has never had licensing laws or trade unions, by means of which women might have been effectively discriminated against. A second reason might be the fact that the specialized technical preparation for photography need not be enormously demanding, so that the medium has been open to those unable to spend long years in formal study. A third possible reason could be that women have a greater natural talent for photography than men do. Discretion (or cowardice) suggests that this hypothesis is best not pursued, since a freely speculative exploration of it might take unpredictable and indefensible lines. One might for example consider the idea that the art of photography is in its nature receptive, or passive, thus suggesting that women are also.

ACQUIRING STYLE

In the preceding pages we said that your writing reveals not only where you stand (your topic) and how you think (the structure of your argument), but also who you are and how you take yourself (your tone). To follow our argument to its limit, we might say that everything in this book—including rules on the comma (where you breathe)—is about style. We do. What more is there to say?

Clarity And Texture

First, a distinction Aristotle makes between two parts of style: that which gives clarity, and that which gives texture. Exact words, concrete illustrations of abstractions, conventional punctuation, and so forth—matters we treat in some detail in the sections on revising and editing—make for clarity. On the whole, this part of style is inconspicuous when present; when absent, the effect ranges from mildly distracting to ruinous. Clarity is the foundation of style. It can be achieved by anyone willing to make the effort.

Among the things that give texture, or individuality, are effective repetition, variety in sentence structure, wordplay, and so forth. This second group of devices, on the whole more noticeable, makes the reader aware of the writer's particular voice. These devices can be learned too, but seldom by effort alone. In fact, playfulness helps here more than doggedness. Students who work at this part of style usually enjoy hanging around words. At the same time, they're likely to feel that when they put words on paper, even in a casual letter to a friend, they're putting themselves on the line. Serious, as most people are about games they really care about, but not solemn, they'll come to recognize the rules of play in John Holmes's advice to young poets: "You must believe that your feelings and your words for your feelings are important. . . . That they are unique is a fact; that you believe they are unique is necessary."

A Repertory of Styles

We make a second distinction: between style as the reader perceives it from the written word, and style as the writer experiences it. The first is static: it's fixed in writing or print; we can point to it, discuss it, analyze it. The second, the writer's experience of his or her own style, changes as the writer changes. In his essay "Why I Write" George Orwell said, "I find that by the time you have perfected any style of writing, you have always outgrown it." An exaggeration that deposits a truth. The essay concludes, however, "Looking back through my work, I see that it is invariably where I lacked a political purpose that I wrote lifeless books and was betrayed into purple passages, sentences without meaning, decorative adjectives and humbug generally." A suggestion surely, that through trial and error, and with maturity, a writer comes to a sense of self, a true style, not static and not constantly changing, but achieved.

Undergraduates seldom know what purpose, in Orwell's sense, they will have. You may be inclined toward some subjects and against others, you may have decided on a career—many times. But if your education is worth anything like the money and time invested in it, your ideas and feelings will change more rapidly in the next few years than ever before in your memory, and perhaps more than they ever will again. Make use of the confusion you're in. Reach out for new experiences to assimilate; make whatever connections you can from your reading to your inner life, reaching back into your past and forward into your future. And keep writing.

To keep pace with your changing ideas—and here is our main point—you'll need to acquire not one style, but a repertory of styles, a store of writing habits on which you can draw as the need arises.

Originality and Imitation

Finally, a paradox: one starts to acquire an individual style by studying and imitating the style of others. The paradox isn't limited to writing. Stylists in all fields begin as apprentices. The young ball player imitates the movements of Reggie Jackson, the potter joins a workshop in California to study under Marguerite Wildenhain, the chess player hangs around the park or club watching the old pros, then finds a book that probably recommends beginning with Ruy Lopez's opening. When Michelangelo was an apprentice he copied works by his predecessors; when Millet was young he copied works by Michelangelo; when Van Gogh was young he copied works by Millet. The would-be writer may be lucky enough to have a teacher, one he can imitate; more likely he will, in W. H. Auden's words, "serve his apprenticeship in the library."

Practice in Acquiring Style

Benjamin Franklin's Exercise   Benjamin Franklin says in his *Autobiography,* "Prose writing has been of great use to me in the course of my life, and was a principal means of my advancement," and he reveals how he acquired his ability in it. (He had just abandoned, at about the age of eleven, his ambition to be a great poet—after his father told him that "verse-makers were generally beggars.")

> About this time I met with an odd volume of the *Spectator.* It was the third. I had never before seen any of them. I bought it, read it over and over, and was much delighted with it. I thought the writing excellent, and wished, if possible, to imitate it. With that view I took some of the papers, and making short hints of the sentiment in each sentence, laid them by a few days, and then, without looking at the book, tried to complete the papers again by expressing each sentiment at length, and as fully as it had been expressed before, in any suitable words that should come to hand. Then I compared my *Spectator* with the original, discovered some of my faults, and corrected them.

A few pages later Franklin confides, with characteristic understatement (which he learned, he thought, by imitating Socrates), "I sometimes had the pleasure of fancying that in certain particulars of small import I had been lucky enough to improve the method or the language."

Exercises

1. Outline, in a list of brief notes, Franklin's exercise.
2. Choose a passage of current prose writing whose style you admire and follow Franklin's method. (Don't forget the last step: where you've improved on your model, congratulate yourself with becoming modesty.)

Paraphrasing   Do not confuse a paraphrase with a summary.

A summary is always much shorter than the original; a paraphrase is sometimes a bit longer. Your sentence should say substantially what the original says, but in your own words, and in a fluent, natural style. Each word or phrase in the sentence you're paraphrasing should be replaced with one of your own. (Articles, pronouns, and conjunctions need not be replaced.) The structure of the sentence should be yours as well. Consider the following sentence by W. H. Auden and the paraphrase that follows it:

> Owing to its superior power as a mnemonic, verse is superior to prose as a medium for didactic instruction.
>
> —W. H. AUDEN

> Because it is more easily memorized and can be retained in the mind for a longer time, poetry is better than prose for teaching moral lessons.

Paraphrasing is useful for several reasons. First, paraphrasing helps you to increase your vocabulary. (Many students say that a limited vocabulary is their chief source of difficulty in writing.) You may know, for example, that "didactic" means "intended for instruction, or instructive." But why then does Auden say "didactic instruction"? Are the words redundant, or is Auden stipulating a kind of instruction? Your dictionary, which may list "tending to teach a moral lesson" as one of three or four meanings of "didactic," will help you understand Auden's sentence. But notice, first, that you'll have to choose the appropriate definition, and second, that you won't be able to insert that definition as is into your sentence. To paraphrase "didactic instruction" you'll have to put "didactic" in your own words. (If you look up "mnemonic" you'll find an even more complex puzzle resolved in our paraphrase.) Paraphrasing, then, expands your vocabulary because to paraphrase accurately and gracefully you must actively understand the use of an unfamiliar word, not simply memorize a synonym for it.

Paraphrasing also helps you to focus your attention on what you read. If you want, for example, to become a better reader of poetry, the best way is to *pay attention,* and the best way of paying attention is to try paraphrasing a line whose meaning escapes you. So too with understanding art history or economics or any specialized study. If you come across a difficult passage, don't just stare at it, paraphrase it. (If you don't have time to stop and puzzle through a sentence that is not entirely clear to you, you can always make time to jot it down on a three-by-five card. As Stanislav Andreski says, "Paper is patient.")

Finally, in paraphrasing, you are observing closely and actively the way another mind works. You are, in effect, serving as an apprentice stylist. (Some masters, of course, are not worth serving or emulating. Be discriminating.)

Exercise

Try paraphrasing the following sentences:

Generally speaking and to a varying extent, scientists follow their temperaments in their choice of problems.

—Charles Hermite

The scholar's mind is a deep well in which are buried aborted feelings that rise to the surface as arguments.

—Natalie Clifford Barney

The more extensive your acquaintance is with the works of those who have excelled, the more extensive will be your powers of invention, and what may appear still more like a paradox, the more original will be your composition.

—Sir Joshua Reynolds

Anyone who has ever struggled with poverty knows how extremely expensive it is to be poor.

—James Baldwin

What is expressed is impressed.

—Aristotle

All the road to heaven is heaven.

—Saint Teresa of Avila

When the shoe fits, the foot is forgotten.

—CHUANG TZU

Imitating the Cumulative Sentence

When you write, you make a point, not by subtracting as though you sharpened a pencil, but by adding. When you put one word after another, your statement should be more precise the more you add. If the result is otherwise, you have added the wrong thing, or you have added more than was needed.

—JOHN ERSKINE

In *Notes Toward a New Rhetoric* Francis Christensen cites "Erskine's principle" and argues that "the cumulative sentence" best fulfills it. The cumulative sentence makes a statement in the main clause; the rest of the sentence consists of modifiers *added* to make the meaning of the statement more precise. The cumulative sentence adds *texture* to writing because as the writer adds modifiers she is examining her impressions, summarized in the main clause. At the same time she reveals to the reader how those impressions impinged on her mind. Here are some of Christensen's examples:

He dipped his hands in the bichloride solution and shook them, a quick shake, fingers down, like the fingers of a pianist above the keys.

—SINCLAIR LEWIS

The jockeys sat bowed and relaxed, moving a little at the waist with the movement of their horses.

—KATHERINE ANNE PORTER

The Texan turned to the nearest gatepost and climbed to the top of it, his alternate thighs thick and bulging in the tight trousers, the butt of the pistol catching and losing the sun in pearly gleams.

—WILLIAM FAULKNER

George was coming down in the telemark position, kneeling, one leg forward and bent, the other trailing, his sticks hanging like some insect's thin legs, kicking up puffs of snow, and finally the whole kneeling, trailing figure coming around in a beautiful right curve like points of light, all in a wild cloud of snow.

—ERNEST HEMINGWAY

Exercise

Try writing a cumulative sentence. First, reread Christensen's sample sentences out loud. Then, during a second reading, try to sense the similarities in structure. For the next few days train yourself to observe people closely, the way they walk, move, gesture, smile, speak. Take notes when you can. Then, after reading the sentences again, try writing one. Either imitate one of the sentences closely, word by word (substituting your own words) or start with your subject, imitating the structure you have detected or have simply absorbed.

ACADEMIC STYLES, ACADEMIC AUDIENCES

When you write an essay for a course, you are to some degree learning how people working in that academic discipline express themselves. To communicate with other people in the discipline, you must adapt your voice to the conventions of the discipline and the audience's expectations about writing within that discipline. Some disciplines call for an abstract at the beginning of the paper, and some do not. Some call for an immediate statement of purpose, and some do not. Some disciplines (literature, for example) frown on passive verbs. But in lab reports in the sciences passive verbs are acceptable—even encouraged—in part because they help focus the reader's attention on the experiment rather than on the person who conducted it, and thereby help to establish authority.

To make matters even more complicated, the conventions are changing, and they vary to some degree from class to class, and instructor to instructor. For example, one literature instructor might accept an essay containing the word "we" (as in "we see here the author's fascination with landscape"); another might object to its use, arguing that the "we" falsely implies that all readers—regardless of race, class, gender, and so on—read all texts in the same way.

These differences make some students frustrated, even cynical. To them, writing an essay becomes a game of figuring out What The Instructor Wants. (For what it's worth, such students can make instructors a bit frustrated too.) It may help both students and instructors to keep in mind that there isn't one *right* style—and that the differences among styles aren't a matter of arbitrary and inscrutable personal taste, but rather a matter of disciplinary convention, and (to some degree) theoretical approach.

It would be impossible to list here all the different conventions you'll encounter in college. You don't need to learn them all anyway. You simply need to be alert to the ways in which people talk to each other in the disciplines within which you're writing, and do your best to follow the conventions you observe. We illustrate a few of these differences below.

Here is the first paragraph of an article from a recent issue of the *Cambridge Journal of Economics.*

In this paper I shall develop a framework which may be used to examine several alternative theories of the rate of interest. The four most widely accepted approaches are the Neoclassical Loanable Funds, Keynes's Liquidity Preference, Neoclassical Synthesis ISLM, and Basil Moore's Horizontalist (or endogenous money). I will use the framework developed here to present a fifth: an integration of liquidity preference theory with an endogenous money approach. I first briefly set forth the primary alternative approaches, then develop an analytical framework based on an asset or stock approach and use it to discuss several theories of the interest rate: those advanced by Keynes, by Moore, by neoclassical theory and the monetarists, by Kregel, and by Tobin. Finally, I shall use the framework to reconcile liquidity preference theory with an endogenous money approach.

—L. RANDALL WRAY

Note the use of the pronoun "I," the direct statement of what the writer will do ("In this paper I shall develop a framework . . ."); and the listing of the steps of his procedure ("I first briefly set forth," and so on). A literary critic would be unlikely to present his or her ideas so methodically, as the next paragraph suggests.

Here is the first paragraph of a chapter from a recent study of Bram Stoker's *Dracula,* in which a literary critic analyzes the novel in its social and political context.

"In obedience to the law as it then stood, he was buried in the centre of a *quadrivium,* or conflux of four roads (in this case four streets), with a stake driven through his heart. And over him drives for ever the uproar of unresting London!" No, not *Dracula* (1897), but the closing lines of a much earlier nineteenth-century work, Thomas De Quincey's bleakly ironic essay "On Murder Considered as One of the Fine Arts" (1854). De Quincey is describing how in 1812 the London populace dealt with the body of one of his prize exhibits, a particularly grisly serial killer who had escaped the gallows by hanging himself in his cell in the dead of night. Yet it is difficult for us to read this gleefully chilling passage today without thinking of Bram Stoker's classic vampire novel. The quirky Christian symbolism, the mandatory staking down of the monster to keep it from roaming abroad, the sense of busily self-absorbed London unaware of its proximity to a murderous presence that haunts its most densely populated byways: together these features seem virtually to define a basic iconography for the vampire Gothic as it achieved canonical status in *Dracula.*

—DAVID GLOVER

Note the absence of the pronoun "I" and the presence of the pronoun "we." Note also the playfulness of the style (the reference to a "gleefully chilling passage" and the "staking down of the monster"), the specificity of the language, and the variety in punctuation and sentence structure.

Finally, here is the opening paragraph of a chemistry student's study of the enzyme calf alkaline phosphatase.

Enzymes, protein molecules that catalyze reactions, are crucial for many biochemical reactions. This research project studies the actions of the enzyme calf alkaline phosphatase on the substrate p-nitrophenyl phosphate. The focus of this research project is the relation of alkaline phosphatase denaturation to temperature. Heat denaturation has been well documented in major biology and chemistry texts, but few textbooks mention how extreme cold affects enzyme structure and function. This study will examine how alkaline phosphatase responds to both high and low temperatures.

—HILARY SUZAWA

Note the absence of personal pronouns (the *research project* "studies"), the orderly and careful presentation of information (including the brief definition of the word "enzymes" in the first sentence), and the clear statement of purpose. (You might compare this writer's first sentence with Glover's—deliberately misleading—opening.)

THE WRITER'S VOICE: SIX EXAMPLES

1. The following passage is the first paragraph from an essay titled "Rape and Modern Sex War." It originally appeared in a newspaper and has been republished in *Sex, Art, and American Culture* (1992), a collection of essays by the author.

> Rape is an outrage that cannot be tolerated in civilized society. Yet feminism, which has waged a crusade for rape to be taken more seriously, has put young women in danger by hiding the truth about sex from them.
>
> —CAMILLE PAGLIA

a. The first sentence says something that presumably everyone agrees with. Why, then, did Paglia bother to say it? Would the paragraph be significantly different if it began, "Feminism, which has waged a crusade . . . ."? Explain.

b. If you had read this paragraph in the newspaper, do you think you would have continued to read the essay? Why? (The entire essay is reprinted in this book, beginning on page 543.)

2. The following paragraph, from an essay called "First Amendment Pixillation," was originally published in *National Review.*

> Freedom of the press is in mortal peril again, this time out in Kansas, where pseudonymous postal officials tricked New York pornographer Al Goldstein into mailing them his brainchildren, *Screw* and *Smut.* Civil libertarians are swarming to the defense of Goldstein and his former partner, one James Buckley (don't even ask), who are now on trial on federal charges of mailing obscene materials. "*Screw* is a despicable publication," says Harvard's Alan Dershowitz, "but that's what the First Amendment was designed to protect." False. That's what the First Amendment is currently *used* to protect, but . . . well, class, let's have a short review.
>
> —WILLIAM F. BUCKLEY

a. Buckley begins by saying that "Freedom of the press is in mortal peril again. . . ." Does he mean what he says? Or is he being ironic? How do you know?

b. In his second sentence Buckley says that civil libertarians "are swarming" to the defense of a pornographer. Why "swarming" rather than, say, "hastening"? What are the connotations of "swarming"?

c. How does Buckley present himself here? As deeply thoughtful? Cocky? Concessive? Or what? Explain.

3. The following paragraph comes from a speech by the British mathematician and philosopher, Alfred North Whitehead:

> Style, in its finest sense, is the last acquirement of the educated mind; it is also the most useful. It pervades the whole being. The administrator with a sense for style hates waste; the engineer with a sense for style economizes his material; the artisan with a sense for style prefers good work. Style is the ultimate morality of mind. . . . With style the end is attained without side issues, without raising undesirable inflammations. With style you attain your end and nothing but your end. With style the effect of your activity is calculable, and foresight is the last gift of Gods to men. With style your power is increased, for your mind is not distracted with irrelevancies, and you are more likely to attain your object.

    a. Suppose that the first sentence of Whitehead's passage began thus: "I want to point out to you today that style may be regarded not only as the last acquirement of what I consider the mind that has been well educated, but it is also the most useful, I definitely believe." What would be lost?

    4. Here is the opening paragraph of a chapter on "apparition belief" from a recent cultural history of eighteenth-century England:

> Why do we no longer believe in ghosts? In his nostalgic celebration *The Book of Dreams and Ghosts* (1897), Andrew Lang blamed the skeptical eighteenth century: "the cock-sure common-sense of the years from 1650 to 1850, or so, regarded everyone who had an experience of a hallucination as a dupe, a lunatic, or a liar." Enlightenment thinking—to put it bluntly—made spirits obsolete. Keith Thomas takes up a similar theme in *Religion and the Decline of Magic* (1971), but develops it rather more ingeniously. Men and women of the eighteenth century "stopped seeing ghosts," he asserts, not so much because ghosts came to seem "intellectually impossible" (though this was certainly the case) but because ghosts gradually lost their "social relevance." In traditional English society, he suggests, the belief in apparitions performed a powerful community function. The idea that spirits of the dead might come back to haunt murderers, locate stolen objects, enforce the terms of legacies, expose adulterers, and so on, functioned as a kind of implicit social control—a restraint on aggression and a "useful sanction for social norms." With the emergence after 1706 of new and bureaucratic forms of surveillance—with the rise of an organized police force, grand juries, insurance companies, and other information-gathering bodies—the need for a spectral monitoring agency, composed of ethereal headless ladies, morose figures in shrouds, and other supernatural busybodies, gradually began to fade.
>
> —TERRY CASTLE

    a. How would you characterize Castle's attitude toward her topic? Her audience? How would you describe her attitude toward the scholars she cites?
    b. Recall the distinction Aristotle makes between the two parts of style: that which gives clarity (exact words, concrete illustrations of abstractions, conventional punctuation), and that which gives texture (effective repetition,

variety in sentence structure, wordplay). Analyze the paragraph in terms of these two "parts": where, for example, does Castle supply "concrete illustrations of abstractions"? Which words and phrases could be described as giving "texture" to the paragraph?

5. Here is the opening paragraph of an essay on Jane Austen's *Pride and Prejudice:*

> In a famous and lovely chapter of *Pride and Prejudice,* Elizabeth Bennet first sees Pemberley, the splendid estate of the splendid Mr. Darcy, whose rather insulting offer of marriage she has rather insultingly refused. Jane Austen reports that Elizabeth felt "an embarrassment impossible to be overcome" when the place's owner, whom she had supposed absent, suddenly appears and finds her, accompanied by relatives whom she thinks *he* thinks beneath his notice, admiring his property like any common tourist. "Embarrassment" seems the right word—she feels confused, ill at ease, disconcerted, flustered, to be discovered rubbernecking at the home of someone she knows as an approximate social equal. But after this first encounter the terms change: Elizabeth now feels "overpowered by shame and vexation" to suppose that she has given Darcy reason to think she has "thrown herself in his way," though his gracious, cordial behavior soon suggests even to her that he thinks no such thing.
>
> —THOMAS R. EDWARDS

a. Read this passage out loud. What is the most noticeable feature of Edwards's style? What effect does it create?

b. How would you describe the writer's tone? How does it differ from Castle's tone in the paragraph on ghosts, above?

6. Following is a passage from *The Alchemy of Race and Rights* (1991) by Patricia J. Williams, a lawyer and professor of law at Columbia University.

> Walking down Fifth Avenue in New York not long ago, I came up behind a couple and their young son. The child, about four or five years old, had evidently been complaining about big dogs. The mother was saying, "But why are you afraid of big dogs?" "Because they're big," he responded with eminent good sense. "But what's the difference between a big dog and a little dog?" the father persisted. "They're *big,*" said the child. "But there's really no difference," said the mother, pointing to a large slathering wolfhound with narrow eyes and the calculated amble of a gangster, and then to a beribboned Pekingese the size of a roller skate, who was flouncing along just ahead of us all, in that little fox-trotty step that keeps Pekingese from ever being taken seriously. "See," said the father. "If you look really closely you'll see there's no difference at all. They're all just dogs."
>
> And I thought: Talk about your iron-clad canon. Talk about a static, unyielding, totally uncompromising point of reference. These people must be lawyers. Where else do people learn so well the idiocies of High Objectivity? How else do people learn to capitulate so uncritically to a norm that refuses to allow for difference? How else do grown-ups sink so deeply into the authoritarianism of their own world view that they can universalize their relative bigness so com-

pletely that they obliterate the subject positioning of their child's relative smallness? (To say nothing of the position of the slathering wolfhound, from whose own narrow perspective I dare say the little boy must have looked exactly like a lamb chop.)

    a. At what point in the first paragraph do you begin to get Williams's attitude toward the little boy? How does the cumulative sentence in the middle of the paragraph convey her attitude toward the boy's parents? (What would be lost if Williams simply said that the mother pointed to a wolfhound and a Pekingese?)

    b. Describe Williams's voice at the beginning of the second paragraph. How does her style express her attitude here?

    c. Paraphrase the sentence in the second paragraph that begins "How else do grown-ups sink so deeply."

PART TWO

The Writer's Materials and Strategies

CHAPTER

Analytic Thinking and Writing

Look at this drawing by Pieter Brueghel the Elder, titled "The Painter and the Connoisseur" (about 1565), and then jot down your responses to the questions that follow.

ANALYZING A DRAWING

1. One figure is given considerably more space than the other. What may be implied by this fact?
2. What is the painter doing (besides painting)?
3. What is the connoisseur doing?
4. What does the face of each figure tell you about the character of each figure? The figures are physically close; are they mentally close? How do you know?

Now consider this brief discussion of the picture.

> The painter, standing in front of the connoisseur and given more than two-thirds of the space, dominates this picture. His hand holds the brush with which he creates, while the connoisseur's hand awkwardly fumbles for money in his purse. The connoisseur apparently is pleased with the picture he is looking at, for he is buying it, but his parted lips give him a stupid expression and his eyeglasses imply defective vision. In contrast, the painter looks away from the picture and fixes his eyes on the model (reality) or, more likely, on empty space, his determined expression suggesting that he possesses an imaginative vision beyond his painting and perhaps even beyond earthly reality.

The author of this paragraph uses analysis to interpret the drawing, to discover its meaning. The paragraph doesn't simply tell us that the picture shows two people close together; it separates the parts of the picture, pointing out that the two figures form a contrast. It explains why one figure gets much more space than the other, and it explains what the contrasting gestures and facial expressions imply. The writer of the comment has "read" or interpreted the drawing by examining how the parts function, that is, how they relate to the whole.

ANALYZING TEXTS

Most of what you read and write in most of your courses is analytical: you read of the various causes of a revolution, of the effects of inflation, or of the relative importance of heredity and environment; you write about the meaning of a short story or painting, the causes and effects of poverty, the strengths and weaknesses of some proposed legislative action. And much (though not all) of this reading and writing is based on the analysis of *texts*. The word "text" derives from the Latin for "woven" (as in textile), and it has come to refer not only to words stitched together into sentences (whether novels or letters or advertisements), but also to all kinds of objects of interpretation: films, paintings, music videos, even food on a plate.

For that reason, much—but not all—of our discussion in this chapter focuses on textual analysis. Of course writing an analysis of a drawing differs from writing an interpretation of a poem (or, for that matter, a legislative proposal or an argument about the causes of inflation). Nevertheless, we believe that there are important similarities between these processes. In all cases, the reader must be able to envision the object under scrutiny, so the writer must summarize it or describe it precisely. In all cases, the writer must be able to explain what the text *means,* so the writer must pay close attention to its details, to its parts—to how they work, to what they imply or suggest, to their relationship to each other and to the whole.

CLASSIFYING AND THINKING

Analysis (literally a separating into parts) is not only the source of much writing that seeks to explain, it is also a way of thinking, a way of arriving at conclusions (generalizations), a way of discovering meaning. One form of analytical thinking, classifying, is, at its simplest, an adult version of sorting out cards with pictures of baseball players on them. Now, if you have identical items—for instance, one hundred bricks to unload from a truck—you can't sort them; you can only divide them for easier handling into groups of, say, ten, or into armloads. But if the items vary in some way you can sort them out. You can, for example, put socks into one drawer, underwear into another, trousers or dresses in a closet—all in an effort to make life a little more manageable.

Thinking, if broadly defined, must include intuitions and even idle reveries, but much of what we normally mean by analysis requires classifying things into categories and seeing how the categories relate to each other. When you think about choosing courses, for example, you classify the courses by subject matter, or by degree of difficulty ("Since I'm taking two hard courses, I ought to look for an easy one"), or by the hour at which they are offered, or by the degree to which they interest you, or by their merit as determined through the grapevine. When you classify, you establish categories by breaking down the curriculum into parts, and by then putting into each category courses that significantly resemble each other but that are not identical. We need categories: we simply cannot get through life treating every object as unique.

In classifying, the categories must be established on a single basis of division: you cannot classify dogs into purebreds and small dogs, for some dogs belong in both categories. You must classify them into consistent, coordinate categories, let's say either by breed or by size. Of course, you can first classify or sort dogs into purebreds and mutts and *then* sort each of these groups into two subordinate categories, dogs under twelve inches at the shoulder and dogs twelve inches or more at the shoulder. The categories, as we shall see, will depend on your purpose. That the categories into which things are sorted should be coordinate is, alas, a principle unknown to the American Kennel Club, which divides dogs into seven groups. The first five seem reasonable enough: (1) sporting dogs (for example, retrievers, pointers, spaniels), (2) hounds (bassets, beagles, whippets), (3) working dogs (Doberman pinscher, Saint Bernards, Rottweilers), (4) terriers (Airedales, Irish terriers, Scottish terriers), (5) herding dogs (German shepherd dogs, collies, corgis). Trouble begins with the sixth classification, toy dogs (Maltese, Chihuahuas, toy poodles), for size has not been a criterion up to now. The seventh category is desperate: nonsporting dogs (chow chows, miniature and standard poodles, Dalmatians). Nonsporting! What a category. Why not nonworking or nonhound? And is a standard poodle really more like a chow

chow than like a toy poodle?* Still, the classifications are by now established. Every purebred must fit into one and only one, and thus every purebred can be measured against all of the dogs that in significant ways are thought to resemble it.

Examples of Classifying

Suppose you were asked to write an essay putting forth your ideas about punishment for killers. You would need to distinguish at least between those killers whose actions are premeditated and those killers whose actions are not. And in the first category you might make further distinctions:

1. Professional killers who carefully contrive a death
2. Killers who are irrational except in their ability to contrive a death
3. Robbers who contrive a property crime and who kill only when they believe that killing is necessary in order to commit that crime

You can hardly talk usefully about capital punishment or imprisonment without making some such analysis of killers. You have, then, taken killers and sorted or *classified* them, not for the fun of inventing complications but for the sake of educating yourself and those persons with whom you discuss the topic. Unless your attitude is the mad Queen of Hearts's "Off with their heads," you will be satisfied with your conclusion only after you have tested it by dividing your topic into parts, each clearly distinguished from the others, and then showed how they are related.

A second example: if you think about examinations—especially if you think about them with the aid of pencil and paper—you may find that they can serve several purposes. Examinations may test knowledge, intelligence, or skill in taking examinations; or they may stimulate learning. Therefore, if you wish to discuss what constitutes a good examination, you must decide what purpose an examination *should* serve. Possibly you will decide that in a particular course an examination should chiefly stimulate learning, but that it should also test the ability to reason. To arrive at a reasonable conclusion, a conclusion worth sharing and, if need be, defending, you must first recognize and sort out the several possibilities.

Often the keenest analytical thinking considers not only what parts are in the whole, but also what is *not* there—what is missing in relation to a larger context that we can imagine. For example, if we analyze the women in the best-known fairy tales, we will find that most are either sleeping beauties or wicked stepmothers. These categories are general: "sleeping beauties" includes all passive women valued only for their appearance, and "wicked stepmothers" includes Cinderella's cruel older sisters. (Fairy godmothers form another category, but they are not human beings.) Analysis helps us to discover the almost total absence of resourceful, productive women. ("Almost total," rather than "total," because there are a few resourceful women in fairy tales, such as Gretel.) You

---

*The American Kennel Club's categories, though, are perhaps a bit more precise than those given in an old Chinese encyclopedia, whose fourteen classifications of dogs (according to Jorge Luis Borges) include "those belonging to the Emperor," "stuffed dogs," "free-running dogs," "those getting madly excited," "those that look like flies from the distance," and "others."

might begin a thoughtful essay with a general statement to this effect and then support the statement with an analysis of "Cinderella," "Little Red Riding Hood," and "Snow White."

CAUSE AND EFFECT

Analytical reasoning from cause to effect is also often expected in academic discussions, which are much given to questions such as the following:

> What part did the Bay of Pigs attack on Cuba play in the Cuban missile crisis of 1962?
>
> What is the effect of labeling on mental patients?
>
> What is the function of Mrs. Linde in Ibsen's *A Doll's House?*
>
> How does the death penalty affect jury verdicts?
>
> Why do people enjoy horror movies?
>
> What are the effects of billboard advertising?

Let's look at the first eight paragraphs of an essay, by the architect Dolores Hayden, that addresses the last question on the list, arguing from cause to effect.

DOLORES HAYDEN

Advertisements, Pornography, and Public Space

Dolores Hayden did her undergraduate work at Mount Holyoke and holds master's degrees from Harvard and Cambridge. A licensed architect, Hayden has taught architecture at the University of California (Berkeley) and at the Massachusetts Institute of Technology. She is currently Professor of Architecture and Urbanism and Professor of American Studies at Yale. She is especially concerned with the political and social implications of public spaces.

1   Americans need to look more consciously at the ways in which the public domain is misused for spatial displays of gender stereotypes: These appear in outdoor advertising, and to a lesser extent in commercial displays, architectural decoration, and public sculpture. While the commercial tone and violence of the American city is often criticized, there is little analysis of the routine way that crude stereotypes appear in public, urban spaces as the staple themes of commercial art. Most Americans are accustomed to seeing giant females in various states of undress smiling and caressing products such as whiskey, food, and records. Male models also sell goods, but they are usually active and clothed—recent ad campaigns aimed at gay men seem to be the first major exception. Several geographers have established that men are most often shown doing active things, posed in the great outdoors; women are shown in reflective postures responding to male demands in interior spaces. As the nineteenth-century sexual double standard is preserved by the urban advertising, many twentieth-century urban men behave as if good women are at home while bad ones adorn the billboards and travel on their own in urban space; at the same time, many urban women are encouraged to think of emotionlessness, war-mongering, and sexual

inexhaustibility as natural to the Marlboro cowboy, war heroes' statues, and every other male adult.

2   This double standard is the result of advertising practices, graphic design, and urban design. Sanctioned by the zoning laws, billboards are approved by the same urban planning boards who will not permit child care centers or mother-in-law apartments in many residential districts. But the problem with billboards is not only aesthetic degradation. By presenting gender stereotypes in the form of nonverbal body language, fifty feet long and thirty feet high, billboards turn the public space of the city into a stage set for a drama starring enticing women and stern men.

3   Let us observe outdoor advertising and other urban design phenomena with similar effects, as they are experienced by two women on an urban commuting trip along the Sunset Strip in Los Angeles in June 1981. Standing on a street corner, the two women are waiting for a bus to go to work. The bus arrives, bearing a placard on the side advertising a local nightclub. It shows strippers doing their act, their headless bodies naked from neck to crotch except for a few blue sequins. The two women get on the bus and find seats for the ride along Sunset Boulevard. They look out the windows. As the bus pulls away, their heads appear incongruously above the voluptuous cardboard female bodies displayed on the side. They ride through a district of record company headquarters and film offices, one of the most prosperous in L.A.

4   Their first views reveal rows of billboards. Silent Marlboro man rides the range; husky, khaki-clad Camel man stares at green hills; gigantic, uniformed professional athletes catch passes and hit home runs on behalf of booze. These are the male images. Then, on a billboard for whiskey, a horizontal blonde in a backless black velvet dress, slit to the thigh, invites men to "Try on a little Black Velvet." Next, a billboard shows a well-known actress, reclining with legs spread, who notes that avocados are only sixteen calories a slice. "Would this body lie to you?" she asks coyly, emphasizing that the body language which communicates blatant sexual availability is only meant to bring attention to her thin figure. Bo Derek offers a pastoral contrast garbed in nothing but a few bits of fur and leather, as she swings on a vine of green leaves, promoting *Tarzan, the Ape Man.*

5   Next the bus riders pass a club called the Body Shop that advertises "live, nude girls." Two reclining, realistic nudes, one in blue tones in front of a moonlight cityscape, one in orange sunshine tones, stretch their thirty-foot bodies along the sidewalk. This is the same neighborhood where a billboard advertising a Rolling Stones' record album called "Black and Blue" made news ten years ago. A manacled, spread-legged woman with torn clothes proclaimed "I'm Black and Blue from the Rolling Stones—and I love it!" Members of a group called Women Against Violence Against Women (WAVAW) arrived with cans of spray paint and climbed the scaffolding to make small, uneven letters of protest: "This is a crime against women." Demonstrations and boycotts eventually succeeded in achieving the removal of that image, but not in eliminating the graphic design problem. "Black and Blue" has been replaced by James Bond in a tuxedo, pistol in hand, viewed through the spread legs and buttocks of a giant woman in a bathing suit and improbably high heels, captioned "For Your Eyes Only."

6   When the two women get off the bus in Hollywood, they experience more gender stereotypes as pedestrians. First, they walk past a department store. In the windows mannequins suggest the prevailing ideals of sartorial elegance. The

male torsos lean forward, as if they are about to clinch a deal. The female torsos, pin-headed, tip backward and sideways, at odd angles, as if they are about to be pushed over onto a bed. The themes of gender advertisements are trumpeted here in the mannequins' body language as well as on billboards. Next, the women pass an apartment building. Two neoclassical caryatids support the entablature over the front door. Their breasts are bared, their heads carry the load. They recall the architecture of the Erechtheum on the Acropolis in Athens, dating from the 5th century B.C., where the sculptured stone forms of female slaves were used as support for a porch in place of traditional columns and capitals. This is an ancient image of servitude.

7   After the neo-classical apartment house, the commuters approach a construction site. Here they are subject to an activity traditionally called "running the gauntlet," but referred to as "girl watching" by urban sociologist William H. Whyte. Twelve workers stop whatever they are doing, whistle, and yell: "Hey, baby!" The women put their heads down, and walk faster, tense with anger. The construction workers take delight in causing exactly this response: "You're cute when you're mad!" Whyte regards this type of behavior as charming, pedestrian fun in "Street Life," where he even takes pleasure in tracing its historic antecedents, but he has never been whistled at, hooted at, and had the dimensions of his body parts analyzed out loud on a public street.[1]

8   Finally, these women get to the office building where they work. It has two statues out front of women. Their bronze breasts culminate in erect nipples. After they pass this last erotic public display of women's flesh, sanctioned as fine art, they walk in the door to begin the day's work. Their journey has taken them through an urban landscape filled with images of men as sexual aggressors and women as submissive sexual objects.

Now let's analyze these paragraphs. In the first paragraph Hayden introduces the question her essay will address: "how do billboards and other outdoor representations of male and female bodies perpetuate gender stereotypes?" (our paraphrase). She points out that there has been "little analysis" of this problem, thus suggesting that it is worth investigating. In the last sentence of the second paragraph, she states an argument: "billboards turn the public space of the city into a stage set for a drama starring enticing women and stern men." Paragraphs 4 through 8 discuss the "causes." We note Hayden classifies these images fairly methodically: paragraphs 4 and 5 focus on billboards representing women as "available"; paragraph 6 focuses first on mannequins that represent women as vulnerable, and then on architectural elements that represent women as subservient; paragraph 8 focuses on bronze statues of female torsos.

In the last four paragraphs of the essay, Hayden discusses the effects of these representations: "women guard themselves," "men assume that ogling is part of normal public life," and the "sexual double standard" is maintained "in a brutal and vulgar way."

[1]William H. Whyte, "Street Life," *Urban Open Spaces* (Summer 1980); for a more detailed critique of hassling: Lindsy Van Gelder, "The International Language of Street Hassling," *Ms.* 9 (May 1981), 15–20, and letters about this article, *Ms.* (September 1981); and Cheryl Benard and Edith Schlaffer, "The Man in the Street: Why He Harasses," *Ms.* 9 (May 1981), 18–19.

9   The transient quality of male and female interaction in public streets makes the behavior provoked by billboards and their public design images particularly difficult to attack. Psychologist Erving Goffman has analyzed both print ads and billboards as *Gender Advertisements* because art directors use exaggerated body language to suggest that consumers buy not products but images of masculinity or femininity.[2] If passers-by are driving at fifty miles per hour, these gender cues cannot be subtle. In *Ways of Seeing,* art historian John Berger describes the cumulative problem that gender stereotypes in advertising create for woman as "split consciousness."[3] While many women guard themselves, some men assume that ogling is part of normal public life. Women are always wary, watching men watch them, and wondering if and when something is going to happen to them.

10   Urban residents also encounter even more explicit sexual images in urban space. Tawdry strip clubs, X-rated films, "adult" bookstores and sex shops are not uncommon sights. Pornographic video arcades are the next wave to come. Pornography is a bigger, more profitable industry in the United States than all legitimate film and record business combined.[4] It spills over into soft-porn, quasi-porn, and tasteless public imagery everywhere. In the midst of this sex-exploitation, if one sees a real prostitute, there is mild surprise. Yet soliciting is still a crime. Of course, the male customer of an adult prostitute is almost never arrested, but the graphic designer, the urban designer, and the urban planner never come under suspicion for their contributions to a commercial public landscape that preserves the sexual double standard in a brutal and vulgar way.

11   Feminist Laura Shapiro calls our society a "rape culture."[5] Adrienne Rich has written of "a world masculinity made unfit for women or men"[6] But surely most Americans do not consciously, deliberately accept public space given over to commercial exploitation, violence and harassment of women. Indeed, the success of the "Moral Majority" displays how a few activists were able to tap public concern effectively about commercialized sexuality, albeit in a narrow, antihumanist way. In contrast, the example of the Women's Christian Temperance Union under Frances Willard's leadership, and the parks movement under Olmsted's,[7] show religious idealism, love of nature, and concern for female safety can be activated into dynamic urban reform movements that enlarge domestic values into urban values, instead of diminishing them into domestic pieties.

---

[2]Erving Goffman, *Gender Advertisements* (New York: Harper Colphon, 1976), pp. 24–27; Nancy Henley, *Body Politics: Power, Sex, and Nonverbal Communication* (Englewood Cliffs, N.J.: Prentice-Hall, 1977), p. 30; Marianne Wex, *Let's Take Back Our Space* (Berlin: Movimento Druck, 1979).

[3]John Berger et al., *Ways of Seeing* (Harmondsworth, England: BBC and Penguin, 1972), pp. 45–64.

[4]Tom Hayden, *The American Future: New Visions Beyond Old Frontiers* (Boston: South End Press, 1980), p. 15.

[5]Laura Shapiro, "Violence: The Most Obscene Fantasy," in Jo Freeman, ed., *Women: A Feminist Perspective,* pp. 469–73.

[6]Ibid., p. 469.

[7]Frederick Law Olmsted (1822–1903) was an American landscape architect. Among his noble works are Central Park in Manhattan and Prospect Park in Brooklyn.

Your writing course may offer you some practice in writing cause and effect analyses; other academic courses, especially in the sciences and social sciences, almost certainly will. You can also practice by noticing patterns as you read assigned academic texts as well as newspapers and magazines. Make it a habit to underline or highlight such phrases as *The three causes everyone agrees on were . . .* , or *Among the most notable effects . . .* , and then number the causes and effects in the margins of the text. When you are studying for a quiz or an exam, make lists of causes and effects; make lists too when your writing calls for an analysis of cause and effect. In the essays at the end of this chapter, see where you can spot this pattern of thinking and writing.

ANALYSIS AND DESCRIPTION

In Chapter 10 we discuss in more detail some strategies for writing effective descriptions. But it's worth noting here that passages of description are commonly used in essays to support analysis. In the preceding essay, for example, a writer asks and answers the question "What are the effects of representations of women in public space?"; as she answers this question, she presents us with brief but vivid descriptions of billboards, mannequins, and architectural elements. Hayden's essay is primarily analytical; reading it, we share the writer's thoughts, but these thoughts are not the random and fleeting notions of reverie. The thoughts have been organized for us; the effects of billboards and other images on both women and men have been classified and presented to us in an orderly and coherent account made vivid by passages of description. Even if we haven't seen the advertisement for the James Bond film or the Rolling Stones album, we can visualize these images because Hayden has made them present to us. Through these passages, we share at least imaginatively in the experiences that gave rise to her thinking. And through description, if the communication between writer and reader has been successful, we are persuaded to share the writer's opinions.

DESCRIPTION AT WORK IN THE ANALYTIC ESSAY

As we suggest above, descriptions are often used in analytic essays: in the essay "Pornography and Public Space," Hayden uses description to support her analysis of the effects of certain kinds of representations of women—the kind of analysis that might be written for a course in a women's studies department, or perhaps for a course in sociology or popular culture.

But description is not analysis, and needless to say, if you are asked to analyze a painting for your art history class or an advertisement for your media studies class, it won't be enough simply to describe the thing in detail. It may be useful, then, to make some distinctions between the two processes, *description* and *analysis*. Hayden *describes* a billboard when she says, "a horizontal blonde in a backless black velvet dress, slit to the thigh, invites men to 'Try on a little Black Velvet'"; she *describes* mannequins in a department store window: "The female torsos, pin-headed, tip backward and sideways, at odd angles." She reports what any viewer might see if he or she looked closely enough. These statements do not offer inferences, and they don't offer evaluations (although of course Hayden's diction and tone—the words "slit" and "pin-headed," for example—do begin to shape our responses to these images). But when Hayden goes on to say that those mannequins look "as if they are about to be pushed over onto a bed" she is making an *inference,* she's telling her readers what the image *implies* or *suggests;* she is *analyzing.* Likewise, she *describes* the caryatids on the front door of an apartment building when she says,

> Their breasts are bared, their heads carry the load.

But she's *analyzing* when she says,

> They recall the architecture of the Erechtheum on the Acropolis in Athens, dating from the 5th century B.C., where the sculptured stone forms of female slaves were used as support for a porch in place of traditional columns and capitals. This is an ancient image of servitude.

She's comparing (a common analytic procedure) the modern caryatids to those on the Acropolis, and she's offering an evaluation, a judgment: the caryatids at the entrance of the modern building present an "image of servitude." In another sense, she's explaining how the caryatids function. She not only answers the question "what do these images mean?" she explains *how* they mean.

 Topics for Critical Thinking and Writing

1. Look closely at the photograph of a migrant farmworker. What would you say about the photograph if you were to describe it for a person who hadn't seen it?

Dorothea Lange, *Migrant Mother, Nipomo, California,* 1936. Gelatin-silver print. (Collection, The Museum of Modern Art, New York)

2. What does the photograph mean? What does it imply or suggest about its subject? You might begin to answer this question by considering how you respond to the woman and children it represents. Do you feel sympathy? hope? horror? admiration?

3. *How* does the photograph mean? How does it make its point? Consider the mother's facial expression, her position, her children's positions in relation to her, their clothes, and so on, as well as the apparent distance between the viewer and the subjects.

4. In an essay of 2–3 pages, describe and analyze Dorothea Lange's *Migrant Mother*.

A NOTE ON THE USE OF SUMMARY IN THE ANALYTIC ESSAY

When a writer analyzes an image, he or she must first describe it, must make it present to the reader. When writers analyze a written text, they must do something similar, and that is provide enough information about the text at hand to enable a reader to follow the discussion. This information often appears in the form of a brief *summary* at or near the beginning of an essay. The word "summary" is related to "sum," the total something adds up to. (We say "adds *up* to" because the Greeks and Romans counted upward, and wrote the total at the top.)

A summary is a condensation or abridgment; it briefly gives the reader the gist of a longer work. Or, to change the figure, it boils down the longer work, resembling the longer work as a bouillon cube resembles a bowl of soup. For example, the student who wrote about Roth's essay on the Newark Public Library, reprinted in Chapter 1 of this book, is *summarizing* when she writes,

> Roth, in his article . . . argues that the closing of the libraries will be a costly mistake, and that the action will be an insult to the citizens of Newark,

She is *summarizing* because she is briefly reporting what Roth said, and of course her readers need to know what he said before they can make sense of what she'll say about it. On the other hand, she is *analyzing* when she writes:

> By overdramatizing the possible reactions, Roth gains the interest of the reader.

In this sentence, the writer is not reporting *what* Roth said but is explaining *how* he achieved an effect.

Most of your writing about other writing will be chiefly analytical, but for the benefit of the reader, it will probably include an occasional sentence or even a paragraph summarizing some of your reading. (And part of your preparation for writing your essay may involve writing summaries as you take notes on the reading you are going to analyze.) Needless to say, if the assignment calls for an analysis, it will not be enough simply to write a summary. (You will find a detailed explanation of how to write a summary on pages 285–86.)

COMPARING

We began this chapter with a brief analysis of a Brueghel drawing. We *compared* Brueghel's handling of the two figures: the amount of space each figure occupied, their activities, their facial expressions, the directions of their gaze; we thereby arrived at an interpretation of the *meaning* of Brueghel's drawing. We might say that the drawing invites the comparison, and in so doing communicates Brueghel's understanding of the artist's vision, or of the value of art.

Writers, too, often use comparisons to explain a concept or idea or to arrive at a judgment or conclusion. As in drawing or painting, the point of a comparison in writing is not simply to list similarities or differences, but to explain something, to illuminate what the similarities and differences add up to. What the comparison—or analysis—adds up to is sometimes referred to as a *synthesis,* literally, a combination of separate elements to form a coherent whole.

Notice in the following paragraph, from an essay titled "England, Your England," written during World War II, how George Orwell clarifies our understanding of one kind of military march, the Nazi goose-step, by calling attention to how it differs from the march used by English soldiers. Notice, too, the point of his comparison, which he makes clear in his second sentence, and which resonates throughout the comparison.

> One rapid but fairly sure guide to the social atmosphere of a country is the parade-step of its army. A military parade is really a kind of ritual dance, something like a ballet, expressing a certain philosophy of life. The goose-step, for instance, is one of the most horrible sights in the world, far more terrifying than a dive-bomber. It is simply an affirmation of naked power; contained in it, quite consciously and intentionally, is the vision of a boot crashing down on a face. Its ugliness is part of its essence, for what it is saying is "Yes, I *am* ugly, and you daren't laugh at me," like the bully who makes faces at his victim. Why is the goose-step not used in England? There are, heaven knows, plenty of army officers who would be only too glad to introduce some such thing. It is not used because the people in the street would laugh. Beyond a certain point, military display is only possible in countries where the common people dare not laugh at the army. The Italians adopted the goose-step at about the time when Italy passed definitely under German control, and, as one would expect, they do it less well than the Germans. The Vichy government, if it survives, is bound to introduce a stiffer parade-ground discipline into what is left of the French army. In the British army the drill is rigid and complicated, full of memories of the eighteenth century, but without definite swagger; the march is merely a formalised walk. It belongs to a society which is ruled by the sword, no doubt, but a sword which must never be taken out of the scabbard.
>
> —GEORGE ORWELL

Organizing Short Comparisons

An essay may be devoted entirely to a comparison, say of two kinds of tribal organization. But such essays are relatively rare. More often, an essay includes only a paragraph or two of comparison—for example, explaining something unfamiliar by comparing it to something familiar. Let's spend a moment discussing how to organize a paragraph that makes a comparison—though the same principles can be applied to entire essays.

The first part may announce the topic, the next part may discuss one of the two items being compared, and the last part may discuss the other. We can call this method *lumping,* because it presents one item in a lump, and then the other in another lump. Thus Orwell says all that he wishes to say about the goose-step in one lump, and then says what he wishes to say about the British parade-step in another lump. But in making a comparison a writer may use a different method, which we'll call *splitting.* The discussion of the two items may run throughout the paragraph, the writer perhaps devoting alternate sentences to each. Because almost all writing is designed to help the reader to see what the writer has in mind, it may be especially useful here to illustrate this second structure, splitting, with a discussion of visible distinctions. The following comparison of a Japanese statue of a Buddha with a Chinese statue of a bodhisattva (a slightly lower spiritual being, dedicated to saving humankind) shows how a comparison can run throughout a paragraph.

> The Buddha sits erect and austere, in the lotus position (legs crossed, each foot with the sole upward on the opposing thigh), in full control of his body. In contrast, the bodhisattva sits in a languid, sensuous posture known as "royal ease," the head pensively tilted downward, one knee elevated, one leg hanging down. The carved folds of the Buddha's garments, in keeping with his erect posture, are severe, forming a highly disciplined pattern, whereas the bodhisattva's garments hang naturalistically. Both figures are spiritual but the Buddha is remote, constrained, and austere; the bodhisattva is accessible, relaxed, and compassionate.

Sakyamuni Buddha. Wood, 33½"; Japanese, late tenth century.

Bodhisattva Kuan Yin. Wood, 56½"; Chinese, twelfth century.

In effect the structure of the paragraph is this:

    the Buddha (posture)
    the bodhisattva (posture)
    the Buddha (garments)
    the bodhisattva (garments)
    the Buddha and the bodhisattva (synthesis)

Notice, again, that although this paragraph on two images is chiefly devoted to offering an analysis, it also offers a *synthesis.* That is, the analytic discussion of the Buddha calls attention to the posture and garments, but it also brings these elements together, seeing the figure as "remote, constrained, austere." Similarly, the discussion of the bodhisattva calls attention to the posture and garments, and synthesizes these, or brings them together, by characterizing the image as "accessible, relaxed, compassionate." And notice, finally, that the paragraph brings the two images together, characterizing both as "spiritual."

As we have said, the paragraph comparing the two Buddhist sculptures illustrates splitting. An outline of that paragraph might look like this:

    The Buddha
        cranial bump
        robe and unadorned head

The bodhisattva
  rich garment

  crown

The Buddha
  color

The bodhisattva
  color

The Buddha
  pose

  carving of garment

The bodhisattva
  pose

  carving of garment

Summary of the two figures

Whether in any given piece of writing you should compare by lumping or by splitting will depend largely on your purpose and on the complexity of the material. We can't even offer the rule that splitting is good for brief, relatively obvious comparisons, lumping for longer, more complex ones, though such a rule usually works. We can, however, give some advice:

1. If you split, in re-reading your draft

   • *imagine your reader,* and ask yourself if it is likely that this reader can keep up with the back-and-forth movement. Make sure (perhaps by a summary sentence at the end) that the larger picture is not obscured by the zigzagging;
   • *don't leave any loose ends.* Make sure that if you call attention to points 1, 2, and 3 in *X,* you mention all of them (not just 1 and 2) in *Y.*

2. If you lump, do not simply comment first on *X* and then on *Y.*

   • *Let your reader know where you are going,* probably by means of an introductory sentence;
   • *Don't be afraid in the second half to remind your reader of the first half.* It is legitimate, and even desirable, to relate the second half of the comparison to the first half. A comparison organized by lumping will not break into two separate halves if the second half develops by reminding the reader how it differs from the first half.

Longer Comparisons

Now let's think about a comparison that extends through two or three paragraphs. If you are comparing the indoor play (for instance, board games or play with toys) and the sports of girls with those of boys, you can, for example, devote one paragraph to the indoor play of girls, a second paragraph to the sports of girls, a third to the indoor play of boys, and a fourth to the sports of boys. If you are thinking in terms of comparing girls and boys, such an organization uses lumps, girls first and then boys (with a transition such as "Boys on the other hand . . ."). But you might split, writing four paragraphs along these lines:

> indoor play of girls
>
> indoor play of boys
>
> sports of girls
>
> sports of boys

Or you might organize the material into two paragraphs:

> play and sports of girls
>
> play and sports of boys

There is no rule, except that the organization and the point of the comparison be clear.

Consider these paragraphs from an essay by Sheila Tobias on the fear of mathematics. The writer's thesis in the essay is that although this fear is more commonly found in females than in males, biology seems not to be the cause. After discussing some findings (for example, that girls compute better than boys in elementary school, and that many girls tend to lose interest in mathematics in junior high school), the writer turns her attention away from the schoolhouse. Notice that whether a paragraph is chiefly about boys or chiefly about girls, the writer keeps us in mind of the overall point: reasons why more females than males fear math.

> Not all the skills that are necessary for learning mathematics are learned in school. Measuring, computing, and manipulating objects that have dimensions and dynamic properties of their own are part of the everyday life of children. Children who miss out on these experiences may not be well primed for math in school.
>
> Feminists have complained for a long time that playing with dolls is one way of convincing impressionable little girls that they may only be mothers or housewives—or, as in the case of the Barbie doll, "pinup girls"—when they grow up. But doll-playing may have even more serious consequences for little girls than that. Do girls find out about gravity and distance and shapes and sizes playing with dolls? Probably not.
>
> A curious boy, if his parents are tolerant, will have taken apart a number of household and play objects by the time he is ten, and, if his parents are lucky, he may even have put them back together again. In all of this he is learning things that will be useful in physics and math. Taking parts out that have to go back in requires some examination of form. Building something that stays up or at least stays put for some time involves working with structure.
>
> Sports is another source of math-related concepts for children which tends to favor boys. Getting to first base on a not very well hit grounder is a lesson in time, speed, and distance. Intercepting a football thrown through the air requires some rapid intuitive eye calculations based on the ball's direction, speed, and trajectory. Since physics is partly concerned with velocities, trajectories, and collisions of objects, much of the math taught to prepare a student for physics deals with relationships and formulas that can be used to express motion and acceleration.

The first paragraph offers a generalization about "children," that is, about boys and girls. The second paragraph discusses the play of girls with dolls, but discusses it in a context of its relevance, really irrelevance, to mathematics. The third paragraph discusses the household play of boys, again in the context of mathematics. The fourth paragraph discusses the outdoor sports of boys, but notice that girls are not forgotten, for its first sentence is "Sports is another source of math-related concepts for children which tends to favor boys." In short, even when there is a sort of seesaw structure, boys on one end and girls on the other, we never lose sight of the thesis that comprises both halves of the comparison.

Ways of Organizing an Essay Devoted to a Comparison

Let's now talk about organizing a comparison or contrast that runs through an entire essay, say a comparison between two political campaigns, or between the characters in two novels. Remember, first of all, one writes such a comparison not as an exercise, but in order to make a point, let's say to demonstrate the superiority of *X* to *Y*.

Probably your first thoughts, after making some jottings, will be to lump rather than to split, that is, to discuss one half of the comparison and then to go on to the second half. We'll discuss this useful method of organization in a moment, but here we want to point out that many instructors and textbooks disapprove of such an organization, arguing that the essay too often breaks into two parts and that the second part involves a good deal of repetition of categories set up in the first part. They prefer splitting. Let's say you are comparing the narrator of *Huckleberry Finn* with the narrator of *The Catcher in the Rye*, in order to show that despite superficial similarities, they are very different, and that the difference is partly the difference between the nineteenth century and the twentieth. An organization often recommended is something like this:

1. first similarity (the narrator and his quest)
    a. Huck
    b. Holden
2. second similarity (the corrupt world surrounding the narrator)
    a. society in *Huckleberry Finn*
    b. society in *The Catcher in the Rye*
3. first differences (degree to which the narrator fulfills his quest and escapes from society)
    a. Huck's plan to "light out" to the frontier
    b. Holden's breakdown

And so on, for as many additional differences as seem relevant. Here is another way of splitting and organizing a comparison:

1. first point: the narrator and his quest
    a. similarities between Huck and Holden
    b. differences between Huck and Holden
2. second point: the corrupt world
    a. similarities between the worlds in *Huck* and *The Catcher*
    b. differences between the worlds in *Huck* and *The Catcher*
3. third point: degree of success
    a. similarities between Huck and Holden
    b. differences between Huck and Holden

But a comparison need not employ either of these methods of splitting. There is even the danger that an essay employing either of them may not come into focus until the essayist stands back from the seven-layer cake and announces, in the concluding paragraph, that the odd layers taste better. In your preparatory thinking you may want to make comparisons in pairs, but you must come to some conclusions about what these add up to before writing the final version. The final version should not duplicate the thought processes; rather, it should be organized so as to make the point clearly and effectively. The point of the essay is not to list pairs of similarities or differences, but to illuminate a topic by making thoughtful comparisons. Although in a long essay you cannot postpone until page 30 a discussion of the second half of the comparison, in an essay of, say, fewer than ten pages, nothing is wrong with setting forth half of the comparison and then, in the light of what you've already said, discussing the second half. True, an essay that uses lumping will break into two unrelated parts if the second half makes no use of the first or fails to modify it; but the essay will hang together if the second half looks back to the first half and calls attention to differences that the new material reveals.

The danger of organizing the essay into two unrelated lumps can be avoided if in formulating your thesis you remember that the point of a comparison is to call attention to the unique features of something by holding it up against something similar but significantly different. If the differences are great and apparent, a comparison is a waste of effort. ("Blueberries are different from elephants. Blueberries do not have trunks. And elephants do not grow on bushes.") Indeed, a comparison between essentially and evidently unlike things can only obscure, for by making the comparison the writer implies there are significant similarities, and readers can only wonder why they do not see them. The essays that do break into two halves are essays that make *un*instructive comparisons: the first half tells the reader five things about baseball, the second half tells the reader five unrelated things about football.

✔ A Checklist for Revising Comparisons

- ✔ Is the point of the comparison—your reason for making it—clear?
- ✔ Do you cover all significant similarities and differences?
- ✔ Is the comparison readable, that is, is it clear and yet not tediously mechanical?
- ✔ Is lumping or is splitting (see page 163) the best way to make this comparison?
- ✔ If you are offering a value judgment, is it fair? Have you overlooked weaknesses in your preferred subject, and strengths in your less preferred subject?

ANALYZING A PROCESS

Popular writing offers many examples of the form of writing known as process analysis. Newspaper articles explain how to acquire a home aquarium or how to "detail" your car to improve its resale value; magazine articles explain how to begin a program of weight training or how to make a safe exit in an airplane emergency. The requirements for writing such an article, sometimes called a *directive process analysis,* can be simply stated. The writer must:

Know the material thoroughly

Keep his or her audience in mind

Set forth the steps clearly, usually in chronological order

Define unfamiliar terms

In addition, in the introductory paragraph or in the conclusion writers often express their pleasure in the process or their sense of its utility or value. But such comments must be brief, must not interrupt the explanation of the process, and must not gush. Surely everyone has one such article to write, and you may be asked to write one.

Explaining a process is common in academic writing too, though usually the explanation is of how something happens or has happened, and it is thus sometimes called an *informative process analysis.* The writer's purpose is for the reader to understand the process, not to perform it. You may find yourself reading or writing about a successful election strategy or a botched military campaign. In an exam you may be explaining your plan to solve a mathematical problem, or you may be explaining how the imagery works in a Shakespearean sonnet. You might write an essay on the camera techniques Hitchcock used in a sequence, or a term paper based on your research in marine biology. Once again, you will need to keep your reader in mind, to organize your explanation clearly and logically, and, of course, to write with expert knowledge of your subject.

We reprint below two process analysis essays. The first, "Tennis Tips for Beginning Players," is a *directive process analysis* written by a student for a college writing class. The second, "It's the Portly Penguin That Gets the Girl, French Biologist Claims" (171–72), reports on a lecture which was, from the evidence, an entertaining example of an *informative process analysis.*

Two Essays Analyzing a Process

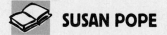 **SUSAN POPE**

Tennis Tips to a Beginning Player

The beginning player needs tennis tips on the two basic skills of tennis: footwork, the way in which you move to prepare to hit the ball, and form, the way in which you hit the ball. The most important coaching command relevant to both skills is "Concentrate and keep your eye on the ball." As soon as you see the opposing player hit the ball, determine where it will land and move quickly to that spot, never taking your eyes from the ball.

Moving requires footwork, the most subtle and often overlooked aspect of tennis. In order to hit the ball well, you must first reach it in plenty of time. When receiving a serve you should stand behind the point where you expect to receive the ball; you may then run smoothly forward to receive it rather than tripping backwards. Stand, facing the net, with your feet shoulder width apart, knees flexed, and holding the neck of your racket lightly in your free hand. This is called the ready position. Bounce up and down on the balls of your feet and prepare to move. The instant the server makes contact with the ball, jump; this enables you to move quickly in any direction. Move laterally by jumping and sliding with your feet parallel; never cross your feet. After completing your swing, return immediately to the center of the backcourt line, assume the ready position, bounce on the balls of your feet, and prepare to move again. If you can predict where your opponent will return the ball, move to this area instead and assume your ready stance. The objective of footwork is to reach the ball quickly so you can prepare to hit it with good form.

Form involves the position and use of the parts of your body as you hit the ball. By the time you have reached the place where you intend to hit the ball, you should have completed your backswing, cocking your racket back until it points behind you. A short backswing resulting from not bringing your racket back soon enough will almost always result in a mistake. On the other hand, by having your racket back, you still may be able to successfully return a ball hit beyond the physical range you can usually reach.

As you wait for the ball with your racket held back, plant your feet firmly, shoulder width apart. If you are using forehand, your left shoulder should be pointing approximately in the direction you wish to hit the ball. Concentrate on firmly gripping the racket handle because a loose grip can result in a wobbly shot. As the ball comes toward you, bend your knees and step with your lead foot toward the ball, the left foot when using forehand. The ball often goes in the net if you hit it standing stiffly. Keep your wrist and elbow rigid as you swing at the ball; using either of these joints for the force of your swing will cause inconsistency in your groundstrokes and promote tennis elbow. Use your arm and shoulder as a unit and twist your torso, throwing the weight of your body onto your lead foot and into your swing. Make your swing quick, snappy, and parallel to the ground. If your stroke is not level, the ball will either be scooped up into the air by a rising swing or be hit directly into the net by a swing directed toward the ground. Stroke through the ball as if it were not there and then follow through with your swing bringing the racket up over your shoulder close to your ear. You will have good control over the ball if you hit it in the middle of your racket, the sweet spot, when it is slightly in front of you. Deviations from these basic coaching instructions may cause problems with your form and weaken your groundstrokes. Try to concentrate on them while you practice until you develop an unconscious, smooth, consistent swing.

5   It requires conscious effort to pinpoint the flaws in your tennis game but often your repeated errors will indicate what you are doing incorrectly. Footwork and form, the basics of the game of tennis may be constantly improved with attention to a few coaching tips. Most important, however, remember to "keep your eye on the ball."

 Topics for Critical Thinking and Writing

1. The essay addresses itself to a beginning player. How successful, for a beginner, would you expect these tips to be?
2. An earlier draft of the essay began with the following paragraph:

   Playing tennis requires determined practice and hard work. There are many well-known coaching suggestions which can help improve the consistency of your groundstrokes and thereby increase your confidence in your game. With practice, you can integrate these coaching prompts until you execute them automatically. Your concentration may then be focused on game strategy, such as how to capitalize on your opponent's weaknesses, and on more difficult strokes, such as the top spin.

Do you agree with the writer's decision to drop the paragraph from her revised essay? Why, or why not?

ANNE HEBALD MANDELBAUM

It's the Portly Penguin That Gets the Girl, French Biologist Claims

The penguin is a feathered and flippered bird who looks as if he's on his way to a formal banquet. With his stiff, kneeless strut and natural dinner jacket, he moves like Charlie Chaplin in his heyday dressed like Cary Grant in his.

But beneath the surface of his tuxedo is a gallant bird indeed. Not only does he fast for 65 days at a time, sleep standing up, and forsake all others in a lifetime of monogamy, but the male penguin also guards, watches over, and even hatches the egg.

We owe much of our current knowledge of the life and loves of the king and emperor penguins to—*bien sûr*—a Frenchman. Twenty-eight-year-old Yvon Le Maho is a biophysiologist from Lyons who visited the University last week to discuss his discoveries and to praise the penguin. He had just returned from 14 months in Antarctica, where he went to measure, to photograph, to weigh, to take blood and urine samples of, to perform autopsies on—in short, to study the penguin.

Although his original intent had been to investigate the penguin's long fasts, Monsieur Le Maho was soon fascinated by the amatory aspect of the penguin. Copulating in April, the female produces the egg in May and then heads out to sea, leaving her mate behind to incubate the egg. The males huddle together, standing upright and protecting the 500-gram (or 1.1-pound) egg with their feet for 65 days. During this time, they neither eat nor stray: each steadfastly stands guard over his egg, protecting it from the temperatures which dip as low as −40 degrees and from the winds which whip the Antarctic wilds with gusts of 200 miles an hour.

5 For 65 days and 65 nights, the males patiently huddle over the eggs, never lying down, never letting up. Then, every year on July 14th—Bastille Day, the national holiday of France—the eggs hatch and thousands of penguin chicks are born, M. Le Maho told his amused and enthusiastic audience at the Biological Laboratories.

The very day the chicks are born—or, at the latest, the following day—the female penguins return to land from their two-and-a-half month fishing expedition. They clamber out of the water and toboggan along the snow-covered beaches toward the rookery and their mates. At this moment, the males begin to emit the penguin equivalent of wild, welcoming cheers—*"comme le cri de trompette,"* M. Le Maho later told the *Gazette* in an interview—"like the clarion call of the trumpet."

And, amid the clamorous thundering of 12,000 penguins, the female recognizes the individual cry of her mate. When she does, she begins to cry to him.

The male then recognizes *her* song, lifts the newborn chick into his feathered arms, and makes a beeline for the female. Each singing, each crying, the males and females rush toward each other, slipping and sliding on the ice as they go, guided all the while by the single voice each instinctively knows.

The excitement soon wears thin for the male, however, who hasn't had a bite to eat in more than two months. He has done his duty and done it unflaggingly, but even penguins cannot live by duty alone. He must have food, and quickly.

Having presented his mate with their newborn, the male abruptly departs, heading out to sea in search of fish. The female, who has just returned from her sea-going sabbatical, has swallowed vast quantities of fish for herself and her chick. Much of what she has eaten she has not digested. Instead, this undigested food becomes penguin baby food. She regurgitates it, all soft and paplike, from her storage throat right into her chick's mouth. The chicks feed in this manner until December, when they first learn to find food on their own.

10   The penguins' reproductive life begins at age five, and the birds live about 25 years. Their fasting interests M. Le Maho because of its close similarities with fasting in human beings. And although many migratory birds also fast, their small size and indeed their flight make it almost impossible to study them closely. With the less-mobile and non-flying penguin, however, the scientist has a relatively accessible population to study. With no damage to the health of the penguin, M. Le Maho told the *Gazette,* a physiobiologist can extract blood from the flipper and sample the urine.

"All fasting problems are the same between man and the penguin," M. Le Maho said. "The penguin uses glucose in the brain, experiences ketosis as does man, and accomplishes gluconeogenesis, too." Ketosis is the build-up of partially burned fatty acids in the blood, usually as a result of starvation; gluconeogenesis is the making of sugar from non-sugar chemicals, such as amino acids. "The penguin can tell as a great deal about how our own bodies react to fasting conditions," M. Le Maho said.

He will return to Antarctica, M. Le Maho said, with the French government-sponsored *Expéditions Polaires Françaises* next December. There he will study the growth of the penguin chick, both inside the egg and after birth; will continue to study their mating, and to examine the penguin's blood sugar during fasting.

During the question-and-answer period following his talk, M. Le Maho was asked what the female penguin looks for in a mate. Responding, M. Le Maho drew himself up to his full five-foot-nine and said, *"La grandeur."*

 Topics for Critical Thinking and Writing

1. In three or four sentences explain the male penguin's role in hatching chicks.
2. Pick out three or four sentences that strike you as especially interesting, and explain what makes them interesting.
3. Addressing an audience pretty much like yourself—say, your classmates— in 300 to 500 words explain a process with which you are familiar but

which is likely to be new to them. Examples: how to perform a card trick, win an argument, make Chinese dumplings, housebreak a puppy, refinish a table, prepare for a marathon, develop a photograph. If you choose a topic you are strongly interested in, you will probably find that an interesting voice emerges, and that the process will engage the reader.

EXPLAINING AN ANALYSIS

As we have suggested, the writer of an analytical essay arrives at a thesis by asking questions and answering them, by separating the topic into parts and by seeing—often through the use of lists and scratch outlines—how those parts relate. Or, we might say, analytic writing presupposes detective work: the writer looks over the evidence, finds some clues, pursues the trail from one place to the next, and makes the arrest. Elementary? Perhaps. Let's observe a famous detective at work. Dr. Watson gives this report.

 ARTHUR CONAN DOYLE

The Science of Deduction

"I wonder what that fellow is looking for?" I asked, pointing to a stalwart, plainly dressed individual who was walking slowly down the other side of the street, looking anxiously at the numbers. He had a large blue envelope in his hand, and was evidently the bearer of a message.

"You mean the retired sergeant of Marines," said Sherlock Holmes.

"Brag and bounce!" thought I to myself. "He knows that I cannot verify his guess."

The thought had hardly passed through my mind when the man whom we were watching caught sight of the number on our door, and ran rapidly across the roadway. We heard a loud knock, a deep voice below, and heavy steps ascending the stair.

5   "For Mr. Sherlock Holmes," he said, stepping into the room and handing my friend the letter.

Here was an opportunity of taking the conceit out of him. He little thought of this when he made that random shot. "May I ask, my lad," I said, in the blandest voice, "what your trade may be?"

"Commissionaire, sir," he said, gruffly. "Uniform away for repairs."

"And you were?" I asked; with a slightly malicious glance at my companion.

"A sergeant, sir, Royal Marine Light Infantry, sir. No answer? Right, sir."

10   He clicked his heels together, raised his hand in salute, and was gone.

I confess that I was considerably startled by this fresh proof of the practical nature of my companion's theories. My respect for his powers of analysis increased wondrously. There still remained some lurking suspicion in my mind, however, that the whole thing was a prearranged episode, intended to dazzle me, though what earthly object he could have in taking me in was past my comprehension.

When I looked at him, he had finished reading the note, and his eyes had assumed the vacant, lack-lustre expression which showed mental abstraction.

"How in the world did you deduce that?" I asked.

"Deduce what?" said he, petulantly.

"Why, that he was a retired sergeant of Marines."

15   "I have no time for trifles," he answered, brusquely; then with a smile, "Excuse my rudeness. You broke the thread of my thoughts; but perhaps it is as well. So you actually were not able to see that that man was a sergeant of Marines?"

"No, indeed."

"It was easier to know it than to explain why I know it. If you were asked to prove that two and two made four, you might find some difficulty, and yet you are quite sure of the fact. Even across the street I could see a great blue anchor tattooed on the back of the fellow's hand. That smacked of the sea. He had a military carriage, however, and regulation side-whiskers. There we have the marine. He was a man with some amount of self-importance and a certain air of command. You must have observed the way in which he held his head and swung his cane. A steady, respectable, middle-aged man, too, on the face of him—all facts which led me to believe that he had been a sergeant."

"Wonderful!" I ejaculated.

"Commonplace," said Holmes, though I thought from his expression that he was pleased at my evident surprise and admiration.

—From *A Study in Scarlet*

Even when, as a writer, after preliminary thinking you have solved a problem—that is, focused on a topic and formulated a thesis—you are, as we have said before, not yet done. It is, alas, not enough simply to present the results of your analytical thinking to a reader who, like Dr. Watson, will surely want to know "How in the world did you deduce that?" And like Holmes, writers are often impatient; we long to say with him "I have no time for trifles." But the real reason for our impatience is, as Holmes is quick to acknowledge, that "It was easier to know it than to explain why I know it." But explaining to readers why or how, presenting both the reasoning that led to a thesis and the evidence that supports the reasoning, is the writer's job.

In your preliminary detective work (that is, in reading, taking notes, musing, jotting down some thoughts, and writing rough drafts) some insights (perhaps including your thesis) may come swiftly, apparently spontaneously, and in random order. You may be unaware that you have been thinking analytically at all. In preparing your essay for your reader, however, you become aware, in part because *you must become aware.* You must persuade *your* Dr. Watson that what you say is not "brag and bounce." To replace your reader's natural suspicion with respect for your analysis (and for yourself), you must, we repeat, explain your reasoning in an orderly and interesting fashion and you must present your evidence.

In the hypothetical example on pages 6–7, we showed a writer of an essay musing over the frequency of the motif of travel in the blues. Perhaps, we imagined, those musings were triggered by a few lines he happened to remember, or to hear. The writer then began to ask himself questions, to listen to some tapes, to jot down some notes. His thesis (which turned out to be that themes of travel are a metaphor for the trip through life) might have been formulated only in a late draft. But it might easily have occurred to the writer much earlier. Perhaps the thesis came almost simultaneously with the writer's first musings. But no matter when or how he arrived at a conclusion interesting enough to offer as the thesis of an essay, he still had the job of explaining to his reader (and perhaps to himself) how he had arrived at it. He probably had to examine his own thought processes carefully—replaying them in slow motion to see each part separately. He would certainly have had to marshal some evidence from available books and tapes. And he would have had to arrange the parts of his analysis and the supporting evidence clearly and interestingly to demonstrate the accuracy of his conclusion to a reader who knew less about the blues than he did.

To turn to another example, notice how Jeff Greenfield, on pages 182–84, solves and presents his case, one involving another famous detective. We will never know in what order the thoughts leading to his thesis came to him. But we can observe how Greenfield organized and supported his analysis. How can we do this? Elementary. By asking questions and answering them.

 ## Topics for Critical Thinking and Writing

1. It is often said that television has had a bad effect on sports. If you believe this, write an essay of 500 to 1000 words setting forth these effects.
2. An aunt has offered to buy you a subscription to *Time* or *Newsweek*. Compare in about 750 words the contents of the current issues, the length and depth with which they are treated, and other special features (photographs, essays, layout). Explain which magazine you prefer. (If neither magazine is of interest, try comparing *Sport* and *Sports Illustrated* or *Cosmopolitan* and *Ms.*)
3. Write a paragraph comparing a magazine advertisement of the 1990s with a counterpart of the 1950s. (You can easily find ads for cars and cigarettes in old copies of *Time* and *Newsweek* in your library.) How are the appeals similar and how are they different? Include copies of the advertisements with your paper.
4. In a paragraph or two, describe and analyze a magazine advertisement that promotes gender stereotypes or one that is aimed at gay men. (See Hayden's first paragraph.)
5. If you are familiar with a sculpture of a female figure in a public space in your neighborhood (perhaps in a plaza or in a public building), in a paragraph set forth what the image "says." Or, compare two sculptures, one of a female and one of a male, and explain what each says.
6. In an essay of two or three pages, describe and analyze two billboards, one featuring a man and one featuring a woman. How do they present the "gender stereotypes" that Hayden discusses in her essay on public space? Your essay should respond to this question with a clearly formulated thesis sentence (see page 16).

Sitting Bull and Buffalo Bill, 1885.

7. The photograph shown here of Sitting Bull and Buffalo Bill was taken in 1885 by William McFarlane Notman. Reread the discussion of Brueghel's drawing on page 152, and then write two or three paragraphs describing and analyzing this photograph, paying special attention to the contrasting poses, expressions, and costumes. Reading brief biographical accounts of Buffalo Bill (William Frederick Cody) and Sitting Bull will help you to understand the photograph. Append a list of "Works Cited" to your paper, and document where appropriate. (See page 332.)

8. Reread the discussion of Brueghel's drawing on page 152, and of the comparison on page 163, and then write a paragraph comparing the photograph of Picasso's son Paul with the painting that Picasso made from it in 1923. Imagine your audience as visitors to a Picasso exhibition at a museum, reading a label on the wall next to the two works.

9. Study the two drawings on the facing page by Francisco Goya (1746–1828). They show a woman holding a dying lover, who has fought a duel for her. The first version is a watercolor; the revision is in chalk. Write a brief essay of two or three paragraphs comparing them.

Pablo Picasso. *Paul, Son of the Artist*, 1923. Gouache, 40 × 52 inches. S.P.A.D.E.M., Paris/V.A.G.A., New York, 1985.

Photographer unknown. *Picasso's Son Paul on a Donkey*, c. 1923. S.P.A.D.E.M., Paris/V.A.G.A., New York, 1985.

Francisco de Goya y Lucientes. Spanish, 1746–1828. *Woman Holding Up Her Dying Lover*. Brush and gray wash, touched with brown wash. $9\frac{1}{4} \times 5\frac{11}{16}$ inches (234 × 145 mm). Gift of Frederick J. Kennedy Memorial Foundation. 1973. Courtesy, Museum of Fine Arts, Boston.

Francisco de Goya y Lucientes, *El amor y la muerte*. (Love and Death) 197 × 141 mm. Courtesy, Museo del Prado, Madrid.

ANALYSIS AT WORK

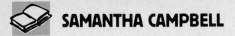 **SAMANTHA CAMPBELL**

My Father's Photograph

Samantha Campbell, a first-year college student, wrote this essay in response to an assignment that called on the student to analyze a family photograph.

Samantha Campbell

Ms. Medina

Writing 125

April 9, 1999

My Father's Photograph

I am asleep. And very little; little and asleep. I am on my back, my little head turned to the side and on my face is the emotionless solemnity of baby dreams. My left hand rests on a little stuffed kangaroo doll, and my right hand is open so you can see all my pretty little fingers. I am wearing a little white terrycloth suit that snaps all the way up the front. My hair looks dark in the black-and-white photograph, but I am told it was quite red when I was just born.

I am the only person in this picture; without the background collage it would be a boring shot, documenting that indeed I did sleep as a newborn child. The precise rows of small photographs on which I lie are what makes the person flipping through my baby book stop to look more closely. There are seven slightly tilted horizontal rows of these identical pictures. If you stare at them long enough they become a series of black-and-white patterns, an oddly frenetic patchwork quilt. They are left-over birth announcements showing the photograph taken in the delivery room minutes after I was born, picturing my mother, my father, and me. In each tiny picture mother is lying down and holding me up; she is smiling at the camera, looking a bit tired but genuinely pleased. My father, standing,

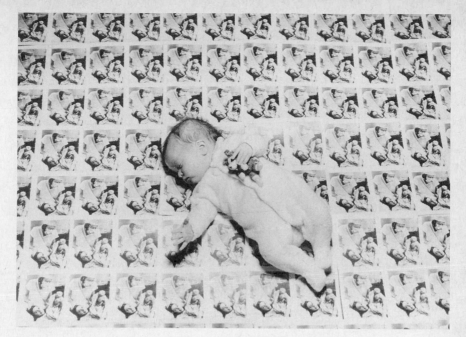

rests his hand on her long, straight, dark hair, and peers down through
his glasses at me, the little baby. He wears antiseptic surgical garb so that
he will not breathe on me or transmit to me any unclean particles that I
should be spared, at least for a while.

It is a nice picture, the birth announcement photo. The doctor
apparently had a good sense of artistic composition: the arrangement is
circular, the figures appear interwoven, bonded and linked. And the entire
shot, me resting on this careful grid-work, is interesting too. Pretty
creative of my father (the biological one)!

But I've never liked it, and I love looking at old pictures of myself
and my family. This photo has always disturbed me in a vague sort of way.
It's hard and it's cold. It's all stark and unflinching lines. The background
must have taken an awfully long time to lay out: I can just see my father,
squinting, leaning over the floor, meticulously spacing the old
announcements so that they are equidistant and straight. Like his bottles

of vitamins and his comb and his brush and his toothbrush and his dental floss and his lotions and his after-shave all perfectly aligned near the bathroom sink that whenever I see them make me want to scream and pound the counter so hard they all jiggle and vibrate and maybe fall over and then finally settle disrupted and just a little bit crooked.

5   I can see him taking me out of my crib when I'm sleeping and gingerly putting me down, very very careful not to disturb his delicate configuration (but I can see that the photo right under my cheek is the tiniest bit misaligned). I'm sure he put the kangaroo under my hand, reached quickly for the camera and took picture after picture. I know he changed my position, gave me different toys to hold, because I have seen similar shots where I, the composition, and the angle have been manipulated, very slightly. One roll of film, two? Photograph after photograph of a little baby asleep on a crafted crazed collage. I don't like it.

It must be the feeling behind it, because in a way I can appreciate the originality. Objectively I like the pictures. But I cannot be objective when it comes to my father because I do not like what he does and I do not like who he is. I have been physically separated from him most of my life, and I grow more apart from him every year. But I cannot be objective because I do not like his constantly calculating mind, his absolute egomania, his entire system of values. And I do not like the way he uses me and talks to me and has ideas about me.

"Blood, Samantha," he says, strong gravelly voice. "That's what it's all about. You see, you can have your friends, that's good, friends are important and other people are important. But you have only one mother and one father. You are connected to your family, your real family, by blood. That's forever, kid." I've heard variations on a blood theme for years and years, especially since my mother remarried and I gained not only a stepfather but also his entire family, to whom I have been very close.

So I know my father loves this picture, because it is dripping with blood. He repeats himself over and over here. "This is you with your mother and father, this is you with your father and mother, this is blood. There you are in the midst of it, on top of it, you sleep with it. This is it." Here is what I say: "No. This is not me who I am, this is me what I was, which is an infant who can be (damn it) used to do whatever a parent wants to do. No, it's not me. And I don't care about the integration of figures here, the circular image of mother father child. I don't care that I have mother's birth blood on my body or yours running through my veins or half your chromosomes or eyebrows shaped like yours I don't care I really don't. And you can't make me."

This is not a picture of love, of adoration of a child just born. It is a picture of cold cleverness and colder ideas. It is manipulated, I am manipulated. I feel used, like I have been before: as a weapon against my mother when he took me away from her (twice), or as the smiling, blond, childish centerpiece of a casual business meeting. He likes to show me off, to show people what he has created, his own blood. This is not love. People tell me, "But he really loves you, look what he sent you, see how he calls you all the time and wants to see you and. . . ." I can't make them understand that this is not love; I know it is not.

10   If you really look at the birth announcement photograph, you see that the circle is not perfect. My mother is the one who holds me. My father, masked, is not touching me; his hand drops to his side. My mother looks outward towards the photographer; she's not trapped here in this circle. And me, well, I'm just a baby. A new, little thing of flesh and yes, blood, but it is me what I was and not me who I am. And I am not part of this photograph, this dead collage with the living child on top of it. This perfect, pretty, artful creation of a man who is only my father.

Topics for Critical Thinking and Writing

1. Is this essay chiefly devoted to analyzing a picture, or is it chiefly devoted to exploring Campbell's feelings about the picture?
2. What is the function of Campbell's opening paragraph? What is the effect on you of the first sentence—very short—and of the second—also short, and market by the repetition of "little." Notice, too, that except for the second sentence, all of the sentences in this paragraph begin with "I am," or with "My." How would you characterize the writer of this paragraph?
3. Do you think that Campbell's interpretation is probably sound, or do you think that she reads too much (or too little) into the picture? Or do you think that our opinion about the validity of the interpretation is irrelevant? Support your view.
4. Evaluate the final paragraph as a final paragraph. (See pages 73–76 for a discussion of final paragraphs.)
5. Campbell wrote her essay in response to the following assignment:

   In an essay of 750 to 1000 words describe and analyze a family photograph, focusing on the relationships of the people as they are revealed in the picture. In an introductory paragraph or a sentence or two you may want to explain the circumstances of the photograph, whether it was posed or candid, and the occasion that it captures or celebrates. If the setting contributes to the meaning of the picture, analyze that as well.

   Following Campbell's example, analyze a family photograph of your own. (See pages 62–65 for another essay written in response to this assignment, Cheryl Lee's "The Story Behind the Gestures.")

 **JEFF GREENFIELD**

Columbo Knows the Butler Didn't Do It

Jeff Greenfield wrote speeches for Robert F. Kennedy and has exchanged sharp words with William F. Buckley on television. He has published essays on sports and on other popular entertainments, and he can be seen regularly on Nightline. *The following essay, which seeks to account for the popularity of the television series* Columbo, *originally appeared in* The New York Times *more than a quarter of a century ago. Reruns of* Columbo *can still be seen every weekday on the Arts and Entertainment Network, and new episodes are broadcast periodically on ABC.*

The popularity of *Columbo* is as intense as it is puzzling. Dinner parties are adjourned, trips to movies postponed, and telephone calls hastily concluded ("It's starting now, I gotta go." "Migod, it's 8:40, what did I miss?"), all for a detective show that tells us whodunit, howhedunit, and whyhedunit all before the first commercial.

Why? Peter Falk's characterization is part of the answer of course; he plays Lieutenant Columbo with sleepy-eyed, slow-footed, crazy-like-a-fox charm. But shtick—even first-class shtick—goes only so far. Nor is it especially fascinating to watch Columbo piece together clues that are often telegraphed far in advance.

No, there is something else which gives *Columbo* a special appeal—something almost never seen on commercial television. That something is a strong, healthy dose of class antagonism. The one constant in *Columbo* is that, with every episode, a working-class hero brings to justice a member of America's social and economic elite.

The homicide files in Columbo's office must contain the highest per-capita income group of any criminals outside of antitrust law. We never see a robber shooting a grocery store owner out of panic or savagery; there are no barroom quarrels settled with a Saturday Night Special; no murderous shoot-outs between drug dealers or numbers runners. The killers in Columbo's world are art collectors, surgeons, high-priced lawyers, sports executives, a symphony conductor of Bernsteinian charisma—even a world chess champion. They are rich and white (if Columbo ever does track down a black killer, it will surely be a famous writer or singer or athlete or politician).

Columbo's villains are not simply rich; they are privileged. They live the lives that are for most of us hopeless daydreams: houses on top of mountains, with pools, servants, and sliding doors; parties with women in slinky dresses, and endless food and drink; plush, enclosed box seats at professional sports events; the envy and admiration of the Crowd. While we choose between Johnny Carson and *Invasion of the Body-Snatchers,* they are at screenings of movies the rest of us wait in line for on Third Avenue three months later.

5   Into the lives of these privileged rich stumbles Lieutenant Columbo—a dweller in another world. His suspects are Los Angeles paradigms: sleek, shiny, impeccably dressed, tanned by the omnipresent sun. Columbo, on the other hand, appears to have been plucked from Queens Boulevard by helicopter, and set down an instant later in Topanga Canyon. His hair is tousled, not styled and sprayed. His chin is pale and stubbled. He has even forgotten to take off his raincoat, a garment thoroughly out of place in Los Angeles eight months of the year. Columbo is also unabashedly stunned by and envious of the life style of his quarry.

"Geez, that is some car," he tells the symphony conductor. "Ya know, I'll bet that car costs more than I make in a year."

"Say, can I ask you something personal?" he says to a suspect wearing $50 shoes. "Ya know where I can buy a pair of shoes like that for $8.95?"

"Boy, I bet this house musta cost—I dunno, hundred, what, hundred fifty thousand?"

His aristocratic adversaries tolerate Columbo at first because they misjudge him. They are amused by him, scornful of his manners, certain that while he possesses the legal authority to demand their cooperation, he has neither the grace nor wit to discover their misdeeds. Only at the end, in a last look of consternation before the final fadeout, do they comprehend that intelligence may indeed find a home in the Robert Hall set. All of them are done in, in some measure, by their contempt for Columbo's background, breeding, and income. Anyone who has worked the wrong side of the counter at Bergdorf's, or who has waited on tables in high-priced restaurants, must feel a wave of satisfaction. ("Yeah, baby, *that's* how dumb we working stiffs are!")

10   Further, Columbo knows about these people what the rest of us suspect: that they are on top not because they are smarter or work harder than we do, but because they are more amoral and devious. Time after time, the motive for murder in *Columbo* stems from the shakiness of the villain's own status in high society. The chess champion knows his challenger is his better; murder is his only

chance to stay king. The surgeon fears that a cooperative research project will endanger his status; he must do in his chief to retain sole credit. The conductor owes his position to the status of his mother-in-law; he must silence his mistress lest she spill the beans and strip him of his wealth and position.

This is, perhaps, the most thorough-going satisfaction *Columbo* offers us: the assurance that those who dwell in marble and satin, those whose clothes, food, cars, and mates are the very best, *do not deserve it.* They are, instead, driven by fear and compulsion to murder. And they are done in by a man of street wit, who is afraid to fly, who can't stand the sight of blood, and who never uses force to take his prey. They are done in by Mosholu Parkway and P. S. 106, by Fordham U. and a balcony seat at Madison Square Garden, by a man who pulls down $11,800 a year and never ate an anchovy in his life.

It is delicious. I wait only for the ultimate episode: Columbo knocks on the door of 1600 Pennsylvania Avenue one day. "Gee, Mr. President, I really hate to bother you again, but there's *just one thing. . . .*"

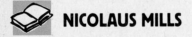

Topics for Critical Thinking and Writing

1. What is Greenfield's thesis? Where does he state it?
2. Describe what Greenfield is doing in his first paragraph; in his second paragraph.
3. Beginning with the third paragraph, Greenfield looks first at the characterization of the hero and villains, then at the underlying conflict, and finally at the implicit meaning of the conflict. Why does he present the parts of his analysis in this order?
4. In an essay of about 750 words, analyze the appeal of a popular television show—*Frasier,* perhaps, or *Law & Order.*

NICOLAUS MILLS

The Endless Autumn

Nicolaus Mills teaches American Studies at Sarah Lawrence College. His most recent book, The Triumph of Meanness, *examines such 1990s cultural phenomena as corporate downsizing, serial killer trading cards, and television talk shows. The following essay was published in* The Nation, *a periodical with a reputation for being somewhat liberal.*

The headline for Adelphi University's full-page *New York Times* ad was apologetic: "Why the Most Interesting University in the Country Stoops So Low as to Advertise Itself." The apology was understandable. Colleges and universities aren't supposed to sell themselves. They are supposed to present themselves—at most in user-friendly fashion—so their future students can make an informed choice.

What Adelphi was doing with its hard sell was, however, similar to what most colleges do now: offer themselves with a Madison Avenue format and treat their students as customers who need to be won over. The change—and with it the rise of firms specializing in institutional promotion and market research—is hardly surprising. Since the baby-boom days of the 1960s the pool of college-age students has shrunk, while in the past ten years the price of a college education has risen by 118 percent at private universities and 82 percent at public ones.

Nonetheless, for most colleges a full-page *New York Times* ad remains too blatant. They prefer a forty- to sixty-page booklet—the viewbook, *a.k.a.* the register or the bulletin. Bigger than a prospectus, smaller than a catalogue, college viewbooks circulate in the millions. For every freshman it accepts, a college often sends out fifty viewbooks. At big schools an annual printing of 100,000 is common.

On these grounds alone, the college viewbook is worth taking seriously. We can no more afford to ignore its mix of rhetoric and social motive than we can that of other mass-circulation publications such as *The Official Boy Scout Handbook* or *The Red Cross First Aid Manual.* But circulation alone is not what makes college viewbooks important. Although the immediate audience is college freshmen and their parents (the paying customers), no other publication so represents college culture as colleges wish it to be seen.

5   What this idealized picture means in 1990 begins with the college code word of the 1980s—diversity. "Diversity is the hallmark of the Harvard/Radcliffe experience," the first sentence in the Harvard University register declares, "Diversity is the virtual core of University life," the University of Michigan bulletin announces. "Diversity is rooted deeply in the liberal arts tradition and is key to our educational philosophy," Connecticut College insists. "Duke's 5,800 undergraduates come from regions which are truly diverse," the Duke University bulletin declares. "Stanford values a class that is both ethnically and economically diverse," the Stanford University bulletin notes. Brown University says, "When asked to describe the undergraduate life at The College—and particularly their first strongest impression of Brown as freshmen—students consistently bring up the same topic: the diversity of the student body."

What diversity means in this context is that a college is doing its best to abolish the idea that it caters to middle-class whites. By focusing on diversity rather than desegregation or some made-up word like "de-eliting," the college sees itself getting a bargain. It doesn't have to own up to a history of bigotry, and by focusing on the variety that diversity implies, the college avoids the charge of social engineering that it would be subject to if it said it was seeking more minority students.

In an era when racial tensions are on the rise and the Supreme Court has put affirmative action beyond the reach of all but the most determined employer, any institution that insists on diversity is noteworthy. In our colleges and universities, faith in diversity is much more than a political stance, however. It is also an expression of faith in their own transforming power, in their ability to create a special world. Connecticut College puts this specialness most extravagantly when it declares that its students are led into "another universe of discourse." Indeed, in 1990 it's impossible for any leading college to imagine that its students won't, as Oberlin College notes with ten banner headlines in the first five pages of its bulletin, "THRIVE."

What thriving means in this context is exemplified by the boxed cameo portraits of superstudents (for example, the Stanford Rhodes scholar who aids battered women and intends to play basketball on the Oxford team) that every viewbook seems to feature. If ever a student undertook a project that failed, it is never mentioned. Nor is there a hint that a project might have caused a student to see humanity less hopefully.

Above all, there is never an indication that students don't mature on schedule. While even in the Ivy League there is a difference between a Columbia University, which requires its students to take a core curriculum, and a Brown, which emphasizes that it has no core curriculum, the guiding assumption in all cases is that by their junior year at the latest students will find their academic path. As Princeton University, which emphasizes the independent work its juniors and seniors do, notes in its viewbook, "A first-rate education is not something that happens to you, but rather is something you yourself make happen." Never in any viewbook do we get a senior who confesses he coasted through too many courses, nor does any student ever worry that four years of study may make a 9-to-5 job unbearably dull.

10   What underlies this faith in the college experience is never systematically argued in any viewbook, but it is not hard to find the philosophical source: It is the virtues of a liberal education. "A liberal education must be the thread that weaves a pattern of meaning into the total learning experience," Brown president Vartan Gregorian writes. "By stressing the value of a liberal education we encourage students to seek the infinitely precious affirmation of their most authentic selves," Dartmouth College president James Freedman states. "A liberally educated person is 'liberated' to the extent that education has deepened his or her capacity and inclination for clear thought, analytical reasoning, comprehension and empathy," Wesleyan University's dean of admission declares.

The result is that while viewbooks may read differently (less so if copy as well as graphics have been turned over to a Madison Avenue firm), they remain remarkably similar in structure. Almost all contain the following:

The Melting-Pot Ideal. In addition to their viewbooks, most colleges now have special brochures for minority students. But in the viewbook itself nothing is more important to convey than a picture of students of all races mixing, and doing so in approximately equal numbers of men and women (a problem at single-sex schools that have only marginally turned coed). The result is the ubiquitous posed group photo in which white, black, Asian and Latino students look into the camera and grin like crazy. The photo, if the college can afford it, will be in color, and if not on the cover of its viewbook, within the first few pages. Significantly, candid photos are not used to make the same point.

The Endless Autumn Motif. Falling yellow leaves at Indiana University. Falling red leaves at Smith College. In the college viewbook autumn never seems to stop. At its simplest the point is that college is a beautiful place. But the real function of the endless autumn motif is to convince students that college is a timeless world where they can forget the day-to-day pressures of ordinary life. Even at Columbia, where campus guards have been attacked by New York City muggers, the viewbook makes the school sound like a utopia. "No traffic rumbles across its paths, no skyscrapers skewer its sunshine, no urban tumult disturbs its placid terraces," the Columbia viewbook declares before going on to conclude that the "Columbia landscape is a classic collegiate stage."

The Small-but-Big Paradox. Its aim is to convince students they can have the best of two possible worlds without sacrificing anything. Wesleyan declares that it "brings together the best features of the liberal arts college and the large university." Duke, with 5,800 undergraduate students in contrast with Wesleyan's 2,600, describes its size as "midway between that of small liberal arts colleges and larger research universities." The key here is for the viewbook never to pose the kinds of questions that make the difference between bigness and smallness clear: What percentage of their students do teachers see in office hours?

Could an unrecruited athlete expect to play on a varsity team? Do teachers give out written student evaluations or only grades?

15   *The Admissions Fudge.* Its intention is to assure prospective students that there is no conflict between selecting a freshman class on merit and opting for a diversity that means, as one admissions dean put it, "We take in more in the groups with weaker credentials and make it harder for those with stronger credentials." There is no attempt to explain why strong board scores will benefit some minorities (blacks) more than other minorities (Asians), or why some minorities (Italian-Americans) are of interest to almost nobody. The result is the kind of admissions statement that, like the following one by Stanford, could mean anything: "The long and labored evaluation process cannot be reduced to a quantifiable formula. . . . While we are focusing on each individual, we also are mindful of putting together a freshman class that cuts across a number of dimensions. Consequently, many factors enter into the process over which individual candidates have no control."

For colleges, even the leading ones, there would of course be a price to pay for turning out a candid viewbook. Harvard, which insists that "good teaching and scholarship go hand in hand," would have to explain why the winners of its 1986 and 1987 Levenson Award for Outstanding Teaching were both rejected for tenure. Yale University, which in its bulletin stresses a folksy concern for student life (you can get Cap'n Crunch for breakfast), would have to explain why it forced clerical employees with an average salary of $13,318 to go through a bitter ten-week strike in 1984 just to get union recognition and improved pay. Stanford, which advertises its social concern with a picture of folk singer Joan Baez at a Stanford antiapartheid rally, would have to explain why so many of its minority students saw its required Western culture courses as racist.

The irony is that in college publications sent to alumni, candor on controversial subjects is usual. In the *Princeton Alumni Weekly* one can read a harrowing account of the rape of a student, and the *Dartmouth Alumni Magazine* carried a series of articles on the racial confrontations that have made Dartmouth national news. Indeed, the assumption our leading colleges make is that the only way to keep the support of students and alumni is to come clean about their troubles. Where they draw the line is with prospective freshmen and their parents.

The closest any viewbook comes to being candid is at Williams College, where the prospectus in its between-the-pages inserts offers such information about the Williams freshman class as the percentage who admit they cheated on a high school test. But even in the Williams viewbook (yearly cost, $100,000) candor is primarily a tactic, part of an overall antihype strategy. In the final analysis the viewbooks of our leading colleges are a sad performance, made sadder still by the fact that, given what it can cost to visit a far-off school, the viewbook remains the most democratic mechanism a college has for reaching new students.

 ## Topics for Critical Thinking and Writing

1. According to Mills, what has caused colleges to advertise themselves through viewbooks and other means? When you were applying to college, were you aware that colleges were selling themselves to you, and if so, what techniques did you notice?

2. For whom are college viewbooks intended? Does Mills suggest why he is analyzing them? If the answer is yes, what reason does he give? Do you find the reason adequate?

3. In paragraph 5, Mills calls diversity "the college code word of the 1980s." First explain what he means and then what attitude the phrase, particularly "code word," reveals.

4. According to Mills, what information will we *not* find in viewbooks? Is he suggesting that this information should be included? If not, what *is* he suggesting?

5. Mills more or less debunks college viewbooks. Does he seem reasonably impartial, or do you think he has an ax to grind? Explain.

6. If your college or university issues a viewbook, examine it to see to what degree it fits Mills's description of a viewbook and to what extent it fairly represents your institution. Or, if your institution has a videotape, describe and analyze the videotape for someone who has not seen it. (Give credit to Mills's article if it provides you with some ideas for your analysis. For information on how to cite and document sources, see pages 323–351.)

EDWARD MENDELSON

The Word and the Web

A Professor of English at Columbia University, Edward Mendelson is also a contributing editor at PC Magazine.

When the Benedictine monks at the Monastery of Christ in the Desert, in New Mexico, created a Web site on the Internet, they claimed to be reviving a tradition that began when monastic scribes created the first illuminated manuscripts. One of the monks told a reporter for *The New York Times* that their work "goes back to the ancient tradition of the scribes, taking information and making it beautiful, into art." But the relation between modern Web sites and medieval scriptoria, or writing rooms, is even closer than these monks may have guessed. The technology that connects all the millions of pages on the World Wide Web derives ultimately from techniques invented by the scribes and scholars who copied out the Bible more than a thousand years ago.

The pages of the Web are connected by a system of hyperlinks—words, phrases or pictures that, when you click on one with a mouse, will summon up another page to your computer screen, perhaps a page on a computer thousands of miles away. Medieval manuscripts of the Bible were the first books to be interconnected by a system of cross-references—marginal notes that directed a reader from one biblical passage to another, perhaps to a passage written at a distance of hundreds of years from the first. The marginal references to the Bible and the hyperlinks of the World Wide Web may be the only two systems ever invented that give concrete expression to the idea that everything in the world holds together, that every event, every fact, every datum is connected to every other. Where the two systems differ drastically is in what their connections mean.

A 10th-century monk reading a manuscript of the Book of Exodus might find a line under the verse "And the Lord went before them by day in a pillar of a cloud, to lead them the way." A note in the margin would refer him to a verse in another manuscript that included Paul's First Letter to the Corinthians: "Our fathers were under the cloud, and all passed through the sea; and were all baptized unto Moses in the cloud and in the sea." This gives a new meaning to the verse from Exodus, but also gives new meaning to verses in the Gospels about baptism, verses that the monk could find by tracing further cross-references in the margin of Paul's letters.

The system of hyperlinks connecting the pages of the World Wide Web suggests a world where connections are everywhere but are mostly meaningless, transient, fragile and unstable. A would-be monk in the 20th century who visits the Web page of the Monastery of Christ in the Desert will find the exhortation "Don't miss our Thanks page." A few clicks, and he arrives at an image by a local artist, which will be replaced on screen automatically and randomly in a few seconds by another, and then another. You can create a link between your own Web page—the "home page" that acts as a table of contents for all the pages linked to it—and someone else's home page, but you have no assurance that the other person's page will display the same content from one day to the next.

5   In a world without tangible bodies or enduring memories, no one can keep promises. No one can even remember why they might be worth keeping. In the Bible, the connections between early and later books signify covenants that a personal God has already kept and promises that will be kept in the future. The connections between pages on the World Wide Web exist independently of space or time. The World Wide Web is touted by its evangelists as a force that will transform society in ways that no political revolution could ever accomplish. Until now the Web's main social achievement has been to provide a cure for spare time.

Another claim for the Web is that it is uniquely non-hierarchical, that it has no beginning and no end, no top or bottom, that it can be entered anywhere and traveled in any direction. In a strictly technical sense, all this is true, but in all practical and social senses, the Web dutifully reproduces all the hierarchies and inequalities of the world outside. Thousands of links point toward Web sites backed by fame, money and power. Far fewer scattered links point toward sites posted by the obscure and impoverished. A thousand students can insert in their home pages a link to the page dedicated to a rock group like Sonic Youth, but Sonic Youth's home page contains no link to any of the students' pages.

Biblical cross-references, unlike most of the links on the World Wide Web, always point in both directions. A link from the Old Testament to the New is mirrored by a link from the New to the Old. Some parts of the Bible are more densely cross-referenced than others—the margins of the dietary laws in Leviticus are mostly blank—but the annotators of the Bible believed that every word was equally inspired, that it was their own fault if they had not yet found all the connections that the Bible contained. Some passages of the Bible were more difficult than others, but all were available to be read and studied. The Web, on the other hand, has secret pages accessible only to those who know a password, and others accessible only to those willing to pay.

The vision of coherence and connectedness that gave rise to biblical cross-references can plausibly be credited with one of the greatest social transformations of all time: the 19th-century abolition of slavery. The movement to ban first the slave trade and then slavery itself in the British Empire came from Quakers and other religious-minded men and women who understood the link between Exodus and Corinthians to mean that they were morally obliged to repeat the work of Moses as long as any individual people were enslaved, that every individual—not only one or another group of people—had been promised liberation by God. The slaves themselves, in their campaign for freedom, found in this connection both a promise of deliverance and an unanswerable rebuke to the slave holders, who so manifestly failed to practice the religion they professed. To accept slavery was to sign up with Pharaoh. To fight against it was to obey the same imperatives that Moses obeyed.

The annotators who marked biblical cross-references in medieval manuscripts and early printed editions were more interested in the text of the Bible than in their marginal commentary on it. No scholar has studied the history of the references. No one seems to have given much thought to them as a form or a medium. The one notably eccentric exception was the Rev. C.I. Scofield, who announced on the title page of his Scofield Reference Bible, first published in 1909, that he had included "a new system of connected topical references to all the greater themes of Scripture," and then devoted much of his introduction to the merits of his new system.

10   The World Wide Web, from the start, has been obsessed with the visual display and invisible technology of its hyperlinks, and the heaviest traffic on the Web seems to consist of computer users in search of new versions of their favorite navigation software. As Kierkegaard wrote in 1839: "It is characteristic of the present time always to be conscious of the medium. It is almost bound to end in madness, like a man who whenever he looked at the sun and the stars was conscious of the world going round."

But the greatest difference between the cross-references in the Bible and the links on the World Wide Web is the difference between words written on parchment or paper in books that were meant to last forever and words written on the transient phosphorescence of a computer screen, where they will soon be effaced by others. This may or may not be the same contrast, written down 1,900 years ago, between the wise man who built his house upon rock and the foolish man who built his house upon sand.

Topics for Critical Thinking and Writing

1. Mendelson defines two terms in his second paragraph. What are they, and how does he define them?
2. How is Mendelson's essay organized? Does he "split" or "lump" his material?
3. In a sentence or two, summarize Mendelson's discussion of the similarities between medieval manuscripts and modern Web sites. In a sentence or two, summarize his discussion of the differences.
4. Mendelson argues that the abolition of slavery can be attributed at least in part to "the vision of coherence and connectedness that gave rise to biblical cross-reference"; he suggests that the World Wide Web is unlikely to have any such positive consequences. ("Until now," he says, "The Web's main social achievement has been to provide a cure for spare time.") Do you agree with him? Does the Web have any "positive social consequences"? Might it have such consequences in the future?
5. In an essay of about 500 words, compare a new technology to an old one. For example, you might compare using e-mail to using the telephone or writing a letter; you might compare using an online library catalog to working with a library card catalog; or you might compare looking up a word in an online (or CD-ROM) version of the *Oxford English Dictionary* to looking up the same word in the printed volume of the *OED*. It may be helpful to keep in mind that the purpose of your comparison is not simply to establish that the new technology is good or bad, but to explore the implications of the differences you identify.

CHAPTER

9

Narrating

THE USES OF NARRATIVE

Usually we think of **narrative** writing as the art of the novelist or short story writer, but narratives are not always fictional. History books, travel books, biographies, and autobiographies are also largely narrative—although they are likely to contain substantial portions of **analysis** and **description** as well. A history of the American Civil War might provide an analysis of the causes of the war and descriptions of devastated battlefields as well as a narrative account of the major battles. An essay that is mostly **persuasive** or analytic might begin with a narrative designed to capture a reader's attention or to illustrate a point. (The narrative introduction reprinted below does both things, we believe.) And even essays that are mostly narrative can make implicit arguments. At the end of this chapter you will find an autobiographical narrative by Zora Neale Hurston. As you read it, ask yourself what point or idea the author communicates by telling the story. (You might ask yourself the same question if you read George Orwell's celebrated narrative essay, "Shooting an Elephant," on pages 538–42.)

Narrative Introductions

Narrative paragraphs frequently appear in analytical essays, to introduce or illuminate an idea. Here is the way Fan Shen introduces an article in a journal whose audience is primarily teachers of college composition courses. She begins with an incident from her life in China:

> One day in June 1975, when I walked into the aircraft factory where I was working as an electrician, I saw many large-letter posters on the walls and many people parading around the workshops shouting slogans like: "Down with the word 'I'!" and "Trust in masses and the Party!" I then remembered that a new political campaign called "Against Individualism" was scheduled to begin that day. Ten years later, I got back my first English composition paper at the University of Nebraska–Lincoln. The professor's first comments were: "Why did you always use 'we' instead of 'I'?" and "Your paper would be stronger if you eliminated some sentences in the passive voice." The clashes between my Chinese background and the requirements of English composition had begun. At the center of

this mental struggle, which has lasted several years and is still not completely over, is the prolonged, uphill battle to recapture "myself."

The two brief narratives, the first introduced by "One day in June 1975" and the
next by "Ten years later," placed one after the other in the opening paragraph,
dramatize Fan Shen's struggle. At the end of the paragraph the word "myself" is
in quotation marks; the two incidents described here have prepared us to understand why.

Here is another *narrative introduction* to an essay. Flannery O'Connor begins "The King of the Birds" (an essay on her passion for collecting and raising
peacocks) with the following story:

> When I was five, I had an experience that marked me for life. Pathé
> News sent a photographer from New York to Savannah to take a pic-
> ture of a chicken of mine. This chicken, a buff Cochin Bantam, had the
> distinction of being able to walk either forward or backward. Her fame
> had spread through the press, and by the time she reached the attention
> of Pathé News, I suppose there was nowhere left for her to go—for-
> ward or backward. Shortly after that she died, as now seems fitting.

What makes this anecdote arresting? First of all, we can hardly read that an
experience marked a person for life without wanting to know what the experience was. We expect to learn something sensational; perhaps, human nature
being what it is, we hope to learn something horrifying. But O'Connor cannily
does not gratify our wish. Instead she treats us to something like a joke. The
chicken, whose fame had "spread through the press," has her picture taken by
Pathé News (one of the companies that made the newsreels shown regularly in
movie theaters before television became popular) and then dies. If the joke is
partly on us, O'Connor takes the sting out of it by turning it around on herself. In
her second paragraph she explains:

> If I put this information in the beginning of an article on peacocks, it is
> because I am always being asked why I raise them, and I have no short
> or reasonable answer.

But of course her answer, contained in the first paragraph, *is* short, and
about as reasonable an explanation as any of us can offer about our passion for
collecting anything. If these opening paragraphs persuade us to keep reading, it
is not because they deliver the melodrama they at first hinted at, but because
O'Connor's irony persuades us that she is entertaining, and that she is honest
about her experience. We want to learn more about her, and we may thereby be
seduced into learning what she wants to teach us about peacocks. Moreover,
O'Connor's explanation that she tells the story because "I have no short or reasonable answer" reveals a profound truth about the impulse to tell stories. When
a writer, even the writer of an essay, tells a story, it is because that story happens
to be the best way to make the particular point he or she wants to make.

Narratives in Other Positions in an Essay

Although writers often use narratives in opening paragraphs of essays (just as
speakers often begin their speeches with anecdotes), narration can be introduced effectively in almost any position in an essay. If you look back at essays
that appear in earlier chapters of this book, you will see that one student, Suki

Hudson, introduces her essay "Two Sides of a Story" (page 35), naturally enough, with a story, but she tells another story (which illuminates the first) in the second half of her essay. In several places in Philip Roth's essay describing his opposition to a plan to close the Newark Public Library (page 9), Roth vividly recalls how he used the library and what it meant to him when he was young. By contrast, the brief essay "A Lesson" (page 18), an account of what a student learned from a boring job, would have been invigorated had the writer included a narrative—an account of what happened during one day or one hour on the job. Not only would we have better understood what the "lesson" was, very likely she would have understood it better herself. Recounting an event or experience, *reliving* it, so that someone else can understand it, deepens our own understanding of it as well.

DISCOVERING STORIES

Some people are more apt to tell stories than others, but we all have stories to tell. We have stories about our childhood, or work, or travel; the beginning of a relationship, the death of a friend. Sometimes a memory is contained in an image, a sense impression, an emotion, even a dream, and we must examine the traces of memory to remember the event and its meaning. Once on the track of a story, you can capture and develop it by writing about it. Try *freewriting,* or *asking yourself questions.* The journalist's questions are specifically designed to elicit stories. They are, you may remember:

- *What* happened?
- *Who* was involved?
- *When* did it happen?
- *Where* did it happen?
- *Why* did it happen?
- *How* did it happen?

NARRATIVE PACE: SCENE AND SUMMARY

In telling a story, you have some decisions to make: will you present it as a scene or will you summarize it? A **scene** brings the characters and actions before the eyes and often, with dialogue, before the ears of your readers. A **summary** briefly comments on an action, giving your readers a synopsis. Brent Staples, in his essay "Just Walk On By: A Black Man Ponders His Power to Alter Public Space" (page 556), begins with a scene, his encounter with a white woman on a deserted street in Hyde Park. The scene dramatizes his first experience of "being perceived as dangerous." Later in the essay he summarizes "the standard unpleasantries with police, doormen, bouncers, cab drivers, and others whose business it is to screen out troublesome individuals *before* there is any nastiness." When you are writing an essay, as opposed to a novel, you can't present everything as a scene. When you read Staples's essay, ask yourself why he summarizes the "unpleasantries" instead of presenting them as scenes.

The general rule is to keep the point of the story in mind and to cut any details or incidents that clog the action or blur the point. Flannery O'Connor describes her chicken only enough to convince us of its reality—it was a "buff

Cochin Bantam." The point of the anecdote lies not in the unremarkable chicken (who achieves her fame and dies in three sentences) but in the effect on the writer of a brief moment of celebrity. On a deeper level, the point of the anecdote is the writer's wish to secure our attention and goodwill.

ORGANIZING A NARRATIVE

The usual way to organize a narrative is chronologically. As the King tells the White Rabbit in *Alice's Adventures in Wonderland:* "Begin at the beginning, and go on till you come to the end: then stop." Sometimes, though, it's effective to start with the end of the action, or somewhere in the middle, and then tell the story through a *flashback.* If on television you have seen *Sunset Boulevard,* a classic film, you will remember the opening scene: as we look down at a man's corpse in a swimming pool, his voice begins the story of how he got there! Narratives, however they are organized, are almost always told in the past tense; and good storytellers help us to follow the succession of events, the passage of time, by using such transitional words as *first, then, next, at last,* and *finally.*

Finally, we reprint a letter to the editor in which a college student, an assault victim, tells her experience. You may observe that the organization is for the most part chronological, made clear by transitions, and framed by the writer's analysis of her experience and her reasons for revealing it. As readers, we may or may not notice these points; gripped by the story being told, we are largely unaware of the techniques of successful writers. As students of writing, however, we study these techniques.

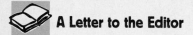 **A Letter to the Editor**

1   I write this letter out of concern for women of the college community. I am one of the two students who were assaulted during the winter recess. I do not feel any shame or embarrassment over what happened. Instead, I want to share some of my experience because in doing so I may help other women to think about rape and rape prevention.

2   First I think it is important for the community to understand what happened to me. At my request, during the vacation a well-intentioned employee let me into my residence hall to collect some things from my room. It was after dark. I was alone in my room when a man appeared at the door with a stocking over his head and a knife in his hand. He said he was going to rape me. I had no intention of submitting, and I struggled with him for about five minutes. One of the reasons why I chose not to submit but to resist was that as a virgin I did not want my first sexual experience to be the horror of rape. While struggling I tried to get him to talk to me, saying such things as "Why do you want to rape me? Don't you understand I want no part of this? I am a woman, not an object. In God's name, please don't rape me." He finally overpowered me and attempted to rape me, but stopped when he realized I had a tampax in. Then at knifepoint he asked me a number of questions. He ended by threatening that if I reported and identified him he would kill me. As he was leaving he made me lie on my bed and count to five hundred, which I started to do. Then as I reached one hundred he returned and told me to start over. Thus it was good I did not get up right after he left.

3   It is impossible to say what should be done in all instances of assault. Each incident is different and requires a different response. I think what helped me

most was my ability to remain calm, assess the situation, and then act firmly. I did struggle, I did talk, but I also did act in such a way as to ensure my own safety at knife point.

4   I believe there are some reasons why I was able to cope with the situation. One is that I had talked with other women about rape and self-defense. As a result I was more aware of the possibility of rape and had thought some about what I might do if confronted with an attacker. Also my active involvement in the women's movement has helped me develop confidence in myself, especially in my strength, both emotional and physical. I believe such confidence helped me not to panic. Another reason why I was able to cope was that I prayed.

5   I think it is important also to share with you the aftermath of the attack. The first thing I did after leaving my room was to report the incident to security and to the campus police. I did not hesitate to report the attack since I realized that reporting it was vital to protect the safety of the college community. The police were efficient and helpful in taking the report and starting search procedures. (The police also told me they did not think I was in further danger, despite the threats on my life. There seemed to be little reason for him to come back.) Also, two female members of the student services staff stayed with me most of the evening. Their presence and support were very helpful to me, especially while I talked to the police. Since the incident, I have also found support from professional staff and from friends. The residence office, the medical and psychiatric staff, the dean's office, and the chaplaincy staff have all been helpful. All have protected my confidentiality.

6   At first I did not realize that I would want or need to seek out people's help, but now I am glad I did. The rape experience goes beyond the assault itself. I have come to understand the importance of dealing with the complex emotions that follow. Also I now know that there is no reason for women to feel ashamed, embarrassed, or scared about seeking help.

7   I hope you now have a greater concern for your own safety after reading about what happened to me. I think this is the most important point of my writing. It never occurred to me that entering an unoccupied residence hall was dangerous. We all have been too accustomed to doing things on and off this campus without considering our own safety or vulnerability to attacks. But we ourselves are our own best security, so please protect yourselves and each other.

8   I am aware I will be working through this experience for a long time to come. I am thankful that there are people in this community to help me do that. I in turn want to be helpful in any way I can. So I invite women who are genuinely concerned about rape and assault to join me in sharing experiences and thoughts next Tuesday, February 18 at 7 P.M. in the Women's Center.

—Name withheld upon request.

 Topics for Critical Thinking and Writing

1. In one or two paragraphs tell a story that illustrates an abstraction, such as anger, courage, endurance, a misunderstanding, a put-down, pride, the generation gap, embarrassment, racism, loneliness. For an example, see "Conceit" (page 128) and the brief discussion following it.
2. In 750 to 1000 words survey your development as a writer and explain your current attitude toward writing. Include a narrative or two contrasting narratives to exemplify what you have learned and how you learned it.

3. For an essay on any topic you choose, write an opening paragraph that includes an anecdote. Don't write the essay, but indicate from the anecdote and, if you wish, an additional sentence or two, the topic of your essay.

4. In 500 to 1000 words narrate an experience in such a way that you communicate not only the experience but also the significance of it. For example, you might tell of an interview for a job that gave you some awareness of the attitude of people with jobs toward those without jobs. Or you might narrate an experience at school that seems to you to illuminate the virtues or defects or assumptions of the school. A variation: John Keats in a letter says, "Nothing ever becomes real till it is experienced— Even a proverb is no proverb to you till your life has illustrated it." Recount an experience that has made you feel the truth of a proverb.

NARRATION AT WORK

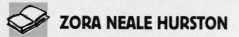 **ZORA NEALE HURSTON**

A Conflict of Interest

Zora Neale Hurston (1891?–1960) was brought up in Eatonville, Florida, a town said to be the first all-black self-governing town in the United States. Her early years were spent working at odd jobs (domestic servant, manicurist, waitress), but she managed to attend Howard University and then, with the aid of a scholarship, entered Barnard College, where she was the first black student. She graduated from Barnard in 1928. At Barnard, influenced by the anthropologists Franz Boas and Ruth Benedict, she set out to study the folklore of Eatonville. Later she published several volumes of folklore, as well as stories, novels, and an autobiography (the source of our selection) called Dust Tracks on a Road *(1942).*

In the 1950s her writing seemed reactionary, almost embarrassing in an age of black protest, and she herself—working as a domestic, a librarian, and a substitute teacher—was almost forgotten. She died in a county welfare home in Florida and was buried in an unmarked grave. In the 1980s Hurston was, so to speak, rediscovered, partly because of the attention given to her by Alice Walker.

An incident happened that made me realize how theories go by the board when a person's livelihood is threatened. A man, a Negro, came into the shop one afternoon and sank down in Banks's chair. Banks was the manager and had the first chair by the door. It was so surprising that for a minute Banks just looked at him and never said a word. Finally, he found his tongue and asked, "What do you want?"

"Hair-cut and shave," the man said belligerently.

"But you can't get no hair-cut and shave here. Mr. Robinson[1] has a fine shop for Negroes on U Street near Fifteenth," Banks told him.

"I know it, but I want one here. The Constitution of the United States—"

---

[1]**Robinson** George Robinson, an African-American, owned a chain of barber shops. Most of his shops catered to whites in Washington, D.C. (Editors' note)

5   But by that time, Banks had him by the arm. Not roughly, but he was helping him out of his chair, nevertheless.

"I don't know how to cut your hair," Banks objected. "I was trained on
straight hair. Nobody in here knows how."

"Oh, don't hand me that stuff!" the crusader snarled. "Don't be such an
Uncle Tom."

"Run on, fellow. You can't get waited on in here."

"I'll stay right here until I do. I know my rights. Things like this have got to
be broken up. I'll get waited on all right, or sue the place."

10   "Go ahead and sue," Banks retorted. "Go on uptown, and get your hair cut,
man. Don't be so hard-headed for nothing."

"I'm getting waited on right here!"

"You're next, Mr. Powell," Banks said to a waiting customer. "Sorry, mister,
but you better go on uptown."

"But I have a right to be waited on wherever I please," the Negro said, and
started towards Updyke's chair which was being emptied. Updyke whirled his
chair around so that he could not sit down and stepped in front of it. "Don't you
touch *my* chair!" Updyke glared. "Go on about your business."

But instead of going, he made to get into the chair by force.

15   "Don't argue with him! Throw him out of here!" somebody in the back
cried. And in a minute, barbers, customers all lathered and hair half cut, and
porters, were all helping to throw the Negro out.

The rush carried him way out into the middle of G Street and flung him
down. He tried to lie there and be a martyr, but the roar of oncoming cars made
him jump up and scurry off. We never heard any more about it. I did not participate in the mêlée, but I wanted him thrown out, too. My business was threatened.

It was only that night in bed that I analyzed the whole thing and realized that
I was giving sanction to Jim Crow, which theoretically, I was supposed to resist.
But here were ten Negro barbers, three porters and two manicurists all stirred
up at the threat of our living through loss of patronage. Nobody thought it out at
the moment. It was an instinctive thing. That was the first time it was called to
my attention that self-interest rides over all sorts of lines. I have seen the same
thing happen hundreds of times since, and now I understand it. One sees it
breaking over racial, national, religious and class lines. Anglo-Saxon against
Anglo-Saxon, Jew against Jew, Negro against Negro, and all sorts of combinations
of the three against other combinations of the three. Offhand, you might say that
we fifteen Negroes should have felt the racial thing and served him. He was one
of us. Perhaps it would have been a beautiful thing if Banks had turned to the
shop crowded with customers and announced that this man was going to be
served like everybody else even at the risk of losing their patronage, with all of
the other employees lined up in the center of the floor shouting, "So say we all!"
It would have been a stirring gesture, and made the headlines for a day. Then we
could all have gone home to our unpaid rents and bills and things like that. I
could leave school and begin my wanderings again. The "militant" Negro who
would have been the cause of it all, would have perched on the smuddled-up
wreck of things and crowed. Nobody ever found out who or what he was. Perhaps he did what he did on the spur of the moment, not realizing that serving
him would have ruined Mr. Robinson, another Negro who had got what he had
the hard way. For not only would the G Street shop have been forced to close,
but the F Street shop and all of his other six downtown shops. Wrecking George

Robinson like that on a "race" angle would have been ironic tragedy. He always helped out any Negro who was trying to do anything progressive as far as he was able. He had no education himself, but he was for it. He would give any Howard University student a job in his shops if they could qualify, even if it was only a few hours a week.

So I do not know what was the ultimate right in this case. I do know how I felt at the time. There is always something fiendish and loathsome about a person who threatens to deprive you of your way of making a living. That is just human-like, I reckon.

Topics for Critical Thinking and Writing

1. Hurston published this account in 1942, and she was writing about an event that had taken place a couple of decades earlier. Given the period, and given Hurston's analysis of her action, do you find her behavior understandable and excusable, or do you think that she is rationalizing cowardice? Explain.
2. Words like "Outrageous," "ironic," "pathetic," and even "tragic" probably can be appropriately applied to this episode. Would you agree, however, that, as Hurston narrates it, it also has comic elements? If so, explain.
3. Hurston argues that self-interest overrides "racial, national, religious, and class lines." Do you agree? Does she persuade you that at least in this incident it was true, or might there have been other reasons for the employees' actions?

LAURA CUNNINGHAM

The Girls' Room

Laura Cunningham was born in 1947. Orphaned at the age of eight, she was brought up by two unmarried uncles, both of whom were writers. She says that she became a writer because she didn't know that one could become anything else. Had she known of other possibilities, she says, she would have become a ballerina. The essay that we reprint appeared originally in The New York Times.

When I heard she was coming to stay with us I was pleased. At age eight I thought of "grandmother" as a generic brand. My friends had grandmothers who seemed permanently bent over cookie racks. They were a source of constant treats and sweets. They were pinchers of cheeks, huggers and kissers. My own grandmother had always lived in a distant state; I had no memory of her when she decided to join the household recently established for me by my two uncles.

But with the example of my friends' grandmothers before me, I could hardly wait to have a grandmother of my own-and the cookies would be nice too. For while my uncles provided a cuisine that ranged from tuna croquettes to Swedish meatballs, they showed no signs of baking anything more elegant than a potato.

My main concern on the day of my grandmother's arrival was: How soon would she start the cookies? I remember her arrival, my uncles flanking her as they walked down the apartment corridor. She wore a hat, a tailored navy blue suit, an ermine stole. She held, tucked under her arm, the purple leather folder that contained her work in progress, a manuscript entitled "Philosophy for

Women." She was preceded by her custom-made white trunk packed with purses, necklaces, earrings, dresses and more purple-inked pages that stress "the spiritual above the material."

She was small—at five feet one inch not much taller than I was—thin and straight, with a pug nose, one brown eye (the good eye) and one blue eye (the bad eye, frosted by cataracts). Her name was "Esther in Hebrew, Edna in English, and Etka in Russian." She preferred the Russian, referring to herself as "Etka from Minsk." It was not at once apparent that she was deaf in her left ear (the bad ear) but could hear with the right (the good ear). Because her good ear happened to be on the opposite side from the good eye, anyone who spoke to her had to run around her in circles, or sway to and fro, if eye contact and audibility were to be achieved simultaneously.

5   Etka from Minsk had arrived not directly from Minsk, as the black-eyed ermine stole seemed to suggest, but after many moves. She entered with the draft of family scandal at her back, blown out of her daughter's home after assaults upon her dignity. She held the evidence: an empty-socketed peacock pin. My cousin, an eleven-year-old boy, had surgically plucked out the rhinestone eyes. She could not be expected to stay where such acts occurred. She had to be among "human beings," among "real people" who could understand. We seemed to understand. We—my two uncles and I—encircled her, studied her vandalized peacock pin and vowed that such things would never happen with "us."

She patted my head—a good sign—and asked me to sing the Israeli national anthem. I did, and she handed me a dollar. My uncles went off to their jobs, leaving me alone with my grandmother for the first time. I looked at her, expecting her to start rolling out the cookie dough. Instead she suggested: "Now maybe you could fix me some lunch?"

It wasn't supposed to be this way, I thought, as I took her order: "toasted cheese and a sliced orange." Neither was she supposed to share my pink and orange bedroom, but she did. The bedroom soon exhibited a dual character— stuffed animals on one side, a hospital bed on the other. Within the household this chamber was soon referred to as "the girls' room." The name, given by Uncle Abe, who saw no incongruity, only the affinity of sex, turned out to be apt, for what went on in the girls' room could easily have been labeled sibling rivalry if she had not been eighty and I eight. I soon found that I had acquired not a traditional grandmother but an aged kid sister.

The theft and rivalry began within days. My grandmother had given me her most cherished possession, a violet beaded bag. In return I gave her my heart-shaped "ivory" pin and matching earrings. That night she stole back the purse but insisted on keeping the pin and earrings. I turned to my uncles for mediation and ran up against unforeseen resistance. They thought my grandmother should keep the beaded bag; they didn't want to upset her.

I burned at the injustice of it and felt the heat of an uncomfortable truth: where I once had my uncles' undivided indulgence, they were now split as my grandmother and I vied for their attention. The household, formerly geared to my little-girl needs, was rearranged to accommodate hers. I suffered serious affronts—my grandmother, in a fit of frugality, scissored all the household blankets, including what a psychiatrist would have dubbed my "security" blanket, in half. "Now," she said, her good eye gleaming, "we have twice as many." I lay under my narrow slice of blanket and stared hopelessly up at the ceiling. I thought evilly of ways of getting my grandmother out of the apartment.

10   Matters worsened, as more and more of my trinkets disappeared. One afternoon I came home from school to find her squeezed into my unbuttoned favorite blouse. Rouged and beribboned, she insisted that the size 3 blouse was
hers. Meanwhile, I was forced to adapt to her idiosyncrasies: she covered everything black—from the dog to the telephone—with white doilies. She left saucers
balanced on top of glasses. She sang nonstop. She tried to lock my dog out of the
apartment.

The word that explained her behavior was "arteriosclerosis." She had forgotten so much that sometimes she would greet me with "You look familiar." At
other times she'd ask, "What hotel is this?" My answer, shouted in her good ear,
was: "We're not in a hotel! This is our apartment!" The response would be a hoot
of laughter: "Then why are we in the ballroom?"

Finally we fought: arm-to-arm combat. I was shocked at her grip, steely as
the bars that locked her into bed at night. Her good eye burned into mine and
she said, "I'll tell." And she did. For the first time I was scolded. She had turned
their love to disapproval, I thought, and how it chafed. Eventually our rivalry
mellowed into conspiracy. Within months we found we had uses for each other.
I provided the lunches and secret, forbidden ice cream sundaes. She rewarded
me with cold cash. She continued to take my clothes; I charged her competitive
prices. I hated school; she paid me not to go. When I came home for lunch I usually stayed.

Our household endured the status quo for eight years: my uncles, my grandmother and I. Within the foursome rivalries and alliances shifted. I became my
grandmother's friend and she became mine. We were the source of all the family
comedy. When she said she wanted a college diploma we gave her one—with
tinfoil stars and a "magna magna summa summa cum laude" inscription. We sang
and performed skits. We talcum-powdered hair and wearing one of her old
dresses, I would appear as her "long-lost friend." We had other themes, including
a pen pal, "The Professor."

Of course, living with an elderly person had its raw aspects. When she was
ill our girls' room took on the stark aura of a geriatrics ward. I imagined, to my
shame, that neighbors could stare in through curtainless windows as I tended to
my grandmother's most personal needs.

15   Yet, in these times of age segregation, with grandmothers sent off to impersonal places, I wonder if the love and the comedy weren't worth the intermittent difficulties. Certainly I learned what it might be to become old. And I took as
much comfort as my grandmother did in a nightly exchange of Russian endear-
ments—"Ya tebya lyublyu," "Ya tebya tozhe lyublyu—"I love you," "I love you,
too."

If I sold my grandmother blouses and baubles, maybe she gave me the truth
in exchange. Once, when we were alone in the girls' room, she turned to me,
suddenly lucid, her good eye as bright as it would ever be—a look I somehow
recognized as her "real" gaze—and said, "My life passes like a dream."

✏ Topics for Critical Thinking and Writing

1. In the second sentence, what does Cunningham mean by "a generic
   brand"?
2. What is the title of Esther's manuscript? What is it about? Do you detect
   any irony in the way Cunningham conveys this information? Explain.

3. In the second sentence of paragraph 4, what is conveyed by putting the names within quotation marks?
4. Is paragraph 4—about Esther's physical disabilities—in bad taste? Explain.
5. In her last paragraph Cunningham says that perhaps her grandmother gave her "the truth." What does she mean?
6. "I burned at the injustice of it and felt the heat of an uncomfortable truth." Where in the narrative does Cunningham say this? What was the "truth"? If you remember a similar experience, write a narrative that discloses both the experience and the truth on which it was based. Or, write an essay of 500 words on your own most potent experience of living with or near an elderly person.

RICHARD MURPHY

Anorexia: The Cheating Disorder

Richard Murphy teaches writing and English at Radford University; his books include The Calculus of Intimacy: A Teaching Life *and* Symbiosis: Writing and an Academic Culture. *The following essay was originally published in the journal* College English.

> I wanted to pray. A part of me would not let myself ask Him for help. I did it to myself. God understood my confusion. I tried to figure out why it was happening to me, and how. It only happens to weak girls, girls who have no self-control, girls who are caught up with society's standards—not me. But was I one of them? It was happening to me, just like the cases I read about in magazines.

This is the first paragraph of an essay I received from a young woman purporting to describe her own experience with anorexia nervosa. Before I had finished reading one page, I suspected it was plagiarized. I cannot easily explain my hunch. Something canned about the writing, its confessional sentiment exactly like the cases in the magazines. I ran a quick search through the *Magazine Index* in the library and then through recent issues of *Teen, McCall's, Glamour,* and *Mademoiselle.* In a half-hour, I had six articles: "Anorexia Nearly Killed Me," "Starving Oneself to Death," "Starving for Attention," "Two Teens," "My Sister and I," and "One Teen's Diet Nightmare." I did not accuse the student of plagiarism on the evidence of this search, but I decided to talk with her before I would comment on or evaluate her paper. I guessed that in our talk she would reveal that she had copied her essay or in some other way falsified it. She did.

I am not inquiring here into the causes of plagiarism among students nor describing how teachers ought to respond to it. I am simply telling two stories in order to convey something of its perversity.

Several years before I received the anorexia paper, a student submitted a brief analysis of James Joyce's "The Dead." As I was reading it, the paper tripped some wire in my mind. It seemed both accomplished and incompetent, full of discontinuities like those in the following two sentences:

> The physical movement of the main character, Gabriel Conroy, from a house in the western part of the city eastward to a hotel at the very center expresses in spatial terms his commitment to the ways and

the doom of his fellow Dubliners. His spiritual movement westward, in our imaginative vision, symbolizes his supremeness of that doom through recognition of its meaning and acceptance of this truth of his inward nature.

Much of the first sentence here is sensible; the character's physical movement expresses his commitment. It is also syntactically sophisticated. The grammatical subject, "movement," is sustained through five prepositional phrases before its meaning is completed by the verb "expresses." The verb itself is modified by a prepositional phrase ("in spatial terms") that parallels and reiterates the adjective "physical." The second sentence, however, is nonsense. The grammatical kernel (movement symbolizes supremeness) is unintelligible. The pronoun sequence creates nothing but blur (his-our-his-that-its-this-his). One sentence, then, is substantial and coherent. The next is gummed with vagueness. So stark is the contrast between the two that it was difficult for me to imagine the same person writing both.

5   When I had assigned the paper, I explicitly restricted the use of secondary sources. I asked students to select a short reading from the literature we had been studying and to write an essay defining and explaining what they considered its central aesthetic purpose. I asked them to write about the work only as it presented itself to them in their reading. They were not to read or refer to any critical or historical background discussions of it.

In spite of the assignment's restriction, however, parts of this student paper about Gabriel Conroy seemed to me surely to have been copied. I scanned several library collections of critical essays on Joyce, browsed in longer works that made reference to *Dubliners,* and then, without having found anything but still persuaded the paper was plagiarized, asked the student to come to my office to talk with me.

"Before I give you credit for this paper," I said, "I need to ask a couple of questions: Did you use any outside materials when you wrote this? Did you read any books or articles about Joyce or about this story?"

To both of these questions he answered, "No," simply and firmly. But the look on his face was perplexed, and I realized once again how difficult it is to confront plagiarism without proof, how important it is not to accuse a student of cheating without sufficient cause. I hurried to soften the impression that I thought he had cheated by saying that my reason for asking was the strange inconsistency in the paper between specific recounting of the story line and abstract discussion of thematic issues. I was trying to understand the combination, I said, and I thought that perhaps he had looked at some outside sources which had influenced what he wrote. He still looked puzzled, but said, "No," again, and our brief conference ended.

Plagiarism irritates, like a thin wood splinter in the edge of one's thumb. With any sort of reasonable perspective, I realize that one student's possibly copying part of one paper on James Joyce is a small matter. In a typical semester, I teach 120 students and read perhaps 600 student papers. In a typical day, I have two classes to prepare and teach, committee meetings to attend, conferences with individual students, the utility bill to pay, a child to pick up from a Cub Scout meeting. But everything I touch rubs the sliver in my thumb and sets its irritation pulsing. As much as I try, I cannot ignore it.

10   So when I happened to be sitting in a colleague's office, waiting for her to finish a phone call, my eye seized upon the book of Joyce criticism on her shelf.

I had to look. It took only a moment. The phrases of the student's jumbled sentences were everywhere. I borrowed the book, took it back to my office, double-checked its lines with the lines of the paper, and then went again to the library.

I wanted to verify that our library collection contained the book and thus that it had actually been available to the writer. It was checked out. "To whom?" I asked. The circulation clerk said that library policy prohibited his divulging that information, but if I wished I could have the book recalled, I did, and reconciled myself to waiting several days for it to arrive.

In order to make the story complete, I have to explain some of the mixture of my feeling during this episode. Though I should not have had time to play detective, I made room among all the duties of my life to pursue this student. I was thrilled by the chase. When I happened on those sentences in my colleague's office, I was exhilarated. They promised the solution to a puzzle that had eluded me. They reinforced my sense of judgment and my sense of self-satisfaction at the thought that, in a small way, I was preserving the integrity of the university.

I was also dismayed, however, and angry at what I came to feel as the obligation to play out this scene, at my exhilaration, at the student's distortion of our whole working relationship. When I thought about his voice, about his poise in denying that he had used any outside sources, I thought too about the other 119 students and wondered what his cheating meant about them. When I went into class in the following days and watched their faces, I realized that I had lost some of my faith in them. For no more reason than my experience with him, I found myself wondering what the rest of them had copied.

The recall notice came shortly afterward. I hurried to the library to pick up the book. When I could not find the sentences I was looking for, I first imagined that I had inadvertently recalled the wrong book. Then I thought that perhaps this was a different edition. I walked away from the circulation desk flipping the pages and wondering—through the electronic gate at the library door, out through the foyer past the philodendrons in their huge pots, onto the columned porch—and then I saw it. The gap in the pagination, page 98 followed immediately by page 113, and, in the fold of the binding so neatly done as to be almost invisible, the seven razor-bladed stumps.

15   He still denied it, first in my office, then in the Dean of Students' office, sitting with his legs crossed in an upholstered armchair next to a whirring tape-recorder. He began by denying that he had even used the book, then that he had damaged it in any way: he went so far as to say that he had noticed the missing pages and reported them to the library himself. He hadn't wanted to be blamed, he said. What kind of person did we think he was, he asked, how did we suppose he had been brought up? He was offended at the very thought of it. But when I finally left the hearing room, he admitted to the Dean both that he had copied and that he had cut out the pages he had used. Within the week he was suspended from the university.

Nearly every year I encounter students who cheat in their writing. Their stories are all different, and all the same: they were worried about their school work, rushed, unclear about the assignment, afraid. My stories are all different, and all the same: an intuition, some feeling on the surface of the page, something about the dye of the ink that whispers this is counterfeit currency; the excitement of judicial self-satisfaction, the slanderous suspicion that all students are cheating. Though particularly vivid, my experience with the *Dubliners* paper is like all the others, obsessive and bilious. Like all the others, it has nothing whatever to do with what the job of teaching should be.

"Did this really happen?" I asked my student when we met to talk about her essay on anorexia. She was already nodding yes when I thought that I shouldn't seem rude in my disbelief. "I mean," I said, trying to make the edge of my question sharp, "I mean, did this happen the way you tell it here?"

"Yes," she nodded again. "Why do you ask?"

"Well, I don't know exactly." I looked up from the paper at her face, then back down to the typed page. "It's sort of vague in places, as if . . . I don't know . . . as if you didn't remember what happened in your own story."

20 Now she was shaking her head. "I don't know what you mean."

She played the correct gambit—my move, force me to commit myself. But I didn't want to move yet. I was after proof, and I needed to go after it slowly. This was a parody of a writing conference. I was asking her about the details of her story, trying to appear helpful, as if I were attempting to help her revise, when in fact I was trying to tease out the insincerity of her paper.

"I mean, I'm sort of confused by your essay," I said. "In the part here on page three where you say you ran to the bathroom to vomit—'I would run to the toilet to vomit, screaming the entire way' and 'The vomiting ceased after awhile'—when did that happen? Did that happen before you went to the hospital or after?"

"After."

"And here where you say, on page two, that your father stroked your hair and rubbed behind your ears, and then on the next page you say that your father was a monster who yelled at you and forced food down your throat constantly. Are you talking about what caused your anorexia or what happened afterward?"

25 She didn't answer this question at all, just sat there looking at me: so I tried a different tack.

What struck me as I read and reread her paper were the seams, the joints, where the parts were pushed together with no bonding. She is lying in a hospital bed staring at the ceiling tiles. She is trying to listen to the doctor talk to her. She is using and abusing a whole series of diet plans. She is flipping through a magazine looking at the pictures of models. She is taking a laxative every night before she goes to bed. She is listening to her father tell her that she is going home.

The effect on me was two-fold. I thought that the details she included were completely credible: only a person who had lain in a hospital bed would think to mark off the ceiling tiles: only a girl whose father actually rubbed behind her ears would think to mention that specific caress. At the same time, the vague and abrupt transitions between these highly individual details seemed to me understandable only if I assumed that she had copied them in fragments from a magazine memoir. My guess was that she had taken them from an article that was too long to copy in its entirety and so had included just selected parts in her essay.

"Did you write this?" I finally asked unexpectedly. I did not plan to say it like that, but I couldn't seem to approach the real point of my questions by just skirting the issue.

Her face looked so blank that I immediately switched to a different question. "Is this story really about you?"

30 She paused for a moment and then asked quietly, "What would happen if it weren't?"

I told her that I could not accept such a paper since the assignment was to write about a personal experience of her own. I told her, too, that it would help explain the vagueness I had been trying to point out to her: if she wrote the paper about someone else's experience, then she would be likely to leave gaps in the story that she couldn't fill.

"What grade would I get on it if it were about someone else?" she asked. To pin me down.

"I wouldn't grade it at all. I wouldn't give you any credit for doing it. It's not the assignment."

"OK," she said. "It's not about me. It's about a friend of mine."

35   My reaction to this admission was complicated. I had been expecting it, in fact working toward it, trying to get her to tell me where the paper had come from. I was glad finally to have its pretense uncovered but disappointed because I knew immediately that I would have to accept this substitute explanation though I didn't believe it either. I was sorry I had not been able to find the magazine story that provided the actual source of her paper and so would have to settle for this second lie about its roots. And I was angry at the whole situation: at the wasted time in the library, at the wasted conference with her, at my own inability to define the fakery of the piece, and at her apparent inability to see the purpose of our work together. I wanted her to write truthfully about her own experience and to use my responses, along with others', to help her convey the meaning of that experience more surely and vividly. As it was, her paper seemed just a hoax.

The deep flux of such feeling is just one of the dimensions for me of the problem of plagiarism. Another is the comic peculiarity of my claiming to be committed to helping students learn but sometimes spending large chunks of everyone's time trying to corner them in a fraud. Then there is the distance, the surprising separation I discover in such situations between myself and students. Because I assume their good will and candor and my own, both their cheating and my response to it shock me. I take for granted that we are working together and thus am amazed each time at the unimagined distance between us.

But even if I had expected the fakery of the anorexia paper, I would not have been prepared for what happened. Even if I had remembered the pages sliced out of the book of Joyce criticism and the self-righteous posturing of that frightened student writer trying to elude me. I would not have anticipated the journal of the woman who had told me that her essay on anorexia was not really about herself but about her friend.

I gave her a zero on the paper. She completed the rest of the semester's assignments, and at the end of the term, as required, she turned in a binder containing all her work for the course. As I was rereading her finished essays and the background notes and drafts she had made while working on them, I came upon the following entries in her journal:

> Feb. 7. My roommates and I did watch the Miss America pageant. I believe pageants are my favorite programs to watch. They are so inspiring. But sometimes that can make you sick.

> Feb. 21. The title of Miss America is such a distinguished title. Who ever is chosen for this honor represents the dreams of millions of young girls.

> Feb. 22. My next paper I am writing about when I had anorexia. The thought of going all through that again scares me but I think it would be a good experience to write about.

Feb. 22. Skinny. Healthy. Slim. Muscle. Diets. Firmness. Roundness. All thoughts of women in today's society. Is this such a healthy attitude to have? Women can be obsessed with these listed thoughts to the point of worshipped, slimness, firmness, healthiness etc.—

Feb. 22.

. . . It really hurt.

"You're fat" my brother said to me.

I looked in the mirror.

You're fat I said to myself.

March 1. Blindness is a scary experience or at least it was for me. I haven't experienced blindness but something close to it. The world diminishes. Your only hope is through touch.

March 2. Scared and alone. I laid in my hospital bed. I wanted to pray. I thought prayer would make me feel closer to the only friend I had left. My situation had done this to me. I thought it only happened to weak girls, girls who have no self-control, girls concerned w'society.

These journal entries astonished and appalled me. Their sincerity was unmistakable. These were not descriptions of a friend's experience. These were not fragments copied from the pages of a popular magazine. They were threads of memory—a brother's teasing, a father's touch. As closely as I can reconstruct it, she and I met in conference to discuss her essay on anorexia nervosa March 12, eighteen days after she began writing it, thirty-three days after she had begun to remember in her journal about her feelings that led both to her sickness and to her writing.

40   What must she have been thinking as I began to ask her those strange questions in our conference? At what point did she catch a glimmer of what I was really doing there? And when she saw it—if she saw it—what must she then have thought about it all—the course, me, the whole project of learning in school? What calculation, what weariness with it all, must have led her to deny her own paper? "Is this paper about you?" I asked her.

"No," she said.

I did not mean for it to come to this.

 ## Topics for Critical Thinking and Writing

1. In paragraph 2, Murphy says, "I am not inquiring here into the causes of plagiarism among students nor describing how teachers ought to respond to it. I am simply telling two stories in order to convey something of its perversity." Why does he tell *two* stories? Who, exactly, is perverse in these stories?

2. Why does Murphy tell first about the essay on *Dubliners,* and then about the essay on anorexia?

3. At the beginning of this chapter we say that a writer may make a point by means of a story. What is Murphy's point? If he had decided to offer an explicit thesis, what might have been his thesis statement?

4. Murphy ends his narrative with a one-sentence paragraph: "I did not mean for it to come to this." To what does the "this" refer?

5. Murphy doesn't discuss at length the causes of plagiarism, but in paragraph 16 he does mention some of the reasons students cheat: they're "worried about their school work, rushed, unclear about the assignment, afraid." What other reasons might there be?

6. Using Murphy's essay as a model, write a narrative about a similar experience, an experience of being wrong—but for complicated reasons.

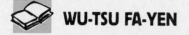 **WU-TSU FA-YEN**

Zen and the Art of Burglary*

Wu-tsu Fa-yen (1025–1104) was a Chinese Zen Buddhist priest. More exactly, he was a Ch'an priest; Zen is Japanese for the Chinese Ch'an.

The practitioner of Zen (to use the more common name) seeks satori, "enlightenment" or "awakening." The awakening is from a world of blind strivings (including those of reason and of morality). The awakened being, free from a sense of the self in opposition to all other things, perceives the unity of all things. Wu-tsu belonged to the branch of Zen that uses "shock therapy, the purpose of which is to jolt the student out of his analytical and conceptual way of thinking and lead him back to his natural and spontaneous faculty" (Kenneth Ch'en, Buddhism in China *[1964, rptd. 1972], p. 359).*

If people ask me what Zen is like, I will say that it is like learning the art of burglary. The son of a burglar saw his father growing older and thought, "If he is unable to carry on his profession, who will be the breadwinner of the family, except myself? I must learn the trade." He intimated the idea to his father, who approved of it.

One night the father took the son to a big house, broke through the fence, entered the house, and, opening one of the large chests, told the son to go in and pick out the clothing. As soon as the son got into it, the father dropped the lid and securely applied the lock. The father now came out to the courtyard and loudly knocked at the door, waking up the whole family; then he quietly slipped away by the hole in the fence. The residents got excited and lighted candles, but they found that the burglar had already gone.

The son, who remained all the time securely confined in the chest, thought of his cruel father. He was greatly mortified, then a fine idea flashed upon him. He made a noise like the gnawing of a rat. The family told the maid to take a candle and examine the chest. When the lid was unlocked, out came the prisoner, who blew out the light, pushed away the maid, and fled. The people ran after him. Noticing a well by the road, he picked up a large stone and threw it into the water. The pursuers all gathered around the well trying to find the burglar drowning himself in the dark hole.

*The title of this story, from The Sayings of Goso Ho¯yen, is the editors'.

In the meantime he went safely back to his father's house. He blamed his father deeply for his narrow escape. Said the father, "Be not offended, my son. Just tell me how you got out of it." When the son told him about his adventures, the father remarked, "There you are, you have learned the art."

 Topics for Critical Thinking and Writing

1. What assumptions about knowledge did the father make? Can you think of any of your own experiences that substantiate these assumptions?
2. Is there anything you have studied or are studying to which Zen pedagogical methods would be applicable? If so, explain by setting forth a sample lesson.

CHAPTER

10
Describing

Looking is not as simple as it looks.

—Ad Reinhardt

OBSERVING DETAILS

Description represents in words our sensory impressions caught in a moment of time. In much descriptive writing visual imagery dominates. Look at the following example, part of a letter Vincent Van Gogh wrote to his brother, Theo.

> Twilight is falling, and the view of the yard from my window is simply wonderful, with that little avenue of poplars—their slender forms and thin branches stand out so delicately against the gray evening sky; and then the old arsenal building in the water—quiet as the "waters of the old pool" in the book of Isaiah—down by the waterside the walls of that arsenal are quite green and weatherbeaten. Farther down is the little garden and the fence around it with the rosebushes, and everywhere in the yard the black figures of the workmen, and also the little dog. Just now Uncle Jan with his long black hair is probably making his rounds. In the distance the masts of the ships in the dock can be seen, in front the Atjeh, quite black, and the gray and red monitors—and just now here and there the lamps are being lit. At this moment the bell is ringing and the whole stream of workmen is pouring towards the gate; at the same time the lamplighter is coming to light the lamp in the yard behind the house.

First, notice that Van Gogh does not attempt to describe the view from the window at all times of day, but only now, when "twilight is falling." Thus, the figures of the workmen, the little dog, the masts in the distance, appear black; the evening sky is gray, and "just now here and there the lamps are being lit."

Second, notice that Vincent tells Theo that he sees not "a row of trees" but a "little avenue of poplars—their slender forms and thin branches stand out so delicately against the gray evening sky." These details, the result of close observation, help the reader to see what Van Gogh saw, and to feel as he felt.

Third, notice that while Van Gogh describes primarily what he *sees* (not surprising in a painter) he also notices and tells Theo what he *hears:* "At this moment the bell is ringing." And through every detail he communicates what he feels about the scene he describes: "the view of the yard from my window is simply wonderful."

We note in Chapter 8 that description is an important strategy in **analytic writing.** An urban planner writing an analysis of billboards must describe them before she can explore their meaning; a student analyzing Buddhist sculptures must describe them before he can compare them. But description is often also a kind of **persuasion.** Writers wish to persuade us to share their judgment that what they describe is beautiful or ugly, noble or ignoble, valuable or worthless.

If we are persuaded, it is not so much because the writer tells us what to feel (often the judgment is not stated, but implied) as it is because the writer skillfully represents to us what he or she sees, or experiences through other senses.

ORGANIZING A DESCRIPTION

Patient observation of details and willingness to search for exactly the right words with which to communicate our impressions are both part of the secret of good descriptive writing. Still another part is organization, the translation of our disorderly, even chaotic, impressions into orderly structures. Limiting the description to what is sensed at a particular moment in time in itself imposes some order. But in addition, our descriptions must have some discernible pattern, such as from left to right, from bottom to top, from general to particular, or, as in Van Gogh's description, from near to far.

Notice this structure, from near to far, as Walt Whitman uses it in his poem "A Farm Picture."

> Through the ample open door of the peaceful country barn,
> A sunlit pasture field with cattle and horses feeding,
> And haze and vista, and the far horizon fading away.

Although the poem is only three lines long, the view is leisurely, beginning where the observer stands, inside the "ample open door," and then stretching slowly out to the "sunlit pasture field," still distinct, because still close up, then to the slightly more general "cattle and horses," and last to the indistinct "far horizon fading away." The leisurely pace persuades us that the scene is indeed "peaceful"; the orderly structure of the poem allows us to feel that it is.

Now look, by contrast, at a description not of a place, but of a phenomenon, a phenomenon not seen but felt, not peaceful, but "uneasy."

> There is something uneasy in the Los Angeles air this afternoon, some unnatural stillness, some tension. What it means is that tonight a Santa Ana will begin to blow, a hot wind from the northeast whining down through the Cajon and San Gorgonio Passes, blowing up sandstorms out along Route 66, drying the hills and the nerves to the flash point. For a few days now we will see smoke back in the canyons, and hear sirens in the night. I have neither heard nor read that a Santa Ana is due, but I know it, and almost everyone I have seen today knows it too. We know it because we feel it. The baby frets. The maid sulks. I rekindle a waning argument with the telephone company, then cut my losses and lie

down, given over to whatever it is in the air. To live with the Santa Ana
is to accept, consciously or unconsciously, a deeply mechanistic view
of human behavior.

—JOAN DIDION

Here the governing pattern of the description is more complex—from the
general to the specific, and back to the general. Didion begins with the relatively
general statement "There is something uneasy in the Los Angeles air this afternoon." She then moves to the specific details that support the generalization: the
visible effects of the unseen wind first on the landscape and then on people (the
baby, the maid, Didion herself). In the final sentence, again a relatively general
one, she summarizes a further effect of what it is "to live with the Santa Ana."
The organization is complex, but the passage is not disorderly. Or, we might say,
it is just disorderly enough to make us feel, with the writer, "something uneasy
in the Los Angeles air."

Specific details and concrete language help us to imagine what the writer
has observed; a suitable organization further assists us in following the writer's
representation of impressions and feelings.

Establishing the Observer's Position

In addition to observing closely, finding the right word, and organizing the material, there is yet another technique that helps persuade the reader to accept the
writer's observations as true, and his or her judgment as sound. This technique
can be discovered by comparing two descriptions of a building on fire. The first
is by a student.

The thick, heavy smoke, that could be seen for miles, filled the blue July

sky. Firemen frantically battled the blaze that engulfed Hempstead High

School, while a crowd of people sadly looked on. Eyes slowly filled up with

tears as the reality of having no school to go to started to sink in. Students

that had once downed everything that the high school stood for and did,

began to realize how much they cared for their school. But it was too late,

it was going up in smoke.

This is surely a competent description, and it is well organized. But compare it to
the second description by a professional writer, a practiced hand.

We were on the porch only a short time when I heard a lot of hollering
coming from toward the field. The hollering and crying got louder and
louder. I could hear Mama's voice over all the rest. It seemed like all the
people in the field were running to our house. I ran to the edge of the
porch to watch them top the hill. Daddy was leading the running
crowd and Mama was right behind him.

"Lord have mercy, my children is in that house!" Mama was
screaming. "Hurry, Diddly!" she cried to Daddy. I turned around and

saw big clouds of smoke booming out of the front door and shooting out of cracks everywhere. "There, Essie Mae is on the porch," Mama said. "Hurry, Diddly! Get Adline outta that house!" I looked back at Adline. I couldn't hardly see her for the smoke.

George Lee was standing in the yard like he didn't know what to do. As Mama got closer, he ran into the house. My first thought was that he would be burned up. I'd often hoped he would get killed, but I guess I didn't really want him to die after all. I ran inside after him but he came running out again, knocking me down as he passed and leaving me lying face down in the burning room. I jumped up quickly and scrambled out after him. He had the water bucket in his hands. I thought he was going to try to put out the fire. Instead he placed the bucket on the edge of the porch and picked up Adline in his arms.

Moments later Daddy was on the porch. He ran straight into the burning house with three other men right behind him. They opened the large wooden windows to let some of the smoke out and began ripping the paper from the walls before the wood caught on fire. Mama and two other women raked it into the fireplace with sticks, broom handles, and anything else available. Everyone was coughing because of all the smoke.

—ANNE MOODY

What can we learn from the professional writer? First notice her patience with detail, the concreteness of the passage. In the first passage we read: "Firemen frantically battled the blaze that engulfed Hempstead High School." Moody, by contrast, shows us individuals and exactly what each does. The first passage generalizes the reaction of the observers—"Eyes slowly filled up with tears" and "Students . . . began to realize how much they cared for their school"—in Moody's passage Mama screams, "Lord have mercy, my children is in that house!"

But equally important, the professional writer captures the reader's attention, and secures the reader's identification with the observer or narrator, by establishing the observer's physical position. At the beginning she is on the porch, looking toward the field. It is only when she hears her mother scream that she turns around and sees the smoke. And notice that she *does have to turn,* and the writer has the patience to tell us "I turned around and saw . . ." We could, if we wished to, place the position of the observer, exactly, throughout the action, as if we were blocking a scene in a play. By contrast, notice that there is no real observer in the student's description. If there were, she would first have to be miles away from the scene and looking up into the sky to see the smoke. Then, in the second sentence she would be across the street, watching the firemen. By the third sentence she'd be closer still—not close to the fire, but close to the other observers. In fact, she'd have to be inside their heads to know what they were thinking. As readers we sense this lack of focus; we have no one to identify with. Though we may find the passage interesting, it will not engage us and we will soon forget it.

Establishing the Observer's Point of View

In addition to the observer's physical location, a good description also provides a consistent psychological position, or *point of view,* with which we can identify ourselves. In the following passage from *Black Elk Speaks,* Black Elk, an Oglala Sioux holy man, is describing the Battle of Little Bighorn (1876).

> The valley went darker with dust and smoke, and there were only shadows and a big noise of many cries and hoofs and guns. On the left side of where I was I could hear the shod hoofs of the soldiers' horses going back into the brush and there was shooting everywhere. Then the hoofs came out of the brush, and I came out and was in among men and horses weaving in and out and going upstream, and everybody was yelling, "Hurry! Hurry!" The soldiers were running upstream and we were all mixed there in the twilight and the great noise. I did not see much; but once I saw a Lakota charge at a soldier who stayed behind and fought and was a very brave man. The Lakota took the soldier's horse by the bridle, but the soldier killed him with a six-shooter. I was small and could not crowd in to where the soldiers were, so I did not kill anybody. There were so many ahead of me, and it was all dark and mixed up.

Black Elk was an old man when he told this story. How old would you guess he was at the time it happened? How do you know?

DESCRIBING AN ACTION

At the beginning of this chapter we defined description as a representation, in words, of sensory impressions caught in a moment of time. Strictly speaking, description is static. The passage from Van Gogh's letter and Whitman's poem most nearly conform to this definition: they each describe a scene caught in a single moment, like a snapshot. Didion's paragraph about the Santa Ana is less static; it implies the passage of time. That time passes is, however, somewhat masked because Didion represents almost everything as happening simultaneously: "The baby frets. The maid sulks. I rekindle a waning argument with the telephone company." By contrast, in Moody's description of a house on fire, we not only hear (with Essie Mae) "a lot of hollering," and see "big clouds of smoke booming out of the front door and shooting out of cracks everywhere," we also know that moments have passed between the first sensory impression and the second, and that several more have passed before the passage ends with all the adults raking the burning wallpaper into the fireplace. The description is thoroughly interwoven with narration. Black Elk's account of the Battle of Little Bighorn is similarly a blend of description and narration.

Long passages of pure description are rare. The reason is simple. A description of a place will be much more interesting if the writer shows us something happening there. Similarly, descriptions of people are seldom (except briefly) static. In real life we seldom observe people at dead rest; we see them in action; we form our impressions of them from how they move, what they do. Good descriptions, then, frequently show us a person performing some action, a particularly revealing action, or a characteristic one. If, for example, you want to suggest a person's height and weight, it's much more interesting to show him maneuvering through a subway turnstile, perhaps laden with packages, than to say, "He was only five feet four but weighed 185 pounds" or "he was short and stocky." Here is Maya Angelou describing Mr. Freeman, a man who lived for a while with her mother.

Mr. Freeman moved gracefully, like a big brown bear, and seldom spoke to us. He simply waited for Mother and put his whole self into the waiting. He never read the paper or patted his foot to the radio. He waited. That was all.

   If she came home before we went to bed, we saw the man come alive. He would start out of the big chair, like a man coming out of sleep, smiling. I would remember then that a few seconds before, I had heard a car door slam; then Mother's footsteps would signal from the concrete walk. When her key rattled the door, Mr. Freeman would have already asked his habitual question, "Hey, Bibbi, have a good time?"

   His query would hang in the air while she sprang over to peck him on the lips. Then she turned to Bailey and me with the lipstick kisses. "Haven't you finished your homework?" If we had and were just reading—"O.K., say your prayers and go to bed." If we hadn't—"Then go to your room and finish . . . then say your prayers and go to bed."

   Mr. Freeman's smile never grew, it stayed at the same intensity. Sometimes Mother would go over and sit on his lap and the grin on his face looked as if it would stay there forever.

Notice how animated this description is, how filled not only with Mr. Freeman's physical presence but also with his mysterious inner life. We have a portrait of Mother, too, reflected in Mr. Freeman's waiting, his concentration on the slam of her car door, her footsteps, her key rattling, and, most of all, in his smile. More subtly and more pervasively, the description is animated by our identification with the observer, the small child watching the man who waits so intently for the woman who is her mother.

✏ Topics for Critical Thinking and Writing

1. In one paragraph, describe what you see from your window. Choose a particular time of day and describe only what you see (or might see) or otherwise sense within a moment or two.
2. In one paragraph, describe something that cannot be seen, or cannot be seen except by the effects it creates. (Something hot, or smelly, or loud?)
3. In one paragraph, describe something from the point of view of a child, or an old person, or someone of the opposite sex. (Note *person*. The point of view of a dog, or stone, or carrot is *out*.)
4. In one paragraph, describe a room—for example, a doctor's waiting room or an elementary school classroom—by showing something happening in it. Your description should reveal (without explicitly stating) your attitude toward it. The reader should be able to sense that the room is, for example, comfortable or sterile or pretentious or cozy or menacing, though no such words are used in the description.
5. First read the following two paragraphs from Saul Bellow's novel *The Victim*. Then answer the questions that follow the paragraphs.

   Leventhal's apartment was spacious. In a better neighborhood, or three stories lower, it would have rented for twice the amount he paid. But the staircase was narrow and stifling and full of turns. Though he went up slowly, he was out of breath when he reached the fourth floor, and his heart beat thickly. He rested before unlocking the door. Entering, he threw down his raincoat and flung himself on the tapestry-covered low bed in the front room. Mary had moved some of the chairs into the corners and covered them with sheets. She could not depend on him to keep the windows shut and the shades and curtains drawn during the day. This afternoon the cleaning woman had been in and there was a pervasive odor of soap powder. He got up and opened a window. The curtains waved once and then were as motionless as before. There was a movie house strung with lights across the street; on its roof a water tank sat heavily uneven on its timbers; the cowls of the chimneys, which rattled in the slightest stir of air, were still.

The motor of the refrigerator began to run. The ice trays were empty and rattled. Wilma, the cleaning woman, had defrosted the machine and forgotten to refill them. He looked for a bottle of beer he had noticed yesterday; it was gone. There was nothing inside except a few lemons and some milk. He drank a glass of milk and it refreshed him. He had already taken off his shirt and was sitting on the bed unlacing his shoes when there was a short ring of the bell. Eagerly he pulled open the door and shouted, "Who is it?" The flat was unbearably empty. He hoped someone had remembered that Mary was away and had come to keep him company. There was no response below. He called out again, impatiently. It was very probable that someone had pushed the wrong button, but he heard no other doors opening. Could it be a prank? This was not the season for it. Nothing moved in the stairwell, and it only added to his depression to discover how he longed for a visitor. He stretched out on the bed, pulling a pillow from beneath the spread and doubling it up. He thought he would doze off. But a little later he found himself standing at the window, holding the curtains with both hands. He was under the impression that he had slept. It was only eight-thirty by the whirring electric clock on the night table, however. Only five minutes had passed.

Questions: How old, approximately, is Leventhal? Of what social or economic class is he? Who is Mary? What do you know of her relationship to Leventhal? What is the weather like? What is Leventhal's mood? How did you know all these things?

6. In one or two paragraphs, describe a person by showing him or her performing some action that takes less than five minutes. From the description we should be able to infer some of the following: the time of day; the weather; and the person's height, weight, age, sex, occupation, economic or educational background, and mood.

7. Describe and analyze an advertisement from a magazine or newspaper in about 500 words. To do this, you will need a thesis, such as "This advertisement appeals to male chauvinism," or "This advertisement plays on our fear that we may lack sex appeal." Include a copy of the advertisement with your essay.

8. Choose a recent political cartoon to describe and analyze. In your first paragraph identify the cartoon (cartoonist's name, place and date of publication) and describe the drawing (including any words in it) thoroughly

enough so that someone who has not seen it can visualize or even draw it fairly accurately. In a second paragraph explain the political message. Don't inject your own opinion; present the cartoonist's point objectively. Submit a copy of the cartoon with your essay. Be sure to choose a cartoon of sufficient complexity to make the analysis worthwhile.

DESCRIPTION AT WORK

 **GINA MEN**

Observing Mrs. Taylor

Gina Men wrote the following essay when she was a first-year college student.

Every morning, she floats into the classroom with her red-striped bookbag cradled in her arms. Swiftly, she arranges her tools, with the textbook in the upper left corner of her table, the notebook in the center, and a mechanical pencil beside it. Explaining some problems from the previous day's assignment, she knows that no matter how hard she tries, her voice is never quite loud enough. And so she articulates each word by shaping her mouth to make sure that we at least <u>see</u> what she is trying to say. Occasionally, she even uses her arms, legs, and torso to construct a graph. For instance, she will uplift her arms to form a parabola (a graph which is symmetrical with respect to the y-axis) with her body acting as the y-axis. Using her stomach as the origin (the center of the graph), she will turn toward us sideways, with one arm uplifted to the left and one leg uplifted to the right in order to represent a tangent graph. (I remember, too, how she demonstrated that the quadratic equation fits perfectly into the melody of "Pop Goes the Weasel.") Although a difficult question from one of us sometimes causes a frown on her face, she always jots the question down immediately and promises to think it over in the evening. Finally, almost buried in the rustle of paper and book-packing, her meek voice rises: "Girls, you ought to learn this lesson in your heart of hearts."

And she is out the door.

✏️ Topics for Critical Thinking and Writing

1. How does Men establish her physical position and point of view? What is the effect of her use of the present tense? How does she organize the description?
2. The description depends largely on visual images. What other sense impressions are evoked?
3. What is Mrs. Taylor's subject? How does Men persuade you that she was an effective teacher?
4. Search your memory for the image of a teacher, religious leader, or coach with a distinctive physical style. Then, in a paragraph, describe your subject at work.

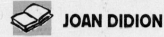 **JOAN DIDION**

Los Angeles Notebook

Joan Didion was born in California in 1934 and educated at the University of California, Berkeley. While she was still a senior she wrote a prize-winning essay for a contest sponsored by Vogue, *and soon she became an associate feature editor for* Vogue. *She has written novels, essays, and screenplays.*

1   There is something uneasy in the Los Angeles air this afternoon, some unnatural stillness, some tension. What it means is that tonight a Santa Ana will begin to blow, a hot wind from the northeast whining down through the Cajon and San Gorgonio Passes, blowing up sandstorms out along Route 66, drying the hills and the nerves to the flash point. For a few days now we will see smoke back in the canyons, and hear sirens in the night. I have neither heard nor read that a Santa Ana is due, but I know it, and almost everyone I have seen today knows it too. We know it because we feel it. The baby frets. The maid sulks. I rekindle a waning argument with the telephone company, then cut my losses and lie down, given over to whatever it is in the air. To live with the Santa Ana is to accept, consciously or unconsciously, a deeply mechanistic view of human behavior.

2   I recall being told, when I first moved to Los Angeles and was living on an isolated beach, that the Indians would throw themselves into the sea when the bad wind blew. I could see why. The Pacific turned ominously glossy during a Santa Ana period, and one woke in the night troubled not by the peacocks screaming in the olive trees but by the eerie absence of surf. The heat was surreal. The sky had a yellow cast, the kind of light sometimes called "earthquake weather." My only neighbor would not come out of her house for days, and there were no lights at night, and her husband roamed the place with a machete. One day he would tell me that he had heard a trespasser, the next a rattlesnake.

3   "On nights like that," Raymond Chandler once wrote about the Santa Ana, "every booze party ends in a fight. Meek little wives feel the edge of the carving knife and study their husbands' necks. Anything can happen." That was the kind of wind it was. I did not know then that there was any basis for the effect it had on all of us, but it turns out to be another of these cases in which science bears out folk wisdom. The Santa Ana, which is named for one of the canyons it rushes through, is a *foehn* wind, like the *foehn* of Austria and Switzerland and the *hamsin* of Israel. There are a number of persistent malevolent winds, perhaps the best known of which are the mistral of France and the Mediterranean sirocco, but a *foehn* wind has distinct characteristics: it occurs on the leeward slope of a mountain range and, although the air begins as a cold mass, it is warmed as it comes down the mountain and appears finally as a hot dry wind. Whenever and wherever a *foehn* blows, doctors hear about headaches and nausea and allergies, about "nervousness," about "depression." In Los Angeles some teachers do not attempt to conduct formal classes during a Santa Ana, because the children become unmanageable. In Switzerland the suicide rate goes up during the *foehn,* and in the courts of some Swiss cantons the wind is considered a mitigating circumstance for crime. Surgeons are said to watch the wind, because blood does not clot normally during a *foehn*. A few years ago an Israeli physicist discovered that not only during such winds, but for the ten or twelve hours which precede them, the air carries an unusually high ratio of positive to negative ions. No one seems to know exactly why that should be; some talk about friction and others suggest solar disturbances. In any case the positive ions are there, and what an excess of positive ions does, in the simplest terms, is make people unhappy. One cannot get much more mechanistic than that.

4   Easterners commonly complain that there is no "weather" at all in Southern California, that the days and the seasons slip by relentlessly, numbingly bland. That is quite misleading. In fact the climate is characterized by infrequent but violent extremes: two periods of torrential subtropical rains which continue for weeks and wash out the hills and send subdivisions sliding toward the sea; about twenty scattered days a year of the Santa Ana, which, with its incendiary dryness, invariably means fire. At the first prediction of a Santa Ana, the Forest Service flies men and equipment from northern California into the southern forests, and the Los Angeles Fire Department cancels its ordinary non-firefighting routines. The Santa Ana caused Malibu to burn the way it did in 1956, and Bel Air in 1961, and Santa Barbara in 1964. In the winter of 1966–67 eleven men were killed fighting a Santa Ana fire that spread through the San Gabriel Mountains.

5   Just to watch the front-page news out of Los Angeles during a Santa Ana is to get very close to what it is about the place. The longest single Santa Ana period in recent years was in 1957, and it lasted not the usual three or four days but fourteen days, from November 21 until December 4. On the first day 25,000 acres of the San Gabriel Mountains were burning, with gusts reaching 100 miles an hour. In town, the wind reached Force 12, or hurricane force, on the Beaufort Scale; oil derricks were toppled and people ordered off the downtown streets to avoid injury from flying objects. On November 22 the fire in the San Gabriels was out of control. On November 24 six people were killed in automobile accidents, and by the end of the week the Los Angeles *Times* was keeping a box score of traffic deaths. On November 26 a prominent Pasadena attorney, depressed about money, shot and killed his wife, their two sons, and himself. On November 27 a South Gate divorcée, twenty-two, was murdered and thrown from a moving car. On November 30 the San Gabriel fire was still out of control, and the wind in

town was blowing eighty miles an hour. On the first day of December four people died violently, and on the third the wind began to break.

6   It is hard for people who have not lived in Los Angeles to realize how radically the Santa Ana figures in the local imagination. The city burning is Los Angeles's deepest image of itself: Nathanael West perceived that, in *The Day of the Locust;* and at the time of the 1965 Watts riots what struck the imagination most indelibly were the fires. For days one could drive the Harbor Freeway and see the city on fire, just as we had always known it would be in the end. Los Angeles weather is the weather of catastrophe, of apocalypse, and, just as the reliably long and bitter winters of New England determine the way life is lived there, so the violence and the unpredictability of the Santa Ana affect the entire quality of life in Los Angeles, accentuate its impermanence, its unreliability. The wind shows us how close to the edge we are.

✎ Topics for Critical Thinking and Writing

1. Paraphrase or explain the last sentence of the first paragraph. What passages in the essay offer the most persuasive evidence supporting the point?
2. Beginning with the third paragraph, Didion defines the Santa Ana. Would the essay have been clearer or more effective if the definition had introduced the essay? Explain.
3. Explain the last sentence, and evaluate it as a conclusion.

 **E. B. WHITE**

Education

E[lwyn] B[rooks] White (1899–1985) wrote poetry and fiction, but he is most widely known as an essayist and as the coauthor (with William Strunk, Jr.) of The Elements of Style. *After a long career at* The New Yorker, *he retired to Maine, but he continued to write until the year before his death at the age of 86.*

1   I have an increasing admiration for the teacher in the country school where we have a third-grade scholar in attendance. She not only undertakes to instruct her charges in all the subjects of the first three grades, but she manages to function quietly and effectively as a guardian of their health, their clothes, their habits, their mothers, and their snowball engagements. She has been doing this sort of Augean task for twenty years, and is both kind and wise. She cooks for the children on the stove that heats the room, and she can cool their passions or warm their soup with equal competence. She conceives their costumes, cleans up their messes, and shares their confidences. My boy already regards his teacher as his great friend, and I think tells her a great deal more than he tells us.

2   The shift from city school to country school was something we worried about quietly all last summer. I have always rather favored public school over private school, if only because in public school you meet a greater variety of children. This bias of mine, I suspect, is partly an attempt to justify my own past (I never knew anything but public schools) and partly an involuntary defense

against getting kicked in the shins by a young ceramist on his way to the kiln. My wife was unacquainted with public schools, never having been exposed (in her early life) to anything more public than the washroom of Miss Winsor's. Regardless of our backgrounds, we both knew that the change in schools was something that concerned not us but the scholar himself. We hoped it would work out all right. In New York our son went to a medium-priced private institution with semi-progressive ideas of education, and modern plumbing. He learned fast, kept well, and we were satisfied. It was an electric, colorful, regimented existence with moments of pleasurable pause and giddy incident. The day the Christmas angel fainted and had to be carried out by one of the Wise Men was educational in the highest sense of the term. Our scholar gave imitations of it around the house for weeks afterward, and I doubt if it ever goes completely out of his mind.

3   His days were rich in formal experience. Wearing overalls and an old sweater (the accepted uniform of the private seminary), he sallied forth at morn accompanied by a nurse or a parent and walked (or was pulled) two blocks to a corner where the school bus made a flag stop. This flashy vehicle was as punctual as death: seeing us waiting at the cold curb, it would sweep to a halt, open its mouth, suck the boy in, and spring away with an angry growl. It was a good deal like a train picking up a bag of mail. At school the scholar was worked on for six or seven hours by half a dozen teachers and a nurse, and was revived on orange juice in mid-morning. In a cinder court he played games supervised by an athletic instructor, and in a cafeteria he ate lunch worked out by a dietitian. He soon learned to read with gratifying facility and discernment and to make Indian weapons of a semi-deadly nature. Whenever one of his classmates fell low of a fever the news was put on the wires and there were breathless phone calls to physicians, discussing periods of incubation and allied magic.

4   In the country all one can say is that the situation is different, and somehow more casual. Dressed in corduroys, sweatshirt, and short rubber boots, and carrying a tin dinner-pail pail, our scholar departs at the crack of dawn for the village school, two and a half miles down the road, next to the cemetery. When the road is open and the car will start, he makes the journey by motor, courtesy of his old man. When the snow is deep or the motor is dead or both, he makes it on the hoof. In the afternoons he walks or hitches all or part of the way home in fair weather, gets transported in foul. The schoolhouse is a two-room frame building, bungalow type, shingles stained a burnt brown with weather-resistant stain. It has a chemical toilet in the basement and two teachers above the stairs. One takes the first three grades, the other the fourth, fifth, and sixth. They have little or no time for individual instruction, and no time at all for the esoteric. They teach what they know themselves, just as fast and as hard as they can manage. The pupils sit still at their desks in class, and do their milling around outdoors during recess.

5   There is no supervised play. They play cops and robbers (only they call it "Jail") and throw things at one another—snowballs in winter, rose hips in fall. It seems to satisfy them. They also construct darts, pinwheels, and "pick-up sticks" (jackstraws), and the school itself does a brisk trade in penny candy, which is for sale right in the classroom and which contains "surprises." The most highly prized surprise is a fake cigarette, made of cardboard, fiendishly lifelike.

6   The memory of how apprehensive we were at the beginning is still strong. The boy was nervous about the change too. The tension, on that first fair morning in September when we drove him to school, almost blew the windows out of the sedan. And when later we picked him up on the road, wandering along with

his little blue lunch-pail, and got his laconic report "All right" in answer to our inquiry about how the day had gone, our relief was vast. Now, after almost a year of it, the only difference we can discover in the two school experiences is that in the country he sleeps better at night—and *that* probably is more the air than the education. When grilled on the subject of school-in-country vs. school-in-city, he replied that the chief difference is that the day seems to go so much quicker in the country. "Just like lightning," he reported.

Topics for Critical Thinking and Writing

1. Which school, public or private, does White prefer? Since White doesn't state his preference outright, from what evidence were you able to infer it?
2. In the first half of paragraph 2 White admits to a bias in favor of public schools, and he speculates, half-seriously, about the origins of his bias. If his intention here is not simply to amuse us, what is it?
3. What is White's strongest argument in favor of the school he prefers? Where in the essay do you find it?

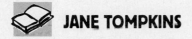

JANE TOMPKINS

At the Buffalo Bill Museum—June 1988

Jane Tompkins is Professor of English at Duke University, where she teaches courses in literature and literary theory, pedagogy, popular culture, and autobiography. She is author of Sensational Designs: The Cultural Work of American Fiction, 1790–1870 *(1985),* West of Everything: The Inner Life of Westerns *(1992), and* A Life in School: What the Teacher Learned *(1996). The following piece, on an exhibit of Frederic Remington's work, is excerpted from an essay originally published in* The South Atlantic Quarterly *and subsequently reprinted in* The Best American Essays 1991.

The video at the entrance to the Buffalo Bill Historical Center tells us that Buffalo Bill was the most famous American of his time, that by 1900 over a billion words had been written about him, and that he had a progressive vision of the West. Buffalo Bill had worked as a cattle driver, a wagoneer, a Pony Express rider, a buffalo hunter for the railroad, a hunting guide, an army scout and sometime Indian fighter; he wrote dime novels about himself and an autobiography at the age of thirty-three, by which time he was already famous; and then he began another set of careers—first he became an actor, performing on the urban stage in wintertime melodramatic representations of what he actually earned a living at in the summer (scouting and leading hunting expeditions), and finally he became the impresario of the Wild West show, a form of entertainment which he invented and carried on as actor, director, and all-round idea man for thirty years. Toward the end of his life he founded the town of Cody, Wyoming, to which he gave, among other things, $200,000. Strangely enough, it was as a progressive civic leader that Bill Cody wanted to be remembered. "I don't want to die," the video at the entrance tells us he said, "and have people say—oh, there goes another old showman. . . . I would like people to say—this is the man who opened Wyoming to the best of civilization."

The best of civilization. This was the phrase that rang in my head as I moved through the museum, which is one of the most disturbing places I have ever visited. It is also a wonderful place. It is four museums in one: the Whitney Gallery of Western Art, which houses art works on western subjects; the Buffalo Bill Museum proper, which memorializes Cody's life; the Plains Indian Museum, which exhibits artifacts of American Indian civilization; and the Winchester Arms Museum, a collection of firearms, historically considered.

The whole operation is extremely well designed and well run, from the video program at the entrance that gives an overview of all four museums, to the fresh-faced young attendants wearing badges that say "Ask Me," to the museum shop stacked with books on western Americana, to the ladies' room—a haven of satiny marble, shining mirrors, and flattering light. Among other things, the museum is admirable for its effort to combat prevailing stereotypes about the so-called "winning of the West," a phrase it self-consciously places in quotation marks. There are placards declaring that all history is a matter of interpretation, and that the American West is a source of "myth." Everywhere except, perhaps, in the Winchester Arms Museum, where the rhetoric is different, you feel the effort of the museum staff to reach out to the public, to be clear, to be accurate, to be fair, not to condescend, in short, to educate in the best sense of the term.

On the day I went, the museum was featuring an exhibition of Frederic Remington's works. There are two facts about these productions that make them different from those of artists one is used to encountering in museums. The first is that Remington's paintings and statues function as a historical record. Their chief attraction has always been that they transcribe scenes and events that have vanished from the earth. The second fact, related to this, is the brutality of their subject matter. Remington's work makes you pay attention to *what is happening* in the painting or the piece of statuary. When you look at his work you cannot escape from its subject.

5   Consequently, as I moved through the exhibit, the wild contortions of the bucking broncos, the sinister expression invariably worn by the Indians, and the killing of animals and men made the placards discussing Remington's use of the "lost wax" process seem strangely disconnected. In the face of unusual violence, or implied violence, their message was: what is important here is technique. Except in the case of paintings showing the battle of San Juan Hill, where white Americans were being killed, the material accompanying Remington's works did not refer to the subject matter of the paintings and statues. Nevertheless, an undertone of disquiet ran beneath the explanations; at least I thought I detected one. Someone had taken the trouble to ferret out Remington's statement of horror at the slaughter on San Juan Hill; someone had also excerpted the judgment of art critics commending Remington for the lyricism, inferiority, and mystery of his later canvases—pointing obliquely to the fascination with bloodshed that preoccupied his earlier work.

The uneasiness of the commentary, and my uneasiness with it, were nothing compared to the blatant contradictions in the paintings themselves. A pastel palette, a sunlit stop-action haze, murderous movement arrested under a lazy sky, flattened onto canvas and fixed in azure and ocher—two opposed impulses nestle here momentarily; the tension that keeps them from splitting apart is what holds the viewer's gaze.

The most excruciating example of what I mean occurs in the first painting in the exhibit. Entitled *His First Lesson*, it shows a horse standing saddled but riderless while a man pierces it just below the shoulder with a sharp instrument. The white of the horse's eye signals his pain. The man who is doing the piercing is simultaneously backing away from the reaction he clearly anticipates, and the man who holds the horse's halter is doing the same. But what can they be afraid of? For the horse's right rear leg is tied a foot off the ground by a rope that is also tied around his neck. He can't move. That is the whole point.

"His First Lesson." Whose? And what lesson, exactly? How to stay still and stand pain? How not to break away when they come at you with sharp instruments? How to be obedient? How to behave? It is impossible not to imagine that Remington's obsession with physical cruelty had roots somewhere in his own experience. Why else, in statue after statue, is the horse rebelling? The bucking bronco—symbol of the state of Wyoming, on every license plate, on every sign for every bar, on every belt buckle, mug, and decal—this image Remington cast in bronze over and over again. There is a wild diabolism in the bronzes; the horse and rider seem one thing, not so much rider and ridden as a single bolt of energy gone crazy and caught somehow, complicatedly, in a piece of metal.

In the paintings it is different, more subtle and bizarre. The cavalry on its way to a massacre, sweetly limned, softly tinted, poetically seized in midcareer, and gently laid on the two-dimensional surface. There is about these paintings of military men in the course of their deadly duty an almost maternal tenderness. The idealization of the cavalrymen in their dusty uniforms on their gallant horses has nothing to do with patriotism; it is pure love.

10   Remington's paintings and statues, as shown in this exhibition, embody everything that was objectionable about his era in American history. They are imperialist and racist; they glorify war and the torture and killing of animals; there are no women in them anywhere. Never the West as garden, never as pastoral, never as home. But in their aestheticizing of violent life Remington's pictures speak (to me at least) of some other desire. The maternal tenderness is not an accident, nor the beauty of the afternoons, nor the warmth of the desert sun. In these paintings Remington plays the part of the preserver, as if by catching the figures in color and line he could save their lives, and absorb some of that life into himself.

In one painting that particularly repulsed and drew me, a moose is outlined against the evening sky at the brink of a lake. He looks expectantly into the distance. Behind him and to one side, hidden from his view, and only just revealed to ours, for it is dark there, is a hunter poised in the back of a canoe, rifle perfectly aimed. We look closer; the title of the picture is *Coming to the Call*. Ah, now we see. This is a sadistic scene. The hunter has lured the moose to his death. But wait a moment. Isn't the sadism really directed at us? First we see the glory of the animal; Remington has made it as noble as he knows how. Then we see what is going to happen. The hunter is one up on the moose but Remington is one up on us. He makes us feel the pain of the anticipated killing, and makes us want to hold it off, to preserve the moose, just as he has done. Which way does the painting cut? Does it go against the hunter—who represents us, after all—or does it go against the moose, who came to the call? Who came, to what call? Did Remington come to the West in response to it—to whatever the moose represents, or to whatever the desire to kill the moose represents? But he hasn't killed it; he has only preserved an image of a white man about to kill it. And what call do we answer when we look at this painting? Who is calling whom? What is being preserved here? That is the question that for me hung over the whole museum.

The Whitney Gallery is an art museum: its allegiance is to "art" as our academic tradition has defined it. In this tradition, we come to understand a painting by having in our possession various bits of information. Something about the technical process used to produce it (pastels, watercolors, woodblock prints, etc.); something about the elements of composition—line and color and movement; something about the artist's life (where born, how educated, by whom influenced, which school belonged to or revolted against); something about his relation to this particular subject, such as how many times he painted it, or whether it contains his favorite model. Occasionally there will be some philosophizing about the themes or ideas the paintings are said to represent.

The problem is, when you're faced with a painter like Remington, these bits of information, while nice to have, don't explain what is there in front of you. They don't begin to give you an account of why a person should have depicted such things. The experience of a lack of fit between the explanatory material and what is there on the wall is one I've had before in museums, when, standing in front of a painting or a piece of statuary, I've felt a huge gap between the information on the little placard and what it is I'm seeing. I realize that "works of art," so-called, all have a subject matter, are all engaged with life, with some piece of life no less significant, no less compelling than Remington's subjects are, if we could only see its force. The idea that art is somehow separate from history, that it somehow occupies a space that is not the same as the space of life, seems out of whack here.

I wander through the gallery thinking these things because right next to it, indeed all around it, in the Buffalo Bill Museum and in the Plains Indian Museum, are artifacts that stand not for someone's expertise or skill in manipulating the elements of an artistic medium, but for life itself; they are the residue of life.

 ## Topics for Critical Thinking and Writing

1. In a sentence or two, characterize Tompkins's response to Remington's work.

2. Tompkins describes Remington's paintings and statues as brutal, bloody, and "bizarre." How does she account for or explain these qualities?

3. Discussing the information presented in placards next to Remington's works, Tompkins says, "the problem is, when you're faced with a painter like Remington, these bits of information, while nice to have, don't explain what is there in front of you." She says further that she's experienced before this "lack of fit between the explanatory material and what is there on the wall." What does she make of this gap, this "lack of fit"?

4. As we note in the chapter on analysis, descriptive passages are commonly used to support analysis. Examine paragraph 11, which begins "In one painting . . . ." Which sentences are primarily descriptive? Which ones are primarily analytic? How exactly does this passage support Tompkins's analysis?

5. Using "At the Buffalo Bill Museum—1988" as a model, write a 750–1000-word essay in which you describe, analyze, and articulate your response to an exhibit at your college or university museum.

11

Defining

THE NEED FOR DEFINITION

To argue a point or to explain an idea, writers frequently need to define words. Defining the terms of an argument is one of the persuasive writer's most useful strategies: a writer making an argument for or against abortion would be likely at some point in her essay to define the term "life." Even a primarily analytic essay may need to define its key terms. A writer analyzing a group of nineteenth-century Gothic stories, for example, might clarify his analysis by defining the term *Gothic tale*:

Though it may be confused with the ghost story, the Gothic tale--despite

its frequent reliance on supernatural elements--is quite distinct. A Gothic

tale is one in which outdated and oppressive conventions confine a

generally helpless victim, who is usually in some way associated with a

decaying family line, and imprisoned in an isolated and deteriorating

house, mansion, or castle.

—Chad Hill

The words may be *specialized* or unfamiliar to the writer's intended audience—for example, the words "venture capitalist" or "enterprise zones." Or, we might define a word that the audience may think it knows but that (in the writer's opinion) the audience may misunderstand. For instance, a writer might argue that the words "guerrilla" and "terrorist" are not synonyms, and then go on to define each word, showing the differences between them.

Often, however, providing a *synonym* is a reasonable strategy. Talking about the word "civilizing" in Roth's argument against closing the Newark Public Library (page 9), a student briefly explained a point by saying, "By 'civilizing,' Roth meant 'socializing.'"

In addition to defining a word because it is specialized ("venture capitalist"), or because we want to distinguish it from another word ("guerrilla" and "terrorist"), or because we may think that a synonym will clarify it ("civilizing" and "socializing"), we may define a word because the word has many meanings, and we want to make sure that readers take the word in a particular way. A word like "ability," for example, may require defining in a discussion of the Scholastic Aptitude Test. To argue that the SAT does or does not measure "academic ability," the writer and reader need, in a sense, to agree on a specific meaning for "ability." This kind of definition, where the writer specifies or stipulates a meaning, is called a *stipulative definition*.

The word "stipulate," by the way, comes from a Latin word meaning "to bargain." Explaining a word's *etymology*, its *history* or its *origin*, as we have just done, is often an aid in definition.

In short, in defining a word or term, writers have many options and they need to take into account both their own purposes in writing and their readers' needs. Let's look at some examples.

KINDS OF DEFINITIONS

Inclusive/Exclusive Definitions

Here is a writer defining a *specialized* term for readers of a Central Florida newspaper:

> Enterprise zones are government-designated areas of severe poverty and high unemployment to which businesses are encouraged to relocate through tax breaks and other incentives. Where once there were vacant lots and boarded-up buildings, the theory goes, new companies attracted by the tax breaks would provide badly needed jobs, and the newly employed residents would spend their earnings on other local businesses, creating a ripple effect that revitalizes an entire community.
>
> —MAX FRIEDMAN

Notice how Friedman defines "enterprise zones." In the first sentence, he places "enterprise zones" in a category or class, "government-designated areas." He next shows how they differ from other members of the class: they are areas "of severe poverty and high unemployment to which businesses are encouraged to relocate through tax breaks and other incentives." Such a definition is sometimes called *inclusive/exclusive* because it *includes* the word in a relevant category (government-designated areas) and then *excludes* other members of that category (for example, "disaster zones" or "postal zones" or "war zones"). Notice too that Friedman's definition uses a parallel form, a noun for a noun: "zones" are "areas." (Avoid saying "enterprise zones are when the government designates.")

Notice, also, that Friedman briefly describes "enterprise zones": they contain "vacant lots and boarded-up buildings." In the rest of the sentence he also describes, with a few details, the presumed effects of enterprise zones. (In the words, "the theory goes," what does he imply about the actual effect of these zones?)

A definition of a specialized term can be very brief, for example: "Venture capitalists, *the specialized firms that raise money for new technological inventions . . . .*" Here the definition is accomplished in a phrase (which we have italicized). A term can be defined in a paragraph, as Friedman does above. But a writer might need the space of an essay to define a word. Notice how, in the following short essay—a book review—the writer begins with a whimsical definition of *caricature* as "a portrait with an attitude," but throughout the review she further defines caricature as "an acerbic and accessible form of social and political criticism" and "a savage mirror that confronts society."

A caricature is a portrait with an attitude, a likeness meant to provoke recognition by its distortions. Although its purpose is often nothing more than to be a visual prank, caricature at its best has often been an acerbic and accessible form of social and political criticism. In *The Savage Mirror: The Art of Contemporary Caricature* (Watson-Guptil, paper, $29.95), Steven Heller, the art director of *The New York Times Book Review,* and Gail Anderson, the deputy art director of *Rolling Stone,* present an overview of contemporary caricature, tracing its evolution from 19th-century France through its powerful resurgence in the United States from the mid–1950's to the mid–1970's. The authors explain the roles that editorial preferences, design fads and technology have played in creating the current scene, which they seem, almost in spite of themselves, to find disappointing. For Ms. Anderson and Mr. Heller, caricaturists have great power—and perhaps even a duty—to address the issues of the day, to use their skills to rouse the public. Today the subjects of caricature are less likely to be political figures than celebrities, who menace our sensibilities more than our freedom. As the book amply illustrates, in changing from pen to airbrush, caricature has gone from inspired anger to dextrous hipness. Ms. Anderson and Mr. Heller clearly believe that a caricature should communicate an idea; as they survey contemporary caricature, they see "little gems of mild distortion" rather than a savage mirror that confronts society with its sorry reflection. This profusely illustrated book provides an excellent introduction to its subject, and the authors are persuasive in their arguments for the importance of caricature.

—ROSEMARY RANCK

Stipulative Definitions

Now let's look at an example of a *stipulative definition.* In "The Morality and Rationality of Suicide," Richard B. Brandt asks his readers to agree on a *neutral* definition of suicide.

"Suicide" is conveniently defined, for our purposes, as doing something which results in one's death, either from the intention of ending one's life or the intention to bring about some other state of affairs (such as relief from pain) which one thinks it certain or highly probable can be achieved only by means of death or will produce death. It may seem odd to classify an act of heroic self-sacrifice on the part of a soldier as suicide. It is simpler, however, not to try to define "suicide" so that an act of suicide is always irrational or immoral in some way; if we adopt a neutral definition like the above we can still proceed to ask when an act of suicide in that sense is rational, morally justifiable, and so on, so that all evaluations anyone might wish to make can still be made.

Notice that Brandt concedes that there are apparent problems with this definition. It would, for example, include a soldier's self-sacrifice. But, he argues, if we adopt the definition he proposes, we can still evaluate a particular act as "rational, morally justifiable, and so on." In *stipulating* this definition of suicide we can see Brandt striking a bargain with his readers.

Striking such bargains is often necessary: although technical words have relatively stable meanings, many of the words that you will be defining—words such as *democracy, identity, family, society*—have so many meanings that your reader won't know what you mean until you explain which definition you are using.

Definition by Origin or History

The passage that follows, from a column called "The Word Watchers," is a *definition by origin and history* of the word "stonewall" used as a verb.

> "Stonewall" as a verb originated in the game of cricket, as a term for playing solely on the defensive. Australian political slang picked it up in the late nineteenth-century, and it was adopted quickly by British politicians.
>
> In America, stonewalling was rarely used: the citation in *Webster's New International Unabridged Dictionary* is a James Reston column of the late fifties, "stonewalling for time in order to close the missile gap." But then Henry Kissinger picked up the term: I first heard him use it in late 1969 as, "The North Vietnamese are stonewalling us."
>
> As a needed figure of speech, the word's usage increased; more stones were added as a strategy of silence was adopted by the Watergaters, and when the President's tapes revealed him to have said "I want you to stonewall it," the word was sealed into the language. Stonewalling has a pejorative connotation today. But long before its scornful use by cricketeers, politicians from Down Under and up above, the figure of speech was used in admiration during our Civil War about one of the Confederacy's greatest generals: "There stands Jackson, like a stone wall!"
>
> Might it be possible, someday, for stonewalling to regain an admirable connotation? The word-watchers will be watching.
>
> —WILLIAM SAFIRE

Safire's engaging discussion comes not only from his zeal for "word-watching" but also, we imagine, from the legwork of a staff of researchers, and an office wall of dictionaries and other reference books. But all writers must become word-watchers, to some degree, and it is fascinating as well as useful to learn word origins and histories. With nothing more than a good desk dictionary, we can learn that "yoga" derives from a Sanskrit word for union, or joining or yoking ("join" and yoke" both come from this same root: yoga seeks to join or yoke the individual's consciousness to its spiritual source); that "Islam" is Arabic for "submission to God," and comes ultimately from an Arabic word for safety; that "science" comes from a Latin verb meaning "to know"; and that "holocaust" comes from a Greek word meaning "completely burnt." Here is the word history that accompanies the definition of "holocaust" in the third edition of *The American Heritage Dictionary of the English Language.*

> Totality of destruction has been central to the meaning of *holocaust* since it first appeared in Middle English in the 14th century and referred to the biblical sacrifice in which a male animal was wholly burnt on the altar in worship of God. *Holocaust* comes from Greek *holokauston* ("that which is completely burnt"), which was a translation of Hebrew *old* (literally "that which goes up," that is, in smoke). In this sense of "burnt sacrifice," *holocaust* is still used in some versions of the Bible. In the 17th century the meaning of *holocaust* broadened to "something totally consumed by fire," and the word eventually was applied to fires of extreme destructiveness. In the 20th century *holocaust* has taken on a variety of figurative meanings, summarizing the effects of war, rioting, storms, epidemic diseases, and even economic failures. Most of these usages arose after World War II, but it is unclear whether they permitted or resulted from the use of *holocaust* in reference to the mass murder of European Jews and others by the Nazis. This application of the word occurred as early as 1942, but the phrase *the Holocaust* did not become established until the late 1950's. Here it parallels and may have been influenced by another Hebrew word, *sho'ah* ("catastrophe"). In the Bible *sho'ah* has a range of meanings including "personal ruin or devastation" and "a wasteland or desert." *Sho'ah* was first used to refer to the Nazi slaughter of Jews in 1939, but its phrase *hasho'ah* ("the catastrophe") only became established after World War II. *Holocaust* has also been used to translate *hurban* ("destruction"), another Hebrew word used to summarize the genocide of Jews by the Nazis. This sense of *holocaust* has since broadened to include the mass slaughter of other peoples, but when capitalized it refers specifically to the destruction of Jews and other Europeans by the Nazis and may also encompass the Nazi persecution of Jews that preceded the outbreak of the war.

THE LIMITS OF DEFINITION BY SYNONYM

A Last Example

Paralyzed by illness, a professor of anthropology reflects on the meaning of the word "disabled." The passage is from his book, *The Body Silent:*

> I was badly damaged, yet just as alive as ever, and I had to make the best of it with my remaining capabilities. It then occurred to me that this is

the universal human condition. We all have to muddle through life within our limitations, and while I had certain physical handicaps, I retained many strengths. My brain was the only part of the central cortex that still worked well, but that also is where I made my living. *Disability* is an amorphous and relativistic term. Some people are unable to do what I do because they lack the mental equipment, and in this sense, they are disabled and I am not. Everybody is disabled in one way or another. And even though my growing paralysis would one day end my active participation in the affairs of the world, I could still sit back and watch them unfold.

—ROBERT F. MURPHY

Without calling attention to it, Murphy takes into account the *origin* of the word disability. "Dis" as a prefix (from Latin) means "not" or "deprived of." What does it mean, he seems to ask, to be deprived of or to not have ability? His discussion acknowledges that "damaged" and "handicapped" are *synonyms* for disabled. But, he argues, "*Disability* is an amorphous and relativistic term." Its meaning, he implies, needs to be *stipulated.* Above all, what his discussion makes clear is that he has a compelling reason to reexamine and explain how he defines the word "disability" and how we all should define it.

A NOTE ON USING A DICTIONARY

A dictionary is for a writer an invaluable resource. If you do not own a recent hardback college dictionary, we advise you to buy one and to keep it handy as you read and write. You will use it to look up the meaning or several meanings of a word you're not sure of, to check its spelling or pronunciation, to see how its form changes in its various functions, to discover its origin. In some dictionaries, you will find usage notes that will tell you, for example, whether a word is considered slang, or obscene, or whether a usage is now generally accepted. We particularly recommend *The American Heritage Dictionary,* Third Edition, for its extensive list of words and its superb notes on word histories and word usage. Any good bookstore will have several other excellent dictionaries, among them, *Webster's New World Dictionary* (third edition), *Merriam-Webster's Collegiate Dictionary* (tenth edition), or *The Random House Dictionary of the English Language: College Edition.*

You should also become acquainted, in the library, with the great multi-volume *Oxford English Dictionary* (*OED*). In it you will find quotations illustrating the meanings of words over the centuries. It is an unparalleled source for shedding light on texts (especially poetry) written before our times.

The *OED* and other dictionaries are now available on CD-ROM; most colleges and universities provide online access to them as well. For information on accessing these resources, consult your institution's reference librarian.

The one use to which you ought *not* put a dictionary is this: Do not introduce an essay with the words "Webster says . . ." or "According to the dictionary . . ." Because the name Webster is no longer copyrighted, it appears on all sorts of dictionaries, bad as well as good. Besides, as we note in our discussion of introductory paragraphs, there is no staler opening.

A Checklist for Revising Definitions

✔ Do you give brief definitions, where needed—for example, of a specialized or technical term?
✔ Do you give sufficient examples to clarify the definition?
✔ Do you distinguish the term from a near synonym—for example communism from socialism, revolution from resistance, terrorism from guerrilla warfare? Will a comparison help to define the term?
✔ Would it be helpful to mention the etymology or origin of the word?
✔ Do you make clear which meaning of a word you are using (stipulating), and why?
✔ Is the need for a definition implied or, in a long definition, do you explain the need?

Topics for Critical Thinking and Writing

1. Define, for an audience unfamiliar with the terms, *bebop, rap, ska, hip-hop, world music,* or *country music,* in 250 to 500 words.
2. Write one paragraph defining one of the following terms: *security blanket, twilight zone, holding pattern, stalking.* Your paragraph should disclose the origin of the term (if you can't find it, make a reasonable guess) and some examples of current use distinct from its original meaning.
3. Write an opening paragraph for an essay in which you stipulate a meaning for *death,* or *vegetarianism,* excluding one or two other meanings. Don't write the essay, just the opening paragraph.
4. In a paragraph explain the difference between "a reason" (for some action) and "an excuse." Provide a specific example, real or invented. Your audience is someone who expects you to offer an excuse.
5. If you are fluent in a language other than English, or in a dialect other than Standard American, write a paragraph defining for native speakers of Standard American a word that stands for some concept. Examples: Spanish *machismo* or *commoción,* Yiddish *haimish* or *chutzpa,* Japanese *shibui,* or African-American English *bad* or *cool.*
6. Write an essay of approximately 500 words on the word *natural* as it is used to advertise products such as cereals, yogurt, cosmetics, and cigarettes. Your essay should stipulate a definition of natural, and should have a thesis. An example of a thesis: "Yogurt may be a wholesome food, but most commercial yogurts are not as 'natural' as we are led to believe."
7. Write an essay defining sexual harassment. Explain the need for definition, what the term includes and excludes, and the relevance of the etymology of *harass.* Use examples of what is and is not sexual harassment to clarify your point.
8. Write an essay (about 500 words) explaining one of the following terms: *horror film, situation comedy, soap opera, junk food, nostalgia, ethnic joke, yuppie.* Your essay will probably include a definition, reference to several examples, and perhaps an extended discussion of one example, explaining the reasons for its popularity, or arguing its merits or lack of merits.

DEFINITION AT WORK

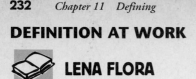 **LENA FLORA**

The Plight of the Politically Correct

In the following brief essay, a student defines the term political correctness.

Political correctness is a style of language, an attitude, and a standard of ethics that people have now been struggling with for years. Part of the reason for this struggle lies in the fact that no one is exactly sure what is and what is not politically correct. The phrase *political correctness* might be defined as "conformity to a body of liberal or radical opinion, especially on social matters." Political correctness also involves the avoidance of anything, even established vocabulary, that might be construed as discriminatory or pejorative. In effect, political correctness seems to mean taking every word in the English language, scrutinizing it for any way that it could possibly offend any one person, and using this criterion to ban its use in day-to-day speech. For example, I can no longer grow up and be a fireman, a policeman, a mailman, or a woman. I may not even be allowed to call myself female. Does this mean that I am fated to call myself testosteronally-challenged, or maybe x-chromosomally gifted? Am I a chauvinist pig if I like to be known as a woman, or if I refer to my daughter as my little girl? By some strict politically correct standards, yes. Also, political correctness forces me to refrain from using many adjectives I might use to describe myself. I am not Oriental, short, or near-sighted. Instead, I am Asian-American, vertically-challenged, and distant-visually-challenged person of feminine gender. I certainly don't feel challenged in any of these areas, only in the area of speaking with political correctness.

 ## Questions for Critical Thinking and Writing

1. Are you persuaded by Flora's definition of *political correctness?* What are two or three strongest points she makes in this paragraph? What points seem weak?
2. Would a person in favor of what Flora calls political correctness be likely to use the term political correctness? Why or why not?
3. If on the whole you disagree with Flora's definition of political correctness, write your own definition of the term.
4. If you agree with her definition, define the term *multiculturalism*.

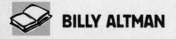 **BILLY ALTMAN**

Country Just Ain't What It Used to Be

Billy Altman currently writes about music and television for the online magazine Addicted to Noise. *This essay, however, appeared in* The New York Times, *in 1993.*

Time was when listeners tuning into a country radio station had a pretty good idea what kind of music they were likely to find. For decades, country songs meant stories of rabble-rousing, working-class everymen loving, cheating on and/or crawling back to strong, understanding girlfriends, wives or mistresses. Throw in an undercurrent of alcohol-soaked, moralistic ruminations about a fixed set of mandatory topics (prison, religion, mom) and certain basic sociopolitical tenets (when in doubt, wave the flag), and there, with few exceptions, was the genre in a shot glass.

Lately, however, country has been redefining itself, particularly when it comes to the relationship between the sexes, and even its supposedly firmest clichés have been dropping off lyric sheets faster than an unsecured payload falling off the back end of an 18-wheeler on the interstate. Garth Brooks's recent album, *The Chase,* for example, found the singer-songwriter using his megastar pulpit to attack some of country's longest-standing attitudes with the anthemic eye-opener "We Shall Be Free." "When we're free to love anyone we choose," he sings, "When this world's big enough for all different views / When we can all worship from our own kind of pew / Then we shall be free." In so doing, he poses a direct challenge to country's traditionally conservative positions on sexual preference, political affiliation and religious persuasion.

"We Shall Be Free" is no isolated statement, either—a fact underscored by other tracks on the album, most notably, "Face to Face," in which a date-rape victim is both supported and encouraged in a courtroom confrontation with her attacker, and "That Summer," in which a young, virginal field hand learns about sex from a widowed farm woman. Put the messages of these songs together and one begins to understand not only why Mr. Brooks is selling millions of albums to country's predominantly female audience, but also why the music is drawing new followers from outside its customary strongholds.

Simply put, the old country song just ain't what it used to be. Yes, there are still hurt-pride hunks like Billy Ray Cyrus pining over their achy-breaky hearts; the homefires-burning housewife that Reba McIntyre sings about will continue to look out the window and wonder "Is There Life Out There?" without ever venturing forth on her own. But at both ends of the gender gap, a growing number of artists are displaying raised consciousnesses about the eternal battle of the sexes and helping to, if not erase, then at least recast many of country's male–female stereotypes into more enlightened models.

5   This updated sensibility is a function of a several factors. For one, country music has been appealing of late to a different breed of fan—adults who grew up on rock and have found in country music the kind of listener-friendly melodies and narrative styles that have been elbowed off the airwaves by youth-oriented grunge, metal and hip-hop. But the standard if-it's-too-loud-you're-too-old argument fails to recognize one crucial point: from its very beginnings, country music has been an adult medium, with an adult tone and addressing adult concerns. Yet nobody saw adults running for country cover during the British Invasion of the 60's or when punk exploded in rock's face in the 70's.

The last time country music captured the public's attention to an even remotely comparable degree was in the "Urban Cowboy" days of the early 80's. But in retrospect, that revival seems to have been more a fashion-driven fad than anything else, with denim jeans replacing polyester leisure suits and the mechanical bull replacing the mirrored ball for the post-disco crowd. The music served merely as a background accessory, created no major stars and carried little import. Not exactly a movement.

What's going on now, though, definitely is a movement. And its leaders—
Mr. Brooks, Clint Black, Rosanne Cash and Mary-Chapin Carpenter—clearly display a different perspective than those of an earlier era. Country's new songs,
like its old songs, still focus on the social currents rumbling through American
life—remember, this is a genre that prides itself on being real people's music.
But the observations being made, and the conclusions being drawn, about such
well-traveled terrain as drinking and carousing, loving and losing and familial responsibilities, reflect the influences of contemporary concerns like feminism,
the men's movement, the environment and AIDS.

For the men, macho swagger is out and ego-secure emotional maturity is in.
Mr. Brooks's "Everytime That It Rains," a ballad about a failed attempt at re-creat-
ing a chance sexual encounter, ends in (of all things) friendship, Clint Black's
1989 debut hit, "A Better Man," avoids tears-in-your-beer self-pity in describing
the breakup of a long-term relationship ("I'm leaving here a better man / Knowing you this way / Things I couldn't do before now I think I can / And I'm leaving here a better man").

Speaking of beer, even erstwhile honky-tonkers like Alan Jackson now know
when to say when. He raised a few eyebrows in 1991 with "Midnight in Montgomery," which invoked the spirit of the legendary Hank Williams Sr., in a de-
mythologized form—"a drunk man in a cowboy hat." And, just in case anybody
missed the message, his latest album includes the all-sobered up with somewhere to go "I Don't Need the Booze (to Get a Buzz On)," which finds the singer
"hooked on my baby's love / There ain't nothing in a jug this strong."

10   The idea of unquestioned male dominance in the home is also taking it on
the chin in songs like Mr. Brooks's "Thunder Rolls." His depiction of a husband's
unwarranted attack on his wife is probably the first song by a male country artist
to confront spousal abuse. For a genre that once gave us Fiddlin' John Carson
singing "It's a Shame to Whip Your Wife on Sunday" ("When you've got Monday,
Tuesday, Wednesday . . ."), the empathy Mr. Brooks exhibits says a lot.

Country's women, meanwhile, are asserting themselves as never before.
The bend-but-don't-break philosophy of Tammy Wynette's late–60's classic,
"Stand By Your Man," is becoming a thing of the past. As Ms. Cash proclaimed on
"The Real Me" a few years ago, "A woman's her own mystery / Not a shadow of
a man."

Similarly, Mary-Chapin Carpenter uses songs on her latest album, *Come On
Come On,* to address a range of women's issues, from men's need to express
their emotions to women's need to have their own emotional space. The
album's pivotal track, "He Thinks He'll Keep Her," describes the plight of a 36-
year-old mother of three who has been taken so completely for granted by her
husband that she wakes up one morning, packs his bags and tosses him out,
without regard for what the future will bring.

Even sexy sirens like Lorrie Morgan are trying to define relationships on
their own terms. On one of her singles, "Watch Me," a lover tells her cheating
man, "If you think I won't go, just watch me." Ms. Morgan's latest song is about
an unescorted woman getting hit on by a stranger at a bar. "I'm not interested in
romance, or what you have in mind," she says without a trace of country-belle
flirtatiousness in her voice. "What part of no don't you understand?"

If country music is a gauge of what Middle America thinks and feels, it's
probably safe to say that happy hour will never be the same—and that, in country music at least, the "kinder, gentler" America envisioned by George Bush may

finally have manifested itself. Country music, nonsexist and politically progressive? Sounds like a cultural elitist's pipe dream.

 ## Topics for Critical Thinking and Writing

1. What is unusual about Altman's first sentence? How do you explain this element?
2. In his first paragraph Altman in effect defines older country music, although he allows for exceptions. If you are familiar with the material, do you think his definition is adequate, or, on the other hand, are the exceptions so numerous or so important that Altman's definition is misleading?
3. In paragraph 2 Altman argues that "country has been redefining itself." In what way or ways does he claim that it has been changing? How (by what methods) does he establish that it has been redefining itself in these ways?
4. *The American Heritage Dictionary of the English Language,* Third Edition, defines country music thus:

   Popular music based on the folkstyle of the southern rural United States or the music of cowboys in the American West. Also called *country and western.*

   Is this a reasonable definition? Why, do you suppose, doesn't Altman quote this or any other dictionary definition?

5. In paragraph 5 Altman mentions "grunge, metal and hip-hop." Define one of these, in a paragraph.
6. Is k. d. lang a country singer? Explain, in a paragraph.

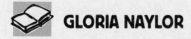 ## GLORIA NAYLOR

A Question of Language

Gloria Naylor, university teacher, essayist, and novelist, holds an M.A. in Afro-American Studies from Yale University. Her first novel, The Women of Brewster Place *(1983), won an American Book Award; her most recent book is the sequel,* The Men of Brewster Place *(1998). This essay originally appeared in* The New York Times.

Language is the subject. It is the written form with which I've managed to keep the wolf away from the door and, in diaries, to keep my sanity. In spite of this, I consider the written word inferior to the spoken, and much of the frustration experienced by novelists is the awareness that whatever we manage to capture in even the most transcendent passages falls far short of the richness of life. Dialogue achieves its power in the dynamics of a fleeting moment of sight, sound, smell, and touch.

I'm not going to enter the debate here about whether it is language that shapes reality or vice versa. That battle is doomed to be waged whenever we seek intermittent reprieve from the chicken and egg dispute. I will simply take the position that the spoken word, like the written word, amounts to a nonsensical arrangement of sounds or letters without a consensus that assigns "meaning." And building from the meanings of what we hear, we order reality. Words themselves are innocuous; it is the consensus that gives them true power.

I remember the first time I heard the word *nigger*. In my third-grade class, our math tests were being passed down the rows, and as I handed the papers to a little boy in back of me, I remarked that once again he had received a much lower mark than I did. He snatched his test from me and spit out that word. Had he called me a nymphomaniac or a necrophiliac, I couldn't have been more puzzled. I didn't know what a nigger was, but I knew that whatever it meant, it was something he shouldn't have called me. This was verified when I raised my hand, and in a loud voice repeated what he had said and watched the teacher scold him for using a "bad" word. I was later to go home and ask the inevitable question that every black parent must face—"Mommy, what does 'nigger' mean?"

And what exactly did it mean? Thinking back, I realize that this could not have been the first time the word was used in my presence. I was part of a large extended family that had migrated from the rural South after World War II and formed a close-knit network that gravitated around my maternal grandparents. Their ground-floor apartment in one of the buildings they owned in Harlem was a weekend mecca for my immediate family, along with countless aunts, uncles, and cousins who brought along assorted friends. It was a bustling and open house with assorted neighbors and tenants popping in and out to exchange bits of gossip, pick up an old quarrel or referee the ongoing checkers game in which my grandmother cheated shamelessly. They were all there to let down their hair and put up their feet after a week of labor in the factories, laundries, and shipyards of New York.

5   Amid the clamor, which could reach deafening proportions—two or three conversations going on simultaneously, punctuated by the sound of a baby's crying somewhere in the back rooms or out on the street—there was still a rigid set of rules about what was said and how. Older children were sent out of the living room when it was time to get into the juicy details about "you-know-who" up on the third floor who had gone and gotten herself "p-r-e-g-n-a-n-t!" But my parents, knowing that I could spell well beyond my years, always demanded that I follow the others out to play. Beyond sexual misconduct and death, everything else was considered harmless for our young ears. And so among the anecdotes of the triumphs and disappointments in the various workings of their lives, the word *nigger* was used in my presence, but it was set within contexts and inflections that caused it to register in my mind as something else.

In the singular, the word was always applied to a man who had distinguished himself in some situation that brought their approval for his strength, intelligence, or drive:

"Did Johnny really do that?"

"I'm telling you, that nigger pulled in $6,000 of overtime last year. Said he got enough for a down payment on a house."

When used with a possessive adjective by a woman—"my nigger"—it became a term of endearment for husband or boyfriend. But it could be more than just a term applied to a man. In their mouths it became the pure essence of manhood—a disembodied force that channeled their past history of struggle and present survival against the odds into a victorious statement of being: "Yeah, that old foreman found out quick enough—you don't mess with a nigger."

10   In the plural, it became a description of some group within the community
that had overstepped the bounds of decency as my family defined it: Parents
who neglected their children, a drunken couple who fought in public, people
who simply refused to look for work, those with excessively dirty mouths or un-
kempt households were all "trifling niggers." This particular circle could forgive
hard times, unemployment, the occasional bout of depression—they had gone
through all of that themselves—but the unforgivable sin was lack of self-respect.

A woman could never be a *nigger* in the singular, with its connotation of
confirming worth. The noun *girl* was its closest equivalent in that sense, but
only when used in direct address and regardless of the gender doing the addressing. *Girl* was a token of respect for a woman. The one-syllable word was
drawn out to sound like three in recognition of the extra ounce of wit, nerve or
daring that the woman had shown in the situation under discussion.

"G-i-r-l, stop. You mean you said that to his face?"

But if the word was used in a third-person reference or shortened so that it
almost snapped out of the mouth, it always involved some element of communal
disapproval. And age became an important factor in these exchanges. It was only
between individuals of the same generation, or from an older person to a
younger (but never the other way around), that "girl" would be considered a
compliment.

I don't agree with the argument that use of the word *nigger* at this social
stratum of the black community was an internalization of racism. The dynamics
were the exact opposite: the people in my grandmother's living room took a
word that whites used to signify worthlessness or degradation and rendered it
impotent. Gathering there together, they transformed *nigger* to signify the varied and complex human beings they knew themselves to be. If the word was to
disappear totally from the mouths of even the most liberal of white society, no
one in that room was naïve enough to believe it would disappear from white
minds. Meeting the word head-on, they proved it had absolutely nothing to do
with the way they were determined to live their lives.

15   So there must have been dozens of times that the word *nigger* was spoken
in front of me before I reached the third grade. But I didn't "hear" it until it was
said by a small pair of lips that had already learned it could be a way to humiliate
me. That was the word I went home and asked my mother about. And since she
knew that I had to grow up in America, she took me in her lap and explained.

✏ Topics for Critical Thinking and Writing

1. Why, according to Naylor (in paragraph 1), is written language inferior to
   spoken language? Can you think of any way or any circumstance in
   which written language is superior? How does Naylor's essay support her
   position here? Or does it?
2. In paragraph 2 Naylor says "Words themselves are innocuous; it is the
   consensus that gives them true power." What does this mean? In the rest
   of the essay Naylor discusses meanings of the word *nigger*. To what extent does her discussion demonstrate that consensus "assigns meaning"
   and gives words power?
3. If as a child you were the victim of an ethnic slur, explain how you reacted to it and how others (perhaps a parent or teacher) reacted to it. Or,
   if you ever delivered an ethnic slur, explain how you felt then, and how
   you feel now, about the incident or incidents.

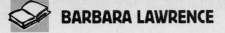

BARBARA LAWRENCE

Four-Letter Words Can Hurt You

Barbara Lawrence was born in Hanover, New Hampshire, and she was educated at Connecticut College and at New York University. She teaches at the State University of New York at Old Westbury. This essay first appeared in The New York Times.

Why should any words be called obscene? Don't they all describe natural human functions? Am I trying to tell them, my students demand, that the "strong, earthy, gut-honest"—or, if they are fans of Norman Mailer, the "rich, liberating, existential"—language they use to describe sexual activity isn't preferable to "phony-sounding, middle-class words like 'intercourse' and 'copulate'?" "Cop You Late!" they say with fancy inflections and gagging grimaces. "Now, what is *that* supposed to mean?"

Well, what is it supposed to mean? And why indeed should one group of words describing human functions and human organs be acceptable in ordinary conversation and another, describing presumably the same organs and functions, be tabooed—so much so, in fact, that some of these words still cannot appear in print in many parts of the English-speaking world?

The argument that these taboos exist only because of "sexual hangups" (middle-class, middle-age, feminist), or even that they are a result of class oppression (the contempt of the Norman conquerors for the language of their Anglo-Saxon serfs), ignores a much more likely explanation, it seems to me, and that is the sources and functions of the words themselves.

The best known of the tabooed sexual verbs, for example, comes from the German *ficken,* meaning "to strike"; combined, according to Partridge's etymological dictionary *Origins,* with the Latin sexual verb *futuere;* associated in turn with the Latin *fustis,* "a staff or cudgel"; the Celtic *buc,* "a point, hence to pierce"; the Irish *bot,* "the male member"; the Latin *battuere,* "to beat"; the Gaelic *batair,* "a cudgeller"; the Early Irish *bualaim,* "I strike"; and so forth. It is one of what etymologists sometimes call "the sadistic group of words for the man's part in copulation."

5   The brutality of this word, then, and its equivalents ("screw," "bang," etc.), is not an illusion of the middle class or a crotchet of Women's Liberation. In their origins and imagery these words carry undeniably painful, if not sadistic, implications, the object of which is almost always female. Consider, for example, what a "screw" actually does to the wood it penetrates; what a painful, even mutilating, activity this kind of analogy suggests. "Screw" is particularly interesting in this context, since the noun, according to Partridge, comes from words meaning "groove," "nut," "ditch," "breeding sow," "scrofula" and "swelling," while the verb, besides its explicit imagery, has antecedent associations to "write on," "scratch," "scarify," and so forth—a revealing fusion of a mechanical or painful action with an obviously denigrated object.

Not all obscene words, of course, are as implicitly sadistic or denigrating to women as these, but all that I know seem to serve a similar purpose: to reduce the human organism (especially the female organism) and human functions (especially sexual and procreative) to their least organic, most mechanical dimension; to substitute a trivializing or deforming resemblance for the complex human reality of what is being described.

Tabooed male descriptives, when they are not openly denigrating to women, often serve to divorce a male organ or function from any significant interaction with the female. Take the word "testes," for example, suggesting "witnesses" (from the Latin *testis*) to the sexual and procreative strengths of the male organ; and the obscene counterpart of this word, which suggests little more than a mechanical shape. Or compare almost any of the "rich," "liberating" sexual verbs, so fashionable today among male writers, with that much-derided Latin word "copulate" ("to bind or join together") or even that Anglo-Saxon phrase (which seems to have had no trouble surviving the Norman Conquest) "make love."

How arrogantly self-involved the tabooed words seem in comparison to either of the other terms, and how contemptuous of the female partner. Understandably so, of course, if she is only a "skirt," a "broad," or a "chick," a "pussycat" or a "piece." If she is, in other words, no more than her skirt, or what her skirt conceals; no more than a breeder, or the broadest part of her; no more than a piece of a human being or a "piece of tail."

The most severely tabooed of all the female descriptives, incidentally, are those like a "piece of tail," which suggest (either explicitly or through antecedents) that there is no significant difference between the female channel through which we are all conceived and born and the anal outlet common to both sexes—a distinction that pornographers have always enjoyed obscuring.

10   This effort to deny women their biological identity, their individuality, their humanness, is such an important aspect of obscene language that one can only marvel at how seldom, in an era preoccupied with definitions of obscenity, this fact is brought to our attention. One problem, of course, is that many of the people in the best position to do this (critics, teachers, writers) are so reluctant today to admit that they are angered or shocked by obscenity. Bored, maybe, unimpressed, aesthetically displeased, but—no matter how brutal or denigrating the material—never angered, never shocked.

And yet how eloquently angered, how piously shocked many of these same people become if denigrating language is used about any minority group other than women; if the obscenities are racial or ethnic, that is, rather than sexual. Words like "coon," "kike," "spic," "wop," after all, deform identity, deny individuality and humanness in almost exactly the same way that sexual vulgarisms and obscenities do.

No one that I know, least of all my students, would fail to question the values of a society whose literature and entertainment rested heavily on racial or ethnic pejoratives. Are the values of a society whose literature and entertainment rest as heavily as ours on sexual pejoratives any less questionable?

✐ Topic for Critical Thinking or Writing

In addition to giving evidence to support her view, what persuasive devices (for example, irony, analogy) does Lawrence use?

📖 WILLIAM IAN MILLER

Darwin's Disgust

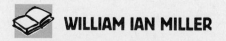

William Ian Miller is Professor of Law at the University of Michigan Law School. The selection that follows is from his recent book The Anatomy of Disgust *(1997), which examines disgust from psychological, social, and political perspectives. Miller's other*

works include Humiliation and Other Essays on Honor, Social Discomfort, and Violence *(1993), and* Law and Literature in Medieval Iceland *(1989).*

1   Modern psychological interest in disgust starts with Darwin, who centers it in the rejection of food and the sense of taste. Consider his account:

> The term "disgust," in its simplest sense, means something offensive to the taste. It is curious how readily this feeling is excited by anything unusual in the appearance, odour, or nature of our food. In Tierra del Fuego a native touched with his finger some cold preserved meat which I was eating at our bivouac, and plainly showed utter disgust at its softness; whilst I felt utter disgust at my food being touched by a naked savage, though his hands did not appear dirty. A smear of soup on a man's beard looks disgusting, though there is of course nothing disgusting in the soup itself. I presume that this follows from the strong association in our minds between the sight of food, however circumstanced, and the idea of eating it.[1]

Darwin is right about the etymology of disgust. It means unpleasant to the taste.[2] But one wonders whether taste would figure so crucially in Darwin's account if the etymology hadn't suggested it. The German *Ekel,* for instance, bears no easily discernible connection to taste. Did that make it easier for Freud to link disgust as readily with the anal and genital as with the oral zone?[3] I suspect that the English word is in some unquantifiable way responsible for the narrow focus on taste, oral incorporation, and rejection of food in psychological treatments of disgust.[4] Before the word disgust entered the English lexicon in the first quarter of the seventeenth century, taste figured distinctly less prominently than foul odors and loathsome sights. Disgust undoubtedly involves taste, but it also involves— not just by extension but at its core—smell, touch, even at times sight and hearing. Above all, it is a moral and social sentiment. It plays a motivating and confirming role in moral judgment in a particular way that has little if any connection with ideas of oral incorporation.[5] It ranks people and things in a kind of cosmic ordering.

2   I use the word to indicate a complex sentiment that can be lexically marked in English by expressions declaring things or actions to be repulsive, revolting, or giving rise to reactions described as revulsion and abhorrence as well as disgust.[6] Disgust names a syndrome in which all these terms have their proper role. They all convey a strong sense of aversion to something perceived as dangerous because of its powers to contaminate, infect, or pollute by proximity, contact, or ingestion. All suggest the appropriateness, but not the necessity, of accompanying nausea or queasiness, or of an urge to recoil and shudder from creepiness.

---

[1]*The Expression of the Emotions in Man and Animals* 256–257.

[2]Disgust comes to English via French via Latin: dis (a negative prefix) + gustus (taste).

[3]See Susan Miller, "Disgust: Conceptualization, Development and Dynamics," 295; see Freud, *Three Essays* II 177–178.

[4]See, among others, the works of Tomkins, Izard, and Rozin in the list of Works Cited.

[5]The moral aspects of disgust have only very recently been recognized in academic psychological literature. See Haidt, McCauley, and Rozin, "Individual Differences in Sensitivity to Disgust," and Haidt, Rozin, et al., "Body, Psyche, and Culture." In the Freudian account disgust is distinctly moral or at least does much the same work as morality; Freud makes reaction formations a trinity of disgust, shame, and morality; see *Three Essays* II 177–178.

3   Disgust, however, is not nausea. Not all disgust need produce symptoms of nausea, nor all nausea mark the presence of disgust. The nausea of the stomach flu is not a sign or consequence of disgust, although, should we vomit as a result, the vomiting and the vomit might themselves lead to sensations of disgust that would be distinguishable from the nausea that preceded it. The nausea of a hangover, however, is more complex, accompanied as it often is by feelings of contamination, poisoning, and self-disgust, as well as shame and embarrassment. On the other side, things or deeds we find disgusting put us in the world of disgust when we have the sense that we would not be surprised should we start feeling queasy or nauseated, whether or not we actually do so. Disgust surely has a feel to it; that feel, however, is not so much of nausea as of the uneasiness, the panic, of varying intensity, that attends the awareness of being defiled.

4   Let us put that aside for now and look more closely at the passage from Darwin. Is it food and taste that elicit disgust as a first-order matter?

> In Tierra del Fuego a native touched with his finger some cold preserved meat which I was eating at our bivouac, and plainly showed disgust at its softness; whilst I felt utter disgust at my food being touched by a naked savage, though his hands did not appear dirty.

In this passage, long before food ever reaches a mouth to raise the issue of its taste, we have suggestions of other categories that implicate disgust: categories of tactility as in cold (meat) vs. hot, soft vs. firm; overt categories of purity such as raw vs. cooked, dirty vs. clean; categories of bodily shame, naked vs. clothed; and broader categories of group definition, Tierra del Fuego vs. England, them vs. us. For the native, it is not ultimately the softness of the preserved meat so much as what eating it means about the person eating it. For Darwin, it is not just that someone touched his food (with clean hands no less), but that the person doing the touching was a *naked savage* who had already offended him. In the first clause the savage is merely a curious native in the two senses of curious: curious because strange and curious subjectively as a dispositional trait that makes him poke at Darwin's food. But once he finds Darwin's food disgusting, Darwin redescribes him downward as a naked savage capable of polluting his food. Before this interaction Darwin could look at the native with the contempt of bemusement or indifference or with a kind of benign contempt that often is itself a component of curiosity. The native, however, gets too close and gives real offense, and the inkling of threat is enough to transform a complacent contempt into disgust.

5   Would Darwin have been as disgusted by the native touching his food if the native had not insulted it by registering his revulsion? Or had the native already discerned Darwin's disgust for him and decided to use it to toy with him by touching his food? Would Darwin have been less disgusted if the native had touched him rather than his food? Food plays a role here, to be sure, and both actors share a deep belief that you pretty much are what you eat. The native recoils at the idea of what manner of man could eat such stuff, whereas Darwin fears ingesting some essence of savagery that has been magically imparted to his food by

---

[6]Wierzbicka argues for the distinctiveness of the notions of revulsion, repulsiveness, and disgust ("Human Emotions," 588–591). Disgust, she supposes, refers to ingestion of, revulsion to contact with, and repulsiveness to proximity to the offensive entity. She underestimates the generality and easy interchangeability of these concepts. Disgust melds notions of ingestion, contact, and proximity.

the finger of the naked savage. But oral ingestion is put in play here only because food is acting as one of a number of possible media by which pollution could be transferred. The issue is the doubts and fears each man's presence elicits in the other and the little battle for security and dominance by which they seek to resolve it; it is a battle of competing disgusts.

6   Less loaded with politics is the smear of soup on a man's beard, "though there is of course nothing disgusting in the soup itself." Again it is not food that is disgusting; Darwin's own explanation says it only becomes disgusting by the "strong association . . . between the sight of food . . . and the idea of eating it." But this can't be right. The sight of the man with his beard befouled is disgusting long before any idea of eating the soup on his beard ever would, if ever it could, occur to us. The association of ideas is not of seeing food in a beard and then imagining eating that food. If the soup is disgusting as food, it is so only because beard hair would be in it. Now that *is* disgusting. We could see this, in accordance with the structural theory of Mary Douglas, as a manifestation of things becoming polluting by being out of place.⁷ That captures some of the problem but doesn't explain the sense that it is more the hair than the soup, more the man than the food, that elicits disgust. The soup on the beard reveals the man as already contaminated by a character defect, a moral failure in keeping himself presentable in accordance with the righteously presented demand that he maintain his public purity and cleanliness of person and not endanger us by his incompetence. It needn't have been soup or bread crumbs that incriminated him; it could just as well have been bits of lint or even soap residue. No doubt, however, the soup would be more disgusting than either lint or soap. The soup, after all, unlike lint or soap, might have fallen onto his beard from his mouth or from a spoon that had already been in his mouth. It is thus not our fear of oral incorporation that makes the soup disgusting to us but his failure to have properly orally incorporated it.

7   Yet suppose that it was not a naked savage who touched Darwin's meat but a cockroach that walked across it. Would the issue then be one primarily of ingesting food? Even here I think the matter is more complex. A roach walking across our arm would elicit disgust too and perhaps even more than if it walked across our food, and we are not about to eat our arm. The roach (and the naked savage) is disgusting before it touches our food; its contaminating powers come from some other source.

✎ Topics for Critical Thinking and Writing

1. Miller quotes Darwin's definition of *disgust* at the beginning of the selection. To what end does he use that definition?
2. In the last sentence of the selection, Miller says that the "contaminating powers" of both the roach and the naked savage "come from some other source." According to Miller, what is that "other source"?
3. Miller distinguishes *disgust* from *nausea.* Look up *nausea* in the *Oxford English Dictionary,* and define the word in a brief essay of about 3–4 paragraphs. Give its etymology, distinguish it from a near synonym (perhaps *queasiness* or *revulsion*), and illustrate it with an example.

⁷*Purity and Danger.*

12

Persuading

There are several ways to persuade. A threat may persuade you to hand over money; an emotional appeal may also persuade you to hand over money. But in this chapter we are also concerned with persuading by means of *evidence* and *reasonable arguments*.

MAKING REASONABLE ARGUMENTS

Persuasive writing that, in addition to offering other evidence, relies chiefly on reasoning (rather than on appeals to the emotions) is usually called *argument*. An argument here is not a wrangle but a *reasoned analysis*. What distinguishes argument from explanation (for instance, the explanation of a process) is this: whereas both consist of statements, in argument some statements are offered as *reasons* for other statements. Another way of characterizing argument is that argument assumes there is or may be substantial disagreement between informed readers. To overcome this disagreement, the writer tries to offer reasons that convince by their validity. Here, for example, is C. S. Lewis arguing against vivisection (experimentation on live animals for scientific research):

> A rational discussion of this subject begins by inquiring whether pain is, or is not, an evil. If it is not, then the case against vivisection falls. But then so does the case for vivisection. If it is not defended on the ground that it reduces human suffering, on what ground can it be defended? And if pain is not an evil, why should human suffering be reduced? We must therefore assume as a basis for the whole discussion that pain is an evil, otherwise there is nothing to be discussed.
>
> Now if pain is an evil then the infliction of pain, considered in itself, must clearly be an evil act. But there are such things as necessary evils. Some acts which would be bad, simply in themselves, may be excusable and even laudable when they are necessary means to a greater good. In saying that the infliction of pain, simply in itself, is bad, we are not saying that pain ought never to be inflicted. Most of us think that it can rightly be inflicted for a good purpose—as in dentistry or just and reformatory punishment. The point is that it always requires justification. On the man whom we find inflicting pain rests the burden of showing why an act which in itself would be simply bad is, in those particular

circumstances, good. If we find a man giving pleasure it is for us to prove (if we criticize him) that his action is wrong. But if we find a man inflicting pain it is for him to prove that his action is right. If he cannot, he is a wicked man.

And here is Supreme Court Justice Louis Brandeis, concluding his justly famous argument that government may not use evidence illegally obtained by wiretapping:

Decency, security and liberty alike demand that government officials shall be subjected to the same rules of conduct that are commands to the citizen. In a government of laws, existence of the government will be imperiled if it fails to observe the law scrupulously. Our Government is the potent, the omnipresent teacher. For good or for ill, it teaches the whole people by its example. Crime is contagious. If the Government becomes a lawbreaker, it breeds contempt for law; it invites every man to become a law unto himself; it invites anarchy. To declare that in the administration of the criminal law the end justifies the means—to declare that the Government may commit crimes in order to secure the conviction of a private criminal—would bring terrible retribution. Against that pernicious doctrine this Court should resolutely set its face.

Notice here that Brandeis's reasoning is highlighted by his forceful style. Note the resonant use of parallel constructions ("Decency, security and liberty," "For good or for ill," "it breeds . . . it invites," "To declare . . . to declare") and the variation between long and short sentences. Note too the wit in his comparisons: government is a teacher, crime is like a disease.

MAKING REASONABLE CLAIMS

You have only a little time—perhaps a few days, and even for a term paper at most a few weeks—to think about and to support your claim. You probably cannot come up with a comprehensive health-care program within that time, and you may not even be able to evaluate the evidence on whether our planet has or has not been undergoing a greenhouse effect, or whether or not elephants are so endangered that a ban on the sale of ivory is needed in order to preserve the species.

On the other hand, maybe you can. You may encounter a good collection of essays, pro and con, on a topic, and you will find that in the course of a day's reading you can become quite an expert. For instance, you may find, after reading a couple of dozen essays on abortion (or gun control, or the death penalty) that a few arguments on each side keep recurring, and you may rightly feel that you are in a position to offer your own point of view—that is, you may be in a position to make a reasonable and perhaps a novel claim.

Finally, we want to mention that what may at first seem to be an unreasonable claim may, after some reflection, become reasonable. Not much more than a century ago it seemed unreasonable to many intelligent people to argue that slavery was immoral. Issues such as those regarding women as priests, women in the armed forces going into combat, gays in the military, and animal experimentation are still matters on which you can take a stand that your opponents regard as utterly unreasonable. It happens that on the day we are writing these pages, the newspaper includes an account of Andrew Martinez, "The Naked Guy," a junior at the University of California, Berkeley, who strolls the campus naked except for his peace-sign, shoes and socks (and on cool days a sweatshirt), eats naked in the dining hall, and attends class naked. Campus police arrested The Naked Guy, but the state of California refused to prosecute him because nudity without "lewd behavior" is not illegal. The university then passed a ban on campus nudity, addressed specifically at Martinez, and suspended him. He hopes to take the matter to the courts. The university's arguments include the charge that his behavior constitutes sexual harassment of women and creates intolerable conditions for students in the "workplace." On the other hand, Martinez says that clothing is part of a middle-class, body-hating, repressive, consumerist society. Can one make a reasonable case for nudism? Can one make a reasonable case against nudism?

Claims of Fact

We can usually distinguish between two kinds of claims, claims of fact and claims of value, and we can sometimes distinguish these from a third kind of claim, claims of policy. *Claims of fact* assert that something is or was or will be. They include, for instance, arguments about cause and effect, correlation, probability, and states of affairs. The following examples can be considered claims of fact:

> Vanilla is the most popular flavor of ice cream in the United States.
>
> Pornography stimulates violence against women.
>
> Pornography has the potential of leading to violence.
>
> Capital punishment reduces crime.
>
> Capital punishment does not reduce crime.
>
> Racial integration of the armed forces was achieved with very little conflict during the Korean War.

To support a claim of this sort, you must provide (probably after defining any terms that may be in doubt) information. Such information might, for instance, be testimony (for instance, your own experience, or statements by men who have said that pornography stimulated them to violence), or it might be statistics (gathered from a report in a scholarly journal). Even if the claim has to do with the future—let's say the claim that gun control will not reduce crime—you try to offer information. For example, you might gather information about the experiences of other countries, or even of certain states, that have adopted strict regulations concerning the sale of guns.

Claims of Value

Claims of value concern what is right or wrong, good or bad, better or worse than something else:

> Country music deserves to be taken seriously.
>
> Rock is better than country music.
>
> Capital punishment is barbaric.
>
> Euthanasia is immoral.

Some claims of value may be mere expressions of taste: "Vanilla is better than chocolate." It is hard to imagine how one could go about supporting such a claim—or refuting it. One probably can do no better than reply with the Latin proverb, "De gustibus non est disputandum." (There is no disputing about tastes.) Notice, however, that the claim that vanilla is better than chocolate is quite different from the claim that most Americans prefer vanilla to chocolate. The last statement is a claim of fact, not of value, and it can be proved or disproved with information—for example, with information provided by the makers of ice cream.

Claims of value that go beyond the mere expression of taste—for instance, claims of morality or claims of artistic value—are usually supported by appeals to standards ("Such-and-such a proposal is bad *because* governments should not restrict the rights of individuals," or "Such-and-such music is good *because* it is complex"—or because it is popular or because it is sincere or whatever). In supporting claims of value, writers usually appeal to standards that they believe are acceptable to their readers. Examples:

> Sex-education programs in schools are inappropriate *because* aspects of moral education should properly be given only by parents.

> Sex-education programs in schools are appropriate *because* society has a duty to provide what most parents obviously are reluctant to provide.

> Doctors should be permitted to end a patient's life if the patient makes such a request, *because* each of us should be free to make the decisions that most concern us.

> Euthanasia is unacceptable *because* only God can give or take life.

In arguing a claim of value, be sure you have clearly in your mind the standards that you believe support the claim. You may find it appropriate to explain *why* you hold these standards, and *how* adherence to these standards will be of benefit.

Claims of Policy

Claims of policy assert that a policy, law, or custom should be initiated or altered or dropped. Such claims usually are characterized by words like "should," "must," and "ought."

> Children should be allowed to vote, if they wish to.

> A course in minority cultures ought to be required.

> The federal tax on gasoline must be raised.

In defending an unfamiliar claim of policy, you may want to begin by pointing out that there is a problem that is usually overlooked. For instance, if you urgently believe that children should have the right to vote—a view almost never expressed—you'll probably first have to convince your audience that there really is an arguable issue here, an issue concerning children's rights, an issue that deserves serious thought.

In defending a claim of policy you will probably find yourself providing information, just as you would do in support of a claim of fact. For instance, if your topic is children and the vote, you might point out that until 1920 women could not vote in the United States, the usual arguments being that they were mentally unfit and that they would vote the way their men told them to vote. Experience has proven that these low estimates of the capabilities of the disenfranchised were absurd.

But in defending a claim of policy you will probably have to consider values as well as facts. Thus, in arguing for an increase in the gasoline tax, you might want not only to provide factual information about how much money a five-cents-per-gallon tax would raise, but also to argue that such an increase is *fairer* than an alternative such as reducing social security benefits.

THREE KINDS OF EVIDENCE: EXAMPLES, TESTIMONY, STATISTICS

Writers of arguments seek to persuade by offering evidence. There are three chief forms of evidence used in argument:

- Examples
- Testimony, the citation of authorities
- Statistics

We'll briefly consider each of these.

Examples

"Example" is from the Latin *exemplum,* which means "something taken out." An example is the sort of thing, taken from among many similar things, that one selects and holds up for view, perhaps after saying "For example," or "For instance."

Three categories of examples are especially common in written arguments:

- Real examples
- Invented instances
- Analogies

Real examples are just what they sound like, instances that have occurred. If, for example, we are arguing that gun control won't work, we point to those states that have adopted gun control laws and that nevertheless have had no reduction in crimes using guns. Or, if we want to support the assertion that a woman can be a capable head of state, we may find ourselves pointing to women who actually served as heads of state, such as Golda Meir and Indira Ghandi (prime ministers of Israel and India) and to Margaret Thatcher (prime minister of England).

The advantage of using real example is, clearly, that they are real. Of course an opponent might stubbornly respond that Golda Meir, Indira Gandhi, and Margaret Thatcher for some reason or other could not function as the head of state in *our* country. Someone might argue, for instance, that the case of Golda Meir proves nothing, since the role of women in Israeli society is different from the role of women in the United States (a country in which a majority of the citizens are Christians). And another person might argue that much of Mrs. Gandhi's power came from the fact that she was the daughter of Nehru, an immensely popular Indian statesman. Even the most compelling real example inevitably will in some ways be special or particular, and in the eyes of some readers may not seem to be a fair example.

Consider, for instance, a student who is arguing that peer review should be part of the writing course. The student points out that he or she found it of great help in high school. An opponent argues that things in college are different—college students should be able to help themselves, even highly gifted college students are not competent to offer college-level instruction, and so on. Still, as the feebleness of these objections (and the objections against Meir and Gandhi indicate), real examples can be very compelling.

Invented instances are exempt from the charge that, because of some detail or other, they are not relevant as evidence. Suppose, for example, you are arguing against capital punishment, on the grounds that if an innocent person is executed, there is no way of even attempting to rectify the injustice. If you point to the case of *X,* you may be met with the reply that *X* was not in fact innocent. Rather than get tangled up in the guilt or innocence of a particular person, it may be better to argue that we can suppose—we can imagine—an innocent person convicted and executed, and we can imagine that evidence later proves the person's innocence.

Invented instances have the advantage of presenting an issue clearly, free from all of the distracting particularities (and irrelevancies) that are bound up with any real instance. But invented instances have the disadvantage of being invented, and they may seem remote from the real issues being argued.

Analogies are comparisons pointing out several resemblances between two rather different things. For instance, one might assert that a government is like a ship, and in times of stress—if the ship is to weather the storm—the authority of the captain must not be questioned.

But don't confuse an analogy with proof. An analogy is an extended comparison between two things: it can be useful in exposition, for it explains the unfamiliar by means of the familiar: "A government is like a ship, and just as a ship has a captain and a crew, so a government has . . ."; "Writing an essay is like building a house; just as an architect must begin with a plan, so the writer must . . ." Such comparisons can be useful, helping to clarify what otherwise might be obscure, but their usefulness goes only so far. Everything is what it is, and not another thing. A government is not a ship, and what is true of a captain's power need not be true of a president's power; and a writer is not an architect. Some of what is true about ships may be roughly true of governments, and some of what is true about architects may be (again, roughly) true of writers, but there are differences too. Consider the following analogy between a lighthouse and the death penalty:

> The death penalty is a warning, just like a lighthouse throwing its beams out to sea. We hear about shipwrecks, but we do not hear about the ships the lighthouse guides safely on their way. We do not have proof of the number of ships it saves, but we do not tear the lighthouse down.
>
> —J. Edgar Hoover

How convincing is Hoover's analogy as an argument, that is, as a reason for retaining the death penalty?

Testimony

Testimony, or the citation of authorities, is rooted in our awareness that some people are recognized as experts. In our daily lives we constantly turn to experts for guidance: we look up the spelling of a word in the dictionary, we listen to weather forecasts on the radio, we take an ailing cat to the vet for a checkup. Similarly, when we wish to become informed about controversial matters, we often turn to experts, first to help educate ourselves, and then to help convince others.

Don't forget that *you* are an authority on many things. For example, today's newspaper includes an article about the cutback in funding for the teaching of the arts in elementary and secondary schools. Art educators are responding that the arts are not a frill, and that in fact the arts provide the analytical thinking, teamwork, motivation, and self-discipline that most people agree are needed to reinvigorate American schools. If you have been involved in the arts in school—for instance, if you studied painting or learned to play a musical instrument—you are in a position to evaluate these claims. Similarly, if you have studied in a bilingual educational program, your own testimony will be invaluable.

There are at least two reasons for offering testimony in an argument. The obvious one is that expert opinion does (and should) carry some weight with any audience; the less obvious one is that a change of voice (if the testimony is not your own) in an essay may afford the reader a bit of pleasure. No matter how engaging your own voice may be, a fresh voice—whether that of Thomas Jefferson, Albert Einstein, or Barbara Jordan—may provide a refreshing change of tone.

But, of course, there are dangers: the chief one is that the words of authorities may be taken out of context or otherwise distorted, and the second is that the authorities may not be authorities on the present topic. Quite rightly we are concerned with what Jefferson said, but it is not entirely clear that his words can be fairly applied, on one side or the other, to such an issue as abortion. Quite rightly we are concerned with what Einstein said, but it is not entirely clear that his eminence as a physicist constitutes him an authority on, say, world peace. In a moment, when we discuss errors in reasoning, we'll have more to say about the proper and improper use of authorities.

Statistics

Statistics, another important form of evidence, are especially useful in arguments concerning social issues. If we want to argue for (or against) raising the driving age, we will probably do some research in the library, and will offer statistics about the number of accidents caused by people in certain age groups.

But a word of caution: The significance of statistics may be difficult to assess. For instance, opponents of gun control legislation have pointed out, in support of the argument that such laws are ineffectual, that homicides in Florida *increased* after Florida adopted gun control laws. Supporters of gun control laws cried "Foul," arguing that in the years after adopting these laws Miami became (for reasons having nothing to do with the laws) the cocaine capital of the United States, and the rise in homicide was chiefly a reflection of murders involved in the drug trade. That is, a significant change in the population has made a comparison of the figures meaningless. This objection seems plausible, and probably the statistics therefore should carry little weight.

HOW MUCH EVIDENCE IS ENOUGH?

If you allow yourself ample time to write your essay, you probably will turn up plenty of evidence to illustrate your arguments, such as examples drawn from your own experience and imagination, from your reading, and from your talks with others. Examples will not only help to clarify and to support your assertions, but they will also provide a concreteness that will be welcome in a paper that might be on the whole fairly abstract. Your sense of your audience will have to guide you in making your selection of examples. Generally speaking, a single example may not fully illuminate a difficult point, and so a second example, a clincher, may be desirable. If you offer a third or fourth example you probably are succumbing to a temptation to include something that tickles your fancy. If it is as good as you think it is, the reader probably will accept the unnecessary example and may even be grateful. But before you heap up examples, try to imagine yourself in your reader's place, and ask if the example is needed. If it is not needed, ask yourself if the reader will be glad to receive the overload.

One other point. On most questions, say on the value of bilingual education or on the need for rehabilitation programs in prisons, it's not possible to make a strictly logical case, in the sense of an absolutely airtight proof. Don't assume that it is your job to make an absolute proof. What you are expected to do is to offer a reasonable argument. Virginia Woolf put it this way: "When a subject is highly controversial . . . one cannot hope to tell the truth. One can only show how one came to hold whatever opinion one does hold."

AVOIDING FALLACIES

Let's further examine writing reasonable arguments by considering some obvious errors in reasoning. In logic these errors are called *fallacies* (from a Latin verb meaning "to deceive"). As Tweedledee says in *Through the Looking-Glass,* "If it were so, it would be; but as it isn't, it ain't. That's logic."

To persuade readers to accept your opinions you must persuade them that you are reliable; if your argument includes fallacies, thoughtful readers will not take you seriously. More important, if your argument includes fallacies, you are misleading yourself. When you search your draft for fallacies, you are searching for ways to improve the quality of your thinking.

1. **False authority.** Don't try to borrow the prestige of authorities who are not authorities on the topic in question—for example, a heart surgeon speaking on politics. Similarly, some former authorities are no longer authorities, because the problems have changed or because later knowledge has superseded their views. Adam Smith, Jefferson, Eleanor Roosevelt, and Einstein remain persons of genius, but an attempt to use their opinions when you are examining modern issues—even in their fields—may be questioned. Remember the last words of John B. Sedgwick, a Union Army general at the Battle of Spotsylvania in 1864: "They couldn't hit an elephant at this dist—." In short, before you rely on an authority, ask yourself if the person in question *is* an authority on the topic. And don't let stereotypes influence your idea of who is an authority. Remember the Yiddish proverb: "A goat has a beard, but that doesn't make him a rabbi."

2. **False quotation.** If you do quote from an authority, don't misquote. For example, you may find someone who grants that "there are strong arguments in favor of abolishing the death penalty"; but if she goes on to argue that, on balance, the arguments in favor of retaining it seem stronger to her, it is dishonest to quote her words so as to imply that she favors abolishing it.

3. Suppression of evidence. Don't neglect evidence that is contrary to your own argument. You owe it to yourself and your reader to present all the relevant evidence. Be especially careful not to assume that every question is simply a matter of *either/or*. There may be some truth on both sides. Take the following thesis: "Grades encourage unwholesome competition, and should therefore be abolished." Even if the statement about the evil effect of grading is true, it may not be the whole truth, and therefore it may not follow that grades should be abolished. One might point out that grades do other things too: they may stimulate learning, and they may assist students by telling them how far they have progressed. One might nevertheless conclude, on balance, that the fault outweighs the benefits. But the argument will be more persuasive now that the benefits of grades have been considered.

Concede to the opposition what is due it, and then outscore the opposition. Failure to confront the opposing evidence will be noticed; your readers will keep wondering why you do not consider this point or that, and may consequently dismiss your argument. However, if you confront the opposition you will almost surely strengthen your own argument. As Edmund Burke said 200 years ago, "He that wrestles with us strengthens our nerves, and sharpens our skill. Our antagonist is our helper."

4. Generalization from insufficient evidence. In rereading a draft of an argument that you have written, try to spot your own generalizations. Ask yourself if a reasonable reader is likely to agree that the generalization is based on an adequate sample.

A visitor to a college may sit in on three classes, each taught by a different instructor, and may find all three stimulating. That's a good sign, but can we generalize and say that the teaching at this college is excellent? Are three classes a sufficient sample? If all three are offered by the Biology Department, and if the Biology Department includes only five instructors, perhaps we can tentatively say that the teaching of biology at this institution is good. If the Biology Department contains twenty instructors, perhaps we can still say, though more tentatively, that this sample indicates that the teaching of biology is good. But what does the sample say about the teaching of other subjects at the college? It probably does say something—the institution may be much concerned with teaching across the board—but then again it may not say a great deal, since the Biology Department may be exceptionally concerned with good teaching.

5. The genetic fallacy. Don't assume that something can necessarily be explained in terms of its birth or origin. "He wrote the novel to make money, so it can't be any good" is not a valid inference. The value of a novel does not depend on the author's motivations in writing it. Indeed, the value or worth of a novel needs to be established by reference to other criteria. Neither the highest nor the lowest motivations guarantee the quality of the product. Another example: "Capital punishment arose in days when men sought revenge, so now it ought to be abolished." Again an unconvincing argument: capital punishment may have some current value; for example, it may serve as a deterrent to crime. But that's another argument, and it needs evidence if it is to be believed. Be on guard, too, against the thoughtless tendency to judge people by their origins: Mr. X has a foreign accent, so he is probably untrustworthy or stupid or industrious.

6. Begging the question and circular reasoning. Don't assume the truth of the point that you should prove. The term "begging the question" is a trifle odd. It means, in effect, "You, like a beggar, are asking me to grant you something at the outset."

"Look, maybe you're right, but for the sake of argument let's assume you're wrong and drop it."

Drawing by Mankoff; © 1983 The New Yorker Magazine, Inc.

Examples: "The barbaric death penalty should be abolished"; "This senseless language requirement should be dropped." Both of these statements assume what they should prove—that the death penalty is barbaric, and that the language requirement is senseless. You can of course make assertions such as these, but you must go on to prove them.

Circular reasoning is usually an extended form of begging the question. What ought to be proved is covertly assumed. Example: "*X* is the best-qualified candidate for the office, because the most informed people say so." Who are the most informed people? Those who recognize *X's* superiority. Circular reasoning, then, normally includes intermediate steps absent from begging the question, but the two fallacies are so closely related that they can be considered one. Another example: "I feel sympathy for her because I identify with her." Despite the "because," no reason is really offered. What follows "because" is merely a restatement, in slightly different words, of what precedes; the shift of words, from "feel sympathy" to "identify with" has misled the writer into thinking she is giving a reason. Other examples: "Students are interested in courses when the subject matter and the method of presentation are interesting"; "There cannot be peace in the Middle East because the Jews and the Arabs will always fight." In each case, an assertion that ought to be proved is reasserted as a reason in support of the assertion.

7. *Post hoc ergo propter hoc* (Latin for "after this, therefore because of this"). Don't assume that because *X* precedes *Y*, *X* must cause *Y*. For example: "He went to college and came back a boozer; college corrupted him." He might have taken up liquor even if he had not gone to college. Another example: "When a fifty-five-mile-per-hour limit was imposed in 1974, after the Arab embargo on oil, the number of auto fatalities decreased sharply, from 55,000 deaths

in 1973 to 46,000 in 1974, so it is evident that a fifty-five-mile-per-hour limit—still adhered to in some states—saves lives." Not quite. Because gasoline was expensive after the embargo, the number of miles traveled decreased. The number of fatalities *per mile* remained constant. The price of gas, not the speed limit, seems responsible for the decreased number of fatalities. Moreover, the national death rate has continued to fall. Why? Several factors are at work: seat-belt and child-restraint laws, campaigns against drunk driving, improved auto design, and improved roads. Medicine, too, may have improved so that today doctors can save accident victims who in 1974 would have died. In short, it probably is impossible to isolate the correlation between speed and safety.

8. ***Argumentum ad hominem*** (Latin for "argument toward the man"). Here the argument is directed toward the person rather than toward the issue. Don't shift from your topic to your opponent. A speaker argues against legalizing abortions and her opponent, instead of facing the merits of the argument, attacks the character or the associations of the opponent: "You're a Catholic, aren't you?"

9. False assumption. Consider the Scot who argued that Shakespeare must have been a Scot. Asked for his evidence, he replied, "The ability of the man warrants the assumption." Or take a statement such as "She goes to Yale, so she must be rich." Possibly the statement is based on faulty induction (the writer knows four Yale students, and all four are rich) but more likely he is just passing on a cliché. The Yale student in question may be on a scholarship, may be struggling to earn the money, or may be backed by parents of modest means who for eighteen years have saved money for her college education. Other examples: "I haven't heard him complain about French 10, so he must be satisfied"; "She's a writer, so she must be well read." A little thought will show how weak such assertions are; they *may* be true, but they may not.

The errors we have discussed are common. In revising, try to spot them and eliminate or correct them. You have a point to make, and you should make it fairly. If it can be made only unfairly, you do an injustice not only to your reader but also to yourself; you should try to change your view of the topic. You don't want to be like the politician whose speech had a marginal note: "Argument weak; shout here."

WIT

In addition to using sound argument and other evidence, writers often use wit, especially irony, to persuade. In irony, the words convey a meaning somewhat different from what they explicitly say. Wry understatement is typical. Here, for instance, is Thoreau explaining why in *Walden*, his book about his two years in relative isolation at Walden Pond, he will talk chiefly about himself:

> In most books, the *I*, or first person, is omitted; in this it will be retained; that, in respect to egotism, is the main difference. We commonly do not remember that it is, after all, always the first person that is speaking. I should not talk so much about myself if there were anybody else whom I knew as well. Unfortunately, I am confined to this theme by the narrowness of my experience.

"Please forgive Edgar. He has no verbal skills."

Notice the wry apology in his justification for talking about himself: he does not know anyone else as well as he knows himself. Similarly, in "unfortunately" ("Unfortunately, I am confined to this theme by the narrowness of my experience") we again hear a wry voice. After all, Thoreau knows, as we know, that *no one* has experience so deep or broad that he or she knows others better than himself or herself. Thoreau's presentation of himself as someone who happens not to have had the luck of knowing others better than himself is engagingly clever.

Avoiding Sarcasm

Because writers must, among other things, persuade readers that they are humane, sarcasm has little place in persuasive writing. Although desk dictionaries usually define sarcasm as "bitter, caustic irony" or "a kind of satiric wit," if you think of a sarcastic comment that you have heard you will probably agree that "a crude, sneering remark" is a better definition. Lacking the wit of good satire and the carefully controlled mockery of irony, sarcasm usually relies on gross overstatement and intends simply to humiliate. *Sarcasm* is derived from a Greek word meaning "to tear flesh" or "to bite the lips in rage," altogether an unattractive business. Sarcasm is unfair, for it dismisses an opponent's arguments with ridicule rather than with reason; it is also unwise, for it turns the reader against you. Readers hesitate to ally themselves with a writer who apparently enjoys humiliating the opposition. A sarcastic remark can turn the hearers against the speaker and arouse sympathy for the victim. In short, sarcasm usually doesn't work.

ORGANIZING AN ARGUMENT

As we have said earlier, writers find out what they think partly by means of the act of putting words on paper. But in presenting arguments for their readers, writers rarely duplicate their own acts of discovery. To put it another way, the process of setting forth ideas, and supporting them, does not follow the productive but untidy, repetitive, often haphazard process of preliminary thinking. For instance, a point that did not strike us until the middle of the third draft may, in the final version, appear in the opening paragraph. Or an example that seemed useful early in our thinking may, in the process of revision, be omitted in favor of a stronger example. Through a series of revisions, large and small, we try to work out the best strategy for persuading our readers to accept our reasoning as sound, our conclusion as valid. Unfortunately, we find, an argument cannot be presented either as it occurs to us or all at once.

Nor is there a simple formula that governs the organization of all effective argumentative essays. An essay may begin by announcing its thesis and then set forth the reasons that support the thesis. Or it may begin more casually, calling attention to specific cases, and then generalize from these cases. Probably it will then go on to reveal an underlying unity that brings the thesis into view, and from here it will offer detailed reasoning that supports the thesis.

As the writer of a persuasive essay, you almost always have to handle, in some sequence or other, the following matters:

- The background (for instance, the need to consider the issue)
- The thesis (claim)
- The evidence that supports the thesis
- The counterevidence
- The response to counterclaims and counterevidence (either a refutation or a concession that there *is* merit to the counterclaims but not as much as to the writer's thesis)
- Some sort of reaffirmation, perhaps that the topic needs attention or that the thesis advanced is the most plausible or the most workable or the most moral, or that the ball is now in the reader's court

Three methods of organizing arguments are fairly common, and one or another may suit an essay you're working on.

1. Begin with the background, then set forth the thesis statement and work from the simplest argument up to the most complex. Such an arrangement will keep your reader with you, step by step.

2. After setting forth the background and your thesis, arrange the arguments in order of increasing strength. The danger in following this plan is that you may lose the reader from the start, because you begin with a weak argument. Avoid this problem by telling your reader that indeed the first argument is relatively weak (if it is terribly weak, it isn't an argument at all, so scrap it), but that you offer it for the sake of completeness or because it is often given, and that you will soon give the reader far stronger arguments. Face the opposition to this initial argument, grant that opposition as much as it deserves, and salvage what is left of the argument. Then proceed to the increasingly strong arguments, devoting at least one paragraph to each. Introduce each argument with an appropriate transition ("another reason," "even more important," "most convincing of all"). State it briefly, summarize the opposing view, and then demolish this opposition. With this organization, your discussion of each of your own arguments ends affirmatively.

3. After sketching the background and stating your thesis in an introductory paragraph, mass all of the opposing arguments, and then respond to them one by one.

In short, when you (1) think you have done your initial thinking and your rethinking, (2) have, if appropriate, consulted some published sources, (3) have talked with friends and perhaps with experts, and (4) have moved from random notes and lists to fairly full drafts, you are not quite done.

You still must check what you hope is your last draft to see if you have found the best possible order for the arguments, have given effective examples, and have furnished transitions. In short, you must check to see that you have produced an argument that will strike a reasonable reader as courteous, clear, and concrete.

✔ A Checklist for Revising Drafts of Persuasive Essays

✔ Are the terms clearly defined?
✔ Is the thesis stated promptly and clearly?
✔ Are the assumptions likely to be shared by your readers? If not, are they reasonably argued rather than merely stated?
✔ Are the facts verifiable? Is the evidence reliable? (No out-of-date statistics, no generalizations from insufficient evidence?)
✔ Is the reasoning sound?
✔ Are the authorities really authorities on this matter?
✔ Are all of the substantial counterarguments recognized and effectively responded to?
✔ Does the essay make use, where appropriate, of concrete examples?
✔ Is the organization effective? Does the essay begin interestingly, keep the thesis in view, and end interestingly?
✔ Is the tone appropriate? (Avoid sarcasm. Present yourself as fair-minded, and assume that those who hold a view opposed to yours are also fair-minded.)

Topics for Critical Thinking and Writing

1. Analyze and evaluate each of the following arguments. If any of the arguments contain fallacies, name the fallacies.
   a. To the Editor:

   The recent senseless murder of a 15-year-old seminary student again emphasizes the insanity of our gun laws. No matter how guilty the 13-year-old boy who shot into the head of the victim, it seems that our congressional leaders are even more guilty by not enacting stricter gun-control laws. They are supposedly sane, rational individuals; and the kindest thing that can be said about them is that they are merely motivated by greed.

   b. To the Editor:

   Your editorial last Wednesday arguing against censorship as an infringement on freedom is full of clever arguments but it overlooks an obvious fact. We have Pure Food and Drug laws to protect us against poison, and no one believes that such laws interfere with the freedom of those who produce food and drugs. The public is entitled, then, to laws that will similarly protect us from the poison that some movie-makers produce.

c. To the Editor:

On Dec. 5 *The Times* published a story saying that colleges have come under pressure to improve the "quality of their teaching." Unfortunately, nobody knows what good teaching is, let alone how to evaluate it.

Unlike scholarship, which has a visible product, namely published reports, the results of teaching are locked in the heads of students and are usually not apparent, even to the students themselves, for a very long period.

One device which is frequently used is a poll of students, the so-called "student evaluation of teachers." This type of measurement has been studied by Rodin and Rodin, who correlated it with how much the students learned, as demonstrated on tests. The correlation was highly negative (−.75). As the Rodins put it, "Students rate most highly instructors from whom they learn least."

What invariably happens is that attempts to reward "good teaching" turn out to reward good public relations.

d. The following paragraph was written by Walter Lippmann shortly after the United States entered World War II:

The Pacific Coast is in imminent danger of a combined attack from within and from without. . . . It is [true] . . . that since the outbreak of the Japanese war there has been no important sabotage on the Pacific Coast. From what we know about the fifth column in Europe, this is not, as some have liked to think, a sign that there is nothing to be feared. It is a sign that the blow is well-organized and that it is held back until it can be struck with maximum effect. . . . I am sure I understand fully and appreciate thoroughly the unwillingness of Washington to adopt a policy of mass evacuation and internment of all those who are technically enemy aliens. But I submit that Washington is not defining the problem on the coast correctly. . . . The Pacific Coast is officially a combat zone: some part of it may at any moment be a battlefield. Nobody's constitutional rights include the right to reside and do business on a battlefield. And nobody ought to be on a battlefield who has no good reason for being there.

2. In July 1984 President Reagan signed a bill that exerted pressure on the states to enact legislation setting the drinking age at twenty-one. The bill allows the government to withhold 5 percent of federal highway construction funds from states that do not set the drinking age at twenty-one by October 1986. If the age is not set at twenty-one by October 1987, 10 percent of the funds can be withheld.

Read the following letter to a newspaper, written in 1986, and then list and evaluate the persuasive devices that it uses.

To the Editor:

Congress and the President are bullying the states into raising the drinking age.

The law is discriminatory because it withholds a right from certain people merely because of their age.

The law is unreasonable, because it seems to say that people who are old enough to vote and to fight for their country are not old enough to drink alcohol.

The law is illogical, because it takes as proof of its value that fact that those states that already have raised the drinking age to twenty-one have had a reduction in the number of nighttime driving accidents by persons under twenty-one. Of course they have—and if the age were raised to thirty-five there would be a similar reduction in the number of driving accidents by persons under thirty-five. Why not set the age at fifty? Or at sixty-five? Or a hundred?

In any case, the statistics prove nothing. The lower percent of accidents may be due to other factors, such as heightened public awareness, or stricter enforcement of speeding laws.

The real problem is not that people between eighteen and twenty-one drink, but that they do not receive adequate driver education—an education that would of course emphasize that one must never drive while intoxicated. Further, the police do not strictly enforce laws against speeding, and thus they in effect contribute to the accident rate.

Yours,
Stephen Ohmann

3. A writer arguing against gun control made the following three points:

More criminals are shot by private citizens each year than by the police. There are twice as many people killed by drunken drivers each year as by handguns (and ten times as many severely injured).

In about half of the handgun murders the people know each other—so they would probably use other weapons if guns were not available.

Trying to put aside your own views about the possession of handguns, make explicit the assumptions that lie beneath the three statements, and then evaluate each of the statements as an argument against outlawing handguns.

4. Read the following passage, from George Will's *The Morning After:*

When a society becomes, like ours, uneasy about calling prisons penitentiaries or penal institutions, and instead calls them "correctional institutions," the society has lost its bearings. If prisoners are "corrected," that is nice but it is an ancillary outcome. The point of imprisonment is punishment. The idea of punishment is unintelligible if severed from the idea of retribution, which is inseparable from the concept of vengeance, which is an expression of anger. No anger, no justice.

Evaluate this selection as a piece of persuasive writing with attention to the aspects of good—or faulty—argumentation reviewed in this chapter.

PERSUASION AT WORK

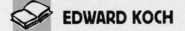 **EDWARD KOCH**

Death and Justice: How Capital Punishment Affirms Life

Edward Koch, born in New York City, was mayor of New York from 1978 to 1989. This essay first appeared in The New Republic.

Last December a man named Robert Lee Willie, who had been convicted of raping and murdering an 18-year-old woman, was executed in the Louisiana state prison. In a statement issued several minutes before his death, Mr. Willie said: "Killing people is wrong. . . . It makes no difference whether it's citizens, countries, or governments. Killing is wrong." Two weeks later in South Carolina, an admitted killer named Joseph Carl Shaw was put to death for murdering two teenagers. In an appeal to the governor for clemency, Mr. Shaw wrote: "Killing is wrong when I did it. Killing is wrong when you do it. I hope you have the courage and moral strength to stop the killing."

It is a curiosity of modern life that we find ourselves being lectured on morality by cold-blooded killers. Mr. Willie previously had been convicted of aggravated rape, aggravated kidnapping, and the murders of a Louisiana deputy and a man from Missouri. Mr. Shaw committed another murder a week before the two for which he was executed, and admitted mutilating the body of the 14-year-old girl he killed. I can't help wondering what prompted these murderers to speak out against killing as they entered the death-house door. Did their newfound reverence for life stem from the realization that they were about to lose their own?

Life is indeed precious, and I believe the death penalty helps to affirm this fact. Had the death penalty been a real possibility in the minds of these murderers, they might well have stayed their hand. They might have shown moral awareness before their victims died, and not after. Consider the tragic death of Rosa Velez, who happened to be home when a man named Luis Vera burglarized her apartment in Brooklyn. "Yeah, I shot her," Vera admitted. "She knew me, and I knew I wouldn't go to the chair."

During my twenty-two years in public service, I have heard the pros and cons of capital punishment expressed with special intensity. As a district leader, councilman, congressman, and mayor, I have represented constituencies generally thought of as liberal. Because I support the death penalty for heinous crimes of murder, I have sometimes been the subject of emotional and outraged attacks by voters who find my position reprehensible or worse. I have listened to their ideas. I have weighed their objections carefully. I still support the death penalty.

The reasons I maintain my position can be best understood by examining the arguments most frequently heard in opposition.

5   1. *The death penalty is "barbaric."* Sometimes opponents of capital punishment horrify with tales of lingering death on the gallows, of faulty electric chairs, or of agony in the gas chamber. Partly in response to such protests, several states such as North Carolina and Texas switched to execution by lethal injection. The condemned person is put to death painlessly, without ropes, voltage, bullets, or gas. Did this answer the objections of death penalty opponents? Of course not. On June 22, 1984, *The New York Times* published an editorial that sarcastically attacked the new "hygienic" method of death by injection, and stated that "execution can never be made humane through science." So it's not the method that really troubles opponents. It's the death itself they consider barbaric.

Admittedly, capital punishment is not a pleasant topic. However, one does not have to like the death penalty in order to support it any more than one must like radical surgery, radiation, or chemotherapy in order to find necessary these attempts at curing cancer. Ultimately we may learn how to cure cancer with a simple pill. Unfortunately, that day has not yet arrived. Today we are faced with the choice of letting the cancer spread or trying to cure it with the methods available, methods that one day will almost certainly be considered barbaric. But to give up and do nothing would be far more barbaric and would certainly delay the discovery of an eventual cure. The analogy between cancer and murder is imperfect, because murder is not the "disease" we are trying to cure. The disease is injustice. We may not like the death penalty, but it must be available to punish crimes of cold-blooded murder, cases in which any other form of punishment would be inadequate and, therefore, unjust. If we create a society in which injustice is not tolerated, incidents of murder—the most flagrant form of injustice—will diminish.

2. *No other major democracy uses the death penalty.* No other major democracy—in fact, few other countries of any description—are plagued by a murder rate such as that in the United States. Fewer and fewer Americans can remember the days when unlocked doors were the norm and murder was a rare and terrible offense. In America the murder rate climbed 122 percent between 1963 and 1980. During that same period, the murder rate in New York City increased by almost 400 percent, and the statistics are even worse in many other cities. A study at M.I.T. showed that based on 1970 homicide rates a person who lived in a large American city ran a greater risk of being murdered than an American soldier in World War II ran of being killed in combat. It is not surprising that the laws of each country differ according to differing conditions and traditions. If other countries had our murder problem, the cry for capital punishment would be just as loud as it is here. And I daresay that any other major democracy where 75 percent of the people supported the death penalty would soon enact it into law.

3. *An innocent person might be executed by mistake.* Consider the work of Hugo Adam Bedau, one of the most implacable foes of capital punishment in this country. According to Mr. Bedau, it is "false sentimentality to argue that the death penalty should be abolished because of the abstract possibility that an innocent person might be executed." He cites a study of the 7,000 executions in this country from 1893 to 1971, and concludes that the record fails to show that such cases occur. The main point, however, is this. If government functioned only when the possibility of error didn't exist, government wouldn't function at all. Human life deserves special protection, and one of the best ways to guarantee that protection is to assure that convicted murderers do not kill again. Only

the death penalty can accomplish this end. In a recent case in New Jersey, a man named Richard Biegenwald was freed from prison after serving 18 years for murder; since his release he has been convicted of committing four murders. A prisoner named Lemuel Smith, who, while serving four life sentences for murder (plus two life sentences for kidnapping and robbery) in New York's Green Haven Prison, lured a woman corrections officer into the chaplain's office and strangled her. He then mutilated and dismembered her body. An additional life sentence for Smith is meaningless. Because New York has no death penalty statute, Smith has effectively been given a license to kill.

But the problem of multiple murder is not confined to the nation's penitentiaries. In 1981, 91 police officers were killed in the line of duty in this country. Seven percent of those arrested in the cases that have been solved had a previous arrest for murder. In New York City in 1976 and 1977, 85 persons arrested for homicide had a previous arrest for murder. Six of these individuals had two previous arrests for murder, and one had four previous murder arrests. During those two years the New York police were arresting for murder persons with a previous arrest for murder on the average of one every 8.5 days. This is not surprising when we learn that in 1975, for example, the median time served in Massachusetts for homicide was less than two and a half years. In 1976 a study sponsored by the Twentieth Century Fund found that the average time served in the United States for first-degree murder is ten years. The median time served may be considerably lower.

10   4. *Capital punishment cheapens the value of human life.* On the contrary, it can be easily demonstrated that the death penalty strengthens the value of human life. If the penalty for rape were lowered, clearly it would signal a lessened regard for the victims' suffering, humiliation, and personal integrity. It would cheapen their horrible experience, and expose them to an increased danger of recurrence. When we lower the penalty for murder, it signals a lessened regard for the value of the victim's life. Some critics of capital punishment, such as columnist Jimmy Breslin, have suggested that a life sentence is actually a harsher penalty for murder than death. This is sophistic nonsense. A few killers may decide not to appeal a death sentence, but the overwhelming majority make every effort to stay alive. It is by exacting the highest penalty for the taking of human life that we affirm the highest value of human life.

5. *The death penalty is applied in a discriminatory manner.* This factor no longer seems to be the problem it once was. The appeals process for a condemned prisoner is lengthy and painstaking. Every effort is made to see that the verdict and sentence were fairly arrived at. However, assertions of discrimination are not an argument for ending the death penalty but for extending it. It is not justice to exclude everyone from the penalty of the law if a few are found to be so favored. Justice requires that the law be applied equally to all.

6. *Thou shalt not kill.* The Bible is our greatest source of moral inspiration. Opponents of the death penalty frequently cite the sixth of the Ten Commandments in an attempt to prove that capital punishment is divinely proscribed. In the original Hebrew, however, the Sixth Commandment reads "Thou shalt not commit murder," and the Torah specifies capital punishment for a variety of offenses. The biblical viewpoint has been upheld by philosophers throughout history. The greatest thinkers of the nineteenth century—Kant, Locke, Hobbes, Rousseau, Montesquieu, and Mill—agreed that natural law properly authorizes the sovereign to take life in order to vindicate justice. Only Jeremy Bentham was ambivalent. Washington, Jefferson, and Franklin endorsed it. Abraham Lincoln

authorized executions for deserters in wartime. Alexis de Tocqueville, who expressed profound respect for American institutions, believed that the death penalty was indispensable to the support of social order. The United States Constitution, widely admired as one of the seminal achievements in the history of humanity, condemns cruel and inhuman punishment, but does not condemn capital punishment.

7. *The death penalty is state-sanctioned murder.* This is the defense with which Messrs. Willie and Shaw hoped to soften the resolve of those who sentenced them to death. By saying in effect, "You're no better than I am," the murderer seeks to bring his accusers down to his own level. It is also a popular argument among opponents of capital punishment, but a transparently false one. Simply put, the state has rights that the private individual does not. In a democracy, those rights are given to the state by the electorate. The execution of a lawfully condemned killer is no more an act of murder than is legal imprisonment an act of kidnapping. If an individual forces a neighbor to pay him money under threat of punishment, it's called extortion. If the state does it, it's called taxation. Rights and responsibilities surrendered by the individual are what give the state its power to govern. This contract is the foundation of civilization itself.

Everyone wants his or her rights, and will defend them jealously. Not everyone, however, wants responsibilities, especially the painful responsibilities that come with law enforcement. Twenty-one years ago a woman named Kitty Genovese was assaulted and murdered on a street in New York. Dozens of neighbors heard her cries for help but did nothing to assist her. They didn't even call the police. In such a climate the criminal understandably grows bolder. In the presence of moral cowardice, he lectures us on our supposed failings and tries to equate his crimes with our quest for justice.

15   The death of anyone—even a convicted killer—diminishes us all. But we are diminished even more by a justice system that fails to function. It is an illusion to let ourselves believe that doing away with capital punishment removes the murderer's deed from our conscience. The rights of society are paramount. When we protect guilty lives, we give up innocent lives in exchange. When opponents of capital punishment say to the state: "I will not let you kill in my name," they are also saying to murderers: "You can kill in your *own* name as long as I have an excuse for not getting involved."

It is hard to imagine anything worse than being murdered while neighbors do nothing. But something worse exists. When those same neighbors shrink back from justly punishing the murderer, the victim dies twice.

🖉 Topics for Critical Thinking and Writing

1. Koch is, of course, writing an argument. He wants to persuade his readers. Beginning with paragraph 5 (Koch's first numbered point), he states the opposition's arguments and tries to refute them. But why did he include his first four paragraphs? What, as persuasion, does each contribute?

2. In paragraph 6 Koch compares our use of capital punishment to our use of "radical surgery, radiation, or chemotherapy." Do you find this analogy impressive—or not—and why? (Note that in this paragraph Koch goes on to say that "the analogy between cancer and murder is imperfect." Should he, then, not have used it?)

3. At the end of paragraph 6 Koch says, "If we create a society in which injustice is not tolerated, incidents of murder—the most flagrant form of injustice—will diminish." Has the earlier part of the paragraph prepared us for this statement?

4. Explain why you are or are not persuaded by Koch's second argument, about the likelihood that other countries would enact the death penalty if they too had high rates of murder.

5. In paragraph 9 Koch speaks of "murder" and then of "homicide." Are these two the same? If not, *why* is Koch bringing in statistics about homicide?

6. In paragraph 12, Koch lists authorities who supported the death penalty. Some of them—for instance, Washington and Jefferson—also supported slavery. What can be said in behalf of, and what can be said against, Koch's use of these authorities?

7. In paragraph 15, Koch puts a sentence into the mouths of his opponents. *Is* this what his opponents are in effect saying or thinking? (For the views of at least one of his opponents, see David Bruck's response to Koch, immediately below.)

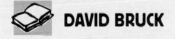 **DAVID BRUCK**

The Death Penalty

David Bruck, born in 1949, holds a law degree from the University of South Carolina. After serving four years as a public defender in South Carolina he entered private practice in order to devote all of his efforts to defending inmates on death row.

This essay was written as a direct response to the essay by Edward Koch, beginning on page 259.

Mayor Ed Koch contends that the death penalty "affirms life." By failing to execute murderers, he says, we "signal a lessened regard for the value of the victim's life." Koch suggests that people who oppose the death penalty are like Kitty Genovese's neighbors, who heard her cries for help but did nothing while an attacker stabbed her to death.

This is the standard "moral" defense of death as punishment: even if executions don't deter violent crime any more effectively than imprisonment, they are still required as the only means we have of doing justice in response to the worst of crimes.

Until recently, this "moral" argument had to be considered in the abstract, since no one was being executed in the United States. But the death penalty is back now, at least in the southern states, where every one of the more than 30 executions carried out over the last two years has taken place. Those of us who live in those states are getting to see the difference between the death penalty in theory, and what happens when you actually try to use it.

South Carolina resumed executing prisoners in January with the electrocution of Joseph Carl Shaw. Shaw was condemned to death for helping to murder two teenagers while he was serving as a military policeman at Fort Jackson, South Carolina. His crime, propelled by mental illness and PCP, was one of terrible brutality. It is Shaw's last words ("Killing was wrong when I did it. It is wrong you do it . . . .") that so outraged Mayor Koch: he finds it "a curiosity of modern life that we are being lectured on morality by cold-blooded killers." And so it is.

5   But it was not "modern life" that brought this curiosity into being. It was capital punishment. The electric chair was J. C. Shaw's platform. (The mayor mistakenly writes that Shaw's statement came in the form of a plea to the governor for clemency: actually Shaw made it only seconds before his death, as he waited, shaved and strapped into the chair, for the switch to be thrown.) It was the chair that provided Shaw with celebrity and an opportunity to lecture us on right and wrong. What made this weird moral reversal even worse is that J. C. Shaw faced his own death with undeniable dignity and courage. And while Shaw died, the TV crews recorded another "curiosity" of the death penalty—the crowd gathered outside the death-house to cheer on the executioner. Whoops of elation greeted the announcement of Shaw's death. Waiting at the penitentiary gates for the appearance of the hearse bearing Shaw's remains, one demonstrator started yelling, "Where's the beef?"

        For those who had to see the execution of J. C. Shaw, it wasn't easy to keep in mind that the purpose of the whole spectacle was to affirm life. It will be harder still when Florida executes a cop-killer named Alvin Ford. Ford has lost his mind during his years of death-row confinement, and now spends his days trembling, rocking back and forth, and muttering unintelligible prayers. This has led to litigation over whether Ford meets a centuries-old legal standard for mental competency. Since the Middle Ages, the Anglo-American legal system has generally prohibited the execution of anyone who is too mentally ill to understand what is about to be done to him and why. If Florida wins its case, it will have earned the right to electrocute Ford in his present condition. If it loses, he will not be executed until the state has nursed him back to some semblance of mental health.

        We can at least be thankful that this demoralizing spectacle involves a prisoner who is actually guilty of murder. But this may not always be so. The ordeal of Lenell Jeter—the young black engineer who recently served more than a year of a life sentence for a Texas armed robbery that he didn't commit—should remind us that the system is quite capable of making the very worst sort of mistake. That Jeter was eventually cleared is a fluke. If the robbery had occurred at 7 P.M. rather than 3 P.M., he'd have had no alibi, and would still be in prison today. And if someone had been killed in that robbery, Jeter probably would have been sentenced to death. We'd have seen the usual execution-day interviews with state officials and the victim's relatives, all complaining that Jeter's appeals took too long. And Jeter's last words from the gurney would have taken their place among the growing literature of death-house oration that so irritates the mayor.

        Koch quoted Hugo Adam Bedau, a prominent abolitionist, to the effect that the record fails to establish that innocent defendants have been executed in the past. But this doesn't mean, as Koch implies, that it hasn't happened. All Bedau was saying was that doubts concerning executed prisoners' guilt are almost never resolved. Bedau is at work now on an effort to determine how many wrongful death sentences may have been imposed: his list of murder convictions since 1900 in which the state eventually *admitted* error is some 400 cases long. Of course, very few of these cases involved actual executions: the mistakes that Bedau documents were uncovered precisely because the prisoner was alive and able to fight for his vindication. The cases where someone is executed are the very cases in which we're least likely to learn that we got the wrong man.

        I don't claim that executions of entirely innocent people will occur very often. But they will occur. And other sorts of mistakes already have. Roosevelt Green was executed in Georgia two days before J. C. Shaw. Green and an accomplice kidnapped a young woman. Green swore that his companion shot her to death after Green had left, and that he knew nothing about the murder. Green's claim was supported by a statement that his accomplice made to a witness after the crime. The jury never resolved whether Green was telling the truth, and when he tried to take a polygraph examination a few days before his scheduled execution, the state of Georgia refused to allow the examiner into the prison. As the pressure for symbolic retribution mounts, the courts, like the public, are losing patience with such details. Green was electrocuted on January 9, while members of the Ku Klux Klan rallied outside the prison.

10   Then there is another sort of arbitrariness that happens all the time. Last October, Louisiana executed a man named Ernest Knighton. Knighton had killed a gas station owner during a robbery. Like any murder, this was a terrible crime. But it was not premeditated, and is the sort of crime that very rarely results in a death sentence. Why was Knighton electrocuted when almost everyone else who committed the same offense was not? Was it because he was black? Was it because his victim and all 12 members of the jury that sentenced him were white? Was it because Knighton's court-appointed lawyer presented no evidence on his behalf at his sentence hearing? Or maybe there's no reason except bad luck. One thing is clear: Ernest Knighton was picked out to die the way a fisherman takes a cricket out of a bait jar. No one cares which cricket gets impaled on the hook.

Not every prisoner executed recently was chosen that randomly. But many were. And having selected these men so casually, so blindly, the death penalty system asks us to accept that the purpose of killing each of them is to affirm the sanctity of human life.

The death penalty states are also learning that the death penalty is easier to advocate than it is to administer. In Florida, where executions have become almost routine, the governor reports that nearly a third of his time is spent reviewing the clemency requests of condemned prisoners. The Florida Supreme Court is hopelessly backlogged with death cases. Some have taken five years to decide, and the rest of the Court's work waits in line behind the death appeals. Florida's death row currently holds more than 230 prisoners. State officials are reportedly considering building a special "death prison" devoted entirely to the isolation and electrocution of the condemned. The state is also considering the creation of a special public defender unit that will do nothing else but handle death penalty appeals. The death penalty, in short, is spawning death agencies.

And what is Florida getting for all of this? The state went through almost all of 1983 without executing anyone: its rate of intentional homicide declined by 17 percent. Last year [1984] Florida executed eight people—the most of any state, and the sixth highest total for any year since Florida started electrocuting people back in 1924. Elsewhere in the U.S. last year, the homicide rate continued to decline. But in Florida, it actually rose by 5.1 percent.

But these are just the tiresome facts. The electric chair has been a centerpiece of each of Koch's recent political campaigns, and he knows better than anyone how little the facts have to do with the public's support for capital punishment. What really fuels the death penalty is the justifiable frustration and rage of people who see that the government is not coping with violent crime. So what if the death penalty doesn't work? At least it gives us the satisfaction of knowing that we got one or two of the sons of bitches.

15   Perhaps we want retribution on the flesh and bone of a handful of convicted murderers so badly that we're willing to close our eyes to all of the demoralization and danger that come with it. A lot of politicians think so, and they may be

right. But if they are, then let's at least look honestly at what we're doing. This lottery of death both comes from and encourages an attitude toward human life that is not reverent, but reckless.

And that is why the mayor is dead wrong when he confuses such fury with justice. He suggests that we trivialize murder unless we kill murderers. By that logic, we also trivialize rape unless we sodomize rapists. The sin of Kitty Genovese's neighbors wasn't that they failed to stab her attacker to death. Justice does demand that murderers be punished. And common sense demands that society be protected from them. But neither justice nor self-preservation demands that we kill men whom we have already imprisoned.

The electric chair in which J. C. Shaw died earlier this year was built in 1912 at the suggestion of South Carolina's governor at the time, Cole Blease. Governor Blease's other criminal justice initiative was an impassioned crusade in favor of lynch law. Any lesser response, the governor insisted, trivialized the loathsome crimes of interracial rape and murder. In 1912 a lot of people agreed with Governor Blease that a proper regard for justice required both lynching and the electric chair. Eventually we are going to learn that justice requires neither.

✏ Topics for Critical Thinking and Writing

1. In paragraph 7 Bruck cites the case of Lenell Jeter in order to show that "the system is quite capable of making the very worst sort of mistake." How relevant, and how convincing, do you find this example?
2. In paragraph 8 Bruck says that of the murder cases in which the state admitted error, "very few . . . involved actual executions." How many do you suppose is "very few"? Why do you think Bruck does not cite the exact number?
3. What precautions, if any, does Bruck take, in the essay, to indicate that he is not soft on crime? Do you regard him as soft on crime? Why, or why not?
4. Bruck argues in paragraphs 10 and 11 that some of the people executed are, in effect, randomly selected from the group of murderers. Do you find paragraph 10 in itself convincing? And, if so, do you take it as a strong argument against the death penalty? If not, why not?
5. Evaluate Bruck's final paragraph as an argument and as a final paragraph.
6. Bruck's article is intended as a refutation of Koch's. Which of Koch's arguments, if any, does Bruck not face?

📖 ROBERT ELLIS SMITH

The True Terror Is in the Card

Robert Ellis Smith is publisher of Privacy Journal *and author of* Our Vanishing Privacy *and* What You Can Do to Protect Yours *(1993). The following essay was originally published in* The New York Times.

Last winter, a friend of mine from Washington was mugged in New York City and had her wallet stolen. Shaken by the experience, she wanted only one thing, to get back home. Luckily, her employer's headquarters is in Manhattan and she was able to borrow cash to get to the airport. But she had some fast explaining to do there because Delta was demanding that passengers produce a driver's license or other ID before boarding the plane. After some trouble, she was finally able to convince the airline of her identity by proving she was a Delta frequent flyer. She would have an even harder time today because airlines are much more stringent since the Olympics and the T.W.A. crash.

Delta, like other airlines, is using a directive from the Federal Aviation Administration to require passengers to provide a Government-issued identification to board an airplane. If it could be shown that this in fact enhances airline safety, then we would all readily accept this invasion of privacy. The Government and the airlines, however, have never shown a connection between the ID card and the prevention of explosives or weapons in luggage.

I object to the requirement on the grounds that it forces me to satisfy the Government that I am a real person before I may exercise the constitutional right to travel within the United States. I object also that it is part of an accelerating trend toward requiring every citizen to carry a Government-issued ID card—in essence, a national identity document.

Attention seems to be focused on asking passengers for more identification rather than on subjecting all carry-on and checked luggage to complete screening for weapons or bombs. The ID requirement, in fact, serves only to lead the public to believe that somehow we are more secure on an airplane if our "papers are in order" before boarding. Probably the only effective consequence of such requirements is to get us used to the idea of presenting identification in all aspects of our lives.

5   I'm shocked that more Americans are not shocked by the idea. Don't we remember the Nazi experience in Europe, where identity documents listing religion and ethnic background facilitated the roundup of Jews? Don't we remember how we condemned South Africa in the 1970's and 80's for using a domestic passport to limit the movements of certain citizens but not others? Don't we realize the dangers of allowing the Government to establish identity and legitimacy? Isn't it, in fact, the responsibility of the citizenry to establish the legitimacy of the Government?

Faced with rising crime, illegal immigration, welfare fraud and absentee parents, many bureaucrats and members of Congress insist that the nation would run more smoothly if we all had counterfeit-proof plastic identity cards. In considering immigration legislation this spring, the House came within a few votes of requiring a national identification card for all working Americans. Congress is about to authorize pilot programs with employers in several states verifying the legal identity of new employees by using central data bases. And it has already established a National Directory of New Hires containing the name, Social Security number and birth date of every person newly hired in the private and public sector.

These are precursors of a national ID card. The machinery, in fact, is now in place. All that is missing is the piece of plastic—and apparently most Americans are ready for it. Senator Dianne Feinstein, Democrat of California, has increased the stakes; she wants to create an identity card with a fingerprint, digitized photo, eye retina scan or some other biometric identity device.

Would an ID card work? It would make it easy to track illicit cash transactions, to discover after the fact all persons at the scene of a crime, to know immediately whether an adult accompanying a child is a parent or legal guardian, to keep a list of suspicious persons in a neighborhood each night, to know who purchased a gun or knife or fertilizer or Satanic books, or to know who carries the H.I.V. virus.

A suspicious police officer could demand to see your identity document and then query an on-line data base that would display identifying information about you. An employer could check the card to see whether you are a citizen or legal alien, have a criminal record or have filed previous workers' compensation claims.

10   But listing possible uses of a national ID card makes evident how it could be a nightmare to each of us. And that's not even considering the errors inevitable in such a data base. Even a remarkably low error rate of 1 percent would impose hardship on 650,000 innocent Americans who would be excluded from work, travel, commerce or schooling if their identity were somehow confused with a criminal's.

And that doesn't take into account the lucrative market in counterfeit ID cards. The advocates of an identity document want us to believe that it would be counterfeit-proof. But experts know there is no such thing.

Many people, charmed by the convenience of credit-card shopping by number over the phone or the Internet, think we already have a national identity system anyway. But that practice is wholly voluntary and doesn't involve centralized Government depositories of information. It is true that Social Security numbers are used in all kinds of ways. But the number is not issued to every person in the country as a national ID number would be.

Nor is a driver's license a true national identity document. While it is issued by a governmental agency, people are not required to have it when they do not drive, a photograph is not always required and a person who moves may apply for a new and different license.

A true national identity document would be mandatory; everyone would have to carry it and present it upon demand. It would be issued to everyone, probably at birth. And the identity of the bearer of each card would be recorded in a national data bank, usually along with other personal history. It would be the universally accepted proof of identity everywhere in the society. Without the card, you would have no acceptable proof of your citizenship.

15   Let's be clear that this is a one-way street. Once having established a requirement to carry photo ID, it will be difficult if not impossible to reverse. It's hard to imagine that the Government can begin issuing an identifying number at birth, then later tell all the agencies that have come to rely on it that they must disregard it.

What would a national ID card mean to American life? By accepting it, we will have removed the spontaneity in our lives. Every time we leave home, it will be necessary for each of us to gather up "our documents"—and those of our children, of course—before we venture out, to jog in a park, stroll in the neighborhood, lounge at the beach, buy a six-pack of beer or cross a state line. We will have empowered police officers to stop citizens engaged in law-abiding activities and demand that they produce proof of identity and "give a good account of themselves." There would be no excuse for not carrying the card—only criminals would not be carrying the card. By acting strangely at any time or by simply passing someone who doesn't like our looks, we can trigger a demand to produce the ID card. This, in turn, will trigger a search of an electronic data base to confirm our identity and perhaps provide other bits of personal data.

For most Americans, this would usually be an occasional inconvenience. For many others, it would be an affront to their dignity—but still nothing worse than a reason to rant at the next forum on civil liberties. But for several segments of our society, it would be truly a nightmare. One includes those whose records in the data base happen to be mixed up or whose identity is being used by a criminal impostor. Another would be those whose mere presence raises suspicions. That might be because of their dress, race, youth or incivility. The lack of an identification card could be the beginning of an ordeal—arrest and possibly criminal charges. Yet another segment would be those on the fringes of society, who may have no permanent residence nor even a safe place on their persons to keep such a document. These are precisely the people who will have difficulty holding on to their cards or explaining a computer error.

After we have come to accept this, politicians will point out that technology allows for other means of establishing identity. Many parents would welcome computer-readable implants to identify their children in the event of kidnapping. Relatives of Alzheimer's disease patients would want these microchip implants too, so that wandering patients could be located.

Laurence N. Gold, a former vice president of Nielsen Marketing Research, has written futuristically about voluntary "devices that can be carried, worn—or even implanted under the skin. These sensors will store and transmit data . . . identifying not only who is in the room but also his or her physiological state in response to both TV programs and advertising messages." Would people stand for it? Gold speculated that, despite "20th century sensibilities, future children may have much different attitudes about this." Well, not my children, I hope. We must draw the line now. Identifying people by a number is dehumanizing, and in the end destructive of a free society.

 Topics for Critical Thinking and Writing

1. Evaluate Smith's opening paragraphs. Why does he begin with a narrative about a friend whose wallet was stolen?
2. In paragraph 5, Smith refers to the use of identity cards in Nazi Germany and in South Africa. Are these examples relevant to the discussion of identity cards in the United States? If so, to what degree? And if not, why not?
3. Smith presents some counterarguments in paragraph 8—he notes that ID cards could help identify, for example, gun purchasers and AIDS carriers—but he doesn't directly refute those counterarguments. Should he have done so? How might they be refuted?
4. In paragraph 16, Smith argues that the national identity card will end "the spontaneity in our lives." Do you find the reasons he presents in this paragraph compelling? Why or why not?
5. Consider Smith's last paragraph. Which of the strategies recommended in the section on concluding paragraphs (pages 73–76) does Smith use here?

 **PATRICIA J. WILLIAMS**

Radio Hoods

A Professor of Law at Columbia University, Patricia J. Williams holds degrees from Wellesley College and Harvard Law School. She writes and teaches about property law, race, gender, and language. Her books include The Alchemy of Race and Rights

(1991) and The Rooster's Egg *(1995), a collection of essays from which the follow-*
ing selection is reprinted. Her most recent book is Seeing a Color-Blind Future: The
Paradox of Race *(1997).*

> *It is a hallmark of Limbaugh's commentary to provide blue-collar translations*
> *of white-collar conservatism, and in doing so to inflect them with tones of*
> *anger and outrage that articulate the resentment of a newly disenfranchised*
> *social formation, one that had its wallets emptied by Reaganomics while Rea-*
> *ganism massaged its egos.*

> *—John Fiske,* Media Matters: Everyday Culture and Political Change

Four years ago, I stood at my sink, washing the dishes and listening to the radio.
Howard Stern was a popular deejay in New York City but I had never heard of
him; he was not the national celebrity he has since become. I was listening to
rock'n'roll so I could avoid thinking about the big news from the day before:
George Bush had just nominated Clarence Thomas to replace Thurgood Marshall
on the Supreme Court. I was squeezing a dot of Lemon Joy into each of the wine-
glasses when I realized that two smoothly radio-cultured voices, a man's and a
woman's, had replaced the music.

"I think it's a stroke of genius on the president's part," said the female voice.

"Yeah," said the male voice. "Then those blacks, those African-Americans,
those Negros—hey, 'Negro' is good enough for Thurgood Marshall—whatever
they can't make up their minds they want to be called—I'm gonna call them
Blafricans. Black Africans. Yeah I like it. Blafricans. Then they can get all upset
because now the president appointed a *Blafrican!*"

"Yeah, well, that's the way those liberals think. It's just crazy."

5   "And then after they turn down his nomination the president can say he
tried to please 'em, and then he can go ahead and appoint someone with some
intelligence."

Back then, this conversation seemed so horrendously unusual, so singularly
hateful, that I picked up a pencil and wrote it down. I was certain that a
firestorm of protest was going to engulf the station and purge those foul radio
mouths with the good clean soap of social outrage.

I am so naive. When I finally rolled my dial around to where everyone else
had been tuned while I was busy watching Cosby reruns, it took me a while to
understand that there's a firestorm all right, but not of protest. In the four years
since Clarence Thomas has assumed his post on the Supreme Court, crude, in-
your-face racism, sexism, anti-Semitism, and homophobia have become commonplace, popularly expressed, and louder in volume than at any time since the
beginning of the civil rights movement. Snide polemical bigotry is everywhere—
among my friends, on the street, on television in toned-down versions. Unleashed as the new freedom of "what people are really thinking," it has reached
its highest pitch in the wildly proliferating phenomenon of right-wing radio
shows. Blaring the battle hymn of the First Amendment, these radio programs
enshrine a crude demagoguery that makes me heartsick; I feel more and more
surrounded by megawatted expressions of hate and discrimination—the coded
epithets, the mocking angry glee, the endless tirades filled with nonspecific,
nonempirically based slurs against "these people" or "those minorities" or "femi-
nazis" or "liberals" or "scumbags" or "pansies" or "jerks" or "sleazeballs" or
"loonies" or "animals" or "foreigners." American popular culture has suddenly
been given a megadose of childish turnaround laced with a very adult kind of
verbal brutality.

At the same time I am not so naive as to suppose that this is something new. In clear-headed moments I realize I am not listening to the radio anymore; I really am listening to a large segment of white America think aloud and ever louder—resurgent thoughts that have generations of historical precedent. It is as if the radio has split open like an egg, Morton Downey's clones and Joe McCarthy's ghost spilling out, broken yolks, a great collective of sometimes clever, sometimes small, but uniformly threatened brains—they have all come gushing out. Just as they were about to pass into oblivion, Jack Benny and his humble black sidekick, Rochester, get resurrected in the ungainly bodies of Howard Stern and his faithful black henchwoman, Robin Quivers. The culture of Amos 'n' Andy has been revived and reassembled in Bob Grant's radio minstrelsy, radio newcomer Darryl Gates's sanctimonious imprecations on behalf of decent white people, and Jerry Springer's racially and homophobically charged Punch and Judy shows. And in striking imitation of Father Coughlin and of Jesse Helms's nearly forgotten days as a radio host, the far Right has found its undisputed king in the personage of Rush Limbaugh—a polished demagogue with a daily radio audience of at least twenty million, a television show that vies for the top ratings with David Letterman and Jay Leno, a newsletter with a circulation of 360,000, and two best-selling books whose combined sales exceed seven million copies.

While it is probably true that the media are a reflection of America in general, I resist the temptation to say that they are *just* a mirror. From Churchill to Hitler to the old Soviet Union, it is quite clear that radio and television have the power to change the course of history, have the power to proselytize and to coalesce not merely the good and the noble but also the very worst in human nature. When Orson Welles made his famous radio broadcast "witnessing" the landing of a spaceship full of hostile Martians, America ought to have learned a lesson about the power of radio to appeal to mass instincts and crowd panic.

10   Radio remains a peculiarly powerful medium even today, its visual emptiness in a world of six trillion flashing images allowing one of the few remaining playgrounds for the aural subconscious. Perhaps its power is attributable to our need for an oral tradition, some conveying of stories, feelings, myths of ancestors, epics of alienation and the need to rejoin ancestral roots, even the ignorant bigoted roots. Perhaps the visual quiescence of radio is related to the popularity of electronic networking. It encourages some deep imaginative blindness of which we are barely aware, the busy embodiment being eliminated from view. Only the voice made manifest, the masked and hooded words that cannot—or dare not?—be seen. Just yet. Nostalgia crystallizing into a dangerous future. The preconscious voice erupting into the expressed, the prime time.

The shape of this electronic voice could be anything. What comes out of the modern radio mouth could be the *Iliad*, the *Rubáiyát*, the griot's song of our times. If indeed radio is a vessel for the American Song of Songs, then what does it mean that a manic, racist, penis-obsessed adolescent named Howard Stern is number one among radio listeners, that Rush Limbaugh's wittily smooth sadism has gone the way of prime-time television, and that these men's books tie for the number one slot on all the best-seller lists—Stern's book having had the largest first printing in publishing history. Professor Andy Herz of Touro College Law School sent me this anecdote:

> In my Jurisprudence class this semester, we were discussing John Stuart Mill's notion that the speech of eccentrics should be protected, even if the majority widely frowns upon their unconventional ideas, because their "ravings" against orthodoxy could ulti-

mately lead society to some deeper understanding. Names like
Galileo, Darwin, Pearl S. Buck and other early environmentalists
were mentioned as good examples. Then someone (seriously) suggested that Howard Stern might fit the same category: a man who
also "rants against orthodoxy" and whose views are looked down
upon and even censored by some in the majority. What a vision:
Howard Stern as the seer of our future society.

I smiled when I first received this letter. But a few weeks later Citizen Stern
became the Libertarian Party's candidate for governor of New York—a candi-
dacy cut blessedly short only by Stern's refusal to disclose his personal finances.

What to make of the stories being told by our modern radio evangelists, and
their tragic unloved choruses of "dittohead" callers? Is it really just a collapsing
economy that spawns this drama of grown people sitting around scaring themselves to death with fantasies of black feminist Mexican able-bodied gay soldiers
earning $100,000 a year on welfare who are so criminally depraved that Hillary's
hen-pecked husband or the Anti-Christ-of-the-moment had no choice but to invite them onto the government payroll so they can run the country?

As I spin the dial on my radio, I can't help thinking that this stuff must be related to that most poignant of fiber-optic phenomena, phone sex with Jessica
Hahn (who now has her own 900 number). Oral sex. Radio racism with a touch
of S&M. High-priest hosts with the power and run-amok ego to discipline listeners, to smack with the verbal back-of-the-hand, to smash the button that shuts
you up for once and for all. "Idiot!" shouts Bob Grant—and then the sound of a
droning telephone emptiness, the voice of dissent dumped out some trapdoor in
the aural space. Rush Limbaugh's "splendidly awful taste" and "delightful offen-
siveness" have been celebrated in the *National Review.* And Howard Stern remains on the air by popular demand at the highest levels of the FCC, thanks to a
seemingly insatiable national appetite for blam! and ker-pow! and make-a-big-
bathroom-sound and the earth shakes and you get to giggle afterward.

As I have listened to a range of such programs around the country what has
struck me as the most unifying theme of this genre is not merely the specific in-
tolerance of such hot topics as race and gender but a much more general contempt for the world, a verbal stoning of anything different. It is like some unusually violent game of "Simon Says," this mockery and shouting down of callers,
this roar of incantations, the insistence on agreement. A disrespect so deep as to
be satisfying, I suppose, all those shouted epithets and dashed receivers, like a
car crash in a movie except you can stay on the safe side of it if only you agree.

15   But, ah, if you *will* only agree, what sweet and safe reward, what soft en-
folding by a stern and angry radio god, oh leader of a righteous nation. And as an
added bonus, the invisible shield of an AM community, a family of fans who are
Exactly Like You, to whom you can express, with sheltering call-in anonymity,
all the filthy stuff you imagine "them" doing to you. The comfort and relief of
being able to ejaculate, to those who understand, about the dark imagined excess overtaking, robbing, needing to be held down and taught a good lesson,
needing to be put in its place before the ravenous demon enervates all that is
true and good and pure in this life.

The panicky exaggeration reminds me of a child's fear . . . *And then, and
then, and then, a huge lion jumped out of the shadows and was about to gob-
ble me up and I can't ever sleep again for a whole week, it was the biggest
most dangerous lion in the whole world* . . . The irresistible thread of a good
story line; a trail of breadcrumbs to an inevitable ending. Yet the panicky exag-

geration is not that of a child but that of millions of adults. And the trail of that story line reminds me of nothing so much as the quietly epic subtitles in that great American cornerstone of the silent screen, *The Birth of a Nation: Drunk with wine and power . . . the negroes and carpetbaggers sweep the state . . . men who knew nothing of the uses of authority, except its insolences . . . want to marry a white woman . . . the town given over to crazed negroes . . . the helpless white minority . . . victims of the black mobs . . . a veritable overthrow of civilization.*

If the statistics are accurate, the audience for this genre of radio flagellation is mostly young, white, and male. (For example, 96 percent of Rush Limbaugh's audience is white, about two-thirds of it white men, and 75 percent of Howard Stern's listeners are white men.) Yet it is hard to take the call-in conversations as a genuine barometer of social relations in any sense other than as a measure of nonrelation and just plain ignorance. Most of the callers, by their own testimony, have spent their lives walling themselves off from any real experience with feminists and gays, they certainly don't have any black neighbors, and they avoid and resent all manner of troublesome "types" in the workplace.

In this regard, it is probably true, as former Secretary of Education William Bennett says, that Rush Limbaugh "tells his audience that what you think inside you can talk about in the marketplace." If only that quality of exorcising "what's inside" were the highlighted feature of that statement. Unfortunately, "what's inside" is then mistaken for what's outside, treated as empirical and political reality. The *National Review* extols Limbaugh's conservative leadership as no less than that of Ronald Reagan, and the Republican Party provides Limbaugh with books, stories, angles, and public support. "People were afraid of censure by gay activists, feminists, environmentalists—now they are not because Rush takes them on," says Bennett. Hooray for the cavalry of bad-boy smash-'em-up audacity, for the cruel cowboy hero gone political.

Our history in the United States has been marked by cycles in which brands of this or that hatred come into fashion and go out again, are unleashed and restrained. If racism, homophobia, jingoism, and woman-hating have been features of national life in pretty much all of modern history, it's probably not worth spending much time wondering if right-wing radio is a symptom or a cause. For at least four hundred years, prevailing attitudes in the West have considered blacks less intelligent than whites. When recent statistics show 53 percent of Americans agreeing that blacks and Hispanics are less intelligent and a majority believing that they are lazy, violent, welfare-dependent, and unpatriotic, it's not as though it's ever been a lot better than that. In other words, it's not as though dittoheads needed Rush Limbaugh to tell them what to think—they can be pretty creative on their own. (Once upon a time, I went on Wisconsin public radio to talk about statistics that showed college-educated black men earning much less than similarly qualified white men. Promptly a male caller phoned in to explain that this was because it took a college degree to bring a black man up to the level of a white high school graduate.)

20   I think that what has made life more or less tolerable for out-groups has been those moments in history when those "inside" feelings were relatively restrained, when angry or bigoted people more or less kept their feelings to themselves. In fact, if I could believe that right-wing radio were only about idiosyncratic, singular, rough-hewn individuals thinking those inside thoughts, I'd be much less concerned. If I could convince myself, as the Columbia University professor Everette Dennis proclaims, that "Stern and Limbaugh make [radio] a more interactive, more personal experience . . . They make it a better, more vibrant

medium. It's the triumph of the individual"—then I'd be much more inclined to agree with *Time* magazine's bottom line that "the fact that either is seriously considered a threat . . . is more worrisome than Stern or Limbaugh will ever be." If, moreover, what I were hearing had even a tad more to do with real oppression, with real depression, with real white *and* black levels of joblessness and homelessness, or with the real problems of real white men, then I wouldn't have bothered to slog my way through hours of Howard Stern's miserable obsessions.

Yet at the heart of my anxiety is the worry that Stern, Limbaugh, Grant, et al. represent the very antithesis of individualism's triumph. As the *National Review* said of Limbaugh's ascent, "It was a feat not only of the loudest voice but also of a keen political brain to round up, as Rush did, the media herd and drive them into the conservative corral." "Rush is God / Rush in '96" reads the body paint slathered across the bare backs of two young male fans pictured in *Time* magazine. And when asked about his political aspirations, New York radio demagogue Bob Grant gloated, "I think I would make rather a good dictator."

Were this only about "conservative" politics, I would not be quite so worried, but Limbaugh's so-called dittohead fans are not really conservative in the best sense of that word. The polemics of right-wing radio are putting nothing less than hate onto the airwaves, into the marketplace, electing it to office, teaching it in schools, and exalting it as freedom. What worries me, in other words, is the increasing-to-constant commerce of retribution, control, and lashing out, fed not by fact but by fantasy and very powerful myth. (The media watchdog organization Fairness and Accuracy in Reporting has issued a series of lists of substantial factual errors purveyed by Limbaugh's show. But is anybody listening to that?)

What worries me is the reemergence, more powerful than at any time since the founding of the Ku Klux Klan and the institution of Jim Crow, of a socio-centered self that excludes "the likes of," well, me for example, from the civic circle, and that would rob me of my worth and claim and identity as a citizen. Dittoheadedess has less the character of individualism (or at least what the conventional political imagination would wish individualism to be) than of a mass-produced group identity that knows itself by denunciation and racialized nationalism. As the *Economist* observes, "Mr. Limbaugh takes a mass market—white, mainly male, middle class, ordinary America—and talks to it as an endangered minority."

I worry about this identity whose external reference is neither family nor religion nor the Constitution but a set of beliefs, ethics, and practices that exclude, restrict, and act in the world on me, on mine, as the perceived if not real enemy. I (that is, the likes of me) am acutely aware of losing *my* mythic shield of protective individualism, in the dittohead cosmos, to the surface shapes of my mythic group fearsomeness as black, as female, as left-wing. "I" merge not fluidly but irretrievably into a category of "them"; I become a suspect self, a moving target of loathsome properties, not merely different but dangerous. And it is precisely this unacknowledged contest of groupness—an Invisible Nation of whites locked in mortal combat with an Evil Empire of rascally carpetbaggers and Know-Nothing Negroes—for which the dominant ideology of individualism has no eyes, no vocabulary, and certainly no remedy, that worries me most.

25 It is interesting, moreover, to note what has happened as Rush Limbaugh has moved from being a small-time talk-show host with lots of noisy callers to a big-time radio host with twenty million listeners willing to be summed up by a pair of ditto marks, to a television personality, seated behind a schoolmaster's desk with an American flag planted on it, with only an applause-metered audi-

ence of onlookers and no call-in voices at all. This is, arguably, a progression away from a conversation among those who styled themselves the Little Guys, on to a mean-spirited populism, and finally to an embodiment of Rush Limbaugh as Über-Little-Guy. And this seems dangerously close to those moments when populism passes into fascism, when the common man is condensed into an aggregation, a mass united in one driving symbol. Limbaugh is hardly just an "irreverent individual" under such circumstances; in invoking the name of the common man, he mines a power that is the "addition of all oneness" and uses it to affirm great, coordinated, lock-step political power.

What happens to the lives of those not in lock step with all this translated license, this permission to be uncivil? What happens to the social space that was supposed to have been opened up by the Reconstruction Amendments' injunction against the badges and incidents of institutionalized stigma, the social space that was supposedly at the sweet mountaintop of the civil rights movement's trail? Can I get a seat on the bus without having to be reminded that I *should* be standing? Did the civil rights movement guarantee us nothing more than the freedom to use public accommodations while surrounded by raving bigots? "They didn't beat this idiot [Rodney King] enough," says Howard Stern in the background.

Not long ago I had the misfortune to hail a taxicab in which the driver was listening to Howard Stern undress some woman. After some blocks, I had to get out. I was, frankly, afraid to ask the driver to turn it off—not because I was afraid of "censoring" him, but because the driver was stripping me too as he leered into the rearview mirror. "Something the matter?" he demanded, still leering, as I asked him to pull over and let me out at the next corner, well short of my destination. (I'll spare you the full story of what happened from there—trying to get another cab, having lots of trouble as cabs speed by me while stopping for all the white businessmen who so much as scratch their heads near the curb; a nice young white man seeing my plight, giving me his cab, having to thank him, he hero, me saved-but-humiliated, cab driver peeved and surly. I fight my way to my destination, arriving in a bad mood, militant black woman, cranky feminazi, gotta watch out for my type, no pleasing that kind.)

When Yeltsin blared rock'n'roll music at his opponents holed up in the Parliament building in Moscow, in imitation of the Marines trying to torture Manuel Noriega in Panama, it occurred to me that it must be like being trapped in a crowded subway car when all the Walkmen are tuned to Bob Grant or Howard Stern. With Howard Stern's voice a tinny, screeching backdrop, with all the faces growing dreamily mean as though some soporifically evil hallucinogen were gushing into their bloodstreams, I'd start clawing at the doors, begging to surrender, for sure.

Surrender to what? Surrender to the laissez-faire resegregation that is the metaphoric significance of the hundreds of Rush Rooms that have cropped up in restaurants around the country; rooms broadcasting Limbaugh's words, rooms for your listening pleasure, rooms where bigots can capture the purity of a Rush-only lunch counter, rooms where all those unpleasant others just "choose" not to eat? Surrender to the naughty luxury of a room in which a Ku Klux Klan meeting could take place in orderly, First Amendment fashion? Everyone's "free" to come in (and a few of you outsiders do), but mostly the undesirable nonconformist non-dittoheads are gently repulsed away. It's a high-tech world of enhanced choice, you see. Whites choose mostly to sit in the Rush Room; feminists, blacks, and gays "choose" to sit elsewhere. No need to buy black votes, you just pay blacks not to vote; no need to insist on white-only schools, you just sell them on the desirability of black-only schools. No need for signs and police to enforce the separation of gay from straight; nonconformist troublemakers will herd themselves nicely in the face of a din of racist, sexist, homophobic babble. Just sit back and watch it work, like those invisible shock shields that keep dogs cowering in their own backyards.

30   How real is the driving perception behind all the Sturm und Drang of this genre of radio harangue—the perception that white men are an oppressed minority, with no power and no opportunity in the land that they made great? While it is true that power and opportunity are shrinking for all but the very wealthy in this country (and would that Limbaugh would take that issue on), white men remain this country's most privileged citizens and market actors, firmly in control of almost all major corporate and political power. In contrast, according to the *Wall Street Journal,* "Blacks were the only racial group to suffer a net job loss during the 1990–91 economic downturn, at the companies reporting to the Equal Employment Opportunity Commission. Whites, Hispanics and Asians, meanwhile, gained thousands of jobs." Three years of black gains were wiped out between July 1990 and March 1991, the dates of the last recession. "While whites gained 71,144 jobs at these companies, Hispanics gained 60,040 and Asians gained 55,104, blacks lost 59,479." And while right-wing radio deejays complain that unqualified minorities are taking all the jobs in academia, that white men need not apply, they ignore the degree to which, as a result of the economy, the pool of available academic jobs itself is what has been shrinking, and not just in the United States. Moreover, the number of minority undergraduate and graduate students is declining dramatically: Stanford University, for example, has suffered a 10 percent decline in minority Ph.D. enrollments since 1988, and that statistic reflects a national decline. In fact, there aren't enough people of color in the world to do justice to that expanding balloon of fear felt by white men who think that they have been dispossessed by hordes of the "less qualified."

It certainly cannot be said that minorities are taking over the jobs of radio disc jockeys. In 1993 the *Los Angeles Times* found "only 12 full-time weekday hosts who are members of minority groups among the 1000 or so general-market talk stations. Three of them are on public radio, which tends to be more liberal." And of that small number, a good portion are conservative blacks, although even conservative blacks have trouble in such a race-conscious market: Ken Hamblin, a conservative disc jockey in Denver who rails against "blacks," "black leaders," and the entire civil rights movement, "mentioned on air he was black. The phone lines suddenly went dead, and he had to filibuster his remaining four hours on air."

I think this reaction may be related to the rather fixed way in which all blacks are seen as allied with "radical" causes, no matter what right-wing claptrap they spout. How else can it be that City College of New York professor Leonard Jeffries, who teaches that blacks are sun people and whites are colder, harder, ice people, was held up to be such a symbol of multiculturalism, for example, when his theories revealed him as nothing if not a committed *mono*culturalist? When Khalid Muhammad (the Nation of Islam's national representative) indulged in his notorious anti-Semitic "bloodsucker" rantings, I was curious about why the mainstream media did not just condemn his words, as of course was proper, but condemned them as symbolic of a fearsome black radical Left— this when, except for the fact that he was black, his message was indistinguishable from that of far right-wingers like David Duke.

Similarly, I wonder why Charles Murray's or Richard Herrnstein's or Michael Levin's Nazi-like sociobiological theories of the inferiority of blacks are always so protected from the political vagaries of either Right or Left and graced as "science." And if we can understand what is so upsetting about Louis Farrakhan's famous excesses, one wonders why Senator Ernest Hollings's calling Africans cannibals—in the *Congressional Record* no less—should be received with barely a ho-hum.

What if whites understood Leonard Jeffries not as a "radical" but as a mirror image of a more general American right-winger with a taste for the delicious power of racial pornography? Perhaps some dawning but wrong-headed recognition of this connection motivated *Time* magazine's odd characterization of the call to black leaders to denounce black anti-Semitism as "just another kind of bigotry"—not because such calls single out only black leaders and only when it is black prejudice that is at issue, but because such efforts are purportedly attempts to "enforc[e] racial correctness." My guess is that the author of this astounding bit of moral dismissiveness also might feel that speaking out against white fraternity brothers who stage a slave auction is just another attempt at "enforcing political correctness." As A. M. Rosenthal observed in the *New York Times,* "Not a word did *Time* print to indicate that it ever crossed its collectivized-journalism mind that black leaders who denounced [anti-Semitic] speech really might despise it, that maybe they stood up because they liked that stance in life." Rather than a movement to pressure the full leadership structure of our entire society to look at itself and condemn all forms of bigotry, the intense reductionism in discourse about First Amendment rights in recent years seems to have resulted in an odd formula according to which groups have a *right* to be as racist as they wannabe, and no one else has a *right* to be offended unless they actually get hit.

Topics for Critical Thinking and Writing

1. This argument begins with a narrative. Does it make for an effective opening? Why or why not?
2. In paragraph 20, Williams presents a counterargument, from Everette Dennis, who claims that "'Stern and Limbaugh make [radio] a more interactive, more personal experience . . . They make it a better, more vibrant medium. It's the triumph of the individual.'" Where does she begin to refute this counterargument, and how does she do it? Could you offer more persuasive support of Stern and Limbaugh?
3. In paragraph 27, Williams tells a story about cutting short a cab ride because the driver was listening to Howard Stern. What do you think of this story? Does it supply evidence for her argument? How does the parenthetical narrative in the second part of the paragraph contribute to the larger point of the essay?
4. Near the end of the essay, in paragraphs 30 and 31, Williams offers statistics that help her dispute the idea that "white men are an oppressed minority, with no power and no opportunity in the land that they made great," an idea that Rush Limbaugh advances. Why does she present these statistics so late in the essay?
5. Is "Radio Hoods" an argument against the First Amendment's protection of free speech? What point about free speech does Williams make in the final paragraph of the essay?

PART THREE

Some Forms of
Academic Writing

CHAPTER

13

Outlining and Summarizing

Outlines come in several forms and serve several purposes. A scratch out-line—a few phrases in a sequence that seems appropriate—can help you get started. A paragraph outline—a topic sentence for each as-yet-unwrit-ten paragraph—can help you shape and develop a work in progress. And a formal outline, presented at the beginning of a long piece of writing, can offer guidance to readers, helping them visualize the relationships among the parts of an essay or report, and functioning as kind of table of contents.

The ability to write an accurate **summary** is necessary for writing essay examinations, laboratory reports, book reviews, and essays on litera-ture; it is also essential for taking notes on research, for incorporating re-search into an essay or report, and for writing abstracts, which present in a paragraph or two the main ideas of report, thesis, or dissertation.

We therefore begin Part 3, on academic writing, with a chapter on outlining and summarizing, skills central to much of work we discuss in the next five chapters.

OUTLINING

When you write an outline, you do pretty much what artists do whey they draw an outline: you give, without detail and shading, the general shape of your subject.

An outline is a kind of blueprint, a diagram showing the arrangement of the parts. It is, then, essentially an analysis of your essay, a classification of its parts. Not all writers use outlines, but those who use them report that an outline helps to make clear to them, before or while they labor through a first draft, what their thesis is, what the main points are, and what the subordinate points are. Outlines can help writers subordinate what is subordinate; outlines can also help writers see if the development from part to part is clear, consistent, and reasonable.

An outline drafted before you write, however, is necessarily tentative. Don't assume that once you have constructed an outline your plan is fixed. If, as you begin to write, previously neglected points come to mind, or if you see that in any way the outline is unsatisfactory, revise or scrap the outline. One other caution: an outline does not indicate connections. In your essay be sure to use transitions like "equally important," "less important but still worth mentioning," and "on the other hand" to make clear the relationships between your points.

Scratch Outline

The simplest outline is a *scratch outline,* half a dozen phrases jotted down, revised, rearranged, listing the topics to be covered in the most effective and logical order. As we suggest in Chapter 1, and as Frances FitzGerald illustrates in Chapter 2, a scratch outline can help a writer get started. In the example shown here, phrases serve as milestones rather than as a road map. Most writers do at least this much.

travel common in blues --
disappointed lover
travel to a job
from the South
fantasy travel
back to the South
life is a trip
~~my first trip out of the state~~
jail

Paragraph Outline

A *paragraph outline* is more developed. It begins with a sentence or a phrase, stating the thesis—this will ensure that you know where you are going—and then it gives the topic sentence (or a phrase summarizing the topic idea) of each paragraph. Thus a paragraph outline of Jeff Greenfield's "Columbo Knows the Butler Didn't Do It" (pages 182–84) might begin like this:

> Thesis: *Columbo* is popular because it shows a privileged, undeserving elite brought down by a fellow like us.
>
> i. *Columbo* is popular.
> ii. Its popularity is largely due to its hostility toward a social and economic elite.
> iii. The killers are all rich and white.
> iv. Their lives are privileged.

And so on, one roman numeral for each remaining paragraph. A paragraph outline has its uses, especially for papers under, say, a thousand words; it can help you to write unified paragraphs, and it can help you to write a reasonably organized essay. But after you write your essay, check to see if your paragraphs really are developments of what you assert to be the topic sentences, and check to see if you have made the organization clear to the reader, chiefly by means of transitional words and phrases (see pages 60–61). If your essay departs from your outline, the departures should be improvements.

As this last point suggests, your first paragraph outline, worked out after some preliminary thinking, should be a guide, not a straitjacket. As you jot down what you think may be your topic sentences, you will probably find that the jottings help you to get further ideas, but once you draft your essay you may find that the outline has served its initial purpose and has been superseded by a better organization than you had originally imagined. Of course, you should then sketch a new outline, one that corresponds to your draft, to make sure that the pattern of the essay as it now stands really is more effective than the earlier pattern.

Even if you don't write from an outline, when you complete your final draft you ought to be able to outline it—you ought to be able to sketch its parts. If you have trouble outlining the draft, your reader will certainly have trouble following your ideas. Even a paragraph outline made from what you hope is your final draft may help to reveal disproportion or faulty organization (for example, an anticlimactic arrangement of the material) that you can remedy before you write your final copy.

Formal Outline

For longer papers, such as a research paper (usually at least eight pages of double-spaced typing), a more complicated outline is usually needed. The *formal outline* shows relationships, distinguishing between major parts of the essay and subordinate parts. Major parts are indicated by capital roman numerals. The parts should clearly bear on the thesis. Chief divisions within a major part are indicated by indented capital letters. Subdivisions within these divisions are indicated by arabic numerals, further indented. Smaller subdivisions are indicated by lowercase letters, indented still further. Still smaller subdivisions—although they are rarely needed, because they are apt to provide too much detail for an outline—are indicated by small roman numerals, again indented.

The point of indenting is to make the relationship among the parts visibly clear to a reader. If you use I, II, and III, you are identifying three major points that are at least roughly equal. Under point I, A and B are parts roughly equal to each other, and so on. The outline is a sort of table of contents.

Note that you cannot have a single subdivision. In the example that follows, part I is divided into parts A and B; it cannot have only a part A. Similarly, part B cannot be "divided" into 1 without there being a 2. In effect, you can't say, as a naturalist did say, "The snakes in this district may be divided into one species— the venomous." If you have a single subdivision, eliminate it and work the material into the previous heading.

Here is a formal outline of Greenfield's "Columbo." Other versions are, of course, possible. In fact, in order to illustrate the form of divisions and subdivisions, we have written a much fuller outline than is usual for such a short essay. We have also not hesitated to mix sentences and phrases, though some authorities require that an outline use only one form or the other.

Thesis: *Columbo* is popular because it shows the undeserving rich brought low by a member of the working class.

I. Popularity of *Columbo*
   A. What it is *not* due to
      1. Acting
      2. Clever detection of surprising criminal plot

    B. What it is due to
        1. Hostility to privileged elite
        2. Columbo is poor and shoddy.
        3. The high are brought low.
            a. No black (minority) villains
            b. The villains live far above us.
  II. The hero
    A. Physical appearance
        1. Dress
        2. Hair, beard
    B. Manner
    C. Success as an investigator
        1. Adversaries mistakenly treat him as negligible.
            a. They assume his lack of wealth indicates lack of intelligence.
            b. They learn too late.
        2. Columbo understands the elite.
            a. They are not superior mentally or in diligence.
            b. They are in a shaky position.
 III. Our satisfaction with the program
    A. The villains do not deserve their privileges.
    B. Villains are undone by a man in the street.
    C. We look forward to an episode when Columbo visits the most privileged house.

There is, of course, no evidence that Greenfield wrote an outline before he wrote his essay. But he may have roughed out something along these lines, thereby providing himself with a ground plan or a road map. And while he looked at it he may have readjusted a few parts to give more emphasis here (changing a subdivision into a major division) or to establish a more reasonable connection there (say, reversing A and B in one of the parts).

SUMMARIZING

As we suggest above, the ability to write an accurate summary (abridgment, condensation) is central to much academic work: taking notes and writing research essays—as well as writing reviews, examinations, and even essays on literature.

    The need to write summaries continues in professional life. Scientists usually begin a scientific paper with an abstract, lawyers write briefs (which are, as the name implies, documents that briefly set forth all the facts and points of law pertinent to a case), and business executives must constantly reduce long memoranda and reports to their essential points.

What a Summary Is

Writing a summary requires that you analyze the text you are summarizing, separating out the main points from the examples and details that support these points.

    Here are a few principles that govern summaries.

1. A summary is much briefer than the original. It is not a paraphrase—a word-by-word translation of someone's words into your own. A summary is rarely longer than one-fourth the original, and often is much briefer. An entire essay may be summarized in a sentence or two.
2. A summary usually omits almost all the concrete details of the original, presenting only the main points of the original.
3. A summary is accurate; it has no value if it misrepresents the point of the original.
4. The writer of a summary need not state the points in the same order as that of the original. If the writer of an essay has delayed revealing the main point until the end of the essay, the summary usually rearranges the order, stating the main point first. Occasionally, when the original author presents an argument in a disorderly or confusing sequence, a summary clarifies the argument by changing the order of statements.
5. A summary normally is written in the present tense because whether the author wrote the piece last year or a hundred years ago, we assume that the piece speaks to us today.

Here is a summary of Barnet, Stubbs, and Bellanca on "summary":

> A summary is a condensation or abridgment. Its chief characteristics are: (1) it is rarely more than one-fourth as long as the original; (2) its brevity is achieved by leaving out most of the details of the original; (3) it is accurate; (4) it may rearrange the organization of the original, especially if rearrangement makes things clearer; (5) it is normally phrased in the present tense.

How to Write a Summary

With the text you intend to summarize before you—let's say a chapter of a book, or an essay—get ready to take notes, on your computer or on a pad of lined paper. Read the text quickly to get the gist of it, then begin rereading, slowly and thoughtfully.

On rereading, jot down, after reading each paragraph, a sentence giving the main point the paragraph makes, leaving out the details and examples that support the point. A very long paragraph may require two sentences; a series of short paragraphs, each illustrating the same point, may require only one sentence. One sentence per paragraph is a rule of thumb.

Here is a student's paragraph-by-paragraph summary of Philip Roth's essay on the Newark Public Library, "Reflections of the Death of a Library" (pages 9–10):

1. If the City Council shuts down the Newark public library will there be looting, sniping, etc.?
2. I hope not; I hope there is respect for Law and Order, even if there is none for thoughtfulness and pleasure.
3. When I was a child in Newark, the knowledge that the books belonged to the public was comforting to me, and it also civilized me by developing in me a sense of my responsibility as a citizen.
4. The library, quiet and tidy, provided a lesson in order, fostering self-restraint and also self-confidence.

5. The City Council thinks it is solving a fiscal problem, but its solution—an insult to the community—may be very costly in frustration, cynicism, and rage.

When you have written your sentence summarizing the last paragraph, you
may have done enough if the summary is intended for your own private use—for
example, if it is to help you review for an examination. But if you are going to use
it as the basis of a summary within an essay you are writing, you will probably
want to reshape it. In an essay of your own, you will seldom want to include a summary longer than three or four sentences, so your job will be to reduce and combine the sentences you have jotted down. Indeed, you may even want to reduce
the summary to a single sentence. One student summarized Roth's essay thus:

Philip Roth, in his article, "Reflections on the Death of a Library,"

argues that the closing of the libraries will be a costly mistake, and that

the action will be an insult to the citizens of Newark.

Notice that, since the summary is intended for a reader, the student has introduced the summary with Roth's name and the title of the article.

A writer who wants to devote a little more space to summarizing Roth's
essay might come up with this summary:

Roth, in his article, "Reflections on the Death of a Library," explains

in some detail how, when he was a child, the public library gave him

confidence and a sense of responsibility. In its orderliness, and in its

demand for quiet, it exerted a civilizing effect. The City Council may think

that by shutting down the library it is solving a fiscal problem, but it is

unaware of the rage that this insult will generate in the citizens (now,

mostly black) in Newark.

How Much Summary Is Enough?

As we suggest above, if you think that your reader needs a summary, you'll also
have to think about how long—that is, how detailed—the summary should be.

If you're writing a review of a book you read for your women's studies class,
you probably shouldn't assume that your reader has already read the book (readers tend not to read reviews of books they've already read!). You'll therefore
have to offer a fairly detailed summary of the text, probably at least a paragraph
or two if the review is five to six paragraphs long. (To see how summary works
in a review, see Jane Brox's review of Alex Johnson's book on pages 290-91.)

If you're analyzing a short story for a literature class, the matter is a bit trickier. In this case, you're probably writing about a text your classmates and instructor (that is to say, your audience) are at least somewhat familiar with. Nevertheless, you can't simply launch into your analysis, because only readers who know the story *very* well would be able to follow your discussion. In this case, the best thing to do is to imagine that your readers are intelligent people who have read the text you're writing about, but that they read it some time ago, and need to be reminded—in passing—about who's who and what happens. (To see how writers use summary in essays on literature, see Beatrice Cody's essay on *The Awakening,* pages 352–62 and Aviva Geiger's essay on "The Yellow Wallpaper," pages 395–400.)

In general, your awareness of your reader's needs as well as your own purpose will guide you as you summarize the material you're writing about.

Exercises

1. If you've just completed a draft of an essay, outline it now, before beginning to revise. Doing so may enable you to see where you need to include more information, where the discussion veers off on a tangent, or where the parts of the argument or analysis need to be reorganized.
2. Read Beatrice Cody's essay on *The Awakening,* reprinted on pages 352–62. Then write a paragraph outline of the essay.
3. Summarize the following paragraph in one or two sentences:

No society, whether human or animal, can exist without communication. Thoughts, desires, appetites, orders—these have to be conveyed from one brain to another, and they can rarely be conveyed directly. Only with telepathy do we find mind speaking straight to mind, without the intermediacy of signs, and this technique is still strange enough to seem a music-hall trick or a property of science fiction. The vast majority of sentient beings—men, women, cats, dogs, bees, horses—have to rely on signals, symbols of what we think and feel and want, and these signals can assume a vast variety of forms. There is, indeed, hardly any limit to the material devices we can use to express what is in our minds: we can wave our hands, screw up our faces, shrug our shoulders, write poems, write on walls, carve signs out of stone or wood, mould signs with clay or butter, scrawl sky-signs with an aircraft, semaphore, heliograph, telephone, run a pirate radio transmitter, stick pins in dolls. A dog will scratch at a door if it wants to be let in; a cat will mew for milk; a hostess will ring a bell for the course to be changed; a pub-customer will rap with a coin for service; a wolf will whistle; the people in the flat upstairs will bang with a stick if our party is too noisy. One can fill pages with such examples, bringing in the language of flowers and the signaling devices of honey-bees, but one will always end up with human speech as the most subtle, comprehensive, and exact system of communication we possess.

—Anthony Burgess

4. Choose a current editorial and summarize it in about one-fourth its number of words. Include a copy of the editorial with your summary.

5. Using the outline of "Columbo Knows the Butler Didn't Do It" (pages 109–10) and the essay itself (pages 182–84), write a summary of the essay, in about 250 words.

CHAPTER

14

Reviewing

Readers turn to reviews when they want to decide on what movie to see or book to buy. But they also turn to reviews when they begin to gather information for a research project, as we discuss in Chapter 16, "The Research Essay." Because they are generally brief and written by experts in their disciplines, book reviews published in such academic journals as *Modern Fiction Studies* and *American Quarterly,* for example, are excellent sources of information about recently published work in the fields of literature and American Studies.

Reviews serve other purposes as well. An engineer might write a review of a research proposal in order to help a committee decide on funding it; a publisher might ask a biologist to review a college biology textbook in order to help its authors make revisions. Editors of academic journals regularly ask experts in their fields to write reviews of articles submitted to them for publication.

Although there are many different kinds of reviews, they all share several features. In general, they

- describe or summarize the thing being reviewed
- point to its strengths and weaknesses, and
- make a judgment about its merit.

In this chapter we focus on writing book reviews. But the skills you'll develop as you learn to review books will be of use in other kinds of reviews—and other kinds of writing—as well.

WRITING A BOOK REVIEW

Because book reviews in newspapers, magazines, and academic journals are usually about a newly published work, reviewers normally assume that their readers will be unfamiliar with the book. Reviewers take it as their job to acquaint readers with the book, its contents, and its value and to help them decide whether or not they wish to read it. Since most reviews are brief (500 to 1500 words) they cannot, like explications, comment on everything. On the other hand they cannot, like analyses, focus on one aspect of the writing; they usually attempt in some way to cover the book. Reviews, then, usually contain more summary and more evaluation than explications or analyses. Nevertheless, reviewers must approach the task analytically if they are to accomplish it in the relatively small space allotted. And if they are to be convincing, they must support their opinion with quotations (usually indispensable), examples, and specific references to the text so that readers may think and feel the way the reviewer thinks and feels.

A review commonly has a structure something like this:

1. An opening paragraph that names the author and the title, gives the reader some idea of the nature and scope of the work (a children's book; a book for the general reader; a book for specialists), and establishes the tone of the review (more about tone in a moment).
2. A paragraph or two of plot summary if the book is a novel; some summary of the contents if it is not.
3. A paragraph on the theme, purpose, idea, or vision embodied in the book, perhaps within the context of related works.
4. A paragraph or two on the strengths, if any (for instance, the book fulfills its purpose).
5. A paragraph or two on the weaknesses, if any.
6. A concluding paragraph in which the reviewer delivers his or her point—but the point in some degree has probably been implied from the beginning, because the concluding paragraph is a culmination rather than a surprise.

Tone, as we suggest elsewhere in this book (see pages 136–38), usually refers to the writer's attitude toward the subject, the readers, and the writer's self. The tone of a review is therefore somewhat dependent on the publication in which it will appear. A review in *Scientific American* will have a different tone from one in *Ms.* Since you have not been commissioned to write your review and are essentially playing a game, you must *imagine* your reader. It's a reasonable idea to imagine that your classmates are your readers, forgetting of course that they may be reviewing the same book you are. And it's always productive to treat both your reader and your subject with respect. This does not mean you need to be solemn or boring; on the contrary, the best way to show your respect for your reader is to write something you would be interested in reading yourself.

Here is a book review from an academic journal. Although this review was published without a title, reviews often are given titles; if you are asked to write a review for one of your classes, you should be sure to title it.

JANE BROX

The Hidden Writer: Diaries and the Creative Life
By Alexandra Johnson

"Whom do I tell when I tell a blank page?" Virginia Woolf asks her diary. In *The Hidden Writer: Diaries and the Creative Life,* Alexandra Johnson searches for the complex and changeable answer as she traces women's diaries, always "the blank-faced old confidante," through two centuries as they work their way into the life of literature to become something for the public eye. An inveterate diarist herself, Johnson opens with a recollection of her own childhood interest in diaries, and ends—writer and teacher of writing—with selections from her adult journal. In between these chapters is a deft, intelligent examination of seven women's diaries beginning with the 1809 Edinburgh journal of Marjory Fleming: six years old, exuberant, testing out words, a nascent diarist. Fleming dies of meningitis just shy of her ninth birthday.

Johnson goes on to examine the private works and overshadowed ambitions of Sonya Tolstoy and Alice James, then continues with the competitive literary friendship of Virginia Woolf and Katherine Mansfield. Ambitions no longer closeted, Woolf's and Mansfield's diaries become companions to their literary accomplishments, pages where they not only set down daily thoughts and observations but sharpen technique and aim for style. Woolf writes in hers: "It strikes me that in this book I practice writing; do my scales; yes and work at certain effects . . . and shall invent my next book here." Her aspirations for a literature that would record "all the traces of the minds passage through the world; & achieve in the end some kind of whole made of shivering fragments . . ." broadens the way for Anaïs Nin and May Sarton. Sarton, on the coast of Maine and late in her life, records just such fragments of solitude and aging in diaries she specifically intends for publication.

With Sarton's *Journal of a Solitude,* Johnson suggests, the diary has made a full journey from the hidden to the public, one that she subtly links to the journey of a more inclusive literature tunneling its way into the world. Diarists—observers, listeners, silent and ambitious—are kin to all those "haunting the corners of creative life . . . centuries of voices that have been lost forever. They are the shadow writers—male and female, white and black—voices beat back in the throat."

Whether she is describing Alice James' room in Leamington, the quiet broken only by the scratch of a pen, or the first meeting over dinner at Hogarth House of Katherine Mansfield, "sensual, wary, bohemian . . . the shock of the new about her," and Virginia Woolf, "tall, patrician, her skin fragile at the temples, her collar bones shimmering like ivory calligraphy," Johnson's clarifying prose, apt and evocative, is a pleasure to read. With each chapter, she sets forth an entire world, and you feel she has found just the right word, just the right phrase to recreate the atmosphere of the times. Her examinations of Sonya Tolstoy and the friendship between Woolf and Mansfield are feats of compression, encapsulating the complexities of these lives as well as the complexities of the place of these lives in the literature of their era.

From the private writings of these seven women, Johnson gleans "a time-lapse study of confidence." Her own comprehensive knowledge of dairies—those of her subjects, and those of well-known diarists such as Ann Frank and Sylvia Plath, and the lesser-known such as Etty Hillesum—gives added depth and continuity to her argument. In *The Hidden Writer* Alexandra Johnson weaves together a smart, graceful account that does honor to diaries, literature, and the creative life.

Topics for Critical Thinking and Writing

1. Characterize or describe the tone of the review.
2. Write a one-sentence summary of each paragraph. Your list of sentences should resemble an outline.

3. How well does your outline correspond with the structure we say reviews commonly have? (See page 290.)

4. If there are discrepancies between what we have said about reviews and the review by Brox, can you offer a reasonable explanation for these discrepancies? Or would you argue that we revise our discussion, or that we choose a different review as an example?

5. Write a book review. Your instructor may give you a list of possibilities. If not, we recommend that you choose a book on a subject that you're familiar with. (In other words, if you're a fan of detective fiction, you might review Patricia A. Cornwell's latest novel; if you're taking a course in the American Civil War, you might review a recent biography of one of the figures you're studying.)

WRITING OTHER REVIEWS

Our suggestions for writing a book review, with obvious modifications, can serve as guidelines for other reviews you may be assigned or choose to write: of an article, a proposal, a play, a movie, a concert, or other performance. Again, it is the reviewer's job to acquaint readers, real or imagined, with a performance they are assumed to be unfamiliar with (although in fact reviews are often read by readers who want to see their own judgments confirmed, or their small talk improved). And again, you must adopt an appropriate tone, suggesting both your own expert knowledge of your topic and your respect for your readers' intelligence and taste.

Your best preparation for writing a review is to read reviews in publications you trust, consciously noting what you find informative, interesting, and persuasive. Then, if you are covering a live event, you'll find it useful to ask to see in advance the promotional material usually in the hands of the organization sponsoring the event. You'll want to be skeptical of some of the rave reviews you'll find quoted (and of course you mustn't use them in your own review without acknowledging their sources), but you may well find biographical and other background information that will prepare you for the performance and make note taking easier. And you must go prepared to take notes—often in the dark—and allow yourself sufficient time immediately after the event to type or rewrite your notes legibly.

Reviewing a compact disc or tape obviously has some advantages. You can listen to it many times, you may have access to the score or lyrics and previous recordings, and you can choose your own time and place for listening. Or perhaps the relaxed and witty style of the review we print below just makes it seem easier. The review was written by a student for a college newspaper.

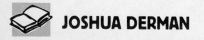 **JOSHUA DERMAN**

Deconstructing Pop: The Halo Benders

There's a piece of conventional wisdom regarding modern art that goes like this: creators of it have no appreciable skills, and they conceal this fact by creating art (music, books) that doesn't resemble anything (isn't tuneful, doesn't make sense).

This sentiment is particularly popular when applied to the scrawling, jagged genre of indie rock. Trace it back to the Sex Pistols, when bad music became chic; or even earlier to the Velvet Underground, whose aggressive feedback and guitar mutilation was so at odds with the bubblegum melodies of the day. In this music scene The Halo Benders' third album, *The Rebels Not In,* is a refreshing dose of accessible art rock. In it, they have created an album whose aural texture achieves musical ends you won't find anywhere in mainstream rock. After but a single hearing, you'll realize that indie rock is more than just about bad haircuts and funny T-shirts.

Judging by the press release that accompanied the album, being an indie rock star is akin to being a pedigree dog—your full name, when mentioned, must be accompanied by a lengthy musical genealogy. In the case of The Halo Benders, this could take pages: the Olympia, Washington-based band is actually a side-project, staffed by the frontmen of other indie groups. Calvin Johnson (Beat Happening), Doug Matsch (Built to Spill), Ralf Youtz (The Feelings) and Wayne Flower (Violent Green).

All the ingredients you've come to love or hate in lo-fi are here for the offering: no verse-chorus structure, stop-and-start guitar solos, lyrics that sound as if they were excerpted from "The Jabberwocky," plus a general air of aggressive avant garde posture. But unlike some lo-fi outfits (i.e. Pavement), The Halo Benders actually sound like a band. There's a full, textured quality to their sound that one usually finds only on heavier-produced albums. Their lo-fi style isn't an affectation or an excuse, but a real aesthetic agenda. The marching of drums across a static soundscape, the simple polyphony of guitar and bass, organic song structure—these features are more expressive, more evocative than any slick Puff Daddy remix.

5   A critic once said of a Bela Bartok violin-and-piano sonata that the composer returned these instruments to their original functions: the violin is for scratching, the piano for banging. The Halo Benders have done something similar for the electric guitar—you won't find any Hendrix-style guitar impersonations on this album, epic screech or distorted wah-wah. Doug Matsch embraces the jangly, plucky sound of the guitar and puts it to his purposes. His stop-and-go solos, breaking in waves over the drum and bass rhythm, owe more to Bach cantatas than to conventional alterna-rock.

The opening measures of the album's first track, "Virginia Reel Around the Fountain," pairs off a guitar and electric bass, whose low-frequency warblings sound like whale songs. "Love Travels Faster," a bitter-sweet spastic ballad, and the very VU-inspired "Turn It My Way" are also notably clever, well-wrought songs. One of the album's best songs is the haunting "Rebels Got a Hole in It" (whatever that means), an epic instrumental that might make a good soundtrack for a post-apocalyptic road movie.

The vocal harmonies of Matsch and Calvin Johnson are an equally distinctive feature of The Halo Benders. Johnson's voice sounds much like that of an extremely bored, medicated Johnny Cash—his basso profundo is a little bit too deep to actually be believed. His singing is weird enough to be interesting at first, but after prolonged exposure its total lack of expression becomes unnerving. Thankfully, Matsch accompanies him on most songs in a higher register, and the resulting vocal harmonies are surprisingly satisfying, in a distinctly atonal kind of way.

As far as lyrics are concerned, *The Rebels Not In* is a mixed bag. The fact that none of the album's lyrics are really quotable out of context says something. (I am reminded of one verse from the first track: "Do a little dance on the kitchen table/Rub your tummy and show your navel.") I take it that the general idea behind this school of song-writing, as exemplified by Pavement's Stephen Malkmus, is that the words should conspire to produce a theme or feeling to accompany the music. If the music's not figurative, the words might as well not be either.

The fact that it's hard to say what the songs are about doesn't detract from the album, but it's sometime difficult to distinguish lyrical avant garde from just plain laziness. It's hard to be taken seriously—which is what The Halo Benders deserve—when your lyrics are that far out in left field.

10   Despite its playfulness, this is an outstanding, inventive album. A far cry from their excellent but obscure 1994 release, *Don't Tell Me Now, The Rebels Not In* has serious cross-genre appeal. So dig the hyperactivity, put on your funny T-shirts and revel in the cerebro-punk vibes.

✎ Topics for Critical Thinking and Writing

1. Characterize the writer's tone. Is it appropriate to his material and his audience? Explain.
2. On the basis of this review, would you buy *The Rebels Not In?* If you didn't have to pay for the album, would you be interested, because of the review, in listening to it? Explain why, or why not.
3. If you saw this writer's byline in your newspaper would you read the article? Explain.
4. Write a review of a current album. Or, attend a concert and review it. In a note appended to your review, define your intended audience.

15

Interviewing

We have all been treated to the television interview with (and perhaps by) a celebrity. Question: "Which game was the toughest that you have ever lost?" Answer: "Uh, well, Marv, that's a tough question." Question: "When did you have your first sexual experience?" Answer: "Oh, Barbara, I knew you'd ask me that!" And we've read similarly inspiring transcriptions in popular magazines (while standing in the checkout line at a supermarket). But the interview is also an important tool of academic research and writing. Sociologists and psychologists regularly use interviews, and biographers and historians often rely heavily on interviews when they write about recent events. Interviews with poets and fiction writers in literary magazines help us to learn not only about the writers and their work but also about the craft of poetry or fiction. For the apprentice writer, interviews provide excellent sources for interesting essays about the person being interviewed or about issues and ideas.

WRITING AN ESSAY BASED ON AN INTERVIEW

A college campus is an ideal place to practice interviewing. Faculties are composed of experts in a variety of fields and distinguished visitors are a regular part of extracurricular life. In the next few pages, we'll offer some advice on conducting interviews and writing essays based on them. If you take our advice, you'll acquire a skill you may well put to further, more specialized use in social science courses; at the same time you'll be developing skill in asking questions and shaping materials relevant to all research and writing.

Before we list the steps for you to follow, we offer two examples, essays based largely on interviews. First read "The Einstein of Happiness." Then answer the questions that follow it.

PATRICIA FREEMAN

The Einstein of Happiness

If the truth be known, being a professor of happiness is no picnic. People deride your research, trivialize your interests—then badger you for the secret of eternal bliss. Nevertheless, Allen Parducci, fifty-seven-year-old professor of psychology at UCLA, has been exploring the fabric of human felicity for over forty years.

Parducci became a happiness scholar because of his father, a stern architectural sculptor in Grosse Pointe, Michigan, who voiced a vexing conviction that "things balance out" between happiness and woe—or, as Mark Twain put it, "Every man is a suffering machine and a happiness machine combined, and for every happiness turned out in one department, the other stands ready to modify it with a sorrow or pain." Young Parducci, wondering why he ought to bother getting out of bed in the morning if that were true, set out to debunk the theory.

He conducted his research everywhere. He quizzed his college roommates as to the completeness of their contentment. He grilled his fellow sailors during World War II: "As the ship rolled back and forth and they retched, I'd ask them, 'How happy are you now? Are you really unhappy?'"

Eventually he received a graduate degree in psychology from Berkeley, where he could finally study the phenomenon scientifically. Today, he is known around the world for his work in "the relativism of absolute judgments"—a fancy phrase meaning that how we evaluate a thing depends on what we compare it to. (Though his work was an outgrowth of his search for the answers to human happiness, hardly anybody in academia has applied it that way.) To back up his ideas, he devised several studies to show that judgments of all kinds depend on the context in which they are made.

5   For one study, he gave a "test" of moral judgments to college students, who were asked to assign each item in a list of behaviors a ranking of from "1—not particularly bad or wrong" to "5—extremely evil." Half of the students were given a list of comparatively mild acts of wrongdoing, including such items as "cheating at solitaire," "wearing shorts on the street where it is illegal" and "stealing towels from a hotel room." The other half were given a much nastier list, including such acts as "selling to a hospital milk from diseased cattle." Both lists contained six of the same items. The crucial feature of the test was that the students were to judge the items according to their own personal values and not to judge them in comparison to one another. Nonetheless, the experiment showed that students' moral judgments depended on how the list was "skewed"—the six acts appearing on both lists were rated more leniently by students who judged them in the context of the nasty list than by those who encountered them on the mild list. "Poisoning a neighbor's barking dog," for example, got a rather harsh score of 4.19 when it appeared along with "playing poker on a Sunday" and a less disapproving 3.65 when it came just after "murdering your mother without justification or provocation."

According to the same principle, which Parducci calls a "negatively skewed distribution," our judgments of personal satisfaction depend on how often we experience the things we deem most satisfying. To demonstrate this, he devised a study in which two groups of students selected cards from two different decks and won money based on the value assigned to each card. One group played with cards marked from 1 cent to 21 cents, with the higher values predominating, and the other groups with cards marked from 7 cents to 27 cents, with low sums predominating. Every player won the same total of money for the series, but group one, which garnered its winnings primarily from the higher end of the scale, reported themselves happier with their winnings.

What does all of this mean for us? It means, Parducci says, that just as the cardplayers were happiest when most of their winnings were close to the maximum that could be earned, we will likely be most satisfied if our lives are arranged so that the best of what we experience happens more frequently. The happy person, who finds "zest, fun and joy in life," says Parducci, is one for whom "the things he's experiencing are high relative to his standards." And conversely, the unhappy person—whose life is marked by "terror, anxiety and misery"—sets inappropriate standards for himself often comparing his life to an impossible ideal.

Parducci will venture a few tips on living the happy life, but only with prodding. If we want to be happy, he says, we ought not to live in the future, thinking that we'd be happy if only we could double our income, marry this person or get that job; instead we should learn to delight in what we have and look forward to things that happen every day. Above all, we should let go of what's impossible.

"We all know people who have had a great love affair break up and their friends say, 'Get it out of your head,' but they can't. But if they could, in effect, drop that relationship out of their context altogether, then the best of their experience with someone new would seem good and wonderful. They could experience the same high even with a lesser person."

10   The happiest person Parducci has ever known (though he doesn't think he's particularly good at telling whether people are happy or not) was a woman who died of cancer in her mid-thirties. "The six months before she died was like a party every night," he recalls. "Her friends would come over, her ex-husbands would visit, and everybody would have a great time. I asked her, 'Joanne, how do you feel about death?' and she said. 'I know I could die any time, but I'm very happy.'" Joanne was married approximately five times if you count both legal and informal spouses. "She'd meet these men anybody would say she shouldn't marry," Parducci says, "and it would be disastrous. She'd see virtues in people that no one else could see. It seemed that she was living in a dream world. I would have said, looking at her life, that she should see things the way they are. But sometimes I think some people are just born to be happy."

Most Americans, in fact, say that they are happy. According to national polls the average citizen gives himself a happiness rating of seven on a scale of one to ten. Parducci gives himself a six, a rating he believes actually makes him significantly more sanguine than most Americans. "People's reports of their own happiness show an astonishing positive bias," he says. He thinks people make themselves out to be happier than they really are because "there's the implication that there's something wrong with you if you can't somehow arrange your life to be satisfying."

In fact, unhappiness seems to be a national personality trait. "The success credo of American business is that you're supposed to always be setting higher standards," Parducci says. "And in setting inappropriately high standards, we can't help but doom ourselves to unhappiness. Society is pyramidal. There's only one position at the top, and if everyone is pushing toward that one position, the great majority must inevitably fall by the wayside." But still we push our children to aim for medical school or sports superstardom.

Does Parducci hope, in some small way, to make the world a happier place to live? "I'm very skeptical about the possibility of doing that," he says. Still, there are those who would make him into a guru of good cheer. But, unlike Leo Buscaglia, psychologist to the masses and a fixture on the best-seller lists, Parducci is uninterested in providing road maps to felicity and pointers to pleasure. "I've been approached by several literary agents," he says. "There's always a pressure toward self-help. You know. 'The Ten Rules for Happiness.' But if it were that simple, it would have been discovered by now."

People tell him that he could make a fortune if only he would become at least a bit of a happiness hawker. "I ask myself, if lightning struck in that way, if I made a million dollars, would I be happier? But friends of mine who have made that kind of money say that it hasn't made them happy," he says.

15   Even though Parducci says he'd like to be "more happy," in the end there's something he considers more important—and that is, "being good." He will readily declare that religion—particularly Christianity—has fostered unhappiness by holding up an ideal of goodness that is impossible to live up to. Still, he says, "I think there are rules that people ought to follow, rules that may be difficult. Suppose Mephistopheles came and said, 'If you kill a few people I'll make you very happy.' I hope I would be strong enough to turn him down. I don't want to be identified with the 'me first' psychology that says we're all out for ourselves."

If he can't make people happier and he doesn't consider happiness the most important thing in the world anyway, why does Parducci press on with his work? "There's a satisfaction," he submits, "in just understanding things. We can understand how the planets move around the sun, though we can't affect them. We get satisfaction out of understanding happiness, even though we can't do much about it."

✎ Topics for Critical Thinking and Writing

1. What homework do you think Patricia Freeman did in preparation for the interview?
2. List the questions Freeman might have posed to elicit the information in each paragraph or group of paragraphs. Were there any paragraphs for which you had difficulty imagining questions? Can you explain why? (Or, what information do you suppose did not come from Professor Parducci's own words? Who or what do you imagine to be the source of this information?)
3. Through much of the article we hear Parducci's voice, either paraphrased or directly quoted. Where do we hear the interviewer's voice as well?
4. Suppose you had begun with only the information that Allen Parducci is a professor of psychology at an American university. What library sources might tell you his age, education, major field of interest, publications, and current academic post? (See if you can find this information in your own library.)

Now read the second article and answer the questions following it.

EILEEN GARRED

Ethnobotanists Race Against Time to Save Useful Plants

Although a white lab coat hangs a bookshelf in his cramped office and an IBM personal computer sits on a nearby table, these are not the tools Mark Plotkin prefers to use. As an ethnobotanist, Plotkin has spent months in the tropical forests of South America, bringing along newspapers and moth balls to press and preserve plant specimens he then hauls back to the Botanical Museum at Harvard.

In annual visits over the past eight years, Plotkin has been patiently cultivating the trust of tribal medicine men in the Suriname jungle in order to learn how the native people use forest plants in their cultures. It is a race against time and the steadily increasing influences of civilization.

Tropical forests the world over are shrinking as deforestation escalates and development spurred by rapid population growth reaches further into the jungle. The Amazon region alone contains approximately 80,000 species of plants, a vast resource of living organisms, many of which are yet unknown to science. Plants of great potential value of medical, agricultural, and industrial uses are vanishing even before they are identified.

Perhaps more important, knowledge about plants long used by native Indians for beneficial purposes is dying out with the witch doctors. "Within one generation after civilization arrives, aboriginal peoples will forget most of their plant lore," predicts Richard Schultes, Director of the Botanical Museum.

5   The Westerners who arrive to build roads or preach the Gospel also bring with them Western medicines. "Our medicines are effective, cheap, and easy to get," Schultes adds. "The natives are not going to run through the forest to look for a leaf their ancestors used to alleviate sickness if they don't have to."

Few of the witch doctors today have young apprentices from the tribe because visiting missionaries have strongly discouraged shamanism. The last of the medicine men in the tribes must be coaxed to reveal their secrets to a new breed of botanist like Plotkin.

Last year, for example, Plotkin returned from Suriname with a small tree limb called doubredwa. The South American Indians scrape the bark into rum and claim the resulting drink is a powerful male aphrodisiac. "The world doesn't need more people," explains Plotkin. "What it needs is a treatment for impotence—and there it is in a woody vine from the Amazon."

Curare, a native arrow poison, has been used for a number of years in hospitals as an anesthetic and muscle relaxant during surgery. Another plant poison that stupefies fish and forces them to the water's surface where they are easy targets for spearfishers is the basis for the pesticide rotenone. Because it is biodegradable, rotenone is widely used in the United States.

Fruit from a common Amazonian palm produces oil that is very similar to olive oil, and the fruit from still another species is extremely rich in vitamins C and A.

10   "The so-called 'wonder drugs,' including penicillin, cortisone, and reserpine, that have revolutionized the practice of medicine came from plants that had some use in primitive societies that called the attention of a chemist to the plant," says Schultes.

According to Schultes, tribes of the northwest Amazon utilize just under 2000 different plant species for "medicinal" purposes. "In these plants there is a tremendous storehouse of new chemicals," he explains. "In the hands of a chemist, a naturally occurring chemical can be changed to form the basis of many new semi-synthetic chemicals. So if you find in a plant one useful chemical, you are finding literally hundreds that chemists can make using that natural structure as a base. How can chemists hope to procure and analyze 80,000 species of plants?

"One shortcut for the chemist is to concentrate on the plants that native peoples by trial and error over thousands of years have found to have some biological activity," he says.

Although it often takes two decades or more of research from discovery of a plant to a packaged drug, ethnobotanists who provide chemists with the material must work quickly since the varieties of jungle plants and the numbers of medicine men who know how to identify and use them are disappearing at an alarming rate.

As a defined field of study, ethnobotany is more than a century old, but it has received greater attention only in recent years. Schultes, a pioneer in the field, lived and worked in Colombia and Peru from 1941 to 1954. During that time, he collected 24,000 plants and filled dozens of field notebooks, which he is still trying to put into publishable form.

15   "We call this work an 'ethnobotanical salvage operation,'" says Plotkin, "which just means that we are documenting the plants the Indians use and the ways in which they use them." The U.S. Division of the World Wildlife Fund is sponsoring Plotkin's work at the Harvard Botanical Museum. As part of the Tropical South American Conservation and Ethnobotany Project, Plotkin has compiled a catalog of more than 1000 useful plant species, which includes Latin and vernacular names, data on distribution, aboriginal use, chemical composition and economic potential. Previously, much of this information was widely scattered and not available to botanists, conservationists and development planners.

Plotkin, whose initial interest in the beneficial uses of plants was cultivated by Schultes, is now primarily concerned with tying ethnobotany to conservation. Money, he says, is the bottom line. In fighting for preservation of the Amazon's tropical forest with its large reserve of natural resources, Plotkin aims to put conservation in economic terms.

"The ill-planned development in the tropics by local governments and transnational corporations is causing serious damage," he says. "But you can't tell Brazil, a country with the largest foreign debt in the world, 'Don't cut down the forest because you've got the cutest little monkey living there.' You have to explain that plant A is worth 'x' number of dollars and plant B, if you manage it right, will be worth 'y' number of dollars."

"You have to convince the government that it is worth more as a forest than as an agricultural area, which is probably going to fail anyway over the long term. Until you can put it in concrete economic terms, it's just talk."

As an example, Plotkin points to the irony that Brazil imports $20 million worth of olive oil a year, although there are millions of the palm trees that produce a similar edible oil within its borders.

20   One of the most common trees in the Amazon, the buriti palm, has a multitude of uses discovered by the Indians. Its fruit is rich in vitamins, an extract from the stem can be used to make bread, the fibers can be used to make twine,

houses are built from its wood, and it grows only in swampy areas that could not otherwise be used for agriculture. However, says Plotkin, the Brazilian government has yet to step in to look for high yielding strains of the buriti, or "tap into what is a potential gold mine" by putting it into plantations.

"Conservation works best if it's in that country's self-interest." says Plotkin. "Ethnobotany"—the study of the use of plants by native peoples who have intimate knowledge of forests and the useful products they contain—"is really in the forefront of international conservation efforts."

"For thousands of years, aboriginal peoples have been living with and depending on the native vegetation. Now civilization is destroying that knowledge," says Schultes. "Much more endangered than any species is the knowledge about plant lore. If we don't pick it up now, we'll never get it."

 ## Topics for Critical Thinking and Writing

1. Is the article primarily about Plotkin or about Schultes? If neither, what is it about?
2. What is ethnobotany? Where in the article is it defined? Should Garred have defined it earlier? Why or why not?
3. Garred is on the editorial staff of the *Harvard Gazette,* a weekly devoted to news of the Harvard community. How do you suppose Garred came upon her story? Reconstruct the steps she probably took to research her article.
4. From what office or offices at your institution might you learn of an activity of more than usual interest engaged in by a faculty member, an administrator, a student, an alumnus, or a trustee? (Check your college catalog and directory for possible leads.)

GUIDELINES FOR CONDUCTING THE INTERVIEW AND WRITING THE ESSAY

As these two essays illustrate, writers use interviews in writing about people, and they also use interviews in writing about issues. For either purpose, an interview produces, and the writer reproduces, more than information. By skillful selection of the most interesting remarks for quotation and by reporting gestures and settings, the writer allows us to experience both the writer's and the speaker's interest in the topic under discussion.

Here are some steps to follow in conducting an interview and writing an essay based on it.

1. Finding a subject for an interview. As with all writing projects, the best place to start is with your own interest. If you are taking a course from a particularly interesting professor, you might end your search, and begin your research, there. Or, you might use an interview as a way of investigating a department you're thinking of majoring in. Your college catalog lists the names of all faculty members, by department.

Scan the list in the department that interests you and begin to ask questions of upperclassmen. Then, with a name or two in mind, check your library for appropriate biographical reference works. *Directory of American Scholars* contains the most names of academicians, but also check various Who's Who volumes. In addition to *Who's Who in America,* you'll also find such works as *Who's Who in the West,* (and similar titles for the East, South, Southwest, and Midwest), *Who's Who Among Black Americans, Who's Who in Religion, Who's Who of American Women.* In addition, the circulation desk or the research librarian may have a list of current publications by faculty members. In some libraries, current publications by faculty and alumni are on display. Department administrators are good sources of information not only about the special interests of the faculty but also about guest speakers scheduled by the department in the near future. Investigate the athletic department if you're interested in sports; or the departments of music, art, and drama, for the names of resident or visiting performing artists. Other sources of newsworthy personalities or events: the publicity office, the president's office, the college newspaper. All are potential sources for information about recent awards, or achievements, or upcoming events that may lead you to a subject for an interview, and a good story.

2. Preliminary work. Find out as much as you can about your potential interviewee's work, from the sources we mentioned above. If the subject of your interview is a faculty member, ask the department secretary if you may see a copy of that person's vita (Latin for "life," and pronounced *vee-ta*). Many departments have these brief biographical sketches on file for publicity purposes. The vita will list, among other things, publications and current research interests.

3. Requesting the interview. In making your request, don't hesitate to mention that you are fulfilling an assignment, but also make evident your own interest in the person's work or area of expertise. (Showing that you already know something about the work, that you've done some preliminary homework, is persuasive evidence of your interest.) Request the interview, preferably in writing, at least a week in advance, and ask for ample time (probably an hour to an hour and a half) for a thorough interview.

4. Preparing thoroughly. If your subject is a writer, read and take notes on the publications that most interest you. Read book reviews, if available; read reviews of performances if your subject is a performing artist. As you read, write out the questions that occur to you. As you work on them, try to phrase your questions so that they require more than a yes or no answer. A "why" or "how" question is likely to be productive, but don't be afraid of a general question such as "Tell me something about . . ."

Revise your questions and put them in a reasonable order. Work on an opening question that you think your subject will find both easy and interesting to answer. "How did you get interested in . . ." is often a good start. Type your questions or write them boldly so that you will find them easy to refer to.

Think about how you will record the interview. Although a tape recorder may seem like a good idea, there are good reasons not to rely on one. First of all, your subject may be made uneasy by its presence and freeze up. Second, the recorder (or the operator) may malfunction, leaving you with a partial record, or nothing at all. Third, even if all goes well, when you prepare to write you will face a mass of material, some of it inaudible, and all of it daunting to transcribe.

If, despite these warnings, you decide (with your subject's permission) to tape, expect to take notes anyway. It's the only way you can be sure you will have a record of what was important to you out of all that was said. Think beforehand, then, of how you will take notes, and if you can manage to, practice by interviewing a friend. You'll probably find that you'll want to devise some system of shorthand, perhaps no more than using initials for names that frequently recur, dropping the vowels in words that you transcribe—whatever assists you to write quickly but legibly. But don't think you must transcribe every word. Be prepared to do a lot more listening than writing.

5. Presenting yourself for the interview. Dress appropriately, bring your prepared questions and a notebook or pad for your notes, and appear on time.

6. Conducting the interview. At the start of the interview, try to engage briefly in conversation, without taking notes, to put your subject at ease. Even important people can be shy. Remembering that will help keep you at ease, too. If you want to use a tape recorder, ask your subject's permission, and if it is granted, ask where the microphone may be conveniently placed.

As the interview proceeds, keep your purpose in mind. Are you trying to gain information about an issue or topic, or are you trying to get a portrait of a personality? Listen attentively to your subject's answers and be prepared to follow up with your own responses and spontaneous questions. Here is where your thorough preparation will pay off.

A good interview develops like a conversation. Keep in mind that your prepared questions, however essential, are not sacred. At the same time don't hesitate to steer your subject, courteously, from apparent irrelevancies (what one reporter calls "sawdust") to something that interests you more. "I'd like to hear a little more about . . ." you can say. Or, "Would you mind telling me about how you . . ." It's also perfectly acceptable to ask your subject to repeat a remark so that you can record it accurately, and if you don't understand something, don't be afraid to admit it. Experts are accustomed to knowing more than others do and are particularly happy to explain even the most elementary parts of their lore to an interested listener.

7. Concluding the interview. Near the end of the time you have agreed upon, ask your subject if he or she wishes to add any material, or to clarify something said earlier. Express your thanks and, at the appointed time, leave promptly.

8. Preparing to write. As soon as possible after the interview, review your notes, amplify them with details you wish to remember but might have failed to record, and type them up. You might have discovered during the interview, or you might see now, that there is something more that you want to read by or about your subject. Track it down and take further notes.

9. Writing the essay. In writing your first draft, think about your audience. Unless a better idea occurs to you, consider your college newspaper or magazine, or a local newspaper, as the place you hope to publish your story. Write with the readers of that publication in mind. Thinking of your readers will help you to be clear—for instance to identify names that have come up in the interview but which may be unfamiliar to your readers.

As with other writing, begin your draft with any idea that strikes you, and write at a fast clip until you have exhausted your material (or yourself).

When you revise, remember to keep your audience in mind; your material should, as it unfolds, tell a coherent and interesting story. Interviews, like conversations, tend to be delightfully circular or disorderly. But an essay, like a story, should reveal its contents in a sequence that captures and holds attention.

If you've done a thorough job of interviewing you may find that you have more notes than you can reasonably incorporate without disrupting the flow of your story. Don't be tempted to plug them in anyway. If they're really interesting, save them, perhaps by copying them into your journal; if not, chuck them out. (For a wretched example of a story that ends with a detail the writer couldn't bear to let go, see "Fish Eat Brazilian Fisherman," page 78).

In introducing direct quotations from your source, choose those that are particularly characteristic, or vivid, or memorable. Paraphrase or summarize the rest of what is usable. Although the focus of your essay is almost surely the person you interviewed, it is your story, and most of it should be in your own words. Even though you must keep yourself in the background, your writing will gain in interest if your reader hears your voice as well as your subject's.

You might want to use a particularly good quotation for your conclusion. (Notice that both essays we've chosen as examples conclude this way.) Now make sure that you have an attractive opening paragraph. Identifying the subject of your interview and describing the setting is one way to begin. (Again, look at the sample essays.) Give your essay an attractive title. Before you prepare your final draft, read your essay aloud. You're almost certain to catch phrases you can improve, and places where a transition will help your reader to follow you without effort. Check your quotations for accuracy; check with your subject any quotations or other details you're in doubt about. Type your final draft, then edit and proofread carefully.

10. Going public. Make two copies of your finished essay, one for the person you interviewed, one for yourself. The original is for your instructor; hand it in on time.

Topic for Writing

Write an essay based on an interview. You needn't be limited in your choice of subject by the examples we've given. A very old person, a recent immigrant, the owner or manager of an interesting store or business, a veteran of the Gulf War, a gardener, are only a few of the possibilities. If you can manage to do so, include a few photographs of your subject, with appropriate captions.

CHAPTER

16

The Research Essay

*Knowledge is of two kinds. We know a subject ourselves, or we know
where we can find information upon it.*

—Samuel Johnson, in a
Conversation in 1775

WHAT RESEARCH IS

Research consists of collecting information to support and develop ideas.
Of course, this does not mean that you collect only the information that
supports your initial ideas. Your ideas will develop, often in unexpected
ways, as you gather information. The information can include facts, opinions, and the ideas of others, recorded in print or in bytes, and in the form
of books, articles, lectures, reports, reviews, and interviews. Research essays are based in part on such material, and you'll write them in many of
your college courses.

Not everyone likes research, of course. There are hours spent reading
books and articles that prove to be contradictory or irrelevant. There is
never enough time to read all the material that's available—or even to get
your hands on it. And some of the books are dull. The poet William Butler
Yeats, though an indefatigable worker on projects that interested him, engagingly expressed an indifference to the obligation that confronts every
researcher: to look carefully at all the available evidence. Running over the
possible reasons why Jonathan Swift did not marry (that he had syphilis,
for instance, or that he feared he would transmit a hereditary madness),
Yeats says: "Mr. Shane Leslie thinks that Swift's relation to Vanessa was not
platonic, and that whenever his letters speak of a cup of coffee they mean
the sexual act; whether the letters seem to bear him out I do not know, for
those letters bore me."

Though research sometimes requires one to read boring things, those
who engage in it feel, at other times, an exhilaration, a sense of triumph at
becoming expert on something. When you study a topic thoroughly, you
are in a position to say: "Here is how other people have thought about this

305

question; their ideas are all very interesting, but I see the matter differently: let me tell you what *I* think."

There can be great satisfaction in knowing enough about a topic to contribute to the store of knowledge and ideas about it. There can also be great satisfaction in simply learning to use the seemingly infinite resources now available to researchers—in print or electronic formats—as well as in learning to document and to acknowledge your research accurately and responsibly.

In this chapter we discuss

- how to find and evaluate sources, both print and electronic,
- how to take useful notes,
- how to use others' ideas to help you develop your own, and
- how to acknowledge your sources.

When you acknowledge sources, giving credit where credit is due for your use of the ideas and words of others, you provide a kind of road map for the researcher who comes after you and who may want to retrace some of your steps. And you publicly thank those who have helped you on your way.

PRIMARY AND SECONDARY MATERIALS

The materials of research are usually divided into two categories, primary and secondary. The primary materials or sources are the real subject of study; the secondary sources are critical and historical accounts written about these primary materials. For example, if you want to know whether Shakespeare's attitude toward Julius Caesar was highly traditional or highly original, or a little of each, you would read *Julius Caesar,* other Elizabethan writings about Caesar, and translations of Latin writings known to the Elizabethans; in addition to these primary materials you would read secondary material such as modern books on Shakespeare and on Elizabethan attitudes toward Rome and toward monarchs.

Similarly, the primary material for an essay on a novel by Kate Chopin, *The Awakening* (1899), is of course the novel itself; the secondary material consists of such things as biographies of Chopin and critical essays on the novel. But the line between these two kinds of sources is not always sharp. For example, if you are concerned with the degree to which *The Awakening* is autobiographical, primary materials include not only the novel and also Chopin's comments on her writing but perhaps also the comments of people who knew her. Thus the essays—based on interviews with Chopin—that two of her friends published in newspapers probably can be regarded as primary material because they were contemporary with the novel and because they give direct access to Chopin's views, while the writings of later commentators constitute secondary material.

DEVELOPING A RESEARCH TOPIC

Your instructor may assign a topic, in which case, you'll be saved some work. (On the other hand, you may find yourself spending a lot of time with material you don't find exciting. On yet another hand, you might become interested in something you'd otherwise never have known about.) More likely, you'll need to develop your own topic, a topic related to the subject of the course for which the research essay has been assigned. Some possibilities:

- Perhaps you've read Maxine Hong Kingston's *The Woman Warrior* (1976) for a Women's Studies course, and you have become interested in Confucian or Buddhist ideas that inform the narrative.
- Perhaps your Government course has touched on the internment of Japanese-Americans during World War II, and you'd like to know more about what happened.
- Perhaps you have read Chopin's *The Awakening* for a literature course, and you're wondering what readers thought about the novel when it was first published.

Any of these interests could well become a topic for a research essay. But how do you begin to find the relevant material?

Getting Started

There's no one right way to start, and of course different topics lend themselves to different kinds of approaches. Nevertheless, one good rule of thumb is to begin with what you already know, with what you already have at hand. For instance, the textbook for your government course may cite official documents on the relocation and internment of Japanese-Americans. Or your edition of Chopin's *The Awakening* may contain an introduction that references some critical essays on the novel; it's also likely to contain a selected bibliography, a list of books and articles about Chopin and her work. If you have already identified a few titles, you can go directly to your library's on-line catalog, and begin your search there. (We'll have more to say about on-line searches in a moment.)

If, however, you know very little about the topic, and haven't yet identified any possible sources (let's say you know nothing or almost nothing about Confucianism, but Maxine Hong Kingston's *The Woman Warrior* has made you want to learn about it), it's not a bad idea to begin with an encyclopedia—the *Encyclopaedia Britannica*, perhaps—which you'll find in the reference area of your college or university library. In addition to providing you with information about your topic, encyclopedia articles will usually include cross-references to other articles within the encyclopedia, as well as suggestions for further reading. These suggestions can help you begin to compose a list of secondary sources for your essay. And of course you need not limit yourself to this one encyclopedia: there are hundreds of invaluable specialized encyclopedias, such as *Encyclopedia of Anthropology*, *Encyclopedia of Crime and Justice*, *Encyclopedia of Psychology*, *Encyclopedia of Religion* (a good place to go for an introduction to Confucianism), and *Kodansha Encyclopedia of Japan*, and many of them are certain to be available in your library's reference area. Encyclopedias are also available on-line, in full-text versions you can access through your library's central information system.

THE LIBRARY'S CENTRAL INFORMATION SYSTEM

It used to be the case that all libraries worked in more or less the same way. Each one had a card catalog, a set of hundreds of little drawers containing thousands (even millions) of alphabetically arranged three-by-five cards. When you wanted a book, you went to the card catalog and looked it up by title, author, or subject. Because books would of course differ from library to library, the cards would also of course differ. But the system in every library was pretty much the same.

In recent years, on-line catalogs have replaced card catalogs in college and university libraries, and in most public libraries as well. And the on-line catalog constitutes only a tiny fraction of the information available to you through your institution's library. From a computer terminal in your library (or from home via a telnet or World Wide Web connection), you can access bibliographies and indexes, full-text versions of encyclopedias and dictionaries and academic journals, the catalogs of *other* libraries—and much more.

Unlike card catalogs, each library's central information system is a bit different. Resources differ from one library to the next. And things change—literally—every day. For these reasons, our discussion of library resources in the following pages can only provide you with a sketch of what's available and a general sense of how to find it. The best advice we can give you about learning to find books and articles in your library is to go to your college or university's research librarian and ask for help.

THE ON-LINE CATALOG

Let's assume that you're at a computer terminal in the library. Let's also assume that you're taking a course in environmental studies, and as a result of one of the course lectures, you've become interested in researching the subject of food additives—that is, chemicals and other substances added to preserve desirable properties (color, flavor, freshness) or to suppress undesirable properties in food. You want to do some reading, and you must now find the books, articles, and reports. Of course, as you do the reading, your focus may narrow, for instance to the potentially dangerous effects, in various foods, of sodium nitrate, or to the controversy over the effects of aspartame (an artificial sweetener), or you may concentrate on so-called enriched bread, which is first robbed of many nutrients by refining and bleaching the flour and is then enriched by the addition of some of the nutrients in synthetic form. But at this point, you don't yet know what your focus will be, and you simply want to begin finding relevant material.

The steps required for searching the on-line catalog vary from system to system, and so we can't tell you exactly how you'll perform a search at your library. Generally speaking, you'll enter into the terminal some information about the source you're looking for (usually the author, title, or subject); the computer will perform the search, and the results will appear on the screen.

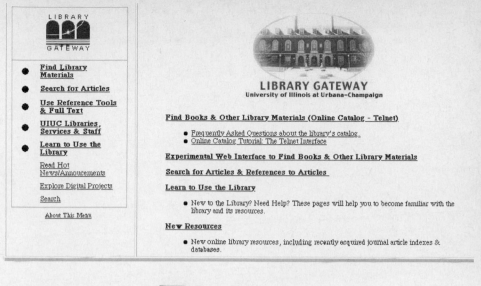

The Library Gateway page for the University of Illinois at Urbana-Champaign (A student at the University of Illinois might connect to this page from home and begin searching the library's resources here). http://www.library.uiuc.edu/

Author and title searches are relatively straightforward. To find works by a particular author, you enter the author's name (beginning with the last name), and a list of his or her works will appear on the screen. To find a particular title, simply type in the title (omitting the initial "the," "an," or "a") at the appropriate prompt, and all the books with that title will likewise be listed on the screen.

Subject searches are more complicated because they often depend on a highly structured language and very specific terms. (If you don't know what subject terms to use, consult four big red volumes entitled *Library of Congress Subject Headings,* available in the reference area of your library.) To find material for the essay on food additives, you would begin with a subject search (since you don't have in mind the titles or authors of any particular books), typing the phrase "food additives"—which happens to be an accepted subject heading term—at the prompt on the computer screen. The computer will search the library's holdings, and a list of more detailed subject headings, such as the following list, will appear on the screen. (We reproduce an image of only the first screen that would appear in one specific library; the complete list of holdings for the subject "food additives" in this library contains 94 items.)

```
HU GUIDE: SUBJECT HEADING LIST  94 items retrieved by your search:

FIND SU FOOD ADDITIVES

---------------------------------------------------------------------

1          FOOD ADDITIVES

43         FOOD ADDITIVES  —ANALYSIS

47         FOOD ADDITIVES  —BIBLIOGRAPHY

50         FOOD ADDITIVES  —CONGRESSES

55         FOOD ADDITIVES  —DICTIONARIES

56         FOOD ADDITIVES  —GREAT BRITAIN

57         FOOD ADDITIVES  —HANDBOOKS MANUALS ETC

58         FOOD ADDITIVES  —HEALTH ASPECTS

61         FOOD ADDITIVES  —ISRAEL —PERIODICALS

62         FOOD ADDITIVES  —LAW AND LEGISLATION

63         FOOD ADDITIVES  —LAW AND LEGISLATION  —AUSTRALIA

64         FOOD ADDITIVES  —LAW AND LEGISLATION  —CANADA

65         FOOD ADDITIVES  —LAW AND LEGISLATION  —DENMARK

66         FOOD ADDITIVES  —LAW AND LEGISLATION  —EUROPE—MISCELLANEA

67         FOOD ADDITIVES  —LAW AND LEGISLATION  —FRANCE

68         FOOD ADDITIVES  —LAW AND LEGISLATION   —GERMANY WEST

OPTIONS: -------------------- More - to see next page ---------------------
                   GUide # - see guide at #th item           Help
                   index # - see list at #th item            Quit
   Help COMMANDS   REDo - edit search   STORe # - save for email  COMment
   COMMAND?
_____
   4-©                     Sess-2                    128.103.60.84
```

Note that the first line of this list says simply "food additives." The other entries are followed by phrases that indicate more specific subject categories, such as "Food additives—Israel—periodicals," categories that may be too specific for your purposes at the very beginning of your research on this topic. In this case, if you now were to enter "1," a second list of 42 items would appear, and this list would contain titles and authors of books on your subject. The first screen of this list, which contains the first 15 of the 42 items, appears on the next page.

FIND SU FOOD ADDITIVES

FOOD ADDITIVES

| 1 | [retrieves related heading: | DIETARY SUPPLEMENTS] |

| 2 | [retrieves related heading: | ENRICHED FOODS] |

| 3 | [retrieves related heading: | FLAVORING ESSENCES] |

| 4 | [retrieves related heading: | FOOD PRESERVATIVES] |

| 5 | [retrieves related heading: | SUCROSE POLYESTER] |

| 6 | [retrieves related heading: | SWEETENERS] |

7   additives guide /hughes christopher c/ 1987 bks

8   alternatives to the current use of nitrite in foods/ 1982 bks

9   bugs in the peanut butter dangers in everyday food /weiner micha/ 1976 bks

10   chemical safety regulation and compliance proceeding /course on/ 1985 bks

11   chemicals we eat /benarde melvin a/ 1971 bks

12   chemicals we eat /benarde melvin a/ 1975 bks

13   eaters digest the consumers fact book of food additi /jacobson m/ 1972 bks

14   eating may be hazardous to your health how your gove /verrett ja/ 1974 bks

15   environmental poisons in our food /millichap j gordon/ 1993 bks

OPTIONS: ------------------- More - to see next page ---------------------

                                                                     Help

GUide   display # - see #th item   Quit

Help COMMANDS   REDo - edit search   STORe # - save for email COMment

COMMAND?

4-©   Sess-2   128.103.60.84

In addition to author, subject, and title searches, most on-line catalogs permit **keyword searches**. Searching by keyword enables you to locate books in your field without requiring you to enter a specific subject heading. The keywords can be drawn from just titles or subject headings, or from a combination of both. To find material on food additives, for example, you might type in the words "chemicals and food" at the title keyword prompt; on the screen would appear a list of all the books in the library whose *titles* contain the words chemicals and food. (Note: the word "and" in this context is an *operator*; it tells the computer to look for books with *both* words in their title fields. Another option would be to use the word "or"; doing so would instruct the computer to locate titles containing either word.)

Why is a keyword search useful? Chiefly for two reasons. First, when you're just beginning your research you won't necessarily know all the right subject headings for the books you want, but you probably will already know some of the words likely to appear in their titles; performing a keyword search will quickly give you a sense of what's available. Second, a keyword search can be a kind of shortcut to finding a group of useful subject headings because the full bibliographic record for each book located by the keyword search will list all the subject headings under which the book is classified.

It's also usually possible to **limit an on-line search**. Let's say the list you retrieved during your initial subject search is very long—too long to browse through in the time you have available. You may be able to generate a shorter and more focused list by telling the computer to limit the search—for example, to books written in English or published during a particular range of years, or to books located in a particular part of your library (or in a library within your university's library system—the science library or the humanities library perhaps).

You may at this point decide to browse through the list you've generated, pausing to read the full catalog record (or "long display") for titles that interest you. Your attention may have been caught, for example, by the title *Safe Food: Eating Wisely in a Risky World*. Reading the full record for this title, illustrated in our third screen image, will tell you the authors' names, the publisher, and the date and place of publication. (This information should enable you to decide if the book may be useful to you.)

HU SHORT DISPLAY page 1 of 1   Item 36 of 94 retrieved by your search:

FIND SU FOOD ADDITIVES

---HU HOLLIS# ALM1510 /bks

AUTHOR:	Jacobson, Michael F.
TITLE:	Safe food : eating wisely in a risky world / Michael F. Jacobson, Lisa Y. Lefferts, Anne Witte Garland.
PUB. INFO:	Los Angeles, Calif. : Living Planet Press, c1991.
DESCRIPTION:	xvi, 234 p. : ill. ; 24 cm.
SUBJECTS:	*S1 Food—Toxicology.
	*S2 Food adulteration and inspection.
	*S3 Food additives.
LOCATION:	Hilles: RA1258.J32 1991x
	C2 - Enter DISPLAY C2 for circulation information
	Schlesinger: 641.5637 J17s

OPTIONS: -----------------------

Display Long		Next - next item	Help
LOCation	TRace *S1 (etc)	PRevious - prev item	Quit
Index	REDo - edit search	STORe - save for email	COMment
COMMAND?			

4-©   Sess-2   128.103.60.84

The record also gives the book's length, call number, location, and availability—in addition to (as we note above) the subject headings under which it is listed. You'll want to keep this information at hand: you'll need the call number in order to find the book on the shelf; you'll need the name of the author and the publication data when you make the Works Cited list or bibliography for your essay. To record all this information you can (obviously) write it on a notecard or piece of paper. But you may also be able simply to print it on one of the library's printers. Alternately, you may be able to email it to yourself or download it onto a computer disk.

SCANNING BOOKS AND BOOK REVIEWS

At this point you can begin to scan some of the books you've located, or you can put off looking at the books until you have found some relevant articles in periodicals. For the moment, let's postpone the periodicals.

Put a bunch of books in front of you, and choose one as an introduction. How do you choose one from half a dozen? Partly by its size—choose a thin one because it's less likely to bury you in details—and partly by other qualities. Roughly speaking, the book you choose should be among the more recent publications, and it should strike you as fair. A pamphlet published by a meat-packers association is desirably thin but you have a hunch that it may be biased. Roger John Williams's *Nutrition in a Nutshell* is published by a well-known commercial press (Doubleday), and it is only 171 pages, but because it was published in 1962 it may not reflect current food chemistry. The book *Safe Food,* published in 1991 and 243 pages long, might be a better place to start.

When you have found the book that you think may serve as your introductory study, do the following:

- **Read the preface** in order to get an idea of the author's purpose and outlook.
- **Scan the table of contents** in order to get an idea of the organization and the coverage.
- **Scan the final chapter or the last few pages,** where you may be lucky enough to find a summary. (You're not reading a novel; skipping to the end isn't against the rules.)

The index, too, may let you know if the book will suit your purpose by showing you what topics are covered and how much coverage they get. If the book still seems suitable, scan it.

At this stage it is acceptable to trust your hunches—you are only going to scan the book, not buy it or even read it—but you may want to look up some book reviews to assure yourself that the book has merit. There are two especially useful general indexes to book reviews:

Book Review Digest (published from 1905 onward)

Book Review Index (1965–)

There are also indexes to specialized fields. Given the topic of food additives, you might want to consult, in order to locate reviews in journals,

Business Periodicals Index (1958–)

General Science Abstracts (1978–)

Most reviews of books will come out in the same year as the book, or within the next two years. If, for example, a book was published in 1995, look in the

1995 volume of the appropriate index and see what is there. If you want some more reviews, look in 1996 and 1997. Begin with *Book Review Digest,* because it includes excerpts from and synopses of the reviews; if it has your book, the excerpts and synopses may be enough, and you won't have to dig out the reviews themselves. But *Book Review Digest* does not have as broad coverage as the other indexes, and you may have to turn to them for citations, and then to the journals to which they refer you. (*Book Review Digest* covers about 200 periodicals; *Book Review Index* covers about 450.) Read the synopses in *Book Review Digest,* or some reviews in journals, and draw some conclusions about the merit of the book in question. Of course, you cannot assume that every review is fair, but a book that on the whole gets good reviews is probably at least good enough for a start.

By quickly reading such a book (take few or no notes at this stage) you will probably get an overview of your topic, and you will begin to see exactly what part of the topic you wish to pursue.

FINDING ARTICLES IN PERIODICALS

Your next step may be to locate articles in periodicals and academic journals. On some topics, especially recent happenings, there may be few or even no books, but there may well be many articles published in newspapers and magazines. Further, it's often the case that scholars publish their work in journals before it is published in book form. You can start thumbing through these publications at random, but such a procedure is monstrously inefficient. Fortunately, there are indexes to periodicals, so you can quickly find the latest writing on your topic. As we note above, many indexes are available on line.

Among the most widely used on-line indexes are

Readers' Guide to Periodical Literature (1900–)

Arts and Humanities Abstracts

Social Science Abstracts

Science Citation Abstracts

Readers' Guide indexes about 200 of the more familiar magazines—such as *Atlantic, Ebony, Nation, Scientific American, Sports Illustrated,* and *Time.* The other three indexes are guides to academic journals in the sciences and humanities. If you were looking for articles on Chopin's novel *The Awakening*, you might begin by doing a search in *Humanities Abstracts.* If you wanted to find articles on food additives, you might check *Science Abstracts.* To search these indexes, at the prompt you simply type terms relevant to your topic.

Keep in mind that indexes we discuss above are only a few of the many, many indexes available. Each discipline has its own specialized index, from *Accountant's Index* to *World Law Index.* To find the indexes most likely to help you find the articles you're looking for, search your library's electronic resources by keyword or subject—or consult a research librarian.

FINDING BIBLIOGRAPHIES

Many researchers have published bibliographies, that is, lists of the works they have consulted. Sometimes the bibliographies appear as articles in scholarly journals or as appendices to books, or even as entire books. All of these kinds of bibliographies are listed in *Bibliographic Index,* a print resource that is issued three times a year and cumulates in an annual volume. Begin, of course, with the most recent issue, check it for your subject, and then work back for a few years. A recent bibliography will probably offer you as many sources as you will have time to consult. You may be able to locate a bibliography of works in your field by performing an on-line catalog subject search (note the third item on the subject heading list on page 310): simply enter your subject heading, then a dash and the word "bibliography." You're also likely to find bibliographies in various disciplines when you consult the list of your library's electronic resources.

A WORD ON THE INTERNET

The Internet, a vast network of interconnected computers, can be a tremendous resource for researchers. But because anyone, anywhere, can post pretty much anything, the information available on the Internet can be difficult to evaluate. When you're working with secondary sources that have been published in journals or in book form, for the most part you're working with material that experts in that field have judged to be worth reading. Before it's published, an article in the journal *College English,* for example, will have been read by a number of reviewers (most or all of them college English professors), as well as by members of an advisory board and several editors. If *College English* is in your institution's library—and we bet it is—it's there in part because librarians have decided it's worth including in the serials collection. An article in *College English* may have weaknesses, but several experts have thought it was pretty good.

Information available on the Internet has not been similarly vetted. Advertisements coexist with course syllabi. One could (if one wanted to) access a chat-group on Leonardo DiCaprio as easily as one could find photographs of people's pets. Or an interview with Jamaica Kincaid. Or the full text of *Romeo and Juliet.* Or an essay on your research topic, written by your professor—or by the person who sits next to you in your biology class.

How do you judge what may be worth considering? In part by using the critical thinking skills we discuss elsewhere in this book. Ask questions of the material:

- Who is the author?
- For whom is the author writing? What is the intended audience?
- Who sponsored the document?
- Can you tell if the author is an authority in the field? (Perhaps the document is linked to the author's homepage.)
- Does he or she reference other critics or writers? Good ones?
- Is the text well written?
- Do arguments seem well supported, or is the document full of vague generalizations?
- Does the author point you toward other resources?
- How current is the piece?

For more on this matter, we recommend (appropriately enough) that you consult documents available on the Web, such as "Evaluating Information Found on the Internet" (http://milton.mse.jhu.edu:8001/research/education/net.html). It *should* still be available—but that's the other problem with Internet sources: what's here today may be gone tomorrow.

READING AND TAKING NOTES ON SECONDARY SOURCES

Almost all researchers—professionals as well as beginners—find that they end up with some notes that are irrelevant, and, on the other hand, find that when drafting the paper they vaguely remember certain material that they now wish they had taken notes on. Especially in the early stages of one's research, when the topic and thesis may still be relatively unfocused, it's hard to know what is noteworthy and what is not. You simply have to flounder a bit.

As we suggest above, it may be helpful to read (or skim) an article or book all the way through the first time around without taking notes. By the time you reach the end, you may find it isn't noteworthy. Or you may find a useful summary near the end that will contain most of what you can get from the piece. Or you will find that, having a sense of the whole, you can now quickly reread the piece and take notes on the chief points.

Even if you do follow this procedure, a certain amount of inefficiency is inevitable; therefore plenty of time should be allowed. And it's worth keeping in mind that different people really do work differently. We list here three strategies; we suspect that, over time, you'll develop your own.

- Take notes using four-by-six-inch cards, writing on one side only, because material on the back of a card is usually neglected when you come to write the paper. (Taking notes by hand offers several advantages—not least of which is that you don't need access to a computer to do it.)

> Verrett, pp. 152-154 ✓   botulism argument
>   search for substitute
> p.152 Industry and gov't approved nitrite as color
> fixer. Now shifting ground, saying it prevents
> botulism. Verrett points out "legal snag." New
> approval needed for new use.
> (Thus public hearing and unwanted attention)
>
> p.154 "... the industry--USDA-FDA coalition seems
> firm in its position that there is no substitute for
> nitrate, now or ever. Their posture is misdirected
> at defending nitrites devising ways to keep it
> in food rather than ways to get it out. ✓
>   Verrett and Carper, Eating May Be Hazardous

- Take notes on your computer, keeping a separate file for each book or article. Material can be easily moved from one file to another as the organization of the essay begins to take shape.
- Don't take notes—or take very few notes. Photocopy secondary material you think you might use, and underline and annotate that material as you read and think about it. (Material from electronic sources can be downloaded and later printed out and annotated as well.) The disadvantage here is obvious: this method uses a lot of paper. But there are two big advantages. Passages from the sources are transcribed (or, in the

cases of downloaded material, moved) only once, into the draft itself, so there's less risk of mistakes and distortions. And the research—the collecting of information—can go very quickly. **A word of caution** though: it's crucial that you think carefully about the material you're collecting and that you annotate it thoroughly. If you don't, you'll find yourself with a pile of paper, and no idea of what to do with it.

A Guide to Note Taking

1. Be sure to record the title and author of the source. If you're using notecards, specify the source in an abbreviated form in the upper left corner; if you're taking notes on your computer, make a separate file for each book or article, and use the author's name and the first significant word of the title to identify the file. If you're using photocopies, make sure that you also photocopy the bibliographic information—which usually appears in full on the title pages of book and often (but not always) appears on the first page of a journal article. (And be sure to make a record of the full span of the article, not just the pages that you have copied.)

2. Write summaries, not paraphrases (that is, write abridgments rather than restatements, which in fact may be as long as or longer than the original). There is rarely any point to paraphrasing. Generally speaking, either quote exactly (and put the passage in quotation marks, with a notation of the source, including the page number or numbers) or summarize, reducing a page or even an entire article or chapter of a book to a few sentences that can be written on a note card, typed into your computer, or squeezed into the margin of a photocopied page. Even when you summarize, record your source (including the page numbers), so that you can give appropriate credit in your essay.

3. Quote sparingly. Of course in your summary you will sometimes quote a phrase or a sentence—putting it in quotation marks—but quote sparingly. You are not simply transcribing what you read; rather you are assimilating knowledge and you are thinking, and so for the most part your source should be digested rather than engorged whole. Thinking now, while taking notes, will also help you later to avoid plagiarism. If, on the other hand, when you take notes you mindlessly copy material at length, later when you are writing the essay you may be tempted to copy it yet again, perhaps without giving credit. Similarly, if you simply photocopy pages from articles or books, and then merely underline some passages without annotating your reading, you probably will not be thinking; you will just be underlining. But if you make a terse summary you will be forced to think and to find your own words for the idea. Quote directly only those passages that are particularly effective, or crucial, or memorable. In your finished essay these quotations will provide authority and emphasis.

4. Quote accurately. After copying a quotation, check your transcription against the original, and correct any misquotation. Verify the page number also. If a quotation runs from the bottom of, say, page 306 to the top of 307, make a distinguishing mark (for instance two backslashes after the last word of the first page), so that if you later use only part of the quotation, you will know the page on which it appeared.

5. Use ellipses (three spaced periods) to indicate the omission of any words within a sentence. If the omitted words are at the end of the quoted sentence, put a period immediately at the point where you end the sentence, and then add three spaced periods to indicate the omission. Example:

> If the . . . words were at the end of the quoted sentence, put a period

immediately at the end. . . .

Use square brackets to indicate your additions to the quotation. Here is an example.

> Here is an [uninteresting] example.

6. *Never* **copy a passage by changing an occasional word,** under the impression that you are thereby putting it into your own words. Notes of this sort may find their way into your essay, your reader will sense a style other than your own, and suspicions (and perhaps even charges) of plagiarism will follow. (For a detailed discussion of plagiarism, see below).

7. **Comment on your notes.** Again, consider it your obligation to *think* about the material as you make your notes, evaluating it and using it as a stimulus to further thought. For example, you may want to say "Tyler seems to be generalizing from insufficient evidence," or "Corsa made the same point five years earlier"; but make certain that later you will be able to distinguish between these comments and the notes summarizing or quoting your source. A suggestion: surround all comments recording your responses with double parentheses, thus: ((. . .)).

8. **Write a keyword on each card or at the beginning of each section of notes in your computer file.** A brief key—for example "effect on infants' blood"—can help you to tell at a glance what is on the card or in the file.

ACKNOWLEDGING SOURCES

Borrowing Without Plagiarizing

As we suggested earlier, respect for your readers and for your sources requires that you acknowledge your indebtedness for material when

1. you quote directly from a work, or
2. you paraphrase or summarize someone's words (the words of your paraphrase or summary are your own, but the points are not), or
3. you appropriate an idea that is not common knowledge.

Most commonly, the words, ideas, and information you'll cite in a research essay will come from printed and electronic sources. But you must also acknowledge the advice of peer editors and ideas that come from lectures and class discussions (unless your instructor tells you not to do so). We give the form for acknowledging peer editors on pages 28–29; we'll tell you how to document all these other sources in the pages that follow.

Let's suppose you are going to make use of William Bascom's comment on the earliest responses of Europeans to African art:

> The first examples of African art to gain public attention were the bronzes and ivories which were brought back to Europe after the sack

of Benin by a British military expedition in 1897. The superb technology of the Benin bronzes won the praise of experts like Felix von Luschan who wrote in 1899, "Cellini himself could not have made better casts, nor anyone else before or since to the present day." Moreover, their relatively realistic treatment of human features conformed to the prevailing European aesthetic standards. Because of their naturalism and technical excellence, it was at first maintained that they had been produced by Europeans—a view that was still current when the even more realistic bronze heads were discovered at Ife in 1912. The subsequent discovery of new evidence has caused the complete abandonment of this theory of European origins of the bronzes of Benin and Ife, both of which are cities in Nigeria.

> —William Bascom, *African Art in Cultural Perspective*
> (New York: Norton, 1973), p. 4

1. Acknowledging a direct quotation. You may want to use some or all of Bascom's words, in which case you will write something like this:

As William Bascom says, when Europeans first encountered Benin and Ife works of art in the late nineteenth century, they thought that Europeans had produced them, but the discovery of new evidence "caused the complete abandonment of this theory of European origins of the bronzes of Benin and Ife, both of which are cities in Nigeria" (4).

Normally, at the end of an essay a page headed Works Cited will give bibliographic information (author, title, place of publication, name of the publisher, and date of publication) for each work cited within the essay, but of course in a relatively informal essay it may be enough merely to mention, in the body of the essay, the author, title, and page number, without later specifying place of publication, publisher, and date. The point here is not that you must use detailed footnotes but that you must give credit. Not to give credit is to plagiarize, which is a serious breach of the rules governing academic work.

2. Acknowledging a paraphrase or summary. Summaries (abridgments) are usually superior to paraphrases (rewordings, of approximately the same length as the original) because summaries are briefer, but occasionally you may find that you cannot abridge a passage in your source and yet you don't want to quote it word for word—perhaps because it is too technical or because it is poorly written. Even though you are changing some or all of the words, you must give credit to the source because the idea is not yours, nor, probably, is the sequence of the presentation.

Here is an example of a summary:

William Bascom, in <u>African Art</u>, points out that the first examples of African art--Benin bronzes and ivories--brought to Europe were thought by Europeans to be of European origin, because of their naturalism and their technical excellence, but evidence was later discovered that caused this

theory to be abandoned.

Not to give Bascom credit is to plagiarize, even though the words are yours. The offense is just as serious as not acknowledging a direct quotation. And, of course, if you say something like this and do not give credit, you are also plagiarizing, even though almost all of the words are your own:

The earliest examples of African art to become widely known in

Europe were bronzes and ivories that were brought to Europe in 1897.

These works were thought to be of European origin, and one expert said

that Cellini could not have done better work. Their technical excellence, as

well as their realism, fulfilled the European standards of the day. The later

discovery of new evidence at Benin and Ife, both in Nigeria, refuted this

belief.

It is pointless to offer this sort of rewording: If there is a point, it is to conceal the source and to take credit for thinking that is not your own.
    3. Acknowledging an idea. Let us say that you have read an essay in which Irving Kristol argues that journalists who pride themselves on being tireless critics of national policy are in fact irresponsible critics because they have no policy they prefer. If this strikes you as a new idea and you adopt it in an essay—even though you set it forth entirely in your own words and with examples not offered by Kristol—you should acknowledge your debt to Kristol. *Not to acknowledge such borrowing is plagiarism.* Your readers will not think the less of you for naming your source; rather, they will be grateful to you for telling them about an interesting writer.

Fair Use of Common Knowledge

If in doubt as to whether or not to give credit (either with formal documentation or merely in a phrase such as "Carol Gilligan says . . ."), give credit. But as you begin to read widely in your field or subject, you will develop a sense of what is considered common knowledge.
    Unsurprising definitions in a dictionary can be considered common knowledge, and so there is no need to say "According to Webster, a novel is a long narrative in prose." (That's weak in three ways: it's unnecessary, it's uninteresting, and it's inexact since "Webster" appears in the titles of several dictionaries, some good and some bad.)
    Similarly, the date of Freud's death can be considered common knowledge. Few can give it when asked, but it can be found out from innumerable sources, and no one need get the credit for providing you with the date. Again, if you simply *know*, from your reading of Freud, that Freud was interested in literature,

you need not cite a specific source for an assertion to that effect, but if you know only because some commentator on Freud said so, and you have no idea whether the fact is well known or not, you should give credit to the source that gave you the information. Not to give credit—for ideas as well as for quoted words—is to plagiarize.

"But How Else Can I Put It?"

If you have just learned—say from an encyclopedia—something that you sense is common knowledge, you may wonder, How can I change into my own words the simple, clear words that this source uses in setting forth this simple fact? For example, if before writing about the photograph of Buffalo Bill and Sitting Bull (page 176), you look up these names in the *Encyclopaedia Britannica,* you will find this statement about Buffalo Bill (William F. Cody): "In 1883 Cody organized his first Wild West exhibition." You cannot use this statement as your own, word for word, without feeling uneasy. But to put in quotation marks such a routine statement of what can be considered common knowledge, and to cite a source for it, seems pretentious. After all, the *Encyclopedia Americana* says much the same thing in the same routine way: "In 1883, . . . Cody organized Buffalo Bill's Wild West." It may be that the word "organized" is simply the most obvious and the best word, and perhaps you will end up using it. Certainly to change "Cody organized" into "Cody presided over the organization of" or "Cody assembled" or some such thing, in an effort to avoid plagiarizing, would be to make a change for the worse and still to be guilty of plagiarism. But you won't get yourself into this mess of wondering whether to change clear, simple wording into awkward wording if in the first place, when you take notes, you *summarize* your sources, thus: "1883: organized Wild West," or "first Wild West: 1883." Later (even if only thirty minutes later), when drafting your paper, if you turn this nugget—probably combined with others—into the best sentence you can, you will not be in danger of plagiarizing, even if the word "organized" turns up in your sentence.

Of course, even when dealing with material that can be considered common knowledge—and even when you have put it into your own words—you probably *will* cite your source if you are drawing more than just an occasional fact from a source. If, for instance, your paragraph on Buffalo Bill uses half a dozen facts from a source, cite the source. You do this both to avoid charges of plagiarism and to protect yourself in case your source contains errors of fact.

WRITING THE ESSAY

When you use sources, you are not merely dumping on the table the contents of a shopping-cart filled at the scholar's supermarket, the library. You are cooking a meal. You must have a point, an opinion, a thesis; you are working toward a conclusion, and your readers should always feel they are moving toward that conclusion (by means of your thoughtful argument and use of sources) rather than reading an anthology of commentary on the topic. You've become an expert on your topic; you now know what others have to say about it, but if you've been *thinking* about what the secondary sources have said about your primary material, it's likely that you've noticed contradictions and gaps, that you agree with some opinions and arguments (and disagree with others), that you've begun to develop your *own* ideas about your topic.

There remains the difficult job of writing the essay. Beyond referring you to the rest of this book, we can offer only seven pieces of advice.

1. With a tentative thesis in mind, begin by rereading your notes and sorting them by topic. Put together what belongs together. Don't hesitate to reject material that—however interesting—now seems irrelevant or redundant. After sorting, resorting, and rejecting, you will have a kind of first draft without writing a draft.

2. From your notes you can make a first outline. Although you can't yet make a paragraph outline, you may find it useful to make a fairly full outline, indicating, for example, not only the sequence of points but also the quotations that you will use. In sketching the outline, of course you will be guided by your *thesis.* As you worked, you probably modified your tentative ideas in the light of what your further research produced, but by now you ought to have a relatively firm idea of what you want to say. Without a thesis you will have only the basis for a *report*, not a potential essay.

3. Transcribe or download quotations, even in the first draft, exactly as you want them to appear in the final version. Of course this takes some time, and the time will be wasted if, as may well turn out, you later see that the quotation is not really useful. (On the other hand, the time has not really been wasted, since it helped you ultimately to delete the unnecessary material.)

If at this early stage you just write a note reminding yourself to include the quotation—something like "here quote Jackson on undecided voters"—when you re-read the draft you won't really know how the page sounds. You won't, for instance, know how much help your reader needs by way of a lead-in to the quotation, or how much discussion should follow. Only if you actually see the quotation are you in the position of your audience—and all good writers try to imagine their audience.

4. Include, right in the body of the draft, all of the relevant citations so that when you come to revise you don't have to start hunting through your notes to find who said what, and where. You can, for the moment, enclose these citations within diagonal lines, or within double parentheses—anything at all to remind you that they will be your documentation.

5. Resist the urge to include every note in your essay. As we suggest in Chapter 1, writing is a way of discovering ideas. Consequently, as you write your first draft, your thesis will inevitably shift, and notes that initially seemed important will now seem irrelevant. Don't stuff them into the draft, even if you're concerned about meeting a page requirement: readers know padding when they see it.

6. Resist the urge to do more research. As you draft, you may also see places where another piece of evidence, another reference to a source, or another example would be useful. And you may feel compelled to head back to the library. We think that for now you should resist that urge too: it may simply be procrastination in disguise. Continue writing this first draft if possible, and plan to incorporate new material in a later draft.

7. As you revise your draft, make sure that you do not merely tell the reader "A says . . . B says . . . C says . . ." Rather, by using such expressions as "A claims," "B provides evidence that," "C gives the usual view," "D concedes that," you help the reader to see the role of the quotation in your paper.

Let your reader know why you are quoting, or how the quotation fits into your organization.

 A Checklist for Reading Drafts

- ✔ Is the tentative title informative and focused?
- ✔ Does the paper make a point, or does it just accumulate other people's ideas?
- ✔ Does it reveal the thesis early?
- ✔ Are generalizations supported by evidence?
- ✔ Are all the *words* and *ideas* of the sources accurately attributed?
- ✔ Are quotations introduced adequately?
- ✔ Are all of the long quotations necessary, or can some of them be effectively summarized?
- ✔ Are quotations discussed adequately?
- ✔ Does the paper advance in orderly stages? Can your imagined reader easily follow your thinking?
- ✔ Is the documentation in the correct form?

DOCUMENTATION

One purpose of documentation is to enable your readers to retrace your steps, to find your source and to read what you read—whether you read it in the library, on the Internet, or in today's newspaper. To make this possible, you must give your readers enough information to locate and identify each source you cite. For printed sources, this information generally includes:

- the author
- the publisher
- the date and place of publication
- a page number

And for electronic sources, this information includes (at minimum):

- the site address
- the date on which you accessed the information.

The way this information is presented varies from discipline to discipline: sociologists, for example, present the date of publication more prominently than do historians; at the end of a research work, engineers usually list their sources by number (in order of their appearance in the text) while literary critics list sources alphabetically by authors' names. In the following pages we discuss in detail two systems of documentation: The Modern Language Association (or MLA) and the American Psychological Association (or APA).

MLA Format

Citations Within the Text Brief parenthetic citations within the body of the essay are made clear by a list of your sources, entitled Works Cited, appended to the essay. Thus, an item in your list of Works Cited will clarify such a sentence in your essay as

> According to Angeline Goreau, Aphra Behn in her novels continually contradicts "the personal politics she had defended from the outset of her career as a writer" (252).

This citation means that the words inside the quotation marks appear on page 252 of a source written by Goreau which will be listed in Works Cited. More often than not the parenthetic citation appears at the end of a sentence, as in the example just given, but it can appear elsewhere in the sentence. Its position will depend in part on your ear, and in part on the requirement that you point clearly to the place where your source's idea ends, and your point begins. (In the following example, the idea that follows the parenthetic citation is not Gardiner's, but the writer's own.)

> Judith Kegan Gardiner, on the other hand, acknowledges that Behn's work "displays its conflicts with patriarchal authority" (215), conflicts that appear most notably in the third volume of Love Letters.

Seven points must be made about these examples:

1. Quotation marks. The closing quotation mark appears after the last word of the quotation, *not* after the parenthetic citation. Since the citation is not part of the quotation, the citation is not included within the quotation marks.

2. Omission of words (ellipsis). If the quoted words are merely a phrase, as in the example above, you do not need to indicate (by three spaced periods) that you are omitting material before or after the quotation, but if the quotation is longer than a phrase, and is not a complete sentence, you must indicate that you are omitting material. If you are omitting material from the beginning of the sentence, after the opening quotation mark put three spaced periods, and then give the quotation. If you are omitting material from the end of the sentence, put three spaced periods after the quoted words, or four periods if you are ending your sentence, one immediately after the last quoted word, the last three spaced, and then close with a quotation mark. (For more on ellipses, see pages 476–77.)

3. Addition of words. On occasion, you'll need to add a word or two to a quotation in order to clarify its meaning. If you must make such an addition—and such additions should be kept to a minimum because they're distracting—then enclose the word or words in square brackets, *not* parentheses. If the quotation contains a misspelling or other error, transcribe it as it appears in the source, and insert the word "sic" (Latin for "thus," as in "thus the word appears in the source; it's not *my* error") in italics and in square brackets, thus: [*sic*].

4. Punctuation with parenthetic citations. Look again at the two examples given a moment ago. Notice that if you follow a quotation with a parenthetic citation, any necessary period, semicolon, or comma *follows* the parenthetic citation. In the first example, a period follows the citation; in the second, a comma. In the next example, notice that the comma follows the citation.

Johnson insists that "these poems can be interpreted as Tory

propaganda" (72), but his brief analysis is not persuasive.

If, however, the quotation itself uses a question mark or an exclamation mark, this mark of punctuation appears *within* the closing quotation mark; even so, a period follows the parenthetic citation.

Jenkins-Smith is the only one to suggest doubt: "How can we accept

such a superficial reading of these works?" (178). He therefore rejects the

entire argument.

5. Two or more titles by one author. If your list of Works Cited includes more than one work by an author, you will have to give additional information (either in your sentence or within the parentheses) in order to indicate *which* of the titles you are referring to. We will go further into this in a moment (on page 326).

6. Long (or "block") quotations. We have been talking about short quotations, which are not set off but are embedded within your own sentences. Long quotations, usually defined as more than four lines of type, are set off, as in the example below.

Janet Todd explains Behn's reverence for the Stuart monarchy:

> She was a passionate supporter of both Charles II and James II
>
> as not simply rulers but as sacred majesties, god-kings on earth,
>
> whose private failings in no way detracted from their high
>
> office. . . . For her, royalty was not patriarchal anachronism as
>
> it would be for liberated women writers a hundred years on, but
>
> a mystical state. (73)

While it is true that Behn expressed "passionate support" in a poem written

in praise of James II (Todd 73), her novels suggest that her attitude toward

the Stuarts was much more complicated.

In introducing a long quotation, keep in mind that a reader will have trouble reading a sentence that consists of a lead-in, a long quotation, and then a continuation of your own sentence. It's better to have a short lead-in ("Janet Todd explains Behn's reverence for the Stuart monarchy"), and then set off a long quotation that is a complete sentence or group of sentences and therefore ends with a period. The quotation that is set off begins on a new line, is double-spaced and indented ten spaces (or one inch) from the left margin, and is *not* enclosed within quotation marks. Put a period at the end of the quotation (since the quotation is a complete sentence or group of sentences and is not embedded within a longer sentence of your own), hit the space bar twice, and then, on the same line, give the citation in parentheses. Do *not* put a period after the parenthetic citation that follows a long quotation.

   7. Citing a summary or a paraphrase. Even if you don't quote a source directly, but use its point in a paraphrase or a summary, you will give a citation:

   Goreau notes (89-90) that Behn participated in public life and in politics

not only as a writer: in the 1660s she went to Antwerp as a spy for

Charles II.

The basic point, then, is that the system of in-text citation gives the documentation parenthetically. Notice that in all but one of the previous examples the author's name is given in the text (rather than within the parenthetic citation). But there are several other ways of giving the citation, and we shall now look at them.

Author and Page Number in Parenthetic Citation

   Heroines who explore their own individuality (with varying degrees

of success and failure) abound in Chopin's work (Shinn 358).

   It doesn't matter whether you summarize (as in this example) or quote directly; the parenthetic citation means that your source is page 358 of a work by Shinn, listed in Works Cited, at the end of your essay.

Title and Page Number in Parentheses If, as we mentioned earlier, your list of Works Cited includes two or more titles by an author, you cannot in the text simply give a name and a page reference; the reader would not know to which of the titles you are referring. Let's assume that Works Cited includes two items by Larzer Ziff. If in a sentence in your essay you don't specify one title—that is, if you don't say something like, "For example, Larzer Ziff, in *The American 1890's,* claims . . ."—you will have to give the title (in a shortened form) in the parenthetic citation:

   Larzer Ziff, for example, claims that the novel "rejected the family as

the automatic equivalent of feminine self-fulfillment . . ." (<u>American</u> 175).

Notice in this example that *American* is a short title for Ziff's book *The American 1890's: Life and Times of a Lost Generation.* The full title is given in Works Cited, as is the title of another work by Ziff, but the short title in the parenthetic citation is enough to direct the reader to page 175 of the correct source in Works Cited.

   Notice also that when a short title and a page reference are given in parentheses, a comma is *not* used after the title.

Author, Title, and Page Number in Parentheses We have just seen that if Works Cited includes two or more works by an author, and if in your lead-in you do not specify which work you are at the moment making use of, you will have to give the title as well as the page number in parentheses. Similarly, if for some reason you do not in your lead-in mention the name of the author, you will have to add this bit of information to the parenthetic citation, thus:

> At least one critic has claimed that the novel "rejected the family as the automatic equivalent of feminine self-fulfillment . . ." (Ziff, American 175).

Notice that, as in the previous example, a comma does *not* separate the title from the page reference; but notice, too, that a comma *does* separate the author's name from the title. (Don't ask us why; ask the Modern Language Association. Or just obey orders.)

A Government Document or a Work of Corporate Authorship Treat the issuing body as the author. Thus, you will probably write something like this:

> The Commission on Food Control, in Food Resources Today, concludes that there is no danger (36-37).

A Work by Two or More Authors If a work is by *two authors,* give the names of both, either in the parenthetic citation (the first example below) or in a lead-in (the second example):

> Where the two other siblings strive compulsively either to correct or create problems, the sibling in the middle passively escapes from her painful family situation by withdrawing into herself (Seixas and Youcha 48-49).

or

> Seixas and Youcha note that where the two other siblings strive compulsively either to correct or create problems, the sibling in the middle passively escapes from her painful family situation by withdrawing into herself (48-49).

If there are more than *three authors,* give the last name of the first author, followed by "et al." (an abbreviation for *et alii,* Latin for "and others"), thus:

Gardner et al. found that . . .

or

Sometimes even higher levels are found (Gardner et al. 83).

Parenthetic Citation of an Indirect Source (Citation of Material That Itself Was Quoted or Summarized in Your Source)   Suppose you are reading a book by Jones, and she quotes Smith, and you wish to use Smith's material. Your citation will be to Jones—the source you are using—but of course you cannot attribute the words to Jones. You will have to make it clear that you are quoting not Jones but Smith, and so your parenthetic citation will look like this:

(qtd. in Jones 84-85)

Parenthetic Citation of Two or More Works

In microorganisms, nitrite enters the blood (Hervey 72; Lederer 195).

Note that a semicolon, followed by a space, separates the two sources.

A Work in More Than One Volume   This is a bit tricky.

1. If you have used only one volume, in Works Cited you will specify the volume, and so in your parenthetic in-text citation you will need to give only a page number—the very sort of thing illustrated by most of the examples that we have been giving.
2. If you have used more than one volume, your parenthetic citation will have to specify the volume as well as the page, thus:

   Landsdale points out that nitrite combines with hemoglobin to

   form a pigment which cannot carry oxygen (2: 370).

   The reference is to page 370 of volume 2 of a work by Landsdale.
3. If, however, you are citing not a page but an entire volume—let's say volume 2—your parenthetic citation would be

   (vol. 2)

   Or, if you did not name the author in your lead-in, it would be

   (Landsdale, vol. 2)

Notice that

- in citing a volume and page, the volume number, like the page number, is given in arabic (not roman) numerals;

- the volume number is followed by a colon, then a space, then the page number;
- abbreviations such as "vol." and "p." and "pg." are *not* used, except when citing a volume number without a page number, as illustrated in the last two examples.

An Anonymous Work For an anonymous work, give the title in your lead-in, or give it in a shortened form in your parenthetic citation:

Official Guide to Food Standards includes a statistical table on

nitrates (362).

or

A statistical table on nitrites is available (Official Guide 362).

But double-check to make sure that the work is truly anonymous. Some encyclopedias, for example, give the authors' names quietly. If initials follow the article, these are the initials of the author's name. Check the alphabetic list of authors given at the front of the encyclopedia.

A Literary Work You will specify the edition of a literary work in Works Cited—let's say Alvin Kernan's edition of *Othello,* or an edition of Conrad's *Heart of Darkness* with a preface by Albert Guerard—but because classic works of literature are widely available, and your reader may have at hand an edition different from the one that you have read, it is customary to use the following forms.

1. A novel. In parentheses give the page number of the edition you specify in Works Cited, followed by a semicolon, a space, and helpful additional information, thus:

(181; ch. 6)

or

(272; part 1, ch. 7).

2. A play. Most instructors want the act, scene, and (if the lines are numbered) the line numbers, rather than a page reference. Thus,

(2.4.18-23)

would refer to lines 18–23 of the fourth scene of the second act.

If you are quoting a few words within a sentence of your own, immediately after closing the brief quotation give the citation (enclosed within parentheses), and, if your sentence ends with the quotation, put the period after the closing parenthesis.

That Macbeth fully understands that killing Duncan is not a manly act but a villainous one is clear from his words to Lady Macbeth: "I dare do all that may become a man" (1.7.46). Moreover, even though he goes on to kill Duncan, he does not go on to deceive himself into thinking that his act was noble.

If, however, your sentence continues beyond the citation, after the parenthetic citation put whatever punctuation may be necessary (for instance, a comma may be needed), complete your sentence, and end it with a period.

This is clear from his words, "I dare do all that does become a man" (1.7.46), and he never loses his awareness of true manliness.

3. A poem. Preferences vary, and you can't go wrong in citing the page, but for a poem longer than, say, a sonnet (fourteen lines), most instructors find it useful if students cite the line numbers, in parentheses, after the quotations. In your first use, preface the numerals with "line" or "lines" (not in quotation marks, of course); in subsequent citations simply give the numerals. For very long poems that are divided into books, such as Homer's *Odyssey,* give the page, a semicolon, a space, the book number, and the line number(s). The following example refers to page 327 of a title listed in Works Cited; it goes on to indicate that the passage occurs in the ninth book of the poem, lines 130–35.

(327; 9.130-35)

Long quotations (more than three lines of poetry) are indented ten spaces. As we explained on page 325, if you give a long quotation, try to give one that can correctly be concluded with a period. After the period, hit the space bar three times, and then, on the same line, give the citation in parentheses.

A Personal Interview Probably you won't need a parenthetic citation, because you'll say something like

Cyril Jackson, in an interview, said . . .

or

According to Cyril Jackson, . . .

and when your readers turn to Works Cited, they will see that Jackson is listed, along with the date of the interview. But if you do not mention the source's name in the lead-in, you will have to give it in the parentheses, thus:

It has been estimated that chemical additives earn the drug

companies well over five hundred million dollars annually (Jackson).

Lectures If you use in your research essay a distinctive phrase, idea, or piece of information, from a class lecture or discussion, you'll want to give the speaker credit for it. If you give a signal phrase, the parenthetic citation should include only the date of the lecture; if you don't give a signal phrase, then include the speaker's name, followed by a comma, followed by the date. For example:

(Cahill, Sept. 20, 1999)

(The entry for the lecture on the Works Cited list will contain the title of the lecture—if there is one—and the place it was given.)

Electronic Sources Follow the format for print sources. In some cases, page numbers will be available; in others, paragraphs will be numbered; in still others; no number at all will be given. Use what you have, indicating the author's name or title where necessary, as determined by context. When giving paragraph numbers, use the abbreviation "pars." (Use a comma to separate the abbreviation from the author's name or title.)

One lawyer argued that Monica Lewinsky was nowhere near the

White House that day (Hedges, pars. 2-3).

A Note on Footnotes in an Essay Using Parenthetic Citations There are two reasons for using footnotes in an essay that chiefly uses parenthetic citations.

1. In a research paper you will of course draw on many sources, but in other kinds of papers you may be using only one source, and yet within the paper you may often want to specify a reference to a page or (for poetry) a line number, or (for a play) to an act, scene, and line number. In such a case, to append a page headed Work Cited, with a single title, is silly; it is better to use a single footnote when you first allude to the source. Such a note can run something like this:

[1]All references are to Mary Shelley, Frankenstein, afterword by

Harold Bloom (New York: Signet, 1965).

Here's another example of this sort of footnote:

[2]All experiments described in this paper were performed in January

1999 in the laboratory of Dr. Jan Pechenik, of Tufts University.

2. Footnotes can also be used in another way in a paper that documents sources by giving parenthetic citations. If you want to include some material that might seem intrusive in the body of the essay, you may relegate it to a footnote. For example, in a footnote you might translate a quotation given in a foreign language, or in a footnote you might write a paragraph—a sort of mini-essay—in which you offer an amplification of some point. By putting the amplification in a footnote you are signaling to the reader that it is dispensable; it is, so to speak, thrown in as something extra, something relevant but not essential to your argument.

A raised arabic numeral indicates in the body of your text that you are adding a footnote at this point. (The "insert" function of your word processing program will insert both the raised numeral and the text of your footnote in the appropriate places in your essay; simply click "insert" at the point in the text where you want the footnote to appear, and follow the program's instructions.)

Joachim Jeremias's <u>The Parables of Jesus</u> is probably the best

example of this sort of book.[1]

Usually the number is put at the end of a sentence, immediately after the period, but put it earlier if clarity requires you to do so.

Helen Cam[1] as well as many lesser historians held this view.

The List of Works Cited   Your parenthetic documentation consists of references that become meaningful when the reader consults a list entitled Works Cited, given at the end of your essay. We give sample entries below, but see also the list of Works Cited at the end of a student's documented paper, on page 361.

The list of Works Cited continues the pagination of the essay; if the last page of text is 10, then the list begins on page 11. Your last name and the page number will appear in the upper right corner, half an inch from the top of the sheet. Next, type "Works Cited," centered, one inch from the top, then double-space and type the first entry. Here are the governing conventions.

Alphabetic Order
1. Arrange the list alphabetically by author, with the author's last name first.
2. List an anonymous work alphabetically under the first word of the title, or under the second word if the first word is *A, An,* or *The,* or a foreign equivalent.
3. If your list includes two or more works by one author, the work whose title comes earlier in the alphabet precedes the work whose title comes later in the alphabet.

Form on the Page
1. Begin each entry flush with the left margin, but if an entry runs to more than one line, indent five spaces for each succeeding line of the entry.
2. Double-space each entry, and double-space between entries.

From here on, things get complicated. We will begin with

> books, then
>
> films, television and radio programs (page 340),
>
> articles in journals and newspapers (pages 340–41), and finally,
>
> electronic sources (pages 341–45).

The forms for books are as follows.

The Author's Name Note that the last name is given first, but otherwise the name is given as on the title page. Do not substitute initials for names written out on the title page.

If your list includes two or more works by an author, the author's name is not repeated for the second title, but is represented by three hyphens followed by a period and two spaces. When you give two or more works by the same author, the sequence is determined by the alphabetic order of the titles, as in the example below, listing two books by Blassingame, where *Black* precedes *Slave*.

Bishop, Robert. American Folk Sculpture. New York: Dutton, 1974.

Blassingame, John W. Black New Orleans, 1860-1880. Chicago: U of

   Chicago P, 1973.

---. The Slave Community: Plantation Life in the Antebellum South. Rev. ed.

   New York: Oxford UP, 1979.

Danto, Arthur. Embodied Meanings. New York: Farrar, 1994.

We have already discussed the treatment of an anonymous work; in a few moments we will discuss books by more than one author, government documents, and works of corporate authorship.

The Title Take the title from the title page, not from the cover or the spine, but disregard any unusual typography—for instance, the use of only capital letters, or the use of & for *and*. Italicize or underline the title and subtitle. (The MLA recommends underlining rather than italicizing in texts submitted in courses or for publication because underlining may be more visible to readers.) If you choose to underline the title, use one continuous underline, but do not underline the period that concludes this part of the entry.) Example:

   Frankenstein: Or, The Modern Prometheus.

A peculiarity: italicizing is used to indicate the title of a book, but if a title of a book itself includes the title of a book (for instance, a book about Mary Shelley's *Frankenstein* might include the title of her novel in its own title), the title-within-the-title is neither italicized nor underlined. Thus the title would be given as (if italicized)

The Endurance of Frankenstein.

If it were underlined, it would be

The Endurance of Frankenstein.

Place of Publication, Publisher, and Date For the place of publication, give the name of the city (you can usually find it either on the title page or on the copyright page, which is the reverse of the title page). If several cities are listed, give only the first. If the city is not likely to be widely known, or if it may be confused with another city of the same name (for instance, Cambridge, Massachusetts, and Cambridge, England), add the name of the state.

The name of the publisher is abbreviated. Usually the first word is enough (Random House becomes Random; Little, Brown and Co. becomes Little), but if the first word is a first name, such as in Alfred A. Knopf, the surname (Knopf) is used instead. University presses are abbreviated thus: Yale UP, U of Chicago P, State U of New York P.

The date of publication of a book is given when known; if no date appears on the book, write but *not* enclosed in quotation marks, "n.d." to indicate "no date."

Here are sample entries, illustrating the points we have covered thus far:

Douglas, Ann. The Feminization of American Culture. New York: Knopf,

1977.

Early, Gerald. One Nation Under a Groove: Motown and American Culture.

Hopewell, N.J.: Echo, 1995.

Feitlowitz, Marguerite. A Lexicon of Terror: Argentina and the Legacies of

Torture. New York: Oxford UP, 1998.

Frye, Northrop. Fables of Identity: Studies in Poetic Mythology. New York:

Harcourt, 1963.

—. Fools of Time: Studies in Shakespearian Tragedy. Toronto: U of

Toronto P, 1967.

Kennedy, Paul. Preparing for the Twenty-First Century. New York:

Random, 1993.

Notice that a period follows the author's name, and another period follows the title. If a subtitle is given, as it is for Feitlowitz's book, it is separated from the title by a colon and a space. A colon follows the place of publication, a comma follows the publisher, and a period follows the date.

A Book by More Than One Author The book is alphabetized under the last name of the first author named on the title page. If there are *two or three authors,* the names of these are given (after the first author's name) in the normal order, *first name first.*

Majors, Richard, and Janet Mancini Billson. Cool Pose: The Dilemmas of

   Black Manhood in America. Lexington, MA: Lexington, 1992.

Notice, again, that although the first author's name is given *last name first,* the second author's name is given in the normal order. Notice, too, that a comma is put after the first name of the first author, separating the authors.

   If there are *more than three authors,* give the name of only the first, and then add (but *not* enclosed within quotation marks) "et al." (Latin for "and others").

Belenky, Mary Field, et al. Women's Ways of Knowing: The Development

   of the Self, Voice, and Mind. New York: Basic Books,

   1986.

Government Documents If the writer is not known, treat the government and the agency as the author. Most federal national documents are issued by the Government Printing Office (abbreviated to GPO) in Washington.

United States Congress. Office of Technology Assessment. Computerized

   Manufacturing Automation Employment, Education and the

   Workplace. Washington: GPO, 1984.

Works of Corporate Authorship Begin the citation with the corporate author, even if the same body is also the publisher, as in the first example:

American Psychiatric Association. Psychiatric Glossary. Washington:

   American Psychiatric Association, 1984.

Carnegie Council on Policy Studies in Higher Education. Giving Youth a

   Better Chance: Options for Education, Work, and Service. San

   Francisco: Jossey, 1980.

A Reprint, for Instance a Paperback Version of an Older Hardback After the title, give the date of original publication (it can usually be found on the copyright page of the reprint you are using), then a period, and then the place, publisher, and date of the edition you are using. The example indicates that Rourke's book was originally published in 1931 and that the student is using the Doubleday reprint of 1953.

Rourke, Constance. <u>American Humor</u>. 1931. Garden City, N.Y. Doubleday,

   1953.

A Book in Several Volumes

Friedel, Frank. <u>Franklin D. Roosevelt</u>. 4 vols. Boston: Little, 1973.

   If you have used more than one volume, in your essay you will (as has been explained on page 328) indicate a reference to, say, page 250 of volume 3 thus: (3: 250).
   If, however, you have used only one volume of the set—let's say volume 3— in your entry in Works Cited write, after the period following the date, "Vol. 3," as in the next entry:

Friedel, Frank. <u>Franklin D. Roosevelt</u>. 4 vols. Boston: Little, 1973.

   Vol. 3.

In this case, the parenthetic citation would be to the page only, not to the volume and page, since a reader will understand that the page reference must be to this volume. But notice that in Works Cited, even though you say you used only volume 3, you also give the total number of volumes.

One Book with a Separate Title in a Set of Volumes Sometimes a set of volumes with a title makes use also of a separate title for each book in the set. If you are listing such a book, use the following form:

Churchill, Winston. <u>The Age of Revolution</u>. Vol. 3 of <u>A History of the</u>

   <u>English-Speaking Peoples</u>. New York: Dodd, 1957.

A Book with an Author and an Editor

Churchill, Winston, and Franklin D. Roosevelt. <u>The Complete</u>

   <u>Correspondence</u>. 3 vols. Ed. Warren F. Kimball. Princeton: Princeton

   UP, 1985.

Shakespeare, William. <u>The Sonnets</u>. Ed. William Burto. New York: NAL,

   1965.

If a book has one editor, the abbreviation is "ed."; if two or more editors, "eds."

If you are making use of the editor's introduction or other editorial material, rather than of the author's work, list the book under the name of the editor, rather than of the author, following the form we give later for "An Introduction, Foreword, or Afterword."

A Revised Edition of a Book

Hall, James. Dictionary of Subjects and Symbols in Art. 2nd ed. New York:

Harper, 1979.

A Translated Book

Franqui, Carlos. Family Portrait with Fidel: A Memoir. Trans. Alfred

MacAdam. New York: Random, 1984.

But if you are discussing the translation itself, as opposed to the book, list the work under the translator's name. Thus

MacAdam, Alfred, trans. Family Portrait with Fidel: A Memoir. By Carlos

Franqui. New York: Random, 1984.

An Introduction, Foreword, or Afterword

Wolff, Cynthia Griffin. Introduction. The House Of Mirth. By Edith

Wharton. New York: Penguin, 1985. vii-xxvi.

Usually a book with an introduction or some such comparable material is listed under the name of the author of the book (here Wharton), rather than under the name of the writer of the introduction (here Wolff), but if you are referring to the apparatus rather than to the book itself, use the form just given. The words Introduction, Preface, Foreword, and Afterword are neither enclosed within quotation marks nor underlined.

A Book with an Editor but No Author Anthologies of literature fit this description, but here we have in mind a book of essays written by various people but collected by an editor (or editors), whose name appears on the collection.

Denevan, William M., ed. The Native Population of the Americas in 1492.

Madison: U of Wisconsin P, 1992.

A Work in a Volume of Works by One Author The following entry indicates that a short work by Susan Sontag—an essay called "The Aesthetics of Science"—appears in a book by Sontag entitled *Styles of Radical Will*. Notice that the inclusive page numbers of the short work are cited—not merely page numbers that you may happen to refer to, but the page numbers of the entire piece.

Sontag, Susan. "The Aesthetics of Science." In Styles of Radical Will. New

York: Farrar, 1969. 3-34.

A Work in an Anthology—That Is, in a Collection of Works by Several Authors
There are several possibilities here. Let's assume, for a start, that you have made use of one work in an anthology. In Works Cited, begin with the author (last name first) and title of the work you are citing, not with the name of the anthologist or the title of the anthology. Here is an entry for Coleridge's poem "Kubla Khan," found on pages 501-03 in the second volume of a two-volume anthology edited by David Damrosch and several others.

Coleridge, Samuel Taylor. "Kubla Khan." The Longman Anthology of

British Literature. Ed. David Damrosch et al. 2 vols. New York:

Longman, 1999. 2: 501-03.

Now let's assume that during the course of your essay you refer to several, rather than to only one, work in this anthology. You can, of course, list each work in the form just given. Or you can have an entry in Works Cited for Damrosch's anthology, under Damrosch's name, and then in each entry for a work in the anthology you can eliminate some of the data by simply referring to Damrosch, thus:

Coleridge, Samuel Taylor. "Kubla Khan." Damrosch 2: 501-03.

Again, this requires that you also list Damrosch's volume, thus:

Damrosch, David et al., eds. The Longman Anthology of British Literature.

2 vols. New York: Longman, 1999.

The advantage of listing the anthology separately is that if you are using a dozen works from the anthology, you can shorten the dozen entries in Works Cited merely by adding one entry, that of the anthology itself. Notice, of course, that in the body of the essay you would still refer to Coleridge and to your other eleven authors, not to the editor of the anthology—but the entries in Works Cited will guide the reader to the book you have used.

A Book Review

Vendler, Helen. Rev. of Essays on Style. Ed. Roger Fowler. Essays in

Criticism 16 (1966): 457-63.

If the review has a title, give it between the period following the reviewer's name and "Rev."

If a review is anonymous, list it under the first word of the title, or under the second word if the first word is *A, An,* or *The.* If an anonymous review has no title, begin the entry with "Rev. of" and then give the title of the work reviewed; alphabetize the entry under the title of the work reviewed.

An Article or Essay—Not a Reprint—in a Collection A book may consist of a collection (edited by one or more persons) of new essays by several authors. Here is a reference to one essay in such a book. (The essay, by Smith, occupies pages 178-94 in a collection edited by Lubiano.)

Smith, David Lionel. "What Is Black Culture?" The House That Race Built.

Ed. Wahneema Lubiano. New York: Vintage, 1998. 178-194.

An Article or Essay Reprinted in a Collection The previous example (Smith's essay in Lubiano's collection) was for an essay written for a collection. But some collections reprint earlier material, for example essays from journals, or chapters from books. The following example cites an essay that was originally printed in a book called *The Cinema of Alfred Hitchcock*. This essay has been reprinted in a later collection of essays on Hitchcock, edited by Arthur J. LaValley, and it was LaValley's collection that the student used.

Bogdanovich, Peter. "Interviews with Alfred Hitchcock." The Cinema of

Alfred Hitchcock. New York: Museum of Modern Art, 1963. 15-18.

Rpt. in Focus on Hitchcock. Ed. Albert J. LaValley. Englewood Cliffs:

Prentice, 1972. 28-31.

The student has read Bogdanovich's essay or chapter, but not in Bogdanovich's book, where it occupied pages 15-18. The material was actually read on pages 28-31 in a collection of writings on Hitchcock, edited by LaValley. Details of the original publication—title, date, page numbers, and so forth—were found in LaValley's collection. Almost all editors will include this information, either on the copyright page or at the foot of the reprinted essay, but sometimes they do not give the original page numbers. In such a case, the original numbers need not be included in the entry.

Notice that the entry begins with the author and the title of the work you are citing (here, Bogdanovich's interviews), not with the name of the editor of the collection or the title of the collection. In the following example, the student used an essay by Arthur Sewell; the essay was originally on pages 53-56 in a book by Sewell entitled *Character and Society in Shakespeare,* but the student encountered the piece on pages 36-38 in a collection of essays, edited by Leonard Dean, on Shakespeare's *Julius Caesar.* Here is how the entry should run:

Sewell, Arthur. "The Moral Dilemma in Tragedy: Brutus." Character and

Society in Shakespeare. Oxford: Clarendon, 1951. 53-56. Rpt. in

Twentieth Century Interpretations of Julius Caesar. Ed. Leonard F.

Dean. Englewood Cliffs: Prentice, 1968. 36-38.

An Encyclopedia or Other Alphabetically Arranged Reference Work The publisher, place of publication, volume number, and page number do *not* have to be given. For such works, list only the edition (if it is given) and the date.

For a *signed* article, begin with the author's last name. (If the article is signed with initials, check the volume for a list of abbreviations—it is usually near the front, but it may be at the rear—which will say what the initials stand for, and use the following form.)

Messer, Thomas. "Picasso." Encyclopedia Americana. 1998 ed.

For an *unsigned article,* begin with the title of the article.

"Picasso, Pablo (Ruiz y)." Encyclopaedia Britannica: Macropaedia. 1985 ed.

"Automation." The Business Reference Book. 1977 ed.

A Film Begin with the director's name (last name first), followed by "dir." Next give the title of the film, underlined, then a period, two spaces, the name of the studio, the date, and a period.

Spielberg, Steven, dir. Saving Private Ryan. Paramount, 1998.

A Television or Radio Program

Sixty Minutes. CBS. 31 Jan. 1999.

An Article in a Scholarly Journal The title of the article is enclosed within quotation marks, and the title of the journal is underlined to indicate italics.

Some journals are paginated consecutively—the pagination of the second issue begins where the first issue leaves off; but other journals begin each issue with page 1. The forms of the citations differ slightly. First, an article in a *journal that is paginated consecutively*:

Jacobus, Mary. "Tess's Purity." Essays in Criticism 26 (1976): 318-38.

Jacobus's article occupies pages 318-38 of volume 26, which was published in 1976. (Note that the volume number is followed by a space, and then by the year, in parentheses, and then by a colon, a space, and the page numbers of the entire article. Because the journal is paginated consecutively, the issue number does *not* need to be specified.

For a *journal that begins each issue with page 1* (there will be four page 1's each year if such a journal is a quarterly), the issue number must be given. After the volume number, type a period and (without hitting the space bar) the issue number, as in the next example.

Spillers, Hortense J. "Martin Luther King and the Style of the Black

Sermon." The Black Scholar 3.1 (1971): 14-27.

Spillers's article appeared in the first issue of volume 3 of *The Black Scholar.*

An Article in a Weekly, Biweekly, or Monthly Publication The date and page numbers are given, but volume numbers and issue numbers are usually omitted for these publications. The first example is for an article in a weekly publication:

McCabe, Bernard. "Taking Dickens Seriously." Commonwealth 14 May

1965: 245-46.

An Article in a Newspaper Because a newspaper usually consists of several sections, a section number or a capital letter may precede the page number. The example indicates that an article begins on page 1 of section 1 and is continued on a later page.

Bennet, James. "Judge Cites Possible Breaches of Ethics Guidelines by

Starr." New York Times 8 Aug. 1998. Sec. 1: 1+.

An Interview The citation gives the name of the person you interviewed, the form of the interview ("personal," "telephone," "E-mail"), and the date.

Curley, Michael. Personal interview. 3 Jul. 1999.

A Lecture In addition to the date of the lecture and the name of the speaker, the citation should include the title of the presentation (if there is one) and the place it was given. If there is no title, use a descriptive word or phrase such as "class lecture," but do not use quotation marks. If the lecture was sponsored by a particular organization or group, give that information before the date.

Cahill, Patricia A. Class lecture on Othello. Emory Univ. 20 Sept. 1999.

McNamara, Eileen. "Truth and Ethics in Writing." The Writers Writing for

a Living Lecture. Wellesley College Writing Program, Wellesley, MA.

10 Feb. 1999.

Portable Database Sources Material obtained from a portable database, such as a CD-ROM, magnetic tape, or diskette, is treated like print material, but with one important difference: you must specify the physical form of the source. This information comes after the underlined title of the source, and before the city of publication.

Database of African-American Poetry, 1760-1900. CD-ROM. Alexandria,

VA: Chadwyck-Healy, 1995.

Gates, Henry Louis, and Kwame Anthony Appiah, eds. Encarta Africana.

   CD-ROM. Redmond, WA: Microsoft, 1999.

If the database is periodically published and updated, then some additional information is required. You must include the original date of publication of the material you're using, as well as the date of publication for the database. And if the source of the information is not also the distributor (the MLA publishes the CD-ROM version of the MLA International Bibliography, for example, but SilverPlatter distributes it), you must include the distributor (or vendor's) name as well.

Odygaard, Floyd D. P. "California's Collodion Artist: The Images of William

   Dunniway." Military Images 1995 16(5): 14-19. America: History and

   Life on Disc. CD-ROM. ABC-Clio. Winter 1997-98.

On-line Sources On-line sources are treated like books and articles, with four major (and many minor) exceptions:

- The **Internet address** of the source is given in angle brackets at the end of the entry.
- The **date accessed**—the date on which *you* found the source—is included in the citation.
- **Page numbers** are included in the citation *only* if the source is paginated. (This is often the case with full-text on-line versions of books and journal articles, in which case the pagination follows that of the print source.)
- Sometime paragraphs are numbered; the citation gives **paragraph numbers** when the sources provides them.

   The basic format for an on-line source follows that of a print source. You give, in the following order,

- author,
- title,
- publication information (including date of original publication, if applicable), and
- page or paragraph numbers if available.

   Then you give additional information—as much as is applicable and available—in the following order.

- name of database, project, periodical, or site (underlined),
- number of volume, issue, or version,
- date of posting,
- name of site sponsor (if applicable),
- date *you* consulted the material, and
- electronic address (or URL) in angle brackets.

Again, keep in mind that one purpose of documentation is to enable your readers to retrace your steps. It may also be useful to keep in mind that like the Internet itself, guidelines for citing electronic sources are continually evolving. Our guidelines are based on the format given in "MLA Style" [20 May 1999] ⟨http://www.mla.org/main_stl.htm#sources⟩.

Here are some examples.

1. A Novel

Jewett, Sarah Orne. The Country of the Pointed Firs. 1910. Bartleby

Archive. Columbia U. 3 June 1999.

⟨http://www.cc.columbia.edu/acis/bartleby/jewett⟩.

2. Journal Article

Fluck, Winfried. "'The American Romance' and the Changing Functions of

the Imaginary." New Literary History 27.3 (1996) 415-457. Project

Muse. JHU. 1 May 1998. ⟨http://muse:jhu.edu:80/journals/new_literary_

history_/v27/27.3fluck.html⟩.

3. Magazine Article (from a Print Source)

Murphy, K. "Do Food Additives Subtract from Health?" Business Week 6

May 1996: 140. Lexis-Nexis. 12 May 1998.

4. Magazine Article (no Print Source)

Green, Laura. "Sexual Harassment Law: Relax and Try to Enjoy It." Salon.

3 March 1998. 14 Aug. 1998

⟨http://www.salon1999.com/mwt/feature/ 1998/03/cov_

03featurea.html⟩

5. Article in a Reference Work

"Chopin, Kate." Britannica Online. Vers 98.1.1. June 1998. Encyclopaedia

Britannica. 14 Aug. 1998.

⟨http://www.eb.com:180/cgi-bin/g?DocF=micro/125/57.html⟩.

Reuben, Paul P. "Chapter 6: 1890-1910: Kate Chopin (1851-1904)." <u>PAL:</u>

　　<u>Perspectives in American Literature--A Research and Reference</u>

　　<u>Guide.</u>⟨http://www.csustan.edu/english/reuben/pal/chap6/chopin

　　.html⟩ 20 March 1998.

6. Personal Website

Mendelsson, Jonathan. Homepage. 8 Jan. 1999.

　　　　⟨http://www.mit.edu/~jrmendel/index.html⟩.

7. E-mail

Maphet, Mercedes. "Re: Kate Chopin Diaries." E-mail to author. 4 May

　　1998.

8. Posting to a Discussion List

Searls, Damion. "Re: Fiction Inspired by Woolf." VWOOLF@lists.acs

　　.ohio-state.edu. On-line posting. 30 Oct. 1998.

　　Although we have covered the most common sources, it is entirely possible that you will come across a source that does not fit any of the categories that we have discussed. For several hundred pages of explanation of these matters, covering the proper way to cite all sorts of troublesome and unbelievable (but real) sources, see Joseph Gibaldi, *MLA Handbook for Writers of Research Papers,* 5th ed. (New York: Modern Language Association of America, 1999). Numerous websites also provide additional information about and discussion of documenting on-line sources. The research skills you've developed will enable you to locate and evaluate these sites, but to get you started, here are a few useful citations.

Harnack, Andrew, and Gene Kleppinger. "Beyond the MLA Handbook:

　　Documenting Electronic Sources on the Internet." 10 June 1996. 2

　　Feb. 1999. ⟨http://english.ttu.edu/kairos/1.2/inbox/

　　mla_ archive.html#citing sites⟩.

Li, Xia, and Nancy Crane. "Electronic Sources: MLA Style of Citation." 29

　　Apr. 1996. 1 Feb. 1999.

　　⟨http://www.uvm.edu/~xli/reference/mla.html⟩.

Walker, Janice R. " MLA-Style Citations of Electronic Source." Ver. 1.0,

Rev. Apr. 1995. 1 Feb. 1999.

⟨http://www.cas.usf.edu/english/walker/mla.html⟩.

APA Format

The MLA style is used chiefly by writers in the humanities. Writers in the social sciences and in business, education, and psychology commonly use a style developed by the American Psychological Association. In the following pages we give the chief principles of the APA style, but for full details the reader should consult the fourth edition (1994) of *Publication Manual of the American Psychological Association.*

An Overview of the APA Format A paper that uses the format prescribed by the American Psychological Association will contain brief parenthetical citations within the text and will end with a page headed "References," which lists all of the author's sources. This list of sources begins on a separate page, continuing the pagination of the last page of the essay itself. Thus, if the text of the essay ends on page 8, the first page of references is page 9.

Here are some general guidelines for formatting both the citations within the text and the list of references at the end of the essay.

Citations Within the Text The APA style emphasizes the date of publication; the date appears not only in the list of references at the end of the paper but also in the paper itself, when you give a brief parenthetic citation of a source that you have quoted or summarized or in any other way used. Here is an example:

Statistics for church attendance are highly unreliable (Catherton,

1991, p. 17).

The title of Catherton's book or article will be given in your list entitled References. By turning to the list, the reader will learn in what publication Catherton made this point.

A Summary of an Entire Work

Catherton (1991) concluded the opposite.

Or

Similar views are easily found (Catherton, 1991; Brinnin and Abse,

1992).

A Reference to a Page or Pages

Catherton (1991, p. 107) argues that "church attendance is
increasing but religious faith is decreasing."

A Reference to an Author Represented by More Than One Work in the References

As we explained in discussing the form of the material in References, if
you list two or more works that an author published in the same year, the works
are listed in alphabetic order, by the first letter of the title. The first work is labeled *a,* the second *b,* and so on. Here is a reference to the second work that
Catherton published in 1991:

Boston is "a typical large Northern city" so far as church attendance
goes (Catherton, 1991b).

The List of References

Form on the Page
1. Begin each entry flush with the left margin, but if an entry runs to more
   than one line, indent five spaces for each succeeding line of the entry.
2. Double-space each entry, and double-space between entries.

Alphabetic Order
1. Arrange the list **alphabetically by author.**
2. Give the **author's last name first,** then the initial *only* of the first and of
the middle name (if any).
3. **If there is more than one author,** name all of the authors, again inverting the name (last name first) and giving only initials for first and middle
names. (But do not invert the editor's name when the entry begins with the
name of an author who has written an article in an edited book. See the example
below, page 348, illustrating "A Work in a Collection of Essays.") When there are
two or more authors, use an ampersand (&) before the name of the last author.
Here is an example of an article in the seventh volume of a journal called *Journal
of Experimental Social Psychology:*

Berscheid, E., Hatfield, E., & Bohrnstett, G. (1971). Physical

attractiveness and dating choice: A test of the matching

hypothesis. Journal of Experimental Social Psychology 7, 173-

89.

4. **If there is more than one work by an author**, list the works in the
order of publication, the earliest first.
If two works by an author were published in the same year, give them in alphabetic order by the first letter of the title, disregarding *A, An,* or *The,* and their

foreign equivalents. Designate the first work as "a," the second as "b." Repeat the author's name at the start of each entry.

If the author of a work or works is also the co-author of other works listed, list the single-author entries first, arranged by date. Following these, list the multiple-author entries, in a sequence determined alphabetically by the second author's name. Thus, in the example below, notice that the works Bem wrote unassisted are listed first, arranged by date, and when two works appear in the same year they are arranged alphabetically by title. These single-author works are followed by the multiple-author works, with the work written with Lenney preceding the work written with Martyna and Watson.

Bem, S. L. (1974). The measurement of psychological androgyny. Journal of Consulting and Clinical Psychology, 42, 155-62.

Bem, S. L. (1981a). The BSRI and gender schema theory: A reply to Spence and Helmreich. Psychological Review, 88, 369-71.

Bem, S. L. (1981b). Gender schema theory: A cognitive account of sex typing. Psychological Review, 88, 354-64.

Bem, S. L., & Lenney, E. (1976). Sex-typing and the avoidance of cross-sex behavior. Journal of Personality and Social Psychology, 33, 48-54.

Bem, S. L., Martyna, W., & Watson, C. (1976). Sex-typing and androgyny: Further exploration of the expressive domain. Journal of Personality and Social Psychology, 34, 1016-23.

Form of Title

1. In references to books, capitalize only the first letter of the first word of the title (and of the subtitle, if any) and capitalize proper nouns. Underline the complete title and type a period after it.

2. In references to articles in periodicals or in edited books, capitalize only the first letter of the first word of the article's title (and subtitle, if any), and all proper nouns. Do not put the title within quotation marks. Type a period after the title of the article. For the title of the journal, and the volume and page numbers, see the next instruction.

3. In references to periodicals, capitalize all important words, as you would usually do. (Note that the rule for the titles of periodicals differs from the rule for books and articles.) Give the volume number in arabic numerals, and underline it. Do *not* use *vol.* before the number, and do not use *p.* or *pg.* before the page numbers.

Sample References

A Book by One Author

Money, J. (1980). Love and love sickness: The science of sex, gender

difference and pair-bonding. Baltimore: Johns Hopkins Press.

A Book by More than One Author

Spence, J. T., & Helmreich, R. L. (1978). Masculinity and femininity.

Austin: University of Texas Press.

A Collection of Essays

Bundy, W. P. (Ed.). (1985). The nuclear controversy. New York: New

American Library.

A Work in a Collection of Essays

Rogers, B. (1985). The Atlantic alliance. In W. P. Bundy (Ed.). The nuclear

controversy (pp. 41-52). New York: New American Library.

Government Documents   If the writer is not known, treat the government and
the agency as the author. Most federal documents are issued by the Government
Printing Office in Washington.

United States Congress. Office of Technology Assessment (1984).

Computerized manufacturing automation: Employment, education,

and the workplace. Washington, DC: U.S. Government Printing

Office.

An Article in a Journal That Paginates Each Issue Separately

Swinton, E. (1993, Winter). New wine in old casks: Sino-Japanese and

Russo-Japanese war prints. Asian Art, 27-49.

The publication is issued four times a year, each issue containing a page 27. It is
necessary, therefore, to tell the reader that this article appears in the winter
issue.

An Article in a Journal with Continuous Pagination

Herdt, G. (1991). Representations of homosexuality. Journal of the History

of Sexuality, 1, 481-504.

An Article from a Monthly or Weekly Magazine

Corliss, R. (1993, March 8). Bill Murray in the driver's seat. Time, p.

67.

An Article in a Newspaper

Perry, T. (1993, 16 February). Election to give Latinos new political clout

in San Diego. Los Angeles Times, sec. A, p. 3.

(*Note:* If no author is given, simply begin with the article title, followed by the date in parentheses.)

A Book Review

Bayme, S. (1993). Tradition or modernity? [Review of Neil Gillman, Sacred

fragments: Recovering theology for the modern Jew.] Judaism, 42,

106-13.

Bayme is the reviewer, not the author of the book. The book under review is called *Sacred Fragments: Recovering Theology for the Modern Jew,* but the review, published in volume 42 of a journal called *Judaism,* had its own title, "Tradition or Modernity?"

If the review does not have a title, type the material in square brackets, then two spaces, then the date (given in parentheses), and proceed as in the example just given.

Electronic Sources References to electronic sources generally follow the format for printed sources. Include

- the author,
- the year of publication (in parentheses),
- the title (and edition, if applicable),

then give

- the medium in brackets (e.g., on-line or CD-ROM);
- the word "Available" followed by the Internet address or the database name or supplier, and
- the date you retrieved the material (in brackets, with the year first).

The examples below follow guidelines set forth by Xia Li and Nancy B. Crane and retrieved from the website "Electronic Sources: APA Style of Citation" [Online] Available: http://www.uvm.edu/~xli/reference/apa.html [1999, Aug. 20].

1. A Professional or Government Site

Edlefsen, M. & Brewer, M. S. (no date). The national food safety database.

Nitrates/Nitrites [Online]. Available:

http://www.foodsafety.org/il/il089.htm [1998, May 6].

National Cancer Institute (1996, June). NCI fact sheet. Food additives.

[online]. Available: http://nisc8a.upenn.edu/pdg_html/6/eng/

600037.html. [1998, May 4].

2. An Encyclopedia Article

Muckraker (journ.). (1994-1998). In Britannica Online [online]. Available:

http://www.eb.com:180cgibin/g?DocF=index/mu/ckr.html [1999, Jan.

2].

3. A Newspaper Article

Legator, M. & Daniel, A. Reproductive systems can be harmed by toxic

exposure. Galveston County Daily News [online]. Available:

http://www.utmb.edu/toxics/newsp.htm#canen [1998, May 6].

Warrick, P. (1994, June 8). A frank discussion. Los Angeles Times

[online], p. E1. Available: Lexis-Nexis [1998, May 6].

4. A Journal Article

Tollefson, C. (1995, May 29). Stability preserved; preservatives; food

additives '95. Chemical Marketing Reporter 247(22), [online] p. SR28.

Available: Lexis-Nexis [May 6, 1998].

5. A book

Riis, J. (1890). How the other half lives. New York: Charles Scribner's

Sons. [Online] David Phillips. Available:

http://www.cis.edu/amstud/inforev/riis/ch#3/html [1998, 14 Sept].

A Note on Other Systems of Documentation

The MLA style is commonly used in the humanities, and the APA style is commonly used in the social sciences, but many other disciplines use their own styles. What follows is a list of handbooks that give the systems used in some other disciplines.

Biology

Council of Biology Editors, Style Manual Committee. *Scientific Style and Format: CBE Style Manual for Authors, Editors, and Publishers in the Biological Sciences.* 6th ed. New York: Cambridge University Press, 1994.

Chemistry

American Chemical Society. *ACS Style Guide: A Manual for Authors and Editors,* 2nd ed. Washington, D. C.: American Chemical Society, 1997.

Geology

U.S. Geological Survey. *Suggestions to Authors of the Reports of the United States Geological Survey.* 8th ed. Washington: GPO, Department of the Interior, 1997.

Law

The Bluebook: A Uniform System of Citation. 16th ed. Cambridge: Harvard Law Review Association, 1996.

Mathematics

American Mathematical Society. *A Manual for Authors of Mathematical Papers.* 8th ed. Providence, R.I.: American Mathematical Society, 1990.

Medicine

American Medical Association, *Manual of Style.* 8th ed. Acton, Mass.: Publishing Sciences Group, 1989.

Physics

American Institute of Physics, *Style Manual for Guidance in the Preparation of Papers,* 4th ed. New York: American Institute of Physics, 1990.

TWO SAMPLE RESEARCH ESSAYS BY STUDENTS

Here are two essays in which students have drawn on the writing of others in developing their ideas. The first, "Politics and Psychology in *The Awakening*," by Beatrice Cody, uses the MLA form of in-text citations, which are clarified by a list headed "Works Cited." The second—Jacob Alexander's "Nitrite: Preservative or Carcinogen?"—uses the APA form of in-text citations, which are clarified by a list headed "References."

MLA Style

Beatrice Cody

Ms. Bellanca

Writing 125

1 April 99

Politics and Psychology in <u>The Awakening</u>

Title announces focus and scope of essay.

At first glance, Kate Chopin's novel <u>The Awakening</u> (1899) poses no problem to the feminist reader. It is the story of Edna Pontellier, a woman living at the turn of

Plot summary helps orient readers unfamiliar with novel.

the century who, partly through a half-realized summer romance, discovers that sensual love, art, and individuality mean more to her than marriage or motherhood. When she concludes that there can be no compromise between her awakened inner self and the stifling shell of her outer life as a wife and mother, she drowns herself. In

←— 1" —→

such a summary, Edna appears to be yet another victim

←— 1" —→

of the "Feminine Mystique" described by Betty Friedan in the 1950's, a mind-numbing malaise afflicting the typical American housewife whose husband and society expected her to care for family at the expense of personal freedom and fulfillment. However, it is possible that the events leading to Edna's tragic death were not caused solely by the expectations of a sexist society pre-dating Friedan's model, in which a wife was not only dutiful to but also the "property" of her husband (Culley

Citation includes title because there are two works by Chopin on Works Cited list.

117), and a mother not only stayed home but also sacrificed even the "essential" for her children (Chopin <u>Awakening</u> 48). Perhaps Edna's suicide resulted from

Clear statement of thesis.

the torments of her individual psyche, her inability to cope with the patriarchal expectations, which most women in fact were able to tolerate.

1"

Cody 2

It is difficult to say how Chopin wished <u>The Awak-</u>
<u>ening</u> to be interpreted. Heroines who explore their own
individuality (with varying degrees of success and failure)
abound in her work (Shinn 358); Chopin herself, though
married, was a rather nontraditional wife who smoked
cigarettes, and, like Edna Pontellier, took walks by herself
(Nissenbaum 333-34). One might think therefore that
Chopin was making a political statement in <u>The Awak-</u>
<u>ening</u> about the position of women in society based on her
own rejection of that position. But aside from slim biographical evidence and the assertions of some critics such
as Larzer Ziff and Daniel S. Rankin that Chopin sympathized with Edna, we have no way of knowing whether
she regarded this protagonist as a victim of sexist
oppression or simply, to quote her family doctor in the
novel itself, as "a sensitive and highly organized woman . . .
[who] is especially peculiar" (66). It is therefore
necessary to explore the two possibilities, using evidence
from the novel to determine whether Edna Pontellier's
awakening is political or peculiarly personal in nature.

It does not take a deeply feminist awareness to
detect the dominant, controlling stance Edna's husband,
Leonce, assumes in their marriage. Throughout the novel
Chopin documents the resulting injustices, both great
and small, which Edna endures. In one instance Leonce
comes home late at night after Edna has fallen asleep,
and, upon visiting their sleeping children, concludes that
both of them are feverish. He wakes Edna so that she may
check on them, despite her assertion that the children are
perfectly well. He chides her for her "inattention" and "habitual neglect of the children" (7)--rather than respecting
her ability as their mother to judge the state of their

*Citation
includes name
because
author isn't
cited in the
sentence itself.*

*Sources are
paraphrased
here. Although
the words of
the sources
aren't used,
ideas must be
acknowledged*

*Brackets
around "who"
indicate that
word has
been added.*

*Citation
includes page
number alone
because title
and author
are clear from
context.*

Cody 3

health or attending to them himself--and reduces her to tears. She defers to his judgment, looking at the boys as he had asked, and, finding them entirely healthy, goes out to the porch where "an indescribable oppression . . . filled her whole being with a vague anguish" (8). Though in some ways inconsequential, actions such as these epitomize Leonce Pontellier's attitude toward women and particularly toward his wife. It is his belief that she has a certain role and specific duties (those of a woman) which must be done well--according to his (a man's) standards. Although he would probably claim to love Edna, he does not seem to regard her as an autonomous individual; she is the mother of his children, the hostess of such "callers" as he deems appropriate (i.e., the ones who will bring him influence and esteem) (51) and essentially another decoration in his impeccably furnished house (50). When Edna's awakening leads her to abandon household chores in favor of painting, Chopin exposes Leonce's sexism:

Three spaced periods indicate that words have been omitted from sentence.

Prose quotations longer than four typed lines are indented one inch from the left margin and double-spaced.

> Mr. Pontellier had been a rather courteous husband so long as he met a certain tacit submissiveness in his wife. But her new and unexpected line of conduct completely bewildered him . . . her absolute disregard for her duties as a wife angered him. (57)

Block quotations do not need quotation marks. Note that the period precedes the parenthetic citation in a block quotation.

It would seem from such evidence that Chopin intended The Awakening to depict the wrongs that women suffered at the hands of men in her society. Taking this cue from Chopin, many twentieth-century critics choose to view it in a political light. Larzer Ziff, for example, claims that the novel "rejected the family as the automatic equivalent of feminine self-fulfillment, and on the very eve of the twentieth century it raised the question of what

Cody 4

Cody quotes opposing views. Note smooth integration of quoted passages. The verbs "claims," "noting," and "states" clearly signal quotations.

woman was to do with the freedom she struggled toward" (175). Winfried Fluck, noting Edna's "preference for semi-conscious states of being . . . sleeping, dreaming, dozing, or the moment of awakening" (435), argues that she is enacting a "a radical retreat from the imprisonment of all social roles" (435). Marie Fletcher states that "[Edna's] suicide is the last in a series of rebellions which structure her life, give it pathos, and make of the novel . . . an interpretation of the 'new woman'" (172)--"the emerging suffragist/woman professional of the late nineteenth century" (Culley 118). Even in 1899 an anonymous reviewer in the New Orleans Times-Democrat noticed the political implications of the novel, declaring in his own conservative way that

> a woman of twenty-eight, a wife and twice a
> mother who is pondering upon her relations to
> the world about her, fails to perceive that the
> relation of a mother to her children is far more
> important than the gratification of a passion
> which experience has taught her is . . . evanes-
> cent, can hardly be said to be fully awake. (150)

These critics lead us to focus on the socio-political implications of the novel, and on the questions it raises about woman's role and responsibility: when if ever does a woman's personal life become more important than her children? or, how does Edna embody the emancipated woman? But I believe that more than just the social pressure and politics of the late nineteenth century were acting on Edna. It was the inherent instability of her own psyche, exacerbated by the oppression she suffered as a woman, that drove her to swim out to her death at the end of The Awakening.

Cody 5

Clear transition ("despite").

Despite the feminist undertones discernible in Chopin's work, a strong sense prevails that Edna's tragedy is unique, a result of her own psychology, not only of societal oppression. Throughout the novel Chopin describes Edna's agitated state of mind and drops hints about her upbringing and family life before marriage. Upon piecing all the clues to her personality together one gets a troubling, stereotypical picture. Edna's widowed father is a stern colonel from Kentucky who "was perhaps unaware that he had coerced his own wife into her grave" (71). From the scenes in which he appears one deduces that he is harsh and authoritative with his family; the narrator's comment about his wife implies that perhaps he was abusive (no doubt psychologically, possibly physically) as well. He gambles compulsively on horseracing (69), which denotes an addictive personality. He also makes his own very strong cocktails--"toddies"--which he drinks almost all day long (71). He retains the appearance of sobriety, however, which indicates a high tolerance built up over much time. From this evidence one may assume that he suffers from alcoholism.

In this paragraph and the next, Cody develops her argument by analyzing the text of the novel.

The rest of Edna's family--two sisters--fit the mold of the dysfunctional family that a violent, alcoholic parent tends to create. Her oldest sister seems to be the hyper-responsible, over-functioning "perfect" daughter. She served as a surrogate mother to Edna and her younger sister, and is described by Edna's husband as the only daughter who "has all the Presbyterianism undiluted" (66). Edna's younger sister is, predictably, exactly the opposite: Leonce Pontellier describes her as a "vixen" (66). She has rebelled against all of the rules and expectations that the eldest daughter obeys and fulfills. Edna,

Cody 6

the middle child, is hence a curious case. Chopin tells us
that "even as a child she had lived her own small life all
within herself" (15). In such family situations the middle
child is usually rather introverted. Where the two other
siblings strive compulsively either to correct or create
problems, the sibling in the middle passively escapes
from her painful family situation by withdrawing into
herself (Seixas and Youcha 48-49).

Evidence from experts offered in support of thesis.

So far this simplistic but relatively reliable delin-
eation of personalities works for Edna's character. Later
in life she perpetuates the patterns of her dysfunctional
family by marrying a man who almost mirrors her father
in personality; he is simply a workaholic rather than an
alcoholic. Edna gives birth to two children, "a responsibility
which she had blindly assumed" (20) in her typically
passive way. The first time she truly examines her role
in this marriage and indeed in the world at large occurs
on Grand Isle, a resort island where she and her family are
vacationing for the summer. There she begins to spend
a great deal of time with a young man named Robert
Lebrun, and a mutual desire gradually arises between
them. This desire, and the general sensuality and open-
ness of the Creole community to which she is exposed,
bring about Edna's sexual, artistic, and individual
awakening. Although the reader is excited and inspired
by this awakening in Edna--a woman learning to shed
the fetters of both her oppressive marriage and society
in general--the way it takes control of her life is
disturbingly reminiscent of mental illness. She becomes
infatuated with Robert, devotes an inordinate amount of
time to painting, and seeks out classical music, which
wracks her soul in a torturous ecstasy.

Cody 7

Throughout her awakening, she experiences myriad moods and feelings that she had never felt before in her docile, passive state. Many of these moods manifest themselves in the form of mysterious, troubling voices: "the voices were not soothing that came to her from the darkness and the sky above and the stars" (53); "she felt like one who has entered and lingered within the portals of some forbidden temple in which a thousand muffled voices bade her begone" (84). Behind the veil of metaphor here one can detect hints of an almost schizoid character. Chopin even describes Edna as two selves, which naturally befits a woman undergoing an emotional transformation, but which also denotes a distinctly schizophrenic state of mind: "she was becoming herself and daily casting aside that fictitious self which we assume like a garment with which to appear before the world" (57); "she could only realize that she herself--her present self--was in some way different from the other self" (41). Chopin phrases her descriptions of Edna in such a way that they could in fact describe either a woman gaining her emotional autonomy or a woman losing her mind.

As compelling as I find the suggestion of Edna's insanity, I must admit that her struggle between self-hood and motherhood is one too common to all women to be passed off as the ravings of a madwoman. As to which interpretation she preferred, Chopin offered few clues. For example, in February 1898 Chopin responded to a question, posed by the society page of the St. Louis Post-Dispatch, about the possible motives for a recent rash of suicides among young high-society women. Rather than the pressure of society as a likely motive, she suggests a "highly nervous" disposition (qtd. in Toth 120). Indeed, she asserts that "leadership in society is a business . . .

Parenthetic reference to an indirect source. (The quotation from Chopin appears on page 120 of Toth's book.)

Cody 8

there is nothing about it that I can see that would tend to
produce an unhealthy condition of mind. On the contrary,
it prevents women from becoming morbid, as they might,
had they nothing to occupy their attention when at leisure"
(qtd. in Toth 120). Perhaps, then, we are to suppose that
a combination of psychic instability and extensive leisure,
rather than the oppression of her society, caused Edna to
take her own life. And yet this same response in the
Post-Dispatch includes a counter-question to the editor:
"Business men commit suicide every day, yet we do not
say that suicide is epidemic in the business world. Why
should we say the feeling is rife among society women,
because half a dozen unfortunates, widely separated,
take their own lives?" (qtd. in Toth 120). Her implicit
criticism of the double standard suggests that Chopin
was aware of the politics of gender relations in her own
society in addition to the existence of an "hysterical
tendency" in some women (qtd. in Toth 120). One cannot
therefore discount the possibility that Chopin meant
Edna's suicide to be in part a reaction to her society's
rigid and limiting expectations of women.

Chopin received such harsh criticism of Edna
Pontellier's sexual freedom and attitude toward family
that, when The Awakening was published, if not before,
she must have had some idea of how controversial the issue
of her protagonist's personal freedom really was: her hometown library banned the book, and Chopin herself was

*Citation of
on-line source.
(Source is
unpaginated,
so citation
gives only the
author's
name.)*

banned from a St. Louis arts club (Reuben). Her critics
tend to believe that she sympathized unreservedly with
her headstrong heroine; but even the retraction she
published soon after her novel does not reveal whether she
viewed Edna as oppressed or mentally ill. Apparently
written for the benefit of her scandalized reviewers, the

Cody 9

retraction ironically relieves Chopin of all responsibility for Edna's "making such a mess of things and working out her own damnation" (159). Again, as in her ambiguous response to the Post-Dispatch, Chopin leaves curious readers unsatisfied, and the motive of Edna's suicide unclear.

It is left to the reader therefore to decide whether Edna is a martyr to a feminist cause—the liberation of the American housewife—or the victim of a psychological disturbance that drives her to suicide. I believe that it is best not to dismiss either possibility. To begin with, one cannot deny that in the nineteenth century few options other than marriage and child-rearing were open to women. These narrow options were the result of a societal structure in which men socially, economically, and sexually dominated women. In the late twentieth century we can look back at Chopin's time and feel confident in condemning this state of affairs, but from contemporary criticism of The Awakening alone, it is clear that this political view was not so widely accepted at the turn of the century. Perhaps Chopin had an unusually clear and untimely insight into what we now consider the sexism of her society, but she chose to condemn it only implicitly by portraying it as a fact of life against which her unbalanced heroine must struggle and perish. As Larzer Ziff puts it, "Edna Pontellier is trapped between her illusions and the condition which society arbitrarily establishes to maintain itself, and she is made to pay" (175). Chopin fused the political and the personal in Edna Pontellier, who, like most women in the world, suffers not only from the pressures of a society run by and for men, but also from her own individual afflictions.

Sources are
listed in
alphabetical
order by
author.

"Works Cited"
is centered.

Three hyphens
indicate
another work
by the author
named
immediately
above.

Second and
subsequent
lines of entry
are indented 5
spaces.

Signed entry
in a reference
work with
alphabetically
arranged
entries.

Journal
article.

Cody 10   Begin Works
Cited list on
new page.
Continue
pagination.

Works Cited

Chopin, Kate. The Awakening. 1899. Ed. Margaret
Culley. New York: Norton, 1976.

– – –. "Retraction." 1899. Rpt. in The Awakening. By
Kate Chopin. 159.

Culley, Margaret. "The Context of The Awakening." In
The Awakening. By Kate Chopin. 17-19.

Fletcher, Marie. "The Southern Woman in the Fiction of
Kate Chopin." Rpt. in The Awakening. By Kate
Chopin. 170-73.

Fluck, Winfried. "'The American Romance' and the
Changing Functions of the Imaginary." New
Literary History 27.3 (1996) 415-457. Project
Muse. JHU. 1 May 1998. http://muse:jhu.edu:80/
journals/new literary history /v27/27.3fluck.html.

"New Publications." New Orleans Times-Democrat. Rpt.
in The Awakening. By Kate Chopin. 150.

Nissenbaum, Stephen. "Chopin, Kate O'Flaherty." Notable
American Women. 1971 ed.

Rankin, Daniel S. "Influences Upon the Novel." Rpt. in
The Awakening. By Kate Chopin. 163-65.

Reuben, Paul P. "Chapter 6: 1890-1910: Kate Chopin
(1851-1904)." PAL: Perspectives in American
Literature--A Research and Reference Guide. 20
Mar. 1998. http://www.csustan.edu/english/
reuben/pal/chap6/chopin.html.

Seixas, Judith S., and Geraldine Youcha. Children of
Alcoholism: A Survivor's Manual. New York:
Harper, 1985.

Shinn, Thelma J. "Kate O'Flaherty Chopin." American
Women Writers. 1979 ed.

Toth, Emily. "Kate Chopin on Divine Love and Suicide:
Two Rediscovered Articles." American Literature.
63 (1991): 115-21.

Ziff, Larzer. Excerpt from The American 1890s: Life and
Times of a Lost Generation, 279-305. Rpt. in The
Awakening. By Kate Chopin. 173-75.

Short form of
citation.
Articles by
Cully and
Fletcher are
reprinted in
the Norton
edition of The
Awakening.
The full
citation for
the volume
appears under
Chopin.

On-line source
(paginated).

On-line source
(unpaginated).

APA Style

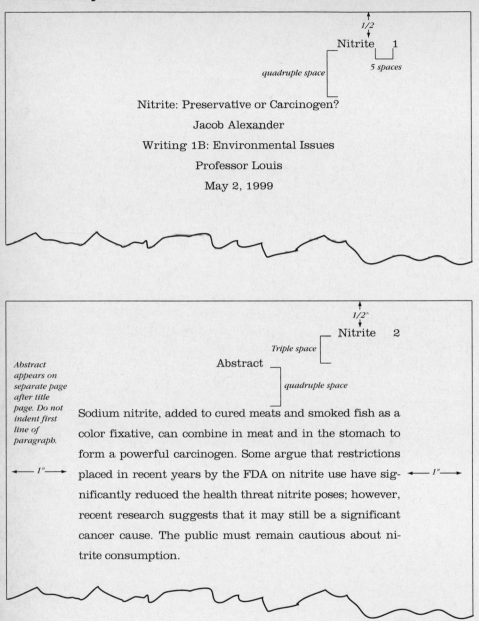

1/2
Nitrite   1
5 spaces

quadruple space

Nitrite: Preservative or Carcinogen?

Jacob Alexander

Writing 1B: Environmental Issues

Professor Louis

May 2, 1999

1/2"
Nitrite   2

Triple space

Abstract

quadruple space

Abstract appears on separate page after title page. Do not indent first line of paragraph.

Sodium nitrite, added to cured meats and smoked fish as a color fixative, can combine in meat and in the stomach to form a powerful carcinogen. Some argue that restrictions placed in recent years by the FDA on nitrite use have significantly reduced the health threat nitrite poses; however, recent research suggests that it may still be a significant cancer cause. The public must remain cautious about nitrite consumption.

← 1" →

← 1" →

Nitrite: Preservative or Carcinogen?

According to Julie Miller Jones, a professor of food and nutrition and the author of <u>Food Safety,</u> "average Americans eat their weight in food additives every year" (cited in Murphy, 1996, p. 140). There are approximately fifteen thousand additives currently in use (National Cancer Institute Fact Sheet [NCI], 1996); many of them are known to be dangerous. Of these, nitrites may be among the most hazardous of all. In this country, ham, bacon, corned beef, salami, bologna, lox, and other cold cuts and smoked fish almost invariably contain sodium nitrite. In fact, one-third of the federally inspected meat and fish we consume--more than seven billion pounds of it every year--contains this chemical (Jacobson, 1987, p. 169).

An indirect reference. Alexander consulted Murphy, who quotes Jones.

Citation gives author because Jacobson is not named in the text. Note format: author, date of publication, and page number preceded by a "p."

Just how dangerous are nitrites, and why--if they really <u>are</u> dangerous--does the food industry still use them? Both questions are difficult to answer. Some experts say that nitrites protect consumers from botulism, a deadly disease that can be caused by spoiled food, and that "the benefits of nitrite additives outweigh the risks" (Edlefsen & Brewer, no date). Others argue that the dangers nitrites once posed have been significantly reduced--even eliminated--by restrictions placed on their use by the Food and Drug Administration. Nevertheless, the evidence has long suggested that nitrites are linked to stomach cancer; recent research has linked nitrites to leukemia and brain tumors as well (Warrick, 1994; Legator & Daniel, 1995). Perhaps the only certain conclusions one can reach are that the effects of nitrite on the human body are still to some degree uncertain--and that to protect themselves, consumers must be cautious and informed.

A reference to two sources. The writer is summarizing whole works, so no pages numbers are given.

Clear statement of thesis.

That nitrite is a poison has been clear for almost three decades. In 1974, Jacqueline Verrett, who worked for the FDA for fifteen years, and Jean Carper reported on several instances of people poisoned by accidental overdoses of nitrites in cured meats:

Quotations of more than forty words must be indented one inch from the left margin.

> In Buffalo, New York, six persons were hospitalized with "cardiovascular collapse" after they ate blood sausage which contained excessive amounts of nitrites . . . In New Jersey, two persons died and many others were critically poisoned after eating fish illegally loaded with nitrites. In New Orleans, ten youngsters between the ages of one and a half and five became seriously ill . . . after eating wieners or bologna overnitrited by a local meat-processing firm; one wiener that was obtained later from the plant was found to contain a whopping 6,570 parts per million. In Florida, a three-year-old boy died after eating hot dogs with three times greater nitrite concentration than the government allows. (pp. 138-139)

The chemical has the unusual and difficult-to-replace quality of keeping meat a fresh-looking pink throughout the cooking, curing, and storage process (Assembly of Life Science, 1982, p. 3). The nitrous acid from the nitrite combines with the hemoglobin in the blood of the meat, fixing its red color so that the meat does not turn the tired brown or gray natural to cured meats.

Unfortunately, it does much the same thing in humans. Although most of the nitrite passes through the body unchanged, a small amount is released into the bloodstream. This combines with the hemoglobin in the

blood to form a pigment called methemoglobin, which
cannot carry oxygen. If enough oxygen is incapacitated,
a person dies. The allowable amount of nitrite in a
quarter pound of meat has the potential to incapacitate
between 1.4 and 5.7 percent of the hemoglobin in an
average-sized adult (Verrett & Carper, 1974, pp. 138-39).
One of the problems with nitrite poisoning is that
infants under a year, because of the quantity and
makeup of their blood, are especially susceptible to it.

If the consumer of nitrite isn't acutely poisoned
(and granted, such poisonings are rare), his or her blood
soon returns to normal and this particular danger
passes: the chemical, however, has long-term effects, as
research conducted in the 1970's clearly established.
Nitrite can cause headaches in people who are especially
sensitive to it, an upsetting symptom considering that in
rats who ate it regularly for a period of time it has
produced lasting "epileptic like" changes in the brain--
abnormalities which showed up when the rats were fed
only a little more than an American fond of cured meats
might eat (Wellford, 1973, p. 173). Experiments with
chickens, cattle, sheep, and rats have shown that nitrite,
when administered for several days, inhibits the ability
of the liver to store vitamin A and carotene (Hunter, 172,
p. 90). And finally, Nobel laureate Joshua Lederberg
points out that, in microorganisms, nitrite enters the
DNA. "If it does the same thing in humans," he says, "it
will cause mutant genes." Geneticist Bruce Ames adds, "If
out of one million people, one person's genes are mutant,
that's a serious problem. . . . If we're filling ourselves now
with mutant genes, they're going to be around for
generations" (cited in Zwerdling, 1971, pp. 34-35).

By far the most alarming characteristic of nitrite,

however, is that in test tubes, in meats themselves, in
animal stomachs, and in human stomachs--wherever a
mildly acidic solution is present--it can combine with
amines to form nitrosamines. And nitrosamines are
carcinogens. Even the food industry and the agencies
responsible for allowing the use of nitrite in foods admit
that nitrosamines cause cancer. Edlefsen and Brewer,
writing recently for the National Food Safety Database,
note that "over 90 percent of the more than 300 known

An on-line source. (The authors and title are named in the sentence; the source has no date or page numbers.)

nitrosamines in foods have been shown to cause cancer in
laboratory animals." They continue: "No case of human
cancer has been shown to result from exposure to
nitrosamines," but they acknowledge that "indirect evidence
indicates that humans would be susceptible" (no date).

It is important to note that nitrite alone, when fed
to rats on an otherwise controlled diet, does not induce
cancer. It must first combine with amines to form
nitrosamines. Considering, however, that the human
stomach has the kind of acidic solution in which amines
and nitrites readily combine, and considering as well
that amines are present in beer, wine, cereals, tea, fish,
cigarette smoke, and a long list of drugs including
antihistamines, tranquilizers, and even oral
contraceptives, it is hardly surprising to find that
nitrosamaines have been found in human stomachs.

When animals are fed amines in combination
with nitrite, they developed cancer with a statistical
consistency that is frightening, even to scientists.
Verrett and Carper report that after feeding animals 250
parts per million (ppm) of nitrites and amines, William
Lijinsky, a scientist at Oak Ridge National Laboratory,
found malignant tumors in 100 percent of the
test animals within six months. . . . "Unheard

Nitrite   7

of," he says. . . . "You'd usually expect to find
50 percent at the most. And the cancers are all
over the place--in the brain, lung, pancreas,
stomach liver, adrenals, intestines. We open up
the animals and they are a bloody mess." [He]
believes that nitrosamines, because of their
incredible versatility in inciting cancer, may
be the key to an explanation for the mass
production of cancer in seemingly dissimilar
populations. In other words, nitrosamines
may be a common factor in cancer that has
been haunting us all these years. (1974, p. 136)

Verrett and Carper (1974, pp. 43-46) list still more
damning evidence. Nitrosamines have caused cancer in
rats, hamsters, mice, guinea pigs, dogs, and monkeys. It
has been proven that nitrosamines of over a hundred
kinds cause cancer. Nitrosamines have been shown to
pass through the placenta from the mother to cause
cancer in the offspring. Even the lowest levels of
nitrosamines ever tested have produced cancer in
animals. When animals are fed nitrite and amines
separately over a period of time, they develop cancers
of the same kind and at the same frequency as animals
fed the corresponding nitrosamines already formed.

To address these problems (and in response to
intense public concern), in 1978, the FDA ruled that a
reducing agent, such as ascorbic acid, must be added
to products containing nitrite; the reducing agent
inhibits the formation of nitrosamines (Edlefsen &
Brewer, no date). And in the last two decades, at least, the
furor over nitrite seems as a consequence to have abated.
In fact, an anonymous Internet posting, dated August
1997, entitled "Nitrite: Keeping Food Safe" celebrates

*This on-line
source did not
provide a date
of publication.*

nitrite as a "naturally-derived" substance that, according to the American Academy of Science, has never been found to cause cancer. On the contrary, the anonymous author states, nitrite does many good things for consumers; it may even help to fight cancer: "it safeguards cured meats against the most deadly foodborne bacterium known to man" and helps with "promoting blood clotting, healing wounds and burns and boosting immune function to kill tumor cells."

No citation is given here because all information is included in the sentence itself.

Other experts are less certain that reducing agents have entirely solved the nitrosamine problem. The Consumer's Dictionary of Food Additives notes that one common agent, sodium ascorbate, which is added to the brine in which bacon is cured, "offers only a partial barrier because ascorbate is soluble in fatty tissues" (Winter, 1994, p. 282). But in the wake of several studies reported in the March 1993 Cancer Causes and Control, it is unclear that "inhibiting" the formation of nitrosamines actually makes nitrites safe to consume.

The Los Angeles Times reports that one of these studies, conducted by John Peters, an epidemiologist at USC, found that "children who eat more than 12 hot dogs per month have nine times the normal risk of developing childood leukemia"'" (Warrick, 1994). Interestingly, the study was focused not on nitrites, but rather on electromagnetic fields. "'Dietary exposure to processed or cured meats was part of a little side questionnaire to our study on (electro)magnetic fields,'" Peters said. "'We were as surprised as anyone by the hot dogs findings. . . . It was the biggest risk for anything we saw in the study--about four times the risk for EMF's'" (cited in Warrick, 1994).

An indirect reference.

In another of these recent studies, hot dogs were linked to brain tumors: researchers found that "children born to mothers who ate at least one hot dog per week

Nitrite   9

while pregnant have twice the risk of developing brain

*Authors are
named in the
sentence and
the on-line
sources isn't
paginated.
Only
publication
date is cited.*
tumors, as do children whose fathers ate too many hot

dogs before conception" (Warrick, 1994). Dr. M. Legator

and Amanda Daniel comment that "these studies confirm

thirty years worth of scientific research on the cancer

causing properties of preserved meats and fish" (1995).

The question, then, is why nitrite continues to be

used in so much of the meat Americans consume.

Although nitrite adds a small amount to flavor, it is used

primarily for cosmetic purposes. Food producers are of

course also quick to point out that nitrite keeps people

safe from botulinum in cured meats, an argument to

which the public may be particularly susceptible because

of a number of recent and serious food scares.

Nevertheless, some evidence suggests that the protection

nitrite offers is both unnecessary and ineffective.

Michael Jacobson explains the preservative action

of nitrite:

> Nitrite makes botulinum spores sensitive to
> heat. When foods are treated with nitrite and
> then heated, any botulinum spores that may
> be present are killed. In the absence of nitrite,
> spores can be inactivated only at temperatures
> that ruin the meat products. . . . Nitrite's
> preservative action is particularly important
> in foods that are not cooked after they leave
> the factory, such as ham, because these offer
> an oxygen-free environment, the kind in
> which botulinum can grow. The toxin does
> not pose a danger in foods that are always
> well cooked, such as bacon, because the toxin
> would be destroyed in cooking.
>
> Laboratory studies demonstrate clearly
> that nitrite can kill botulinum, but whether it

actually does in commercially processed meat
has been called into question. Frequently, the
levels used may be too low to do anything but
contribute to the color. (1987, p. 165)

Bratwurst and breakfast sausage are manufactured now
without nitrite because they don't need to be colored pink;
bacon is always cooked thoroughly enough to kill off
any botulinum spores present. Certainly there are other
ways of dealing with botulism. High or low temperature
prevents botulism. What nitrite undoubtedly does lower,
however, is the level of care and sanitation necessary in
handling meat.

Clearly, the use of nitrite adds immeasurably to the
profit-making potential of the meat industry, but why
does the federal government allow this health hazard in
our food? In the first place, nitrite and nitrate have been
used for so long that it is hard for lawmakers to get past
their instinctive reaction, "But that's the way we've
always done it." Indeed, the Romans used saltpeter, a
nitrate, to keep meat and, as early as 1899, scientists
discovered that the nitrate breaks down into nitrite and
that it is the nitrite which actually preserves the red color

*Note that a
reference to a
single page is
preceded by
"p." and that
a reference to
two or more
pages is
preceded by
"pp."*

in meats (Jacobson, 1987, pp. 164-65). Thus, by the time
the U.S. Department of Agriculture and the Food and
Drug Administration got into the business of regulating
food, they tended to accept nitrite and nitrate as givens.

A second reason for the inadequacy of regulation is
that government mechanisms for protecting the consumer
are full of curious loopholes. In 1958 Congress passed the
Food Additive Amendment, including the Delaney Clause,
which clearly states that additives should be banned if
they induce cancer in laboratory animals. Unfortunately,
however, the amendment does not apply to additives

Nitrite   11

that were in use before it was passed, so, since nitrite and nitrate had already been in use for a long time, they were automatically included on the list of chemicals "Generally Recognized as Safe." To complicate matters further, nitrite in meat is regulated by the USDA, while nitrite in fish is under the jurisdiction of the FDA. And these agencies generally leave it to industry--the profit-maker--to establish whether or not an additive is safe. The final irony in this list of governmental errors is that the FDA depends heavily, for "independent" research and advice, on the food committees of the National Academy of Sciences which Daniel Zwerdling claims are "like a Who's Who of the food and chemical industry" (1971, p. 34). (This, of course, is the organization cited in the anonymous web posting quoted above, the organization that holds that "nitrite levels in cured meat have not been linked to the development of human cancers.")

Because the author is named in the sentence, the citation gives only the date and page number.

Clearly, consumers need to be informed; clearly, it is unwise to count on government agencies for protection against the dangers food additives may pose. Some experts continue to argue that nitrite is safe enough; Edelfson and Brewer, for example, cite a 1992 study by J. M. Jones that suggests that drinking beer exposes a consumer to more nitrite than does eating bacon—and that new car interiors are a significant source of nitrite as well.[1] Others recommend caution. One expert advises: "If you must eat nitrite-laced meats, include a food or drink high in vitamin C at the same time--for example, orange juice, grapefruit juice, cranberry juice, or lettuce" (Winter, 1994, p. 282). And, in fact, a study by a committee

An explanatory footnote.

[1]Presumably the exposure here results from contact, not ingestion.

organized by the National Academy of Science strongly
implies (Assembly, 1982, p. 12) that the government
should develop a safe alternative to nitrites.

In the meantime, the chemical additive industry
doesn't seem very worried that alternatives, such as
biopreservatives, will pose a threat to its profits. An
industry publication, "Chemical Marketing Reporter,"
recently reassured its readers by announcing that "around
82.5 million pounds of preservatives, valued at $133
million, were consumed in the US in 1991." The report
also stated that "though the trend toward phasing out
controversial preservatives like sulfites, nitrates and
nitrites continues, natural substitutes remain expensive
and often less than effective, making biopreservatives a
distant threat" (Tollefson, 1995).

Nitrite   13

References

References begin on new page

Assembly of Life Science. (1982). Alternatives to the current use of nitrite in food. Washington: National Academy Press.

Second and subsequent lines of entries are indented five spaces

Edlefsen, M. & Brewer, M. S. (no date). The national food safety database. Nitrates/Nitrites [Online]. Available: http://www.foodsafety.org/il/il089.htm [1998, May 6].

A book. Capitalize only the first word in book and article titles.

Hunter, B. T. (1972). Fact/book on food additives and your health. New Canaan, Conn.: Keats.

Jacobson, M. F. (1987). Eater's digest. Washington: Center for Science in the Public Interest.

An on-line version of a printed newspaper article. Capitalize all important words in newspaper and periodical titles.

Legator, M. & Daniel, A. Reproductive systems can be harmed by toxic exposure. Galveston County Daily News [online]. Available: http://www.utmb.edu/toxics/newsp.htm#canen. [1998, May 6].

Murphy, K. (1996, May 6). Do food additives subtract from health? Business Week [online], p. 140. Available: Lexis-Nexis [1998, July 30].

An on-line version of printed magazine article. Note that the year precedes the month and date in the parentheses following the author; the date of access appears in brackets at end of entry.

National Cancer Institute (1996, June). NCI fact sheet. Food additives. [online]. Available: http://nisc8a.upenn.edu/pdghtml/6/eng/600037.html. [1998, May 4].

Tollefson, C. (1995, May 29). Stability preserved; preservatives; food additives '95. Chemical Marketing Reporter 247(22), [online] p. SR28. Available: Lexis-Nexis [1998, May 6].

A book by two authors. Note use of ampersand between authors' names.

Verritt, J., & Carper, J. (1974). Eating may be hazardous to your health. New York: Simon and Schuster.

Warrick, P. (1994, June 8). A frank discussion. Los Angeles Times [online], p. E1. Available: Lexis-Nexis [May 6, 1998].

Winter, R. (1994). A consumer's dictionary of food additives (Updated Fourth Edition). New York. Crown.

Use "p." or "pp." when citing books or newspapers, but not periodicals.
Ramparts is a periodical.

Zwerdling, D. (1971, June). Food pollution. Ramparts 9(11), 31-37, 53-54.

Exercises

1. If you have trouble finding material in the library, don't hesitate to ask a librarian for assistance. But you will soon learn to solve many of the most common problems yourself. Here are a few.

   a. You want to do some research for a paper on Sicilian immigrants in the United States. You perform a title keyword search of the on-line catalog, entering the phrase "Sicilian immigrants" at the prompt, and find only one citation, reprinted here. How can you find other books on the subject?

   FIND KW SICILIAN IMMIGRANTS

   --HU HOLLIS# AFC6151 /bks

AUTHOR:	Mangione, Jerre Gerlando, 1909-
TITLE:	Mount Allegro : a memoir of Italian American life / Jerre Mangione; introduction by Herbert J. Gans.
EDITION:	Columbia University Press Morningside ed.
PUB. INFO:	New York : Columbia University Press, 1981.
DESCRIPTION:	xiii, 309 p. ; 21 cm.
SUBJECTS:	*S1 Mangione, Jerre Gerlando, 1909-
	*S2 Italian Americans—New York (State)—Rochester—Social life and customs.
	*S3 Italian Americans—New York (State)—Rochester—Biography.
	*S4 Rochester (N.Y.)—Biography.
	*S5 Rochester (N.Y.)—Social life and customs.
LOCATION:	Hilles: F129.R79 I85 1981
	C2 - Enter DISPLAY C2 for circulation information

   OPTIONS: -------------------- More - to see next page ----------------------

Display Long			Help
LOCation	TRace *S1 (etc)	PRevious - prev item	Quit
Index	REDo - edit search	STORe - save for email	COMment

   b. You want to do a paper on Richard Wright's short stories, and the on-line catalog lists several relevant books, but when you check the stacks you find none of these books is on the shelf. What might you do next, short of abandoning the topic or going to another library?

   c. You need reviews of a film released a few months ago. How might you use electronic resources to locate them?

   d. You are looking for an issue of a journal published a few months ago. It is not on the shelf with the current issues, and it is not on the shelf with the bound volumes. Where is it? What might you do next to locate the article you want?

   e. You want to write a paper on bilingual education, or, more exactly, on bilingual education of Mexican Americans. How do you locate books on this subject in the on-line catalog? To locate articles on this subject, what indexes might you consult?

2. Using the MLA form, list the following items in Works Cited.

a. A book entitled *Areas of Challenge for Soviet Foreign Policy,* with an introduction by Adam B. Ulam. The book, published in 1985 by the Indiana University Press, in Bloomington, is written by three authors: Gerrit W. Gong, Angela E. Stent, and Rebecca V. Strode. Write *two* entries for Works Cited, the first entry indicating that you referred only to Ulam's introduction, the second entry indicating that you referred to material written by the three authors of the book.

b. *Journal of Political and Military Strategy* paginates its issues continuously; the second issue takes up where the first issue leaves off. The issues of 1984 constitute volume 12. Issue number 2 (the fall issue) contains an article that runs from page 229 to page 241. The article, written by James Burke, is entitled "Patriotism and the All-Volunteer Force."

c. *International Security* begins the pagination of each issue with page 1. The issues of 1985 constitute volume 9. Issue number 4 (the spring issue) contains an article that runs from page 79 to page 98. The article, written by Klaus Knorr, is entitled "Controlling Nuclear War."

d. On page 198 of the book you are now holding in your hand you will find an essay by Laura Cunningham. How would you list the essay in Works Cited?

3. Go to your library and prepare entries for Works Cited for any five of the following:

A signed article in a recent issue of a journal devoted to some aspect of psychology.

A signed article in a newspaper.

A signed article in a recent issue of *Time.*

A signed journal article retrieved with an information service.

An unsigned article in a recent issue of *Newsweek.*

A signed article in an on-line version of a recent issue of *Newsweek.*

An unsigned article from the Macropaedia portion of *Encyclopaedia Britannica.*

A signed article from the Micropaedia portion of *Encyclopaedia Britannica.*

An unsigned article from *Britannica Online.*

A catalog from your college.

An E-mail message.

A web site.

A book (one of your textbooks will do) written by one author.

4. Read the following paragraph, by Mark Edmundson, from his book *Nightmare on Main Street: Angels, Sadomasochism, and the Culture of the Gothic* (1997).

Gothic is the art of haunting, and in two senses. Gothic shows time and again that life, even at its most ostensibly innocent, is possessed, that the present is in thrall to the past. All are guilty. All must, in time, pay up. And Gothic also sets out to haunt its audience, possess them so they can think of nothing else. They have to read it—or see it—again and again to achieve some peace. (Repetition, Freud claimed, is the way we attempt to master a trauma.) For a work to be Gothic, the critic Chris Baldick says, it "should combine a fearful

sense of inheritance in time with a claustrophobic sense of enclo-
sure in space, these two dimensions reinforcing one another to produce an impression of sickening descent into disintegration." When
a culture teems with such work and cannot produce persuasive alternatives, its prognosis is anything but favorable.

a. Write a paragraph in which you imitate someone who is plagiarizing
   the passage.
b. Write a paragraph that acknowledges the author but nevertheless illustrates plagiarism.
c. Write a paragraph in which you quote from and acknowledge Edmundson, but distort his point or otherwise misrepresent what he
   says. (The paragraph need not contain plagiarism.)
d. Write a paragraph in which you make honest use of Edmundson's
   material.

17
Writing About Literature

RESPONDING TO LITERARY TEXTS

One important difference between literary and nonliterary texts is the literary author's concern with presenting experience concretely, with *showing* rather than with *telling*. Let's consider the briefest literary form, the proverb. Take this example: "A rolling stone gathers no moss." Of course the statement says something—it offers an assertion—but its concreteness helps to make it memorable.

Compare the original, for instance, with this unmemorable **paraphrase** or restatement, "If a stone is always moving around, vegetation won't have a chance to grow on it." The original version seems more real, more present, more convincing; it offers a small but complete world, hard (stone) and soft (moss), inorganic and organic, at rest and in motion.

The shapeliness of the proverb also makes it memorable. This shapeliness is perhaps *felt* rather than consciously recognized, but a close look reveals that each of the nouns in the sentence (*stone* and *moss*) has one syllable, and each of the two words of motion (*rolling, gathers*) has two syllables, with the accent on the first of the two. The world of the proverb is complex but it is also unified into a whole by such relationships as these.

And generally speaking, this is the way most poets, fiction writers, and dramatists work. They present scenes (for instance, a lover eagerly anticipating a meeting with the beloved) that are memorable for their vividness, their shapeliness, and their rich implications. "John loves Mary," written on a wall, is information—mere *telling* rather than *showing*. Literature is something else; it is, as Robert Frost said, "a performance in words."

Although literary texts are especially compact or rich and dense, and are especially shapely (interestingly patterned or organized), when you respond to a literary text you are not doing something essentially different from what you do when you respond to *any* text—for instance, a psychology textbook or an argument about capital punishment. You experience a variety of responses; you agree or disagree, you feel pleasure or irritation or puzzlement or boredom. And since your writing will be in large measure a report of your responses, your first reading of a work (which starts the responses) is the beginning of the writing process.

READING FICTION

Fiction can range from the short story of a page or two to the thousand-page novel. Let's begin with a very short story, an anonymous tale from nineteenth-century Japan.

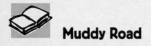 **Muddy Road**

Two monks, Tanzan and Ekido, were once traveling together down a muddy road. A heavy rain was still falling.

Coming around a bend, they met a lovely girl in a silk kimono and sash, unable to cross the intersection.

"Come on, girl," said Tanzan at once. Lifting her in his arms, he carried her over the mud.

Ekido did not speak again until that night when they reached a lodging temple. Then he no longer could restrain himself. "We monks don't go near females," he told Tanzan, "especially not young and lovely ones. It is dangerous. Why did you do that?"

"I left the girl there," said Tanzan. "Are you still carrying her?"

A superb story. The opening paragraph, though simple and matter-of-fact, conveys the sense that something interesting is going to happen during this journey along a muddy road on a rainy day. The references to the mud and the rain seem to suggest as well that the journey itself rather than the travelers' destination will be the heart of the story. The first paragraph of this **third-person narrative** also of course introduces the two **characters** (Tanzan and Ekido) and the **setting** (a muddy road); the second paragraph introduces a **complication** (the encounter with the girl) into the **plot** (the sequence of events or happenings). Still, there is apparently no **conflict,** though "Ekido did not speak again until that night" suggests an unspoken conflict, an action (or, in this case, an inaction) that must be explained, an imbalance that must be righted before the story can end. At last Ekido, no longer able to contain his thoughts, lets his indignation burst out: "We monks don't go near females . . . especially not young and lovely ones. It is dangerous. Why did you do that?" His words reveal not only his moral principles but also his insecurity and the anger that grows from it. And now, when the conflict is out in the open, comes the brief reply that reveals Tanzan's very different character as clearly as the outburst revealed Ekido's. This reply—though initially, perhaps, surprising—feels exactly right, bringing the story to a satisfying end. It provides the **denouement** (literally, the "unknotting"), or resolution. A longer story might offer **foreshadowing**—hints of what is to come, or early details that later gain in significance—but "Muddy Road" is so brief that there is hardly space or need for such significant anticipations. (When you read Charlotte Perkins Gilman's "The Yellow Wallpaper" on pages 380–390, you probably will be surprised by the ending, but if you then reread it you will notice that the narrator's first description of the wallpaper in her bedroom and perhaps even the way she discusses her illness in the beginning of the story serve as foreshadowing.)

What is the story about, what is its subject or **theme?** We do not want to reduce the story to a neat moral, but we can say that some idea holds it together. There is plenty of room for a difference of opinion about what that idea is; probably no two people will use exactly the same words in discussing what a given literary text is about. But perhaps we can say this story concerns the difference between living according to the spirit of the monastic law (free from attachment to things of this world), and, on the other hand, living according to the letter of the law (complying only outwardly with the law). More briefly, we might say that the story concerns spirituality. Or perhaps its theme is understanding, understanding others and oneself.

What does the story add up to, what is its point or **meaning?** This is a somewhat different question. To ask it is to begin to develop an **argument** about the text, the kind of argument that usually forms the **thesis** or main point of an analytic essay on a work of literature. To put the question another way, we might ask: What is the story *saying about* the theme with which it is concerned? What is it saying about spirituality, or about understanding, or about living by the spirit (versus the letter) of the law? Again, different readers may answer this question in different ways, but one might say that the point of "Muddy Road" is to suggest the limitations of purely legalistic behavior, of living by the letter of the law.

That interpretation would probably seem right, even natural, to a reader familiar with the New Testament precept, "the letter [of the law] killeth, the spirit giveth life." It's worth noting though, that the story is a Zen story, and that a Zen interpretation, while harmonious with what we have said above, would significantly differ from it. Zen emphasizes "nothingness," "a state of no-mind." A Zen interpretation of "Muddy Road" would probably note that one monk brings rational or categorical thinking (rules, women, monks) to the encounter with the lovely girl. The other, bringing "no-mind" to the encounter, is unaffected by it; after helping the woman, he leaves, as he came, in a state of "no-mind."

Is one interpretation better, or more right, than the other? No. Evidence supports both readings; both readings are grounded in the details of the text. But each interpretation of "Muddy Road" is shaped by the context within which the story is read. Your sense of the meaning of the texts you're asked to write about will likewise be shaped by your background, beliefs, and experiences; how you interpret what you read may also be affected by the ideas you've begun to explore in your reading for other courses (psychology, perhaps, or history or women's studies) and by the influence of your teachers in both high school and college. To help you begin to develop some perspective on the literary interpretation you'll be doing in your college courses, we offer on pages 406–407 of this chapter a very brief overview of some of the most important current approaches to literary criticism. For an example of a student essay that uses several different kinds of critical material, see Beatrice Cody's essay on Kate Chopin's novel *The Awakening*, reprinted in Chapter 16, "The Research Essay," pages 352–361.

But first, let's look at another story.

CHARLOTTE PERKINS GILMAN

The Yellow Wallpaper

First published in New England Magazine in 1892, "The Yellow Wallpaper" is based in part on Gilman's own experience with depression in the years following the birth of her daughter Katharine. Her physician, Dr. Weir Mitchell, prescribed bed rest for female patients suffering from what was then called "nervous prostration": "in some cases" he wrote, *"for four or five weeks, I do not permit the patient to sit up, or to sew or write or read, or to use the hands in any active way except to clean the teeth."* As the story suggests, Gilman did not find his treatment effective.

It is very seldom that mere ordinary people like John and myself secure ancestral halls for the summer.

A colonial mansion, a hereditary estate, I would say a haunted house, and reach the height of romantic felicity—but that would be asking too much of fate!

Still I will proudly declare that there is something queer about it.

Else, why should it be let so cheaply? And why have stood so long untenanted?

5   John laughs at me, of course, but one expects that in marriage.

John is practical in the extreme. He has no patience with faith, an intense horror of superstition, and he scoffs openly at any talk of things not to be felt and seen and put down in figures.

John is a physician, and *perhaps*—(I would not say it to a living soul, of course, but this is dead paper and a great relief to my mind)—*perhaps* that is one reason I do not get well faster.

You see he does not believe I am sick!

And what can one do?

10   If a physician of high standing, and one's own husband, assures friends and relatives that there is really nothing the matter with one but temporary nervous depression—a slight hysterical tendency—what is one to do?

My brother is also a physician, and also of high standing, and he says the same thing.

So I take phosphates or phosphites—whichever it is, and tonics, and journeys, and air, and exercise, and am absolutely forbidden to "work" until I am well again.

Personally, I disagree with their ideas.

Personally, I believe that congenial work, with excitement and change, would do me good.

15   But what is one to do?

I did write for a while in spite of them; but it *does* exhaust me a good deal—having to be so sly about it, or else meet with heavy opposition.

I sometimes fancy that in my condition if I had less opposition and more society and stimulus—but John says the very worst thing I can do is to think about my condition, and I confess it always makes me feel bad.

So I will let it alone and talk about the house.

The most beautiful place! It is quite alone, standing well back from the road, quite three miles from the village. It makes me think of English places that you read about, for there are hedges and walls and gates that lock, and lots of separate little houses for the gardeners and people.

20   There is a *delicious* garden! I never saw such a garden—large and shady, full of box-bordered paths, and lined with long grape-covered arbors with scats under them.

There were greenhouses, too, but they are all broken now.

There was some legal trouble, I believe, something about the heirs and co-heirs; anyhow, the place has been empty for years.

That spoils my ghostliness, I am afraid, but I don't care—there is something strange about the house—I can feel it.

I even said so to John one moonlight evening, but he said what I felt was a *draught,* and shut the window.

25   I get unreasonably angry with John sometimes. I'm sure I never used to be so sensitive. I think it is due to this nervous condition.

     But John says if I feel so, I shall neglect proper self-control; so I take pains to control myself—before him, at least, and that makes me very tired.

     I don't like our room a bit. I wanted one downstairs that opened on the piazza and had roses all over the window, and such pretty old-fashioned chintz hangings! but John would not hear of it.

     He said there was only one window and not room for two beds, and no near room for him if he took another.

     He is very careful and loving, and hardly lets me stir without special direction.

30   I have a schedule prescription for each hour in the day; he takes all care from me, and so I feel basely ungrateful not to value it more.

     He said we came here solely on my account, that I was to have perfect rest and all the air I could get. "Your exercise depends on your strength, my dear," said he, "and your food somewhat on your appetite; but air you can absorb all the time." So we took the nursery at the top of the house.

     It is a big, airy room, the whole floor nearly, with windows that look all ways, and air and sunshine galore. It was nursery first and then playroom and gymnasium, I should judge; for the windows are barred for little children, and there are rings and things in the walls.

     The paint and paper look as if a boys' school had used it. It is stripped off— the paper—in great patches all around the head of my bed, about as far as I can reach, and in a great place on the other side of the room low down. I never saw a worse paper in my life.

     One of those sprawling flamboyant patterns committing every artistic sin.

35   It is dull enough to confuse the eye in following, pronounced enough to constantly irritate and provoke study, and when you follow the lame uncertain curves for a little distance they suddenly commit suicide—plunge off at outrageous angles, destroy themselves in unheard of contradictions.

     The color is repellent, almost revolting; a smouldering unclean yellow, strangely faded by the slow-turning sunlight.

     It is a dull yet lurid orange in some places, a sickly sulphur tint in others.

     No wonder the children hated it! I should hate it myself if I had to live in this room long.

     There comes John, and I must put this away,—he hates to have me write a word.

40   We have been here two weeks, and I haven't felt like writing before, since that first day.

     I am sitting by the window now, up in this atrocious nursery, and there is nothing to hinder my writing as much as I please, save lack of strength.

     John is away all day, and even some nights when his cases are serious.

     I am glad my case is not serious!

     But these nervous troubles are dreadfully depressing.

45   John does not know how much I really suffer. He knows there is no *reason* to suffer, and that satisfies him.

     Of course it is only nervousness. It does weigh on me so not to do my duty in any way!

     I meant to be such a help to John, such a real rest and comfort, and here I am a comparative burden already!

     Nobody would believe what an effort it is to do what little I am able,—to dress and entertain, and order things.

It is fortunate Mary is so good with the baby. Such a dear baby!

50 And yet I *cannot* be with him, it makes me so nervous.

I suppose John never was nervous in his life. He laughs at me so about this wall-paper!

At first he meant to repaper the room, but afterwards he said that I was letting it get the better of me, and that nothing was worse for a nervous patient than to give way to such fancies.

He said that after the wall-paper was changed it would be the heavy bedstead, and then the barred windows, and then that gate at the head of the stairs, and so on.

"You know the place is doing you good," he said, "and really, dear, I don't care to renovate the house just for a three months' rental."

55 "Then do let us go downstairs," I said, "there are such pretty rooms there."

Then he took me in his arms and called me a blessed little goose, and said he would go down to the cellar, if I wished, and have it whitewashed into the bargain.

But he is right enough about the beds and windows and things.

It is an airy and comfortable room as any one need wish, and, of course, I would not be so silly as to make him uncomfortable just for a whim.

I'm really getting quite fond of the big room, all but that horrid paper.

60 Out of one window I can see the garden, those mysterious deep-shaded arbors, the riotous old-fashioned flowers, and bushes and gnarly trees.

Out of another I get a lovely view of the bay and a little private wharf belonging to the estate. There is a beautiful shaded lane that runs down there from the house. I always fancy I see people walking in these numerous paths and arbors, but John has cautioned me not to give way to fancy in the least. He says that with my imaginative power and habit of story-making, a nervous weakness like mine is sure to lead to all manner of excited fancies, and that I ought to use my will and good sense to check the tendency. So I try.

I think sometimes that if I were only well enough to write a little it would relieve the press of ideas and rest me.

But I find I get pretty tired when I try.

It is so discouraging not to have any advice and companionship about my work. When I get really well, John says we will ask Cousin Henry and Julia down for a long visit; but he says he would as soon put fireworks in my pillow-case as to let me have those stimulating people about now.

65 I wish I could get well faster.

But I must not think about that. This paper looks to me as if it *knew* what a vicious influence it had!

There is a recurrent spot where the pattern lolls like a broken neck and two bulbous eyes stare at you upside down.

I get positively angry with the impertinence of it and the everlastingness. Up and down and sideways they crawl, and those absurd, unblinking eyes are everywhere. There is one place where two breadths didn't match, and the eyes go all up and down the line, one a little higher than the other.

I never saw so much expression in an inanimate thing before, and we all know how much expression they have! I used to lie awake as a child and get more entertainment and terror out of blank walls and plain furniture than most children could find in a toy-store.

70 I remember what a kindly wink the knobs of our big, old bureau used to have, and there was one chair that always seemed like a strong friend.

I used to feel that if any of the other things looked too fierce I could always hop into that chair and be safe.

The furniture in this room is no worse than inharmonious, however, for we had to bring it all from downstairs. I suppose when this was used as a playroom they had to take the nursery things out, and no wonder! I never saw such ravages as the children have made here.

The wall-paper, as I said before, is torn off in spots, and it sticketh closer than a brother—they must have had perseverance as well as hatred.

Then the floor is scratched and gouged and splintered, the plaster itself is dug out here and there, and this great heavy bed which is all we found in the room, looks as if it had been through the wars.

75   But I don't mind it a bit—only the paper.

There comes John's sister. Such a dear girl as she is, and so careful of me! I must not let her find me writing.

She is a perfect and enthusiastic housekeeper, and hopes for no better profession. I verily believe she thinks it is the writing which made me sick!

But I can write when she is out, and see her a long way off from these windows.

There is one that commands the road, a lovely shaded winding road, and one that just looks off over the country. A lovely country, too, full of great elms and velvet meadows.

80   This wall-paper has a kind of sub-pattern in a different shade, a particularly irritating one, for you can only see it in certain lights, and not clearly then.

But in the places where it isn't faded and where the sun is just so—I can see a strange, provoking, formless sort of figure, that seems to skulk about behind that silly and conspicuous front design.

There's sister on the stairs!

Well, the Fourth of July is over! The people are all gone and I am tired out. John thought it might do me good to see a little company, so we just had mother and Nellie and the children down for a week.

Of course I didn't do a thing. Jennie sees to everything now.

But it tired me all the same.

85   John says if I don't pick up faster he shall send me to Weir Mitchell in the fall.

But I don't want to go there at all. I had a friend who was in his hands once, and she says he is just like John and my brother, only more so!

Besides, it is such an undertaking to go so far.

I don't feel as if it was worth while to turn my hand over for anything, and I'm getting dreadfully fretful and querulous.

I cry at nothing, and cry most of the time.

90   Of course I don't when John is here, or anybody else, but when I am alone.

And I am alone a good deal just now. John is kept in town very often by serious cases, and Jennie is good and lets me alone when I want her to.

So I walk a little in the garden or down that lovely lane, sit on the porch under the roses, and lie down up here a good deal.

I'm getting really fond of the room in spite of the wall-paper. Perhaps *because* of the wall-paper.

It dwells in my mind so!

95   I lie here on this great immovable bed—it is nailed down, I believe—and follow that pattern about by the hour. It is as good as gymnastics, I assure you. I

start, we'll say, at the bottom, down in the corner over there where it has not been touched, and I determine for the thousandth time that I *will* follow that pointless pattern to some sort of a conclusion.

I know a little of the principle of design, and I know this thing was not arranged on any laws of radiation, or alternation, or repetition, or symmetry, or anything else that I ever heard of.

It is repeated, of course, by the breadths, but not otherwise.

Looked at in one way each breadth stands alone, the bloated curves and flourishes—a kind of "debased Romanesque" with *delirium tremens*—go waddling up and down in isolated columns of fatuity.

But, on the other hand, they connect diagonally, and the sprawling outlines run off in great slanting waves of optic horror, like a lot of wallowing seaweeds in full chase.

100   The whole thing goes horizontally, too, at least it seems so, and I exhaust myself in trying to distinguish the order of its going in that direction.

They have used a horizontal breadth for a frieze, and that adds wonderfully to the confusion.

There is one end of the room where it is almost intact, and there, when the crosslights fade and the low sun shines directly upon it, I can almost fancy radiation after all,—the interminable grotesques seem to form around a common center and rush off in headlong plunges of equal distraction.

It makes me tired to follow it. I will take a nap I guess.

I don't know why I should write this.

105   I don't want to.

I don't feel able.

And I know John would think it absurd. But I *must* say what I feel and think in some way—it is such a relief!

But the effort is getting to be greater than the relief.

Half the time now I am awfully lazy, and lie down ever so much.

110   John says I mustn't lose my strength, and has me take cod liver oil and lots of tonics and things, to say nothing of ale and wine and rare meat.

Dear John! He loves me very dearly, and hates to have me sick. I tried to have a real earnest reasonable talk with him the other day, and tell him how I wish he would let me go and make a visit to Cousin Henry and Julia.

But he said I wasn't able to go, nor able to stand it after I got there; and I did not make out a very good case for myself, for I was crying before I had finished.

It is getting to be a great effort for me to think straight. Just this nervous weakness I suppose.

And dear John gathered me up in his arms, and just carried me upstairs and laid me on the bed, and sat by me and read to me till it tired my head.

115   He said I was his darling and his comfort and all he had, and that I must take care of myself for his sake, and keep well.

He says no one but myself can help me out of it, that I must use my will and self-control and not let any silly fancies run away with me.

There's one comfort, the baby is well and happy, and does not have to occupy this nursery with the horrid wall-paper.

If we had not used it, that blessed child would have! What a fortunate escape! Why, I wouldn't have a child of mine, an impressionable little thing, live in such a room for worlds.

I never thought of it before, but it is lucky that John kept me here after all, I can stand it so much easier than a baby, you see.

120   Of course I never mention it to them any more—I am too wise,—but I keep watch of it all the same.

There are things in that paper that nobody knows but me, or ever will.

Behind that outside pattern the dim shapes get clearer every day.

It is always the same shape, only very numerous.

And it is like a woman stooping down and creeping about behind that pattern. I don't like it a bit. I wonder—I begin to think—I wish John would take me away from here!

125   It is so hard to talk with John about my case, because he is so wise, and because he loves me so.

But I tried it last night.

It was moonlight. The moon shines in all around just as the sun does.

I hate to see it sometimes, it creeps so slowly, and always comes in by one window or another.

John was asleep and I hated to waken him, so I kept still and watched the moonlight on that undulating wall-paper till I felt creepy.

130   The faint figure behind seemed to shake the pattern, just as if she wanted to get out.

I got up softly and went to feel and see if the paper *did* move, and when I came back John was awake.

"What is it, little girl?" he said. "Don't go walking about like that—you'll get cold."

I thought it was a good time to talk, so I told him that I really was not gaining here, and that I wished he would take me away.

"Why darling!" said he, "our lease will be up in three weeks, and I can't see how to leave before."

135   "The repairs are not done at home, and I cannot possibly leave town just now. Of course if you were in any danger, I could and would, but you really are better, dear, whether you can see it or not. I am a doctor, dear, and I know. You are gaining flesh and color, your appetite is better, I feel really much easier about you."

"I don't weigh a bit more," said I, "nor as much; and my appetite may be better in the evening when you are here, but it is worse in the morning when you are away!"

"Bless her little heart!" said he with a big hug, "she shall be as sick as she pleases! But now let's improve the shining hours by going to sleep, and talk about it in the morning!"

"And you won't go away?" I asked gloomily.

"Why, how can I, dear? It is only three weeks more and then we will take a nice little trip of a few days while Jennie is getting the house ready. Really dear you are better!"

140   "Better in body perhaps—" I began, and stopped short, for he sat up straight and looked at me with such a stern, reproachful look that I could not say another word.

"My darling," said he, "I beg of you, for my sake and for our child's sake, as well as for your own, that you will never for one instant let that idea enter your mind! There is nothing so dangerous, so fascinating, to a temperament like yours. It is a false and foolish fancy. Can you not trust me as a physician when I tell you so?"

So of course I said no more on that score, and we went to sleep before long. He thought I was asleep first, but I wasn't, and lay there for hours trying to decide whether that front pattern and the back pattern really did move together or separately.

On a pattern like this, by daylight, there is a lack of sequence, a defiance of law, that is a constant irritant to a normal mind.

The color is hideous enough, and unreliable enough, and infuriating enough, but the pattern is torturing.

145 You think you have mastered it, but just as you get well underway in following, it turns a back-somersault and there you are. It slaps you in the face, knocks you down, and tramples upon you. It is like a bad dream.

The outside pattern is a florid arabesque, reminding one of a fungus. If you can imagine a toadstool in joints, an interminable string of toadstools, budding and sprouting in endless convolutions—why, that is something like it.

That is, sometimes!

There is one marked peculiarity about this paper, a thing nobody seems to notice but myself, and that is that it changes as the light changes.

When the sun shoots in through the east window—I always watch for that first long, straight ray—it changes so quickly that I never can quite believe it.

150 That is why I watch it always.

By moonlight—the moon shines in all night when there is a moon—I wouldn't know it was the same paper.

At night in any kind of light, in twilight, candle light, lamplight, and worst of all by moonlight, it becomes bars! The outside pattern I mean, and the woman behind it is as plain as can be.

I didn't realize for a long time what the thing was that showed behind, that dim sub-pattern, but now I am quite sure it is a woman.

By daylight she is subdued, quiet. I fancy it is the pattern that keeps her so still. It is so puzzling. It keeps me quiet by the hour.

155 I lie down ever so much now. John says it is good for me, and to sleep all I can.

Indeed he started the habit by making me lie down for an hour after each meal.

It is a very bad habit I am convinced, for you see I don't sleep.

And that cultivates deceit, for I don't tell them I'm awake—O no!

The fact is I am getting a little afraid of John.

160 He seems very queer sometimes, and even Jennie has an inexplicable look.

It strikes me occasionally, just as a scientific hypothesis,—that perhaps it is the paper!

I have watched John when he did not know I was looking, and come into the room suddenly on the most innocent excuses, and I've caught him several times *looking at the paper!* And Jennie too. I caught Jennie with her hand on it once.

She didn't know I was in the room, and when I asked her in a quiet, a very quiet voice, with the most restrained manner possible, what she was doing with the paper—she turned around as if she had been caught stealing, and looked quite angry—asked me why I should frighten her so!

Then she said that the paper stained everything it touched, that she had found yellow smooches on all my clothes and John's, and she wished we would be more careful!

165 Did not that sound innocent? But I know she was studying that pattern, and I am determined that nobody shall find it out but myself!

Life is very much more exciting now than it used to be. You see I have something more to expect, to look forward to, to watch. I really do eat better, and am more quiet than I was.

John is so pleased to see me improve! He laughed a little the other day, and said I seemed to be flourishing in spite of my wall-paper.

I turned it off with a laugh. I had no intention of telling him it was *because* of the wall-paper—he would make fun of me. He might even want to take me away.

I don't want to leave now until I have found it out. There is a week more, and I think that will be enough.

170   I'm feeling ever so much better! I don't sleep much at night, for it is so interesting to watch developments; but I sleep a good deal in the daytime.

In the daytime it is tiresome and perplexing.

There are always new shoots on the fungus, and new shades of yellow all over it. I cannot keep count of them, though I have tried conscientiously.

It is the strangest yellow, that wall-paper! It makes me think of all the yellow things I ever saw—not beautiful ones like buttercups, but old foul, bad yellow things.

But there is something else about that paper—the smell! I noticed it the moment we came into the room, but with so much air and sun it was not bad. Now we have had a week of fog and rain, and whether the windows are open or not, the smell is here.

175   It creeps all over the house.

I find it hovering in the dining-room, skulking in the parlor, hiding in the hall, lying in wait for me on the stairs.

It gets into my hair.

Even when I go to ride, if I turn my head suddenly and surprise it—there is that smell!

Such a peculiar odor, too! I have spent hours in trying to analyze it, to find what it smelled like.

180   It is not bad—at first, and very gentle, but quite the subtlest, most enduring odor I ever met.

In this damp weather it is awful, I wake up in the night and find it hanging over me.

It used to disturb me at first. I thought seriously of burning the house—to reach the smell.

But now I am used to it. The only thing I can think of that it is like is the *color* of the paper! A yellow smell.

There is a very funny mark on this wall, low down, near the mopboard. A streak that runs round the room. It goes behind every piece of furniture, except the bed, a long, straight, even *smooch,* as if it had been rubbed over and over.

185   I wonder how it was done and who did it, and what they did it for. Round and round and round—round and round and round—it makes me dizzy!

I really have discovered something at last.

Through watching so much at night, when it changes so, I have finally found out.

The front pattern *does* move—and no wonder! The woman behind shakes it!

Sometimes I think there are a great many women behind, and sometimes only one, and she crawls around fast, and her crawling shakes it all over.

190   Then in the very bright spots she keeps still, and in the very shady spots she just takes hold of the bars and shakes them hard.

And she is all the time trying to climb through. But nobody could climb through that pattern—it strangles so; I think that is why it has so many heads.

They get through, and then the pattern strangles them off and turns them upside down, and makes their eyes white!

If those heads were covered or taken off it would not be half so bad.

I think that woman gets out in the daytime!

195   And I'll tell you why—privately—I've seen her!

I can see her out of every one of my windows!

It is the same woman, I know, for she is always creeping, and most women do not creep by daylight.

I see her on that long road under the trees, creeping along, and when a carriage comes she hides under the blackberry vines.

I don't blame her a bit. It must be very humiliating to be caught creeping by daylight!

200   I always lock the door when I creep by daylight. I can't do it at night, for I know John would suspect something at once.

And John is so queer now, that I don't want to irritate him. I wish he would take another room! Besides, I don't want anybody to get that woman out at night but myself.

I often wonder if I could see her out of all the windows at once.

But, turn as fast as I can, I can only see out of one at one time.

And though I always see her, she *may* be able to creep faster than I can turn!

205   I have watched her sometimes away off in the open country, creeping as fast as a cloud shadow in a high wind.

If only that top pattern could be gotten off from the under one! I mean to try it, little by little.

I have found out another funny thing, but I shan't tell it this time! It does not do to trust people too much.

There are only two more days to get this paper off, and I believe John is beginning to notice. I don't like the look in his eyes.

And I heard him ask Jennie a lot of professional questions about me. She had a very good report to give.

210   She said I slept a good deal in the daytime.

John knows I don't sleep very well at night, for all I'm so quiet!

He asked me all sorts of questions, too, and pretended to be very loving and kind.

As if I couldn't see through him!

Still, I don't wonder he acts so, sleeping under this paper for three months.

215   It only interests me, but I feel sure John and Jennie are secretly affected by it.

Hurrah! This is the last day, but it is enough. John to stay in town over night, and won't be out until this evening.

Jennie wanted to sleep with me—the sly thing! but I told her I should undoubtedly rest better for a night all alone.

That was clever, for really I wasn't alone a bit! As soon as it was moonlight and that poor thing began to crawl and shake the pattern, I got up and ran to help her.

I pulled and she shook, I shook and she pulled, and before morning we had peeled off yards of that paper.

220   A strip about as high as my head and half around the room.

And then when the sun came and that awful pattern began to laugh at me, I declared I would finish it to-day!

We go away to-morrow, and they are moving all my furniture down again to leave things as they were before.

Jennie looked at the wall in amazement, but I told her merrily that I did it out of pure spite at the vicious thing.

She laughed and said she wouldn't mind doing it herself, but I must not get tired.

225   How she betrayed herself that time!

But I am here, and no person touches this paper but me,—not *alive!*

She tried to get me out of the room—it was too patent! But I said it was so quiet and empty and clean now that I believed I would lie down again and sleep all I could; and not to wake me even for dinner—I would call when I woke.

So now she is gone, and the servants are gone, and the things are gone, and there is nothing left but that great bedstead nailed down, with the canvas mattress we found on it.

We shall sleep downstairs tonight, and take the boat home tomorrow.

230   I quite enjoy the room, now it is bare again.

How those children did tear about here!

This bedstead is fairly gnawed!

But I must get to work.

I have locked the door and thrown the key down into the front path.

235   I don't want to go out, and I don't want to have anybody come in, till John comes.

I want to astonish him.

I've got a rope up here that even Jennie did not find. If that woman does get out, and tries to get away, I can tie her!

But I forgot I could not reach far without anything to stand on!

This bed will *not* move!

240   I tried to lift and push it until I was lame, and then I got so angry I bit off a little piece at one corner—but it hurt my teeth.

Then I peeled off all the paper I could reach standing on the floor. It sticks horribly and the pattern just enjoys it! All those strangled heads and bulbous eyes and waddling fungus growths just shriek with derision!

I am getting angry enough to do something desperate. To jump out of the window would be admirable exercise, but the bars are too strong even to try.

Besides I wouldn't do it. Of course not. I know well enough that a step like that is improper and might be misconstrued.

I don't like to *look* out of the windows even—there are so many of those creeping women, and they creep so fast.

245   I wonder if they all come out of that wall-paper as I did?

But I am securely fastened now by my well-hidden rope—you don't get *me* out in the road there!

I suppose I shall have to get back behind the pattern when it comes night, and that is hard!

It is so pleasant to be out in this great room and creep around as I please!

I don't want to go outside. I won't, even if Jennie asks me to.

250   For outside you have to creep on the ground, and everything is green instead of yellow.

But here I can creep smoothly on the floor, and my shoulder just fits in that long smooch around the wall, so I cannot lose my way.

Why there's John at the door!

It is no use, young man, you can't open it!

How he does call and pound!

255   Now he's crying for an axe.

It would be a shame to break down that beautiful door!

"John dear!" said I in the gentlest voice, "the key is down by the front steps, under a plantain leaf!"

That silenced him for a few moments.

Then he said—very quietly indeed, "Open the door, my darling!"

260   "I can't," said I. "The key is down by the front door under a plantain leaf!"

And then I said it again, several times, very gently and slowly, and said it so often that he had to go and see, and he got it of course, and came in. He stopped short by the door.

"What is the matter?" he cried. "For God's sake, what are you doing!"

I kept on creeping just the same, but I looked at him over my shoulder.

"I've got out at last," said I, "in spite of you and Jane. And I've pulled off most of the paper, so you can't put me back!"

265   Now why should that man have fainted? But he did, and right across my path by the wall, so that I had to creep over him every time!

A Student's Response to "The Yellow Wallpaper": Aviva Geiger's Preliminary Exercises and Final Draft

In the final weeks of her composition class, Aviva was asked to write a critical analysis and interpretation of "The Yellow Wallpaper." The first step of a process was a brief exercise: students were asked to summarize the story and to identify its themes, to say what the story seemed to be about; then they were to write down their questions about the story—to articulate what puzzled them or disturbed them, to try to say what didn't make sense or add up. The second step required students to choose one of the questions they'd formulated—the question that seemed most interesting after they'd read the story several times—and then to begin gathering passages from the text that might help them to answer the question they'd chosen. (As we suggest on pages 400–401, asking questions and answering them is one way to begin to shape an initial response into an essay topic.) Here is what Aviva wrote for the first exercise.

Exercise #1: Thoughts on "The Yellow Wallpaper" by Charlotte Perkins

Gilman

The story is a first-person account of a woman's decline into insanity,

brought on by the confinement she feels from a male-dominated society.

One of its themes is the narrowness of a woman's role in society; the story

suggests the harm that is done by enforcing that role. It also deals with

the issue of insanity and the repercussions insanity can have for an entire
family when it touches any one member of the family.

Questions:

Why does the narrator repeatedly refer to the act of creeping as she sinks
into insanity? What does the creeping symbolize to her?

> She first brings it up while describing the wallpaper at night, when
> she says: "Behind that outside pattern the dim shapes get clearer
> every day . . . [I]t is like a woman stooping down and creeping about
> behind that pattern. I don't like it a bit" (385). Later on, she starts to
> hallucinate about a woman creeping around outdoors, saying: "I can
> see her out of every one of my windows! It is the same woman, I
> know, for she is always . . . creeping along, and when a carriage
> comes she hides . . . I don't blame her a bit. It must be very
> humiliating to be caught creeping by daylight!" (388). Finally, at
> the end of the story, the narrator "becomes" the woman in the
> wallpaper and creeps around as well. The question is why the
> narrator uses the verb "to creep" over and over again, and
> eventually feels compelled to start creeping herself.

Why does the narrator ignore her own baby throughout the story?

> She refers to her inability to mother her child when she says, "It is
> fortunate Mary is so good with the baby. Such a dear baby! And yet
> I <u>cannot</u> be with him, it makes me so nervous" (382). In fact, even at
> the beginning of the story before her delusions start, the narrator
> seems much more preoccupied with inanimate objects such as
> furniture and wallpaper than she is with her own child.
> Nevertheless, the narrator appears to care about her baby. She says
> later on: "There's one comfort, the baby is well and happy, and does
> not have to occupy the nursery with the horrid wall-paper. . . . Why,

I wouldn't have a child of mine, an impressionable little thing, live

in such a room for worlds" (384). Even in this statement, however,

the narrator refers to her child in the abstract ("a child of mine").

Throughout the entire story, she never even mentions its name.

So perhaps the real question is: why does the narrator seem incapable of

dealing with the idea of being a mother?

A good start. Aviva has identified some important themes: the story, she says, is about "confinement" and "insanity" brought on by "male-dominated society," and about the consequences of insanity on all the members of a family. (Note, though, that Aviva's sense of what the story is about will change as she continues to ponder it. She comes to realize, for example, that "The Yellow Wallpaper" doesn't actually say much about how the narrator's insanity affects the rest of her family, and so she drops that point in the next exercise.) And she asks two main questions—the first, about why the narrator "creeps," and the second, about why she is incapable of taking care of her child. Both questions are good questions, in part because the story *doesn't* offer clear and easy answers to them. (If the questions were easy to answer, anyone could answer them, and there wouldn't be much reason to analyze the story or to write the essay.) In the next stage of the sequence, Aviva chooses to explore the second question and begins considering more passages, passages that help to complicate and to focus her sense of what the story is saying about the narrator's relationship to her child.

Exercise #2: Topic for Essay on "The Yellow Wallpaper"

Why does the narrator keep mentioning children while she can

hardly bring herself to think about her own child? From the first time she

mentions children, when describing the bedroom and the wallpaper, the

narrator's words imply that she identifies herself with children. The

narrator tells us the bedroom "was nursery first and then playroom

and gymnasium, I should judge; for the windows are barred for little

children . . ." (381). Furthermore, she says of the wallpaper: "No wonder

the children hated it! I should hate it myself if I had to live in this room

long" (381). Of course, the narrator is only guessing that the room was

ever inhabited by children, and she projects her own dislike of the

wallpaper onto the children she has imagined.

The question is why the narrator subconsciously projects her own emotions onto children in particular. Her comment about barred windows in the above passage provides a possible explanation. The narrator identifies with children because they are restricted and confined in much the same way that she is by her husband John. For example, she describes how John patronizes her and restricts her freedom when she says:

> Dear John! He loves me very dearly, and hates to have me sick. I tried to have a real earnest reasonable talk with him the other day, and tell him how I wish he would let me go and make a visit to Cousin Henry and Julia.

> But he said I wasn't able to go, nor able to stand it when I got there; and I didn't make out a very good case for myself, for I was crying before I had finished. (384)

In several other passages, she tells of how John supervises her and "hardly lets me stir without special direction" (381). Therefore, it seems likely that the narrator keeps mentioning children because she feels she is treated like a child by her husband.

In a larger sense, however, it is not John who restricts and confines the narrator as much as a male-dominated society that defines an extremely narrow role for wives. This role basically consists of acting as a companion for the husband, organizing the household, and mothering the children. In the following passage, the narrator describes how she cannot bring herself to fulfill any one of these three wifely duties:

> I meant to be such a help to John, such a rest and comfort, and here I am a comparative burden already!

> Nobody would believe what an effort it is to do what little I am able,—to dress and entertain, and order things.

It is fortunate Mary is so good with the baby. Such a

dear baby!

And yet I cannot be with him, it makes me so nervous.

(382)

Thus, the narrator's inability to deal with her own child seems to be a symptom of her inability to perform the general tasks expected of a wife. It is not that the narrator dislikes her child, but allowing herself to be a good mother would symbolize her submission to the behavioral constraints of society placed on married women.

The narrator clearly expresses her love for the baby when she says:

There's one comfort, the baby is well and happy, and

does not have to occupy this nursery with the horrid wall-

paper. . . .

Why, I wouldn't have a child of mine, an impressionable

little thing, live in such a room for worlds.

I never thought of it before, but it is lucky that John kept

me here after all, I can stand it so much easier than a baby,

you see. (384)

This passage shows that the narrator truly is concerned for her child's welfare despite the lack of attention she seems to pay him. It also reinforces the idea that the narrator unconsciously equates her own marital situation with an adult's treatment of a child. She tries to kid herself that she can stand the constraints placed on her "so much more easily than a baby," but at the same time, she describes how John kept her in the nursery instead of the baby. Thus, John's treatment of his wife and his treatment of his child are basically interchangeable. However, John does not do this out of cruelty; he is merely acting as his society dictates a husband should act. In the end, the narrator's loss of touch with reality shows that society's restrictive treatment is actually much harder on a rational adult than it would be on a child. Through the

narrator's references to children, therefore, the author conveys the

message that children should be treated as children but grown women

should not.

This exercise gave Aviva the basis for the draft of her essay. It doesn't yet contain the main point or thesis that will be developed in the final revision (that "the inherent conflict between the needs of the narrator's child and the expectations of her husband precipitates her eventual decline into madness"), and it lacks the focus of the revision (the last sentence of the exercise, for example, is a bit flat). Nevertheless, it does contain some of the main points and a good deal of the evidence found in the revision, reprinted below.

The Narrator's Dilemma in

Charlotte Perkins Gilman's "Yellow Wallpaper"

Charlotte Perkins Gilman's short story "The Yellow Wallpaper"

appears to be a straightforward feminist critique of the oppression of

married women in the nineteenth century. Reported by an unnamed first-

person narrator, "The Yellow Wallpaper" tells the story of a depressed

woman whose husband, John, keeps her so confined that she becomes

obsessed with the wallpaper in her bedroom and experiences a mental

breakdown. But a careful reading of Gilman's references to children and

childhood throughout the story suggests that her critique of women's

oppression is much more focused and complex than it would at first seem.

Although the narrator hardly mentions her own newborn baby at all, her

mind returns to the notion of children in the abstract again and again.

Gradually it becomes clear that her attitude toward children actually

illustrates a paradox in the unstated duties of a married woman. She

realizes that, as a mother, she can serve no greater purpose than to act as

a caretaker and protector for her child, but in order to fulfill her role as a

wife, she is required to act like a child herself. The inherent conflict

between the needs of the narrator's child and the expectations of her

husband precipitates her eventual decline into madness.

Although the narrator only mentions her baby twice, the two references clearly convey the anxiety and guilt that motherhood has created for her. She sighs: "It does weigh on me so not to do my duty in any way! . . . It is fortunate Mary is so good with the baby. Such a dear baby! And yet I <u>cannot</u> be with him, it makes me so nervous" (382).[1] The narrator understands that as a new mother, she should naturally want to love and nurture her son, but for some reason, she seems to find the prospect of acting like a mother too frightening to face. Later in the story, she attempts to overcome these qualms by asserting:

> There's one comfort, the baby is well and happy, and does not have to occupy this nursery with the horrid wallpaper. . . .
>
> Why, I wouldn't have a child of mine, an impressionable little thing, live in such a room for worlds.
>
> I never thought of it before, but it is lucky that John kept me here after all, I can stand it so much easier than a baby. . . .
>
> (384)

The narrator's tone here suggests that she is trying to convince herself that she <u>can</u> fill the role of a proper mother and that she <u>does</u> look out for her child's welfare. Despite all her attempts at maternal sentiment, however, her concern for her son seems insincere. She still only thinks of her baby in the abstract--"a child of mine"--and she sounds more like she is reciting from a script than speaking from the heart.

Perhaps the narrator has difficulty with behaving like a mother because she is treated like a child herself throughout the story. From the very first page, the narrator's husband, John, consistently exhibits the

---

[1]All page references are to Charlotte Perkins Gilman, "The Yellow Wallpaper," reprinted in <u>The Practical Guide to Writing</u>, Eighth Edition (New York: Addison Wesley Longman, 2000), p. 380-90.

philosophy that a man can expect no more logic or self-knowledge
from his wife than he could from a small child. Accordingly, John
dictates nearly every aspect of the narrator's daily life. In one instance,
she describes how her husband and her brother take responsibility
for her health. She says she takes, on their orders, "phosphates
or phosphites—whichever it is, and tonics, and journeys, and air,
and exercise, and am absolutely forbidden to 'work' until I am
well again" (380), even though she maintains: "Personally, I disagree
with their ideas. Personally, I believe that congenial work, with
excitement and change, would do me good" (380). Her words give the
impression that John would brazenly proceed according to his own
theories of mental health care in the face of any protest that the
narrator might put forth.

The temptation, of course, is to blame John for the fact that his
regime fails to pull the narrator out of her depression and, instead, drives
her deeper into mental illness. However, at some points in the story, the
narrator's childish behavior seems to justify his patronizing attitude
toward her. The narrator reports a conversation, for example, in which her
own conduct could have done nothing but confirm John's suspicions about
the irrational nature of womankind:

> I tried to have a real earnest reasonable talk with him the
> other day, and tell him how I wish he would let me go and
> make a visit to Cousin Henry and Julia.
>
> But he said I wasn't able to go, nor able to stand it when I
> got there; and I didn't make out a very good case for myself,
> for I was crying before I had finished. (384)

Although John does come across as dictatorial in his control of his
wife's activities, this exchange also demonstrates the narrator's childishly
inconsistent behavior. Only the page before, she had complained: "I don't

feel as if it was worth while to turn my hand over for anything" (383), describing how the company of visitors tired her. No wonder, then, that John believes his wife will change her mind and wish to return home again if he allows her to visit her friends. The narrator's own indecisiveness creates the need for John to make decisions on her behalf.

Furthermore, the narrator herself seems to believe in her husband's notions about the similarities between wives and children. She mentions children repeatedly over the course of the story, and each time, she gives the impression that she identifies with them. When first describing her bedroom, she says: "It was nursery first and then playroom and gymnasium, I should judge; for the windows are barred for little children . . ." (381), and of the wallpaper she exclaims: "No wonder the children hated it! I should hate it myself if I had to live in this room long" (381). Although the narrator really only assumes that children ever inhabited her room, her wind wanders back to images of children again and again. More important, the narrator seems to project her own instinctual distaste for the wallpaper onto the children she has imagined, suggesting she agrees with her husband's implicit belief that the opinions and thought processes of a woman are as immature and irrational as those of small children.

To some extent, then, the narrator's behavior does confirm her husband's expectations. Nevertheless, her increasingly severe delusions, which contain clear symbols of restraint and confinement, show that she feels terribly constrained by her husband's domineering attitude. In her description of the bedroom, she mentions that "the windows are barred for little children" (381), and she reiterates the image of the bars later on through her hallucinations about the wallpaper. While watching the paper at night, she says of its pattern: "by moonlight, it becomes bars! The outside pattern I mean, and the woman behind it is as plain as can be" (386). Clearly,

the bars symbolize the narrator's own feeling of confinement at the hands
of her husband. Of course, the previous owners of the house put bars in
their windows to protect their children, not to confine them, and John is
equally well-intentioned in the constraints he places on his wife.
Nevertheless, despite the narrator's apparent willingness to conform to her
husband's image of a child-like wife, her delusions surrounding the bars
reveal the long-buried resentment that has resulted from John's
patronizing treatment.

Thus, the narrator feels torn between the two conflicting roles that
marriage and motherhood have created for her. She finds the prospect of
maturing into a loving and responsible caretaker for her baby so
frightening that she cannot stand to spend any time with him, but at the
same time, she seems to know that by continuing to act like a child
herself, she will never be permitted the freedom for which she yearns. It is
this baffling conflict to which she addresses the refrain: "But what is one
to do?" (380). Stripped of the distractions that writing and social
interaction once provided, the narrator finds herself confronted with an
intractable dilemma. The reader can only guess whether a character with
more mental toughness could have successfully wrangled with this
dilemma; for, instead of taking on the struggle, the narrator loses herself
in a new distraction: the yellow wallpaper of her nursery/bedroom.

For this reason, it seems that Gilman does not find John's demeaning
treatment entirely at fault in the narrator's mental breakdown. While
John's insistence on coddling the narrator does create a difficult paradox
for her to face as a new mother, it is the narrator's inability to cope with
the paradox that eventually leads her to insanity. In this way, Gilman's
theme takes the form of a double-edged sword. She condemns John and the
male-dominated society he represents for their patronizing attitude toward

married women. Nevertheless, she also suggests that wives must take

responsibility for their own well-being and force themselves to face the

painful conflicts that marriage and motherhood create.

GETTING IDEAS FOR WRITING ABOUT FICTION

Here are some questions that may help to stimulate responses and therefore ideas about stories. Not every question is, of course, relevant to every story, but if after reading a story and thinking about it, you then run your eye over this checklist, you will probably find some questions that will help you to think further about the story—in short, that will help you to get ideas.

It's best to do your thinking with a pen or pencil in hand or in front of your word processor. If some of the following questions seem to you to be especially relevant to the story you will be writing about, jot down—freely, without worrying about spelling—your initial responses, interrupting your writing only to glance again at the story when you feel the need to check the evidence.

✔ Checklist: Asking Questions About Fiction

- ✔ What happens in the story? Summarize the **plot**. (Think about what your summary *leaves out*.)
- ✔ Is the story told in chronological order or are there flashbacks, or flashforwards? On rereading, what **foreshadowing** of events do you detect?
- ✔ What **conflicts** does the story include?
- ✔ With which **character** or characters do you sympathize? How does the writer reveal character? How does the author create sympathy for some characters but not for others? Are the characters and their actions plausible? What motivates them? Do their names suggest anything about their characters or functions in the story? What do minor characters contribute to the story?
- ✔ Who tells the story? Is the story narrated by a **first-person narrator** (as was the case in "The Yellow Wallpaper")? If so, is that narrator the main character or **protagonist**? If the narrator is a character in the story, how reliable does he or she appear to be? Or is the story told by a **third-person narrator** (as was the case in "Muddy Road")? If so, does the narrator represent the action primarily through the thoughts and actions of one of the characters? Or does the narrator seem to stand entirely outside of the characters, to be neutral? Try to assess your response to or the effect on you of the **point of view.**
- ✔ Where and when does the story take place? What is the relation of the **setting** to the **plot** and **characters**?
- ✔ Do certain characters seem to you to stand for something in addition to themselves; that is, are they **symbolic**? Does the **setting**—a house, a farm, a landscape, a town, a period—have an extra dimension? (Trust your responses to a story. If you don't sense a symbolic overtone in a character or action, move on. Don't let a hunt for symbols distract you from enjoying and thinking about the story.)

✔ Is the **title** informative? Did its meaning seem to change after you read the story?

✔ What do you especially like or dislike about the story? Do you think your responses are in large degree unique, or do you think that most readers share them? Why?

✔ What is the story about? What is its **theme?** Does the theme concern values you hold, or does it challenge them?

✔ What does the story seem to be *saying about* its theme? What point does the author seem to be making? (About what?) What is the **meaning** of the story?

READING POETRY

Let's begin with an example. The following short poem is by Langston Hughes (1902–67), an African-American writer. The poem, first published in 1951, provided Lorraine Hansberry with the title of her well-known play, *A Raisin in the Sun.*

Harlem

What happens to a dream deferred?

Does it dry up
like a raisin in the sun?
Or fester like a sore—
And then run?
Does it stink like rotten meat?
Or crust and sugar over—
like a syrupy sweet?

Maybe it just sags
like a heavy load.

Or does it explode?

Reread the poem, this time thinking about its effect on you. Are there words or ideas that puzzle you, please you, displease you, or what?

Of course, different readers will respond at least somewhat differently to any work. On the other hand, since poets and storytellers, like psychologists, historians, and all other writers, want to communicate, they try to control their readers' responses, and they count on their readers to understand the meanings of words as the writers themselves understand them. Thus Hughes could assume that his readers knew that Harlem was the site of a large African-American community in New York City, and further, that the phrase "dream deferred" refers to the unfulfilled hopes of African-Americans who live in a predominantly white society. But Hughes does not say (as we have just said) "hopes"; rather, he says "dream." And he does not say "unfulfilled"; rather, he says "deferred." You might ask yourself exactly what differences there are between these words. Next, when you reread the poem, you might think about which expression is better in the context, "unfulfilled hopes" or "dream deferred," and why?

This sort of questioning of the words of the text, or, rather, questioning your responses to the words of the text, is at the heart of writing about literature—just as it is at the heart of writing about any sort of complicated text. If after a second reading of a literary text you still feel short of responses—but don't forget that being puzzled is itself a response worth studying—you will almost surely be able to generate responses by using the invention devices that we mention in our first chapter: free writing, listing, clustering, keeping a journal, and asking questions. (At the end of this section, we will suggest some additional strategies for generating responses to poetry.)

A Student Thinks About "Harlem": Richard Taub's Annotations, Journal Entries, Notes, and Final Draft

Let's turn to an analysis of the poem, an examination of how the parts fit. As you look at the poem, thinks about the parts, and jot down whatever notes come to mind. After you have written you own notes, consider the annotations of one student, Richard Taub.

```
                        Harlem              Odd—does not
                                            begin by
  set off                                   describing
  sticks out (What happens to a dream deferred?   Harlem
                                            black hopes?

           ( Does it dry up
           ( like a raisin in the sun?
           ( or fester like a sore—
      ugh. ( And then run?                    4 comparisons
           ( Does it stink like rotten meat?
           ( Or crust and sugar over—
           ( like a syrupy sweet?             not so bad

             Maybe it just sags   Not a question. Strange
             like a heavy load.

  note—                                rhyme
  italics—   Or does it explode?   Ends with a question.
  emphasis—                         (Begins with a question
  also a line                       too)
  by itself.   But does the question mark make
  Very emphatic.   the ending not so emphatic?
```

Taub's annotations chiefly get at the **structure** of the poem, the relationship of the parts. He notices that the poem begins with a line set off by itself and ends with a line set off by itself, and he also notices that each of these lines is a question. Further, he indicates that each of these two lines is emphasized in other ways: The first begins further to the left than any of the other lines—as though the other lines are subheadings or are in some way subordinate—and the last is italicized.

Taub later wrote an entry in his journal:

Feb. 18. Since the title is "Harlem," it's obvious that the "dream" is by African-American people. Also, obvious that Hughes thinks that if the "dream" doesn't become real there may be riots ("explode"). I like "raisin in the sun" (maybe because I like the play), and I like the business about "a syrupy sweet"--much more pleasant than the festering sore and the rotten meat. But if the dream becomes "sweet," what's wrong with that? Why should something "sweet" explode?

Feb. 21. Prof. McCabe said to think of structure or form of a poem as a sort of architecture, a building with a foundation, floors, etc. topped by a roof--but since we read a poem from top to bottom, it's like a building upside down. Title or first line is foundation (even though it's at top); last line is roof, capping the whole. As you read, you add layers. Foundation of "Harlem" is a question (first line). Then, set back a bit from foundation, or built on it by white space, a tall room (7 lines high, with 4 questions); then, on top of this room, another room (two lines, one statement, not a question). Funny; I thought that in poems all stanzas are the same number of lines. Then--more white space, so another unit--the roof. Man this roof is going to fall in-- "explode." Not just the roof, maybe the whole house.

Feb. 21, p.m. I get it; one line at start, one line at end; both are questions, but the last sort of says (because it is in italics) that it is the most likely answer to the question of the first line. The last line is also a question, but it's still an answer. The big stanza (7 lines) has 4 questions: 2 lines, 2 lines, 1 line, 2 lines. Maybe the switch to 1 line is to give some variety, so as not to be dull? It's exactly in the middle of the poem. I get the progress from raisin in the sun (dried, but not so terrible), to festering sore and to stinking meat, but I still don't see what's so bad about "a syrupy sweet." Is Hughes saying that after things are very bad they will get better? But why, then, the explosion at the end?

Feb. 23. "Heavy load" and "sags" in next-to-last stanza seems to me to suggest slaves with bales of cotton, or maybe poor cotton pickers dragging big sacks of cotton. Or maybe people doing heavy labor in Harlem. Anyway, very tired. Different from running sore and stinking meat earlier; not disgusting, but pressing down, deadening. Maybe worse than a sore or rotten meat--a hard, hopeless life. And then the last line. Just one line, no fancy (and disgusting) simile. Boom! Not just pressed down and tired, like maybe some racist whites think (hope?) blacks will be? Bang! Will there be survivors?

Drawing chiefly on these notes, Taub jotted down some key ideas to guide him through a draft of an analysis of the poem. In organizing his draft, Taub followed the organization of the poem. On the following pages we give his notes and final draft.

11 lines; short, but powerful; explosive
Question (first line)
Answers (set off by space, & also indented)
"raisin in the sun": shrinking ⎫
"sore"   ⎬ disgusting
"rotten meat"   ⎭
"syrupy sweet": relief from disgusting comparisons
Final question (last line): explosion?
    explosive (powerful) because:
        short, condensed, packed
        in italics
        stands by self — like first line
        no fancy comparison; very direct

An Analysis of Langston Hughes's "Harlem"

"Harlem" is a poem that is only eleven lines long, but it is charged with power. It explodes. Hughes sets the stage, so to speak, by telling us in the title that he is talking about Harlem, and then he begins by asking "What happens to a dream deferred?" The rest of the poem is set off by being indented, as though it is the answer to his question. This answer is in three parts (three stanzas, of different lengths).

In a way, it's wrong to speak of the answer, since the rest of the poem consists of questions, but I think Hughes means that each question (for instance, does a "deferred" hope "dry up / like a raisin in the sun?") really is an answer, something that really has happened and that will happen again. The first question, "Does it dry up / like a raisin in the sun?" is a famous line. To compare hope to a raisin dried in the sun is to suggest a terrible shrinking. The next two comparisons are to a "sore" and to "rotten meat." These comparisons are less clever, but they are very effective because they are disgusting. Then, maybe because of the disgusting comparisons, he gives a comparison that is not at all disgusting. In this comparison he says that maybe the "dream deferred" will "crust over-- / like a syrupy sweet."

The seven lines with four comparisons are followed by a stanza of two lines with just one comparison:

Maybe it just sags

like a heavy load.

So if we thought that this postponed dream might finally turn into something "sweet," we were kidding ourselves. Hughes comes down to earth, in a short stanza, with an image of a heavy load, which probably also calls to mind images of people bent under heavy loads, maybe of cotton, or maybe just any sort of heavy load carried by African-Americans in Harlem and elsewhere.

The opening question ("What happens to a dream deferred?") was followed by four questions in seven lines, but now, with "Maybe it just sags / like a heavy load" we get a statement, as though the poet at last has found an answer. But at the end we get one more question, set off by itself and in italics: "Or does it explode?" This line itself is explosive for three reasons: it is short, it is italicized, and it is a stanza in itself. It's also interesting that this line, unlike the earlier lines, does not use a simile. It's almost as though Hughes is saying, "O.K., we've had enough fancy ways of talking about this terrible situation; here it is, straight."

GETTING IDEAS FOR WRITING ABOUT POETRY

If you are going to write about a fairly short poem (say, under thirty lines), copy out the poem, writing or typing it double-spaced. By writing it out you will be forced to notice details, down to the punctuation. After you have copied the poem, proofread it carefully against the original. Catching an error—even the addition or omission of a comma—may help you to notice a detail in the original that you might otherwise have overlooked. And of course, now that you have the poem with ample space between the lines, you have a worksheet with room for jottings.

A good essay is based on a genuine response to a poem; a response may be stimulated in part by first reading the poem aloud and then considering the following questions.

 ## Checklist: Asking Questions About Poems

- ✔ What was your first response? On rereading, what parts interest or puzzle you? What words seem especially striking or unusual? (Consult a dictionary for the several meanings of words you're unsure of.)
- ✔ How would you describe the **speaker** of the poem? What persona or voice is suggested? What **tone** or emotion do you detect—for example, remorse, regret, affection, irony, sorrow?
- ✔ What is the **structure** of the poem? Are there stanzas? Are there rhymes or repeated sounds? Do the lines vary in length or echo each other? Are there unexpected stresses or pauses? How do they affect you?
- ✔ What is the poem about? Is the **theme** stated or implied? How might you state it in a sentence?
- ✔ What **images** do you find? (An image recalls a sensation of sight, sound, taste, touch, or smell.) What does the poem suggest **symbolically** as well as literally?
- ✔ What do you especially like or dislike about the poem? Do you think your responses are in large degree unique, or do you think that most readers share them? Why?

A RANGE OF CRITICAL APPROACHES

It's probably impossible to write an essay on a piece of literature without writing from some critical position, even if that position isn't explicit or acknowledged.* An essay might concern a short story, say, and make no reference to the author's gender or biography, or to the time and place of its writing, or to the economic conditions that influenced its production; even so, that essay would still be informed by certain assumptions about how literature works and about how it ought to be read. In fact, **formalist criticism**—also known as the **New Criticism** of the 1930s to 1970s—takes precisely the approach outlined above, emphasizing the work as a self-contained unity to be studied in itself, not as part of an historical context or an author's life. Formalist critics emphasize the *form* of the work, the relationships between the parts: the construction of the plot, the contrasts between characters, the functions of rhymes, the point of view, and so on.

Critics since the 1970s have challenged the principles of formalist criticism, especially the idea that a work can be read in isolation. (Even so, students are often asked to do just that—especially at the beginning of the semester in lower-level literature courses—in part because such assignments can focus on the close-reading skills at the heart of all literary analysis.) For example, **reader-response criticism** focuses on the relationship between texts and readers, arguing that meaning is not something that an author embeds in a work, but that it is something that a reader creates in responding to a work. Early **feminist criticism**, which grew out of the women's movement of the 1960s, challenged the principles of formalism from another direction. Feminist critics have emphasized and explored the differences between women and men, and (generally speaking) argued that literature written by men is different from literature written by women, which is seen to embody the experiences of a group marginalized by the dominant male culture. Feminist criticism has been concerned with the depiction of women and men in a male-determined literary canon and with women's responses to these images; it has also been concerned with women's writing and the connections between the woman writer's biography and her work. When it explores such connections, it is making use of a form of **historical criticism** (see below) known as **biographical criticism**, which interprets a given work in the context of its author's life as revealed through autobiographies, diaries, journals, letters, and the like. (**Psychological** or **psychoanalytic criticism** is related to biographical criticism: the psychoanalytic critic examines the author and his or her work through the lens of psychology, usually Freudian; works of art, like dreams, are interpreted as disguised versions of repressed wishes.)

Lesbian criticism, gay criticism, and (most recently) **queer theory**, all have their roots in feminist theory. Lesbian and gay criticism addresses such questions as: (1) How have straight writers portrayed lesbians and gays, and how have lesbian and gay writers portrayed straight women and men? (2) What strategies did lesbian and gay writers use to make their work acceptable to a general public in an age when lesbian and gay behavior was unmentionable? Whereas

---

*The discussion that follows is a condensed version of Chapter 16, "Writing about Literature: An Overview," in Barnet et al., *Literature for Composition: Essays, Fiction, Poetry, and Drama,* Fourth Edition (New York: HarperCollins, 1996), pages 430–52.

lesbian and gay criticism has tended to examine the effects of an author's—or a character's—sexual identity, queer theorists question the concept of sexual identity itself; Judith Butler, for example, argues that various categories of identity ("heterosexual," "homosexual") are socially constructed and represent ways of defining human beings that are distinct to particular cultures and historical periods.

Like all the approaches discussed above, **historical criticism** and **New Historicism** also consider the literary text in context, but these two critical approaches differ greatly from each other. Historical criticism assumes that an understanding of how people thought and felt in the past can contribute to an understanding of a particular work. (**Marxist criticism**, a form of historical criticism, sees history primarily as a struggle between socioeconomic classes, and it sees literature as the product of the economic forces of the period, a product of work that also *does* work—serving to assure the society that produces it that the society's values are solid, even universal.) New historicism, which emerged in the 1980s and is especially associated with Stephen Greenblatt, insists that there is no "history" in the sense of a narrative of indisputable past events, and suggests that an understanding of how people thought and felt in the past isn't really possible to achieve. Rather, New Historicism holds that there is only *our* version—our narrative, our representation—of the past. Each age projects its own preconceptions on the past. **Post-colonial criticism** shares with New Historicism and Marxism a concern with history and politics and is linked with the work of Edward Said and Gayatri Spivak. It focuses in large part on work produced in former British colonies and expands the notion of English literature to include writing produced by sub-altern (or subordinate) peoples.

At the other end of the spectrum, more or less, is **deconstruction** or **post-structural criticism**, which (like formalist criticism) pays rigorous attention to the text, but which (unlike formalist criticism) assumes that the world is unknowable and that language is unstable, elusive, unfaithful. Deconstructionists hold that literary "texts" inevitably are self-contradictory; they also believe that authors are "socially constructed" from the "discourses of power" or "signifying practices" that surround them. Despite the differences between deconstruction and other critical approaches, deconstructionist thinking has powerfully influenced literary criticism in the last three decades. Jacques Derrida's *Of Grammatology* (1967, trans. 1976) is the seminal document, an influence on perhaps all the theory and criticism that came after it.

For a student essay that makes use of a range of critical approaches—biographical, feminist, psychological, historical—see Beatrice Cody's "Politics and Psychology in *The Awakening*," reprinted in Chapter 16, "The Research Essay."

THREE SHORT WORKS OF FICTION

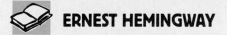 **ERNEST HEMINGWAY**

Cat in the Rain

Ernest Hemingway (1899–1961) was born in Oak Park, Illinois. After graduating from high school in 1917 he worked on the Kansas City Star, *but left to serve as a volunteer ambulance driver in Italy, where he was wounded in action. In 1922 he settled in Paris, where he moved in a circle of American expatriates that included Ezra Pound, Gertrude Stein, and F. Scott Fitzgerald. It was in Paris that he wrote stories and novels about what Gertrude Stein called a "lost generation" of rootless Americans in Europe.*

There were only two Americans stopping at the hotel. They did not know any of the people they passed on the stairs on their way to and from their room. Their room was on the second floor facing the sea. It also faced the public garden and the war monument. There were big palms and green benches in the public garden. In the good weather there was always an artist with his easel. Artists liked the way the palms grew and the bright colors of the hotels facing the gardens and the sea. Italians came from a long way off to look up at the war monument. It was made of bronze and glistened in the rain. It was raining. The rain dripped from the palm trees. Water stood in pools on the gravel paths. The sea broke in a long line in the rain and slipped back down the beach to come up and break again in a long line in the rain. The motor cars were gone from the square by the war monument. Across the square in the doorway of the café a waiter stood looking out at the empty square.

The American wife stood at the window looking out. Outside right under their window a cat was crouched under one of the dripping green tables. The cat was trying to make herself so compact that she would not be dripped on.

"I'm going down and get that kitty," the American wife said.

"I'll do it," her husband offered from the bed.

5   "No, I'll get it. The poor kitty out trying to keep dry under a table."

The husband went on reading, lying propped up with the two pillows at the foot of the bed.

"Don't get wet," he said.

The wife went downstairs and the hotel owner stood up and bowed to her as she passed the office. His desk was at the far end of the office. He was an old man and very tall.

"Il piove,"[1] the wife said. She liked the hotel-keeper.

10   "Si, si, Signora, brutto tempo. It is very bad weather."

He stood behind his desk in the far end of the dim room. The wife liked him. She liked the deadly serious way he received any complaints. She liked his dignity. She like the way he wanted to serve her. She liked the way he felt about being a hotel-keeper. She liked his old, heavy face and big hands.

Liking him she opened the door and looked out. It was raining harder. A man in a rubber cape was crossing the empty square to the café. The cat would be around to the right. Perhaps she could go along under the eaves. As she stood in the doorway an umbrella opened behind her. It was the maid who looked after their room.

"You must not get wet," she smiled, speaking Italian. Of course, the hotel-keeper had sent her.

With the maid holding the umbrella over her, she walked along the gravel path until she was under their window. The table was there, washed bright green in the rain, but the cat was gone. She was suddenly disappointed. The maid looked up at her.

15   "Ha perduto qualque cosa, Signora?"[2]

"There was a cat," said the American girl.

"A cat?"

[1]It's raining (Italian).
[2]Have you lost something, Madam?

"Si, il gatto."

"A cat?" the maid laughed. "A cat in the rain?"

20 "Yes," she said, "under the table." Then, "Oh, I wanted it so much. I wanted a kitty."

When she talked English the maid's face tightened.

"Come Signora," she said. "We must get back inside. You will be wet."

"I suppose so," said the American girl.

They went back along the gravel path and passed in the door. The maid stayed outside to close the umbrella. As the American girl passed the office, the padrone bowed from his desk. Something felt very small and tight inside the girl. The padrone made her feel very small and at the same time really important. She had a momentary feeling of being of supreme importance. She went on up the stairs. She opened the door of the room. George was on the bed, reading.

25 "Did you get the cat?" he asked, putting the book down.

"It was gone."

"Wonder where it went to," he said, resting his eyes from reading.

She sat down on the bed.

"I wanted it so much," she said. "I don't know why I wanted it so much. I wanted that poor kitty. It isn't any fun to be a poor kitty out in the rain."

30 George was reading again.

She went over and sat in front of the mirror of the dressing table looking at herself with the hand glass. She studied her profile, first one side and then the other. Then she studied the back of her head and her neck.

"Don't you think It would be a good idea if I let my hair grow out?" she asked, looking at her profile again.

George looked up and saw the back of her neck, clipped close like a boy's.

"I like it the way it is."

35 "I get so tired of it," she said. "I get so tired of looking like a boy."

George shifted his position in the bed. He hadn't looked away from her since she started to speak.

"You look pretty darn nice," he said.

She laid the mirror down on the dresser and went over to the window and looked out. It was getting dark.

"I want to pull my hair back tight and smooth and make a big knot at the back that I can feel," she said. "I want to have a kitty to sit on my lap and purr when I stroke her."

40 "Yeah?" George said from the bed.

"And I want to eat at a table with my own silver and I want candles. And I want it to be spring and I want to brush my hair out in front of a mirror and I want a kitty and I want some new clothes."

"Oh, shut up and get something to read," George said. He was reading again.

His wife was looking out of the window. It was quite dark now and still raining in the palm trees.

"Anyway, I want a cat," she said, "I want a cat. I want a cat now. If I can't have long hair or any fun, I can have a cat."

45 George was not listening. He was reading his book. His wife looked out of the window where the light had come on in the square.

Someone knocked at the door.

"Avanti,"[3] George said. He looked up from his book.

---

[3]Come in.

In the doorway stood the maid. She held a big tortoise-shell cat pressed tight against her and swung down against her body.

"Excuse me," she said, "the padrone asked me to bring this for the Signora."

✏️ Topics for Critical Thinking and Writing

1. One student argued that the cat represents the child that the girl wants to have. Do you think there is something to this idea? How might you support or refute it?
2. Would it make any difference if the animal were a dog instead of a cat?
3. Can we be certain that the cat at the end of the story is the cat that the woman saw in the rain? (When we first hear about the cat in the rain we are not told anything about its color, and at the end of the story we are not told that the tortoise-shell cat is wet.) Does it matter if there are two cats?
4. What do you suppose Hemingway's attitude was toward each of the three chief characters? How might you support your hunch?
5. Hemingway wrote the story in Italy, when his wife Hadley was pregnant. In a letter to F. Scott Fitzgerald he said,

   Cat in the Rain wasn't about Hadley. . . . When I wrote that we were at Rapallo but Hadley was 4 months pregnant with Bumby. The Inn Keeper was the one at Cortina D'Ampezzo. . . . Hadley never made a speech in her life about wanting a baby because she had been told various things by her doctor and I'd—no use going into all that. (*Letters,* p. 180)

   According to some biographers, the story shows that Hemingway knew his marriage was going on the rocks (Hemingway and Hadley divorced). Does knowing that Hemingway's marriage turned out unhappily help you to understand the story? Does it make the story more interesting? And do you think that the story tells a biographer something about Hemingway's life?

6. It is sometimes said that a good short story does two things at once: It provides a believable picture of the surface of life, and it also illuminates some moral or psychological complexity that we feel is part of the essence of human life. This dual claim may not be true, but for the moment accept it. Do you think that Hemingway's story fulfills either or both of these specifications? Support your view.

📖 JAMAICA KINCAID

Girl

Jamaica Kincaid was born in 1949 in Saint John's, Antigua, in the West Indies. She was educated at the Princess Margaret School in Antigua and, briefly, at Westchester Community College and Franconia College. Before becoming a writer, she worked as an au pair in Westchester County, New York.

Kincaid is the author of At the Bottom of the River *(1983), a collection of short pieces, including "Girl";* Annie John *(1985), a second book recording a girl's growth;*

A Small Place (1988), a passionate essay about the destructive effects of colonialism; and Lucy *(1990), a short novel about a young woman who comes to the United States from the West Indies. Her most recent novel is* The Autobiography of My Mother *(1996).* My Brother, *published in 1997, is a memoir of her return to Antigua to nurse her brother, who was dying of AIDS.*

Wash the white clothes on Monday and put them on the stone heap; wash the color clothes on Tuesday and put them on the clothesline to dry; don't walk barehead in the hot sun; cook pumpkin fritters in very hot sweet oil; soak your little clothes right after you take them off; when buying cotton to make yourself a nice blouse, be sure that it doesn't have gum on it, because that way it won't hold up well after a wash; soak salt fish overnight before you cook it; is it true that you sing benna[1] in Sunday School?; always eat your food in such a way that it won't turn someone else's stomach; on Sundays try to walk like a lady and not like the slut you are so bent on becoming; don't sing benna in Sunday School; you mustn't speak to wharf-rat boys, not even to give directions; don't eat fruits on the street—flies will follow you; *but I don't sing benna on Sundays at all and never in Sunday school;* this is how to sew on a button; this is how to make a buttonhole for the button you have just sewed on; this is how to hem a dress when you see the hem coming down and so to prevent yourself from looking like the slut I know you are so bent on becoming; this is how you iron your father's khaki shirt so that it doesn't have a crease; this is how you iron your father's khaki pants so that they don't have a crease; this is how you grow okra— far from the house, because okra tree harbors red ants; when you are growing dasheen, make sure it gets plenty of water or else it makes your throat itch when you are eating it; this is how you sweep a corner; this is how you sweep a whole house; this is how you sweep a yard; this is how you smile to someone you don't like too much; this is how you set a table for dinner with an important guest; this is how you smile to someone you don't like at all; this is how you smile to someone you like completely; this is how you set a table for tea; this is how you set a table for dinner; this is how you set a table for lunch; this is how you set a table for breakfast; this is how to behave in the presence of men who don't know you very well, and this way they won't recognize immediately the slut I have warned you against becoming; be sure to wash every day, even if it is with your own spit; don't squat down to play marbles—you are not a boy, you know; don't pick people's flowers—you might catch something; don't throw stones at blackbirds, because it might not be a blackbird at all; this is how to make a bread pudding; this is how to make doukona;[2] this is how to make pepper pot; this is how to make a good medicine for a cold; this is how to make a good medicine to throw away a child before it even becomes a child; this is how to catch a fish; this is how to throw back a fish you don't like, and that way something bad won't fall on you; this is how to bully a man; this is how a man bullies you; this is how to love a man, and if this doesn't work there are other ways, and if they don't work don't feel too bad about giving up; this how to spit up in the air if you feel like it, and this is how to move quick so that it doesn't fall on you; this how to make ends meet; always squeeze bread to make sure it's fresh; *but what if the baker won't let me feel the bread?;* you mean to say that after all you are really going to be the kind of woman who the baker won't let near the bread?

[1]Calypso music.
[2]Spicy pudding made of plantains.

Topics for Critical Thinking and Writing

1. Identify the two characters whose voices we hear in this story. Explain what we know about them (their circumstances and their relationship). How old, approximately, is "girl"? Cite specific evidence from the text.
2. What do we learn about the relationship from frequent repetition of "this is how"? Are there other words or phrases frequently repeated? If so, what are they?
3. Imitating the structure of "Girl," compose a comparable piece, based on some repeated conversation in your family.

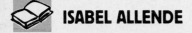 **ISABEL ALLENDE**

If You Touched My Heart

The Chilean writer Isabel Allende is author of several novels, among them The House of Spirits *(1981),* Of Love and Shadows *(1984), and* Eva Luna *(1989), as well as a collection of short fiction,* The Stories of Eva Luna *(1990), from which the following story is reprinted.*

Allende left Chile following the coup that resulted in the deposition of her uncle, socialist president Salvador Allende. She currently lives in Marin County, California. Her most recent work, Aphrodite *(1998), is a meditation on food and sex.*

Amadeo Peralta was raised in the midst of his father's gang and, like all the men of his family, grew up to be a ruffian. His father believed that school was for cissies; you don't need books to get ahead in life, he always said, just balls and quick wits, and that was why he trained his boys to be rough and ready. With time, nevertheless, he realized that the world was changing very rapidly and that his business affairs needed to be more firmly anchored. The era of undisguised plunder had been replaced by one of corruption and bribery; it was time to administer his wealth by using modern criteria, and to improve his image. He called his sons together and assigned them the task of establishing friendships with influential persons and of learning the legal tricks that would allow them to continue to prosper without danger of losing their impunity. He also encouraged them to find sweethearts among the old-line families and in this way see whether they could cleanse the Peralta name of all its stains of mud and blood. By then Amadeo was thirty-two years old; the habit of seducing girls and then abandoning them was deeply ingrained; the idea of marriage was not at all to his liking but he did not dare disobey his father. He began to court the daughter of a wealthy landowner whose family had lived in the same place for six generations. Despite her suitor's murky reputation, the girl accepted, for she was not very attractive and was afraid of ending up an old maid. Then began one of those tedious provincial engagements. Wretched in a white linen suit and polished boots, Amadeo came every day to visit his fiancée beneath the hawk-like eye of his future mother-in-law or some aunt, and while the young lady served coffee and *guayabá* sweets he would peek at his watch, calculating the earliest moment to make his departure.

A few weeks before the wedding, Amadeo Peralta had to make a business trip through the provinces and found himself in Agua Santa, one of those towns where nobody stays and whose name travellers rarely recall. He was walking down a narrow street at the hour of the siesta, cursing the heat and the oppressive, cloying odour of mango marmalade in the air, when he heard a crystalline sound like water purling between stones; it was coming from a modest house with paint flaked by the sun and rain like most of the houses in that town. Through the ornamental iron grille he glimpsed an entryway of dark paving stones and whitewashed walls, then a patio and, beyond, the surprising vision of a young girl sitting cross-legged on the ground and cradling a blond wood psaltery on her knees. For a while he stood and watched her.

"Come here, sweet thing," he called, finally. She looked up, and despite the distance he could see the startled eyes and uncertain smile in a still-childish face. "Come with me," Amadeo asked—implored—in a hoarse voice.

She hesitated. The last notes lingered like a question in the air of the patio. Peralta called again. The girl stood up and walked towards him; he slipped his hand through the iron grille, shot the bolt, opened the gate, and seized her hand, all the while reciting his entire repertoire of seduction: he swore that he had seen her in his dreams, that he had been looking for her all his life, that he could not let her go, and that she was the woman fate had meant for him—all of which he could have omitted because the girl was simple and even though she may have been enchanted by the tone of his voice she did not understand the meaning of his words. Hortensia was her name and she had just turned fifteen; her body was turned for its first embrace, though she was unable to put a name to the restlessness and tremors that shook it. It was so easy for Peralta to lead her to his car and drive to a nearby clearing that an hour later he had completely forgotten her. He did not recognize her even when a week later she suddenly appeared at his house, one hundred and forty kilometres away, wearing a simple yellow cotton dress and canvas espadrilles, her psaltery under her arm, and inflamed with the fever of love.

5   Forty-seven years later, when Hortensia was rescued from the pit in which she had been entombed and newspapermen travelled from every corner of the nation to photograph her, not even she could remember her name or how she had got there.

The reporters accosted Amadeo Peralta: 'Why did you keep her locked up like a miserable beast?'

'Because I felt like it,' he replied calmly. By then he was eighty, and as lucid as ever; he could not understand this belated outcry over something that had happened so long ago.

He was not inclined to offer explanations. He was a man of authority, a patriarch, a great-grandfather; no one dared look him in the eye; even priests greeted him with bowed head. During the course of his long life he had multiplied the fortune he inherited from his father; he had become the owner of all the land from the ruins of the Spanish fort to the state line, and then had launched himself on a political career that made him the most powerful cacique in the territory. He had married the landowner's ugly daughter and sired nine legitimate descendants with her and an indefinite number of bastards with other women, none of whom he remembered since he had a heart hardened to love. The only woman he could not entirely discard was Hortensia; she stuck in his consciousness like a persistent nightmare. After the brief encounter in the tall grass of an empty lot, he had returned to his home, his work, and his insipid, well-bred fiancée. It was Hortensia who had searched until she found *him;* it was she who had planted herself before him and clung to his shirt with the terrifying submission of a slave. This is a fine kettle of fish, he had thought; here I am about to get married with all this hoopla and to-do, and now this idiot girl turns up on my doorstep. He wanted to be rid of her, and yet when he saw her in her yellow dress, with those entreating eyes, it seemed a waste not to take advantage of the opportunity, and he decided to hide her while he found a solution.

And so, by carelessness, really, Hortensia ended up in the cellar of an old sugar mill that belonged to the Peraltas, where she was to remain for a lifetime. It was a large room, dank, and dark, suffocating in summer and in the dry season often cold at night, furnished with a few sticks of furniture and a straw pallet. Amadeo Peralta never took time to make her more comfortable, despite his occasionally feeding a fantasy of making the girl a concubine from an oriental tale, clad in gauzy robes and surrounded with peacock feathers, brocade tented ceilings, stained-glass lamps, gilded furniture with spiral feet, and thick rugs where he could walk barefoot. He might actually have done it had Hortensia reminded him of his promises, but she was like a wild bird, one of those blind guacharos that live in the depths of caves: all she needed was a little food and water. The yellow dress rotted away and she was left naked.

10   "He loves me; he has always loved me," she declared when she was rescued by neighbours. After being locked up for so many years she had lost the use of words and her voice came out in spurts like the croak of a woman on her deathbed.

For a few weeks, Amadeo had spent a lot of time in the cellar with her, satisfying an appetite he thought insatiable. Fearing that she would be discovered, and jealous even of his own eyes, he did not want to expose her to daylight and allowed only a pale ray to enter through the tiny hole that provided ventilation. In the darkness, they coupled frenziedly, their skin burning and their hearts impatient as carnivorous crabs. In that cavern all odours and tastes were heightened to the extreme. When they touched, each entered the other's being and sank into the other's most secret desires. There, voices resounded in repeated echoes; the walls returned amplified murmurs and kisses. The cellar became a sealed flask in which they wallowed like playful twins swimming in amniotic fluid, two swollen, stupefied foetuses. For days they were lost in an absolute intimacy they confused with love.

When Hortensia fell asleep, her lover went out to look for food and before she awakened returned with renewed energy to resume the cycle of caresses. They should have made love to each other until they died of desire; they should have devoured one another or flamed like mirrored torches, but that was not to be. What happened instead was more predictable and ordinary, much less grandiose. Before a month had passed, Amadeo Peralta tired of the games, which they were beginning to repeat; he sensed the dampness eating into his joints, and he began to feel the attraction of things outside the walls of that grotto. It was time to return to the world of the living and to pick up the reins of his destiny.

"You wait for me here. I'm going out and get very rich. I'll bring you gifts and dresses and jewels fit for a queen," he told her as he said goodbye.

"I want children," said Hortensia.

15   "Children, no; but you shall have dolls."

In the months that followed, Peralta forgot about the dresses, the jewels, and the dolls. He visited Hortensia when he thought of her, not always to make love, sometimes merely to hear her play some old melody on her psaltery; he liked to watch her bent over the instrument, strumming chords. Sometimes he was in such a rush that he did not even speak; he filled her water jugs, left her a sack filled with provisions, and departed. Once he forgot about her for nine days, and found her on the verge of death; he realized then the need to find someone to help care for his prisoner, because his family, his travels, his business, and his social engagements occupied all his time. He chose a tight-mouthed Indian woman to fill that role. She kept the key to the padlock, and regularly came to clean the cell and scrape away the lichens growing on Hortensia's body like pale delicate flowers almost invisible to the naked eye and redolent of tilled soil and neglected things.

'Weren't you ever sorry for that poor woman?' they asked when they arrested her as well, charging her with complicity in the kidnapping. She refused to answer but stared straight ahead with expressionless eyes and spat a black stream of tobacco.

No, she had felt no pity for her; she believed the woman had a calling to be a slave and was happy being one, or else had been born an idiot and like others in her situation was better locked up than exposed to the jeers and perils of the street. Hortensia had done nothing to change her jailer's opinion; she never exhibited any curiosity about the world, she made no attempt to be outside for fresh air, and she complained about nothing. She never seemed bored; her mind had stopped at some moment in her childhood, and solitude in no way disturbed her. She was, in fact, turning into a subterranean creature. There in her tomb her senses grew sharp and she learned to see the invisible; she was surrounded by hallucinatory spirits who led her by the hand to other universes. She left behind a body huddled in a corner and travelled through starry space like a messenger particle, living in a dark land beyond reason. Had she had a mirror, she would have been terrified by her appearance; as she could not see herself, however, she was not witness to her deterioration: she was unaware of the scales sprouting from her skin, or the silkworms that had spun a nest in her long, tangled hair, or the lead-coloured clouds covering eyes already dead from peering into shadows. She did not feel her ears growing to capture external sounds, even the faintest and most distant, like the laughter of children at school recess, the ice-cream vendor's bell, birds in flight, or the murmuring river. Nor did she realize that her legs, once graceful and firm, were growing twisted as they adjusted to moving in that confined space, to crawling, nor that her toenails were thickening like an animal's hooves, her bones changing into tubes of glass, her belly caving in, and a hump forming on her back. Only her hands, forever occupied with the psaltery, maintained their shape and size, although her fingers had forgotten the melodies they had once known and now extracted from the instrument the unvoiced sob trapped in her breast. From a distance, Hortensia resembled a tragic circus monkey; on closer view, she inspired infinite pity. She was totally ignorant of the malignant transformations taking place; in her mind she held intact the image of herself as the young girl she had last seen reflected in the window of Amadeo Peralta's automobile the day he had driven her to this lair. She believed she was as pretty as ever, and continued to act as if she were; the memory of beauty crouched deep inside her and only if someone approached very close would he have glimpsed it beneath the external façade of a prehistoric dwarf.

All the while, Amadeo Peralta, rich and feared, cast the net of his power across the region. Every Sunday he sat at the head of a long table occupied by his sons and nephews, cronies and accomplices, and special guests such as politicians and generals whom he treated with a hearty cordiality tinged with sufficient arrogance to remind everyone who was master here. Behind his back, people whispered about his victims, about how many he had ruined or caused to disappear, about bribes to authorities; there was talk that he had made half his fortune from smuggling, but no one was disposed to seek the proof of his transgressions. It was also rumoured that Peralta kept a woman prisoner in a cellar. That aspect of his black deeds was repeated with more conviction even than stories of his crooked dealings; in fact, many people knew about it, and with time it became an open secret.

20   One afternoon on a very hot day, three young boys played hookey from school to swim in the river. They spent a couple of hours splashing around on the muddy bank and then wandered off towards the old Peralta sugar mill that had been closed two generations earlier when cane ceased to be a profitable crop. The mill had the reputation of being haunted; people said you could hear sounds of devils, and many had seen a dishevelled old witch invoking the spirits of dead slaves. Excited by their adventure, the boys crept onto the property and approached the mill. Soon they were daring enough to enter the ruins; they ran through large rooms with thick adobe walls and termite-riddled beams; they picked their way through weeds growing from the floor, mounds of rubbish and dog shit, rotted roof tiles, and snakes' nests. Making jokes to work up their courage, egging each other on, they came to the huge roofless room that contained the ruined sugar presses; here rain and sun had created an impossible garden, and the boys thought they could detect a lingering scent of sugar and sweat. Just as they were growing bolder they heard, clear as a bell, the notes of a monstrous song. Trembling, they almost retreated, but the lure of horror was stronger than their fear, and they huddled there, listening, as the last note drilled into their foreheads. Gradually, they were released from their paralysis; their fear evaporated and they began looking for the source of those weird sounds so different from any music they had ever known. They discovered a small trap door in the floor, closed with a lock they could not open. They rattled the wood planks that sealed the entrance and were struck in the face by an indescribable odour that reminded them of a caged beast. They called but no one answered; they heard only a hoarse panting on the other side. Finally they ran home to shout the news that they had discovered the door to hell.

The children's uproar could not be stilled, and thus the neighbours finally proved what they had suspected for decades. First the boys' mothers came to peer through the cracks in the trap door; they, too, heard the terrible notes of the psaltery, so different from the banal melody that had attracted Amadeo Peralta the day he had paused in a small alley in Agua Santa to dry the sweat from his forehead. The mothers were followed by throngs of curious and, last of all, after a crowd had already gathered, came the police and firemen, who chopped open the door and descended into the hole with their lamps and equipment. In the cave they found a naked creature with flaccid skin hanging in pallid folds; this apparition had tangled grey hair that dragged the floor, and moaned in terror of the noise and light. It was Hortensia, glowing with a mother-of-pearl phosphorescence under the steady beams of the firefighters' lanterns; she was nearly blind, her teeth had rotted away, and her legs were so weak she could barely stand. The only sign of her human origins was the ancient psaltery clasped to her breast.

The news stirred indignation throughout the country. Television screens and newspapers displayed pictures of the woman rescued from the hole where she had spent her life, now, at least, half-clothed in a cloak someone had tossed around her shoulders. In only a few hours, the indifference that had surrounded the prisoner for almost half a century was converted into a passion to avenge and succour her. Neighbours improvised lynch parties for Amadeo Peralta; they stormed his house, dragged him out, and had the Guard not arrived in time, would have torn him limb from limb in the plaza. To assuage their guilt for having ignored Hortensia for so many years, everyone wanted to do something for her. They collected money to provide her a pension, they gathered tons of clothing and medicine she did not need, and several welfare organizations were given the task of scraping the filth from her body, cutting her hair, and outfitting her from head to toe, so she looked like an ordinary old lady. The nuns offered her a bed in a shelter for indigents, and for several months kept her tied up to prevent her from running back to her cellar, until finally she grew accustomed to daylight and resigned to living with other human beings.

Taking advantage of the public furore fanned by the press, Amadeo Peralta's numerous enemies finally gathered courage to launch an attack against him. Authorities who for years had overlooked his abuses fell upon him with the full fury of the law. The story occupied everyone's attention long enough to see the former caudillo in prison, and then faded and died away. Rejected by family and friends, a symbol of all that is abominable and abject, harassed by both jailers and companions-in-misfortune, Peralta spent the rest of his days in prison. He remained in his cell, never venturing into the courtyard with the other inmates. From there, he could hear the sounds from the street.

Every day at ten in the morning, Hortensia, with the faltering step of a madwoman, tottered down to the prison where she handed the guard at the gate a warm saucepan for the prisoner.

25

"He almost never left me hungry," she would tell the guard in an apologetic tone. Then she would sit in the street to play her psaltery, wresting from it moans of agony impossible to bear. In the hope of distracting her or silencing her, some passers-by gave her money.

Crouched on the other side of the wall, Amadeo Peralta heard those sounds that seemed to issue from the depths of the earth and course through every nerve in his body. This daily castigation must mean something, but he could not remember what. From time to time he felt something like a stab of guilt, but immediately his memory failed and images of the past evaporated in a dense mist. He did not know why he was in that tomb, and gradually he forgot the world of light and lost himself in his misfortune.

✐ Topics for Critical Thinking and Writing

1. Why does Amadeo Peralta imprison Hortensia in the cellar?
2. Why doesn't Hortensia try to leave?
3. What passages suggest that Allende holds the townspeople to some degree responsible for what happens to Hortensia?
4. Hortensia brings Amadeo food when he is imprisoned at the end of the story; she also plays her psaltry ("wresting from it moans of agony impossible to bear"). How do you explain these actions?

THREE POEMS

 ## WILLIAM SHAKESPEARE

Sonnet 73

*William Shakespeare (1564–1616) is widely regarded as the world's greatest drama-
tist, but he also wrote nondramatic poetry, including 154 sonnets. The sonnets were
published in 1609 but probably were written from about 1598 to 1605 or so. The fourteen lines of Shakespeare's sonnets can be divided into three quatrains (units of four
lines each) and a couplet (a pair of rhyming lines). In each quatrain, the first and third
lines rhyme with each other, and the second and fourth lines rhyme. The rhyme scheme
thus may be formulated as ababcdcdefefgg.*

> That time of year thou mayst in me behold
> When yellow leaves, or none, or few, do hang
> Upon those boughs which shake against the cold,
> Bare ruined choirs° where late the sweet birds sang.   4
> In me thou see'st the twilight of such day
> As after sunset fadeth in the west,
> Which by-and-by black night doth take away,
> Death's second self that seals up all in rest,   8
> In me thou see'st the glowing of such fire
> That on the ashes of his youth doth lie,
> As the deathbed whereon it must expire,
> Consumed with that which it was nourished by.   12
>> This thou perceiv'st, which makes thy love more strong,
>> To love that well which thou must leave ere long.

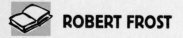 ### Topics for Critical Thinking and Writing

1. Paraphrase—that is, put into your own words—the entire poem.
2. To what does the poet compare himself in the first quatrain? In the second? In the third?
3. What would be gained or lost if the sequence of quatrains were reversed,
   that is, if the poem began with the last quatrain and ended with the first?

 ## ROBERT FROST

Stopping by Woods on a Snowy Evening

*Robert Frost (1874–1963) in his early years farmed in New Hampshire, published a few
poems in local newspapers, left the farm and taught school, and in 1912 left for England, where he hoped to achieve more popular success as a writer. By 1915 he had won
a considerable reputation, and he returned to the United States, settling on a farm in*

---

[4]The part of the church where services were sung.

*New Hampshire and cultivating the image of the country-wise farmer–poet. In fact he
was well read in the classics, the Bible, and English and American literature.*

*Among Frost's many comments about literature, here are three: "Writing is unbor-
ing to the extent that it is dramatic"; "Every poem is . . . a figure of the will braving
alien entanglements"; and, finally, a poem "begins in delight and ends in wisdom. . . .
It runs a course of lucky events, and ends in a clarification of life—not necessarily a
great clarification, such as sects and cults are founded on, but in a momentary stay
against confusion."*

Whose woods these are I think I know.
His house is in the village though;
He will not see me stopping here
To watch his woods fill up with snow.   4

My little horse must think it queer
To stop without a farmhouse near
Between the woods and frozen lake
The darkest evening of the year.   8

He gives his harness bells a shake
To ask if there is some mistake.
The only other sound's the sweep
Of easy wind and downy flake.   12

The woods are lovely, dark and deep.
But I have promises to keep,
And miles to go before I sleep,
And miles to go before I sleep.   16

✏️ Topics for Critical Thinking and Writing

1. Line 5 originally read: "The steaming horses think it queer." Line 7 read:
   "Between a forest and a lake." Evaluate the changes.
2. How would you describe the pattern of rhymes in the first stanza? In the
   second and third stanzas? The pattern changes in the fourth. Describe
   this pattern too, and then offer at least one suggestion as to why Frost
   may have departed from the earlier pattern.
3. Hearing that the poem had been interpreted as a "death poem," Frost
   said. "I never intended that, but I did have the feeling it was loaded with
   ulteriority." What do you understand "ulteriority" to mean in regard to
   this poem? For example, what significance do you attach to the time of
   day and year?
4. How does the horse's attitude contrast with the man's?

 **PAT MORA**

Immigrants

*Pat Mora did her undergraduate work at Texas Western College, and then earned a
master's degree at the University of Texas at El Paso, where she then served as*

Assistant to the Vice President for Academic Affairs, Director of the University Museum, and then from 1981 to 1989 Assistant to the President. She has published essays on Hispanic culture as well as a children's book, Tomás and the Library Lady, *but she is best known for her books of poems. Mora has received several awards, including one from the Southwest Council of Latin American Studies.*

Immigrants
wrap their babies in the American flag,
feed them mashed hot dogs and apple pie,
name them Bill and Daisy,
buy them blonde dolls that blink blue   5
eyes or a football and tiny cleats
before the baby can even walk,
speak to them in thick English,
    hallo, babee, hallo.
whisper in Spanish or Polish   10
when the babies sleep, whisper
in a dark parent bed, that dark
parent fear, "Will they like
our boy, our girl, our fine american
boy, our fine american girl?"

 Topics for Critical Thinking and Writing

1. To say that someone—for example, a politician—"wraps himself in the
    American flag" is to suggest disapproval or even anger or contempt.
    What behavior does the phrase usually describe? What does Mora mean
    when she says that immigrants "wrap their babies in the American flag"?
2. What do you suppose is Mora's attitude toward the immigrants? Do you
    think the poet fully approves of their hopes? On what do you base your
    answer? Speaking generally, do they seek to assimilate to an Anglo-Amer-
    ican culture?
3. Does Mora's description of the behavior of immigrants ring true of the
    immigrant group you are part of or know best? Speaking generally, do
    such groups seek to assimilate to an Anglo-American culture? What is
    your attitude toward these efforts or their efforts to retain their culture?
    Explain in an essay of 750 to 1000 words.

18

Writing Essay Examinations

WHAT EXAMINATIONS ARE

An examination not only measures learning and thinking but stimulates them. Even so humble an examination as a short-answer quiz—chiefly a device to coerce the student to do the assigned reading—is a sort of push designed to move the student forward. Of course internal motivation is far superior to external, but even such crude external motivation as a quiz can have a beneficial effect. Students know this; indeed they often seek external compulsion, choosing a course "because I want to know something about it, and I know that I won't do the reading on my own." (Teachers often teach a new course for the same reason; we want to become knowledgeable about, say, communism in China, and we know that despite our lofty intentions we may not seriously confront the subject unless we are under the pressure of facing a class.) In short, however ignoble it sounds, examinations force the student to acquire learning and then to convert learning into thinking.

Sometimes it is not until preparing for the final examination that the student—rereading the chief texts and classroom notes—sees what the course was really about; until this late stage, the trees obscured the forest, but now, as the student reviews and sorts things out, a pattern emerges. The experience of reviewing and then of writing an examination, though fretful, can be highly exciting as connections are made and ideas take on life. Such discoveries about the whole subject matter of a course can almost never be made by writing critical essays on topics of one's own construction, for such topics rarely require a view of the whole. Furthermore, most of us are more likely to make imaginative leaps when trying to answer questions that other people pose to us than when we are trying to answer questions we pose to ourselves. And although questions posed by others cause anxiety, when they have been confronted and responded to on an examination students often make yet another discovery—a self-discovery, a sudden and satisfying awareness of powers they didn't know they had.

WRITING ESSAY ANSWERS

We assume that before the examination you have read the assigned material, made notes in the margins of your books, made summaries of the reading and of the classroom comments, reviewed all of this material, and had a decent night's sleep. Now you are facing the examination sheet.

Here are eight obvious but important practical suggestions.

1. Take a moment to jot down, as a kind of outline or source of further inspiration, a few ideas that strike you after you have thought a little about the question. You may at the outset realize there are three points you want to make: unless you jot these down—three key words will do—you may spend all the allotted time on only one.
2. Don't bother to copy the question in the examination booklet, but if you have been given a choice of questions do indicate the question number, or write a word or two that will serve as a cue to the reader.
3. Answer the question. Consider this question: "Fromm and Lorenz try to explain aggression. Compare their theories, and discuss the extent to which they assist us in understanding the Arab-Israeli conflict." Notice that you must compare—not just summarize—two theories, and that you must also evaluate their relevance to a particular conflict. In short, take seriously such words as *compare, define, evaluate,* and *summarize.* And don't waste time generalizing about aggression; again, answer the question.
4. You can often get a good start merely be turning the question into an affirmation, for example by turning "In what ways is the poetry of Allen Ginsberg influenced by Whitman?" into "The poetry of Ginsberg is influenced by Whitman in at least . . . ways."
5. Don't waste time summarizing at length what you have read, unless asked to do so—but of course occasionally you may have to give a brief summary in order to support a point. The instructor wants to see that you can *use* your reading, not merely that you have done the reading.
6. Budget your time. Do not spend more time on a question than the allotted time—at least, not *much* more.
7. Be concrete. Illustrate your arguments with facts—names, dates, and quotations if possible.
8. Leave space for last minute additions. Either skip a page between essays, or write only on the right-hand pages so that on rereading you can add material at the appropriate place on the left-hand pages.

Beyond these general suggestions, we can best talk about essay examinations by looking at specific types of questions.

Questions on Literature

The most common questions encountered in literature examinations can be sorted into five categories:

1. A passage to explicate
2. A historical question, such as "Trace T. S. Eliot's religious development," "Trace the development of Shakespeare's conception of the tragic hero," or "What are Virginia Woolf's contributions to feminist criticism?"

3. A critical quotation to be evaluated
4. A comparison, such as "Compare the dramatic monologues of Browning with those of T. S. Eliot"
5. A wild question, such as "What would Dickens think of Stephen King?" or "What would Juliet do if she were in Ophelia's position?"

A few remarks on each of these types may be helpful:

1. An explication is a commentary describing what is going on in a poem or in a short passage of prose. As a short rule, look carefully at the tone (speaker's attitude toward self, subject, and audience) and at the implications of the words (the connotations or associations), and see if there is a pattern of imagery. For example, religious language ("adore," "saint") in a secular love poem may define the nature of the lover and of the beloved. Remember, *an explication is not a paraphrase* (a putting into other words) but an attempt to show the relations of the parts, especially by calling attention to implications. Organization of such an essay is rarely a problem, since most explications begin with the first line and go on to the last.

2. A good essay on a historical question will offer a nice combination of argument and evidence; the thesis will be supported by concrete details (names, dates, perhaps even brief quotations). A discussion of Eliot's movement toward the Church of England cannot be convincing if it does not specify certain works as representative of Eliot in certain years. If you are asked to relate a writer or a body of work to an earlier writer or period, list the chief characteristics of the earlier writer or the period and then show *specifically* how the material you are discussing is related to these characteristics. And if you can quote some relevant lines from the works, your reader will feel that you know not only titles and stock phrases but also the works themselves.

3. If you are asked to evaluate a critical quotation, read it carefully and in your answer take account of *all* of the quotation. If the critic has said, "Eliot in his plays always . . . but in his poems rarely . . ." you will have to write about both the plays and the poems; it will not be enough to talk only about the plays (unless, of course, the instructions on the examination ask you to take only as much of the quotation as you wish). Watch especially for words like "always," "for the most part," "never"; although the passage may on the whole approach the truth, you may feel that some important qualifications are needed. This is not being picky; true thinking involves making subtle distinctions, yielding assent only so far and no further. And, again, be sure to give concrete details, supporting your argument with evidence.

4. Comparisons are discussed on pages 161–68. Because comparisons are especially difficult to write, be sure to take a few moments to jot down a sort of outline so that you can know where you will be going. A comparison of Browning's and Eliot's monologues might treat three poems by each, devoting alternate paragraphs to one author; or it might first treat one author's poems and then turn to the other. But if it adopts this second strategy, the essay may break into two parts. You can guard against this weakness by announcing at the outset that you will treat the authors separately, then by reminding your reader during your treatment of the first author that certain points will be picked up when you get to the second author, and again by briefly reminding your reader during the second part of the essay of certain points already made.

5. Curiously, a wild question such as "What would Dickens think of Stephen King?" or "What would Juliet do in Ophelia's position?" usually produces tame answers: a half dozen ideas about Dickens or Juliet are neatly applied to King or Ophelia, and the gross incompatibilities are thus revealed. But, as the previous paragraph suggests, it may be necessary to do more than to set up bold and obvious oppositions. The interest in such a question and in the answer to it may largely be in the degree to which superficially different figures *resemble* each other in some important ways. And remember that the wildness of the question does not mean that all answers are equally acceptable; as usual, a good answer will be supported by concrete details.

Questions on the Social Sciences

First, an obvious statement: courses in the social sciences almost always require lots of reading. Do the reading when it is assigned, rather than try to do it the night before the examination. Second, when confronted with long reading assignments, you probably will read more efficiently if you scan the table of contents of a book to see the layout of the material, and then read the first and last chapters, where the authors usually summarize their theses. Books and articles on history, psychology, and sociology are not whodunits; there is nothing improper about knowing at the start how it will all turn out. Indeed, if at the start you have a clear grasp of the author's thesis, you may have the pleasure of catching the author perpetrating the crime of arguing from insufficient evidence. The beginning and the end of an article in a journal also may offer summaries that will assist you to read the article with relative ease. But only a reading of the entire work (perhaps with a little skimming) will offer you all of the facts and—no less important—the fully developed view or approach that the instructor believes is essential to an understanding of the course.

The techniques students develop in answering questions on literature may be transferred to examinations in the social sciences. A political science student, for example, can describe through explication the implicit tone or attitude in some of the landmark decisions of the Supreme Court. Similarly, the student of history who has learned to write an essay with a good combination of argument and evidence will not simply offer generalizations or present a list of facts unconnected by some central thesis, but will use relevant facts to support a thesis. The student who is able to evaluate a critical quotation or to compare literary works can also evaluate and compare documents in all the social sciences. Answers to wild questions can be as effective or as trite in the social sciences as in literature. "You are the British ambassador in Petrograd in November 1918. Write a report to your government about the Bolshevik revolution of that month" is to some instructors and students an absurd question but to others it is an interesting and effective way of ascertaining whether a student has not only absorbed the facts of an event but has also learned how to interpret them.

Questions on the Physical Sciences and Mathematics

Although the answer to an examination question in the physical sciences usually requires a mathematical computation, a few sentences may be useful in explaining the general plan of the computation, the assumptions involved, and sometimes the results.

It is particularly valuable to set down at the outset in a brief statement, probably a single sentence, your plan for solving the problem posed by the examination question. The statement is equivalent to the topic sentence of a paragraph. For instance, if the examination question is "What is the time required for an object to fall from the orbit of the moon to the earth?" the statement of your plan might be: "The time required for an object to fall from the orbit of the moon to the earth can be obtained by integration from Newton's law of motion, taking account of the increasing gravitational force as the object approaches the earth." Explicitly setting down your plan in words is useful first in clarifying your thought: is the plan a complete one leading to the desired answer? Do I know what I need to know to implement the plan? If your plan doesn't make sense, you can junk it right away before wasting more time on it.

The statement of plan is useful also in communicating with the instructor. Your plan of solution, although valid, may be a surprise to the instructor (who may have expected a solution to the problem posed above starting from Kepler's laws without any integration). When this is so, the instructor will need your explanation to become oriented to your plan, and to properly assess its merits. Then if you botch the subsequent computation or can't remember how the gravitational force varies with the distance, you will still have demonstrated that you have some comprehension of the problem. If on the other hand you present an erroneous computation without any explanation, the instructor will see nothing but chaos in your effort.

It may also be useful to explain assumptions or simplifications: "I assume the body is released with zero velocity and accordingly set $b = 0$," or "The third term is negligible and I drop it."

Finally, the results of your computation should be summarized or interpreted in words to answer the question asked. "The object will fall to the earth in five days." (The correct answer, for those who are curious.) Or, if you arrive at the end of your computation and of the examination hour and find you have a preposterous result, you can still exit gracefully (and increase your partial credit) with an explanation: "The answer of 53 days is clearly erroneous since the fall time of an object from the moon's orbit must be less than the seven days required for the moon to travel a quarter orbit."

PART FOUR

A Writer's Handbook

CHAPTER

19
Punctuation

Speakers can raise or lower the volume or pitch of their voices; they can speak a phrase slowly and distinctly and then (making a parenthetical remark, perhaps) quicken the pace. They can wave their arms, pound a table, or pause, meaningfully. But writers, physically isolated from their audience, can do none of these things. Nevertheless, they can embody some of the tones and gestures of speech—in the patterns of their written sentences, and in the dots, hooks, and dashes of punctuation that clarify those patterns.

Punctuation clarifies, first of all, by removing or reducing ambiguity. Consider this headline from a story in a newspaper:

SQUAD HELPS DOG BITE VICTIM

Of course, there is no real ambiguity here—only a laugh—because the stated meaning is so clearly absurd, and on second reading we supply the necessary hyphen in *dog-bite*. But other ill-punctuated sentences may be troublesome rather than entertaining. Take the following sentence:

He arrived late for the rehearsal didn't end until midnight.

Almost surely you stumbled in the middle of the sentence, thinking that it was about someone arriving tardily at a rehearsal, and then, since what followed made no sense, you probably went back and mentally added the comma (by pausing) at the necessary place:

He arrived late, for the rehearsal didn't end until midnight.

Punctuation helps to keep the reader on the right path. And the path is your train of thought. If your punctuation is faulty, you unintentionally point the reader off your path and toward dead-end streets and quagmires.

Even when punctuation is not the key to meaning, it usually helps you get your meaning across neatly. Consider the following sentence:

There are two kinds of feminism—one is the growing struggle of women to understand and change the shape of their lives and the other is a narrow ideology whose adherents are anxious to clear away whatever does not conform to their view.

The sentence is clear enough, but by changing the punctuation it can be sharpened. Because a dash usually indicates an abrupt interruption—it usually precedes a sort of afterthought—a colon would be better. The colon, usually the signal of an amplification of what precedes it, here would suggest that the two classifications are not impromptu thoughts but carefully considered ones. Second, and more important, in the original version the two classifications are run together without any intervening punctuation, but since the point is that the two are utterly different, it is advisable to separate them by inserting a comma or semicolon, indicating a pause. A comma before "and the other" would do, but probably a semicolon (without the "and") is preferable because it is a heavier pause, thereby making the separation clearer. Here is the sentence, revised:

> There are two kinds of feminism: one is the growing struggle of women to understand and change the shape of their lives; the other is a narrow ideology whose adherents are anxious to clear away whatever does not conform to their view.

The right punctuation enables the reader to move easily through the sentence.

Now, although punctuation helps a reader to move through a sentence, it must be admitted that some of the rules of punctuation do not contribute to meaning or greatly facilitate reading. For example, in American usage a period never comes immediately after quotation marks; it precedes quotation marks, thus:

> "If you put the period inside the closing quotation mark," the writing instructor said, "I will give you an A."

If you put the period after the closing quotation mark, the meaning remains the same, but you are also informing your reader that you don't know the conventions of American usage—conventions all writers in the United States are expected to adhere to. A pattern of such errors will diminish your authority as a writer: your reader, noticing that you don't know where to put the period in relation to the quotation mark, may well begin to wonder what else you don't know. Conversely, demonstrating that you know the rules will help to gain your reader's confidence and establish your authority as a writer.

A Word on Computer Grammar and Punctuation Checks

Word-processing programs now include a tool that can check grammar and punctuation. At your request, the program will flag sentences that look faulty and offer suggestions for correcting mistakes. These programs can be very helpful: they can draw your attention to sentence fragments, to problems with plurals and possessives, even to passive verbs. But they don't catch everything, and they don't always know how to fix the problems they identify: there are forty-nine faulty sentences in the first nine exercises at the end of this chapter; a computer check of these sentences flagged fourteen of them, and offered correct editing suggestions on only six.

Our advice: use the tool if you have it, but don't let it do your editing for you. Check the program's suggestions against your own knowledge and the advice offered in this book.

THREE COMMON ERRORS: FRAGMENTS, COMMA SPLICES, AND RUN-ON SENTENCES

Fragments and How to Correct Them

A fragment is a part of a sentence set off as if it were a complete sentence: *Because I didn't care. Being an accident. Later in the week. For several reasons. My oldest sister.* Fragments are common in speech, but they are used sparingly in writing, for particular effects (see page 132). A fragment used carelessly in writing often looks like an afterthought—usually because it *was* an afterthought, that is, an explanation or other addition that belongs to the previous sentence.

With appropriate punctuation (and sometimes with no punctuation at all) a fragment can usually be connected to the previous sentence.

Incorrect

Many nineteenth-century horror stories have been made into films. Such as *Dracula* and *Frankenstein.*

Correct

Many nineteenth-century horror stories have been made into films, such as *Dracula* and *Frankenstein.*

Incorrect

Many schools are putting renewed emphasis on writing. Because SAT scores have declined for ten years.

Correct

Many schools are putting renewed emphasis on writing because SAT scores have declined for ten years.

Incorrect

She wore only rope sandals. Being a strict vegetarian.

Correct

Being a strict vegetarian, she wore only rope sandals.

She wore only rope sandals because she was a strict vegetarian.

Incorrect

A fragment often looks like an afterthought. Perhaps because it *was* an afterthought.

Correct

A fragment often looks like an afterthought—perhaps because it *was* an afterthought.

Incorrect

He hoped to get credit for two summer courses. Batik and Hang-Gliding.

Correct

He hoped to get credit for two summer courses: Batik and Hang-Gliding.

Notice in the examples above that, depending upon the relationship between the two parts, the fragment and the preceding statement can be joined by a comma, a dash, a colon, or by no punctuation at all.

Notice also that unintentional fragments often follow subordinating conjunctions, such as *because* and *although*. Subordinating conjunctions introduce a subordinate (dependent) clause; such a clause cannot stand as a sentence. Here is a list of the most common subordinating conjunctions.

after	though
although	unless
because	until
before	when
if	where
provided	whereas
since	while

Fragments also commonly occur when the writer, as in the third example, mistakenly uses *being* as a main verb.

Comma Splices and Run-on Sentences, and How to Correct Them

An error known as a *comma splice* or *comma fault* results when a comma is mistakenly placed between two independent clauses that are not joined by a co-ordinating conjunction: *and, or, nor, but, for, yet, so*. If the comma is omitted, the error is called a *run-on sentence*.

Examples of the two errors:

- *Comma splice* (or *comma fault*): In the second picture the man leans on the woman's body, he is obviously in pain.
- *Run-on sentence:* In the second picture the man leans on the woman's body he is obviously in pain.

Run-on sentences and comma splices may be corrected in five principal ways:

1. Use a **period** to create two sentences.

In the second picture the man leans on the woman's body. He is obviously in pain.

2. Use a **semicolon.**

In the second picture the man leans on the woman's body; he is obviously in pain.

3. Use a **comma and a coordinating conjunction** (*and, or, nor, but, for, yet, so*).

In the second picture the man leans on the woman's body, and he is obviously in pain.

4. Make one of the clauses dependent (subordinate). **Use a subordinating conjunction** such as *after, although, because, before, if, provided, since, though, unless, until, when, where, whereas, while.*

In the second picture the man leans on the woman's body because he is in pain.

5. Reduce one of the independent clauses to a phrase, or even to a single word.

In the second picture the man, obviously in pain, leans on the woman's body.

Run-on sentences and comma splices are especially common in sentences containing transitional words or phrases such as the following:

also	however
besides	indeed
consequently	in fact
for example	nevertheless
furthermore	therefore
hence	whereas

When these words join independent clauses, the clauses cannot be linked by a comma.

Incorrect

She argued from faulty premises, however the conclusions happened to be correct.

Here are five correct revisions, following the five rules we have just given. (In the first two revisions we place "however" after, rather than before, "the conclusions" because we prefer the increase in emphasis, but the grammatical point is the same.)

1. She argued from faulty premises. The conclusions, however, happened to be correct. (Two sentences)
2. She argued from faulty premises; the conclusions, however, happened to be correct. (Semicolon)
3. She argued from faulty premises, but the conclusions happened to be correct. (Coordinating conjunction)
4. Although she argued from faulty premises, the conclusions happened to be correct. (Subordinating conjunction)
5. She argued from faulty premises to correct conclusions. (Reduction of an independent clause to a phrase)

The following sentence contains a comma splice:

The husband is not pleased, in fact, he is embarrassed.

How might it be repaired?

THE PERIOD

1. Periods are used to mark the ends of sentences (or intentional sentence fragments) other than questions and exclamations.

> A sentence normally ends with a period.
> She said, "I'll pass."
> Yes.
> Once more, with feeling.

But a sentence within a sentence is punctuated according to the needs of the longer sentence. Notice, in the following example, that a period is *not* used after "pass."

> She said, "I'll pass," but she said it without conviction.

2. Periods are used with abbreviations of titles and terms of reference.

> Dr., Mr., Mrs., Ms.
> p., pp. (for "page" and "pages"), i.e., e.g., etc.

But when the capitalized initial letters of the words naming an organization are used in place of the full name, the periods are commonly omitted:

> CBS, CORE, IBM, NBA, UCLA, UNICEF, USAF

3. Periods are also used to separate chapter from verse in the Bible.

> Genesis 3.2, Mark 6.10

For further details on references to the Bible, see page 478.

THE QUESTION MARK

Use a question mark after a direct question:

> Did Bacon write Shakespeare's plays?

Do not use a question mark after an indirect question, or after a polite request:

> He asked if Bacon wrote Shakespeare's plays.
> Would you please explain what the support for Bacon is really all about.

THE COLON

The colon has four uses:

- To introduce a list or series of examples
- To introduce an amplification or explanation of what precedes the colon
- To introduce a quotation (though a quotation can be introduced by other means)
- To indicate time.

Now let's look at each of those four uses.

1. The colon may introduce a list or series.

Students are required to take one of the following sciences: biology, chemistry, geology, physics.

2. The colon may introduce an explanation. It is almost equivalent to *namely,* or *that is.* What is on one side of the colon more or less equals what is on the other side. The material on either side of the colon can stand as a separate sentence.

She explained her fondness for wrestling: she did it to shock her parents.

The forces which in China created a central government were absent in Japan: farming had to be on a small scale, there was no need for extensive canal works, and a standing army was not required to protect the country from foreign invaders.

Many of the best of the Civil War photographs must be read as the fossils of earlier events: The caissons with their mud-encrusted wheels, the dead on the field, the empty landscapes, all speak of deeds already past.

—JOHN SZARKOWSKI

Notice in this last example that the writer uses a capital letter after the colon; the usage is acceptable when a complete sentence follows the colon, as long as that style is followed consistently throughout a paper. But most students find it easier to use lower case letters after colons, the prevalent style in writing today.

3. The colon, like the comma, may be used to introduce a quotation; it is more formal than the comma, setting off the quotation to a greater degree.

The black sculptor Ed Wilson tells his students: "Malcolm X is my brother, Martin Luther King is my brother, Eldridge Cleaver is my brother! But Michelangelo is my grandfather!"

—ALBERT E. ELSEN

4. A colon is used to separate the hour from the minutes when the time is given in figures.

9:15, 12:00

Colons (like semicolons) go outside of closing quotation marks if they are not part of the quotation.

"There is no such thing as a free lunch": the truth of these words is confirmed every day.

THE SEMICOLON

There are four main uses of the semicolon. Sheridan Baker (in *The Practical Stylist*) summed them up in this admirable formula: "Use a semicolon where you could also use a period, unless desperate." Correctly used, the semicolon can add precision to your writing; it can also help you out of some tight corners.

1. You may use a semicolon instead of a period between closely related independent clauses not joined by a coordinating conjunction.

All happy families resemble one another; every unhappy family is unhappy in its own fashion.

—Leo Tolstoy

The demands that men and women make on marriage will never be fully met; they cannot be.

—Jessie Bernard

In our fractured culture, we cannot agree on morals; we cannot even agree that moral matters should come before literary ones when there is a conflict between them.

—Flannery O'Connor

When a cat washes its face it does not move its paw; it moves its face.

In each of the examples the independent clauses might have been written as sentences separated by periods; the semicolon pulls the statements together, emphasizing their relationship. Alternatively, the statements might have been linked by coordinating conjunctions (*and, or, nor, but, for, yet, so*). For example:

The demands made upon marriage will never be fully met *for* they cannot be.

When a cat washes its face it does not move its paw *but* it moves its face.

The sentences as originally written, using semicolons, have more bite.

2. You *must* use a semicolon (rather than a comma) if you use a *conjunctive adverb* to connect independent clauses. (A conjunctive adverb is a transitional word such as *also, consequently, furthermore, however, moreover, nevertheless, therefore.*)

His hair was black and wavy; however, it was false.

We don't like to see our depressed relative cry; nevertheless, tears can provide a healthy emotional outlet.

She said "I do"; moreover, she repeated the words.

Take note of the following three points:

- A comma goes after the conjunctive adverb.
- Semicolons (like colons) go outside of closing quotation marks if they are not part of the quotation.
- A conjunctive adverb requires a semicolon to join independent clauses. A comma produces a comma splice:

Incorrect

His hair was black and wavy, however, it was false.

3. You may use a semicolon to separate a series of phrases with internal punctuation.

He had a car, which he hadn't paid for; a wife, whom he didn't love; and a father, who was unemployed.

4. Use a semicolon between independent clauses linked by coordinating conjunctions if the sentence would otherwise be difficult to read, because it is long and complex or because it contains internal punctuation.

In the greatest age of painting, the nude inspired the greatest works; and even when it ceased to be a compulsive subject it held its position as an academic exercise and a demonstration of mastery.

(Often it is preferable to break such sentences up, or to recast them.)

THE COMMA

The comma (from a Greek word meaning "to cut") indicates a relatively slight pause within a sentence. If after checking the rules you are still uncertain of whether or not to use a comma in a given sentence, read the sentence aloud and see if it sounds better with or without a pause; you can then add or omit the comma. A women's shoe store in New York has a sign on the door:

NO MEN PLEASE.

If the proprietors would read the sign aloud, they might want to change it to

NO MEN, PLEASE

When you are typing, always follow a comma with a space.

For your reference, here is an outline for the following pages, which summarize the correct uses of the comma:

1. Independent clauses (unless short) joined by a coordinating conjunction *(and, or, nor, but, for, yet, so)* **take a comma before the conjunction.**

Most students see at least a few football games, and many go to every game of the season.

Most students seem to have an intuitive sense of when to use a comma, but in fact the "intuition" is the result of long training.

If the introductory independent clause is short, the comma is usually omitted:

> She dieted but she continued to gain weight.

2. An **introductory subordinate clause or long phrase** is usually followed by a comma.

> Having revised his manuscript for the third time, he went to bed.
>
> In order to demonstrate her point, the instructor stood on her head.

If the introductory subordinate clause or phrase is short, say four words or fewer, the comma may be omitted, provided no ambiguity results from the omission.

> Having left he soon forgot.

But compare this last example with the following:

> Having left, the instructor soon forgot.

If the comma is omitted, the sentence is misread. Where are commas needed in the following sentences?

> Instead of discussing the book she wrote a summary.
>
> When Shakespeare wrote comedies were already popular.
>
> While he ate his poodle would sit by the table.
>
> As we age small things become killers.

3. A **subordinate clause or long modifying phrase tacked on as an afterthought is usually preceded by a comma.**

> I have decided not to be nostalgic about the 1950s, despite the hoopla over Elvis.
>
> Buster Keaton fell down a flight of stairs without busting, thereby gaining his nickname from Harry Houdini.
>
> By the time he retired, Hank Aaron had 755 home runs, breaking Babe Ruth's record by 41.

With afterthoughts, the comma may be omitted if there is a clear sequence of cause and effect, signaled by such words as *because, for,* and *so.* Compare the following examples:

> In 1601 Shakespeare wrote *Hamlet,* probably his best-known play.
>
> In 1601 Shakespeare wrote *Hamlet* because revenge tragedy was in demand.

4. A **pair of commas can serve as a pair of unobtrusive parentheses.** Be sure not to omit the second comma.

> Doctors, I think, have an insufficient knowledge of acupuncture.
>
> The earliest known paintings of Christ, dating from the third century, are found in the catacombs outside of Rome.
>
> Medicare and Medicaid, the chief sources of federal support for patients in nursing homes, are frequently confused.

Under this heading we can include a conjunctive adverb (a transitional adverb such as *also, besides, consequently, however, likewise, nevertheless, therefore*) inserted within a sentence. These transitional words are set off between a pair of commas.

Her hair, however, was stringy.

If one of these words begins a sentence, the comma after it is optional. Notice, however, that the presence of such a word as "however" is not always a safeguard against a run-on sentence or comma splice; if the word occurs between two independent clauses and it goes with the second clause, you need a semicolon before it and a comma after it.

His hair was black and wavy; however, it was false.

(See the discussion of comma splices on pages 432–33.)

5. Use a comma to set off a nonrestrictive modifier. A nonrestrictive modifier, as the following examples will make clear, is a sort of parenthetical addition; it gives supplementary information about the subject, but it can be omitted without changing the subject. A restrictive modifier, however, is not supplementary but essential; if a restrictive modifier is omitted, the subject becomes more general. In Dorothy Parker's celebrated poem,

Men seldom make passes
At girls who wear glasses,

"who wear glasses" is a restrictive modifier, narrowing or restricting the subject down from "girls" to a particular group of girls, "girls who wear glasses."
Here is a *non*restrictive modifier:

For the majority of immigrants, who have no knowledge of English, language is the chief problem.

Now a restrictive modifier:

For the majority of immigrants who have no knowledge of English, language is the chief problem.

The first version says—in addition to its obvious message that language is the chief problem—that the majority of immigrants have no knowledge of English. The second version makes no such assertion; it talks not about the majority of immigrants but only about a more restricted group—those immigrants who have no knowledge of English.
Other examples:

Shakespeare's shortest tragedy, *Macbeth,* is one of his greatest plays.

In this sentence, *"Macbeth"* is nonrestrictive because the subject is already as restricted as possible; Shakespeare can have written only one "shortest tragedy." That is, *"Macbeth"* is merely an explanatory equivalent of "Shakespeare's shortest tragedy" and it is therefore enclosed in commas. (A noun or noun phrase serving as an explanatory equivalent to another, and in the same syntactical relation to other elements in the sentence, is said to be in apposition.) But compare

Shakespeare's tragedy *Macbeth* is one of his greatest plays.

with the misleadingly punctuated sentence,

> Shakespeare's tragedy, *Macbeth,* is one of his greatest plays.

The first of these is restrictive, narrowing or restricting the subject "tragedy" down to one particular tragedy, and so it rightly does not separate the modifier from the subject by a comma. The second, punctuated so that it is nonrestrictive, falsely implies that *Macbeth* is Shakespeare's only tragedy. Here is an example of a nonrestrictive modifier correctly punctuated:

> Women, who constitute 51.3 percent of the population and 53 percent of the electorate, constitute only 2.5 percent of the House of Representatives and 1 percent of the Senate.

In the next two examples, the first illustrates the correct use of commas after a nonrestrictive appositive, and the second illustrates the correct omission of commas after a restrictive appositive.

> Hong Yee Chiu, a Chinese-American physicist, abbreviated the compound adjective *quasi-stellar* to *quasar.*

> The Chinese-American physicist Hong Yee Chiu abbreviated the compound adjective *quasi-stellar* to *quasar.*

6. Words, phrases, and clauses in series take a comma after each item except the last. The comma between the last two items may be omitted if there is no ambiguity.

> Photography is a matter of eyes, intuition, and intellect.

> She wrote plays, poems, and stories.

> He wrote plays, sang songs, and danced jigs.

> She wrote a wise, witty, humane book.

But adjectives in a series may cause difficulty. The next two examples correctly omit the commas.

> a funny silent film

> a famous French professor

In each of these last two examples, the adjective immediately before the noun forms with the noun a compound that is modified by the earlier adjective. That is, the adjectives are not a coordinate series (what is funny is not simply a film but a silent film, what is famous is not simply a professor but a French professor) and so commas are not used. Compare:

> a famous French professor

> a famous, arrogant French professor

In the second example, only "famous" and "arrogant" form a coordinate series. If in doubt, see if you can replace the commas with "and"; if you can, the commas are correct. In the example given, you could insert "and" between "famous" and "arrogant," but not between "arrogant" and "French."

Commas are not needed if all the members of the series are connected by conjunctions.

He ate steak for breakfast and lunch and supper.

7. Use a comma to set off direct discourse.

"It's a total failure," she said.
She said, "It's a total failure."

But do not use a comma for indirect discourse.

She said that it is a total failure.
She said it is a total failure.

8. Use a comma to set off "yes" and "no."

Yes, he could take Writing 125 at ten o'clock.

9. Use a comma to set off words of address.

Look, Bill, take Writing 125 at ten o'clock.

10. Use a comma to separate a geographical location within another geographical location.

She was born in Brooklyn, New York, in 1895.

Another way of putting it is to say that a comma is used after each unit of an address, except that a comma is *not* used between the name of the state and the zip code.

11. Use a comma to set off the year from the month or day.

He was born on June 10, 1980.

No comma is needed if you use the form "10 June 1980."

12. Note the position of the comma when used with other punctuation: if a comma is required with parenthetic material, it follows the second parenthesis.

Because Japan was secure from invasion (even the Mongols were beaten back), its history is unusually self-contained.

The only time a comma may precede a parenthesis is when parentheses surround a digit or letter used to enumerate a series.

Questions usually fall into one of three categories: (1) true-false, (2) multiple choice, (3) essay.

A comma always goes inside closing quotation marks unless the quotation is followed by a parenthesis.

"Sayonara," he said.
"Sayonara" (Japanese for "goodbye"), he said.

THE DASH

A dash is made by typing two hyphens without hitting the space-bar before, between, or after. It indicates an abrupt break or pause.

1. The material within dashes may be something like parenthetic material (material that is not essential), though by setting it within dashes—an emphatic form of punctuation—the writer gives the material more emphasis than it would get within parentheses.

> The bathroom—that private place—has rarely been the subject of scholarly study.

> The Great Wall of China forms a continuous line over 1400 miles long—the distance from New York to Kansas City—running from Peking to the edge of the mountains of Central Asia.

> The old try to survive by cutting corners—eating less, giving up small pleasures like tobacco and movies, doing without warm clothes—and pay the price of ill-health and a shortened life-span.
>
> —SHARON R. CURTIN

Notice that when two dashes are used, if the material within them is deleted the remainder still forms a grammatical sentence.

2. A dash can serve, somewhat like a colon, as a pause before a series. It is more casual than a colon.

> The earliest Shinto holy places were natural objects—trees, boulders, mountains, islands.

> Each of the brothers had his distinct comic style—Groucho's double-talk, Chico's artfully stupid malapropisms, Harpo's horseplay.
>
> —GERALD MAST

A dash is never used next to a comma, and it is used before a period only to indicate that the sentence is interrupted.

Overuse of the dash—even only a little overuse—gives writing an unpleasantly agitated—even explosive—quality.

PARENTHESES

Let's begin with a caution: avoid using parentheses to explain pronouns: "In his speech he (Hamlet) says . . ." If "he" needs to be explained by "Hamlet," omit the "he" and just say "Hamlet."

1. Parentheses subordinate material; what is in parentheses is almost a casual aside, less essential than similar material set off in commas, less vigorously spoken than similar material set off in dashes.

> While guest curator for the Whitney (he has since returned to the Denver Art Museum), Feder assembled a magnificent collection of masks, totems, paintings, clothing, and beadwork.

Another caution: avoid an abundance of these interruptions, and avoid a long parenthesis within a sentence (you are now reading a simple example of this annoying but common habit of writers who have trouble sticking to the point) because the reader will lose track of the main sentence.

2. Use parentheses to enclose digits or letters in a list that is given in running text.

The exhibition included: (1) decorative screens, (2) ceramics, (3) ink paintings, (4) kimonos.

3. Do not confuse parentheses with square brackets, which are used around material you add to a quotation. See page 476.

4. For the use of parentheses in documentation, see Chapter 16, "The Research Essay."

5. Note the position of other punctuation with a parenthesis: the example under rule number 2, of commas preceding parentheses enclosing digits or letters in a list given in running text, is the rare exception to the rule that within a sentence, punctuation other than quotation marks never immediately precedes an opening parenthesis. Notice that in the example under rule number 1, the comma *follows* the closing parenthesis:

> While guest curator for the Whitney (he has since returned to the Denver Art Museum), Feder assembled a magnificent collection of masks, totems, paintings, clothing, and beadwork.

If an entire sentence is in parentheses, put the final punctuation (period, question mark, or exclamation mark) inside the closing parenthesis.

ITALICS

In typewritten material <u>underlining</u> is the equivalent of *italic* type.

> *This sentence is printed in italic type.*
>
> <u>This sentence is understood to be printed in italic type.</u>

1. Underline the name of a plane, ship, train, movie, radio or television program, record album, musical work, statue, painting, play, pamphlet, and book. Do not underline names of sacred works such as the Bible, the Koran, or Acts of the Apostles, or political documents such as the Magna Carta and the Declaration of Independence. Notice that when you write of *The New York Times,* you underline *New York* because it is part of the title, but when you write of the London *Times,* you do not underline "London" because "London" is not part of the title, only information added for clarity. Similarly, when you refer to *Time* magazine do not underline "magazine."

2. Use italics only sparingly for emphasis. Sometimes, however, this method of indicating your tone of voice is exactly right.

> In 1911 Jacques Henri Lartigue was not merely as unprejudiced as a child; he *was* a child.
>
> —JOHN SZARKOWSKI

3. Use italics for foreign words that have not become a part of the English language.

> Acupuncture aims to affect the *ch'i,* a sort of vital spirit which circulates through the bodily organs.

But:

> He ate a pizza.
>
> She behaved like a prima donna.
>
> Avoid clichés.

4. You may use italics in place of quotation marks to identify a word:

Honolulu means "safe harbor."

5. You may also use italics to identify a word or term to which you wish to call special attention.

> Clause Lévi-Strauss tells us that one of the great purposes of art is that of *miniaturization.* He points out that most works of art are miniatures, being smaller (and therefore more easily understood) than the objects they represent.

CAPITAL LETTERS

Certain obvious conventions—the use of a capital for the first word in a sentence, for names (of days of the week, holidays, months, people, countries), and for words derived from names (such as pro-French)—need not be discussed here.

1. Titles of works in English are usually given according to the following formula. Use a capital for the first letter of the first word, for the first letter of the last word, and for the first letter of all other words that are not articles, conjunctions, or prepositions.

> *The Merchant of Venice*
>
> *A Midsummer Night's Dream*
>
> *Up and Out*
>
> "The Short Happy Life of Francis Macomber"
>
> *The Oakland Bee*

2. Use a capital for a quoted sentence within a sentence, but not for a quoted phrase (unless it is at the beginning of your sentence) and not for indirect discourse.

> He said, "You can even fool some of the people all of the time."
>
> He said you can fool some people "all of the time."
>
> He said that you can even fool some of the people all of the time.

3. Use a capital for a rank or title preceding a proper name or for a title substituting for a proper name.

> She said she was Dr. Perez.
>
> He told President Clinton that the Vice President was away.

But:

Why would anyone wish to be president?

Washington was the first president.

4. Use a capital when the noun designating a family relationship is used as a substitute for a proper noun.

If Mother is busy, ask Tim.

But:

Because my mother was busy, I asked Tim.

5. Formal geographical locations (but not mere points on the compass) are capitalized.

North America

Southeast Asia

In the Southwest, rain sometimes evaporates before touching the ground.

Is Texas part of the South?

The North has its share of racism.

But:

The wind came from the south.

Texas is bordered on the north by Arkansas, Oklahoma, and New Mexico.

Do *not* capitalize the names of the seasons.

spring, summer, winter, fall

THE HYPHEN

The hyphen has five uses, all drawing on the etymology of the word *hyphen,* which comes from the Greek for "in one," "together."

1. Use a hyphen to attach certain prefixes to root words. *All-, pro-, ex-,* and *self-* are the most common of these ("all-powerful," "ex-wife," "pro-labor," "self-made"), but note that even these prefixes are not always followed by a hyphen. If in doubt, check a dictionary. Prefixes before proper names are always followed by a hyphen:

anti-Semite, pro-NATO, un-American

Prefixes ending in *i* are hyphenated before a word beginning with *i:*

anti-intellectual, semi-intelligible

A hyphen is normally used to break up a triple consonant resulting from the addition of a prefix:

ill-lit

2. Use a hyphen to tie compound adjectives into a single visual unit:

out-of-date theory, twenty-three books, a no-smoking area

eighteenth- and nineteenth-century novels

The sea-tossed raft was a common nineteenth-century symbol of the human tragic condition.

But if a compound modifier follows the modified term, it is usually not hyphenated, thus:

The theory was out of date.

3. Use a hyphen to join some compound nouns:

Scholar-teacher, philosopher-poet

4. Use a hyphen to indicate a span of dates or page numbers: 1957–59, pp. 162–68.

THE APOSTROPHE

Use an apostrophe to indicate the possessive, to indicate a contraction, and to form certain unusual plurals.

1. The most common way to indicate the possessive of a singular noun is to add an apostrophe and then an *s*.

A dog's life, a week's work

a mouse's tail, Keats's poems, Marx's doctrines

But some authorities suggest that for a proper noun of more than one syllable that ends in *s* or another sibilant (*-cks, -x, -z*), it is better to add only an apostrophe:

Jesus' parables, Sophocles' plays, Chavez' ideas

When in doubt, say the name aloud and notice if you are adding an *s*. If you are adding an *s* when you say it, add an apostrophe and an *s* when you write it. Our own strong preference, however, is to add an apostrophe and an *s* to all proper nouns:

Jones's book

Kansas's highways

Possessive pronouns, such as *his, hers, its, theirs, ours,* do not take an apostrophe

his book, its fur

The book is hers, not ours.

The book is theirs.

(*Exception:* indefinite pronouns take an apostrophe, as in "one's hopes" and "others' opinions.")

For plurals ending in *s,* add only an apostrophe to indicate the possessive:

the boys' father, the Smiths' house, the Joneses' car

If the plural does not end in *s,* add an apostrophe and an *s*.

women's clothing, mice's eyes

Don't try to form the possessive of the title of a work (for example, of a play, a book, or a film): Write "the imagery in *The Merchant of Venice*" rather than "*The Merchant of Venice*'s imagery." Using an apostrophe gets you into the problem of whether or not to italicize the *s;* similarly, if you use an apostrophe for a work normally enclosed in quotation marks (for instance, a short story), you can't put the apostrophe and the *s* after the quotation marks, but you can't put it inside either.

2. Use an apostrophe to indicate the omitted letters or numbers in contractions.

She won't.

It's time to go.

the class of '87

3. Until recently an apostrophe was used to make plurals of words that do not usually have a plural, and (this is optional) to make the plurals of digits and letters.

Her speech was full of if's and and's and but's.

Ph.D.'s don't know everything.

Mind your p's and q's. I got two A's and two B's.

He makes his 4's in two ways.

the 1920's

This use of the apostrophe is no longer standard, but it remains acceptable.

ABBREVIATIONS

In general, avoid abbreviations except in footnotes and except for certain common ones listed below. And don't use an ampersand (&) unless it appears in material you are quoting, or in a title. Abundant use of abbreviations makes an essay sound like a series of newspaper headlines. Usually, for example, *United States* is better than *U.S.*

1. Abbreviations, with the first letter capitalized, are used before a name.

Dr. Bellini, Ms. Smith, St. Thomas

But: The doctor took her temperature and eighty dollars.

2. Degrees that follow a name are abbreviated:

B.A., D.D.S., M.D., Ph.D.

3. Other acceptable abbreviations include:

A.D., B.C., A.M., P.M., e.g., i.e.

(By the way, *e.g.* means *for example; i.e.* means *that is.* The two ought not to be confused. See pages 459 and 461.)

4. The name of an agency or institution (for instance, the Congress of Racial Equality; International Business Machines; Southern Methodist University) may be abbreviated by using the initial letters, capitalized and usually without periods (e.g., CORE), but it is advisable to give the name in full when first mentioning it (not everyone knows that AARP means American Association of Retired Persons, for instance), and to use the abbreviation in subsequent references.

NUMBERS

1. Write numbers out if you can do so in fewer than three words; otherwise, use figures.

> sixteen, seventy-two, ten thousand, one sixth
>
> 10,200; 10,200,000
>
> There are 336 dimples on a golf ball.

But write out round millions and billions, to avoid a string of zeroes.

> a hundred and ten million

For large round numbers you can also use a combination of figures and words.

> The cockroach is about 250 million years old.

Note, however, that because a figure cannot be capitalized, if a number begins a sentence it should always be written out:

> Two hundred and fifty million years ago the cockroach first appeared on earth.

2. Use figures in dates, addresses, decimals, percentages, page numbers, and hours followed by A.M. or P.M.

> February 29, 1900; .06 percent; 6 percent; 8:16 A.M.

But hours unmodified by minutes are usually written out, followed by *o'clock*.

> Executions in England regularly took place at eight o'clock.

3. Use an apostrophe to indicate omitted figures.

> class of '98
>
> the '90s (but: the nineties)

4. Use a hyphen to indicate a span.

> 1975-79
>
> 10-20

In giving inclusive numbers, give the second number in full for the numbers up through ninety-nine (2-5, 8-11, 28-34). For larger numbers, give only the last two digits of the second number (101-06; 112-14) unless the full number in necessary (198-202).

5. Dates can be given with the month first, followed by numerals, a comma, and the year

> February 10, 1999

or they can be given with the day first, then the month and then the year (without a comma after the day or month)

10 February 1999

6. BC (no periods and no space between the letters) follows the year, but AD precedes it.

10 BC

AD 200

7. Roman numerals are less used than formerly. Capital roman numerals were used to indicate a volume number, but volume numbers are now commonly given in arabic numerals. Capital roman numerals still are used, however, for the names of individuals in a series (Elizabeth II) and for the primary divisions of an outline; lowercase roman numerals are used for the pages in the front matter (table of contents, foreword, preface, etc.) of a book. The old custom of citing acts and scenes of a play in roman numerals and lines in arabic numerals (II.iv.17–25) is still preferred by many instructors, but the use of arabic numerals throughout (2.4.17–25) is gaining acceptance.

Exercises

1. Correct the following sentence fragments. You may join fragments to independent clauses, or you may recast them as complete sentences.
   a. He left the sentence fragments in the final version of his essay. Instead of trying to fix them.
   b. Her associate left the country. Although their project was unfinished.
   c. Philip Roth argues that closing Newark's libraries will be a costly mistake. That the action will be an insult to Newark's citizens.
   d. He made corrections on the final copy of his essay by hand. Being unwilling to print out the whole paper again.
   e. She spent three hours waiting in line in the rain to buy tickets to his concert. Since she was an irrepressibly enthusiastic Springsteen fan.
2. Determine which of the following sentences are run-ons and which contain comma splices. Label them accordingly and correct them appropriately—using any of the five methods shown on pages 432–33.
   a. *A Prayer for Owen Meany* is one of his favorite books, he's reading it now for the fifth time.
   b. Don't write run-on sentences they are not acceptable.
   c. The quarterback was intercepted on fourteen consecutive passes, he was traded the following season.
   d. Ambiguously punctuated sentences are usually confusing often they are humorous.
   e. There are those who warn that computers are dehumanizing students, however such people have produced no verifiable evidence.
3. Correct the following sentences, inserting the necessary colons and semicolons.
   a. I signed up for four courses this semester Spanish, geology, women's studies, and composition.
   b. "Every dark cloud has a silver lining" I've found that the cliché doesn't always hold true.

c. The semicolon is tricky it can be effective, but it is often misused.

d. I finished my final papers three weeks early consequently, I had nothing to do while everyone else was working.

e. The case for nuclear power has always rested on two claims that reactors were reasonably safe, and that they were indispensable as a source of energy.

f. Dinner was a disaster he broiled fish, which he burned he steamed broccoli, which came out soggy and he baked a soufflé, which fell.

4. In these sentences insert commas where necessary to set off phrases and clauses.

a. While she was cooking the cat jumped onto the refrigerator.

b. Geometry is a prerequisite for trigonometry and calculus is a prerequisite for physics.

c. He wanted to go to Europe in the summer so he had to take a part-time job.

d. Although she's aware of the dangers of smoking it seems impossible for her to quit.

e. Final exams they thought were a waste of time.

f. Turner's painting *The Slave Ship* probably his greatest work was donated to Boston's Museum of Fine Arts.

5. Insert commas to make the restrictive elements in the following sentences nonrestrictive. Be prepared to explain how changing the punctuation changes each sentence's meaning.

a. My uncle who owns a farm breeds racehorses.

b. The circus which returns to New York every winter is attended by thousands.

c. Teachers who are the ones chiefly entrusted with educating people formally should concentrate more heavily on developing their students' analytical skills.

d. Athletes who ought to know better sometimes play while injured.

6. Punctuate these sentences using the instructions given in items 6–11 on pages 440–41 as guidelines.

a. A lone masked silent gunman robbed the only bank in Albuquerque New Mexico on March 10, 1885.

b. Yes it's a sentimental story but I like it.

c. "You have no taste" he said.

d. The plot of his detective novel was flimsy weak and unoriginal.

e. I would prefer not to receive a partridge in a pear tree two French hens three turtle doves and all that other stuff again this Christmas.

7. Place commas correctly in the following sentences.

a. "Don't write sentence fragments" the instructor said "they are unacceptable."

b. Arguing with him was useless (he was most stubborn when he was wrong) so she decided to drop the subject.

c. To revise Mrs. Beeton's famous recipe: you must (1) find your hare (2) catch it (3) cook it.

d. "A Good Man Is Hard to Find" "Petrified Man" and "A Rose for Emily" are three of his favorite short stories.

8. Correct the following sentences, adding apostrophes where needed. Label each word you correct to indicate whether it is a possessive, a contraction, or an unusual plural.

a. Its easy to learn to use apostrophes.

b. The boys books are on their shelves, under their beds, and in their closets.

c. There are three copies of James *Portrait of a Lady* in the professors office.

d. My copys falling apart

e. In the 1940s ones dollars went farther.

9. In the following sentences, decide what punctuation is needed, and then add it. If the sentence is correctly punctuated, place a check mark to the left of it.

a. Around his neck is a scarf knotted in front and covering his head is a wide brimmed hat.

b. Buffalo Bill radiates confidence in his bold stance and looks self assured with his head held high.

c. The demands that men and women make on marriage will never be fully met they cannot be.

d. The Polish painter Oskar Kokoschka once said to a man who had posed for a portrait those who know you wont recognize you but those who dont will.

e. Boys on the whole do not keep diaries.

f. Children are unwelcome in most New York restaurants that are not Chinese.

g. Shlomo a giraffe in the Tel Aviv zoo succumbed to the effects of falling down after efforts to raise him with ropes and pulleys were unsuccessful.

h. Character like a photograph develops in darkness.

i. In a grief reaction especially when the person has suffered a loss crying comes easily and produces a healthy release from pent up emotion.

10. We reprint below the fourth paragraph of Jeff Greenfield's essay, "Columbo Knows the Butler Didn't Do It," but without punctuation. Go through the paragraph, adding the punctuation you find necessary. Check your work against the original paragraph on page 183. If you find differences between your punctuation and Greenfield's, try to explain why Greenfield made the choices he did.

columbos villains are not simply rich they are privileged they live the lives that are for most of us hopeless daydreams houses on top of mountains with pools servants and sliding doors parties with women in slinky dresses and endless food and drink plush enclosed box seats at professional sports events the envy and admiration of the crowd while we choose between johnny carson and *invasion of the body snatchers* they are at screenings of movies the rest of us wait in line for on third avenue three months later.

11. Here are the first two paragraphs—but without punctuation—of Raymond A. Sokolov's review of a book by Sarah Stage, *Female Complaints: Lydia Pinkham and the Business of Women's Medicine.* Add the necessary punctuation.

home at the range victorian women in america suffered in shame from all manner of female complaints too intimate to name many of them were the fault of men gonorrhea or men doctors prolapsed uterus and women shrewdly kept shy of the ineffectual and often positively harmful doctors of their day instead they doctored themselves with so called patent medicines the most famous of these was lydia pinkhams vegetable compound mrs pinkham actually existed in lynn mass a center of the progressive spirit hotbed of abolition and feminism sarah stage who has taught american history at williams college had the acuity to see that lydia pinkham was more than a quaint picture on a label that she was a paradigm of the independent woman of her day building a big business with a home remedy to save her family from bankruptcy caused by a neer do well husband she saw furthermore that many of the important themes and forces of american society before world war I clustered around the medicine itself which was largely alcoholic but respectably bitter

CHAPTER

20
Usage

Some things are said or written and some are not. More precisely, anything can be said or written, but only some things are acceptable to the ears and minds of many readers. "I don't know nothing about it" has been said and will be said again, but many readers who encounter this expression might judge the speaker as a person with nothing of interest to say—and immediately tune out.

Although such a double negative today is not acceptable, it used to be: Chaucer's courteous Knight never spoke no baseness, and Shakespeare's courtly Mercutio, in *Romeo and Juliet,* "will not budge for no man." But things have changed; what was acceptable in the Middle Ages and the Renaissance (for example, emptying chamber pots into the gutter) is not always acceptable now. And some of what was once unacceptable has become acceptable. At the beginning of the twentieth century, grammarians suggested that one cannot use *drive* in speaking of a car; one drives (forces into motion) an ox, or even a person ("He drove her to distraction"), but not a machine. Some eighty years of usage, however, have erased all objections.

This chapter presents a list of expressions that, although commonly used, set many teeth on edge. Seventy years from now some of these expressions may be as acceptable as "drive a car"; but we are writing for today, and we might as well try to hold today's readers by following today's taste in language.

A NOTE ON IDIOMS

An idiom (from a Greek word meaning "peculiar") is a fixed group of words, peculiar to a given language. Thus in English we say, "I took a walk," but Germans "make a walk," Spaniards "give a walk," and Japanese "do a walk." (If we think the German, Spanish, and Japanese expressions are odd, we might well ask ourselves where it is that we take a walk to.) If a visitor from Argentina says, in English, that she "gave a walk," she is using *un*idiomatic English, just as anyone who says he knows a poem "at heart" instead of "by heart" is using unidiomatic English.

Probably most unidiomatic expressions use the wrong preposition. Examples:

Unidiomatic	*Idiomatic*
comply to	comply with
superior with	superior to

Sometimes while we write, or even while we speak, we are unsure of the idiom and we pause to try an alternative—"parallel with?" "parallel to?"—and we don't know which sounds more natural, more idiomatic. At such moments, more often than not, either is acceptable, but if you are in doubt, check a dictionary. (The *American Heritage Dictionary* has notes on usage following the definitions of hundreds of its words.)

In any case, if you are a native speaker of English, when you read your draft you will probably detect unidiomatic expressions such as *superior with;* that is, you will hear something that sounds odd, and so you will change it to something that sounds familiar, idiomatic—here, *superior to.* If any unidiomatic expressions remain in your essay, the trouble may be that an effort to write impressively has led you to use unfamiliar language. A reader who sees such unidiomatic language may sense that you are straining for an effect. Try rewriting the passage in your own voice.

If English is not your first language and you are not yet fluent in it, plan to spend extra time revising and editing your work. Check prepositional phrases with special care. In addition to using a college edition of an English language dictionary, consult reference works designed with the international or bilingual student in mind. One compact book our students find particularly useful is Michael Swan's *Practical English Usage,* published by Oxford University Press. But don't neglect another invaluable resource: students who are native speakers. They will usually be able to tell you whether or not a phrase "sounds right," though they may not know why.

GLOSSARY

a, an   Use *a* before words beginning with a consonant ("a book") or with a vowel sounded as a consonant ("a one-way ticket," "a university"). Use *an* before words beginning with a vowel or a vowel sound, including those beginning with a silent *h* ("an egg," "an hour"). If an initial *h* is pronounced but the accent is not on the first syllable, *an* is acceptable, as in "*an* historian" (but "*a* history course").

above   Try to avoid writing *for the above reasons, in view of the above,* or *as above.* These expressions sound unpleasantly legalistic. Substitute *for these reasons,* or *therefore,* or some such expression or word.

academics   Only two meanings of this noun are widely accepted: (1) "members of an institution of higher learning," and (2) "persons who are academic in background or outlook." Avoid using it to mean "academic subjects," as in "A student should pay attention not only to academics but also to recreation."

accept, except   *Accept* means "to receive with consent." *Except* means "to exclude" or "excluding."

affect, effect   *Affect* is usually a verb, meaning (1) "to influence, to produce an effect, to impress," or (2) "to pretend, to put on," as in "He affected an English accent." Psychologists use it as a noun for "feeling," e.g., "The patient experienced no affect." *Effect,* as a verb, means "to bring about" ("The workers effected the rescue in less than an hour"). As a noun, *effect* means "result" ("The effect was negligible").

African American, African-American   Both forms are acceptable to denote an American of African ancestry. In recent years these words have been preferred to *black.*

aggravate   "To worsen, to increase for the worse," as in "Smoking aggravated the irritation." Although it is widely used to mean "annoy" ("He aggravated me"), many readers are annoyed by such a use.

all ready, already   *All ready* means "everything is ready." *Already* means "by this time."

all right, alright   The first of these is the preferable spelling; for some readers it is the only acceptable spelling.

all together, altogether   *All together* means that members of a group act or are gathered together ("They voted all together"); *altogether* is an adverb meaning "entirely," "wholly" ("This is altogether unnecessary").

allusion, reference, illusion   An *allusion* is an implied or indirect reference. "As Lincoln says" is a *reference* to Lincoln, but "As a great man has said," along with a phrase quoted from the Gettysburg Address, constitutes an *allusion* to Lincoln. *Allusion* has nothing to do with *illusion* (a deception). Note the spelling (especially the second *i*) in "disillusioned" (left without illusions, disenchanted).

almost   See *most.*

a lot   Two words (not *alot*).

among, between   See *between.*

amount, number   *Amount* refers to bulk or quantity: "A small amount of gas was still in the tank." Use *number,* not *amount,* to refer to separate (countable) units: "A large number of people heard the lecture" (not "a large amount of people"). Similarly, "an amount of money," but "a number of dollars."

analyzation   Unacceptable; use *analysis.*

and/or   Acceptable, but a legalism and unpleasant-sounding. Often *or* by itself will do, as in "students who know Latin or Italian." When *or* is not enough ("The script was written by Groucho and/or Harpo") it is better to recast ("The script was written by Groucho or Harpo, or both").

and etc.   Because *etc.* is an abbreviation for *et cetera* ("and others"), the *and* in *and etc.* is redundant. (See also the entry on *et cetera.*)

ante, anti   *Ante* means "before" (*antebellum,* "before the Civil War"); *anti* means "against" *(antivivisectionist).* Hyphenate *anti* before capitals *(anti-Semitism)* and before *i (anti-intellectual).*

anxious   Best reserved for uses that suggest anxiety ("He was anxious before the examination"), though some authorities now accept it in the sense of "eager" ("He was anxious to serve the community").

anybody   One word ("Do you know anybody here?"). If two words *(any body),* you mean any corpse ("Several people died in the fire, but the police cannot identify any body").

any more, anymore   *Any more* is used as an adjective: "I don't want any more meat" (here *any more* says something about meat). *Anymore* (one word) is used as an adverb: "I don't eat meat anymore" (here *anymore* says something about eating).

anyone   One word ("Why would anyone think that?"), unless you mean "any one thing," as in "Here are three books; you may take any one." *Anyone* is an indefinite singular pronoun meaning *any person:* "If anyone has a clue, he or she should call the police." In an astounding advertisement, the writer moved from *anyone* (singular) to *their* (third person plural) to *your* (second person): "Anyone who thinks a Yonex racquet has improved their game, please raise your hand."

area of   Like *field of* and *topic of* ("the field of literature," "the topic of politics"), *area of* can usually be deleted. "The area of marketing" equals "marketing."

around   Avoid using *around* in place of *about:* "He wrote it in about three hours." See also *centers on.*

as, like   *As* is a conjunction; use it in forming comparisons, to introduce clauses. (A clause has a subject and a verb.)

> You can learn to write, as you can learn to swim.
> Huck speaks the truth as he sees it.

Like is a preposition; use it to introduce prepositional phrases:

> He looks like me.

> Like Hamlet, Laertes has lost a father.
> She thinks like a lawyer.

A short rule: use *like* when it introduces a noun *not* followed by a verb: "Nothing grabs people like *People.*"

Writers who are fearful of incorrectly using *like* resort to cumbersome evasions: "He eats in the same manner that a pig eats." But there's nothing wrong with "He eats like a pig."

Asian, Oriental   *Asian* as a noun and as an adjective is the preferred word. *Oriental* (from *oriens,* "rising sun," "east") is in disfavor because it implies a Eurocentric view—that is, that things "oriental" are east of the European colonial powers who invented the term. Similarly, **Near East, Middle East, and Far East** are terms that are based on a Eurocentric view. No brief substitute has been agreed on for *Near East* and *Middle East,* but *East Asia* is now regarded as preferable to *Far East.*

as of now   Best deleted, or replaced by *now.* Not "As of now I don't smoke" but "Now I don't smoke" or "I don't smoke now" or "I don't smoke."

aspect   Literally, "a view from a particular point," but it has come to mean *topic,* as in "There are several aspects to be considered." Try to get a sharper word; for example, "There are several problems to be considered," or "There are several consequences to be considered."

as such   Often meaningless, as in "Tragedy as such evokes pity."

as to   Usually *about* is preferable. Not "I know nothing as to the charges," but "I know nothing about the charges."

bad, badly   *Bad* used to be only an adjective ("a bad movie"), and *badly* was an adverb ("she sings badly"). In "I felt bad," *bad* describes the subject, not the verb. (Compare "I felt happy," or "I felt good about getting a raise." After verbs of appearing, such as "feel," "look," "seem," "taste," an adjective, not an adverb is used. If you are in doubt, substitute a word for *bad,* for instance *sad,* and see what you say. Since you would say "I feel sad about his failure," you can say "I feel bad . . . .") But "badly" is acceptable and even preferred by many. Note, however, this distinction: "This meat smells bad" (an adjective describing the meat), and "Because I have a stuffed nose I smell badly" (an adverb describing my ability to smell something).

being   Do not use *being* as a main verb, as in "The trouble being that his reflexes were too slow." The result is a sentence fragment. See pages 431–33.

being that, being as A sentence such as "Being that she was a stranger . . ." sounds like an awkward translation from the Latin. Use *because.*

beside, besides *Beside* means "at the side of." Because *besides* can mean either "in addition to" or "other than," it is ambiguous, as in "Something besides TB caused his death." It is best, then, to use *in addition to* or *other than,* depending on what you mean.

between Only English teachers who have had a course in Middle English are likely to know that between comes from *by twain.* And only English teachers and editors are likely to object to its use (and to call for *among*) when more than two are concerned, as in "among the three of us." Note, too, that even conservative usage accepts *between* in reference to more than two when the items are at the moment paired: "Negotiations *between* Israel and Egypt, Syria, and Lebanon seem stalled." *Between,* a preposition, takes an object ("between you and me"): not "between you and I".

biannually, bimonthly, biweekly Every two years, every two months, every two weeks (*not* twice a year, etc.). Twice a year is *semiannually.* Because *biannually, bimonthly,* and *biweekly* are commonly misunderstood, it is best to avoid them and to say "every two . . ."

Black, black Although one sometimes sees the word capitalized when it refers to race, most publishers use a lowercase letter, making it consistent with *white,* which is never capitalized. See also *African American.*

can, may When schoolchildren asked "Can I leave the room?" their teachers used to correct them thus: "You *can* leave the room if you have legs, but you *may not* leave the room until you receive permission." In short, *can* indicates physical possibility, *may* indicates permission. But because "you may not" and "why mayn't I?" sound not merely polite but stiff, *can* is usually preferred except in formal contexts.

capital, capitol A *capital* is a city that is a center of government. *Capital* can also mean wealth ("It takes capital to start a business"). A *capitol* is a building in which legislators meet. Notice the distinction in the following sentence: "Washington, D.C., is the nation's capital; the capitol ought to have a gold dome."

centers on, centers around Use *centers on,* because *center* refers to a point, not to a movement around.

Chicana, Chicano A Mexican-American (female or male, respectively; the male plural, *Chicanos,* is used for a group consisting of males and females). Although the term sometimes was felt to be derogatory, today it usually implies ethnic pride.

collective nouns A collective noun, singular in form, names a collection of individuals. Examples: *audience, band, committee, crowd, jury, majority, minority, team.* When you are thinking chiefly of the whole as a unit, use a singular verb (and a singular pronoun, if any): "The majority rules"; "The jury is announcing its verdict." But when you are thinking of the individuals, use a plural verb (and pronoun, if any): "The majority are lawyers"; "The jury are divided and they probably cannot agree." If the plural sounds odd, you can usually rewrite: "The jurors are divided and they probably cannot agree."

compare, contrast To *compare* is to note likenesses or differences: "Compare a motorcycle with a bicycle." To *contrast* is to emphasize differences.

complement, compliment *Complement* as a noun means "that which completes"; as a verb, "to fill out, to complete." *Compliment* as a noun is an expression of praise; as a verb it means "to offer praise."

comprise   "To include, contain, consist of": "The university comprises two colleges and a medical school" (not "is comprised of"). Conservative authorities hold that "to be comprised of" is always incorrect, and they reject the form one often hears: "Two colleges and a medical school comprise the university." Here the word should be *compose,* not *comprise.*

concept   Should often be deleted. For "The concept of the sales tax is regressive" write "The sales tax is regressive."

contact   Because it is vague, avoid using *contact* as a verb. *Not* "I contacted him" but "I spoke with him" or "I wrote to him," or whatever.

continual, continuous   Conservative authorities hold that *continuous* means "uninterrupted," as in "It rained continuously for six hours"; *continually* means "repeated often, recurring at short intervals," as in "For a year he continually wrote letters to her."

contrast, compare   See *compare.*

could have, could of   See *of.*

criteria   Plural of *criterion;* hence it is always incorrect to speak of "a criteria," or to say "The criteria is . . ."

data   Plural of *datum.* Although some social scientists speak of "this data," "these data" is preferable: "These data are puzzling." Because the singular, *datum,* is rare and sounds odd, it is best to substitute *fact* or *figure* for *datum.*

different from   Prefer it to *different than,* unless you are convinced that in a specific sentence *different from* sounds terribly wrong, as in "These two books are more different than I had expected." (In this example, "more," not "different," governs "than." But this sentence, though correct, is awkward and therefore it should be revised: "These two books differ more than I had expected.")

dilemma   A situation requiring a choice between equally undesirable alternatives; not every difficulty or plight or predicament is a *dilemma.* Not "Her dilemma was that she had nowhere to go," but "Her dilemma was whether to go out or to stay home: one was frightening, the other was embarrassing." And note the spelling (two *m's,* no *n*).

disinterested   Though the word is often used to mean "indifferent," "unconcerned," "uninterested," reserve it to mean "impartial": "A judge should be disinterested."

due to   Some people, holding that *due to* cannot modify a verb (as in "He failed due to illness"), tolerate it only when it modifies a noun or pronoun ("His failure was due to illness"). They also insist that it cannot begin a sentence ("Due to illness, he failed"). In fact, however, daily usage accepts both. But because it almost always sounds stiff, try to substitute *because of,* or *through.*

due to the fact that   Wordy for *because.*

each   Although many authorities hold that *each,* as a subject, is singular, even when followed by "them" ("Each of them is satisfactory"), some authorities accept and even favor the plural ("Each of them are satisfactory"). But it is usually better to avoid the awkwardness by substituting *all* for *each:* "All of them are satisfactory." When *each* refers to a plural subject, the verb must be plural: "They each have a book"; "We each are trying." *Each* cannot be made into a possessive; you cannot say "Each's opinion is acceptable."

effect   See *affect.*

e.g. Abbreviation for *exempli gratia,* meaning "for example." It is thus different from *i.e.* (an abbreviation for *id est,* meaning "that is"). E.g. (not italicized) introduces an example: i.e. (also not italicized) introduces a definition. Because these two abbreviations of Latin words are often confused, it may be preferable to avoid them and use their English equivalents.

either . . . or, neither . . . nor If the subjects are singular, use a singular verb: "Either the boy or the girl is lying." If one of the subjects joined by *or* or *nor* is plural, most grammarians say that the verb agrees with the nearer subject, thus: "A tree or two shrubs are enough," or "Two shrubs or a tree is enough." But because the singular verb in the second of these sentences may sound odd, follow the first construction; that is, put the plural subject nearer to the verb and use a plural verb. Another point about *either . . . or.* In this construction, "either" serves as advance notice that two equal possibilities are in the offing. Beware of putting "either" too soon, as in "Either he is a genius or a lunatic." Better: "He is either a genius or a lunatic."

enthuse Objectionable to many readers. For "He enthused," say "He was enthusiastic." Use *enthuse* only in the sense of "to be excessively enthusiastic," "to gush."

et cetera, etc. Latin for "and other things"; if you mean "and other people," you need *et al.,* short for *et alii.* Because *etc.* is vague, its use is usually inadvisable. Not "He studied mathematics, etc." but "He studied mathematics, history, economics, and French." Or, if the list is long, cut it by saying something a little more informative than *etc.*—for example, "He studied mathematics, history, and other liberal arts subjects." Even *and so forth* or *and so on* is preferable to *etc.* Confine etc. (and most other abbreviations, including *et al.*) to footnotes, and even in footnotes try to avoid it.

Eurocentric language Language focused on Europe—for instance, the word *Hispanic* when used to refer not to persons from Spain but persons from Mexico and Central and South America, who may in fact have little or no Spanish heritage. (The Latin name for Spain was Hispania.) Similarly, the terms *Near East* and *Far East* represent a European point of view (near to, and far from Europe), objectionable to many persons not of European heritage. See *Asian* and *Hispanic.*

everybody, everyone These take a singular verb ("Everybody is here"), and a pronoun referring to them is usually singular ("Everybody thinks his problems are suitable topics of conversation"), but use a plural pronoun if the singular would seem unnatural ("Everybody was there, weren't they?"). To avoid the sexism of "Everybody thinks his problems . . ." revise to "All people think their problems . . ."

examples, instances See *instances.*

except See *accept.*

exists Often unnecessary and a sign of wordiness. Not "The problem that *exists* here is" but "The problem here is."

expound Usually pretentious for *explain* or *say.* To *expound* is to give a methodical explanation of theological matters.

facet Literally "little face," especially one of the surfaces of a gem. Don't use it (and don't use *aspect* or *factor* either) to mean "part" or "topic." It is most acceptable when, close to its literal meaning, it suggests a new appearance, as when a gem is turned: "Another *facet* appears when we see this law from the taxpayer's point of view."

the fact that   Usually wordy. "Because of the fact that boys played female roles in Elizabethan drama" can be reduced to "Because boys played female roles in Elizabethan drama."

factor   Strictly speaking, a *factor* helps to produce a result. Although *factor* is often used in the sense of "point" ("Another factor to be studied is . . .), such use is often wordy. "The possibility of plagiarism is a factor that must be considered" simply adds up to "The possibility of plagiarism must be considered." *Factor* is almost never the precise word: "the factors behind Gatsby's actions" are, more precisely, "Gatsby's motives."

famous, notorious   See *notorious.*

Far East   See *Asian.*

farther, further   Some purists claim that *farther* always refers to distance and *further* to time ("The gymnasium is farther than the library"; "Let us think further about this").

fatalistic, pessimistic   *Fatalistic* means "characterized by the belief that all events are predetermined and therefore inevitable"; *pessimistic,* "characterized by the belief that the world is evil," or, less gloomily, "expecting the worst."

fewer, less   See *less.*

field of   See *area of.*

firstly, secondly   Acceptable, but it is better to use *first, second.*

former, latter   These words are acceptable, but they are often annoying because they force the reader to reread earlier material in order to locate what *the former* and *the latter* refer to. The expressions are legitimately used in order to avoid repeating lengthy terms, but if you are talking about an easily repeated subject—say, Lincoln and Grant—don't hesitate to replace *the former* and *the latter* with their names. The repetition will clarify rather than bore.

good, well   *Good* is an adjective ("a good book"). *Well* is usually an adverb ("She writes well"). Standard English does not accept "She writes good." But Standard English requires *good* after verbs of appearing, such as "seems," "looks," "sounds," "tastes": "it looks good," "it sounds good." *Well* can also be an adjective meaning "healthy": "I am well."

graduate, graduate from   Use *from* if you name the institution or if you use a substitute word as in "She graduated from high school"; if the institution (or substitute) is not named, *from* is omitted: "She graduated in 1983." The use of the passive ("She was graduated from high school") is acceptable but sounds fussy to many.

he or she, his or her   These expressions are awkward, but the implicit male chauvinism in the generic use of the male pronoun ("A citizen should exercise his right to vote") may be more offensive than the awkwardness of *he or she* and *his or her.* Moreover, sometimes the male pronoun, when used for males and females, is ludicrous, as in "The more violence a youngster sees on television, regardless of his age or sex, the more aggressive he is likely to be." Do what you can to avoid the dilemma. Sometimes you can use the plural *their:* "Students are expected to hand in their papers on Monday" (instead of "The student is expected to hand in his or her paper on Monday"). Or eliminate the possessive: "The student must hand in a paper on Monday." See also *man, mankind.*

Hispanic, Latina, Latino   A person who traces his or her origin to a Spanish-speaking country is a *Hispanic.* (Hispania was the Latin name for Spain.) But some people object to the term when applied to persons in the western hemisphere, arguing that it overemphasizes the European influence on ethnic identity and neglects the indigenous and black heritages. Many who object to *Hispanic* prefer to call a person of Latin-American descent a *Latina* (the feminine form) or a *Latino* (the masculine form), partly because these words are themselves Latin-American words. (The male plural, *Latinos,* commonly is used for a group consisting of males and females.) But many people object that these words too obscure the unique cultural heritages of, say, Mexican-Americans, Cuban-Americans, and Puerto Ricans.

hopefully   Commonly used to mean "I hope" or "It is hoped" (*"Hopefully,* the rain will stop soon"), but it is best to avoid what some consider a dangling modifier. After all, the rain itself is not hopeful. If you mean "I hope the rain will stop soon," say exactly that. Notice, too, that *hopefully* is often evasive; if the president of the college says, "Hopefully tuition will not rise next year," don't think that you have heard a promise to fight against an increase; you only have heard someone evade making a promise. In short, confine *hopefully* to its adverbial use, meaning "in a hopeful manner": "Hopefully he uttered a prayer."

however   Independent clauses (for instance, "He tried" and "He failed") should not be linked with a *however* preceded by a comma. *In*correct: "He tried, however he failed." What is required is a period ("He tried. However, he failed") or a semicolon before *however* ("He tried; however, he failed).

the idea that   Usually dull and wordy. Not "The idea that we grow old is frightening," but "That we grow old is frightening," or (probably better) "Growing old is frightening."

identify   When used in the psychological sense, "to associate oneself closely with a person or an institution," it is preferable to include a reflexive pronoun, thus: "He identified himself with Hamlet," *not* "He identified with Hamlet."

i.e.   Latin for *id est,* "that is." The English words are preferable to the Latin abbreviation. On the distinction between *i.e.* and *e.g.,* see *e.g.*

immanent, imminent   *Immanent,* "remaining within, intrinsic"; *imminent,* "likely to occur soon, impending."

imply, infer   The writer or speaker *implies* (suggests); the perceiver *infers* (draws a conclusion): "Karl Marx implied that . . . but his modern disciples infer from his writings that . . ." Although *infer* is widely used for *imply,* preserve the distinction.

incidence, incident   The *incidence* is the extent or frequency of an occurrence: "The incidence of violent crime in Tokyo is very low." The plural, *incidences,* is rarely used: "The incidences of crime and of fire in Tokyo . . . ." An *incident* is one occurrence: "The incident happened yesterday." The plural is *incidents:* "The two incidents happened simultaneously."

individual   Avoid using the word to mean only "person": "He was a generous individual." But it is precise when it implicitly makes a contrast with a group: "In a money-mad society, he was a generous individual"; "Although the faculty did not take a stand on this issue, faculty members as individuals spoke out."

instances   Instead of *in many instances* use *often.* Strictly speaking an *instance* is not an object or incident in itself but one offered as an example. Thus "another instance of his failure to do his duty" (not "In three instances he failed to do his duty").

irregardless   Unacceptable; use *regardless.*

it is   Usually this expression needlessly delays the subject: "It is unlikely that many students will attend the lecture" could just as well be "Few students are likely to attend the lecture."

its, it's   The first is a possessive pronoun ("The flock lost its leader"); the second is a contraction of *it is* ("It's a wise father that knows his child."). You'll have no trouble if you remember that the possessive pronoun *its,* like other possessive pronouns such as *our, his, their,* does *not* use an apostrophe.

kind of   Singular, as in "That kind of movie bothers me." (*Not:* "Those kind of movies bother me.") If, however, you are really talking about more than one kind, use *kinds* and be sure that the demonstrative pronoun and the verb are plural: "Those kinds of movies bother me." Notice also that the phrase is *kind of,* not *kind of a.* Not "What *kind of a* car does she drive?" but "What *kind of* car does she drive?"

Latina, Latino   See *Hispanic.*

latter   See *former.*

lay, lie   To *lay* means "to put, to set, to cause to rest." It takes an object: "May I lay the coats on the table?" The past tense and the participle are *laid:* "I laid the coats on the table"; "I have laid the coats on the table." To *lie* means "to recline," and it does not take an object: "When I am tired I lie down." The past tense is *lay,* the participle is *lain:* "Yesterday I lay down"; "I have lain down hundreds of times without wishing to get up."

lend, loan   The usual verb is *lend:* "Lend me a pen." The past tense and the participle are both *lent. Loan* is a noun: "This isn't a gift, it's a loan." But, curiously, *loan* as a verb is acceptable in past forms: "I loaned him my bicycle." In its present form ("I often loan money") it is used chiefly by bankers.

less, fewer   *Less* (as an adjective) refers to bulk amounts (also called mass nouns): less milk, less money, less time. *Fewer* refers to separate (countable) items: fewer glasses of milk, fewer dollars, fewer hours.

lifestyle, life-style, life style   All three forms are acceptable, but because many readers regard the expression as imprecise, try to find a substitute such as *values.*

like, as   See *as.*

literally   It means "strictly in accord with the primary meaning; not metaphorically." It is not a mere intensive. "He was literally dead" means that he was a corpse; if he was merely exhausted, *literally* won't do. You cannot be "literally stewed" (except by cannibals), "literally tickled pink," or "literally head over heels in love."

loose, lose   *Loose* is an adjective ("The nail is loose"); *lose* is a verb ("Don't lose the nail").

the majority of   Usually a wordy way of saying *most.* Of course if you mean "a bare majority," say so; otherwise *most* will usually do. Certainly "The majority of the basement is used for a cafeteria" should be changed to "Most of the basement is used for a cafeteria." *Majority* can take either a singular verb or a plural verb. When *majority* refers to a collection—for example, a group acting as a body—the verb is singular, as in "The majority has withdrawn its support from the mayor." But when *majority* refers to members of a group acting as individuals, as in "The majority of voters in this district vote Republican," a plural verb (here, "vote") is usually preferred. If either construction sounds odd, use "most," with a plural verb: "Most voters in this district vote Republican."

man, mankind The use of these words in reference to males and females sometimes is ludicrous, as in "Man, being a mammal, breastfeeds his young." But even when not ludicrous the practice is sexist, as in "man's brain" and "the greatness of mankind." Consider using such words as *human being, person, humanity, people.* Similarly, for "manmade," *artificial* or *synthetic* may do.

may, can See *can.*

me The right word in such expressions as "between you and me" and "They gave it to John and me." It is the object of verbs and of prepositions. In fact, *me* rather than *I* is the usual form after any verb, including the verb *to be;* "It is me" is nothing to be ashamed of. See the entry on *myself.*

medium, media *Medium* is singular, *media* is plural: "TV is the medium to which most children are most exposed. Other media include film, radio, and publishing," It follows, then, that *mass media* takes a plural verb: "The mass media exert an enormous influence."

Middle East See *Asian.*

might of, might have; must of, must have *Might of* and *must of* are colloquial for *might have* and *must have.* In writing, use the *have* form: "He might have cheated; in fact, he must have cheated."

more Avoid writing a false (incomplete) comparison such as: "His essay includes several anecdotes, making it more enjoyable." Delete "more" unless there really is a comparison with another essay. On false comparisons see also the entry on *other.*

most, almost Although it is acceptable in speech to say "most everyone" and "most anybody," it is preferable in writing to use "almost everyone," "almost anybody." But of course: "Most students passed."

myself *Myself* is often mistakenly used for *I* or *me,* as in "They praised Tony and myself," or "Prof. Chen and myself examined the dead rat." In the first example, *me* is the word to use; after all, if Tony hadn't been there the sentence would say, "They praised me." (No one would say, "They praised myself.") Similarly, in the second example if Prof. Chen were not involved, the sentence would run, "I examined the dead rat," so what is needed here is simply "Prof. Chen and I examined . . . ."

In general, use *myself* only when (1) it refers to the subject of the sentence ("I look out for myself"; "I washed myself") or (2) when it is an intensive: ("I myself saw the break-in"; "I myself have not experienced racism").

nature You can usually delete *the nature of,* as in "The nature of my contribution is not political but psychological."

Near East See *Asian.*

needless to say The reader may well wonder why you go on to say it. Of course this expression is used to let readers know that they are probably familiar with what comes next, but usually *of course* will better serve as this sign.

Negro Capitalized, whether a noun or an adjective, though *white* is not. In recent years *Negro* has been replaced by *black* or African-American.

neither . . , nor See *either . . . or.*

nobody, no one, none *Nobody* and *no one* are singular, requiring a singular verb ("Nobody believes this," "No one knows"); but they can be referred to by a plural pronoun: "Nobody believes this, do they?" "No one knows, do they?" *None,* though it comes from *no one,* almost always requires a plural verb when it refers to people ("Of the ten people present, none are students") and a singular verb when it refers to things ("Of the five assigned books, none is worth reading").

not only . . . but also   Keep in mind these two points: (1) many readers object to the omission of "also" in such a sentence as "She not only brought up two children but practiced law," and (2) all readers dislike a faulty parallel, as in "She not only is bringing up two children but practices law." ("Is bringing up" needs to be paralleled with "is also practicing.")

notorious   Widely and unfavorably known; not merely famous, but famous for some discreditable trait or deed.

not . . . un-   Such an expression as "not unfamiliar" is useful only if it conveys something different from the affirmative. Compare the frostiness of "I am not unfamiliar with your methods" with "I am familiar with your methods." If the negative has no evident advantage, use the affirmative.

number, amount   See *amount.*

a number of   requires a plural verb: "A number of women are presidents of corporations." But when *number* is preceded by *the* it requires a singular verb: "The number of women who are presidents is small." (The plural noun after *number* of course may require a plural verb, as in "women are," but *the number* itself remains singular; hence its verb is singular, as in "is small.")

of   Be careful not to use *of* when *have* is required. Not "He might of died in the woods," but "He might have died in the woods." Note that what we often hear as "would've" or "should've" or "must've" or "could've" is "would have" or "should have" or "must have" or "could have," *not* "would of," etc.

off of   Use *off* or *from:* "Take if off the table"; "He jumped from the bridge."

often-times   Use *often* instead.

old-fashioned, old-fashion   Only the first is acceptable.

one   British usage accepts the shift from *one* to *he* in "One begins to die the moment he is born," but American usage prefers "One begins to die the moment one is born." A shift from *one* to *you* ("One begins to die the moment you are born") is unacceptable. As a pronoun, *one* can be useful in impersonal statements such as the sentence about dying, at the beginning of this entry, where it means "a person," but don't use it as a disguise for yourself ("One objects to Smith's argument"). Try to avoid *one;* one *one* usually leads to another, resulting in a sentence that, in James Thurber's words, "sounds like a trombone solo" ("If one takes oneself too seriously, one begins to . . ."). See also *you.*

one of   Takes a plural noun, and if this is followed by a clause, the preferred verb is plural: "one of those students who are," "one of those who feel." Thus, in such a sentence as "One of the coaches who have resigned is now seeking reinstatement," notice that "have" is correct; the antecedent of "who" (the subject of the verb) is "coaches," which is plural. Coaches have resigned, though "one . . . is seeking reinstatement." But in such an expression as "one out of a hundred," the following verb may be singular or plural ("One out of a hundred is," "One out of a hundred are").

only   Be careful where you put it. The classic textbook example points out that in the sentence "I hit him in the eye," *only* can be inserted in seven places (beginning in front of "I" and ending after "eye") with at least six different meanings. Try to put it just before the expression it qualifies. Thus, not

"Presidential aides are only responsible to one person," but "Presidential aides are responsible to only one person" (or "to one person only").

oral, verbal See *verbal.*

Oriental see *Asian.*

other Often necessary in comparisons. "No American president served as many terms as Franklin Roosevelt" falsely implies that Roosevelt was not an American president. The sentence should be revised to "No other American president served as many terms as Franklin Roosevelt."

per Usually it sounds needlessly technical ("twice per hour") or disturbingly impersonal ("as per your request"). Preferable: "twice an hour," "according to your request," or "as you requested."

per cent, percent, percentage The first two of these are interchangeable; both mean "per hundred," "out of a hundred," as in "Ninety per cent (or percent) of the students were white." *Per cent* and *percent* are always accompanied by a number (written out, or in figures). It is usually better to write out *per cent* or *percent* than to use a per cent sign (12%), except in technical or statistical papers. *Percentage* means "a proportion or share in relation to the whole," as in "A very large percentage of the student body is white." Many authorities insist that *percentage* is never preceded by a number. Do not use percentage to mean "a few," as in "Only a percentage of students attended the lecture"; a percentage can be as large as 99.99. It is usually said that with *per cent, percent,* and *percentage,* whether the verb is singular or plural depends on the number of the noun that follows the word, thus: "Ninety percent of his books are paperbacks"; "Fifty percent of his library is worthless"; "A large percentage of his books are worthless." But some readers (including the authors of this book) prefer a singular verb after *percentage* unless the resulting sentence is as grotesque as this one: "A large percentage of the students is unmarried." Still, rather than say a "percentage . . . are," we would recast the sentence: "A large percentage of the student body is unmarried," or "Many (or "Most," or whatever) of the students are unmarried."

per se Latin for "by itself." Usually sounds legalistic or pedantic, as in "Meter per se has an effect."

pessimistic See *fatalistic.*

phenomenon, phenomena The plural is *phenomena;* thus, "these phenomena" but "this phenomenon."

plus Unattractive and imprecise as a noun meaning "asset" or "advantage" ("When he applied for the job, his appearance was a plus"), and equally unattractive as a substitute for *moreover* ("The examination was easy, plus I had studied") or as a substitute for *and* ("I studied the introduction plus the first chapter").

politics Preferably singular ("Ethnic politics has been a strong force for a century") but a plural verb is acceptable.

precede, proceed To *precede* is to go before or ahead ("X precedes Y"). To *proceed* is to go forward ("The spelling lesson proceeded smoothly").

prejudice, prejudiced *Prejudice* is a noun: "It is impossible to live entirely without prejudice." But use the past participle *prejudiced* as an adjective: "He was prejudiced against me from the start."

preventative, preventive Both are acceptable but the second form is the form now used by writers on medicine ("preventive medicine"); *preventative* therefore has come to seem amateurish.

principal, principle   *Principal* is (1) an adjective meaning "main," "chief," "most important" ("The principal arguments against IQ testing are three"), and (2) a noun meaning "the chief person" ("Ms. Murphy was the principal of Jefferson High") or "the chief thing" ("She had so much money she could live on the interest and not touch the principal"). *Principle* is always a noun meaning "rule" or "fundamental truth" ("It was against his principles to eat meat").

prior to   Pretentious for *before.*

protagonist   Literally, the first actor, and, by extension, the chief actor. It is odd, therefore, to speak of "the protagonists" in a single literary work or occurrence. Note also that the prefix is *proto,* "first," not *pro,* "for"; it does *not* mean one who strives for something.

quite   Usually a word to delete, along with *definitely, pretty, rather,* and *very. Quite* used to mean "completely" ("I quite understand") but it has come also to mean "to a considerable degree," and so it is ambiguous as well as vague.

quotation, quote   Quotation is a noun, quote is a verb. "I will quote Churchill" is fine, but not "these quotes from Churchill." And remember, you may *quote* one of Hamlet's speeches, but Hamlet does not *quote* them; he says them.

rather   Avoid use with strong adjectives. "Rather intelligent" makes sense, but "rather tremendous" does not. "Rather brilliant" probably means "bright"; "rather terrifying" probably means "frightening," "rather unique" probably means "unusual." Get the right adjective, not *rather* and the wrong adjective.

the reason ... is because   Usually *because* is enough (not "The reason they fail is because they don't study," but simply "They fail because they don't study"). Similarly, *the reason why* can usually be reduced to *why.* Notice, too, that because *reason* is a noun, it cannot neatly govern a *because* clause: not "The reason for his absence is because he was sick," but "The reason for his absence was illness."

rebut, refute   To rebut is to argue against, but not necessarily successfully. If you mean "to disprove," use *disprove* or *refute.*

in regard to, with regard to   Often wordy for *about, concerning,* or *on,* and sometimes even these words are unnecessary. Compare: "He knew a great deal in regard to jazz"; "He knew a great deal about jazz." Compare: "Hemingway's story is often misunderstood with regard to Robert Wilson's treatment of Margot Macomber"; "In Hemingway's story, Robert Wilson's treatment of Margot Macomber is often misunderstood."

relate to   Usually a vague expression, best avoided, as in "I can relate to Hedda Gabler." Does it mean "respond favorably to," "identify myself with," 'interact with" (and how can a reader "interact with" a character in a play?). Use *relate to* only in the sense of "have connection with" (as in "How does your answer relate to my question?"); even in such a sentence a more exact expression is preferable.

repel, repulse   Both verbs mean "to drive back," but only *repel* can mean "to cause distaste," "to disgust," as in "His obscenities repelled the audience."

respectfully, respectively   *Respectfully* means "with respect, showing respect" ("Japanese students and teachers bow respectfully to each other"). *Respectively* means "each in turn" ("Professors Arnott, Bahktian, and Cisneros teach, respectively, chemistry, business, and biology").

sarcasm   Heavy, malicious sneering ("Oh you're really a great friend, aren't you?" addressed to someone who won't lend the speaker ten dollars). If the apparent praise, which really communicates dispraise, is at all clever, conveying, say, a delicate mockery or wryness, it is irony, not sarcasm.

seem   Properly it suggests a suspicion that appearances may be deceptive: "He seems honest (but . . .)." Don't say "The book seems to lack focus" if you believe it does lack focus.

semiannually, semimonthly, semiweekly   See *biannually.*

sexist language   Language that takes males as the norm. For example, the use of *he* with reference to females as well as to males ("When a legislator votes, he takes account of his constituency"), like the use of *man* for all human beings ("Man is a rational animal"), is now widely perceived as subtly (or not so subtly) favoring males. See the entries on *he or she, man, mankind,* and *s/he.*

shall, will, should, would   The old principle held that in the first person *shall* is the future indicative of *to be* and *should* the conditional ("I shall go," "We should like to be asked"); and that *will* and *would* are the forms for the second and third persons. When the forms are reversed ("I will go," "Government of the people . . . shall not perish from the earth"), determination is expressed. But today almost nobody adheres to these principles. Indeed, *shall* (except in questions) sounds stilted to many ears.

s/he   This new gender-free pronoun ("As soon as the student receives the forms, s/he should fill them out") is sometimes used in place of *he or she* or *she or he,* which are used to avoid the sexism implied when the male pronoun "he" is used to stand for women as well as men ("As soon as the student receives the forms, he should fill them out"). Other, less noticeable ways of avoiding sexist writing are suggested under *he or she.*

simplistic   Means "falsely simplified by ignoring complications." Do not confuse it with *simplified,* whose meanings include "reduced to essentials" and "clarified."

since, because   Traditional objections to *since,* in the sense of "because," have all but vanished. Note, however, that when *since* is ambiguous and may also refer to time ("Since he joined the navy, she found another boyfriend") it is better to say *because* or *after,* depending on which you mean.

situation   Overused, vague, and often unnecessary. "His situation was that he was unemployed" adds up to "He was unemployed." And "an emergency situation" is probably an emergency.

split infinitives   The infinitive is the verb form that merely names the action, without indicating when or by whom performed ("walk," rather than "walked" or "I walk"). Grammarians, however, developed the idea that the infinitive was "to walk," and they held that one cannot separate or split the two words: "to quickly walk." But James Thurber says this idea is "of a piece with the sentimental and outworn notion that it is always wrong to strike a lady." Notice, however, that often the inserted word can be deleted ("to really understand" is "to understand"), and that if many words are inserted between *to* and the verb, the reader may get lost ("to quickly and in the remaining few pages before examining the next question conclude").

stanza   See *verse.*

subjunctive   For the use of the subjunctive with conditions contrary to fact (for instance, "If I were you"), see the entry on *was/were.* The subjunctive is also used in *that* clauses followed by verbs demanding, requesting, or recommending: "He asked that the students be prepared to take a test." But because this last sort of sentence sounds stiff, it is better to use an alternate construction, such as "He asked the students to prepare for a test."

than, then   *Than* is used chiefly in making comparisons ("German is harder than French"), but also after "rather," "other," and "else" ("I'd rather take French than German"; "He thinks of nothing other than sex"). *Then* commonly indicates time ("She took German then, but now she takes French"; "Until then, I'll save you a seat"), but it may also mean "in that case" ("It's agreed, then, that we'll all go"), or "on the other hand" ("Then again, she may find German easy"). The simplest guide: use *than* after comparisons and after "rather," "other," "else"; otherwise use *then.*

that, which, who   Many pages have been written on these words; opinions differ, but you will offend no one if you observe the following principles. (1) Use *that* in restrictive (that is, limiting) clauses: "The rocking chair that creaks is on the porch." (2) Use *which* in nonrestrictive (in effect, parenthetic) clauses: "The rocking chair, which creaks, is on the porch." (See pages 439–40.) The difference between these two sentences is this: in the first, one rocking chair is singled out from several—the one that creaks; in the second, the fact that the rocking chair creaks is simply tossed in, and is not added for the purpose of identifying the one chair out of several. (3) Use *who* for people, in restrictive and in nonrestrictive clauses: "The men who were playing poker ignored the women"; "The men, who were playing poker, ignored the women." But note that often *that, which,* and *who* can be omitted: "The creaky rocking chair is on the porch"; "The men, playing poker, ignored the women." In general, omit these words if the sentence remains clear. See page 92.

their, there, they're   The first is possessive pronoun: "Chaplin and Keaton made their first films before sound tracks were developed." The second, *there,* sometimes refers to a place ("Go there," "Do you live there?"), and sometimes is what is known in grammar as an introductory expletive ("There are no solutions to this problem"). The third, *they're,* is a contraction of "they are" ("They're going to stay for dinner").

this   Often refers vaguely to "what I have been saying." Does it refer to the previous sentence, the previous paragraph, the previous page? Try to modify it by being specific: "This last point"; "This clue gave the police all they needed."

thusly   Unacceptable; *thus* is an adverb and needs no adverbial ending.

till, until   Both are acceptable, but *until* is preferable because *till*—though common in speech—looks literary in print. The following are *not* acceptable: *til, 'til, 'till.*

to, too, two   *To* is toward; *too* is either "also" ("She's a lawyer, too") or "excessively" ("It's too hot"); *two* is one more than one ("Two is company").

topic of   See *area of.*

toward, towards   Both are standard English; *toward* is more common in the United States, *towards* in Great Britain.

type   Often colloquial (and unacceptable in most writing) for *type of,* as in "this type teacher." But *type of* is not especially pleasing either. Better to write "this kind of teacher." And avoid using *type* as a suffix: "essay-type examinations" are essay examinations; "natural-type ice cream" is natural ice cream. Sneaky manufacturers make "Italian-type cheese," implying that their domestic cheese is imported and at the same time protecting themselves against charges of misrepresentation.

unique   The only one of its kind. Someone or something cannot be "rather unique" or "very unique" or "somewhat unique," any more than a woman can be somewhat pregnant. Instead of saying "rather unique," then, say *rare,* or *unusual,* or *extraordinary,* or whatever seems to be the best word.

U.S., United States   Generally, *United States* is preferable to *U.S.;* similarly, *the Soviet Union* is preferable to *the U.S.S.R.*

usage   Don't use *usage* where *use* will do, as in "Here Vonnegut completes his usage of dark images." *Usage* properly implies a customary practice that has created a standard: "Usage has eroded the difference between 'shall' and 'will.'"

use of   The use of *use of* is usually unnecessary. "Through the use of setting he conveys a sense of foreboding" may be reduced to "The setting conveys . . ." or "His setting conveys . . ."

utilize, utilization   Often inflated for *use* and *using,* as in "The infirmary has noted that it is sophomores who have most utilized the counseling service." But when one means "find an effective use for," *utilize* may be the best word, as in (here we borrow from *The American Heritage Dictionary*), "The teachers were unable to utilize the new computers," where *use* might wrongly suggest that the teachers could not operate the computers.

verbal   Often used where *oral* would be more exact. *Verbal* simply means "expressed in words," and thus a *verbal agreement* may be either written or spoken. If you mean spoken, call it an *oral agreement.*

verse, stanza   A *verse* is a single line of a poem; a *stanza* is a group of lines, commonly bound by a rhyme scheme. But in speaking or writing about songs, usage sanctions *verse* for *stanza,* as in "Second verse, same as the first."

viable   A term from physiology, meaning "capable of living" (for example, referring to a fetus at a stage of its development). Now pretentiously used and overused, especially by politicians and journalists, to mean "workable," as in "a viable presidency." Avoid it.

was, were   Use the subjunctive form—*were* (rather than *was*)—in expressing a wish ("I wish I were younger") and in "if-clauses" that are contrary to fact ("If I were rich," "If I were you . . .").

we   If you mean *I,* say *I.* Not "The first fairy tale we heard" but "the first fairy tale I heard." (But of course *we* is appropriate in some statements: "We have all heard fairy tales"; "If we look closely at the evidence, we can agree that . . . .") The rule: don't use *we* as a disguise for *I.* See pages 110–11.

well   See *good.*

well known, widely known   Athletes, performers, politicians, and such folk are not really *well known* except perhaps by a few of their friends and their relatives; use *widely known* if you mean they are known (however slightly) to many people.

which   Often can be deleted. "Students are required to fill out scholarship applications which are lengthy" can be written "Students are required to fill out lengthy scholarship applications." Another example: "*The Tempest,* which is Shakespeare's last play, was written in 1611"; "*The Tempest,* Shakespeare's last play, was written in 1611," or "Shakespeare wrote his last play, *The Tempest,* in 1611." For the distinction between *which* and *that,* see also the entry on *that.*

while Best used in a temporal sense, meaning "during the time": "While I was speaking, I suddenly realized that I didn't know what I was talking about." While it is not wrong to use *while* in a nontemporal sense, meaning "although" (as at the beginning of this sentence), it is better to use *although* in order to avoid any ambiguity. Note the ambiguity in: "While he was fond of movies he chiefly saw westerns." Does it mean "Although he was fond of movies," or does it mean "During the time when he was fond of movies"? Another point: do not use *while* if you mean *and;* "Freshmen take English 1–2, while sophomores take English 10–11" (substitute *and* for *while*).

who, whom Strictly speaking, *who* must be used for subjects, even when they look like objects: "He guessed who would be chosen." (Here *who* is the subject of the clause "who would be chosen.") *Whom* must be used for the objects of a verb, verbal (gerund, participle), or preposition: "Whom did he choose?"; "Whom do you want me to choose?"; "To whom did he show it?" We may feel stuffy in writing "Whom did he choose?" or "Whom are you talking about?" but to use *who* is certain to annoy some reader. Often you can avoid the dilemma by rewriting: "Who was chosen?"; "Who is the topic of conversation?" See also the entry on *that.*

whoever, whomever The second of these is the objective form. It is often incorrectly used as the subject of a clause. "Open the class to whomever wants to take it" is incorrect. The object of "to" is not "whomever" but is the entire clause—"whoever wants to take it"—and of course "whoever" is the subject of "wants."

who's, whose The first is a contraction of *who is* ("I'm everybody who's nobody"). The second is a possessive pronoun: "Whose book is it?" "I know whose it is."

will, would See *shall* and also *would.*

would "I would think that" is a wordy version of "I think that." (On the mistaken use of *would of* for *would have,* see also the entry on *of.*

you In relatively informal writing, *you* is ordinarily preferable to the somewhat stiff *one:* "If you are addicted to cigarettes, you may find it helpful to join Smokenders." (Compare: "If one is addicted to cigarettes, one may . . .") But because the direct address of *you* may sometimes descend into nagging, it is usually better to write: "Cigarette addicts may find it helpful . . ." Certainly a writer (you?) should not assume that the reader is guilty of vices ("You should not molest children") unless the essay is clearly aimed at an audience that admits to these vices, say a pamphlet directed to child molesters who are seeking help. Thus, it is acceptable to say, "If you are a poor speller," but it is not acceptable to say, to the general reader, "You should improve your spelling"; the reader's spelling may not need improvement. And avoid *you* when the word cannot possibly apply to the reader: "A hundred years ago you were faced with many diseases that now have been eradicated." Something like "A hundred years ago people were faced . . ." is preferable.

your, you're The first is a possessive pronoun ("your book"); the second is a contraction of *you are* ("You're mistaken").

21

Manuscript Form

BASIC MANUSCRIPT FORM

When you submit a piece of writing to your instructor (or to anyone else), make sure it looks good. You want to convey the impression that you care about what you've written, that you've invested yourself and your time in it, that the details matter to you.

Much of what follows is ordinary academic procedure. Unless your instructor specifies something different, you can adopt these principles as a guide.

1. Print your essay on 8½-by-11-inch paper of good weight. If your printer uses continuous-feed paper, remove the perforated strips from each side of the paper and separate the sheets before you hand in the essay.

2. Make sure that the printer has enough ink and that the print is dark and clear. One sure way to irritate your instructor is to turn in an essay with nearly invisible print.

3. Do not use a fancy font. Unless your instructor specifies something else, stick to Times or Courier. And use a reasonable point size: generally a 12-point font will do.

4. Print your essay on one side of the paper only. If for some reason you have occasion to submit a handwritten copy, use lined paper and write on every other line in black or dark blue ink.

5. Set the line spacing at "double." The essay (even the heading—see item 6 below) should be double-spaced—not single-spaced, not triple-spaced.

6. In the upper left-hand corner, one inch from the top, put your name, your instructor's name, the course number, and the date. Put your last name before the page number (in the upper right-hand corner) of each subsequent page, so the instructor can easily reassemble your essay if somehow a page gets detached and mixed with other papers.

7. Titles. Use this form for your title: hit the "enter" (or "return") key *once* after the date and then center the title of your essay. We give instructions for punctuating titles in Chapter 19, but we'll reiterate the most important points here. Capitalize the first letter of the first and last words of your title, the first word after a semicolon or colon if you use either one, and the first letter of all the other words except articles, conjunctions, and prepositions, thus:

Two Kinds of Symbols in <u>To Kill a Mockingbird</u>

Notice that your own title is neither underlined nor enclosed in quotation marks. (If, as here, your title includes material that would normally be italicized or in quotation marks, that material continues to be so written.) If the title runs more than one line, double-space between the lines.

8. Begin the essay just below the title. (Again, you'll hit "enter" or "return" only once.) If your instructor prefers a title page, begin the essay on the next page and number it 1. The title page is not numbered.

9. Margins. Except for page numbers, which should appear one-half inch from the top of the page, leave a one-inch margin at top, bottom, and sides of text.

10. Number the pages consecutively, using arabic numerals in the upper right-hand corner, half an inch from the top. Do not put a period or a hyphen after the numeral, and do not precede the numeral with "page" or "p." (Again, if you give the title on a separate sheet, the page that follows it is page 1. Do not number the title page.)

11. Paragraphs. Indent the first word of each paragraph five spaces from the left margin.

12. Proofreading. Check for typographical errors, and check spelling. Use your word processor's spell-check program—but don't rely on it exclusively. This program will flag words that are not in its dictionary and offer suggestions for correcting mistakes. (A misspelled word is of course not in the dictionary and thus flagged.) But a word flagged is not necessarily misspelled; it may simply not be in the program's dictionary. Proper names, for example, regularly get flagged. Keep in mind also that most programs cannot distinguish between homophones *(to, too, two; there, their, alter, altar),* nor can they tell you that you should have written *accept* instead of *except.*

13. Print a copy of your essay for yourself and keep it until the original has been returned. It is a good idea to keep notes and drafts too. They may prove helpful if you are asked to revise a page, substantiate a point, or supply a source you omitted.

14. Fasten the pages of your paper with a paper clip in the upper left-hand corner. Stiff binders are unnecessary; indeed, they are a nuisance to the instructor, adding bulk and making it awkward to write annotations.

1"

Double space

Your Name — *Font is Times*

Your Instructor's Name

Writing 127

April 1, 1999 — *Capitalize main words in title*

Formatting Your Essays: The Right Way to Do It   *Center title*

Print your essay on 8–1/2-by–11-inch paper of good weight, and make sure that the printer has enough ink and that the print is dark and clear. Do not use a fancy font. Unless your instructor specifies something else, stick to Times or Courier. And use a reasonable point size: generally a 12-point font will do. The essay (even the heading) should be double-spaced--not single-spaced, not triple-spaced--and it should be printed on one side of the paper only.

5 spaces, or tab

1"

In the upper left-hand corner, one inch from the top, put your name, your instructor's name, the course number, and the date, all on separate lines. Put your last name before the page number (in the upper right-hand corner) of each subsequent page, so the instructor can easily reassemble your essay if somehow a page gets detached and mixed with other papers. Hit the "enter" (or "return") key *once* after the date and then center the title of your essay. Capitalize the first letter of the first and last words of your title, the first word after a semicolon or colon if you use either one, and the first letter of all the other words except articles, conjunctions, and prepositions. Notice that your own title is neither underlined nor enclosed in quotation marks. If the title runs more than one line, double-space between the lines. Begin the essay just below the title. (Again, you'll hit "enter" or "return" only once.) If your instructor prefers a title page, begin the essay on the next page and number it 1.

Except for page numbers, which should appear one-half inch from the top of the page, leave a one-inch margin at top, bottom, and sides of text. Number the pages consecutively, using

1"

Your name 2

arabic numerals in the upper right-hand corner, half an inch from

the top. Do not put a period or a hyphen after the numeral, and

do not precede the numeral with "page" or "p."

Indent the first word of each paragraph five spaces from

the left margin.

Fasten the pages of your paper with a paper clip in the

upper left-hand corner. Stiff binders are unnecessary; indeed, they

are a nuisance because they add bulk and make essays difficult to

annotate. Spell-check your essay and proofread it carefully; make

a copy for yourself, and then turn the essay in.

USING QUOTATIONS (AND PUNCTUATING QUOTATIONS CORRECTLY)

If you are writing about a text, or about an interview, quotations from your material or subject are indispensable. They not only let your readers know what you are talking about, they give your readers the material you are responding to, thus letting them share your responses. But quote sparingly and quote briefly. Use quotations as evidence, not as padding. If the exact wording of the original is crucial, or especially effective, quote it directly, but if it is not, don't bore the reader with material that can be effectively reduced either by summarizing or by cutting. And make sure, by a comment before or after a quotation, that your reader understands why you find the quotation relevant. Don't count on a quotation to make your point for you.

Here are some additional matters to keep in mind, especially as you revise.

1. Identify the speaker or writer of the quotation. Usually this identification precedes the quoted material (e.g., "Smith says, . . .") in accordance with the principle of letting readers know where they are going. But occasionally it may follow the quotation, especially if the name will provide a meaningful surprise. For example, in a discussion of a proposed tax reform, you might quote a remark hostile to it and then reveal that the author of the proposal was also the author of the remark.

2. When you introduce a quotation, consider using verbs other than "says." Depending on the context—that is, on the substance of the quotation and its place in your essay—it might be more accurate to say "Smith argues," "adds," "contends," "points out," "admits," or "comments." Or, again with just the right verb, you might introduce the quotation with a transitional phrase: "In another context Smith had observed that . . ." or "To clarify this point Smith refers to . . ." or "In an apparent contradiction Smith suggests . . ." But avoid such inflated words as "opines," "avers," and "is of the opinion that." The point is not to add "elegant variation" (see page 119) to your introduction of someone

else's words, but accuracy and grace. A verb often used *in*accurately is "feels."
Ralph Linton does not "feel" that "the term *primitive art* has come to be used
with at least three distinct meanings." He "points out," "writes," "observes," or
"says" so.

3. Distinguish between short and long quotations and treat each appropriately.

Enclose *short quotations,* four (or fewer) lines of typing, within quotation
marks:

Anne Lindbergh calls the harrowing period of the kidnapping and

murder of her first child the "hour of lead." "Flying," she wrote, "was

freedom and beauty and escape from crowds."

Set off *long quotations* (more than four lines of typing). Do *not* enclose
them within quotation marks. To set off a quotation, begin a new line, indent ten
spaces from the left margin, and type the quotation double-spaced:

The last paragraphs of Five Years of My Life contain Dreyfus's words

when he was finally freed:

The Government of the Republic gives me back my liberty. It is

nothing to me without honor. Beginning with today, I shall unremittingly

strive for the reparation of the frightful judicial error of which I am still

the victim. I want all France to know by a final judgment that I am

innocent.

But he was never to receive that judgment.

Note that long quotations are usually introduced by a sentence ending with
a colon (as in the above example) or by an introductory phrase, such as "Dreyfus
wrote:"

**4. Don't try to introduce a long quotation into the middle of one of
your own sentences.** It is too difficult for the reader to come out of the quotation and to pick up your thread. Instead, introduce the quotation, as we did
above, set the quotation off, and then begin a new sentence of your own.

**5. An embedded quotation (that is, a quotation embedded into a sen-
tence of your own) must fit grammatically into the sentence of which it
is a part.** For example, suppose you want to use Othello's line "I have done the
state some service."

Incorrect

Near the end of the play Othello says that he "have done the state

some service."

Correct

Near the end of the play Othello says that he has "done the state some service."

Correct

Near the end of the play, Othello says, "I have done the state some service."

6. Quote exactly. Check your quotation for accuracy at least twice. If you need to edit a quotation—for example, in order to embed it grammatically, or to inform your reader of a relevant point—observe the following rules:

To add or to substitute words, enclose the words in square brackets—not parentheses.

"In the summer of 1816 we [Mary Wollstonecraft and Percy Bysshe Shelley] visited Switzerland and became the neighbors of Lord Byron."

Trotsky became aware that "Stalin would not hesitate a moment to organize an attempt on [his] life."

Indicate the omission of material with ellipses (three periods, with a space between periods and before and after each period).

The New York Times called it "the most intensive man-hunt . . . in the country's history" (3 March 1932).

If your sentence ends with the omission of the last part of the original sentence, use four periods: one immediately after the last word quoted, and three (spaced) to indicate the omission.

The manual says, "If your sentence ends with the omission of the last part of the original sentence, use four spaced periods. . . ."

Notice that if you begin the quotation with the beginning of a sentence (in the example we have just given "If your" is the beginning of a quoted sentence) you do *not* indicate that material preceded the words you are quoting. Similarly, if you end your quotation with the end of the quoted sentence, you give only a single period, not an ellipsis, although of course the material from which you are quoting may have gone on for many more sentences. But if you begin quoting from the middle of a sentence, or end quoting before you reach the end of a sentence in your source, it is customary to indicate the omissions. But even such omissions need not be indicated when the quoted material is obviously incomplete—when, for instance, it is a word or phrase.

7. Use punctuation accurately. There are three important rules to observe:

Commas and periods go inside the quotation marks.

"The land," Nick Thompson observes, "looks after us."

Semicolons and colons go outside quotation marks.

He turned and said, "Learn the names of all these places"; it sounded

like an order.

Question marks, exclamation points, and dashes go inside if they are part of the quotation, outside if they are your own.

Amanda ironically says to her daughter, "How old are you, Laura?"

(The question mark is part of the quotation and therefore goes inside the quotation marks.)

In the following example, why is the question mark placed outside of the quotation marks?

Is it possible to fail to hear Laura's weariness in her reply, "Mother,

you know my age"?

8. Use single quotation marks for a quotation within a quotation.

The student told the interviewer, "I ran back to the dorm and I called

my boyfriend and I said, 'Listen, this is just incredible,' and I told him all

about it."

9. Enclose titles of short works in quotation marks. Short works include: chapters in books, short stories, essays, short poems, songs, lectures, speeches, and unpublished works (even if long).

Underline, or use italic type, for titles of long works. (Underlining indicates *italic* type, used in print and available on computers but ordinarily not available on typewriters.) Underline (or italicize) titles of published book-length works: novels, plays, periodicals, collections of essays, anthologies, pamphlets, textbooks, and long poems (such as *Paradise Lost*). Underline (or italicize) also titles of films, record albums, tapes, television programs, ballets, operas, works of art, and the names of planes, ships, and trains.

Exception: titles of sacred works (for example, the New Testament, the Hebrew Bible, Genesis, Acts, the Gospels, the Koran) are neither underlined nor enclosed within quotation marks. To cite a book of the Bible with chapter and verse, give the name of the book, then a space, then an arabic numeral for the chapter, a period, and an arabic numeral (*not* preceded by a space) for the verse, thus: Exodus 20.14–15. Standard abbreviations for the books of the Bible (for example, Chron.) are permissible in footnotes and in parenthetic citations within the text.

10. Use quotation marks to identify a word or term to which you wish to call special attention. (But italics, indicated by underlining, may be used instead of quotation marks.)

By "comedy" I mean not only a funny play, but any play that ends

happily.

11. Do not use quotation marks to enclose slang or a term that you fear is too casual; use the term or don't use it, but don't apologize by putting it in quotation marks, as in these examples.

Incorrect

Because of "red tape" it took three years.

Incorrect

At last I was able to "put in my two cents."

In both of these sentences the writers are signaling their uneasiness; in neither is there any cause for uneasiness.

12. Do not use quotation marks to convey sarcasm, as in the following sentence:

These "politicians" are nothing but thieves.

Sarcasm, usually a poor form of argument, is best avoided. But of course there are borderline cases when you may want to convey your dissatisfaction with a word used by others.

African sculpture has a long continuous tradition, but this tradition

has been jeopardized by the introduction of "civilization" to Africa.

Perhaps the quotation marks here are acceptable, because the writer's distaste has not yet become a sneer and because she is, in effect, quoting. But it is probably better to change "civilization" to "western culture," omitting the quotation marks.

13. Do not enclose the title of your own essay in quotation marks, and do not underline or italicize it.

CORRECTIONS IN THE FINAL COPY

Extensive revisions should have been made in your drafts, but minor last-minute revisions may be made on the finished copy. Proofreading may catch some typographical errors, and you may notice some small weaknesses. You can make corrections with the following proofreader's symbols. If you did not find an error in each triangle, look again.

1. *Changes* in wording may be made by crossing through words and rewriting just above them, either on the typewriter or by hand in pen:

When I first moved to the United States at the age of nine, I had ~~few~~ *no*

doubts as to my identity.

2. *Additions* should be made above the line, with a caret (^) below the line at the appropriate place:

When I first moved to the United States at the age ^*of* nine, I had no doubts

as to my identity.

3. *Transpositions* of letters may be made thus:

When I fi̶r̶st moved to the United States at the age of nine, I had no

doubts as to my identity.

4. *Deletions* are indicated by a horizontal line through the word or words to be deleted. Delete a single letter by drawing a vertical or diagonal line through it.

When I first moved to the United States at ~~at~~ the age of nine, I had no

doub̸ts as to my identity.

5. *Separation* of words accidentally run together is indicated by a vertical line, *closure* by a curved line connecting the things to be closed up.

When I first moved to the United states at the age of nine, I had no

dou bts as to my identity.

6. *Paragraphing* may be indicated by the paragraph symbol before the word that is to begin the new paragraph.

When I first moved to the United States at the age of nine, I had no

doubts as to my identity. Within a year, however, . . .

PART FIVE

Readings

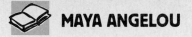 **MAYA ANGELOU**

Maya Angelou, born in Saint Louis, Missouri, in 1938, grew up in Arkansas and California. She studied music, dance, and drama (she received an Emmy nomination for her role in the televised version of Alex Haley's Roots*), and she is now a professor of American studies at Wake Forest University. She has also worked as a cook, streetcar conductor, and waitress. In addition to writing books of poetry, she has written five autobiographical volumes.*

"Graduation" comes from her first autobiography, I Know Why the Caged Bird Sings *(1969).*

Graduation*

The children in Stamps trembled visibly with anticipation. Some adults were excited too, but to be certain the whole young population had come down with graduation epidemic. Large classes were graduating from both the grammar school and the high school. Even those who were years removed from their own day of glorious release were anxious to help with preparations as a kind of dry run. The junior students who were moving into the vacating classes' chairs were tradition-bound to show their talents for leadership and management. They strutted through the school and around the campus exerting pressure on the lower grades. Their authority was so new that occasionally if they pressed a little too hard it had to be overlooked. After all, next term was coming, and it never hurt a sixth grader to have a play sister in the eighth grade, or a tenth-year student to be able to call a twelfth grader Bubba. So all was endured in a spirit of shared understanding. But the graduating classes themselves were the nobility. Like travelers with exotic destinations on their minds, the graduates were remarkably forgetful. They came to school without their books, or tablets or even pencils. Volunteers fell over themselves to secure replacements for the missing equipment. When accepted, the willing workers might or might not be thanked, and it was of no importance to the pregraduation rites. Even teachers were respectful of the now quiet and aging seniors, and tended to speak to them, if not as equals, as beings only slightly lower than themselves. After tests were returned and grades given, the student body, which acted like an extended family, knew who did well, who excelled, and what piteous ones had failed.

Unlike the white high school, Lafayette County Training School distinguished itself by having neither lawn, nor hedges, nor tennis court, nor climbing ivy. Its two buildings (main classrooms, the grade school and home economics) were set on a dirt hill with no fence to limit either its boundaries or those of bordering farms. There was a large expanse to the left of the school which was used alternately as a baseball diamond or a basketball court. Rusty hoops on the swaying poles represented the permanent recreational equipment, although bats and balls could be borrowed from the P.E. teacher if the borrower was qualified and if the diamond wasn't occupied.

*Editors' title

Over this rocky area relieved by a few shady tall persimmon trees the graduating class walked. The girls often held hands and no longer bothered to speak to
the lower students. There was a sadness about them, as if this old world was not
their home and they were bound for higher ground. The boys, on the other
hand, had become more friendly, more outgoing. A decided change from the
closed attitude they projected while studying for finals. Now they seemed not
ready to give up the old school, the familiar paths and classrooms. Only a small
percentage would be continuing on to college—one of the South's A & M (agricultural and mechanical) schools, which trained Negro youths to be carpenters,
farmers, handymen, masons, maids, cooks and baby nurses. Their future rode
heavily on their shoulders, and blinded them to the collective joy that had per-
vaded the lives of the boys and girls in the grammar school graduating class.

Parents who could afford it had ordered new shoes and ready-made clothes
for themselves from Sears and Roebuck or Montgomery Ward. They also engaged the best seamstresses to make the floating graduating dresses and to cut
down secondhand pants which would be pressed to a military slickness for the
important event.

5 Oh, it was important, all right. Whitefolks would attend the ceremony, and
two or three would speak of God and home, and the Southern way of life, and
Mrs. Parsons, the principal's wife, would play the graduation march while the
lower-grade graduates paraded down the aisles and took their seats below the
platform. The high school seniors would wait in empty classrooms to make their
dramatic entrance.

In the Store I was the person of the moment. The birthday girl. The center.
Bailey had graduated the year before, although to do so he had had to forfeit all
pleasures to make up for his time lost in Baton Rouge.

My class was wearing butter-yellow piqué dresses, and Momma launched
out on mine. She smocked the yoke into tiny crisscrossing puckers, then shirred
the rest of the bodice. Her dark fingers ducked in and out of the lemony cloth as
she embroidered raised daisies around the hem. Before she considered herself
finished she had added a crocheted cuff on the puff sleeves, and a pointy crocheted collar.

I was going to be lovely. A walking model of all the various styles of fine
hand sewing and it didn't worry me that I was only twelve years old and merely
graduating from the eighth grade. Besides, many teachers in Arkansas Negro
schools had only that diploma and were licensed to impart wisdom.

The days had become longer and more noticeable. The faded beige of former times had been replaced with strong and sure colors. I began to see my
classmates' clothes, their skin tones, and the dust that waved off pussy willows.
Clouds that lazed across the sky were objects of great concern to me. Their
shiftier shapes might have held a message that in my new happiness and with a
little bit of time I'd soon decipher. During that period I looked at the arch of
heaven so religiously my neck kept a steady ache. I had taken to smiling more
often, and my jaws hurt from the unaccustomed activity. Between the two physical sore spots, I suppose I could have been uncomfortable, but that was not the
case. As a member of the winning team (the graduating class of 1940) I had out-
distanced unpleasant sensations by miles. I was headed for the freedom of open
fields.

10 Youth and social approval allied themselves with me and we trammeled
memories of slights and insults. The wind of our swift passage remodeled my fea-

tures. Lost tears were pounded to mud and then to dust. Years of withdrawal were brushed aside and left behind, as hanging ropes of parasitic moss.

My work alone had awarded me a top place and I was going to be one of the first called in the graduating ceremonies. On the classroom blackboard, as well as on the bulletin board in the auditorium, there were blue stars and white stars and red stars. No absences, no tardinesses, and my academic work was among the best of the year. I could say the preamble to the Constitution even faster than Bailey. We timed ourselves often: "WethepeopleoftheUnited- Statesinordertoform- amoreperfect union . . ." I had memorized the Presidents of the United States from Washington to Roosevelt in chronological as well as alphabetical order.

My hair pleased me too. Gradually the black mass had lengthened and thickened, so that it kept at last to its braided pattern, and I didn't have to yank my scalp off when I tried to comb it.

Louise and I had rehearsed the exercises until we tired out ourselves. Henry Reed was class valedictorian. He was a small, very black boy with hooded eyes, a long, broad nose and an oddly shaped head. I had admired him for years because each term he and I vied for the best grades in our class. Most often he bested me, but instead of being disappointed I was pleased that we shared top places between us. Like many Southern Black children, he lived with his grandmother, who was as strict as Momma and as kind as she knew how to be. He was courteous, respectful and soft-spoken to elders, but on the playground he chose to play the roughest games. I admired him. Anyone, I reckoned, sufficiently afraid or sufficiently dull could be polite. But to be able to operate at a top level with both adults and children was admirable.

His valedictory speech was entitled "To Be or Not to Be." The rigid tenth-grade teacher had helped him to write it. He'd been working on the dramatic stresses for months.

15 The weeks until graduation were filled with heady activities. A group of small children were to be presented in a play about buttercups and daisies and bunny rabbits. They could be heard throughout the building practicing their hops and their little songs that sounded like silver bells. The older girls (non-graduates, of course) were assigned the task of making refreshments for the night's festivities. A tangy scent of ginger, cinnamon, nutmeg and chocolate wafted around the home economics building as the budding cooks made samples for themselves and their teachers.

In every corner of the workshop, axes and saws split fresh timber as the woodshop boys made sets and stage scenery. Only the graduates were left out of the general bustle. We were free to sit in the library at the back of the building or look in quite detachedly, naturally, on the measures being taken for our event.

Even the minister preached on graduation the Sunday before. His subject was, "Let your light so shine that men will see your good works and praise your Father, Who is in Heaven." Although the sermon was purported to be addressed to us, he used the occasion to speak to backsliders, gamblers, and general ne'er-do-wells. But since he had called our names at the beginning of the service we were mollified.

Among Negroes the tradition was to give presents to children going only from one grade to another. How much more important this was when the person was graduating at the top of the class. Uncle Willie and Momma had sent away for a Mickey Mouse watch like Bailey's. Louise gave me four embroidered handkerchiefs. (I gave her three crocheted doilies.) Mrs. Sneed, the minister's wife, made me an underskirt to wear for graduation, and nearly every customer gave me a nickel or maybe even a dime with the instruction "Keep on moving to higher ground," or some such encouragement.

Amazingly the great day finally dawned and I was out of bed before I knew it. I threw open the back door to see it more clearly, but Momma said, "Sister, come away from that door and put your robe on."

20   I hoped the memory of that morning would never leave me. Sunlight was itself still young, and the day had none of the insistence maturity would bring it in a few hours. In my robe and barefoot in the backyard, under cover of going to see about my new beans, I gave myself up to the gentle warmth and thanked God that no matter what evil I had done in my life He had allowed me to live to see this day. Somewhere in my fatalism I had expected to die, accidentally, and never have the chance to walk up the stairs in the auditorium and gracefully receive my hard-earned diploma. Out of God's merciful bosom I had won reprieve.

Bailey came out in his robe and gave me a box wrapped in Christmas paper. He said he had saved his money for months to pay for it. It felt like a box of chocolates, but I knew Bailey wouldn't save money to buy candy when we had all we could want under our noses.

He was as proud of the gift as I. It was a soft-leather-bound copy of a collection of poems by Edgar Allan Poe, or, as Bailey and I called him, "Eap." I turned to "Annabel Lee" and we walked up and down the garden rows, the cool dirt between our toes, reciting the beautifully sad lines.

Momma made a Sunday breakfast although it was only Friday. After we finished the blessing, I opened my eyes to find the watch on my plate. It was a dream of a day. Everything went smoothly and to my credit. I didn't have to be reminded or scolded for anything. Near evening I was too jittery to attend to chores, so Bailey volunteered to do all before his bath.

Days before, we had made a sign for the Store and as we turned out the lights Momma hung the cardboard over the doorknob. It read clearly: CLOSED. GRADUATION.

25   My dress fitted perfectly and everyone said that I looked like a sunbeam in it. On the hill, going toward the school, Bailey walked behind with Uncle Willie, who muttered, "Go on, Ju." He wanted him to walk ahead with us because it embarrassed him to have to walk so slowly. Bailey said he'd let the ladies walk together, and the men would bring up the rear. We all laughed, nicely.

Little children dashed by out of the dark like fireflies. Their crepe-paper dresses and butterfly wings were not made for running and we heard more than one rip, dryly, and the regretful "uh uh" that followed.

The school blazed without gaiety. The windows seemed cold and unfriendly from the lower hill. A sense of ill-fated timing crept over me, and if Momma hadn't reached for my hand I would have drifted back to Bailey and Uncle Willie, and possibly beyond. She made a few slow jokes about my feet getting cold, and tugged me along to the now-strange building.

Around the front steps, assurance came back. There were my fellow "greats," the graduating class. Hair brushed back, legs oiled, new dresses and pressed pleats, fresh pocket handkerchiefs and little handbags, all homesewn. Oh, we were up to snuff, all right. I joined my comrades and didn't even see my family go in to find seats in the crowded auditorium.

The school band struck up a march and all classes filed in as had been rehearsed. We stood in front of our seats, as assigned, and on a signal from the choir director, we sat. No sooner had this been accomplished than the band started to play the national anthem. We rose again and sang the song, after which we recited the pledge of allegiance. We remained standing for a brief minute before the choir director and the principal signaled to us, rather desperately I thought, to take our seats. The command was so unusual that our carefully rehearsed and smooth-running machine was thrown off. For a full minute we fumbled for our chairs and bumped into each other awkwardly. Habits change or solidify under pressure, so in our state of nervous tension we had been ready to follow our usual assembly pattern: the American National Anthem, then the pledge of allegiance, then the song every Black person I knew called the Negro National Anthem. All done in the same key, with the same passion and most often standing on the same foot.

30   Finding my seat at last, I was overcome with a presentiment of worse things to come. Something unrehearsed, unplanned, was going to happen, and we were going to be made to look bad. I distinctly remember being explicit in the choice of pronoun. It was "we," the graduating class, the unit, that concerned me then.

The principal welcomed "parents and friends" and asked the Baptist minister to lead us in prayer. His invocation was brief and punchy, and for a second I thought we were getting back on the high road to right action. When the principal came back to the dais, however, his voice had changed. Sounds always affected me profoundly and the principal's voice was one of my favorites. During assembly it melted and lowed weakly into the audience. It had not been in my plan to listen to him, but my curiosity was piqued and I straightened up to give him my attention.

He was talking about Booker T. Washington, our "late great leader," who said we can be as close as the fingers on the hand, etc. . . . Then he said a few vague things about friendship and the friendship of kindly people to those less fortunate than themselves. With that his voice nearly faded, thin, away. Like a river diminishing to a stream and then to a trickle. But he cleared his throat and said, "Our speaker tonight, who is also our friend, came from Texarkana to deliver the commencement address, but due to the irregularity of the train schedule, he's going to, as they say, 'speak and run.'" He said that we understood and wanted the man to know that we were most grateful for the time he was able to give us and then something about how we were willing always to adjust to another's program, and without more ado—"I give you Mr. Edward Donleavy."

Not one but two white men came through the door offstage. The shorter one walked to the speaker's platform, and the tall one moved over to the center seat and sat down. But that was our principal's seat, and already occupied. The dislodged gentleman bounced around for a long breath or two before the Baptist minister gave him his chair, then with more dignity than the situation deserved, the minister walked off the stage.

Donleavy looked at the audience once (on reflection, I'm sure that he wanted only to reassure himself that we were really there), adjusted his glasses and began to read from a sheaf of papers.

35   He was glad "to be here and to see the work going on just as it was in the other schools."

At the first "Amen" from the audience I willed the offender to immediate death by choking on the word. But Amen's and Yes, sir's began to fall around the room like rain through a ragged umbrella.

He told us of the wonderful changes we children in Stamps had in store. The Central School (naturally, the white school was Central) had already been granted improvements that would be in use in the fall. A well-known artist was coming from Little Rock to teach art to them. They were going to have the newest microscopes and chemistry equipment for their laboratory. Mr. Donleavy didn't leave us long in the dark over who made these improvements available to Central High. Nor were we to be ignored in the general betterment scheme he had in mind.

He said that he had pointed out to people at a very high level that one of the first-line football tacklers at Arkansas Agricultural and Mechanical College had graduated from good old Lafayette County Training School. Here fewer Amen's were heard. Those few that did break through lay dully in the air with the heaviness of habit.

He went on to praise us. He went on to say how he had bragged that "one of the best basketball players at Fisk sank his first ball right here at Lafayette County Training School."

40   The white kids were going to have a chance to become Galileos and Madame Curies and Edisons and Gauguins, and our boys (the girls weren't even in on it) would try to be Jesse Owenses and Joe Louises.

Owens and the Brown Bomber were great heroes in our world, but what school official in the white-goddom of Little Rock had the right to decide that those two men must be our only heroes? Who decided that for Henry Reed to become a scientist he had to work like George Washington Carver, as a bootblack, to buy a lousy microscope? Bailey was obviously always going to be too small to be an athlete, so which concrete angel glued to what country seat had decided that if my brother wanted to become a lawyer he had to first pay penance for his skin by picking cotton and hoeing corn and studying correspondence books at night for twenty years?

The man's dead words fell like bricks around the auditorium and too many settled in my belly. Constrained by hard-learned manners I couldn't look behind me, but to my left and right the proud graduating class of 1940 had dropped their heads. Every girl in my row had found something new to do with her handkerchief. Some folded the tiny squares into love knots, some into triangles, but most were wadding them, then pressing them flat on their yellow laps.

On the dais, the ancient tragedy was being replayed. Professor Parsons sat, a sculptor's reject, rigid. His large, heavy body seemed devoid of will or willingness, and his eyes said he was no longer with us. The other teachers examined the flag (which was draped stage right) or their notes, or the windows which opened on our now-famous playing diamond.

Graduation, the hush-hush magic time of frills and gifts and congratulations and diplomas, was finished for me before my name was called. The accomplishment was nothing. The meticulous maps, drawn in three colors of ink, learning and spelling decasyllabic words, memorizing the whole of *The Rape of Lucrece*—it was nothing. Donleavy had exposed us.

45   We were maids and farmers, handymen and washerwomen, and anything higher that we aspired to was farcical and presumptuous. Then I wished that Gabriel Prosser and Nat Turner had killed all whitefolks in their beds and that Abraham Lincoln had been assassinated before the signing of the Emancipation Proclamation, and that Harriet Tubman had been killed by that blow on her head and Christopher Columbus had drowned in the *Santa Maria*.

It was awful to be Negro and have no control over my life. It was brutal to be young and already trained to sit quietly and listen to charges brought against my color and no chance of defense. We should all be dead. I thought I should like to see us all dead, one on top of the other. A pyramid of flesh with the white-folks on the bottom, as the broad base, then the Indians with their silly toma-hawks and teepees and wigwams and treaties, the Negroes with their mops and recipes and cotton sacks and spirituals sticking out of their mouths. The Dutch children should all stumble in their wooden shoes and break their necks. The French should choke to death on the Louisiana Purchase (1803) while silkworms ate all the Chinese with their stupid pigtails. As a species, we were an abomina-tion. All of us.

Donleavy was running for election, and assured our parents that if he won we could count on having the only colored paved playing field in that part of Arkansas. Also—he never looked up to acknowledge the grunts of acceptance—also, we were bound to get some new equipment for the home economics build-ing and the workshop.

He finished, and since there was no need to give any more than the most perfunctory thank-you's, he nodded to the men on the stage, and the tall white man who was never introduced joined him at the door. They left with the atti-tude that now they were off to something really important. (The graduation cer-emonies at Lafayette County Training School had been a mere preliminary.)

The ugliness they left was palpable. An uninvited guest who wouldn't leave. The choir was summoned and sang a modern arrangement of "Onward, Christ-ian Soldiers," with new words pertaining to graduates seeking their place in the world. But it didn't work. Elouise, the daughter of the Baptist minister, recited "Invictus," and I could have cried at the impertinence of "I am the master of my fate, I am the captain of my soul."

50   My name had lost its ring of familiarity and I had to be nudged to go and re-ceive my diploma. All my preparations had fled. I neither marched up to the stage like a conquering Amazon, nor did I look in the audience for Bailey's nod of approval. Marguerite Johnson, I heard the name again, my honors were read, there were noises in the audience of appreciation, and I took my place on the stage as rehearsed.

I thought about colors I hated: ecru, puce, lavender, beige and black.

There was shuffling and rustling around me, then Henry Reed was giving his valedictory address, "To Be or Not to Be." Hadn't he heard the whitefolks? We couldn't *be,* so the question was a waste of time. Henry's voice came out clear and strong. I feared to look at him. Hadn't he got the message? There was no "no-bler in the mind" for Negroes because the world didn't think we had minds, and they let us know it. "Outrageous fortune"? Now, that was a joke. When the cere-mony was over I had to tell Henry Reed some things. That is, if I still cared. Not "rub," Henry, "erase." "Ah, there's the erase." Us.

Henry had been a good student in elocution. His voice rose on tides of promise and fell on waves of warnings. The English teacher had helped him to create a sermon winging through Hamlet's soliloquy. To be a man, a doer, a builder, a leader, or to be a tool, an unfunny joke, a crusher of funky toadstools. I marveled that Henry could go through with the speech as if we had a choice.

I had been listening and silently rebutting each sentence with my eyes closed; then there was a hush, which in an audience warns that something un-planned is happening. I looked up and saw Henry Reed, the conservative, the proper, the A student, turn his back to the audience and turn to us (the proud graduating class of 1940) and sing, nearly speaking,

Lift ev'ry voice and sing
Till earth and heaven ring
Ring with the harmonies of Liberty ...

It was the poem written by James Weldon Johnson. It was the music composed by J. Rosamond Johnson. It was the Negro National Anthem. Out of habit we were singing it.

55 Our mothers and fathers stood in the dark hall and joined the hymn of encouragement. A kindergarten teacher led the small children onto the stage and the buttercups and daisies and bunny rabbits marked time and tried to follow:

Stony the road we trod
Bitter the chastening rod
Felt in the days when hope, unborn, had died.
Yet with a steady beat
Have not our weary feet
Come to the place for which our fathers sighed?

Every child I knew had learned that song with his ABC's and along with "Jesus Loves Me This I Know." But I personally had never heard it before. Never heard the words, despite the thousands of times I had sung them. Never thought they had anything to do with me.

On the other hand, the words of Patrick Henry had made such an impression on me that I had been able to stretch myself tall and trembling and say, "I know not what course others may take, but as for me, give me liberty or give me death."

And now I heard, really for the first time:

We have come over a way that with tears has been watered,
We have come, treading our path through the blood of the slaughtered.

While echoes of the song shivered in the air, Henry Reed bowed his head, said "Thank you," and returned to his place in the line. The tears that slipped down many faces were not wiped away in shame.

60 We were on top again. As always, again. We survived. The depths had been icy and dark, but now a bright sun spoke to our souls. I was no longer simply a member of the proud graduating class of 1940; I was a proud member of the wonderful, beautiful Negro race.

Oh, Black known and unknown poets, how often have your auctioned pains sustained us? Who will compute the lonely nights made less lonely by your songs, or the empty pots made less tragic by your tales?

If we were a people much given to revealing secrets, we might raise monuments and sacrifice to the memories of our poets, but slavery cured us of that weakness. It may be enough, however, to have it said that we survive in exact relationship to the dedication of our poets (include preachers, musicians and blues singers).

 Topics for Critical Thinking and Writing

1. In paragraph 1 notice such overstatements as "glorious release," "the graduating classes themselves were the nobility," and "exotic destinations." Find further examples in the next few pages. What do you think is the function of this diction?

2. Characterize the writer as you perceive her through paragraph 28. Support your characterization with references to specific passages. Next, characterize her in paragraph 46, which begins "It was awful to be Negro." Next, characterize her on the basis of the entire essay. Finally, in a sentence, try to describe the change, telling the main attitudes or moods that she goes through.

3. How would you define "poets" as Angelou uses the word in the last sentence?

 **MARGARET ATWOOD**

Margaret Atwood, born in 1939 in Ottawa, Ontario, Canada, did her undergraduate work at Victoria College and graduate work at Radcliffe College. She has worked as a cashier, waitress, film writer, and teacher, but she began writing as a child and established herself as a writer before she was thirty. In addition to writing films, stories, novels, poetry, and criticism, she has edited anthologies of Canadian literature.

The essay that we reprint comes from the second volume of a collection entitled The Writer on Her Work, *edited by Janet Sternberg, in which writers give their responses to questions about writing.*

Nine Beginnings

1. *Why do you write?*

I've begun this piece nine times. I've junked each beginning.

I hate writing about my writing. I almost never do it. Why am I doing it now? Because I said I would. I got a letter. I wrote back *no.* Then I was at a party and the same person was there. It's harder to refuse in person. Saying *yes* had something to do with being nice, as women are taught to be, and something to do with being helpful, which we are also taught. Being helpful to women, giving a pint of blood. With not claiming the sacred prerogatives, the touch-me-not self-protectiveness of the artist, with not being selfish. With conciliation, with doing your bit, with appeasement. I was well brought up. I have trouble ignoring social obligations. Saying you'll write about your writing is a social obligation. It's not an obligation to the writing.

2. *Why do you write?*

I've junked each of nine beginnings. They seemed beside the point. Too assertive, too pedagogical, too frivolous or belligerent, too falsely wise. As if I had some special self-revelation that would encourage others, or some special knowledge to impart, some pithy saying that would act like a talisman for the driven, the obsessed. But I have no such talismans. If I did, I would not continue, myself, to be so driven and obsessed.

3. *Why do you write?*

I hate writing about my writing because I have nothing to say about it. I have nothing to say about it because I can't remember what goes on when I'm doing it. That time is like small pieces cut out of my brain. It's not time I myself have lived. I can remember the details of the rooms and places where I've written, the circumstances, the other things I did before and after, but not the process itself. Writing about writing requires self-consciousness; writing itself requires the abdication of it.

4. *Why do you write?*

There are a lot of things that can be said about what goes on around the edges of writing. Certain ideas you may have, certain motivations, grand designs that don't get carried out. I can talk about bad reviews, about sexist reactions to my writing, about making an idiot of myself on television shows. I can talk about books that failed, that never got finished, and about why they failed. The one that had too many characters, the one that had too many layers of time, red herrings that diverted me when what I really wanted to get at was something else, a certain corner of the visual world, a certain voice, an inarticulate landscape.

I can talk about the difficulties that women encounter as writers. For instance, if you're a woman writer, sometime, somewhere, you will be asked: *Do you think of yourself as a writer first, or as a woman first?* Look out. Whoever asks this hates and fears both writing and women.

Many of us, in my generation at least, ran into teachers or male writers or other defensive jerks who told us women could not really write because they couldn't be truck drivers or Marines and therefore didn't understand the seamier side of life, which included sex with women. We were told we wrote like housewives, or else we were treated like honorary men, as if to be a good writer was to suppress the female.

Such pronouncements used to be made as if they were the simple truth. Now they're questioned. Some things have changed for the better, but not all. There's a lack of self-confidence that gets instilled very early in many young girls, before writing is even seen as a possibility. You need a certain amount of nerve to be a writer, an almost physical nerve, the kind you need to walk a log across a river. The horse throws you and you get back on the horse. I learned to swim by being dropped into the water. You need to know you can sink, and survive it. Girls should be allowed to play in the mud. They should be released from the obligations of perfection. Some of your writing, at least, should be as evanescent as play.

A ratio of failures is built into the process of writing. The wastebasket has evolved for a reason. Think of it as the altar of the Muse Oblivion, to whom you sacrifice your botched first drafts, the tokens of your human imperfection. She is the tenth Muse, the one without whom none of the others can function. The gift she offers you is the freedom of the second chance. Or as many chances as you'll take.

5. *Why do you write?*

In the mid-eighties I began a sporadic journal. Today I went back through it, looking for something I could dig out and fob off as pertinent, instead of writing this piece about writing. but it was useless. There was nothing in it about the actual composition of anything I've written over the past six years. Instead there are exhortations to myself—to get up earlier, to walk more, to resist lures and distractions. *Drink more water,* I find. *Go to bed earlier.* There were lists of how many pages I'd written per day, how many I'd retyped, how many yet to go. Other than that, there was nothing but descriptions of rooms, accounts of what we'd cooked and/or eaten and with whom, letters written and received, notable sayings of children, birds and animals seen, the weather. What came up in the garden. Illnesses, my own and those of others. Deaths, births. Nothing about writing.

January 1, 1984. Blakeny, England. As of today, I have about 130 pp. of the novel done and it's just beginning to take shape & reach the point at which I feel that it exists and can be finished and may be worth it. I work in the bedroom of the big house, and here, in the sitting room, with the wood fire in the fireplace and the coke fire in the dilapidated Roeburn in the kitchen. As usual I'm too cold, which is better than being too hot—today is grey, warm for the time of year, damp. If I got up earlier maybe I would work more, but I might just spend more time procrastinating—as now.

And so on.

6. *Why do you write?*

You learn to write by reading and writing, writing and reading. As a craft it's acquired through the apprentice system, but you choose your own teachers. Sometimes they're alive, sometimes dead.

As a vocation, it involves the laying on of hands. You receive your vocation and in your turn you must pass it on. Perhaps you will do this only through your work, perhaps in other ways. Either way, you're part of a community, the community of writers, the community of storytellers that stretches back through time to the beginning of human society.

As for the particular human society to which you yourself belong—sometimes you'll feel you're speaking for it, sometimes—when it's taken an unjust form—against it, or for that other community, the community of the oppressed, the exploited, the voiceless. Either way, the pressures on you will be intense; in other countries, perhaps fatal. But even here—speak "for women," or for any other group which is feeling the boot, and there will be many at hand, both for and against, to tell you to shut up, or to say what they want you to say, or to say it a different way. Or to save them. The billboard awaits you, but if you succumb to its temptations you'll end up two-dimensional.

Tell what is yours to tell. Let others tell what is theirs.

7. *Why do you write?*

Why are we so addicted to causality? *Why do you write?* (Treatise by child psychologist, mapping your formative traumas. Conversely: palm-reading, astrology and genetic studies, pointing to the stars, fate, heredity.) *Why do you write?* (That is, why not do something useful instead?) If you were a doctor, you could tell some acceptable moral tale about how you put Band-Aids on your cats as a child, how you've always longed to cure suffering. No one can argue with that. But writing? What is it *for?*

Some possible answers: *Why does the sun shine? In the face of the absurdity of modern society, why do anything else? Because I'm a writer. Because I want to discover the patterns in the chaos of time. Because I must. Because someone has to bear witness. Why do you read?* (This last is tricky: maybe they don't.) *Because I wish to forge in the smithy of my soul the uncreated conscience of my race. Because I wish to make an axe to break the frozen sea within.*[1] (These have been used, but they're good.)

If at a loss, perfect the shrug. Or say: *It's better than working in a bank.* Or say: *For fun.* If you say this, you won't be believed, or else you'll be dismissed as trivial. Either way, you'll have avoided the question.

8. *Why do you write?*

---

[1]The passage about the smithy is from the end of James Joyce's novel, *A Portrait of the Artist as a Young Man* (1916). The next sentence, about an axe to break the frozen sea within us, is from a letter (1904) by Franz Kafka. Each passage is offered by the author as an explanation of why he writes. (Editors' note)

Not long ago, in the course of clearing some of the excess paper out of my workroom, I opened a filing cabinet drawer I hadn't looked into for years. In it was a bundle of loose sheets, folded, creased, and grubby, tied up with leftover string. It consisted of things I'd written in the late fifties, in high school and the early years of university. There were scrawled, inky poems, about snow, despair, and the Hungarian Revolution. There were short stories dealing with girls who'd had to get married, and dispirited, mousy-haired high-school English teachers— to end up as either was at that time my vision of Hell—typed finger-by-finger on an ancient machine that made all the letters half-red.

There I am, then, back in grade twelve, going through the writers' magazines after I'd finished my French Composition homework, typing out my lugubrious poems and my grit-filled stories. (I was big on grit. I had an eye for lawn-litter and dog turds on sidewalks. In these stories it was usually snowing damply, or raining; at the very least there was slush. If it was summer, the heat and humidity were always wiltingly high and my characters had sweat marks under their arms; if it was spring, wet clay stuck to their feet. Though some would say all this was just normal Toronto weather.)

In the top right-hand corners of some of these, my hopeful seventeen-year-old self had typed, "First North American Rights Only." I was not sure what "First North American Rights" were; I put it in because the writing magazines said you should. I was at that time an aficionado of writing magazines, having no one else to turn to for professional advice.

If I were an archeologist, digging through the layers of old paper that mark the eras in my life as a writer, I'd have found, at the lowest or Stone Age level— say around ages five to seven—a few poems and stories, unremarkable precursors of all my frenetic later scribbling. (Many children write at that age, just as many children draw. The strange thing is that so few of them go on to become writers or painters.) After that there's a great blank. For eight years, I simply didn't write. Then, suddenly, and with no missing links in between, there's a wad of manuscripts. One week I wasn't a writer, the next I was.

Who did I think I was, to be able to get away with this? What did I think I was doing? How did I get that way? To these questions I still have no answers.

9. *Why do you write?*

There's the blank page, and the thing that obsesses you. There's the story that wants to take you over and there's your resistance to it. There's your longing to get out of this, this servitude, to play hooky, to do anything else: wash the laundry, see a movie. There are words and their inertias, their biases, their insufficiencies, their glories. There are the risks you take and your loss of nerve, and the help that comes when you're least expecting it. There's the laborious revision, the scrawled-over, crumpled-up pages that drift across the floor like spilled litter. There's the one sentence you know you will save.

Next day there's the blank page. You give yourself up to it like a sleepwalker. Something goes on that you can't remember afterwards. You look at what you've done. It's hopeless.

You begin again. It never gets any easier.

✏ Topics for Critical Thinking and Writing

1. In her first try, Atwood doesn't answer the question "Why do you write?" What question does she answer and how does she answer it?

2. The beginning of her second try, like the beginning of her first, tells us that she began nine times and "junked each of nine beginnings." But we can see that there are nine beginnings here. What is going on? Why has she not "junked" these?

3. Atwood says in her third try, "Writing about writing requires self-consciousness; writing itself requires the abdication of it." What does it mean to abdicate self-consciousness? How do you think abdicating self-consciousness affects or would affect your writing?

4. In her sixth try, Atwood says, "You learn to write by reading and writing, writing and reading." To what extent do you agree? What have you learned about writing by reading or by writing? What have you learned about writing—and writers—from reading "Nine Beginnings?"

5. Why does Atwood write?

 # BLACK ELK

Black Elk, a wichasha wakon (holy man) of the Oglala Sioux, as a small boy witnessed the Battle of Little Bighorn (1876). He lived to see his people all but annihilated and his hopes for them extinguished. In 1931, toward the end of his life, he told his life story to the poet and scholar John G. Neihardt in order to preserve a sacred vision given him. "High Horse's Courting" provides a comic interlude in a predominantly tragic memoir.

High Horse's Courting

You know, in the old days, it was not so very easy to get a girl when you wanted to be married. Sometimes it was hard work for a young man and he had to stand a great deal. Say I am a young man and I have seen a young girl who looks so beautiful to me that I feel all sick when I think about her. I can not just go and tell her about it and then get married if she is willing. I have to be a very sneaky fellow to talk to her at all, and after I have managed to talk to her, that is only the beginning.

Probably for a long time I have been feeling sick about a certain girl because I love her so much, but she will not even look at me, and her parents keep a good watch over her. But I keep feeling worse and worse all the time; so maybe I sneak up to her tepee in the dark and wait until she comes out. Maybe I just wait there all night and don't get any sleep at all and she does not come out. Then I feel sicker than ever about her.

Maybe I hide in the brush by a spring where she sometimes goes to get water, and when she comes by, if nobody is looking, then I jump out and hold her and just make her listen to me. If she likes me too, I can tell that from the way she acts, for she is very bashful and maybe will not say a word or even look at me the first time. So I let her go, and then maybe I sneak around until I can see her father alone, and I tell him how many horses I can give him for his beautiful girl, and by now I am feeling so sick that maybe I would give him all the horses in the world if I had them.

Well, this young man I am telling about was called High Horse, and there was a girl in the village who looked so beautiful to him that he was just sick all over from thinking about her so much and he was getting sicker all the time. The girl was very shy, and her parents thought a great deal of her because they were not young any more and this was the only child they had. So they watched her all day long, and they fixed it so that she would be safe at night too when they were asleep. They thought so much of her that they had made a rawhide bed for her to sleep in, and after they knew that High Horse was sneaking around after her, they took rawhide thongs and tied the girl in bed at night so that nobody could steal her when they were asleep, for they were not sure but that their girl might really want to be stolen.

5　　　Well, after High Horse had been sneaking around a good while and hiding and waiting for the girl and getting sicker all the time, he finally caught her alone and made her talk to him. Then he found out that she liked him maybe a little. Of course this did not make him feel well. It made him sicker than ever, but now he felt as brave as a bison bull, and so he went right to her father and said he loved the girl so much that he would give two good horses for her—one of them young and the other one not so very old.

But the old man just waved his hand, meaning for High Horse to go away and quit talking foolishness like that.

High Horse was feeling sicker than ever about it; but there was another young fellow who said he would loan High Horse two ponies and when he got some more horses, why, he could just give them back for the ones he had borrowed.

Then High Horse went back to the old man and said he would give four horses for the girl—two of them young and the other two not hardly old at all. But the old man just waved his hand and would not say anything.

So High Horse sneaked around until he could talk to the girl again, and he asked her to run away with him. He told her he thought he would just fall over and die if she did not. But she said she would not do that; she wanted to be bought like a fine woman. You see she thought a great deal of herself too.

10　　　That made High Horse feel so very sick that he could not eat a bite, and he went around with his head hanging down as though he might just fall down and die any time.

Red Deer was another young fellow, and he and High Horse were great comrades, always doing things together. Red Deer saw how High Horse was acting, and he said: "Cousin, what is the matter? Are you sick in the belly? You look as though you were going to die."

Then High Horse told Red Deer how it was, and said he thought he could not stay alive much longer if he could not marry the girl pretty quick.

Red Deer thought awhile about it, and then he said: "Cousin, I have a plan, and if you are man enough to do as I tell you, then everything will be all right. She will not run away with you; her old man will not take four horses; and four horses are all you can get. You must steal her and run away with her. Then afterwhile you can come back and the old man cannot do anything because she will be your woman. Probably she wants you to steal her anyway."

So they planned what High Horse had to do, and he said he loved the girl so much that he was man enough to do anything Red Deer or anybody else could think up.

15　　　So this is what they did.

That night late they sneaked up to the girl's tepee and waited until it sounded inside as though the old man and the old woman and the girl were sound asleep. Then High Horse crawled under the tepee with a knife. He had to cut the rawhide thongs first, and then Red Deer, who was pulling up the stakes around that side of the tepee, was going to help drag the girl outside and gag her.

After that, High Horse could put her across his pony in front of him and hurry out of there and be happy all the rest of his life.

When High Horse had crawled inside, he felt so nervous that he could hear his heart drumming, and it seemed so loud he felt sure it would 'waken the old folks. But it did not, and afterwhile he began cutting the thongs. Every time he cut one it made a pop and nearly scared him to death. But he was getting along all right and all the thongs were cut down as far as the girl's thighs, when he became so nervous that his knife slipped and stuck the girl. She gave a big, loud yell. Then the old folks jumped up and yelled too. By this time High Horse was outside, and he and Red Deer were running away like antelope. The old man and some other people chased the young men but they got away in the dark and nobody knew who it was.

Well, if you ever wanted a beautiful girl you will know how sick High Horse was now. It was very bad the way he felt, and it looked as though he would starve even if he did not drop over dead sometime.

Red Deer kept thinking about this, and after a few days he went to High Horse and said: "Cousin, take courage! I have another plan, and I am sure, if you are man enough, we can steal her this time." And High Horse said: "I am man enough to do anything anybody can think up, if I can only get that girl."

20   So this is what they did.

They went away from the village alone, and Red Deer made High Horse strip naked. Then he painted High Horse solid white all over, and after that he painted black stripes all over the white and put black rings around High Horse's eyes. High Horse looked terrible. He looked so terrible that when Red Deer was through painting and took a good look at what he had done, he said it scared even him a little.

"Now," Red Deer said, "if you get caught again, everybody will be so scared they will think you are a bad spirit and will be afraid to chase you."

So when the night was getting old and everybody was sound asleep, they sneaked back to the girl's tepee. High Horse crawled in with his knife, as before, and Red Deer waited outside, ready to drag the girl out and gag her when High Horse had all the thongs cut.

High Horse crept up by the girl's bed and began cutting at the thongs. But he kept thinking, "If they see me they will shoot me because I look so terrible." The girl was restless and kept squirming around in bed, and when a thong was cut, it popped. So High Horse worked very slowly and carefully.

25   But he must have made some noise, for suddenly the old woman awoke and said to her old man: "Old Man, wake up! There is somebody in this tepee!" But the old man was sleepy and didn't want to be bothered. He said: "Of course there is somebody in this tepee. Go to sleep and don't bother me." Then he snored some more.

But High Horse was so scared by now that he lay very still and as flat to the ground as he could. Now, you see, he had not been sleeping very well for a long time because he was so sick about the girl. And while he was lying there waiting for the old woman to snore, he just forgot everything, even how beautiful the girl was. Red Deer who was lying outside ready to do his part, wondered and wondered what had happened in there, but he did not dare call out to High Horse.

Afterwhile the day began to break and Red Deer had to leave with the two ponies he had staked there for his comrade and girl, or somebody would see him.

So he left.

Now when it was getting light in the tepee, the girl awoke and the first thing she saw was a terrible animal, all white with black stripes on it, lying asleep beside her bed. So she screamed, and then the old woman screamed and the old man yelled. High Horse jumped up, scared almost to death, and he nearly knocked the tepee down getting out of there.

30   People were coming running from all over the village with guns and bows and axes, and everybody was yelling.

By now High Horse was running so fast that he hardly touched the ground at all, and he looked so terrible that the people fled from him and let him run. Some braves wanted to shoot at him, but the others said he might be some sacred being and it would bring bad trouble to kill him.

High Horse made for the river that was near, and in among the brush he found a hollow tree and dived into it. Afterwhile some braves came there and he could hear them saying that it was some bad spirit that had come out of the water and gone back in again.

That morning the people were ordered to break camp and move away from there. So they did, while High Horse was hiding in his hollow tree.

Now Red Deer had been watching all this from his own tepee and trying to look as though he were as much surprised and scared as all the others. So when the camp moved, he sneaked back to where he had seen his comrade disappear. When he was down there in the brush, he called, and High Horse answered, because he knew his friend's voice. They washed off the paint from High Horse and sat down on the river bank to talk about their troubles.

35   High Horse said he never would go back to the village as long as he lived and he did not care what happened to him now. He said he was going to go on the war-path all by himself. Red Deer said: "No, cousin, you are not going on the war-path alone, because I am going with you."

So Red Deer got everything ready, and at night they started out on the war-path all alone. After several days they came to a Crow camp just about sundown, and when it was dark they sneaked up to where the Crow horses were grazing, killed the horse guard, who was not thinking about enemies because he thought all the Lakotas were far away, and drove off about a hundred horses.

They got a big start because all the Crow horses stampeded and it was probably morning before the Crow warriors could catch any horses to ride. Red Deer and High Horse fled with their herd three days and nights before they reached the village of their people. Then they drove the whole herd right into the village and up in front of the girl's tepee. The old man was there, and High Horse called out to him and asked if he thought maybe that would be enough horses for his girl. The old man did not wave him away this time. It was not the horses that he wanted. What he wanted was a son who was a real man and good for something.

So High Horse got his girl after all, and I think he deserved her.

 ## Topics for Critical Thinking and Writing

1. The story "High Horse's Courting" is told by Black Elk, an Oglala Sioux holy man. Though High Horse's behavior is amusing and at times ridiculous, how does Black Elk make it clear that he is not ridiculing the young man, but is instead sympathetic with him? Consider the following questions:

a. What is the effect of the first three paragraphs? Consider the first two sentences, and then the passage beginning "Say I am a young man . . ." and ending ". . . I would give him all the horses in the world if I had them."

b. Describe the behavior of the young girl, and of her father and mother. How do they contribute to the comedy? How does their behavior affect your understanding of Black Elk's attitude toward High Horse?

c. What is the function of Red Deer?

d. The narrative consists of several episodes. List them in the order in which they occur, and then describe the narrative's structure. How does the structure of the narrative affect the tone?

e. What is the effect of the last two sentences?

2. What similarities, if any, are there between the courting customs and attitudes toward courting that Black Elk describes and those you are familiar with? Consider the behavior and attitudes not only of High Horse, the girl, her parents, and his friend, but also of the old man who tells the story.

 **SISSELA BOK**

Sissela Bok has taught courses in philosophy at Brandeis and in medical ethics and in decision making at the Harvard Medical School. A scholar with wide-ranging interests, she is currently a Distinguished Fellow at the Harvard Center for Population and Development Studies. Her most recent book is Mayhem: Violence as Public Entertainment. *The following selection is from* Lying, *a book concerned with such problems as whether or not to lie to people for their own good.*

To Lie or Not to Lie?—The Doctor's Dilemma

Should doctors ever lie to benefit their patients—to speed recovery or to conceal the approach of death? In medicine as in law, government, and other lines of work, the requirements of honesty often seem dwarfed by greater needs: the need to shelter from brutal news or to uphold a promise of secrecy; to expose corruption or to promote the public interest.

What should doctors say, for example, to a forty-six-year-old man coming in for a routine physical checkup just before going on vacation with his family who, though he feels in perfect health, is found to have a form of cancer that will cause him to die within six months? Is it best to tell him the truth? If he asks, should the doctors deny that he is ill, or minimize the gravity of the prognosis? Should they at least conceal the truth until after the family vacation?

Doctors confront such choices often and urgently. At times, they see important reasons to lie for the patient's own sake; in their eyes, such lies differ sharply from self-serving ones.

Studies show that most doctors sincerely believe that the seriously ill do not want to know the truth about their condition, and that informing them risks destroying their hope, so that they may recover more slowly, or deteriorate faster, perhaps even commit suicide. As one physician wrote: "Ours is a profession which traditionally has been guided by a precept that transcends the virtue of uttering the truth for truth's sake, and that is 'as far as possible do no harm.'"

5   Armed with such a precept, a number of doctors may slip into deceptive practices that they assume will "do no harm" and may well help their patients. They may prescribe innumerable placebos, sound more encouraging than the facts warrant, and distort grave news, especially to the incurably ill and the dying.

But the illusory nature of the benefits such deception is meant to bestow is now coming to be documented. Studies show that, contrary to the belief of many physicians, an overwhelming majority of patients do want to be told the truth, even about grave illness, and feel betrayed when they learn that they have been misled. We are also learning that truthful information, humanely conveyed, helps patients cope with illness: helps them tolerate pain better, need less medication, and even recover faster after surgery.

Not only do lies not provide the "help" hoped for by advocates of benevolent deception; they invade the autonomy of patients and render them unable to make informed choices concerning their own health, including the choice of whether to *be* a patient in the first place. We are becoming increasingly aware of all that can befall patients in the course of their illness when information is denied or distorted.

Dying patients especially—who are easiest to mislead and most often kept in the dark—can then not make decisions about the end of life: about whether or not to enter a hospital, or to have surgery; about where and with whom to spend their remaining time; about how to bring their affairs to a close and take leave.

Lies also do harm to those who tell them: harm to their integrity and, in the long run, to their credibility. Lies hurt their colleagues as well. The suspicion of deceit undercuts the work of the many doctors who are scrupulously honest with their patients; it contributes to the spiral of litigation and of "defensive medicine," and thus it injures, in turn, the entire medical profession.

10   Sharp conflicts are now arising. Patients are learning to press for answers. Patients' bills of rights require that they be informed about their condition and about alternatives for treatment. Many doctors go to great lengths to provide such information. Yet even in hospitals with the most eloquent bill of rights, believers in benevolent deception continue their age-old practices. Colleagues may disapprove but refrain from remonstrating. Nurses may bitterly resent having to take part, day after day, in deceiving patients, but feel powerless to take a stand.

There is urgent need to debate this issue openly. Not only in medicine, but in other professions as well, practitioners may find themselves repeatedly in straits where serious consequences seem avoidable only through deception. Yet the public has every reason to be wary of professional deception, for such practices are peculiarly likely to become ingrained, to spread, and to erode trust. Neither in medicine, nor in law, government, or the social sciences can there be comfort in the old saw, "What you don't know can't hurt you."

✎ Topics for Critical Thinking and Writing

1. Is there anything in Bok's opening paragraph that prepares the reader for Bok's own position on whether or not lying is ever justifiable?
2. List the reasons Bok offers on behalf of telling the truth to patients. Are some of these reasons presented more convincingly than others? If any are unconvincing, rewrite them to make them more convincing.

3. Suppose Bok's last sentence was revised to read thus: "In medicine, law, government, and the social sciences, what you don't know *can* hurt you." Which version do you prefer, and why?
4. "What you don't know can't hurt you." Weigh the truth of this assertion in your own life. Were there instances of a truth being withheld from you that did hurt you? Were there occasions when you were told a truth that you now judge would have been better withheld? On the whole, do you come out in favor of the assertion, against it, or somewhere in between?
5. How much should adopted children be told about their biological parents? Consider reasons both for and against telling all. Use not only your own experiences and opinions but those of others, such as friends and classmates.

 **DEBRA DICKERSON**

A former officer in the U. S. Air Force and a graduate of Harvard Law School, Debra Dickerson has published articles in The Nation, Good Housekeeping, Washington Post Book World, *and other periodicals. "Who Shot Johnny?" originally appeared in* The New Republic; *it was reprinted in* The Best American Essays 1997.

Who Shot Johnny?

Given my level of political awareness, it was inevitable that I would come to view the everyday events of my life through the prism of politics and the national discourse. I read *The Washington Post, The New Republic, The New Yorker, Harper's, The Atlantic Monthly, The Nation, National Review, Black Enterprise,* and *Essence* and wrote a weekly column for the Harvard Law School *Record* during my three years just ended there. I do this because I know that those of us who are not well-fed white guys in suits must not yield the debate to them, however well-intentioned or well-informed they may be. Accordingly, I am unrepentant and vocal about having gained admittance to Harvard through affirmative action; I am a feminist, stoic about my marriage chances as a well-educated, thirty-six-year-old black woman who won't pretend to need help taking care of herself. My strength flags, though, in the face of the latest role assigned to my family in the national drama. On July 27, 1995, my sixteen-year-old nephew was shot and paralyzed.

Talking with friends in front of his house, Johnny saw a car he thought he recognized. He waved boisterously—his trademark—throwing both arms in the air in a full-bodied, hip-hop Y. When he got no response, he and his friends sauntered down the walk to join a group loitering in front of an apartment building. The car followed. The driver got out, brandished a revolver, and fired into the air. Everyone scattered. Then he took aim and shot my running nephew in the back.

Johnny never lost consciousness. He lay in the road, trying to understand what had happened to him, why he couldn't get up. Emotionlessly, he told the story again and again on demand, remaining apologetically firm against all demands to divulge the missing details that would make sense of the shooting but obviously cast him in a bad light. Being black, male, and shot, he must apparently

be involved with gangs or drugs. Probably both. Witnesses corroborate his version of events.

Nearly six months have passed since that phone call in the night and my
nightmarish headlong drive from Boston to Charlotte. After twenty hours behind
the wheel, I arrived haggard enough to reduce my mother to fresh tears and to
find my nephew reassuring well-wishers with an eerie sang-froid.

5   I take the day shift in his hospital room; his mother and grandmother, a clerk
and cafeteria worker, respectively, alternate nights there on a cot. They don
their uniforms the next day, gaunt after hours spent listening to Johnny moan in
his sleep. How often must his subconscious replay those events and curse its
host for saying hello without permission, for being carefree and young while a
would-be murderer hefted the weight of his uselessness and failure like Jacob
Marley's chains? How often must he watch himself lying stubbornly immobile on
the pavement of his nightmares while the sound of running feet syncopate his attacker's taunts?

I spend these days beating him at gin rummy and Scrabble, holding a basin
while he coughs up phlegm and crying in the corridor while he catheterizes himself. There are children here much worse off than he. I should be grateful. The
doctors can't, or won't, say whether he'll walk again.

I am at once repulsed and fascinated by the bullet, which remains lodged in
his spine (having done all the damage it can do, the doctors say). The wound is
undramatic—small, neat, and perfectly centered—an impossibly pink pit surrounded by an otherwise undisturbed expanse of mahogany. Johnny has asked
me several times to describe it but politely declines to look in the mirror I hold
for him.

Here on the pediatric rehab ward, Johnny speaks little, never cries, never
complains, works diligently to become independent. He does whatever he is
told; if two hours remain until the next pain pill, he waits quietly. Eyes blood-
shot, hands gripping the bed rails. During the week of his intravenous feeding,
when he was tormented by the primal need to masticate, he never asked for
food. He just listened while we counted down the days for him and planned his
favorite meals. Now required to dress himself unassisted, he does so without
demur, rolling himself back and forth valiantly on the bed and shivering afterward, exhausted. He "ma'am"s and "sir"s everyone politely. Before his "accident," a simple request to take out the trash could provoke a firestorm of
teenage attitude. We, the women who have raised him, have changed as well;
we've finally come to appreciate those boxer-baring, over-sized pants we used to
hate—it would be much more difficult to fit properly sized pants over his diaper.

He spends a lot of time tethered to rap music still loud enough to break my
concentration as I read my many magazines. I hear him try to soundlessly mouth
the obligatory "mothafuckers" over-laying the funereal dirge of the music tracks.
I do not normally tolerate disrespectful music in my or my mother's presence,
but if it distracts him now . . .

10   "Johnny," I ask later, "do you still like gangster rap?" During the long pause
I hear him think loudly, I'm paralyzed, Auntie, not stupid. "I mostly just listen to
hip-hop," he says evasively into his *Sports Illustrated.*

Miserable though it is, time passes quickly here. We always seem to be jerking
awake in our chairs just in time for the next pill, his every-other-night bowel program, the doctor's rounds. Harvard feels a galaxy away—the world revolves

around Family Members Living with Spinal Cord Injury class, Johnny's urine output, and strategizing with my sister to find affordable, accessible housing. There is always another long-distance uncle in need of an update, another church member wanting to pray with us, or Johnny's little brother in need of some attention.

We Dickerson women are so constant a presence the ward nurses and cleaning staff call us by name and join us for cafeteria meals and cigarette breaks. At Johnny's birthday pizza party, they crack jokes and make fun of each other's husbands (there are no men here). I pass slices around and try not to think, Seventeen with a bullet.

Oddly, we feel little curiosity or specific anger toward the man who shot him. We have to remind ourselves to check in with the police. Even so, it feels pro forma, like sending in those $2 rebate forms that come with new pantyhose: you know your request will fall into a deep, dark hole somewhere, but still, it's your duty to try. We push for an arrest because we owe it to Johnny and to ourselves as citizens. We don't think about it otherwise—our low expectations are too ingrained. A Harvard aunt notwithstanding, for people like Johnny, Marvin Gaye was right that only three things are sure: taxes, death, and trouble. At least it wasn't the second.

We rarely wonder about or discuss the brother who shot him because we already know everything about him. When the call came, my first thought was the same one I'd had when I'd heard about Rosa Parks's beating: a brother did it. A non-job-having, middle-of-the-day malt-liquor-drinking, crotch-clutching, loud-talking brother with many neglected children born of many forgotten women. He lives in his mother's basement with furniture rented at an astronomical interest rate, the exact amount of which he does not know. He has a car phone, an $80 monthly cable bill, and every possible phone feature but no savings. He steals Social Security numbers from unsuspecting relatives and assumes their identities to acquire large TV sets for which he will never pay. On the slim chance that he is brought to justice, he will have a colorful criminal history and no coherent explanation to offer for his act. His family will raucously defend him and cry cover-up. Some liberal lawyer just like me will help him plea-bargain his way to yet another short stay in a prison pesthouse that will serve only to add another layer to the brother's sociopathology and formless, mindless nihilism. We know him. We've known and feared him all our lives.

15   As a teenager, he called, "Hey, baby, gimme somma that boodie!" at us from car windows. Indignant at our lack of response, he followed up with, "Fuck you, then, 'ho!" He called me a "white-boy-lovin' nigger bitch oreo" for being in the gifted program and loving it. At twenty-seven, he got my seventeen-year-old sister pregnant with Johnny and lost interest without ever informing her that he was married. He snatched my widowed mother's purse as she waited in predawn darkness for the bus to work and then broke into our house while she soldered on an assembly line. He chased all the small entrepreneurs from our neighborhood with his violent thievery and put bars on our windows. He kept us from sitting on our own front porch after dark and laid the foundation for our periodic bouts of self-hating anger and racial embarrassment. He made our neighborhood a ghetto. He is the poster fool behind the maddening community knowledge that there are still some black mothers who raise their daughters but merely love their sons. He and his cancerous carbon copies eclipse the vast majority of us who are not sociopaths and render us invisible. He is the Siamese twin who has died but cannot be separated from his living, vibrant sibling;

which of us must attract more notice? We despise and disown this anomalous loser, but for many he *is* black America. We know him, we know that he is outside the fold, and we know that he will only get worse. What we didn't know is that, because of him, my little sister would one day be the latest hysterical black mother wailing over a fallen child on TV.

Alone, lying in the road bleeding and paralyzed but hideously conscious, Johnny had lain helpless as he watched his would-be murderer come to stand over him and offer this prophecy: "Betch'ou won't be doin' nomo' wavin', mothafucker."

Fuck you, asshole. He's fine from the waist up. You just can't do anything right, can you?

 ## Topics for Critical Thinking and Writing

1. Characterize Dickerson's tone in the last lines of the essay.
2. Upon hearing that her nephew had been shot, Dickerson says (paragraph 14) she knew immediately that "a brother did it." She goes on to describe the shooter as a "non-job-having, middle-of the day malt-liquor-drinking, crotch-clutching, loud-talking brother with many neglected children born of many forgotten women." Is this description racist? Why or why not?
3. Do you think that this essay perpetuates racial stereotypes—or not?
4. This essay, a narrative account, does not contain an explicit argument or thesis. What is its *implicit* argument?

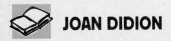 ## JOAN DIDION

Joan Didion was born in California in 1934 and educated at the University of California, Berkeley. While she was a senior in college she wrote a prize-winning essay for a contest sponsored by Vogue, *and soon she became an associate feature editor for* Vogue. *She has written novels, essays, and screenplays.*

On Keeping a Notebook

"'That woman Estelle,'" the note reads, "'is partly the reason why George Sharp and I are separated today.' *Dirty crepe-de-Chine wrapper, hotel bar, Wilmington RR, 9:45 a.m. August Monday morning.*"

Since the note is in my notebook, it presumably has some meaning to me. I study it for a long while. At first I have only the most general notion of what I was doing on an August Monday morning in the bar of the hotel across from the Pennsylvania Railroad station in Wilmington, Delaware (waiting for a train? missing one? 1960? 1961? why Wilmington?), but I do remember being there. The woman in the dirty crepe-de-Chine wrapper had come down from her room for a beer, and the bartender had heard before the reason why George Sharp and she were separated today. "Sure," he said, and went on mopping the floor. "You told me." At the other end of the bar is a girl. She is talking, pointedly, not to the man beside her but to a cat lying in the triangle of sunlight cast through the open door. She is wearing a plaid silk dress from Peck & Peck, and the hem is coming down.

Here is what it is: the girl has been on the Eastern Shore, and now she is going back to the city, leaving the man beside her, and all she can see ahead are the viscous summer sidewalks and the 3 a.m. long-distance calls that will make her lie awake and then sleep drugged through all the steaming mornings left in August (1960? 1961?). Because she must go directly from the train to lunch in New York, she wishes that she had a safety pin for the hem of the plaid silk dress, and she also wishes that she could forget about the hem and the lunch and stay in the cool bar that smells of disinfectant and malt and make friends with the woman in the crepe-de-Chine wrapper. She is afflicted by a little self-pity, and she wants to compare Estelles. That is what that was all about.

In fact I have abandoned altogether that kind of pointless entry; instead I tell what some would call lies. "That's simply not true," the members of my family frequently tell me when they come up against my memory of a shared event. "The party was *not* for you, the spider was *not* a black widow, *it wasn't that way at all.*" Very likely they are right, for not only have I always had trouble distinguishing between what happened and what merely might have happened, but I remain unconvinced that the distinction, for my purposes, matters. The cracked crab that I recall having for lunch the day my father came home from Detroit in 1945 must certainly be embroidery, worked into the day's pattern to lend verisimilitude; I was ten years old and would not now remember the cracked crab. The day's events did not turn on cracked crab. And yet it is precisely that fictitious crab that makes me see the afternoon all over again, a home movie run all too often, the father bearing gifts, the child weeping, an exercise in family love and guilt. Or that is what it was to me. Similarly, perhaps it never did snow that August in Vermont; perhaps there never were flurries in the night wind, and maybe no one else felt the ground hardening and summer already dead even as we pretended to bask in it, but that was how it felt to me, and it might as well have snowed, could have snowed, did snow.

5   *How it felt to me:* that is getting closer to the truth about a notebook. I sometimes delude myself about why I keep a notebook, imagine that some thrifty virtue derives from preserving everything observed. See enough and write it down, I tell myself, and then some morning when the world seems drained of wonder, some day when I am only going through the motions of doing what I am supposed to do, which is write—on that bankrupt morning I will simply open my notebook and there it will all be, a forgotten account with accumulated interest, paid passage back to the world out there: dialogue overheard in hotels and elevators and at the hat-check counter in Pavillon (one middle-aged man shows his hat check to another and says, "That's my old football number"); impressions of Bettina Aptheker and Benjamin Sonnenberg and Teddy ("Mr. Acapulco") Stauffer; careful *aperçus* about tennis bums and failed fashion models and Greek shipping heiresses, one of whom taught me a significant lesson (a lesson I could have learned from F. Scott Fitzgerald, but perhaps we all must meet the very rich for ourselves) by asking, when I arrived to interview her in her orchid-filled sitting room on the second day of a paralyzing New York blizzard, whether it was snowing outside.

Why did I write it down? In order to remember, of course, but exactly what was it I wanted to remember? How much of it actually happened? Did any of it? Why do I keep a notebook at all? It is easy to deceive oneself on all those scores. The impulse to write things down is a peculiarly compulsive one, inexplicable to those who do not share it, useful only accidentally, only secondarily, in the way that any compulsion tries to justify itself. I suppose that it begins or does not begin in the cradle. Although I have felt compelled to write things down since I was five years old, I doubt that my daughter ever will, for she is a singularly blessed and accepting child, delighted with life exactly as life presents itself to her, unafraid to go to sleep and unafraid to wake up. Keepers of private notebooks are a different breed altogether, lonely and resistant rearrangers of things, anxious malcontents, children afflicted apparently at birth with some presentiment of loss.

My first notebook was a Big Five tablet, given to me by my mother with the sensible suggestion that I stop whining and learn to amuse myself by writing down my thoughts. She returned the tablet to me a few years ago; the first entry is an account of a woman who believed herself to be freezing to death in the Arctic night, only to find, when day broke, that she had stumbled onto the Sahara Desert, where she would die of the heat before lunch. I have no idea what turn of a five-year-old's mind could have prompted so insistently "ironic" and exotic a story, but it does reveal a certain predilection for the extreme which has dogged me into adult life; perhaps if I were analytically inclined I would find it a truer story than any I might have told about Donald Johnson's birthday party or the day my cousin Brenda put Kitty Litter in the aquarium.

So the point of my keeping a notebook has never been, nor is it now, to have an accurate factual record of what I have been doing or thinking. That would be a different impulse entirely, an instinct for reality which I sometimes envy but do not possess. At no point have I ever been able successfully to keep a diary; my approach to daily life ranges from the grossly negligent to the merely absent, and on those few occasions when I have tried dutifully to record a day's events, boredom has so overcome me that the results are mysterious at best. What is this business about "shopping, typing piece, dinner with E, depressed"? Shopping for what? Typing what piece? Who is E? Was this "E" depressed, or was I depressed? Who cares?

I imagine, in other words, that the notebook is about other people. But of course it is not. I have no real business with what one stranger said to another at the hat-check counter in Pavillon; in fact I suspect that the line "That's my old football number" touched not my own imagination at all, but merely some memory of something once read, probably "The Eighty-Yard Run." Nor is my concern with a woman in a dirty crepe-de-Chine wrapper in a Wilmington bar. My stake is always, of course, in the unmentioned girl in the plaid silk dress. *Remember what it was to be me:* that is always the point.

10   It is a difficult point to admit. We are brought up in the ethic that others, any others, all others, are by definition more interesting than ourselves; taught to be diffident, just this side of self-effacing. ("You're the least important person in the room and don't forget it," Jessica Mitford's governess would hiss in her ear on the advent of any social occasion: I copied that into my notebook because it is only recently that I have been able to enter a room without hearing some such phrase in my inner ear.) Only the very young and the very old may recount their dreams at breakfast, dwell upon self, interrupt with memories of beach picnics and favorite Liberty lawn dresses and the rainbow trout in a creek near Colorado Springs. The rest of us are expected, rightly, to affect absorption in other people's favorite dresses, other people's trout.

And so we do. But our notebooks give us away, for however dutifully we record what we see around us, the common denominator of all we see is always, transparently, shamelessly, the implacable "I." We are not talking here about the kind of notebook that is patently for public consumption, a structural conceit for binding together a series of graceful *pensées;* we are talking about something private, about bits of the mind's string too short to use, an indiscriminate and erratic assemblage with meaning only for its maker.

And sometimes even the maker has difficulty with the meaning. There does not seem to be, for example, any point in my knowing for the rest of my life that, during 1964, 720 tons of soot fell on every square mile of New York City, yet there it is in my notebook, labeled "FACT." Nor do I really need to remember that Ambrose Bierce liked to spell Leland Stanford's name "£eland $tanford" or that "smart women almost always wear black in Cuba," a fashion hint without much potential for practical application. And does not the relevance of these notes seem marginal at best?:

> In the basement museum of the Inyo County Courthouse in Independence, California, sign pinned to a mandarin coat: "This Mandarin Coat was often worn by Mrs. Minnie S. Brooks when giving lectures on her TEAPOT COLLECTION."

> Redhead getting out of car in front of Beverly Wilshire Hotel, chinchilla stole, Vuitton bags and tags reading:
> MRS. LOU FOX
> HOTEL SAHARA
> VEGAS

Well, perhaps not entirely marginal. As a matter of fact, Mrs. Minnie S. Brooks and her MANDARIN COAT pull me back into my own childhood, for although I never knew Mrs. Brooks and did not visit Inyo County until I was thirty, I grew up in just such a world, in houses cluttered with Indian relics and bits of gold ore and ambergris and the souvenirs my Aunt Mercy Farnsworth brought back from the Orient. It is a long way from that world to Mrs. Lou Fox's world, where we all live now, and is it not just as well to remember that? Might not Mrs. Minnie S. Brooks help me to remember what I am? Might not Mrs. Lou Fox help me to remember what I am not?

But sometimes the point is harder to discern. What exactly did I have in mind when I noted down that it cost the father of someone I know $650 a month to light the place on the Hudson in which he lived before the Crash? What use was I planning to make of this line by Jimmy Hoffa: "I may have my faults, but being wrong ain't one of them"? And although I think it interesting to know where the girls who travel with the Syndicate have their hair done when they find themselves on the West Coast, will I ever make suitable use if it? Might I not be better off just passing it on to John O'Hara? What is a recipe for sauerkraut doing in my notebook? What kind of magpie keeps this notebook? "*He was born the night the* Titanic *went down.*" That seems a nice enough line, and I even recall who said it, but is it not really a better line in life than it could ever be in fiction?

15   But of course that is exactly it: not that I should ever use the line, but that I should remember the woman who said it and the afternoon I heard it. We were on her terrace by the sea, and we were finishing the wine left from lunch, trying to get what sun there was, a California winter sun. The woman whose husband was born the night the *Titanic* went down wanted to rent her house, wanted to go back to her children in Paris. I remember wishing that I could afford the

house, which cost $1,000 a month. "Someday you will," she said lazily. "Someday it all comes." There in the sun on her terrace it seemed easy to believe in someday, but later I had a low-grade afternoon hangover and ran over a black snake on the way to the supermarket and was flooded with inexplicable fear when I heard the checkout clerk explaining to the man ahead of me why she was finally divorcing her husband. "He left me no choice," she said over and over as she punched the register. "He has a little seven-month-old baby by her, he left me no choice." I would like to believe that my dread then was for the human condition, but of course it was for me, because I wanted a baby and did not then have one and because I wanted to own a house that cost $1,000 a month to rent and because I had a hangover.

It all comes back. Perhaps it is difficult to see the value in having one's self back in that kind of mood, but I do see it: I think we are well advised to keep on nodding terms with the people we used to be, whether we find them attractive company or not. Otherwise they turn up unannounced and surprise us, come hammering on the mind's door at 4 a.m. of a bad night and demand to know who deserted them, who betrayed them, who is going to make amends. We forget all too soon the things we thought we could never forget. We forget the loves and the betrayals alike, forget what we whispered and what we screamed, forget who we were. I have already lost touch with a couple of people I used to be: one of them, a seventeen-year-old, presents little threat, although it would be of some interest to me to know again what it feels like to sit on a river levee drinking vodka-and-orange-juice and listening to Les Paul and Mary Ford and their echoes sing "How High the Moon" on the car radio. You see I still have the scenes, but I no longer perceive myself among those present, no longer could even improvise the dialogue. The other one, a twenty-three-year-old, bothers me more. She was always a good deal of trouble, and I suspect she will reappear when I least want to see her, skirts too long, shy to the point of aggravation, always the injured party, full of recriminations and little hurts and stories I do not want to hear again, at once saddening me and angering me with her vulnerability and ignorance, an apparition all the more insistent for being so long banished.

It is a good idea, then, to keep in touch, and I suppose that keeping in touch is what notebooks are all about. And we are all on our own when it comes to keeping those lines open to ourselves: your notebook will never help me, nor mine you. "*So what's new in the whiskey business?*" What could that possibly mean to you? To me it means a blonde in a Pucci bathing suit sitting with a couple of fat men by the pool at the Beverly Hills Hotel. Another man approaches, and they all regard one another in silence for a while. "So what's new in the whiskey business?" one of the fat men finally says by way of welcome, and the blonde stands up, arches one foot and dips it in the pool, looking all the while at the cabaña where Baby Pignatari is talking on the telephone. That is all there is to that, except that several years later I saw the blonde coming out of Saks Fifth Avenue in New York with her California complexion and a voluminous mink coat. In the harsh wind that day she looked old and irrevocably tired to me, and even the skins in the mink coat were not worked the way they were doing them that year, not the way she would have wanted them done, and there is the point of the story. For a while after that I did not like to look in the mirror, and my eyes would skim the newspapers and pick out only the deaths, the cancer victims, the premature coronaries, the suicides, and I stopped riding the Lexington Avenue IRT because I noticed for the first time that all the strangers I had seen for years—the man with the Seeing Eye dog, the spinster who read the classified pages every day, the fat girl who always got off with me at Grand Central—looked older than they once had.

It all comes back. Even that recipe for sauerkraut: even that brings it back. I was on Fire Island when I first made that sauerkraut, and it was raining, and we drank a lot of bourbon and ate the sauerkraut and went to bed at ten, and I listened to the rain and the Atlantic and felt safe. I made the sauerkraut again last night and it did not make me feel any safer, but that is, as they say, another story.

Topics for Critical Thinking and Writing

1. In the sixth paragraph, beginning "Why did I write it down?" Didion says that "it is easy to deceive oneself" about the reasons for keeping a notebook. What self-deceptive reasons does she go on to give? What others can be added? And exactly why *does* she keep a notebook? (Didion in her last three paragraphs—and especially in the first two of these—makes explicit her reasons, but try to state her reasons in a paragraph of your own.)

2. In paragraph 5 Didion refers to a lesson she might have learned from F. Scott Fitzgerald and goes on to say, "but perhaps we all must meet the very rich for ourselves." If you have read a book by Fitzgerald, explain (in a paragraph) the point to someone who doesn't get it.

3. In paragraph 13 Didion says, "It is a long way from that world to Mrs. Lou Fox's world, where we all live now." What does she mean?

4. If you keep a notebook (or diary or journal), explain in one to three paragraphs why you keep it. Following Didion's example, use one entry or two to illustrate the notebook's usefulness to you. If you don't keep a notebook, explain in one to three paragraphs why you don't, and explain what effect, if any, Didion's essay had on you. Do you now think it would be a good idea to keep a notebook? Or did the essay reinforce your belief that there's nothing useful in it for you? Explain.

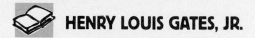 **HENRY LOUIS GATES, JR.**

Henry Louis Gates Jr., born in West Virginia in 1950, did his undergraduate work at Yale University (summa cum laude) and his graduate work (M.A. and Ph.D.) at Cambridge University. He has taught at Yale, Cornell, and Duke, and now at Harvard, where he is the director of the Afro-American Studies program. Gates is the author of several books, including Black Literature and Literary Theory *and* The Signifying Monkey: A Theory of African-American Literary Criticism. *The essay that we reprint originally appeared in* The New York Times Book Review.

Malcolm, the Aardvark and Me

One of the most gratifying effects of Spike Lee's film *Malcolm X* is that its success has prompted the restoration of Malcolm's autobiography to the best-seller lists. The country is *reading* the 1965 book once again, as avidly, it seems, as it is seeing Mr. Lee's movie. For 17 weeks *The Autobiography of Malcolm X*, written with the assistance of Alex Haley, has been on the *New York Times* paperback best-seller list, and for 10 of those weeks it was No. 1. Today, on the 28th anniversary of his assassination, Malcolm's story has become as American—to borrow H. Rap Brown's famous aphorism—as violence and cherry pie.

Malcolm first came into my life some three decades ago, when I was 9 years old and Mike Wallace and CBS broadcast a documentary about the Nation of Islam. It was called *The Hate That Hate Produced,* and it showed just about the scariest black people I had ever seen: black people who talked right into the faces of white people, telling them off without even blinking. While I sat in our living room, I happened to glance over at my mother. A certain radiance was slowly transforming her soft brown face, as she listened to Malcolm naming the white man as the devil. "Amen," she said, quietly at first. "All right now," she continued, much more emphatically. All this time and I had not known just how deeply my mother despised white people. The revelation was terrifying but thrilling.

The book came into my life much later.

I was almost 17, a junior in high school, and I was slowly and pleasurably devouring *Ebony* magazine. More precisely, I was reading a profile of the Roman Catholic basketball player Lew Alcindor, who was then a star at U.C.L.A. and who later became a legend with the Los Angeles Lakers as the Muslim basketball player Kareem Abdul-Jabbar. In the profile he said that *The Autobiography of Malcolm X* had meant more to him than any other book, and that *all* black Americans should read it—*today.*

Today was not possible for me, since I lived in a village in the hills of West Virginia where nobody carried such things. I had to go down to Red Bowl's newsstand, make a deposit and wait while they sent away for it. But when the book arrived, I read it straight through the night, as struck by its sepia-colored photograph of a dangerous-looking, gesticulating Malcolm as I was by the contents, the riveting saga of a man on the run, from whites (as the son of a Garveyite father) and blacks (his former mentors and colleagues at the Nation of Islam, after his falling-out with Elijah Muhammad).

I loved the hilarious scene in which Malcolm is having his hair "conked," or "processed" ("relaxed" remains the euphemism); unable to rinse out the burning lye because the pipes in his home are frozen, he has no recourse but to dunk his head in a toilet bowl. A few months before, the benignly parochial principal of our high school had "paddled" my schoolmate Arthur Galloway when Arthur told him that his processed hairstyle was produced by a mixture of eggs, mashed potatoes and lye. "Don't lie to me, boy," the principal was heard saying above Arthur's protests.

What I remember most, though, is Malcolm's discussion of the word "aardvark."

"I saw that the best thing I could do was get hold of a dictionary—to study. . . . I spent two days just riffling uncertainly through the dictionary's pages. I'd never realized so many words existed! . . . Funny thing, from the dictionary's first page right now, that 'aardvark' springs to my mind. The dictionary had a picture of it, a long-tailed, long-eared, burrowing African mammal, which lives off termites caught by sticking out its tongue as an anteater does for ants."

Years later, near the end of his life, Malcolm found himself heading to the American Museum of Natural History in New York to learn more about that exotic creature, even while trying to figure out how to avoid an almost certain Muslim death sentence. "Boy! I never will forget that old aardvark!" he had mused to Alex Haley. What manner of politician was this, I wondered, in this the year that

Stokely Carmichael and Rap Brown, Eldridge Cleaver and Huey P. Newton, Ron Karenga and Amiri Baraka, simultaneously declared themselves to be the legitimate sons of Malcolm the father, to linger with aardvarks when his world was collapsing around him?

10   Although Malcolm proudly avowed that he read no fiction (he says he read only one novel "since I started serious reading," and that was *Uncle Tom's Cabin*), he still loved fiction—"fiction" defined as a making, a creating, with words. His speeches—such as the oft-repeated "Ballot or the Bullet" or "Bandung Conference"—are masterpieces of the rhetorical arts. More than Martin Luther King Jr., more than any of the black nationalists or the neo-Marxists, Malcolm X was a *writer,* a wordsmith.

In 1968, my English teacher told me that in years to come, long after the civil rights struggle was a footnote in history, this man would be remembered—like St. Augustine, like Benjamin Franklin, like Henry Adams—because of his gift with words. High praise: and yet the teacher's observation, I must confess, didn't go down well with me at the time. Imagining the book stretched on the autopsy slab of purely literary analysis, I somehow felt that the overriding immediacy of Malcolm's experience—and my special relation to it—had been diminished. Despite Malcolm's cautious if heartfelt moves toward universalism, I felt that part of him would always belong to African mammals like aardvarks, like me.

 ## Topics for Critical Thinking and Writing

1. What was the occasion for Gates's article, and where does Gates refer to it?
2. Read the last sentence of the first paragraph. How would you describe its tone? (H. Rap Brown, a militant black power leader, said—we are quoting from memory, assisted by Gates—that "violence is as American as cherry pie.")
3. The third paragraph is only one sentence long. Why do you suppose Gates isolated the sentence, instead of beginning the next paragraph with it? What effect does he create?
4. What magazine, if any, was especially important to you in high school (Gates remembers "slowly and pleasurably devouring *Ebony*")? Why was it important?
5. If you have a "special relation" (Gates's words, in his final paragraph) with any book (or film) write an essay of 500 words, giving the reader some idea of what this relation may be. (Notice how Gates uses examples—of the "sepia-colored photographs," of a "hilarious scene," of the surprising discussion of "aardvark." Try to be just as specific in your discussion.)

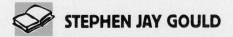 ## STEPHEN JAY GOULD

Stephen Jay Gould, born in 1941, is a professor of geology at Harvard University, where he teaches paleontology, biology, and the history of science. The essays he has written for the magazine Natural History *have been collected in a series of highly readable books.*

Women's Brains

In the Prelude to *Middlemarch,* George Eliot lamented the unfulfilled lives of talented women:

> Some have felt that these blundering lives are due to the inconvenient indefiniteness with which the Supreme Power has fashioned the natures of women: if there were one level of feminine incompetence as strict as the ability to count three and no more, the social lot of women might be treated with scientific certitude.

Eliot goes on to discount the idea of innate limitation, but while she wrote in 1872, the leaders of European anthropometry were trying to measure "with scientific certitude" the inferiority of women. Anthropometry, or measurement of the human body, is not so fashionable a field these days, but it dominated the human sciences for much of the nineteenth century and remained popular until intelligence testing replaced skull measurement as a favored device for making invidious comparisons among races, classes, and sexes. Craniometry, or measurement of the skull, commanded the most attention and respect. Its unquestioned leader, Paul Broca (1824–80), professor of clinical surgery at the Faculty of Medicine in Paris, gathered a school of disciples and imitators around himself. Their work, so meticulous and apparently irrefutable, exerted great influence and won high esteem as a jewel of nineteenth-century science.

Broca's work seemed particularly invulnerable to refutation. Had he not measured with the most scrupulous care and accuracy? (Indeed, he had. I have the greatest respect for Broca's meticulous procedure. His numbers are sound. But science is an inferential exercise, not a catalog of facts. Numbers, by themselves, specify nothing. All depends upon what you do with them.) Broca depicted himself as an apostle of objectivity, a man who bowed before facts and cast aside superstition and sentimentality. He declared that "there is no faith, however respectable, no interest, however legitimate, which must not accommodate itself to the progress of human knowledge and bend before truth." Women, like it or not, had smaller brains than men and, therefore, could not equal them in intelligence. This fact, Broca argued, may reinforce a common prejudice in male society, but it is also a scientific truth. L. Manouvrier, a black sheep in Broca's fold, rejected the inferiority of women and wrote with feeling about the burden imposed upon them by Broca's numbers:

> Women displayed their talents and their diplomas. They also invoked philosophical authorities. But they were opposed by *numbers* unknown to Condorcet or to John Stuart Mill. These numbers fell upon poor women like a sledge hammer, and they were accompanied by commentaries and sarcasms more ferocious than the most misogynist imprecations of certain church fathers. The theologians had asked if women had a soul. Several centuries later, some scientists were ready to refuse them a human intelligence.

Broca's argument rested upon two sets of data: the larger brains of men in modern societies, and a supposed increase in male superiority through time. His most extensive data came from autopsies performed personally in four Parisian hospitals. For 292 male brains, he calculated an average weight of 1,325 grams; 140 female brains averaged, 1,144 grams for a difference of 181 grams, or 14 percent of the male weight. Broca understood, of course, that part of this difference could be attributed to the greater height of males. Yet he made no attempt to measure the effect of size alone and actually stated that it cannot account for the entire difference because we know, a priori, that women are not as intelligent as men (a premise that the data were supposed to test, not rest upon):

> We might ask if the small size of the female brain depends exclusively upon the small size of her body. Tiedemann has proposed this explanation. But we must not forget that women are, on the average, a little less intelligent than men, a difference which we should not exaggerate but which is, nonetheless, real. We are therefore permitted to suppose that the relatively small size of the female brain depends in part upon her physical inferiority and in part upon her intellectual inferiority.

5   In 1873, the year after Eliot published *Middlemarch,* Broca measured the cranial capacities of prehistoric skulls from L'Homme Mort cave. Here he found a difference of only 99.5 cubic centimeters between males and females, while modern populations range from 129.5 to 220.7. Topinard, Broca's chief disciple, explained the increasing discrepancy through time as a result of differing evolutionary pressures upon dominant men and passive women:

> The man who fights for two or more in the struggle for existence, who has all the responsibility and the cares of tomorrow, who is constantly active in combating the environment and human rivals, needs more brain than the woman whom he must protect and nourish, the sedentary woman, lacking any interior occupations, whose role is to raise children, love, and be passive.

In 1879, Gustave Le Bon, chief misogynist of Broca's school, used these data to publish what must be the most vicious attack upon women in modern scientific literature (no one can top Aristotle). I do not claim his views were representative of Broca's school, but they were published in France's most respected anthropological journal. Le Bon concluded:

> In the most intelligent races, as among the Parisians, there are a large number of women whose brains are closer in size to those of gorillas than to the most developed male brains. This inferiority is so obvious that no one can contest it for a moment; only its degree is worth discussion. All pyschologists who have studied the intelligence of women, as well as poets and novelists, recognize today that they represent the most inferior forms of human evolution and that they are closer to children and savages than to an adult, civilized man. They excel in fickleness, inconstancy, absence of thought and logic, and incapacity to reason. Without doubt there exist some distinguished women, very superior to the average man, but they are as exceptional as the birth of any monstrosity, as, for example, of a gorilla with two heads; consequently, we may neglect them entirely.

Nor did Le Bon shrink from the social implications of his views. He was horrified by the proposal of some American reformers to grant women higher education on the same basis as men:

> A desire to give them the same education, and, as a consequence, to propose the same goals for them, is a dangerous chimera. . . . The day when,

misunderstanding the inferior occupations which nature has given her, women leave the home and take part in our battles; on this day a social revolution will begin, and everything that maintains the sacred ties of the family will disappear.

Sound familiar?[1]

I have reexamined Broca's data, the basis for all this derivative pronouncement, and I find his numbers sound but his interpretation ill-founded, to say the least. The data supporting his claim for increased difference through time can be easily dismissed. Broca based his contention on the samples from L'Homme Mort alone—only seven male and six female skulls in all. Never have so little data yielded such far ranging conclusions.

In 1888, Topinard published Broca's more extensive data on the Parisian hospitals. Since Broca recorded height and age as well as brain size, we may use modern statistics to remove their effect. Brain weight decreases with age, and Broca's women were, on average, considerably older than his men. Brain weight increases with height, and his average man was almost half a foot taller than his average woman. I used multiple regression, a technique that allowed me to assess simultaneously the influence of height and age upon brain size. In an analysis of the data for women, I found that, at average male height and age, a woman's brain would weigh 1,212 grams. Correction for height and age reduces Broca's measured difference of 181 grams by more than a third, to 113 grams.

10   I don't know what to make of this remaining difference because I cannot assess other factors known to influence brain size in a major way. Cause of death has an important effect: degenerative disease often entails a substantial diminution of brain size. (This effect is separate from the decrease attributed to age alone.) Eugene Schreider, also working with Broca's data, found that men killed in accidents had brains weighing, on average, 60 grams more than men dying of infectious diseases. The best modern data I can find (from American hospitals) records a full 100-gram difference between death by degenerative arteriosclerosis and by violence or accident. Since so many of Broca's subjects were very elderly women, we may assume that lengthy degenerative disease was more common among them than among the men.

More importantly, modern students of brain size still have not agreed on a proper measure for eliminating the powerful effect of body size. Height is partly adequate, but men and women of the same height do not share the same body build. Weight is even worse than height, because most of its variation reflects nutrition rather than intrinsic size—fat versus skinny exerts little influence upon the brain. Manouvrier took up this subject in the 1880s and argued that muscular mass and force should be used. He tried to measure this elusive property in various ways and found a marked difference in favor of men, even in men and women of the same height. When he corrected for what he called "sexual mass," women actually came out slightly ahead in brain size.

Thus, the corrected 113-gram difference is surely too large; the true figure is probably close to zero and may as well favor women as men. And 113 grams, by

---

[1]When I wrote this essay, I assumed that Le Bon was a marginal, if colorful, figure. I have since learned that he was a leading scientist, one of the founders of social psychology, and best known for a seminal study on crowd behavior, still cited today (*La psychologie des foules,* 1895), and for his work on unconscious motivation.

the way, is exactly the average difference between a 5 foot 4 inch and a 6 foot 4 inch male in Broca's data. We would not (especially us short folks) want to ascribe greater intelligence to tall men. In short, who knows what to do with Broca's data? They certainly don't permit any confident claim that men have bigger brains than women.

To appreciate the social role of Broca and his school, we must recognize that his statements about the brains of women do not reflect an isolated prejudice toward a single disadvantaged group. They must be weighed in the context of a general theory that supported contemporary social distinctions as biologically ordained. Women, blacks, and poor people suffered the same disparagement, but women bore the brunt of Broca's argument because he had easier access to data on women's brains. Women were singularly denigrated but they also stood as surrogates for other disenfranchised groups. As one of Broca's disciples wrote in 1881: "Men of the black races have a brain scarcely heavier than that of white women." This juxtaposition extended into many other realms of anthropological argument, particularly to claims that, anatomically and emotionally, both women and blacks were like white children—and that white children, by the theory of recapitulation, represented an ancestral (primitive) adult stage of human evolution. I do not regard as empty rhetoric the claim that women's battles are for all of us.

Maria Montessori did not confine her activities to educational reform for young children. She lectured on anthropology for several years at the University of Rome, and wrote an influential book entitled *Pedagogical Anthropology* (English edition, 1913). Montessori was no egalitarian. She supported most of Broca's work and the theory of innate criminality proposed by her compatriot Cesare Lombroso. She measured the circumference of children's heads in her schools and inferred that the best prospects had bigger brains. But she had no use for Broca's conclusions about women. She discussed Manouvrier's work at length and made much of his tentative claim that women, after proper correction of the data, had slightly larger brains than men. Women, she concluded, were intellectually superior, but men had prevailed heretofore by dint of physical force. Since technology has abolished force as an instrument of power, the era of women may soon be upon us: "In such an epoch there will really be superior human beings, there will really be men strong in morality and in sentiment. Perhaps in this way the reign of women is approaching, when the enigma of her anthropological superiority will be deciphered. Woman was always the custodian of human sentiment, morality and honor."

15   This represents one possible antidote to "scientific" claims for the constitutional inferiority of certain groups. One may affirm the validity of biological distinctions but argue that the data have been misinterpreted by prejudiced men with a stake in the outcome, and that disadvantaged groups are truly superior. In recent years, Elaine Morgan has followed this strategy in her *Descent of Woman,* a speculative reconstruction of human prehistory from the woman's point of view—and as farcical as more famous tall tales by and for men.

I prefer another strategy. Montessori and Morgan followed Broca's philosophy to reach a more congenial conclusion. I would rather label the whole enterprise of setting a biological value upon groups for what it is: irrelevant and highly injurious. George Eliot well appreciated the special tragedy that biological labeling imposed upon members of disadvantaged groups. She expressed it for people like herself—women of extraordinary talent. I would apply it more widely—not only to those whose dreams are flouted but also to those who never realize that they may dream—but I cannot match her prose. In conclusion, then, the rest of Eliot's prelude to *Middlemarch:*

> The limits of variation are really much wider than anyone would imagine from the sameness of women's coiffure and the favorite love stories in prose and verse. Here and there a cygnet is reared uneasily among the ducklings in the brown pond, and never finds the living stream in fellowship with its own oary-footed kind. Here and there is born a Saint Theresa, foundress of nothing, whose loving heartbeats and sobs after an unattained goodness tremble off and are dispersed among hindrances instead of centering in some long-recognizable deed.

 Topics for Critical Thinking and Writing

1. In paragraph 3, what does Gould mean when he says, "But science is an inferential exercise, not a catalog of facts"?
2. Gould quotes (paragraph 5) Topinard's explanation for the increasing discrepancy in the size of brains. Given your own understanding of evolution, what do you think of Topinard's explanation?
3. In paragraph 9 Gould says, "Brain weight decreases with age." Do you believe this? Why? How would one establish the truth or falsity of the assertion?
4. In paragraph 12 Gould says, "Thus, the corrected 113-gram difference is surely too large; the true figure is probably close to zero and may as well favor women as men." Why "thus"? What evidence or what assumptions prompt Gould to say that the figure is surely too large?
5. In paragraph 13 Gould says, "I do not regard as empty rhetoric the claim that women's battles are for all of us." What does this mean?
6. Also in paragraph 13 Gould refers to the "social role of Broca and his school." What does he mean by that? On the basis of this essay (and other essays of Gould's you may have read) try to formulate in a sentence or two the social role of Gould.

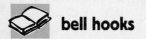 **bell hooks**

bell hooks (Gloria Watkins) teaches English and Women's Studies at Oberlin College. She is the author of more than a dozen books, among them Feminist Theory: From Margin to Center *(1984),* Talking Back *(1989),* Yearning: Race, Gender and Culture *(1990), and* Wounds of Passion: A Writing Life *(1998).*

Talking Back

In the world of the southern black community I grew up in "back talk" and "talking back" meant speaking as an equal to an authority figure. It meant daring to disagree and sometimes it just meant having an opinion. In the "old school" children were meant to be seen and not heard. My great-grandparents, grandparents, and parents were all from the old school. To make yourself heard, if you were a child, was to invite punishment, the backhand lick, the slap across the face that would catch you unaware, or the feel of switches stinging your arms and legs.

To speak then when one was not spoken to was a courageous act—an act of risking and daring. And yet it was hard not to speak in warm rooms where heated discussions began at the crack of dawn, women's voices filling the air, giving orders, making threats, fussing. Black men may have excelled in the art of poetic preaching in the male dominated church but in the church of the home where the everyday rules of how to live and how to act were established it was black women who preached. There, black women spoke in a language so rich, so poetic, that it felt to me like being shut off from life, smothered to death if one was not allowed to participate.

It was in that world of woman talk (the men were often silent, often absent) that was born in me the craving to speak, to have a voice, and not just any voice but one that could be identified as belonging to me. To make my voice I had to speak, to hear myself talk—and talk I did—darting in and out of grown folk's conversations and dialogues, answering questions that were not directed at me, endlessly asking questions, making speeches. Needless to say, the punishments for these acts of speech seemed endless. They were intended to silence me—the child—and more particularly the girl child. Had I been a boy they might have encouraged me to speak believing that I might someday be called to preach. There was no "calling" for talking girls, no legitimized rewarded speech. The punishments I received for "talking back" were intended to suppress all possibility that I would create my own speech. That speech was to be suppressed so the "right speech of womanhood" would emerge.

Within feminist circles silence is often seen as the sexist defined "right speech of womanhood"—the sign of woman's submission to patriarchal authority. This emphasis on woman's silence may be an accurate remembering of what has taken place in the households of women from WASP backgrounds in the United States but in black communities (and in other diverse ethnic communities) women have not been silent. Their voices can be heard. Certainly for black women our struggle has not been to emerge from silence into speech but to change the nature and direction of our speech. To make a speech that compels listeners, one that is heard.

5 Our speech, "the right speech of womanhood," was often the soliloquy, the talking into thin air, the talking to ears that do not hear you—the talk that is simply not listened to. Unlike the black male preacher whose speech was to be heard, who was to be listened to, whose words were to be remembered, the voices of black women—giving orders, making threats, fussing—could be tuned out, could become a kind of background music, audible but not acknowledged as significant speech. Dialogue, the sharing of speech and recognition, took place not between mother and child or mother and male authority figure but with other black women. I can remember watching, fascinated, as our mother talked with her mother, sisters, and women friends. The intimacy and intensity of their speech—the satisfaction they received from talking to one another, the pleasure, the joy. It was in this world of woman speech, loud talk, angry words, women with tongues quick and sharp, tender sweet tongues, touching our world with their words, that I made speech my birthright—and the right to voice, to authorship, a privilege I would not be denied. It was in that world and because of it that I came to dream of writing, to write.

Writing was a way to capture speech, to hold onto it, to keep it close. And so I wrote down bits and pieces of conversations, confessing in cheap diaries that soon fell apart from too much handling, expressing the intensity of my sorrow, the anguish of speech—for I was always saying the wrong thing, asking the wrong questions. I could not confine my speech to the necessary corners and concerns of life. These writings I hid under my bed, in pillow stuffings, among faded underwear. When my sisters found and read them, they ridiculed and mocked me—poking fun. I felt violated, ashamed, as if the secret parts of my self had been exposed, brought into the open, and hung like newly clean laundry, out in the air for everyone to see. The fear of exposure, the fear that one's deepest emotions and innermost thoughts would be dismissed as mere nonsense, felt by so many young girls keeping diaries, keeping and hiding speech, seems to me now one of the barriers that women have needed and need to destroy so that we are no longer pushed into secrecy or silence.

Despite my feelings of violation, of exposure, I continued to speak and write, choosing my hiding places well, learning to destroy work when no safe place could be found. Rather than teaching me absolute silence I was taught that it was important to speak but to talk a talk that was in itself a silence. Taught to speak and yet to beware of the betrayal of too much heard speech, I experienced intense confusion and deep anxiety in my efforts to speak and write. Reciting poems at Sunday afternoon church service might be rewarded speech. Writing a poem (when one's time could be "better" spent sweeping, ironing, learning to cook) was luxurious activity, indulged in at the expense of others. Questioning authority, raising issues that were not deemed appropriate subjects, brought pain, punishments—like telling mama I wanted to die before her because I could not live without her—that was crazy talk, crazy speech, the kind that would lead you to end up in a mental institution. "Little girl," I would be told, "if you don't stop all this crazy talk and crazy acting you are going to end up right out there at Western State."

Madness too then, not just physical abuse, was the punishment for too much talk if you were female. Yet even as this fear of madness haunted me, hung over my writing like a monstrous shadow, I could not stop the words, making thought, writing speech. For this terrible madness which I feared, which I was sure was the destiny of daring women born to intense speech (after all the authorities emphasized this point daily), was not as threatening as imposed silence, as suppressed speech.

Safety and sanity were to be sacrificed if I was to experience defiant speech. Though I risked the two, deep-seated fears and anxieties characterized my childhood days. I would speak, but I would not ride a bike, play hard ball, or hold the gray kitten. Writing about the ways we are hurt by negative traumas in our growing-up years, psychoanalyst Alice Miller makes the point in *For Her Own Good* that it is not clear why wounding in childhood becomes for some folk an opportunity to grow, to move forward in the process of self-realization rather than a retardation of that process. Certainly, when I reflect on the trials of my growing-up years, the many punishments, I can see now that in resistance I learned then to be vigilant in the nourishment of my spirit, to be tough, to courageously protect that spirit from forces that would break it.

10   While punishing me, my parents often spoke about the necessity of breaking my spirit. Now when I ponder the silences, the voices that are not heard, the voices of those wounded and/or oppressed individuals who do not speak or write, I contemplate the acts of persecution, torture—the terrorism that breaks spirits, that makes creativity impossible. I write these words to bear witness to

the primacy of struggle in any situation of domination (even within family life), to the strength and power that emerges from sustained resistance, and the profound conviction that these forces can be healing, can protect us from dehumanization and despair.

These early trials, wherein I learned to stand my ground, to keep my spirit intact, came vividly to mind after I published *Ain't I a Woman* and the work was sharply and harshly criticized. While I had expected a climate of critical dialogue, I was not expecting a critical avalanche that had the power in its intensity to crush spirit, to push one into silence. Since that time I have heard stories about black women, about women of color, who write and publish, having nervous breakdowns (even when the work is quite successful), being made mad because they cannot bear the harsh responses of family, friends, and unknown critics, or becoming silent, unproductive. Surely, the absence of a humane critical response has tremendous impact on the writer from any group, but especially for those writers from oppressed, colonized groups who endeavor to speak. For us, true speaking is not solely an expression of creative power, it is an act of resistance, a political gesture that challenges the politics of domination that would render us nameless and voiceless. As such it is a courageous act; as such it represents a threat. To those who wield oppressive power that which is threatening must necessarily be wiped out, annihilated, silenced.

Recent efforts by black women writers to call attention to our work serve to highlight both our presence and absence. Whenever I peruse women's bookstores I am struck not by the rapidly growing body of feminist writing by black women but by the paucity of available published material. Those of us who write and are published remain few in number. The context of silence is varied and multi-dimensional. Most obvious are the ways racism, sexism, and class exploitation act as agents to suppress and silence. Less obvious are the inner struggles, the effort made to gain necessary confidence to write, to rewrite, to fully develop craft and skill, the extent to which such efforts fail.

Although I have wanted writing to be a life work for me since childhood, it has been difficult for me to claim "writer" as part of that which identifies and shapes my everyday reality. Even after publishing books I would often speak of wanting to be a writer as though these works did not exist. And though I would be told, "you are a writer," I was not ready yet to affirm fully this truth. Part of myself was still held captive by domineering forces of history, of familial life that had charted a map of silence, of right speech. I had not completely let go the fear of saying the wrong thing, of being punished. Somewhere in the deep recesses of my mind I believed I could avoid both responsibility and punishment if I did not declare myself a writer.

One of the many reasons I chose to write using the pseudonym bell hooks, a family name (mother to Sarah Oldham, grandmother to Rosa Bell Oldham, great-grandmother to me) was to construct a writer identity that would challenge and subdue all impulses that would lead me away from speech into silence. I was a young girl buying bubble gum at the corner store when I first "really" heard the full name Bell Hooks: I had just "talked back" to a grown person. Even now I can recall the surprised look, the mocking tones that informed me I must be kin to Bell Hooks—a sharp-tongued woman, a woman who spoke her mind, a woman who was not afraid to talk back. I claimed this legacy of defiance, of will, of courage, affirming my link to female ancestors who were bold and daring in their speech. Unlike my bold and daring mother and grandmother, who were not supportive of talking back, even though they were assertive and powerful in their speech, Bell Hooks, as I discovered, claimed, and invented her, was my ally, my support.

15   The initial act of talking back outside the home was an empowering moment. It was the first of many acts of defiant speech that would make it possible for me to emerge as independent thinker and writer. Seen in retrospect, "talking back" became for me a rite of initiation, testing my courage, strengthening my commitment, preparing me for the days ahead—the days when writing seems impossible but necessary, rejection notices, periods of silence, publication, ongoing development.

    Moving from silence into speech is for the oppressed, the colonized, the exploited, and those who stand and struggle side by side, a gesture of defiance that heals, that makes new life, and new growth possible. It is that act of speech, of "talking back" that is no mere gesture of empty words, that is the expression of moving from object to subject, that is the liberated voice.

Topics for Critical Thinking and Writing

1. hooks makes it clear, in her first paragraph, that in her family children were not expected to speak to adults unless they were spoken to. Nevertheless, and despite frequent punishment, she insisted on speaking. Where and how does hooks suggest why she so needed to speak?
2. How did the speech of men and women differ in hooks's family and community? When you were a child, what differences between the speech of men and women were you aware of?
3. What was the connection for hooks between her desire to speak and her beginnings as a writer?
4. In paragraph 6, writing about her diaries, hooks describes her "fear of exposure," a feeling shared by many young girls. She assumes here that only girls, not boys, keep diaries. Do you think that is true, and if so, why is it true? Under what circumstances might boys as well as girls experience "the fear of exposure" from their writing, and how do you account for it?
5. In paragraph 11 hooks speaks of writers of "oppressed, colonized groups" and characterizes their writing as "an act of resistance, a political gesture." What connects her observations here and in the next paragraph with what she has told us of her experience as a child?
6. If you have sometimes "talked back" in bell hooks's sense, in an essay of 750 words describe a particular occasion, and indicate whether it empowered you (paragraph 15) or not.

 **MARY KARR**

Mary Karr is a poet and essayist who has won numerous prizes, awards, and grants for her work. In The Liars' Club *(1995), she describes a troubled and at times traumatic childhood with her parents and sister in East Texas. Critics have called her work "dazzling" and "wickedly funny."*

Karr teaches literature and creative writing at Syracuse University.

Texas, 1961

Maybe it's wrong to blame the arrival of Grandma Moore for much of the worst hurt in my family, but she was such a ring-tailed bitch that I do. She sat like some dissipated empress in Mother's huge art deco chair (mint-green vinyl with square black arms), which she turned to face right out of our front picture window like she was about to start issuing proclamations any minute.

All day, she doled out criticisms that set my mother to scurrying around with her face set so tight her mouth was a hyphen. The drapes were awful; let's make some new. When was the last time we'd cleaned our windows? (Never.) Had Mother put on weight? She seemed pudged up. I looked plumb like a wet-back I was so dark. (Lecia had managed to come out blond like her people, but Grandma never got over my looking vaguely Indian like Daddy.) And I was *pore-looking,* a term she reserved for underfed farm animals and the hookworm-ridden Cajun kids we saw trying to catch crawfish on summer afternoons on the edge of Taylor's Bayou. (Marvalene Seesacque once described her incentive for crawdadding all day: "You don't catch, you don't eat.")

In a house where I often opened a can of tamales for breakfast and ate them cold (I remember sucking the cuminy tomato sauce off the paper each one was wrapped in) Grandma cut out a *Reader's Digest* story on the four major food groups and taped it to the refrigerator. Suddenly our family dinners involved dishes you saw on TV, like meatloaf—stuff you had to light the oven to make, which Mother normally didn't even bother doing for Thanksgiving.

Our family's habit of eating meals in the middle of my parents' bed also broke overnight. Mother had made the bed extra big by stitching two mattresses together and using coat hangers to hook up their frames. She'd said that she needed some spread-out space because of the humidity, a word Lecia and I misheard for a long time as *stupidity.* (Hence, our tendency to say, *It ain't the heat, it's the stupidity.*) It was the biggest bed I ever saw, and filled their whole bedroom wall-to-wall. She had to stitch up special sheets for it, and even the chest of drawers had to be put out in the hall. The only pieces of furniture that still fit next to the bed were a standing brass ashtray shaped like a Viking ship on Daddy's side and a tall black reading lamp next to a wobbly tower of hardback books on Mother's.

5   Anyway, the four of us tended to eat our family meals sitting cross-legged on the edges of that bed. We faced opposite walls, our backs together, looking like some four-headed totem, our plates balanced on the spot of quilt between our legs. Mother called it picnic-style, but since I've been grown, I recall it as just plain odd. I've often longed to take out an ad in a major metropolitan paper and ask whether anybody else's family ate back-to-back in the parents' bed, and what such a habit might signify.

With Grandma there, we used not just the table but table linens. Mother hired a black woman named Mae Brown to wash and iron the tablecloth and napkins when they got greased up. And we couldn't just come in out of the heat at midday and pull off our clothes anymore with Grandma there. We'd had this habit of stripping down to underwear or putting on pajamas in the house, no matter what the time. In the serious heat, we'd lie for hours half-naked on the wooden floor in front of the black blade-fan sucking chipped ice out of wadded-up dish towels. Now Grandma even tried to get us to keep shoes and socks on. Plus we had to take baths every night. One of these first baths ended with the old woman holding me in a rough towel on her lap while she scrubbed at my neck with fingernail-polish remover. (It had supposedly accumulated quite a crust.)

She undertook to supervise our religious training, which had until then consisted of sporadic visits to Christian Science Sunday school alternating with the exercises from a book Mother had on yoga postures. (I could sustain a full-lotus position at five.) Grandma bought Lecia and me each white leather Bibles that zipped shut. "If you read three chapters a day and five on Sunday, you can read the Holy Bible in one year," she said. I don't remember ever unzipping mine once after unwrapping it, for Grandma was prone to abandoning any project that came to seem too daunting, as making us into Christians must have seemed.

Much later, when Mother could be brought to talk about her own childhood, she told stories about how peculiar her mother's habits had been. Grandma Moore didn't sound like such a religious fanatic back then. She just seemed like a fanatic in general. For instance, she had once sent away for a detective-training kit from a magazine. The plan was for her and Mother to spy on their neighbors—this, back when the Lubbock population still fit into three digits. According to Mother, this surveillance went on for weeks. Grandma would stirrup Mother up to the parson's curtained windows—and not because of any suspected adultery or flagrant sinning, but to find out whether his wife did her cakes from scratch or not. She kept the answers to these kinds of questions in an alphabetized log of prominent families. She would also zero in on some particular person who troubled her and keep track of all his comings and goings for weeks on end. She knew the procedure for taking fingerprints and kept Mother's on a recipe card, in case she was ever kidnapped. Grandma even began to collect little forensic envelopes of hair and dust that she found on people's furniture when she visited them. Mother said that for the better part of a year, they'd be taking tea at some lady's house, when her mother would suddenly sneak an envelope with something like a dustball in it into the pocket of her pinafore. Whatever became of this *evidence* Mother couldn't say. The whole detective-training deal got dropped as abruptly as it had been undertaken.

When Grandma came to our house, she brought with her that same kind of slightly deranged scrutiny. Before, our lives had been closed to outsiders. The noise of my parents' fights might leak out through the screens at night, and I might guess at the neighbors' scorn, but nobody really asked after our family, about Mother's being Nervous. We didn't go to church. No one came to visit. We probably seemed as blurry to the rest of the neighborhood as bad TV. Suddenly Grandma was staring at us with laser-blue eyes from behind her horn rims, saying *Can I make a suggestion?* or beginning every sentence with *Why don't you . . . ?*

10   Also, she was herself secretive. She bustled around as if she had some earnest agenda, but God knows what it was. She carried, for instance, an enormous black alligator doctor's bag, which held, along with the regular lady stuff in there—cosmetics and little peony-embroidered hankies—an honest-to-God hacksaw. It was the kind you see only in B movies, when criminals need it to saw through jail bars. Lest you think I fabricate, Lecia saw it, too. We even had a standing joke that we were keeping Grandma prisoner, and she was planning to bust out.

I had always thought that what I lacked in my family was some attentive, brownie-baking female to keep my hair curled and generally Donna-Reed over me. But my behavior got worse with Grandma's new order. I became a nail-biter.

My tantrums escalated to the point where even Daddy didn't think they were funny anymore. I tore down the new drapes they'd hung across the dining room windows and clawed scratch marks down both of Lecia's cheeks. Beating me didn't seem to discourage me one whit. Though I was a world-famous crybaby, I refused to cry during spankings. I still can recall Daddy holding a small horse quirt, my calves striped with its imprint and stinging and my saying, "Go on and hit me then, if it makes you feel like a man to beat on a little girl like me." End of spanking.

Lecia was both better-tempered and better at kissing ass than I was, so she fared better. But the pressure must have gotten to her too. It was during Grandma's residency that my sister stuffed me struggling into the clothes hamper that pulled out from the bathroom wall, and left me screaming among the mildewed towels till Mae Brown came back from getting groceries. Also, she took to plastering down her bangs with so much hair spray that neither wind nor rain could move them. (I called her Helmethead.) And she lengthened all her skirts so her knees didn't show anymore. In pictures from then, she looks like a child trying to impersonate an adult and coming out some strange gargoyle neither adult nor child. Once she even had me climb up on her shoulders, then draped a brown corduroy painter's smock to hang from my shoulders to her knees. We staggered from house to house pretending we were some lady collecting for the American Cancer Society. I remember holding a coffee can out to various strangers as I listed side to side on her shoulders. We didn't clear a dime.

In fairness to Grandma, she was dying of cancer at fifty, which can't do much for your disposition. Still, I remember not one tender feeling for or from her. Her cheek was withered like a bad apple and smelled of hyacinth. I had to be physically forced to kiss this cheek, even though I was prone to throwing my arms around the neck of any vaguely friendly grown-up—vacuum-cleaner salesman, mechanic, checkout lady.

The worst part wasn't all the change she brought, but the silence that came with it. Nobody said anything about how we'd lived before. It felt as if the changes themselves had just swept over us like some great wave, flattening whatever we'd once been. I somehow knew that suggesting a dinner in the middle of the bed, or stripping down when I came in from playing, would have thrown such a pall of shame over the household that I couldn't even consider it. Clearly, we had, all this time, been doing everything all wrong.

Topics for Critical Thinking and Writing

1. In the opening sentence of this section of her memoir, Karr calls Grandma Moore "a ring-tailed bitch." Do you remember how you felt, reading that description? Were you surprised? How do you explain your reaction, whatever it was?
2. How did Mary feel about her parents? About her sister? What passages best reveal how she felt about them?
3. Karr doesn't reveal until her next-to-last paragraph that her grandmother was dying of cancer. Should she have revealed this earlier? What does the narrative gain (or lose) by her postponing this revelation?
4. Imagine that you were a social worker in East Texas and the Karrs were on your case list. In three or four sentences, describe the family.

5. How does Karr feel about her childhood? Is she angry? Regretful? Stoic? Note some instances of humor in her account. How do they help you to understand her feelings?

6. A writing assignment: Think of a relative or close family friend whom you disliked or who made you uncomfortable when you were very young. Write a narrative about that person, including two or three incidents that reveal the person as you then perceived him or her. (For guidance on writing a narrative, see Chapter 9, "Narrating.")

 **MARTIN LUTHER KING, JR.**

Martin Luther King Jr. (1929–68), clergyman and civil rights leader, achieved national fame in mid–1950s when he led the boycott against segregated bus lines in Montgomery, Alabama. In 1964 he was awarded the Nobel Peace Prize, but he continued to encounter strong opposition. On April 4, 1968, while in Memphis to support striking sanitation workers, he was shot and killed.

Nonviolent Resistance

Oppressed people deal with their oppression in three characteristic ways. One way is acquiescence: the oppressed resign themselves to their doom. They tacitly adjust themselves to oppression, and thereby become conditioned to it. In every movement toward freedom some of the oppressed prefer to remain oppressed. Almost 2800 years ago Moses set out to lead the children of Israel from the slavery of Egypt to the freedom of the promised land. He soon discovered that slaves do not always welcome their deliverers. They become accustomed to being slaves. They would rather bear those ills they have, as Shakespeare pointed out, than flee to others that they know not of. They prefer the "fleshpots of Egypt" to the ordeals of emancipation.

There is such a thing as the freedom of exhaustion. Some people are so worn down by the yoke of oppression that they give up. A few years ago in the slum areas of Atlanta, a Negro guitarist used to sing almost daily: "Ben down so long that down don't bother me." This is the type of negative freedom and resignation that often engulfs the life of the oppressed.

But this is not the way out. To accept passively an unjust system is to cooperate with that system; thereby the oppressed become as evil as the oppressor. Noncooperation with evil is as much a moral obligation as is cooperation with good. The oppressed must never allow the conscience of the oppressor to slumber. Religion reminds every man that he is his brother's keeper. To accept injustice or segregation passively is to say to the oppressor that his actions are morally right. It is a way of allowing his conscience to fall asleep. At this moment the oppressed fails to be his brother's keeper. So acquiescence—while often the easier way—is not the moral way. It is the way of the coward. The Negro cannot win the respect of his oppressor by acquiescing; he merely increases the oppressor's arrogance and contempt. Acquiescence is interpreted as proof of the Negro's inferiority. The Negro cannot win the respect of the white people of the South or the peoples of the world if he is willing to sell the future of his children for his personal and immediate comfort and safety.

A second way that oppressed people sometimes deal with oppression is to resort to physical violence and corroding hatred. Violence often brings about momentary results. Nations have frequently won their independence in battle. But in spite of temporary victories, violence never brings permanent peace. It solves no social problem; it merely creates new and more complicated ones.

5   Violence as a way of achieving racial justice is both impractical and immoral. It is impractical because it is a descending spiral ending in destruction for all. The old law of an eye for an eye leaves everybody blind. It is immoral because it seeks to humiliate the opponent rather than win his understanding; it seeks to annihilate rather than to convert. Violence is immoral because it thrives on hatred rather than love. It destroys community and makes brotherhood impossible. It leaves society in monologue rather than dialogue. Violence ends by defeating itself. It creates bitterness in the survivors and brutality in the destroyers. A voice echoes through time saying to every potential Peter, "Put up your sword." History is cluttered with the wreckage of nations that failed to follow this command.

If the American Negro and other victims of oppression succumb to the temptation of using violence in the struggle for freedom, future generations will be the recipients of a desolate night of bitterness, and our chief legacy to them will be an endless reign of meaningless chaos. Violence is not the way.

The third way open to oppressed people in their quest for freedom is the way of nonviolent resistance. Like the synthesis in Hegelian philosophy, the principle of nonviolent resistance seeks to reconcile the truths of two opposites—acquiescence and violence—while avoiding the extremes and immoralities of both. The nonviolent resister agrees with the person who acquiesces that one should not be physically aggressive toward his opponent; but he balances the equation by agreeing with the person of violence that evil must be resisted. He avoids the nonresistance of the former and the violent resistance of the latter. With nonviolent resistance, no individual or group need submit to any wrong, nor need anyone resort to violence in order to right a wrong.

It seems to me that this is the method that must guide the actions of the Negro in the present crisis in race relations. Through nonviolent resistance the Negro will be able to rise to the noble height of opposing the unjust system while loving the perpetrators of the system. The Negro must work passionately and unrelentingly for full stature as a citizen, but he must not use inferior methods to gain it. He must never come to terms with falsehood, malice, hate, or destruction.

Nonviolent resistance makes it possible for the Negro to remain in the South and struggle for his rights. The Negro's problem will not be solved by running away. He cannot listen to the glib suggestion of those who would urge him to migrate en masse to other sections of the country. By grasping his great opportunity in the South he can make a lasting contribution to the moral strength of the nation and set a sublime example of courage for generations yet unborn.

10   By nonviolent resistance, the Negro can also enlist all men of good will in his struggle for equality. The problem is not a purely racial one, with Negroes set against whites. In the end, it is not a struggle between people at all, but a tension between justice and injustice. Nonviolent resistance is not aimed against oppressors but against oppression. Under its banner consciences, not racial groups, are enlisted.

If the Negro is to achieve the goal of integration, he must organize himself into a militant and nonviolent mass movement. All three elements are indispensable. The movement for equality and justice can only be a success if it has both a mass and militant character; the barriers to be overcome require both. Nonviolence is an imperative in order to bring about ultimate community.

A mass movement of militant quality that is not at the same time committed to nonviolence tends to generate conflict, which in turn breeds anarchy. The support of the participants and the sympathy of the uncommitted are both inhibited by the threat that bloodshed will engulf the community. This reaction in turn encourages the opposition to threaten and resort to force. When, however, the mass movement repudiates violence while moving resolutely toward its goal, its opponents are revealed as the instigators and practitioners of violence if it occurs. Then public support is magnetically attracted to the advocates of nonviolence, while those who employ violence are literally disarmed by overwhelming sentiment against their stand.

 ## Topics for Critical Thinking and Writing

1. Analysis is a term from science, and to some people it suggests coldness, a dispassionate clinical examination. Point to passages in this essay where King communicates his warmth, or sympathy, or passion.

2. In the first paragraph the passage about Moses and the children of Israel is not strictly necessary; the essential idea of the paragraph is stated in the previous sentence. Why, then, does King add this material? And why the quotation from Shakespeare?

3. Pick out two or three sentences that seem to you to be especially effective, and analyze the sources of their power. You can choose either isolated sentences or (because King often effectively links sentences with repetition of words or of constructions) consecutive ones.

4. In a paragraph, set forth your understanding of what nonviolent resistance is. Use whatever examples from your own experience or reading you find useful. In a second paragraph, explain how Maya Angelou's "Graduation" (pages 483–90) offers an example of nonviolent resistance.

 ## STEPHEN KING

Stephen King, with more than 100 million copies of his books in print, is one of America's most popular authors. King was born in Portland, Maine, in 1947. After graduating from the University of Maine he taught high school English until he was able to devote himself full-time to writing. In addition to writing stories and novels—some of which have been made into films—he has written Danse Macabre, *a book that, like the essay we reprint here, discusses the appeal of horror.*

Why We Crave Horror Movies

I think that we're all mentally ill; those of us outside the asylums only hide it a little better—and maybe not all that much better, after all. We've all known people who talk to themselves, people who sometimes squinch their faces into horrible grimaces when they believe no one is watching, people who have some hysterical fear—of snakes, the dark, the tight place, the long drop . . . and, of course, those final worms and grubs that are waiting so patiently underground.

When we pay our four or five bucks and seat ourselves at tenth-row center in a theater showing a horror movie, we are daring the nightmare.

Why? Some of the reasons are simple and obvious. To show that we can, that we are not afraid, that we can ride this roller coaster. Which is not to say that a really good horror movie may not surprise a scream out of us at some point, the way we may scream when the roller coaster twists through a complete 360 or plows through a lake at the bottom of the drop. And horror movies, like roller coasters, have always been the special province of the young; by the time one turns 40 or 50, one's appetite for double twists or 360-degree loops may be considerably depleted.

We also go to re-establish our feelings of essential normality; the horror movie is innately conservative, even reactionary. Freda Jackson as the horrible melting woman in *Die, Monster, Die!* confirms for us that no matter how far we may be removed from the beauty of a Robert Redford or a Diana Ross, we are still light-years from true ugliness.

5   And we go to have fun.

Ah, but this is where the ground starts to slope away, isn't it? Because this is a very peculiar sort of fun, indeed. The fun comes from seeing others menaced—sometimes killed. One critic has suggested that if pro football has become the voyeur's version of combat, then the horror film has become the modern version of the public lynching.

It is true that the mythic, "fairy-tale" horror film intends to take away the shades of gray. . . . It urges us to put away our more civilized and adult penchant for analysis and to become children again, seeing things in pure blacks and whites. It may be that horror movies provide psychic relief on this level because this invitation to lapse into simplicity, irrationality and even outright madness is extended so rarely. We are told we may allow our emotions a free rein . . . or no rein at all.

If we are all insane, then sanity becomes a matter of degree. If your insanity leads you to carve up women like Jack the Ripper or the Cleveland Torso Murderer, we clap you away in the funny farm (but neither of those two amateur-night surgeons was ever caught, heh-heh-heh); if, on the other hand, your insanity leads you only to talk to yourself when you're under stress or to pick your nose on your morning bus, then you are left alone to go about your business . . . though it is doubtful that you will ever be invited to the best parties.

The potential lyncher is in almost all of us (excluding saints, past and present; but then, most saints have been crazy in their own ways), and every now and then, he has to be let loose to scream and roll around in the grass. Our emotions and our fears form their own body, and we recognize that it demands its own exercise to maintain proper muscle tone. Certain of these emotional muscles are accepted—even exalted—in civilized society; they are, of course, the emotions that tend to maintain the status quo of civilization itself. Love, friendship, loyalty, kindness—these are all the emotions that we applaud, emotions that have been immortalized in the couplets of Hallmark cards and in the verses (I don't dare call it poetry) of Leonard Nimoy.

10   When we exhibit these emotions, society showers us with positive reinforcement; we learn this even before we get out of diapers. When, as children, we hug our rotten little puke of a sister and give her a kiss, all the aunts and uncles smile and twit and cry, "Isn't he the sweetest little thing?" Such coveted

treats as chocolate-covered graham crackers often follow. But if we deliberately slam the rotten little puke of a sister's fingers in the door, sanctions follow—angry remonstrance from parents, aunts and uncles; instead of a chocolate-covered graham cracker, a spanking.

But anticivilization emotions don't go away, and they demand periodic exercise. We have such "sick" jokes as, "What's the difference between a truckload of bowling balls and a truckload of dead babies?" (You can't unload a truckload of bowling balls with a pitchfork . . . a joke, by the way, that I heard originally from a ten-year-old). Such a joke may surprise a laugh or a grin out of us even as we recoil, a possibility that confirms the thesis: If we share a brotherhood of man, then we also share an insanity of man. None of which is intended as a defense of either the sick joke or insanity but merely as an explanation of why the best horror films, like the best fairy tales, manage to be reactionary, anarchistic, and revolutionary all at the same time.

The mythic horror movie, like the sick joke, has a dirty job to do. It deliberately appeals to all that is worst in us. It is morbidity unchained, our most base instincts let free, our nastiest fantasies realized . . . and it all happens, fittingly enough, in the dark. For those reasons, good liberals often shy away from horror films. For myself, I like to see the most aggressive of them—*Dawn of the Dead,* for instance—as lifting a trap door in the civilized forebrain and throwing a basket of raw meat to the hungry alligators swimming around in that subterranean river beneath.

Why bother? Because it keeps them from getting out, man. It keeps them down there and me up here. It was Lennon and McCartney who said that all you need is love, and I would agree with that.

As long as you keep the gators fed.

Topics for Critical Thinking and Writing

1. In paragraph 6 King, paraphrasing an unnamed critic, suggests that "the horror film has become the modern version of the public lynching." In your opinion, why did some people find excitement in a lynching? Does the horror film offer somewhat similar excitement(s)?

2. King suggests in paragraph 11 that we have within us a stock of "anticivilization emotions [that] don't go away, and they demand periodic exercise." What, if any, evidence are you aware of that supports this view?

3. In paragraph 11 King tells a joke about dead babies. He suggests that jokes of this sort "may surprise a laugh or a grin out of us even as we recoil." Analyze your own response to the joke, or to similar jokes. Did you laugh, or grin? Or was your response utterly different? If so, what was it?

4. In paragraphs 12 and 13 King says that horror movies serve a valuable social purpose. Do you think he has proved this point? What are the strengths (if any) and the weaknesses (if any) of his argument?

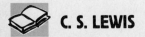 **C. S. LEWIS**

C[live] S[taples] Lewis (1898–1963) taught medieval and Renaissance literature at Oxford and later at Cambridge. In addition to writing about literature, he wrote fiction

(including The Chronicles of Narnia*), poetry, and numerous essays and books on moral and religious topics.*

Vivisection

It is the rarest thing in the world to hear a rational discussion of vivisection. These who disapprove of it are commonly accused of "sentimentality," and very often their arguments justify the accusation. They paint pictures of pretty little dogs on dissecting tables. But the other side lies open to exactly the same charge. They also often defend the practice by drawing pictures of suffering women and children whose pain can be relieved we are assured only by the fruits of vivisection. The one appeal, quite as clearly as the other, is addressed to emotion, to the particular emotion we call pity. And neither appeal proves anything. If the thing is right—and if right at all, it is a duty—then pity for the animal is one of the temptations we must resist in order to perform that duty. If the thing is wrong, then pity for human suffering is precisely the temptation which will most probably lure us into doing that wrong thing. But the real question—*whether* it is right or wrong—remains meanwhile just where it was.

A rational discussion of this subject begins by inquiring whether pain is, or is not, an evil. If it is not, then the case against vivisection falls. But then so does the case for vivisection. If it is not defended on the ground that it reduces human suffering, on what ground can it be defended? And if pain is not an evil, why should human suffering be reduced? We must therefore assume as a basis for the whole discussion that pain is an evil, otherwise there is nothing to be discussed.

Now if pain is an evil then the infliction of pain, considered in itself, must clearly be an evil act. But there are such things as necessary evils. Some acts which would be bad, simply in themselves, may be excusable and even laudable when they are necessary means to a greater good. In saying that the infliction of pain, simply in itself, is bad, we are not saying that pain ought never to be inflicted. Most of us think that it can rightly be inflicted for a good purpose—as in dentistry or just and reformatory punishment. The point is that it always requires justification. On the man whom we find inflicting pain rests the burden of showing why an act which in itself would be simply bad is, in those particular circumstances, good. If we find a man giving pleasure it is for us to prove (if we criticize him) that his action is wrong. But if we find a man inflicting pain it is for him to prove that his action is right. If he cannot, he is a wicked man.

Now vivisection can only be defended by showing it to be right that one species should suffer in order that another species should be happier. And here we come to the parting of the ways. The Christian defender and the ordinary "scientific" (i.e., naturalistic) defender of vivisection, have to take quite different lines.

5 The Christian defender, especially in the Latin countries, is very apt to say that we are entitled to do anything we please to animals because they "have no souls." But what does this mean? If it means that animals have no consciousness, then how is this known? They certainly behave as if they had, or at least the higher animals do. I myself am inclined to think that far fewer animals than is supposed have what we should recognize as consciousness. But that is only an opinion. Unless we know on other grounds that vivisection is right we must not take the moral risk of tormenting them on a mere opinion. On the other hand, the statement that they "have no souls" may mean that they have no moral re-

sponsibilities and are not immortal. But the absence of "soul" in that sense makes the infliction of pain upon them not easier but harder to justify. For it means that animals cannot deserve pain, nor profit morally by the discipline of pain, nor be recompensed by happiness in another life for suffering in this. Thus all the factors which render pain more tolerable or make it less totally evil in the case of human beings will be lacking in the beasts. "Soullessness," in so far as it is relevant to the question at all, is an argument against vivisection.

The only rational line for the Christian vivisectionist to take is to say that the superiority of man over beast is a real objective fact, guaranteed by Revelation, and that the propriety of sacrificing beast to man is a logical consequence. We are "worth more than many sparrows,"[1] and in saying this we are not merely expressing a natural preference for our own species simply because it is our own but conforming to a hierarchical order created by God and really present in the universe whether any one acknowledges it or not. The position may not be satisfactory. We may fail to see how a benevolent Deity could wish us to draw such conclusions from the hierarchical order He has created. We may find it difficult to formulate a human right of tormenting beasts in terms which would not equally imply an angelic right of tormenting men. And we may feel that though objective superiority is rightly claimed for men, yet that very superiority ought partly to *consist in* not behaving like a vivisector: that we ought to prove ourselves better than the beasts precisely by the fact of acknowledging duties to them which they do not acknowledge to us. But on all these questions different opinions can be honestly held. If on grounds of our real, divinely ordained, superiority a Christian pathologist thinks it right to vivisect, and does so with scrupulous care to avoid the least dram or scruple of unnecessary pain, in a trembling awe at the responsibility which he assumes, and with a vivid sense of the high mode in which human life must be lived if it is to justify the sacrifices made for it, then (whether we agree with him or not) we can respect his point of view.

But of course the vast majority of vivisectors have no such theological background. They are most of them naturalistic and Darwinian. Now here, surely, we come up against a very alarming fact. The very same people who will most contemptuously brush aside any consideration of animal suffering if it stands in the way of "research" will also, on another context, most vehemently deny that there is any radical difference between man and the other animals. On the naturalistic view the beasts are at bottom just the same *sort* of thing as ourselves. Man is simply the cleverest of the anthropoids. All the grounds on which a Christian might defend vivisection are thus cut from under our feet. We sacrifice other species to our own not because our own has any objective metaphysical privilege over others, but simply because it is ours. It may be very natural to have this loyalty to our own species, but let us hear no more from the naturalists about the "sentimentality" of antivivisectionists. If loyalty to our own species, preference for man simply because we are men, is not a sentiment, then what is? It may be a good sentiment or a bad one. But a sentiment it certainly is. Try to base it on logic and see what happens!

But the most sinister thing about modern vivisection is this. If a mere sentiment justifies cruelty, why stop at a sentiment for the whole human race? There is also a sentiment for the white man against the black, for a *Herrenvolk*[2] against

---

[1]Matthew x.31
[2]German for "master race" (editors' note)

the non-Aryans, for "civilized" or "progressive" peoples against "savages" or "backward" peoples. Finally, for our own country, party or class against others. Once the old Christian idea of a total difference in kind between man and beast has been abandoned, then no argument for experiments on animals can be found which is not also an argument for experiments on inferior men. If we cut up beasts simply because they cannot prevent us and because we are backing our own side in the struggle for existence, it is only logical to cut up imbeciles, criminals, enemies or capitalists for the same reasons. Indeed, experiments on men have already begun. We all hear that Nazi scientists have done them. We all suspect that our own scientists may begin to do so, in secret, at any moment.

The alarming thing is that the vivisectors have won the first round. In the nineteenth and eighteenth centuries a man was not stamped as a "crank" for protesting against vivisection. Lewis Carroll protested, if I remember his famous letter correctly, on the very same ground which I have just used.[3] Dr. Johnson— a man whose mind had as much *iron* in it as any man's—protested in a note on *Cymbeline* which is worth quoting in full. In Act I, scene v, the Queen explains to the Doctor that she wants poisons to experiment on "such creatures as We count not worth the hanging,—but none human."[4] The Doctor replies:

Your Highness
Shall from this practice but make hard your heart.[5]

Johnson comments: "The thought would probably have been more amplified, had our author lived to be shocked with such experiments as have been published in later times, by a race of men that have practised tortures without pity, and related them without shame, and are yet suffered to erect their heads among human beings."[6]

10   The words are his, not mine, and in truth we hardly dare in these days to use such calmly stern language. The reason why we do not dare is that the other side has in fact won. And though cruelty even to beasts is an important matter, their victory is symptomatic of matters more important still. The victory of vivisection marks a great advance in the triumph of ruthless, non-moral, utilitarianism over the old world of ethical law; a triumph in which we, as well as animals, are already the victims, and of which Dachau and Hiroshima mark the more recent achievements. In justifying cruelty to animals we put ourselves also on the animal level. We choose the jungle and must abide by our choice.

You will notice I have spent no time in discussing what actually goes on in the laboratories. We shall be told, of course, that there is surprisingly little cruelty. That is a question with which, at present, I have nothing to do. We must first decide what should be allowed: after that it is for the police to discover what is already being done.

---

[3]"Vivisection as a Sign of the Times," *The Works of Lewis Carroll,* ed Roger Lancelyn Green (London, 1965), pp. 1089–92. See also "Some Popular Fallacies about Vivisection," ibid., pp. 1092–1100.
[4]Shakespeare, *Cymbeline,* I, v, 19–20.
[5]Ibid., 23.
[6]*Johnson on Shakespeare: Essays and Notes Selected and Set Forth with an Introduction* by Sir Walter Raleigh (London, 1908), p. 181.

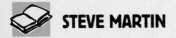

Topics for Critical Thinking and Writing

1. What purpose does Lewis's first paragraph serve? Is his implied definition of sentimentality adequate for his purpose?
2. By the end of the second paragraph are you willing to agree, at least for the sake of argument, that pain is an evil?
3. In the third paragraph Lewis gives two examples (dentistry and reformatory punishment) to prove that the infliction of pain "always requires justification." Are these two examples adequate and effective?
4. By the end of the fifth paragraph (the paragraph beginning "The Christian defender") are we more or less convinced that Lewis is fully aware of both sides of the argument? Do we feel he is fairly presenting both sides?
5. Characterize the tone (Lewis's attitude) implied in "The position may not be satisfactory" (paragraph 6). Notice also the effect of the repetition (in the same paragraph) of "We may fail to see," "We may find it difficult." "And we may feel. . . ." How tentative do you think Lewis really is?
6. The eighth paragraph begins, "But the most sinister thing about modern vivisection is this." How surprising is the word "sinister"? And why does Lewis bring in (drag in?) racist and religious persecution?
7. Late in his essay (paragraph 9) Lewis quotes Lewis Carroll, Shakespeare, and Dr. Johnson. Except for a phrase from the Bible, these are the first quotations he uses. Should he have introduced these quotations, or others, earlier?
8. Analyze the final paragraph. Is Lewis correct in dismissing the question of how much cruelty there is in laboratories? Characterize the tone of the last sentence.

STEVE MARTIN

Steve Martin is an actor, writer, and comedian. This essay originally appeared in The New Yorker.

Studies in the New Causality

> *A 27-year-old Michigan man, who complained that a rear-end auto collision had turned him into a homosexual, has been awarded $200,000 by a jury.*
>
> *—"Ann Landers," July 30, 1998*

Recent discoveries in the legal profession have left scientists, many of whom still linger romantically in the Newtonian world, scrambling to catch up in the field of New Causality. In a case last month, a judge in Sacramento ruled in favor of changing the value of pi, thus acquitting a tire manufacturer of making tires that were not fully round. An appeal by scientists was thrown out for lack of evidence when the small courtroom could not physically accommodate a fully expressed representation of pi. The oblong tires in question were produced at the retrial, the judge said they looked round to him, the defense played the race card, and the value of pi was changed to 2.9.

Cause and effect have traditionally been expressed by the example of one billiard ball hitting another billiard ball, the striking billiard ball being the "cause" and the struck billiard ball being the "effect." However, in the new legal parlance the cause of the second billiard ball's motion is unclear, depending on whether you're prosecuting or defending the first billiard ball. If you are suing the first billiard ball, it is entirely conceivable that striking the second billiard ball harmed your chances of becoming Miss Paraguay. If you're defending the first billiard ball, the motion of the second billiard ball could be an unrelated coincidence.

It's easy to understand how one physical thing can influence another physical thing: my car hit your car because I was blinded by your shiny hair barrette. But what about emotional causality? Can my harsh words affect your mood, costing you millions of dollars that you would have earned behind the counter at Burger King? Apparently so. Several months ago, a male office worker was awarded sixty-seven thousand dollars because a female co-worker asked him if he would like her to drop his "package" off at the post office; he was further awarded fifty thousand dollars after arguing that she was also in constant possession of a vagina, the knowledge of which rendered him unable to concentrate.

A more difficult causality to prove, however, is physical to emotional. Can being struck from behind in a car accident cause someone to become a homosexual? Obviously the answer is yes, evidenced by the large award in the lawsuit cited above. Even more interesting is a little-known case in which a man was awarded thirty-six thousand dollars after a driver *failed* to collide with his car, causing him to become a *latent* homosexual.

5   The New Causality guidelines have redefined many of the basic concepts with which the scientific world has struggled for centuries. They are:

The "Ninety-seven Steps" Rule: It used to be accepted that one event caused another one event to happen. No longer so. It is now acceptable to have up to ninety-seven causality links:

Your dog ate my philodendron which depressed my mother who in a stupor voted for Marion Barry causing an upswing in crack sales that allowed Peru to maintain an embassy and accumulate parking tickets, encouraging me to stay a meter maid rather than become an Imagineer. And so on.

Semantic Causality: Semantic causality occurs when a word or phrase in the cause is the same as a word or phrase in the effect. "You failed to install my client's *sink* properly, causing her to *sink* into a depression." In the case cited earlier, the plaintiff's lawyer might say that the "party" driving the Camaro collided with his client's car, and isn't a "party" where homosexuals gather and socialize with one another?

After-the Fact Causality: This simple law states that having sex with an intern can cause a financial misdealing to occur twenty years prior.

Universal Causality: This is the law that has the legal world most excited. It rests on the proposition that "anything can cause anything," or, more simply put, the "Bill Gates gave my dog asthma" principle. If the law of Universal Causality bears out, the economy will receive an invigorating boost when everyone sues everyone else for everything. Everything actionable that ever happened to you will be the fault of your next-door neighbor, who, in turn, will sue Bill Gates, who, in turn, will sue himself.

10   These advancements in the legal world mean for science that a large stellar object is no longer the *cause* of the bending of light rays that pass nearby but its *blame.* Scientists everywhere are scurrying to make sense of the New Causality, with Newtonians turning into Einsteinians, and Einsteinians turning into Cochranians. Meanwhile, astronomers have discovered new and distant objects in the farthest reaches of the universe. Are they protogalaxies forming near the beginning of time? The courts will decide.

Topics for Critical Thinking and Writing

1. At what point, exactly, do you realize that the essay is satirical?
2. Who or what is Martin's primary target?
3. As precisely as possible, explain what makes "Studies in the New Causality" funny.
4. In paragraphs 6–9 Martin lists four basic concepts of the New Causality: "The 'Ninety-seven Steps' Rule," "Semantic Causality," "After-the-Fact Causality," and "Universal Causality." In a paragraph or so, set out a fifth concept of your own.

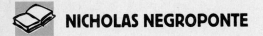 **NICHOLAS NEGROPONTE**

Nicholas Negroponte, born in 1943, holds degrees in architecture from the Massachusetts Institute of Technology, where he now teaches. Among his influential books are The Architecture Machine *and (the source of the following brief essay)* Being Digital *(1995).*

Being Asynchronous

A face-to-face or telephone conversation is real time and synchronous. Telephone tag is a game played to find the opportunity to be synchronous. Ironically, this is often done for exchanges, which themselves require no synchrony whatsoever, and could just as well be handled by non-real-time message passing. Historically, asynchronous communication, like letter writing, has tended to be more formal and less off-the-cuff exchanges. This is changing with voice mail and answering machines.

I have met people who claim they cannot understand how they (and we all) lived without answering machines at home and voice mail at the office. The advantage is less about voice and more about off-line processing and time shifting. It is about leaving messages versus engaging somebody needlessly in on-line discussion. In fact, answering machines are designed slightly backward. They should not only activate when you are not there or don't want to be there, but they should *always* answer the telephone and give the caller the opportunity to simply leave a message.

One of the enormous attractions of e-mail is that it is not interruptive like a telephone. You can process it at your leisure, and for this reason you may reply to messages that would not stand a chance in hell of getting through the secretarial defenses of corporate, telephonic life.

E-mail is exploding in popularity because it is *both* an asynchronous and a computer-readable medium. The latter is particularly important, because interface agents will use those bits to prioritize and deliver messages differently. Who sent the message and what it is about could determine the order in which you see it—no different from the current secretarial screening that allows a call from your six-year-old daughter to go right through, while the CEO of the XYZ Corporation is put on hold. Even on a busy workday, personal e-mail messages might drift to the top of the heap.

5   Not nearly as much of our communications need to be contemporaneous or in real time. We are constantly interrupted or forced into being punctual for things that truly do not merit such immediacy or promptness. We are forced into regular rhythms, not because we finished eating at 8:59 p.m., but because the TV program is about to start in one minute. Our great-grandchildren will understand our going to the theater at a given hour to benefit from the collective presence of human actors, but they will not understand the synchronous experiencing of television signals in the privacy of our home—until they look at the bizarre economic model behind it.

Topics for Critical Thinking and Writing

1. Paraphrase Negroponte's first sentence. How might his obscure diction be explained or justified?
2. Do you agree with Negroponte that "answering machines . . . should *always* answer the telephone"? Explain.
3. Whom is Negroponte addressing in paragraph 3? Does the attraction of e-mail he cites apply to anyone else? Explain.
4. When did you start to use e-mail? How do you currently use it? What advantages or disadvantages do you find in "being asynchronous"?

 **FLANNERY O'CONNOR**

Flannery O'Connor (1925–1964) was born in Georgia and spent most of her short life there. The Complete Stories of Flannery O'Connor *received the National Book Award for fiction in 1971; another posthumous volume,* Mystery and Manners, *includes essays on literature and an account of her experiences raising peacocks in Georgia.*

Total Effect and the Eighth Grade

In two recent instances in Georgia, parents have objected to their eighth- and ninth-grade children's reading assignments in modern fiction. This seems to happen with some regularity in cases throughout the country. The unwitting parent picks up his child's book, glances through it, comes upon passages of erotic detail or profanity, and takes off at once to complain to the school board. Sometimes, as in one of the Georgia cases, the teacher is dismissed and hackles rise in liberal circles everywhere.

The two cases in Georgia, which involved Steinbeck's *East of Eden* and John Hersey's *A Bell for Adano,* provoked considerable newspaper comment. One columnist, in commending the enterprise of the teachers, announced that students do not like to read the fusty works of the nineteenth century, that their attention can best be held by novels dealing with the realities of our own time, and that the Bible, too, is full of racy stories.

Mr. Hersey himself addressed a letter to the State School Superintendent in behalf of the teacher who had been dismissed. He pointed out that his book is not scandalous, that it attempts to convey an earnest message about the nature of democracy, and that it falls well within the limits of the principle of "total effect," that principle followed in legal cases by which a book is judged not for isolated parts but by the final effect of the whole book upon the general reader.

I do not want to comment on the merits of these particular cases. What concerns me is what novels ought to be assigned in the eighth and ninth grades as a matter of course, for if these cases indicate anything, they indicate the haphazard way in which fiction is approached in our high schools. Presumably there is a state reading list which contains "safe" books for teachers to assign; after that it is up to the teacher.

5   English teachers come in Good, Bad, and Indifferent, but too frequently in high schools anyone who can speak English is allowed to teach it. Since several novels can't easily be gathered into one textbook, the fiction that students are assigned depends upon their teacher's knowledge, ability, and taste: variable factors at best. More often than not, the teacher assigns what he thinks will hold the attention and interest of the students. Modern fiction will certainly hold it.

Ours is the first age in history which has asked the child what he would tolerate learning, but that is a part of the problem with which I am not equipped to deal. The devil of Educationism that possesses us is the kind that can be "cast out only by prayer and fasting." No one has yet come along strong enough to do it. In other ages the attention of children was held by Homer and Virgil, among others, but, by the reverse evolutionary process, that is no longer possible; our children are too stupid now to enter the past imaginatively. No one asks the student if algebra pleases him or if he finds it satisfactory that some French verbs are irregular, but if he prefers Hersey to Hawthorne, his taste must prevail.

I would like to put forward the proposition, repugnant to most English teachers, that fiction, if it is going to be taught in the high schools, should be taught as a subject and as a subject with a history. The total effect of a novel depends not only on its innate impact, but upon the experience, literary and otherwise, with which it is approached. No child needs to be assigned Hersey or Steinbeck until he is familiar with a certain amount of the best work of Cooper, Hawthorne, Melville, the early James, and Crane, and he does not need to be assigned these until he has been introduced to some of the better English novelists of the eighteenth and nineteenth centuries.

The fact that these works do not present him with the realities of his own time is all to the good. He is surrounded by the realities of his own time, and he has no perspective whatever from which to view them. Like the college student who wrote in her paper on Lincoln that he went to the movies and got shot, many students go to college unaware that the world was not made yesterday; their studies began with the present and dipped backward occasionally when it seemed necessary or unavoidable.

There is much to be enjoyed in the great British novels of the nineteenth century, much that a good teacher can open up in them for the young student.

There is no reason why these novels should be either too simple or too difficult for the eighth grade. For the simple, they offer simple pleasures; for the more precocious, they can be made to yield subtler ones if the teacher is up to it. Let the student discover, after reading the nineteenth-century British novel, that the nineteenth-century American novel is quite different as to its literary characteristics, and he will thereby learn something not only about these individual works but about the sea-change which a new historical situation can effect in a literary form. Let him come to modern fiction with this experience behind him, and he will be better able to see and to deal with the more complicated demands of the best twentieth-century fiction.

10   Modern fiction often looks simpler than the fiction that preceded it, but in reality it is more complex. A natural evolution has taken place. The author has for the most part absented himself from direct participation in the work and has left the reader to make his own way amid experiences dramatically rendered and symbolically ordered. The modern novelist merges the reader in the experience; he tends to raise the passions he touches upon. If he is a good novelist, he raises them to effect by their order and clarity a new experience—the total effect— which is not in itself sensuous or simply of the moment. Unless the child has had some literary experience before, he is not going to be able to resolve the immediate passions the book arouses into any true, total picture.

It is here the moral problem will arise. It is one thing for a child to read about adultery in the Bible or in *Anna Karenina,* and quite another for him to read about it in most modern fiction. This is not only because in both the former instances adultery is considered a sin, and in the latter, at most, an inconvenience, but because modern writing involves the reader in the action with a new degree of intensity, and literary mores permit him to be involved in any action a human being can perform.

In our fractured culture, we cannot agree on morals; we cannot even agree that moral matters should come before literary ones when there is a conflict between them. All this is another reason why the high schools would do well to return to their proper business of preparing foundations. Whether in the senior year students should be assigned modern novelists should depend both on their parents' consent and on what they have already read and understood.

The high-school English teacher will be fulfilling his responsibility if he furnishes the student a guided opportunity, through the best writing of the past, to come, in time, to an understanding of the best writing of the present. He will teach literature, not social studies or little lessons in democracy or the customs of many lands.

And if the student finds that this is not to his taste? Well, that is regrettable. Most regrettable. His taste should not be consulted; it is being formed.

Topics for Critical Thinking and Writing

1. What is the function of the first three paragraphs of "Total Effect and the Eighth Grade"? Can you justify O'Connor's abrupt dismissal ("I do not want to comment on the merits of these particular cases") of the opposing argument summarized in the second and third paragraphs? How?
2. "English teachers come in Good, Bad, and Indifferent, but too frequently in high schools anyone who can speak English is allowed to teach it." Can you, from your own experience, support this view?

3. Is the tone of the sixth paragraph, beginning "Ours is the first age," sarcastic? If not, how would you characterize it?

4. Which of O'Connor's arguments might be used to support the rating of movies X, R, PG, and G? Are you for or against these ratings? How would you support your position?

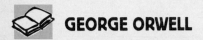 **GEORGE ORWELL**

George Orwell (1903–50), an Englishman, adopted this name; he was born Eric Blair, in India. He was educated at Eton, in England, but in 1921 he went to Burma, where he served for five years as a police officer. He then returned to Europe, doing odd jobs while writing novels and stories. In 1936 he fought in the Spanish Civil War on the side of the Republicans, an experience reported in Homage to Catalonia *(1938). His last years were spent writing in England.*

Shooting an Elephant

In Moulmein, in Lower Burma, I was hated by large numbers of people—the only time in my life that I have been important enough for this to happen to me. I was sub-divisional police officer of the town, and in an aimless, petty kind of way anti-European feeling was very bitter. No one had the guts to raise a riot, but if a European woman went through the bazaars alone somebody would probably spit betel juice over her dress. As a police officer I was an obvious target and was baited whenever it seemed safe to do so. When a nimble Burman tripped me up on the football field and the referee (another Burman) looked the other way, the crowd yelled with hideous laughter. This happened more than once. In the end the sneering yellow faces of young men that met me everywhere, the insults hooted after me when I was at a safe distance, got badly on my nerves. The young Buddhist priests were the worst of all. There were several thousands of them in the town and none of them seemed to have anything to do except stand on street corners and jeer at Europeans.

All this was perplexing and upsetting. For at that time I had already made up my mind that imperialism was an evil thing and the sooner I chucked up my job and got out of it the better. Theoretically—and secretly, of course—I was all for the Burmese and all against their oppressors, the British. As for the job I was doing, I hated it more bitterly than I can perhaps make clear. In a job like that you see the dirty work of Empire at close quarters. The wretched prisoners huddling in the stinking cages of the lockups, the grey, cowed faces of the long-term convicts, the scarred buttocks of the men who had been flogged with bamboos—all these oppressed me with an intolerable sense of guilt. But I could get nothing into perspective. I was young and ill-educated and I had had to think out my problems in the utter silence that is imposed on every Englishman in the East. I did not even know that the British Empire is dying, still less did I know that it is a great deal better than the younger empires that are going to supplant it. All I knew was that I was stuck between my hatred of the empire I served and my rage against the evil-spirited little beasts who tried to make my job impossible. With one part of my mind I thought of the British Raj as an unbreakable tyranny, as something clamped down, in *saecula saeculorum,*[1] upon the will of prostrate peoples; with another part I thought that the greatest joy in the world would be to drive a bayonet into a Buddhist priest's guts. Feelings like these are the normal by-products of imperialism; ask any Anglo-Indian official, if you can catch him off duty.

One day something happened which in a roundabout way was enlightening. It was a tiny incident in itself, but it gave me a better glimpse than I had had before of the real nature of imperialism—the real motives for which despotic governments act. Early one morning the sub-inspector at a police station at the other end of the town rang me up on the 'phone and said that an elephant was ravaging the bazaar. Would I please come and do something about it? I did not know what I could do, but I wanted to see what was happening and I got onto a pony and started out. I took my rifle, an old .44 Winchester and much too small to kill an elephant, but I thought the noise might be useful *in terrorem.*[2] Various Burmans stopped me on the way and told me about the elephant's doings. It was not, of course, a wild elephant, but a tame one which had gone "must." It had been chained up, as tame elephants always are when their attack of "must" is due, but on the previous night it had broken its chain and escaped. Its mahout, the only person who could manage it when it was in that state, had set out in pursuit, but had taken the wrong direction and was now twelve hours' journey away, and in the morning the elephant had suddenly reappeared in the town. The Burmese population had no weapons and were quite helpless against it. It had already destroyed somebody's bamboo hut, killed a cow and raided some fruit-stalls and devoured the stock; also it had met the municipal rubbish van and, when the driver jumped out and took to his heels, had turned the van over and inflicted violences upon it.

The Burmese sub-inspector and some Indian constables were waiting for me in the quarter where the elephant had been seen. It was a very poor quarter, a labyrinth of squalid bamboo huts, thatched with palmleaf, winding all over a steep hillside. I remember that it was a cloudy, stuffy morning at the beginning of the rains. We began questioning the people as to where the elephant had gone and, as usual, failed to get any definite information. That is invariably the case in the East; a story always sounds clear enough at a distance, but the nearer you get to the scene of events the vaguer it becomes. Some of the people said that the elephant had gone in one direction, some said that he had gone in another, some professed not even to have heard of any elephant. I had almost made up my mind that the whole story was a pack of lies, when we heard yells a little distance away. There was a loud, scandalized cry of "Go away, child! Go away this instant!" and an old woman with a switch in her hand came round the corner of a hut, violently shooing away a crowd of naked children. Some more women followed, clicking their tongues and exclaiming; evidently there was something that the children ought not to have seen. I rounded the hut and saw a man's dead body sprawling in the mud. He was an Indian, a black Dravidian coolie, almost naked, and he could not have been dead many minutes. The people said that the elephant had come suddenly upon him round the corner of the hut, caught him with its trunk, put its foot on his back and ground him into the earth. This was the rainy season and the ground was soft, and his face had scored

[1]For world without end.
[2]As a warning.

a trench a foot deep and a couple of yards long. He was lying on his belly with arms crucified and head sharply twisted to one side. His face was coated with mud, the eyes wide open, the teeth bared and grinning with an expression of unendurable agony. (Never tell me, by the way, that the dead look peaceful. Most of the corpses I have seen look devilish.) The friction of the great beast's foot had stripped the skin from his back as neatly as one skins a rabbit. As soon as I saw the dead man I sent an orderly to a friend's house nearby to borrow an elephant rifle. I had already sent back the pony, not wanting it to go mad with fright and throw me if it smelt the elephant.

5   The orderly came back in a few minutes with a rifle and five cartridges, and meanwhile some Burmans had arrived and told us that the elephant was in the paddy fields below, only a few hundred yards away. As I started forward practically the whole population of the quarter flocked out of the houses and followed me. They had seen the rifle and were all shouting excitedly that I was going to shoot the elephant. They had not shown much interest in the elephant when he was merely ravaging their homes, but it was different now that he was going to be shot. It was a bit of fun to them, as it would be to an English crowd; besides they wanted the meat. It made me vaguely uneasy. I had no intention of shooting the elephant—I had merely sent for the rifle to defend myself if necessary—and it is always unnerving to have a crowd following you. I marched down the hill, looking and feeling a fool, with the rifle over my shoulder and an ever-growing army of people jostling at my heels. At the bottom, when you got away from the huts, there was a metalled road and beyond that a miry waste of paddy fields a thousand yards across, not yet ploughed but soggy from the first rains and dotted with coarse grass. The elephant was standing eight yards from the road, his left side towards us. He took not the slightest notice of the crowd's approach. He was tearing up bunches of grass, beating them against his knees to clean them and stuffing them into his mouth.

I had halted on the road. As soon as I saw the elephant I knew with perfect certainty that I ought not to shoot him. It is a serious matter to shoot a working elephant—it is comparable to destroying a huge and costly piece of machinery—and obviously one ought not to do it if it can possibly be avoided. And at that distance, peacefully eating, the elephant looked no more dangerous than a cow. I thought then and I think now that his attack of "must" was already passing off; in which case he would merely wander harmlessly about until the mahout came back and caught him. Moreover, I did not in the least want to shoot him. I decided that I would watch him for a little while to make sure that he did not turn savage again, and then go home.

But at that moment I glanced round at the crowd that had followed me. It was an immense crowd, two thousand at the least and growing every minute. It blocked the road for a long distance on either side. I looked at the sea of yellow faces above the garish clothes—faces all happy and excited over this bit of fun, all certain that the elephant was going to be shot. They were watching me as they would watch a conjurer about to perform a trick. They did not like me, but with the magical rifle in my hands I was momentarily worth watching. And suddenly I realized that I should have to shoot the elephant after all. The people expected it of me and I had got to do it; I could feel their two thousand wills pressing me forward, irresistibly. And it was at this moment, as I stood there with the rifle in my hands, that I first grasped the hollowness, the futility of the white man's dominion in the East. Here was I, the white man with his gun, standing in front of the unarmed native crowd—seemingly the leading actor of the piece; but in reality I was only an absurd puppet pushed to and fro by the will of those yellow faces behind. I perceived in this moment that when the white man turns tyrant it is his own freedom that he destroys. He becomes a sort of hollow, posing dummy, the conventionalized figure of a sahib. For it is the condition of his rule that he shall spend his life in trying to impress the "natives," and so in every crisis he has got to do what the "natives" expect of him. He wears a mask, and his face grows to fit it. I had got to shoot the elephant. I had committed myself to doing it when I sent for the rifle. A sahib has got to act like a sahib; he has got to appear resolute, to know his own mind and do definite things. To come all that way, rifle in hand, with two thousand people marching at my heels, and then to trail feebly away, having done nothing—no, that was impossible. The crowd would laugh at me. And my whole life, every white man's life in the East, was one long struggle not to be laughed at.

But I did not want to shoot the elephant. I watched him beating his bunch of grass against his knees, with that preoccupied grandmotherly air that elephants have. It seemed to me that it would be murder to shoot him. At that age I was not squeamish about killing animals, but I had never shot an elephant and never wanted to. (Somehow it always seems worse to kill a *large* animal.) Besides, there was the beast's owner to be considered. Alive, the elephant was worth at least a hundred pounds; dead, he would only be worth the value of his tusks, five pounds, possibly. But I had got to act quickly. I turned to some experienced-looking Burmans who had been there when we arrived, and asked them how the elephant had been behaving. They all said the same thing: he took no notice of you if you left him alone, but he might charge if you went too close to him.

It was perfectly clear to me what I ought to do. I ought to walk up to within, say, twenty-five yards of the elephant and test his behavior. If he charged, I could shoot; if he took no notice of me, it would be safe to leave him until the mahout came back. But also I knew that I was going to do no such thing. I was a poor shot with a rifle and the ground was soft mud into which one would sink at every step. If the elephant charged and I missed him, I should have about as much chance as a toad under a steam-roller. But even then I was not thinking particularly of my own skin, only of the watchful yellow faces behind. For at that moment, with the crowd watching me, I was not afraid in the ordinary sense, as I would have been if I had been alone. A white man mustn't be frightened in front of "natives"; and so, in general, he isn't frightened. The sole thought in my mind was that if anything went wrong those two thousand Burmans would see me pursued, caught, trampled on and reduced to a grinning corpse like that Indian up the hill. And if that happened it was quite probable that some of them would laugh. That would never do. There was only one alternative. I shoved the cartridges into the magazine and lay down on the road to get a better aim.

10   The crowd grew very still, and a deep, low, happy sigh, as of people who see the theatre curtain go up at last, breathed from innumerable throats. They were going to have their bit of fun after all. The rifle was a beautiful German thing with cross-hair sights. I did not then know that in shooting an elephant one would shoot to cut an imaginary bar running from ear-hole to ear-hole. I ought, therefore, as the elephant was sideways on, to have aimed straight at his ear-hole; actually I aimed several inches in front of this, thinking the brain would be further forward.

When I pulled the trigger I did not hear the bang or feel the kick—one never does when a shot goes home—but I heard the devilish roar of glee that went up from the crowd. In that instant, in too short a time, one would have thought, even for the bullet to get there, a mysterious, terrible change had come over the elephant. He neither stirred nor fell, but every line of his body had altered. He looked suddenly stricken, shrunken, immensely old, as though the frightful impact of the bullet had paralysed him without knocking him down. At last, after what seemed a long time—it might have been five seconds, I dare say—he sagged flabbily to his knees. His mouth slobbered. An enormous senility seemed to have settled upon him. One could have imagined him thousands of years old. I fired again into the same spot. At the second shot he did not collapse but climbed with desperate slowness to his feet and stood weakly upright, with legs sagging and head drooping. I fired a third time. That was the shot that did for him. You could see the agony of it jolt his whole body and knock the last remnant of strength from his legs. But in falling he seemed for a moment to rise, for as his hind legs collapsed beneath him he seemed to tower upward like a huge rock toppling, his trunk reaching skywards like a tree. He trumpeted, for the first and only time. And then down he came, his belly towards me, with a crash that seemed to shake the ground even where I lay.

I got up. The Burmans were already racing past me across the mud. It was obvious that the elephant would never rise again, but he was not dead. He was breathing very rhythmically with long rattling gasps, his great mound of a side painfully rising and falling. His mouth was wide open. I could see far down into caverns of pale pink throat. I waited a long time for him to die, but his breathing did not weaken. Finally I fired my two remaining shots into the spot where I thought his heart must be. The thick blood welled out of him like red velvet, but still he did not die. His body did not even jerk when the shots hit him, the tortured breathing continued without a pause. He was dying, very slowly and in great agony, but in some world remote from me where not even a bullet could damage him further. I felt I had got to put an end to that dreadful noise. It seemed dreadful to see the great beast lying there, powerless to move and yet powerless to die, and not even to be able to finish him. I sent back for my small rifle and poured shot after shot into his heart and down his throat. They seemed to make no impression. The tortured gasps continued as steadily as the ticking of a clock.

In the end I could not stand it any longer and went away. I heard later that it took him half an hour to die. Burmans were bringing dahs and baskets even before I left, and I was told they had stripped his body almost to the bones by the afternoon.

Afterwards, of course, there were endless discussions about the shooting of the elephant. The owner was furious, but he was only an Indian and could do nothing. Besides, legally I had done the right thing, for a mad elephant has to be killed, like a mad dog, if its owner fails to control it. Among the Europeans opinion was divided. The older men said I was right, the younger men said it was a damn shame to shoot an elephant for killing a coolie, because an elephant was worth more than any damn Coringhee coolie. And afterwards I was very glad that the coolie had been killed; it put me legally in the right and it gave me a sufficient pretext for shooting the elephant. I often wondered whether any of the others grasped that I had done it solely to avoid looking a fool.

 ## Topics for Critical Thinking and Writing

1. How does Orwell characterize himself at the time of the events he describes? What evidence in the essay suggests that he wrote it some years later?

2. Orwell says the incident was "enlightening." What does he mean? Picking up this clue, state in a sentence or two the thesis or main point of the essay.
3. Compare Orwell's description of the dead coolie (in the fourth paragraph) with his description of the elephant's death (in the eleventh and twelfth paragraphs). Why does Orwell devote more space to the death of the elephant?
4. How would you describe the tone of the last paragraph, particularly of the last two sentences? Do you find the paragraph an effective conclusion to the essay? Explain.

 **CAMILLE PAGLIA**

Camille Paglia, born in Endicott, New York, in 1947, and educated at the State University of New York at Binghamton and at Yale University, teaches humanities at the University of the Arts, in Philadelphia. Paglia achieved fame in 1990 with the publication of a book entitled Sexual Personae, *a study of pornographic, voyeuristic, and sadistic elements in literature. She considers herself a feminist but she has sharply criticized many other feminists, and in turn she has been sharply criticized. As she said in the preface to* Sexual Personae, *"My stress on the truth in sexual stereotypes and on the biologic basis of sex difference is sure to cause controversy." We reprint an especially controversial essay that was first printed in a popular journal,* New York Newsday, *in 1992, and has been reprinted in a collection of Paglia's essays,* Sex, Art, and American Culture. *Paglia writes regularly for the on-line magazine* Salon.

Rape and Modern Sex War

Rape is an outrage that cannot be tolerated in civilized society. Yet feminism, which has waged a crusade for rape to be taken more seriously, has put young women in danger by hiding the truth about sex from them.

In dramatizing the pervasiveness of rape, feminists have told young women that before they have sex with a man, they must give consent as explicit as a legal contract's. In this way, young women have been convinced that they have been the victims of rape. On elite campuses in the Northeast and on the West Coast, they have held consciousness-raising sessions, petitioned administrations, demanded inquests. At Brown University, outraged, panicky "victims" have scrawled the names of alleged attackers on the walls of women's rest rooms. What marital rape was to the Seventies, "date rape" is to the Nineties.

The incidence and seriousness of rape do not require this kind of exaggeration. Real acquaintance rape is nothing new. It has been a horrible problem for women for all of recorded history. Once fathers and brothers protected women from rape. Once the penalty for rape was death. I come from a fierce Italian tradition where, not so long ago in the motherland, a rapist would end up knifed, castrated, and hung out to dry.

But the old clans and small rural communities have broken down. In our cities, on our campuses far from home, young women are vulnerable and defenseless. Feminism has not prepared them for this. Feminism keeps saying the sexes are the same. It keeps telling women they can do anything, go anywhere, say anything, wear anything. No, they can't. Women will always be in sexual danger.

One of my male students recently slept overnight with a friend in a passageway of the Great Pyramid in Egypt. He described the moon and sand, the ancient silence and eerie echoes. I will never experience that. I am a woman. I am not stupid enough to believe I could ever be safe there. There is a world of solitary adventure I will never have. Women have always known these somber truths. But feminism, with its pie-in-the-sky fantasies about the perfect world, keeps young women from seeing life as it is.

We must remedy social injustice whenever we can. But there are some things we cannot change. There are sexual differences that are based in biology. Academic feminism is lost in a fog of social constructionism. It believes we are totally the product of our environment. This idea was invented by Rousseau. He was wrong. Emboldened by dumb French language theory, academic feminists repeat the same hollow slogans over and over to each other. Their view of sex is naïve and prudish. Leaving sex to the feminists is like letting your dog vacation at the taxidermist's.

The sexes are at war. Men must struggle for identity against the overwhelming power of their mothers. Women have menstruation to tell them they are women. Men must do or risk something to be men. Men become masculine only when other men say they are. Having sex with a woman is one way a boy becomes a man.

College men are at their hormonal peak. They have just left their mothers and are questing for their male identity. In groups, they are dangerous. A woman going to a fraternity party is walking into Testosterone Flats, full of prickly cacti and blazing guns. If she goes, she should be armed with resolute alertness. She should arrive with girlfriends and leave with them. A girl who lets herself get dead drunk at a fraternity party is a fool. A girl who goes upstairs alone with a brother at a fraternity party is an idiot. Feminists call this "blaming the victim." I call it common sense.

For a decade, feminists have drilled their disciples to say, "Rape is a crime of violence but not of sex." This sugar-coated Shirley Temple nonsense has exposed young women to disaster. Misled by feminism, they do not expect rape from the nice boys from good homes who sit next to them in class.

Aggression and eroticism are deeply intertwined. Hunt, pursuit, and capture are biologically programmed into male sexuality. Generation after generation, men must be educated, refined, and ethically persuaded away from their tendency toward anarchy and brutishness. Society is not the enemy, as feminism ignorantly claims. Society is woman's protection against rape. Feminism, with its solemn Carry Nation[1] repressiveness, does not see what is for men the eroticism or fun element in rape, especially the wild, infectious delirium of gang rape. Women who do not understand rape cannot defend themselves against it.

The date-rape controversy shows feminism hitting the wall of its own broken promises. The women of my Sixties generation were the first respectable girls in history to swear like sailors, get drunk, stay out all night—in short, to act like men. We sought total sexual freedom and equality. But as time passed, we

---

[1]Carry Nation, American temperance crusader (1846–1911), known for destroying bottles of liquor and barroom furniture with a hatchet.

woke up to cold reality. The old double standard protected women. When anything goes, it's women who lose.

Today's young women don't know what they want. They see that feminism has not brought sexual happiness. The theatrics of public rage over date rape are their way of restoring the old sexual rules that were shattered by my generation. Because nothing about the sexes has really changed. The comic film *Where the Boys Are* (1960), the ultimate expression of Fifties man-chasing, still speaks directly to our time. It shows smart, lively women skillfully anticipating and fending off the dozens of strategies with which horny men try to get them into bed. The agonizing date-rape subplot and climax are brilliantly done. The victim, Yvette Mimieux, makes mistake after mistake, obvious to the other girls. She allows herself to be lured away from her girlfriends and into isolation with boys whose character and intentions she misreads. *Where the Boys Are* tells the truth. It shows courtship as a dangerous game in which the signals are not verbal but subliminal.

Neither militant feminism, which is obsessed with politically correct language, nor academic feminism, which believes that knowledge and experience are "constituted by" language, can understand preverbal or nonverbal communication. Feminism, focusing on sexual politics, cannot see that sex exists in and through the body. Sexual desire and arousal cannot be fully translated into verbal terms. This is why men and women misunderstand each other.

Trying to remake the future, feminism cut itself off from sexual history. It discarded and suppressed the sexual myths of literature, art, and religion. Those myths show us the turbulence, the mysteries and passions of sex. In mythology we see men's sexual anxiety, their fear of woman's dominance. Much sexual violence is rooted in men's sense of psychological weakness toward women. It takes many men to deal with one woman. Woman's voracity is a persistent motif. Clara Bow, it was rumored, took on the USC football team on weekends. Marilyn Monroe, singing "Diamonds Are a Girl's Best Friend," rules a conga line of men in tuxes. Half-clad Cher, in the video for "If I Could Turn Back Time," deranges a battleship of screaming sailors and straddles a pink-lit cannon. Feminism, coveting social power, is blind to woman's cosmic sexual power.

15   To understand rape, you must study the past. There never was and never will be sexual harmony. Every woman must take personal responsibility for her sexuality, which is nature's red flame. She must be prudent and cautious about where she goes and with whom. When she makes a mistake, she must accept the consequences and, through self-criticism, resolve never to make that mistake again. Running to Mommy and Daddy on the campus grievance committee is unworthy of strong women. Posting lists of guilty men in the toilet is cowardly, infantile stuff.

The Italian philosophy of life espouses high-energy confrontation. A male student makes a vulgar remark about your breasts? Don't slink off to whimper and simper with the campus shrinking violets. Deal with it. On the spot. Say, "Shut up, you jerk! And crawl back to the barnyard where you belong!" In general, women who project this take-charge attitude toward life get harassed less often. I see too many dopey, immature, self-pitying women walking around like melting sticks of butter. It's the Yvette Mimieux syndrome: make me happy. And listen to me weep when I'm not.

The date-rape debate is already smothering in propaganda churned out by the expensive Northeastern colleges and universities, with their overconcentration of boring, uptight academic feminists and spoiled, affluent students. Beware of the deep manipulativeness of rich students who were neglected by their parents. They love to turn the campus into hysterical psychodramas of sexual transgression, followed by assertions of parental authority and concern. And don't look for sexual enlightenment from academe, which spews out mountains of books but never looks at life directly.

As a fan of football and rock music, I see in the simple, swaggering masculinity of the jock and in the noisy posturing of the heavy-metal guitarist certain fundamental, unchanging truths about sex. Masculinity is aggressive, unstable, combustible. It is also the most creative cultural force in history. Women must reorient themselves toward the elemental powers of sex, which can strengthen or destroy.

The only solution to date rape is female self-awareness and self-control. A woman's number one line of defense is herself. When a real rape occurs, she should report it to the police. Complaining to college committees because the courts "take too long" is ridiculous. College administrations are not a branch of the judiciary. They are not equipped or trained for legal inquiry. Colleges must alert incoming students to the problems and dangers of adulthood. Then colleges must stand back and get out of the sex game.

✎ Topics for Critical Thinking and Writing

1. In her first paragraph Paglia says that "feminism . . . has put young women in danger by hiding the truth about sex from them." What evidence does her essay offer to support this assertion?

2. In paragraph 7 Paglia asserts that "the sexes are at war," and she offers a brief explanation here and in paragraph 10 of why men behave as they do (or as she thinks they do). Do you find her explanation adequate? If not, why not?

3. In paragraph 17 Paglia refers to "the date-rape" debate. From this essay, or from your own experience, what issues would you say are being debated and by whom?

4. How would you define date rape? If a friend told you she had been raped on a date by another student, what would you advise her to do? What would Paglia advise her to do, or not do?

5. In her final paragraph Paglia mentions "real rape." What do you think she means by this term? What do you think she would include and what not include?

6. Also in her final paragraph Paglia says "Colleges must alert incoming students to the problems and dangers of adulthood." How can colleges fulfill this responsibility? In your experience, how do they fulfill this responsibility? What do you think they should or should not do?

 **KATHA POLLITT**

Katha Pollitt (b. 1949) writes chiefly on literary, political, and social topics. In addition to writing essays, she writes poetry; her first collection of poems, Antarctic Traveler *(1982), won the National Book Critics Circle Award. She publishes widely, especially in* The Nation, The New Yorker, *and* The New York Times. *We reprint here an article that originally appeared in* The New York Times.

Why Boys Don't Play with Dolls

It's twenty-eight years since the founding of NOW,[1] and boys still like trucks and girls still like dolls. Increasingly, we are told that the source of these robust preferences must lie outside society—in prenatal hormonal influences, brain chemistry, genes—and that feminism has reached its natural limits. What else could possibly explain the love of preschool girls for party dresses or the desire of toddler boys to own more guns than Mark from Michigan?

True, recent studies claim to show small cognitive differences between the sexes: He gets around by orienting himself in space; she does it by remembering landmarks. Time will tell if any deserve the hoopla with which each is invariably greeted, over the protests of the researchers themselves. But even if the results hold up (and the history of such research is not encouraging), we don't need studies of sex-differentiated brain activity in reading, say, to understand why boys and girls still seem so unalike.

The feminist movement has done much for some women, and something for every woman, but it has hardly turned America into a playground free of sex roles. It hasn't even got women to stop dieting or men to stop interrupting them.

Instead of looking at kids to "prove" that differences in behavior by sex are innate, we can look at the ways we raise kids as an index to how unfinished the feminist revolution really is, and how tentatively it is embraced even by adults who fully expect their daughters to enter previously male-dominated professions and their sons to change diapers.

5   I'm at a children's birthday party. "I'm sorry," one mom silently mouths to the mother of the birthday girl, who has just torn open her present—Tropical Splash Barbie. Now, you can love Barbie or you can hate Barbie, and there are feminists in both camps. But *apologize* for Barbie? Inflict Barbie, against your own convictions, on the child of a friend you know will be none too pleased?

Every mother in that room had spent years becoming a person who had to be taken seriously, not least by herself. Even the most attractive, I'm willing to bet, had suffered over her body's failure to fit the impossible American ideal. Given all that, it seems crazy to transmit Barbie to the next generation. Yet to reject her is to say that what Barbie represents—being sexy, thin, stylish—is unimportant, which is obviously not true, and children know it's not true.

Women's looks matter terribly in this society, and so Barbie, however ambivalently, must be passed along. After all, there are worse toys. The Cut and Style Barbie styling head, for example, a grotesque object intended to encourage "hair play." The grown-ups who give that probably apologize, too.

How happy would most parents be to have a child who flouted sex conventions? I know a lot of women, feminists, who complain in a comical, eyeball-rolling way about their sons' passion for sports: the ruined weekends, obnoxious coaches, macho values. But they would not think of discouraging their sons from participating in this activity they find so foolish. Or do they? Their husbands are sports fans, too, and they like their husbands a lot.

Could it be that even sports-resistant moms see athletics as part of manliness? That if their sons wanted to spend the weekend writing up their diaries, or reading, or baking, they'd find it disturbing? Too antisocial? Too lonely? Too gay?

---

[1]National Organization for Women (editor's note)

10   Theories of innate differences in behavior are appealing. They let parents off the hook—no small recommendation in a culture that holds moms, and sometimes even dads, responsible for their children's every misstep on the road to bliss and success.

They allow grown-ups to take the path of least resistance to the dominant culture, which always requires less psychic effort, even if it means more actual work: Just ask the working mother who comes home exhausted and nonetheless finds it easier to pick up her son's socks than make him do it himself. They let families buy for their children, without *too* much guilt, the unbelievably sexist junk that the kids, who have been watching commercials since birth, understandably crave.

But the thing the theories do most of all is tell adults that the *adult* world—in which moms and dads still play by many of the old rules even as they question and fidget and chafe against them—is the way it's supposed to be. A girl with a doll and a boy with a truck "explain" why men are from Mars and women are from Venus, why wives do housework and husbands just don't understand.

The paradox is that the world of rigid and hierarchical sex roles evoked by determinist theories is already passing away. Three-year-olds may indeed insist that doctors are male and nurses female, even if their own mother is a physician. Six-year-olds know better. These days, something like half of all medical students are female, and male applications to nursing school are inching upward. When tomorrow's three-year-olds play doctor, who's to say how they'll assign the roles?

With sex roles, as in every area of life, people aspire to what is possible, and conform to what is necessary. But these are not fixed, especially today. Biological determinism may reassure some adults about their present, but it is feminism, the ideology of flexible and converging sex roles, that fits our children's future. And the kids, somehow, know this.

15   That's why, if you look carefully, you'll find that for every kid who fits a stereotype, there's another who's breaking one down. Sometimes it's the same kid—the boy who skateboards *and* takes cooking in his afterschool program; the girl who collects stuffed animals *and* A-pluses in science.

Feminists are often accused of imposing their "agenda" on children. Isn't that what adults always do, consciously and unconsciously? Kids aren't born religious, or polite, or kind, or able to remember where they put their sneakers. Inculcating these behaviors, and the values behind them, is a tremendous amount of work, involving many adults. We don't have a choice, really, about *whether* we should give our children messages about what it means to be male and female—they're bombarded with them from morning till night.

✎ Topics for Critical Thinking and Writing

1. In a paragraph, summarize Pollitt's answer to the question her title raises.
2. In paragraph 7 Pollitt says, "Women's looks matter terribly in this society." Do you agree with this generalization? If they do matter "terribly," do they matter more than men's? What evidence can you give, one way or the other? Set forth your answer in an essay of about 250 words.
3. In paragraph 14 Pollitt says that "the ideology of flexible and converging sex roles" is the one that "fits our children's future." What would be ex-

amples of "flexible and converging sex roles"? And do you agree that this ideology is the one that suits the immediate future? Why?

4. Do you believe that you have been influenced by Barbie or by any other toy? Explain.

5. In her final paragraph Pollitt says that adults always impose an "agenda" on their children, consciously or unconsciously. What agenda did your parents, or other adults charged with your upbringing, impose or try to impose? What was your response? As you think back on it, were the agenda and the responses appropriate? Present your answer in an essay of 500–750 words.

6. If you have heard that "brain chemistry" or "genes" (paragraph 1) account for "innate differences in behavior" (paragraph 10) in boys and girls, in a paragraph set forth the view, and in another paragraph evaluate it, drawing perhaps on your reading of Pollitt's essay.

 **ROBERT B. REICH**

Robert B. Reich was born in Scranton, Pennsylvania, in 1946, and educated at Dartmouth College, Oxford University (he was a Rhodes Scholar), and Yale Law School. After working for the federal government he taught at Harvard University's John F. Kennedy School of Government, when President Clinton chose him as Secretary of Labor. (He describes his years in the Department of Labor in an engaging book, Locked in the Cabinet.) After leaving Washington, Reich accepted a post at Brandeis University, in the Heller School, Graduate Studies in Social Welfare.

This essay, originally a memorandum circulated to undergraduate students in 1989, has been slightly revised for wider publication.

The Future of Work

It's easy to predict what jobs you *shouldn't* prepare for. Thanks to the wonders of fluoride, America, in the future, will need fewer dentists. Nor is there much of a future in farming. The federal government probably won't provide long-term employment unless you aspire to work in the Pentagon or the Veterans Administration (the only two departments accounting for new federal jobs in the last decade). And think twice before plunging into higher education. The real wages of university professors have been declining for some time, the hours are bad, and all you get are complaints.

Moreover, as the American economy merges with the rest of the world's, anyone doing relatively unskilled work that could be done more cheaply elsewhere is unlikely to prosper for long. Imports and exports now constitute 26 percent of our gross national product (up from 9 percent in 1950), and barring a new round of protectionism, the portion will move steadily upward. Meanwhile, 10,000 people are added to the world's population every hour, most of whom, eventually, will happily work for a small fraction of today's average American wage.

This is good news for most of you, because it means that you'll be able to buy all sorts of things far more cheaply than you could if they were made here (provided, of course, that what your generation does instead produces even more value). The resulting benefits from trade will help offset the drain on your income resulting from paying the interest on the nation's foreign debt and financing the retirement of aging baby boomers like me. The bad news, at least for some of you, is that most of America's traditional, routinized manufacturing jobs will disappear. So will routinized service jobs that can be done from remote locations, like keypunching of data transmitted by satellite. Instead, you will be engaged in one of two broad categories of work: either complex services, some of which will be sold to the rest of the world to pay for whatever Americans want to buy from the rest of the world, or person-to-person services, which foreigners can't provide for us because (apart from new immigrants and illegal aliens) they aren't here to provide them.

Complex services involve the manipulation of data and abstract symbols. Included in this category are insurance, engineering, law, finance, computer programming, and advertising. Such activities now account for almost 25 percent of our GNP, up from 13 percent in 1950. They already have surpassed manufacturing (down to about 20 percent of GNP). Even *within* the manufacturing sector, executive, managerial, and engineering positions are increasing at a rate almost three times that of total manufacturing employment. Most of these jobs, too, involve manipulating symbols.

5   Such endeavors will constitute America's major contribution to the rest of the world in the decades ahead. You and your classmates will be exporting engineering designs, financial services, advertising and communications advice, statistical analyses, musical scores and film scripts, and other creative and problem-solving products. How many of you undertake these sorts of jobs, and how well you do at them, will determine what goods and services America can summon from the rest of the world in return, and thus—to some extent—your generation's standard of living.

You say you plan to become an investment banker? A lawyer? I grant you that these vocations have been among the fastest growing and most lucrative during the past decade. The securities industry in particular has burgeoned. The crash of October 1987 temporarily stemmed the growth, but by mid–1988 happy days were here again. Nor have securities workers had particular difficulty making ends met. (But relatively few security workers have enjoyed majestic compensation. The high average is due to a few thousand high-rolling partners in Wall Street investment banks.)

Work involving securities and corporate law has been claiming one-quarter of all new private sector jobs in New York City and more than a third of all the new office space in that industrious town. Other major cities are not too far behind. A simple extrapolation of the present trend suggests that by 2020 one out of every three American college graduates will be an investment banker or a lawyer. Of course, this is unlikely. Long before that milestone could be achieved, the nation's economy will have dried up like a raisin, as financiers and lawyers squeeze out every ounce of creative, productive juice. Thus my advice: Even if you could bear spending your life in such meaningless but lucrative work, at least consider the fate of the nation before deciding to do so.

Person-to-person services will claim everyone else. Many of these jobs will not require much skill, as is true of their forerunners today. Among the fastest growing in recent years: custodians and security guards, restaurant and retail workers, day-care providers. Secretaries and clerical workers will be as numerous as now, but they'll spend more of their time behind and around electronic machines (imported from Asia) and have fancier titles, such as "paratechnical assistant" and "executive paralegal operations manager."

Teachers will be needed (we'll be losing more than a third of our entire corps of elementary- and high-school teachers through attrition over the next seven years), but don't expect their real pay to rise very much. Years of public breast-beating about the quality of American education notwithstanding, the average teacher today earns $28,000—only 3.4 percent more, in constant dollars, than he or she earned fifteen years ago.

10   Count on many jobs catering to Americans at play—hotel workers, recreation directors, television and film technicians, aerobics instructors (or whatever their twenty-first-century equivalents will call themselves). But note that Americans will have less leisure time to enjoy these pursuits. The average American's free time has been shrinking for more than fifteen years, as women move into the work force (and so spend more of their free time doing household chores) and as all wage earners are forced to work harder just to maintain their standard of living. Expect the trend to continue.

The most interesting and important person-to-person jobs will be in what is now unpretentiously dubbed "sales." Decades from now most salespeople won't be just filling orders. Sales-people will be helping customers define their needs, then working with design and production engineers to customize products and services in order to address those needs. This is because standardized (you can have it in any color as long as it's black) products will be long gone. Flexible manufacturing and the new information technologies will allow a more tailored fit—whether it's a car, machine tool, insurance policy, or even a college education. Those of you who will be dealing directly with customers will thus play a pivotal role in the innovation process, and your wages and prestige will rise accordingly.

But the largest number of personal-service jobs will involve health care, which already consumes about 12 percent of our GNP, and that portion is rising. Because every new medical technology with the potential to extend life is infinitely valuable to those whose lives might be extended—even for a few months or weeks—society is paying huge sums to stave off death. By the second decade of the next century, when my generation of baby boomers will have begun to decay, the bill will be much higher. Millions of corroding bodies will need doctors, nurses, nursing-home operators, hospital administrators, technicians who operate and maintain all the fancy machines that will measure and temporarily halt the deterioration, hospice directors, home-care specialists, directors of outpatient clinics, and euthanasia specialists, among many others.

Most of these jobs won't pay very much because they don't require much skill. Right now the fastest growing job categories in the health sector are nurse's aides, orderlies, and attendants, which compose about 40 percent of the health-care work force. The majority are women; a large percentage are minorities. But even doctors' real earnings show signs of slipping. As malpractice insurance rates skyrocket, many doctors go on salary in investor-owned hospitals, and their duties are gradually taken over by physician "extenders" such as nurse-practitioners and midwives.

What's the best preparation for one of these careers?

15   Advice here is simple: You won't be embarking on a career, at least as we currently define the term, because few of the activities I've mentioned will proceed along well-defined paths to progressively higher levels of responsibility. As the economy evolves toward services tailored to the particular needs of clients and customers, hands-on experience will count for more than formal rank. As technologies and markets rapidly evolve, moreover, the best preparation will be through cumulative learning on the job rather than formal training completed years before.

This means that academic degrees and professional credentials will count for less; on-the-job training, for more. American students have it backwards. The courses to which you now gravitate—finance, law, accounting, management, and other practical arts—may be helpful to understand how a particular job is *now* done (or, more accurately, how your instructors did it years ago when they held such jobs or studied the people who held them), but irrelevant to how such a job *will* be done. The intellectual equipment needed for the job of the future is an ability to define problems, quickly assimilate relevant data, conceptualize and reorganize the information, make deductive and inductive leaps with it, ask hard questions about it, discuss findings with colleagues, work collaboratively to find solutions, and then convince others. And *these* sorts of skills can't be learned in career-training courses. To the extent they can be found in universities at all, they're more likely to be found in subjects such as history, literature, philosophy, and anthropology—in which students can witness how others have grappled for centuries with the challenge of living good and productive lives. Tolstoy and Thucydides are far more relevant to the management jobs of the future, for example, than are Hersey and Blanchard (*Management of Organizational Behavior,* Prentice-Hall, 5th Edition, 1988).

Questions for Critical Thinking and Writing

1. Consider Reich's first three paragraphs. Has he taken account of his audience? What sort of personality does his voice reveal in these paragraphs?

2. In paragraph 7 Reich suggests that one should think twice before spending one's "life in . . . meaningless but lucrative work." What makes any sort of work "meaningless"? For instance is sorting or delivering mail meaningless work? Is working as a butcher in a supermarket? Being a criminal defense lawyer? Breeding or grooming dogs? Designing bathing suits? Explain.

3. Assuming that much of your career as a worker is in the future, how much of a role does prediction of the future play in your plans for a career?

4. In paragraph 11 Reich says that "Salespeople will be helping customers define their needs, then working with design and production engineers to customize products and services in order to address these needs." If you are old enough to have seen some jobs change in this direction, in 500 words provide evidence that supports Reich's point. Or interview an older person, to gain information about what Reich is saying. (For advice on conducting interviews, see Chapter 15, "Interviewing.")

5. In his final paragraph Reich sets forth what he thinks is "the intellectual equipment needed for the job of the future." Read this paragraph care-

fully, and then ask yourself (1) if you think he is probably right about the skills that will be needed; (2) if you think his suggestion about how those skills may be developed in college is probably right; and (3) if you plan in any way to act on his suggestions. Present your answers in an essay of about 500 words.

 **NANCY SAKAMOTO**

Nancy Masterson Sakamoto, professor of Buddhism at the University of Hawaii, lived for a while in Osaka, where she taught English to Japanese people. This essay is a chapter from a textbook written in English, used by Japanese students taking a course in conversational English.

Conversational Ballgames

After I was married and had lived in Japan for a while, my Japanese gradually improved to the point where I could take part in simple conversations with my husband and his friends and family. And I began to notice that often, when I joined in, the others would look startled, and the conversational topic would come to a halt. After this happened several times, it became clear to me that I was doing something wrong. But for a long time, I didn't know what it was.

Finally, after listening carefully to many Japanese conversations, I discovered what my problem was. Even though I was speaking Japanese, I was handling the conversation in a western way.

Japanese-style conversations develop quite differently from western-style conversations. And the difference isn't only in the languages. I realized that just as I kept trying to hold western-style conversations even when I was speaking Japanese, so my English students kept trying to hold Japanese-style conversations even when they were speaking English. We were unconsciously playing entirely different conversational ballgames.

A western-style conversation between two people is like a game of tennis. If I introduce a topic, a conversational ball, I expect you to hit it back. If you agree with me, I don't expect you simply to agree and do nothing more. I expect you to add something—a reason for agreeing, another example, or an elaboration to carry the idea further. But I don't expect you always to agree. I am just as happy if you question me, or challenge me, or completely disagree with me. Whether you agree or disagree, your response will return the ball to me.

5   And then it is my turn again. I don't serve a new ball from my original starting line. I hit your ball back again from where it has bounced. I carry your idea further, or answer your questions or objections, or challenge or question you. And so the ball goes back and forth, with each of us doing our best to give it a new twist, an original spin, or a powerful smash.

And the more vigorous the action, the more interesting and exciting the game. Of course, if one of us gets angry, it spoils the conversation, just as it spoils a tennis game. But getting excited is not at all the same as getting angry. After all, we are not trying to hit each other. We are trying to hit the ball. So long as we attack only each other's opinions, and do not attack each other personally, we don't expect anyone to get hurt. A good conversation is supposed to be interesting and exciting.

If there are more than two people in the conversation, then it is like doubles in tennis, or like volleyball. There's no waiting in line. Whoever is nearest and quickest hits the ball, and if you step back, someone else will hit it. No one stops the game to give you a turn. You're responsible for taking your own turn.

But whether it's two players or a group, everyone does his best to keep the ball going, and no one person has the ball for very long.

A Japanese-style conversation, however, is not at all like tennis or volleyball. It's like bowling. You wait for your turn. And you always know your place in line. It depends on such things as whether you are older or younger, a close friend or a relative stranger to the previous speaker, in a senior or junior position, and so on.

10   When your turn comes, you step up to the starting line with your bowling ball, and carefully bowl it. Everyone else stands back and watches politely, murmuring encouragement. Everyone waits until the ball has reached the end of the alley, and watches to see if it knocks down all the pins, or only some of them, or none of them. There is a pause, while everyone registers your score.

Then, after everyone is sure that you have completely finished your turn, the next person in line steps up to the same starting line, with a different ball. He doesn't return your ball, and he does not begin from where your ball stopped. There is no back and forth at all. All the balls run parallel. And there is always a suitable pause between turns. There is no rush, no excitement, no scramble for the ball.

No wonder everyone looked startled when I took part in Japanese conversations. I paid no attention to whose turn it was, and kept snatching the ball halfway down the alley and throwing it back at the bowler. Of course the conversation died. I was playing the wrong game.

This explains why it is almost impossible to get a western-style conversation or discussion going with English students in Japan. I used to think that the problem was their lack of English language ability. But I finally came to realize that the biggest problem is that they, too, are playing the wrong game.

Whenever I serve a volleyball, everyone just stands back and watches it fall, with occasional murmurs of encouragement. No one hits it back. Everyone waits until I call on someone to take a turn. And when that person speaks, he doesn't hit my ball back. He serves a new ball. Again, everyone just watches it fall.

15   So I call on someone else. This person does not refer to what the previous speaker has said. He also serves a new ball. Nobody seems to have paid any attention to what anyone else has said. Everyone begins again from same starting line, and all the balls run parallel. There is never any back and forth. Everyone is trying to bowl with a volleyball.

And if I try a simpler conversation, with only two of us, then the other person tries to bowl with my tennis ball. No wonder foreign English teachers in Japan get discouraged.

Now that you know about the difference in the conversational ballgames, you may think that all your troubles are over. But if you have been trained all your life to play one game, it is no simple matter to switch to another, even if you know the rules. Knowing the rules is not at all the same thing as playing the game.

Even now, during a conversation in Japanese I will notice a startled reaction, and belatedly realize that once again I have rudely interrupted by instinctively trying to hit back the other person's bowling ball. It is no easier for me to "just listen" during a conversation, than it is for my Japanese students to "just relax" when speaking with foreigners. Now I can truly sympathize with how hard they must find it to try to carry on a western-style conversation.

If I have not yet learned to do conversational bowling in Japanese, at least I have figured out one thing that puzzled me for a long time. After his first trip to America, my husband complained that Americans asked him so many questions and made him talk so much at the dinner table that he never had a chance to eat. When I asked him why he couldn't talk and eat at the same time, he said that Japanese do not customarily think that dinner, especially on fairly formal occasions, is a suitable time for extended conversation.

20 Since westerners think that conversation is an indispensable part of dining, and indeed would consider it impolite not to converse with one's dinner partner, I found this Japanese custom rather strange. Still, I could accept it as a cultural difference even though I didn't really understand it. But when my husband added, in explanation, that Japanese consider it extremely rude to talk with one's mouth full, I got confused. Talking with one's mouth full is certainly not an American custom. We think it very rude, too. Yet we still manage to talk a lot and eat at the same time. How do we do it?

For a long time, I couldn't explain it, and it bothered me. But after I discovered the conversational ballgames, I finally found the answer. Of course! In a western-style conversation, you hit the ball, and while someone else is hitting it back, you take a bite, chew, and swallow. Then you hit the ball again, and then eat some more. The more people there are in the conversation, the more chances you have to eat. But even with only two of you talking, you still have plenty of chances to eat.

Maybe that's why polite conversation at the dinner table has never been a traditional part of Japanese etiquette. Your turn to talk would last so long without interruption that you'd never get a chance to eat.

✐ Topics for Critical Thinking and Writing

1. This essay, by an American woman married to a Japanese man, comes from a textbook designed to teach Japanese students to read English and to learn about American culture. Strictly speaking, the first two paragraphs are not necessary to the points that follow. Do they serve any function?

2. The writer is chiefly seeking to tell her Japanese students something about Western habits of conversation. Why, then, does she also tell them about Japanese habits?

3. Why does Sakamoto bother to use a metaphor (or figurative comparison), seeing conversations as ballgames?

4. If you are familiar with a culture other than what can be called Anglo-American, what metaphor might you use to clarify differences between some Anglo-American social act—say, eating, or talking, or child care, or courting—and the corresponding act in the other culture?

5. For the next few days eavesdrop and try to take notes on a particularly lively conversation you happen to hear. As soon as possible, try to reconstruct the entire conversation in writing. Then analyze it. Does it follow the "rules" Sakamoto describes for either a Western-style or a Japanese-style conversation? Or does it resemble something other than a game,

perhaps a musical composition? Whatever you find, record your observations in a paragraph. (A suggestion: if you can manage to do so, record a conversation—and the accompanying gestures—between preschool children.)

BRENT STAPLES

Brent Staples, born in 1951, holds a Ph.D. from the University of Chicago. He is a member of the editorial board of The New York Times *and the author of a memoir,* Parallel Time: Growing Up in Black and White *(1994).*
   This essay originally appeared in Ms. *magazine.*

Just Walk On By: A Black Man Ponders His Power to Alter Public Space

My first victim was a woman—white, well dressed, probably in her early twenties. I came upon her late one evening on a deserted street in Hyde Park, a relatively affluent neighborhood in an otherwise mean, impoverished section of Chicago. As I swung onto the avenue behind her, there seemed to be a discreet, uninflammatory distance between us. Not so. She cast back a worried glance. To her, the youngish black man—a broad six feet two inches with a beard and billowing hair, both hands shoved into the pockets of a bulky military jacket—seemed menacingly close. After a few more quick glimpses, she picked up her pace and was soon running in earnest. Within seconds she disappeared into a cross street.

That was more than a decade ago. I was 22 years old, a graduate student newly arrived at the University of Chicago. It was in the echo of that terrified woman's footfalls that I first began to know the unwieldy inheritance I'd come into—the ability to alter public space in ugly ways. It was clear that she thought herself the quarry of a mugger, a rapist, or worse. Suffering a bout of insomnia, however, I was stalking sleep, not defenseless wayfarers. As a softy who is scarcely able to take a knife to a raw chicken—let alone hold it to a person's throat—I was surprised, embarrassed, and dismayed all at once. Her flight made me feel like an accomplice in tyranny. It also made it clear that I was indistinguishable from the muggers who occasionally seeped into the area from the surrounding ghetto. That first encounter, and those that followed, signified that a vast, unnerving gulf lay between nighttime pedestrians—particularly women—and me. And I soon gathered that being perceived as dangerous is a hazard in itself. I only needed to turn a corner into a dicey situation, or crowd some frightened, armed person in a foyer somewhere, or make an errant move after being pulled over by a policeman. Where fear and weapons meet—and they often do in urban America—there is always the possibility of death.

In that first year, my first away from my hometown, I was to become thoroughly familiar with the language of fear. At dark, shadowy intersections in Chicago, I could cross in front of a car stopped at a traffic light and elicit the *thunk, thunk, thunk, thunk* of the driver—black, white, male, or female—hammering down the door locks. On less traveled streets after dark, I grew accustomed to but never comfortable with people who crossed to the other side of the street rather than pass me. Then there were the standard unpleasantries with police, doormen, bouncers, cab drivers, and others whose business it is to screen out troublesome individuals *before* there is any nastiness.

I moved to New York nearly two years ago and I have remained an avid night walker. In central Manhattan, the near-constant crowd cover minimizes tense one-on-one street encounters. Elsewhere—visiting friends in SoHo, where sidewalks are narrow and tightly spaced buildings shut out the sky—things can get very taut indeed.

5   Black men have a firm place in New York mugging literature. Norman Podhoretz in his famed (or infamous) 1963 essay, "My Negro Problem—And Ours," recalls growing up in terror of black males; they "were tougher than we were, more ruthless," he writes—and as an adult on the Upper West Side of Manhattan, he continues, he cannot constrain his nervousness when he meets black men on certain streets. Similarly, a decade later, the essayist and novelist Edward Hoagland extols a New York where once "Negro bitterness bore down mainly on other Negroes." Where some see mere panhandlers, Hoagland sees "a mugger who is clearly screwing up his nerve to do more than just *ask* for money." But Hoagland has "the New Yorker's quick-hunch posture for broken-field maneuvering," and the bad guy swerves away.

I often witness that "hunch posture," from women after dark on the warrenlike streets of Brooklyn where I live. They seem to set their faces on neutral and, with their purse straps strung across their chests bandolier style, they forge ahead as though bracing themselves against being tackled. I understand, of course, that the danger they perceive is not a hallucination. Women are particularly vulnerable to street violence, and young black males are drastically overrepresented among the perpetrators of that violence. Yet these truths are no solace against the kind of alienation that comes of being ever the suspect, against being set apart, a fearsome entity with whom pedestrians avoid making eye contact.

It is not altogether clear to me how I reached the ripe old age of 22 without being conscious of the lethality nighttime pedestrians attributed to me. Perhaps it was because in Chester, Pennsylvania, the small, angry industrial town where I came of age in the 1960s, I was scarcely noticeable against a backdrop of gang warfare, street knifings, and murders. I grew up one of the good boys, had perhaps a half-dozen fist fights. In retrospect, my shyness of combat has clear sources.

Many things go into the making of a young thug. One of those things is the consummation of the male romance with the power to intimidate. An infant discovers that random flailings send the baby bottle flying out of the crib and crashing to the floor. Delighted, the joyful babe repeats those motions again and again, seeking to duplicate the feat. Just so, I recall the points at which some of my boyhood friends were finally seduced by the perception of themselves as tough guys. When a mark cowered and surrendered his money without resistance, myth and reality merged—and paid off. It is, after all, only manly to embrace the power to frighten and intimidate. We, as men, are not supposed to give an inch of our lane on the highway; we are to seize the fighter's edge in work and in play and even in love; we are to be valiant in the face of hostile forces.

Unfortunately, poor and powerless young men seem to take all this nonsense literally. As a boy, I saw countless tough guys locked away; I have since buried several, too. They were babies, really—a teenage cousin, a brother of 22, a childhood friend in his mid-twenties—all gone down in episodes of bravado played out in the streets. I came to doubt the virtues of intimidation early on. I chose, perhaps even unconsciously, to remain a shadow—timid, but a survivor.

10   The fearsomeness mistakenly attributed to me in public places often has a perilous flavor. The most frightening of these confusions occurred in the late 1970s and early 1980s when I worked as a journalist in Chicago. One day, rushing into the office of a magazine I was writing for with a deadline story in hand, I was mistaken for a burglar. The office manager called security and, with an ad hoc posse, pursued me through the labyrinthine halls, nearly to my editor's door. I had no way of proving who I was. I could only move briskly toward the company of someone who knew me.

Another time I was on assignment for a local paper and killing time before an interview. I entered a jewelry store on the city's affluent Near North Side. The proprietor excused herself and returned with an enormous red Doberman pinscher straining at the end of a leash. She stood, the dog extended toward me, silent to my questions, her eyes bulging nearly out of her head. I took a cursory look around, nodded, and bade her good night. Relatively speaking, however, I never fared as badly as another black male journalist. He went to nearby Waukegan, Illinois, a couple of summers ago to work on a story about a murderer who was born there. Mistaking the reporter for the killer, police hauled him from his car at gunpoint and but for his press credentials would probably have tried to book him. Such episodes are not uncommon. Black men trade tales like this all the time.

In "My Negro Problem—And Ours," Podhoretz writes that the hatred he feels for blacks makes itself known to him through a variety of avenues—one being his discomfort with that "special brand of paranoid touchiness" to which he says blacks are prone. No doubt he is speaking here of black men. In time, I learned to smother the rage I felt at so often being taken for a criminal. Not to do so would surely have led to madness—via that special "paranoid touchiness" that so annoyed Podhoretz at the time he wrote the essay.

I began to take precautions to make myself less threatening. I move about with care, particularly late in the evening. I give a wide berth to nervous people on subway platforms during the wee hours, particularly when I have exchanged business clothes for jeans. If I happen to be entering a building behind some people who appear skittish, I may walk by, letting them clear the lobby before I return, so as not to seem to be following them. I have been calm and extremely congenial on those rare occasions when I've been pulled over by the police.

And on late-evening constitutionals along streets less traveled by, I employ what has proved to be an excellent tension-reducing measure: I whistle melodies from Beethoven and Vivaldi and the more popular classical composers. Even steely New Yorkers hunching toward nighttime destinations seem to relax, and occasionally they even join in the tune. Virtually everybody seems to sense that a mugger wouldn't be warbling bright, sunny selections from Vivaldi's *Four Seasons*. It is my equivalent of the cowbell that hikers wear when they know they are in bear country.

Topics for Discussion and Writing

1. What did Staples learn, from the first experience that he narrates, about other people? What did he learn about himself?

2. In paragraph 3 Staples gives a second example (the response of people in cars) of the effect that he has on others. Why do you suppose he bothered to give a second example, since it illustrates a point already made by the first example?

3. In paragraph 12 Staples quotes Norman Podhoretz's remark about the "special brand of paranoid touchiness" that Podhoretz finds in many blacks. What would you say is Staples's view of Podhoretz's idea?

4. In paragraph 13 Staples discusses the "precautions" he takes to make himself "less threatening." Are these precautions reasonable? Or do they reveal that he is, in Podhoretz's word, "paranoid"? Do you think he ought to be less concerned with taking precautions? Why, or why not?

5. Evaluate Staples's final paragraph as a way of ending the essay.

6. The success of a narrative as a piece of writing often depends on the reader's willingness to identify with the narrator. From an analysis of "Just Walk On By," what explanation can you give for your willingness (or unwillingness) to identify yourself with Staples?

 **JONATHAN SWIFT**

Jonathan Swift (1667–1745) was born in Ireland of an English family. He was ordained in the Church of Ireland in 1694, and in 1714 he became dean of Saint Patrick's Cathedral, Dublin. He wrote abundantly on political and religious topics, often motivated (in his own words) by "savage indignation." It is ironic that Gulliver's Travels, *the masterpiece by this master of irony, is most widely thought of as a book for children.*

From the middle of the sixteenth century the English regulated the Irish economy so that it would enrich England. Heavy taxes and other repressive legislation impoverished Ireland, and in 1728, the year before Swift wrote "A Modest Proposal," Ireland was further weakened by a severe famine. Swift, deeply moved by the injustice, the stupidity, and the suffering that he found in Ireland, adopts the disguise or persona of an economist and offers an ironic suggestion on how Irish families may improve their conditions.

A Modest Proposal

For Preventing the Children of Poor People in Ireland from Being a Burden to Their Parents or Country, and for Making Them Beneficial to the Public

It is melancholy object to those who walk through this great town or travel in the country, when they see the streets, the roads, and cabin doors, crowded with beggars of the female sex, followed by three, four, or six children, all in rags and importuning every passenger for an alms. These mothers, instead of being able to work for their honest livelihood, are forced to employ all their time in strolling to beg sustenance for their helpless infants: who as they grow up either turn thieves for want of work, or leave their dear native country to fight for the pretender in Spain, or sell themselves to the Barbadoes.

I think it is agreed by all parties that this prodigious number of children in the arms, or on the backs, or at the heels of their mothers, and frequently of their fathers, is in the present deplorable state of the kingdom a very great additional grievance; and, therefore, whoever could find out a fair, cheap, and easy method of making these children sound, useful members of the commonwealth, would deserve so well of the public as to have his statue set up for a preserver of the nation.

But my intention is very far from being confined to provide only for the children of professed beggars; it is of a much greater extent, and shall take in the whole number of infants at a certain age who are born of parents in effect as little able to support them as those who demand our charity in the streets.

As to my own part, having turned my thoughts for many years upon this important subject, and maturely weighed the several schemes of our projectors, I have always found them grossly mistaken in their computation. It is true, a child just dropped from its dam may be supported by her milk for a solar year, with little other nourishment; at most not above the value of 2s.,[1] which the mother may certainly get, or the value in scraps, by her lawful occupation of begging; and it is exactly at one year old that I propose to provide for them in such a manner as instead of being a charge upon their parents or the parish, or wanting food and raiment for the rest of their lives, they shall on the contrary contribute to the feeding, and partly to the clothing, of many thousands.

5 There is likewise another great advantage in my scheme, that it will prevent those voluntary abortions, and that horrid practice of women murdering their bastard children, alas! too frequent among us! sacrificing the poor innocent babes I doubt more to avoid the expense than the shame, which would move tears and pity in the most savage and inhuman breast.

The number of souls in this kingdom being usually reckoned one million and a half, of these I calculate there may be about 200,000 couple whose wives are breeders; from which number I subtract 30,000 couple who are able to maintain their own children (although I apprehend there cannot be so many, under the present distress of the kingdom); but this being granted, there will remain 170,000 breeders. I again subtract 50,000 for those women who miscarry, or whose children die by accident or disease within the year. There only remain 120,000 children of poor parents annually born. The question therefore is, how this number shall be reared and provided for? which, as I have already said, under the present situation of affairs, is utterly impossible by all the methods hitherto proposed. For we can neither employ them in handicraft or agriculture; we neither build houses (I mean in the country) nor cultivate land; they can very seldom pick up a livelihood by stealing, till they arrive at six years old, except where they are of towardly parts; although I confess they learn the rudiments much earlier; during which time they can, however, be properly looked upon only as probationers; as I have been informed by a principal gentleman in the county of Cavan, who protested to me that he never knew above one or two instances under the age of six, even in a part of the kingdom so renowned for the quickest proficiency in that art.

I am assured by our merchants, that a boy or a girl before twelve years old is no saleable commodity; and even when they come to this age they will not yield above 3*l*. or 3*l*.2s.6d. at most on the exchange; which cannot turn to account either to the parents or kingdom, the charge of nutriment and rags having been at least four times that value.

---

[1]Two shillings. Later, "*l*" is an abbreviation for pounds and "d" for pence.

I shall now therefore humbly propose my own thoughts, which I hope will not be liable to the least objection.

I have been assured by a very knowing American of my acquaintance in London, that a young healthy child well nursed is at a year old a most delicious, nourishing, and wholesome food, whether stewed, roasted, baked, or broiled; and I make no doubt that it will equally serve in a fricassee or a ragout.

10   I do therefore humbly offer it to public consideration that of the 120,000 children already computed, 20,000 may be reserved for breed, whereof only one-fourth part to be males; which is more than we allow to sheep, black cattle, or swine; and my reason is, that these children are seldom the fruits of marriage, a circumstance not much regarded by our savages; therefore one male will be sufficient to serve four females. That the remaining 100,000 may, at a year old, be offered in sale to the persons of quality and fortune through the kingdom; always advising the mother to let them suck plentifully in the last month, so as to render them plump and fat for a good table. A child will make two dishes at an entertainment for friends; and when the family dines alone, the fore or hind quarter will make a reasonable dish, and seasoned with a little pepper or salt will be very good boiled on the fourth day, especially in winter.

I have reckoned upon a medium that a child just born will weigh 12 pounds, and in a solar year, if tolerably nursed, will increase to 28 pounds.

I grant this food will be somewhat dear, and therefore very proper for landlords, who, as they have already devoured most of the parents, seem to have the best title to the children.

Infant's flesh will be in season throughout the year, but more plentiful in March, and a little before and after: for we are told by a grave author, an eminent French physician, that fish being a prolific diet, there are more children born in Roman Catholic countries about nine months after Lent than at any other season; therefore, reckoning a year after Lent, the markets will be more glutted than usual, because the number of popish infants is at least three to one in this kingdom: and therefore it will have one other collateral advantage, by lessening the number of papists among us.

I have already computed the charge of nursing a beggar's child (in which list I reckon all cottagers, laborers, and four-fifths of the farmers) to be about 2s. per annum, rags included; and I believe no gentleman would repine to give 10s. for the carcass of a good fat child, which, as I have said, will make four dishes of excellent nutritive meat, when he has only some particular friend or his own family to dine with him. Thus the squire will learn to be a good landlord, and grow popular among the tenants; the mother will have 8s. net profit, and be fit for work till she produces another child.

15   Those who are more thrifty (as I must confess the times require) may flay the carcass; the skin of which artificially dressed will make admirable gloves for ladies, and summer boots for fine gentlemen.

As to our city of Dublin, shambles may be appointed for this purpose in the most convenient parts of it, and butchers we may be assured will not be wanting: although I rather recommend buying the children alive, and dressing them hot from the knife as we do roasting pigs.

A very worthy person, a true lover of his country, and whose virtues I highly esteem, was lately pleased in discoursing on this matter to offer a refinement upon my scheme. He said that many gentlemen of this kingdom, having of late destroyed their deer, he conceived that the want of venison might be well supplied by the bodies of young lads and maidens, not exceeding fourteen years of age nor under twelve; so great a number of both sexes in every country being now ready to starve for want of work and service; and these to be disposed of by their parents, if alive, or otherwise by their nearest relations. But with due deference to so excellent a friend and so deserving a patriot, I cannot be altogether in his sentiments; for as to the males, my American acquaintance assured me from frequent experience that their flesh was generally tough and lean, like that of our schoolboys by continual exercise, and their taste disagreeable; and to fatten them would not answer the charge. Then as to the females, it would, I think, with humble submission be a loss to the public, because they soon would become breeders themselves: and besides, it is not improbable that some scrupulous people might be apt to censure such a practice (although indeed very unjustly), as a little bordering upon cruelty; which, I confess, has always been with me the strongest objection against any project, how well soever intended.

But in order to justify my friend, he confessed that this expedient was put into his head by the famous Psalmanazar, a native of the island Formosa, who came from thence to London about twenty years ago: and in conversation told my friend, that in his country when any young person happened to be put to death, the executioner sold the carcass to persons of quality as a prime dainty; and that in his time the body of a plump girl of fifteen, who was crucified for an attempt to poison the emperor, was sold to his imperial majesty's prime minister of state, and other great mandarins of the court, in joints from the gibbet, at 400 crowns. Neither indeed can I deny, that if the same use were made of several plump young girls in this town, who without one single groat to their fortunes cannot stir abroad without a chair, and appear at the playhouse and assemblies in foreign fineries which they never will pay for, the kingdom would not be the worse.

Some persons of a desponding spirit are in great concern about that vast number of poor people, who are aged, diseased, or maimed, and I have been desired to employ my thoughts what course may be taken to ease the nation of so grievous an encumbrance. But I am not in the least pain upon that matter, because it is very well known that they are every day dying and rotting by cold and famine, and filth and vermin, as fast as can be reasonably expected. And as to the young laborers, they are now in as hopeful a condition: they cannot get work, and consequently pine away for want of nourishment, to a degree that if at any time they are accidentally hired to common labor, they have not strength to perform it; and thus the country and themselves are happily delivered from the evils to come.

20   I have too long digressed, and therefore shall return to my subject. I think the advantages by the proposal which I have made are obvious and many, as well as of the highest importance.

For first, as I have already observed, it would greatly lessen the number of papists, with whom we are yearly overrun, being the principal breeders of the nation as well as our most dangerous enemies; and who stay at home on purpose to deliver the kingdom to the Pretender, hoping to take their advantage by the absence of so many good Protestants, who have chosen rather to leave their country than stay at home and pay tithes against their conscience to an Episcopal curate.

Secondly, The poor tenants will have something valuable of their own, which by law may be made liable to distress and help to pay their landlord's rent, their corn and cattle being already seized, and money a thing unknown.

Thirdly, Whereas the maintenance of 100,000 children from two years old and upward, cannot be computed at less than 10s. a-piece per annum, the nation's stock will be thereby increased £50,000 per annum, beside the profit of a new dish introduced to the tables of all gentlemen of fortune in the kingdom who have any refinement in taste. And the money will circulate among ourselves, the goods being entirely of our own growth and manufacture.

Fourthly, The constant breeders beside the gain of 8s. sterling per annum by the sale of their children, will be rid of the charge of maintaining them after the first year.

Fifthly, This food would likewise bring great custom to taverns, where the vintners will certainly be so prudent as to procure the best receipts for dressing it to perfection, and consequently have their houses frequented by all the fine gentlemen, who justly value themselves upon their knowledge in good eating; and a skilful cook who understands how to oblige his guests, will contrive to make it as expensive as they please.

Sixthly, This would be a great inducement to marriage, which all wise nations have either encouraged by rewards or enforced by laws and penalties. It would increase the care and tenderness of mothers toward their children, when they were sure of a settlement for life to the poor babes, provided in some sort by the public, to their annual profit instead of expense. We should see an honest emulation among the married women, which of them would bring the fattest child to the market. Men would become as fond of their wives during the time of their pregnancy as they are now of their mares in foal, their cows in calf, their sows when they are ready to farrow; nor offer to beat or kick them (as is too frequent a practice) for fear of a miscarriage.

Many other advantages might be enumerated. For instance, the addition of some thousand carcasses in our exportation of barreled beef, the propagation of swine's flesh, and improvement in the art of making good bacon, so much wanted among us by the great destruction of pigs, too frequent at our table; which are no way comparable in taste or magnificence to a well-grown, fat, yearling child, which roasted whole will make a considerable figure at a lord mayor's feast or any other public entertainment. But this and many others I omit, being studious of brevity.

Supposing that 1,000 families in this city would be constant customers for infants' flesh, besides others who might have it at merry-meetings, particularly at weddings and christenings, I compute that Dublin would take off annually about 20,000 carcasses; and the rest of the kingdom (where probably they will be sold somewhat cheaper) the remaining 80,000.

I can think of no one objection that will possibly be raised against this proposal, unless it should be urged that the number of people will be thereby much lessened in the kingdom. This I freely own, and it was indeed one principal design in offering it to the world. I desire the reader will observe, that I calculate my remedy for this one individual kingdom of Ireland and for no other that ever was, is, or I think ever can be upon earth. Therefore let no man talk to me of other expedients: of taxing our absentees at 5s. a pound: of using neither clothes nor household furniture except what is of our own growth and manufacture: of utterly rejecting the materials and instruments that promote foreign luxury: of curing the expensiveness of pride, vanity, idleness,and gaming in our women: of introducing a vein of parsimony, prudence, and temperance: of learning to love our country, in the want of which we differ even from Laplanders and the inhabitants of Topinamboo: of quitting our animosities and factions, nor acting any longer like the Jews, who were murdering one another at the very moment their city was taken: of being a little cautious not to sell our country and conscience for nothing: of teaching landlords to have at least one degree of mercy toward their tenants: lastly, of putting a spirit of honesty, industry, and skill into our shopkeepers; who, if a resolution could now be taken to buy only our native goods, would immediately unite to cheat and exact upon us in the price, the measure, and the goodness, nor could ever yet be brought to make one fair proposal of just dealing, though often and earnestly invited to it.

30   Therefore, I repeat, let no man talk to me of these and the like expedients, till he has at least some glimpse of hope that there will be ever some hearty and sincere attempt to put them in practice.

But as to myself, having been wearied out for many years with offering vain, idle, visionary thoughts, and at length utterly despairing of success, I fortunately fell upon this proposal; which, as it is wholly new, so it has something solid and real, of no expense and little trouble, full in our own power, and whereby we can incur no danger in disobliging England. For this kind of commodity will not bear exportation, the flesh being of too tender a consistence to admit a long continuance in salt, although perhaps I could name a country which would be glad to eat up our whole nation without it.

After all, I am not so violently bent upon my own opinion as to reject any offer proposed by wise men, which shall be found equally innocent, cheap, easy, and effectual. But before something of that kind shall be advanced in contradiction to my scheme, and offering a better, I desire the author or authors will be pleased maturely to consider two points. First, as things now stand, how they will be able to find food and raiment for 100,000 useless mouths and backs. And secondly, there being a round million of creatures in human figure throughout this kingdom, whose subsistence put into a common stock would leave them in debt 200,000,000*l*. sterling, adding those who are beggars by profession to the bulk of farmers, cottagers, and laborers, with the wives and children who are beggars in effect; I desire those politicians who dislike my overture, and may perhaps be so bold as to attempt an answer, that they will first ask the parents of these mortals, whether they would not at this day think it a great happiness to have been sold for food at a year old in the manner I prescribe, and thereby have avoided such a perpetual scene of misfortunes as they have since gone through by the oppression of landlords, the impossibility of paying rent without money or trade, the want of common sustenance, with neither house nor clothes to cover them from the inclemencies of the weather, and the most inevitable prospect of entailing the like or greater miseries upon their breed for ever.

I profess, in the sincerity of my heart, that I have not the least personal interest in endeavoring to promote this necessary work, having no other motive than the public good of my country, by advancing our trade, providing for infants, relieving the poor, and giving some pleasure to the rich. I have no children by which I can propose to get a single penny; the youngest being nine years old, and my wife past child-bearing.

 ## Topics for Critical Thinking and Writing

1. Characterize the pamphleteer (not Swift but his persona) who offers his "modest proposal." What sort of man does he think he is? What sort of man do we regard him as? Support your assertions with evidence.

2. In the first paragraph the speaker says that the sight of mothers begging is "melancholy." In this paragraph what assumption does the speaker make about women that in part gives rise to this melancholy? Now that

you are familiar with the entire essay, explain Swift's strategy in his first paragraph.

3. Explain the function of the "other expedients" (listed in paragraph 29).
4. How might you argue that although this satire is primarily ferocious, it also contains some playful touches? What specific passages might support your argument?

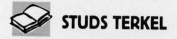 **STUDS TERKEL**

Studs Terkel was born Louis Terkel in New York City in 1912. He was brought up in Chicago and graduated from the University of Chicago. Terkel has been an actor, playwright, columnist, and disc jockey, but he is best known as the man who makes books out of tape recordings of people he gets to talk. We print an interview from American Dreams: Lost and Found *(1980).*

Stephen Cruz

He is thirty-nine.

"The family came in stages from Mexico. Your grandparents usually came first, did a little work, found little roots, put together a few bucks, and brought the family in, one at a time. Those were the days when controls at the border didn't exist as they do now."

You just tried very hard to be whatever it is the system wanted of you. I was a good student and, as small as I was, a pretty good athlete. I was well liked, I thought. We were fairly affluent, but we lived down where all the trashy whites were. It was the only housing we could get. As kids, we never understood why. We did everything right. We didn't have those Mexican accents, we were never on welfare. Dad wouldn't be on welfare to save his soul. He woulda died first. He worked during the depression. He carries that pride with him, even today.

Of the five children, I'm the only one who really got into the business world. We learned quickly that you have to look for opportunities and add things up very quickly. I was in liberal arts, but as soon as Sputnik went up, well, golly, hell, we knew where the bucks were. I went right over to the registrar's office and signed up for engineering. I got my degree in '62. If you had a master's in business as well, they were just paying all kinds of bucks. So that's what I did. Sure enough, the market was super. I had fourteen job offers. I could have had a hundred if I wanted to look around.

5   I never once associated these offers with my being a minority. I was aware of the Civil Rights Act of 1964, but I was still self-confident enough to feel they wanted me because of my abilities. Looking back, the reason I got more offers than the other guys was because of the government edict. And I thought it was because I was so goddamned brilliant. (Laughs.) In 1962, I didn't get as many offers as those who were less qualified. You have a tendency to blame the job market. You just don't want to face the issue of discrimination.

I went to work with Procter & Gamble. After about two years, they told me I was one of the best supervisors they ever had and they were gonna promote me. Okay, I went into personnel. Again, I thought it was because I was such a brilliant guy. Now I started getting wise to the ways of the American Dream. My office was glass-enclosed, while all the other offices were enclosed so you couldn't see into them. I was the visible man.

They made sure I interviewed most of the people that came in. I just didn't really think there was anything wrong until we got a new plant manager, a southerner. I received instructions from him on how I should interview blacks. Just check and see if they smell, okay? That was the beginning of my training program. I started asking: Why weren't we hiring more minorities? I realized I was the only one in a management position.

I guess as a Mexican I was more acceptable because I wasn't really black. I was a good compromise. I was visibly good. I hired a black secretary, which was *verboten.* When I came back from my vacation, she was gone. My boss fired her while I was away. I asked why and never got a good reason.

Until then, I never questioned the American Dream. I was convinced if you worked hard, you could make it. I never considered myself different. That was the trouble. We had been discriminated against a lot, but I never associated it with society. I considered it an individual matter. Bad people, my mother used to say. In '68 I began to question.

10   I was doing fine. My very first year out of college, I was making twelve thousand dollars. I left Procter & Gamble because I really saw no opportunity. They were content to leave me visible, but my thoughts were not really solicited. I may have overreacted a bit, with the plant manager's attitude, but I felt there's no way a Mexican could get ahead here.

I went to work for Blue Cross. It's 1969. The Great Society is in full swing. Those who never thought of being minorities before are being turned on. Consciousness raising is going on. Black programs are popping up in universities. Cultural identity and all that. But what about the one issue in this country: economics? There were very few management jobs for minorities, especially blacks.

The stereotypes popped up again. If you're Oriental, you're real good in mathematics. If you're Mexican, you're a happy guy to have around, pleasant but emotional. Mexicans are either sleeping or laughing all the time. Life is just one big happy kind of event. *Mañana.* Good to have as part of the management team, as long as you weren't allowed to make decisions.

I was thinking there were two possibilities why minorities were not making it in business. One was deep, ingrained racism. But there was still the possibility that they were simply a bunch of bad managers who just couldn't cut it. You see, until now I believed everything I was taught about the dream: the American businessman is omnipotent and fair. If we could show these turkeys there's money to be made in hiring minorities, these businessmen—good managers, good decision makers—would respond. I naïvely thought American businessmen gave a damn about society, that given a choice they would do the right thing. I had that faith.

I was hungry for learning about decision-making criteria. I was still too far away from top management to see exactly how they were working. I needed to learn more. Hey, just learn more and you'll make it. That part of the dream hadn't left me yet. I was still clinging to the notion of work your ass off, learn more than anybody else, and you'll get in that sphere.

15   During my fifth year at Blue Cross, I discovered another flaw in the American Dream. Minorities are as bad to other minorities as whites are to minorities. The strongest weapon the white manager had is the old divide and conquer routine. My mistake was thinking we were all at the same level of consciousness.

I had attempted to bring together some blacks with the other minorities. There weren't too many of them anyway. The Orientals never really got involved. The blacks misunderstood what I was presenting, perhaps I said it badly. They were on the cultural kick: a manager should be crucified for saying "Negro" instead of "black." I said as long as the Negro or the black gets the job, it doesn't mean a damn what he's called. We got into a huge hassle. Management, of course, merely smiled. The whole struggle fell flat on its face. It crumpled from divisiveness. So I learned another lesson. People have their own agenda. It doesn't matter what group you're with, there is a tendency to put the other guy down regardless.

The American Dream began to look so damn complicated, I began to think: Hell, if I wanted, I could just back away and reap the harvest myself. By this time, I'm up to twenty-five thousand dollars a year. It's beginning to look good, and a lot of people are beginning to look good. And they're saying: "Hey, the American Dream, you got it. Why don't you lay off?" I wasn't falling in line.

My bosses were telling me I had all the "ingredients" for top management. All that was required was to "get to know our business." This term comes up all the time. If I could just warn all minorities and women whenever you hear "get to know our business," they're really saying "fall in line." Stay within that fence, and glory can be yours. I left Blue Cross disillusioned. They offered me a director's job at thirty thousand dollars before I quit.

All I had to do was behave myself. I had the "ingredients" of being the good Chicano, the equivalent of the good nigger. I was smart. I could articulate well. People didn't know by my speech patterns that I was of Mexican heritage. Some tell me I don't look Mexican, that I have a certain amount of Italian, Lebanese, or who knows. (Laughs.)

20   One could easily say: "Hey, what's your bitch? The American Dream has treated you beautifully. So just knock it off and quit this crap you're spreading around." It was a real problem. Every time I turned around, America seemed to be treating me very well.

Hell, I even thought of dropping out, the hell with it. Maybe get a job in a factory. But what happened? Offers kept coming in. I just said to myself: God, isn't this silly? You might as well take the bucks and continue looking for the answer. So I did that. But each time I took the money, the conflict in me got more intense, not less.

Wow, I'm up to thirty-five thousand a year. This is a savings and loan business. I have faith in the executive director. He was the kind of guy I was looking for in top management: understanding, humane, also looking for the formula. Until he was up for consideration as executive v.p. of the entire organization. All of a sudden everything changed. It wasn't until I saw this guy flip-flop that I realized how powerful vested interests are. Suddenly he's saying: "Don't rock the boat. Keep a low profile. Get in line." Another disappointment.

Subsequently, I went to work for a consulting firm. I said to myself: Okay, I've got to get close to the executive mind. I need to know how they work. Wow, a consulting firm.

Consulting firms are saving a lot of American businessmen. They're doing it in ways that defy the whole notion of capitalism. They're not allowing these businesses to fail. Lockheed was successful in getting U.S. funding guarantees because of the efforts of consulting firms working on their behalf, helping them look better. In this kind of work, you don't find minorities. You've got to be a proven success in business before you get there.

25   The American Dream, I see now, is governed not by education, opportunity, and hard work, but by power and fear. The higher up in the organization you go, the more you have to lose. The dream is *not* losing. This is the notion pervading America today: Don't lose.

When I left the consulting business, I was making fifty-five thousand dollars a year. My last performance appraisal was: You can go a long way in this business, you can be a partner, but you gotta know our business. It came up again. At this point, I was incapable of being disillusioned any more. How easy it is to be swallowed up by the same set of values that governs the top guy. I was becoming that way. I was becoming concerned about losing that fifty grand or so a year. So I asked other minorities who had it made. I'd go up and ask 'em: "Look, do you owe anything to others?" The answer was: "We owe nothing to anybody." They drew from the civil rights movement but felt no debt. They've quickly forgotten how it happened. It's like I was when I first got out of college. Hey, it's really me, I'm great. I'm as angry with these guys as I am with the top guys.

Right now, it's confused. I've had fifteen years in the business world as "a success." Many Anglos would be envious of my progress. Fifty thousand dollars a year puts you in the one or two top percent of all Americans. Plus my wife making another thirty thousand. We had lots of money. When I gave it up, my cohorts looked at me not just as strange, but as something of a traitor. "You're screwing it up for all of us. You're part of our union, we're the elite, we should govern. What the hell are you doing?" So now I'm looked at suspiciously by my peer groups as well.

I'm teaching at the University of Wisconsin at Platteville. It's nice. My colleagues tell me what's on their minds. I got a farm next-door to Platteville. With farm prices being what they are (laughs), it's a losing proposition. But with university work and what money we've saved, we're gonna be all right.

The American Dream is getting more elusive. The dream is being governed by a few people's notion of what the dream is. Sometimes I feel it's a small group of financiers that gets together once a year and decides all the world's issues.

30   It's getting so big. The small-business venture is not there any more. Business has become too big to influence. It can't be changed internally. A counter-power is needed.

✎ Topics for Critical Thinking and Writing

1. In paragraph 11, Cruz refers to "The Great Society." What is (or was) "The Great Society" and how is it relevant to Cruz's story? If you aren't sure what The Great Society was, what can you learn about it from this pararaph, or others in Cruz's account?

2. In paragraphs 14 and 15 Cruz says he discovered that "minorities are as bad to other minorities as whites are to minorities." Does this view come as a surprise to you? Or have you had experiences that tend to confirm it? Conversely, have you had experiences that tend to refute it? Explain.

3. In paragraph 18 Cruz says, "If I could just warn all minorities and women whenever you hear 'get to know the business,' they're really saying 'fall in line.' Stay within that fence . . . ." If someone were to tell you "get to know the business" how else might you interpret it? Do you agree with

Cruz that the message you were being given would depend on whether or not you were a member of a minority culture or a woman?

4. Cruz frequently cites the American Dream. What is Cruz's idea of the American Dream and what has disillusioned him with it? Do you find yourself in sympathy with his complaints? Why or why not?

5. Suppose you were in a position to offer Cruz a job in management. How would you evaluate him as a candidate? You might try to do this by writing a memo to your supervisor, arguing Cruz's strengths and weaknesses and making a recommendation to hire or not. (You can take as much license as you need to invent the company, your position in it, the job opening, and the resumé Cruz has presented.)

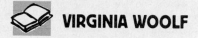 **VIRGINIA WOOLF**

Virginia Woolf (1882–1941) was born in London into an upper-middle-class literary family. In 1912 she married a writer, and with him she founded The Hogarth Press, whose important publications included not only books by T.S. Eliot but her own novels.

Professions for Women[1]

When your secretary invited me to come here, she told me that your Society is concerned with the employment of women and she suggested that I might tell you something about my own professional experiences. It is true I am a woman; it is true I am employed; but what professional experiences have I had? It is difficult to say. My profession is literature; and in that profession there are fewer experiences for women than in any other, with the exception of the stage—fewer, I mean, that are peculiar to women. For the road was cut many years ago—by Fanny Burney, by Aphra Behn, by Harriet Martineau, by Jane Austen, by George Eliot—many famous women, and many more unknown and forgotten, have been before me, making the path smooth, and regulating my steps. Thus, when I came to write, there were very few material obstacles in my way. Writing was a reputable and harmless occupation. The family peace was not broken by the scratching of a pen. No demand was made upon the family purse. For ten and sixpence one can buy paper enough to write all the plays of Shakespeare—if one has a mind that way. Pianos and models, Paris, Vienna and Berlin, masters and mistresses, are not needed by a writer. The cheapness of writing paper is, of course, the reason why women have succeeded as writers before they have succeeded in the other professions.

But to tell you my story—it is a simple one. You have only got to figure to yourselves a girl in a bedroom with a pen in her hand. She had only to move that pen from left to right—from ten o'clock to one. Then it occurred to her to do what is simple and cheap enough after all—to slip a few of those pages into an envelope, fix a penny stamp in the corner, and drop the envelope into the red

[1]This essay was originally a talk delivered in 1931 to the Women's Service League (editors' note)

box at the corner. It was thus that I became a journalist; and my effort was rewarded on the first day of the following month—a very glorious day it was for
me—by a letter from an editor containing a check for one pound ten shillings
and sixpence. But to show you how little I deserve to be called a professional
woman, how little I know of the struggles and difficulties of such lives, I have to
admit that instead of spending that sum upon bread and butter, rent, shoes and
stockings, or butcher's bills, I went out and bought a cat—a beautiful cat, a Persian cat, which very soon involved me in bitter disputes with my neighbors.

What could be easier than to write articles and to buy Persian cats with the
profits? But wait a moment. Articles have to be about something. Mine, I seem to
remember, was about a novel by a famous man. And while I was writing this review, I discovered that if I were going to review books I should need to do battle
with a certain phantom. And the phantom was a woman, and when I came to
know her better I called her after the heroine of a famous poem, The Angel in
the House. It was she who used to come between me and my paper when I was
writing reviews. It was she who bothered me and wasted my time and so tormented me that at last I killed her. You who come of a younger and happier generation may not have heard of her—you may not know what I mean by the Angel
in the House. I will describe her as shortly as I can. She was intensely sympathetic. She was immensely charming. She was utterly unselfish. She excelled in
the difficult arts of family life. She sacrificed herself daily. If there was chicken,
she took the leg; if there was a draught she sat in it—in short she was so constituted that she never had a mind or a wish of her own, but preferred to sympathize always with the minds and wishes of others. Above all—I need not say it—
she was pure. Her purity was supposed to be her chief beauty—her blushes, her
great grace. In those days—the last of Queen Victoria—every house had its
Angel. And when I came to write I encountered her with the very first words.
The shadow of her wings fell on my page; I heard the rustling of her skirts in the
room. Directly, that is to say, I took my pen in hand to review that novel by a famous man, she slipped behind me and whispered: "My dear, you are a young
woman. You are writing about a book that has been written by a man. Be sympathetic; be tender; flatter; deceive; use all the arts and wiles of our sex. Never
let anybody guess that you have a mind of your own. Above all, be pure." And
she made as if to guide my pen. I now record the one act for which I take some
credit to myself, though the credit rightly belongs to some excellent ancestors of
mine who left me a certain sum of money—shall we say five hundred pounds a
year?—so that it was not necessary for me to depend solely on charm for my living. I turned upon her and caught her by the throat. I did my best to kill her. My
excuse, if I were to be had up in a court of law, would be that I acted in self-defense. Had I not killed her she would have killed me. She would have plucked
the heart out of my writing. For, as I found, directly I put pen to paper, you cannot review even a novel without having a mind of your own, without expressing
what you think to be the truth about human relations, morality, sex. And all
these questions, according to the Angel in the House, cannot be dealt with freely
and openly by women; they must charm, they must conciliate, they must—to
put it bluntly—tell lies if they are to succeed. Thus, whenever I felt the shadow
of her wing or the radiance of her halo upon my page, I took up the inkpot and
flung it at her. She died hard. Her fictitious nature was of great assistance to her.
It is far harder to kill a phantom than a reality. She was always creeping back
when I thought I had despatched her. Though I flatter myself that I killed her in
the end, the struggle was severe; it took much time that had better have been

spent upon learning Greek grammar; or in roaming the world in search of adventures. But it was a real experience; it was an experience that was bound to befall all women writers at the time. Killing the Angel in the House was part of the occupation of a woman writer.

But to continue my story. The Angel was dead; what then remained? You may say that what remained was a simple and common object—a young woman in a bedroom with an inkpot. In other words, now that she had rid herself of falsehood, that young woman had only to be herself. Ah, but what is "herself"? I mean, what is a woman? I assure you, I do not know. I do not believe that you know. I do not believe that anybody can know until she has expressed herself in all the arts and professions open to human skill. That indeed is one of the reasons why I have come here—out of respect for you, who are in process of showing us by your experiments what a woman is, who are in process of providing us, by your failures and successes, with that extremely important piece of information.

5   But to continue the story of my professional experiences. I made one pound ten and six by my first review; and I bought a Persian cat with the proceeds. Then I grew ambitious. A Persian cat is all very well, I said; but a Persian cat is not enough. I must have a motor car. And it was thus that I became a novelist— for it is a very strange thing that people will give you a motor car if you will tell them a story. It is a still stranger thing that there is nothing so delightful in the world as telling stories. It is far pleasanter than writing reviews of famous novels. And yet, if I am to obey your secretary and tell you my professional experiences as a novelist, I must tell you about a very strange experience that befell me as a novelist. And to understand it you must try first to imagine a novelist's state of mind. I hope I am not giving away professional secrets if I say that a novelist's chief desire is to be as unconscious as possible. He has to induce in himself a state of perpetual lethargy. He wants life to proceed with the utmost quiet and regularity. He wants to see the same faces, to read the same books, to do the same things day after day, month after month, while he is writing, so that nothing may break the illusion in which he is living—so that nothing may disturb or disquiet the mysterious nosings about, feelings round, darts, dashes and sudden discoveries of that very shy and illusive spirit, the imagination. I suspect that this state is the same both for men and women. Be that as it may, I want you to imagine me writing a novel in a state of trance. I want you to figure to yourselves a girl sitting with a pen in her hand, which for minutes, and indeed for hours, she never dips into the inkpot. The image that comes to my mind when I think of this girl is the image of a fisherman lying sunk in dreams on the verge of a deep lake with a rod held out over the water. She was letting her imagination sweep unchecked round every rock and cranny of the world that lies submerged in the depths of our unconscious being. Now came the experience, the experience that I believe to be far commoner with women writers than with men. The line raced through the girl's fingers. Her imagination had rushed away. It had sought the pools, the depths, the dark places where the largest fish slumber. And then there was a smash. There was an explosion. There was foam and confusion. The imagination had dashed itself against something hard. The girl was roused from her dream. She was indeed in a state of the most acute and difficult distress. To speak without figure she had thought of something, something about the body, about the passions which it was unfitting for her as a woman to say. Men, her reason told her, would be shocked. The consciousness of what men will say of a woman who speaks the truth about her passions had roused her from her artist's state of unconsciousness. She could write no more. This I believe to be a very

common experience with women writers—they are impeded by the extreme conventionality of the other sex. For though men sensibly allow themselves great freedom in these respects, I doubt that they realize or can control the extreme severity with which they condemn such freedom in women.

These then were two very genuine experiences of my own. These were two of the adventures of my professional life. The first—killing the Angel in the House—I think I solved. She died. But the second, telling the truth about my own experiences as a body, I do not think I solved. I doubt that any woman has solved it yet. The obstacles against her are still immensely powerful—and yet they are very difficult to define. Outwardly, what is simpler than to write books? Outwardly, what obstacles are there for a woman rather than for a man? Inwardly, I think, the case is very different; she has still many ghosts to fight, many prejudices to overcome. Indeed it will be a long time still, I think, before a woman can sit down to write a book without finding a phantom to be slain, a rock to be dashed against. And if this is so in literature, the freest of all professions for women, how is it in the new professions which you are now for the first time entering?

Those are the questions that I should like, had I time, to ask you. And indeed, if I have laid stress upon these professional experiences of mine, it is because I believe that they are, though in different forms, yours also. Even when the path is nominally open—when there is nothing to prevent a woman from being a doctor, a lawyer, a civil servant—there are many phantoms and obstacles, as I believe, looming in her way. To discuss and define them is I think of great value and importance; for thus only can the labor be shared, the difficulties be solved. But besides this, it is necessary also to discuss the ends and the aims for which we are fighting, for which we are doing battle with these formidable obstacles. Those aims cannot be taken for granted; they must be perpetually questioned and examined. The whole position, as I see it—here in this hall surrounded by women practising for the first time in history I know not how many different professions—is one of extraordinary interest and importance. You have won rooms of your own in the house hitherto exclusively owned by men. You are able, though not without great labor and effort, to pay the rent. You are earning your five hundred pounds a year. But this freedom is only a beginning; the room is your own, but it is still bare. It has to be furnished; it has to be decorated; it has to be shared. How are you going to furnish it, how are you going to decorate it? With whom are you going to share it, and upon what terms? These, I think, are questions of the utmost importance and interest. For the first time in history you are able to ask them; for the first time you are able to decide for yourselves what the answers should be. Willingly would I stay and discuss those questions and answers—but not tonight. My time is up; and I must cease.

 ## Topics for Critical Thinking and Writing

1. The first two paragraphs seem to describe the ease with which women enter writing as a profession. What difficulties or obstacles for women do these paragraphs imply?

2. Try to characterize Woolf's tone, especially her attitude toward her subject and herself, in the first paragraph.

3. What do you think Woolf means when she says, near the end of paragraph 3, "It is far harder to kill a phantom than a reality"?

4. Woolf conjectures (paragraph 6) that she has not solved the problem of "telling the truth about my own experiences as a body." Is there any reason to believe that today a woman has more difficulty than a man in telling the truth about the experiences of the body?

5. In her final paragraph, Woolf suggests that phantoms as well as obstacles impede women from becoming doctors and lawyers. What might some of these phantoms be?

6. This essay is highly metaphoric. Speaking roughly (or, rather, as precisely as possible), what is the meaning of the metaphor of "rooms" in the final paragraph? What does Woolf mean when she says, "The room is your own, but it is still bare. . . . With whom are you going to share it, and upon what terms?"

7. Explain, to a reader who doesn't understand it, the analogy making use of fishing in paragraph 5.

8. Evaluate the last two sentences. Are they too abrupt and mechanical? Or do they provide a fitting conclusion to the speech?

LAST WORDS

A rich patron once gave money to the painter Chu Ta, asking him to paint a picture of a fish. Three years later, when he still had not received the painting, the patron went to Chu Ta's house to ask why the picture was not done. Chu Ta did not answer, but dipped a brush in ink and with a few strokes drew a splendid fish. "If it is so easy," asked the patron, "why didn't you give me the picture three years ago?" Again Chu Ta did not answer. Instead, he opened the door of a large cabinet. Thousands of pictures of fish tumbled out.

Literary Credits

Allende, Isabel. "If You Touched My Heart," pp. 81–91 from THE STORIES OF EVA LUNA, translated from the Spanish by Margaret Sayers Peden. Copyright © 1989 Isabel Allende. English translation copyright © 1992 Macmillan Publishing Company. Reprinted with the permission of Scribner, a division of Simon & Schuster.

Altman, Billy. "Pop View: Country Just Ain't What It Used to Be." *The New York Times.* January 31, 1993. Copyright © 1993 by The New York Times Company. Reprinted by permission.

Angelou, Maya. "Graduation" from I KNOW WHY THE CAGED BIRD SINGS. Copyright © 1969 by Maya Angelou. Reprinted by permission of Random House, Inc.

Atwood, Margaret. "Nine Beginnings" from THE WRITER ON HER WORK, II, edited by Janet Sternberg, pp. 150–156. Copyright © 1991 by Margaret Atwood. Reprinted by permission of the author.

Barnet, Sylvan. "Writing About Literature: An Overview" from LITERATURE FOR COMPOSITION: Essays, Fiction, Poetry, and Drama, Fourth Edition, pp. 430–452. Copyright © 1996. Reprinted by permission of Addison Wesley Educational Publishers, Inc.

Bly, Robert. "Love Poem" in IRON JOHN: A BOOK OF MEN, p. 133. Copyright © 1990 by Robert Bly. Reprinted by permission of Perseus Books Publishers, a member of Perseus Books, L.L.C.

Bok, Sissela. "To Lie or Not to Lie?–The Doctor's Dilemma," *The New York Times,* 18 April 1978. Copyright © 1978 by The New York Times Company. Reprinted by permission.

Borges, Jorge Luis. "The Gaucho and the City: Stories of Horsemen" first printed in *The New Republic*, May 19, 1982. Copyright © 1982 Jorge Luis Borges. Reprinted with the permission of the Wylie Agency, Inc.

Bruck, David. "The Death Penalty." THE NEW REPUBLIC, May 20, 1985. Copyright © 1985 by The New Republic. Reprinted by permission.

Campbell, Samantha. "My Father's Photograph" in *The Little, Brown Reader,* Seventh Edition. Reprinted by permission of Addison Wesley Educational Publishers, Inc.

Cunningham, Laura. "The Girl's Room," originally appeared in *The New York Times*, September 10, 1981. No part of this material may be reproduced in whole or part without the express written permission of the author or her agent.

Derman, Josh. "Deconstruction Pop: The Halo Benders" from *Harvard Crimson*, April 3, 1998. Reprinted by permission of the author.

Dickerson, Debra. "Who Shot Johnny?" First appeared in *The New Republic*, 1977. Reprinted with permission of the author.

Didion, Joan. "Los Angeles Notebook" from SLOUCHING TOWARDS BETHLEHEM. Copyright © 1966, 1968 and copyright renewed © 1996 by Joan Didion. Reprinted by permission of Farrar, Straus and Giroux, Inc.

Didion, Joan. "On Keeping a Notebook" from SLOUCHING TOWARDS BETHLEHEM. Copyright © 1966, 1968 and copyright renewed © 1996 by Joan Didion. Reprinted by permission of Farrar, Straus and Giroux, Inc.

Doyle, Arthur Conan. "The Science of Deduction" from A STUDY IN SCARLET. Copyright © 1996 The Sir Arthur Conan Doyle Copyright Holders. Reprinted by kind permission of Jonathan Clowes Ltd., London, on behalf of Andrea Plunket, Administrator of the Sir Arthur Conan Doyle Copyrights.

Elk, Black. "High Horse's Courting" from BLACK ELK SPEAKS by John G. Neihardt. Copyright © 1959, 1961 John G. Neihardt Trust; published by University of Nebraska Press. Reprinted by permission.

Fa-Yen, Wu-tsu. "Zen and the Art of Burglary" from ZEN AND JAPANESE CULTURE by Daisetz T. Suzuki. Copyright © 1959 and renewed 1987 by Princeton University Press. Reprinted by permission of Princeton University Press.

Photo Credits

Page 13: Printed with the permission of The Poetry/Rare Books Collection, University Libraries, SUNY at Buffalo; p. 39: From the Frances FitzGerald Collection, Dept. of Special Collections, Boston University; pp. 42-48: From the Frances FitzGerald Collection, Dept. of Special Collections, Boston University; p. 57: Alinari/Art Resource, NY; p. 59: *Spaghetti* from MAZES II by Vladimir Koziakin. Copyright 1972 by Vladimir Koziakin. Reprinted by permission of the Berkley Publishing Group; p. 63: Cheryl Lee, *The Story Behind the Gestures: A Family Photograph*. Reprinted by permission of the author, Cheryl Lee Rim; p. 81: Copyright, 1972. G.B. Trudeau. Reprinted by permission of Universal Press Syndicate. All rights reserved; p. 91: The New Yorker Collection 1971 Rossi from Cartoonbank.com. All Rights Reserved; p. 99: The New Yorker Collection 1976 Richter from Cartoonbank.com. All Rights Reserved; p. 100: Reprinted with permission of King Features Syndicate; p. 105: DILBERT reprinted by permission of United Feature Syndicate, Inc.; p. 107: The New Yorker Collection 1972 Handelsman from Cartoonbank.com. All Rights Reserved; p. 108: © 1979 Jules Feiffer. Reprinted with permission of Universal Press Syndicate. All rights reserved; p. 151: Graphische Sammlung Albertina, Wien; p. 160: Collection, The Museum of Modern Art, New York; p. 163: Courtesy, Museum of Fine Arts, Boston, Denman Waldo Ross Collection; p. 164: Courtesy, Museum of Fine Arts, Boston, Harvey Edward Wetzel Fund.; p. 176: Courtesy, Notman Photographic Archives, McCord Museum, McGill University; p. 177 (top left): S.P.A.D.E.M., Paris/V.A.G.A., New York 1985; p. 177 (top right): S.P.A.D.E.M., Paris/V.A.G.A., New York 1985; p. 177 (bottom left): Gift of Frederick J. Kennedy Memorial Foundation. 1973. Courtesy, Museum of Fine Arts, Boston; p. 177 (bottom right): Courtesy Museo del Prado, Madrid; 179: *My Father's Photograph*. Courtesy Samantha Campbell, in *The Little, Brown Reader*, Seventh Edition. Reprinted by permission of Addison Wesley Educational Publishers, Inc.; p. 252: The New Yorker Collection1983 Mankoff from Cartoonbank.com. All Rights Reserved; p. 254: The New Yorker Collection 1980 Lee Lorenz from Cartoonbank.com. All Rights Reserved; p. 309: University of Illinois at Urbana-Champaign Library Gateway Homepage. Screen grab from website www.library.uiuc.edu. Reprinted by permission

Index